MW00581751

Contact: Lionel Rolfe
213/413-8400 or fax: 213/484-6100
(Please send tearsheets of any mention or review you run. Call if you want to arrange for author interview).

Violin Virtuosos: From Paganini to the 21st Century
396 pages, 8 1/2 x 11
ISBN 1-879395-15-0 $29.95 (paperback)
ISBN 1-879395-18-5 $44.95 (hardcover)

Publication Date: March 1, 1997

The violin is the archetypical musical instrument. Its singing tone and wide range have made it the cornerstone of music since time immemorial. In *Violin Virtuosos: From Paganini to the 21st Century*, violinist/music critic Henry Roth has created a work of rare insight into this most singular instrument.

A professional violinist as well as a widely published writer with over thirty years' experience in music criticism, Roth imparts the intricacies of violin playing to the reader in brilliant and readable style. Presenting a historical pageant of the violin over a span of centuries, Roth explains and pinpoints the strengths, weaknesses, and artistic achievements of hundreds of great and near-great violinists. Roth handles the entire gamut of violin performance with meticulous attention to detail and journalistic flair. A truly encyclopedic volume, with 278 rare photographs and illustrations, *Violin Virtuosos: From Paganini to the 21st Century* belongs in the library of every violinist, violin fancier, and music lover. Portions of this book appeared in Roth's earlier volumes, *Master Violinists in Performance*, and *Great Violinists in Performance*.

The Author

Henry Roth, a prominent Los Angeles violinist, pedagogue and writer, has concertized throughout the United States and Mexico with his pianist-wife Esther, and was employed as a recording artist in the Hollywood film and recording industry over a 50-year period. He has been a regularly published music critic for two Los Angeles weekly newspapers for 27 years, as well as a contributor to *The Strad* magazine of London for 25 years. Roth's unique lecture-concerts and violin masterclasses have been enthusiastically received by teachers, students, and violin fanciers in leading conservatories and universities throughout the United States and in Europe, China, Hong Kong, and Singapore. He was the featured contributor to the book *Heifetz* and co-author of eight of the immensely popular *The Way They Play* series.

Highly sought after as a juror for major international violin competitions, Dr. Roth has served in that capacity for the Indianapolis, Hanover (Joachim), Szeryng, Francescatti, Kreisler, and Taipei competitions, among others.

He is the recipient of an honorary doctorate of music degree from the prestigious Cleveland Institute of Music.

Praise for Henry Roth's *Violin Virtuosos*

"I was captivated by the living portraits described by the author, both as to their performance and personality. His description at times is so alive that the artist under discussion seems to be playing for me. Every detail is analyzed with microscopic precision, and never for a moment does the narrative fail to convey the overall dimensions of the artist's life, the time in which he lived and his place in musical history. Roth's encyclopedic knowledge, profound powers of evaluation, uncompromising honesty and boundless enthusiasm place him among the top writers dealing with the art of violin playing.

"I loved reading this extraordinary book which I am sure will be read with interest and joy by violin lovers, be they professionals or amateurs.

As a document to our beloved violin, it is unique...."

Josef Gingold

"I have been acquainted with the music critiques and writings of Henry Roth for some years, and have always recognized their content to be erudite and articulate.."

– JASCHA HEIFETZ

"I was deeply impressed with Henry Roth's Kreisler lecture and presentation... It was conceived with precision, and reveals some unknown or so far unnoticed facets of this great beloved Master. The audience, which included violinists, critics and musicologists as well as the general public, was enraptured by his 'interpretation' of Kreisler's personality, his life and work. The music world should indeed be thankful to Mr. Roth for giving us all enlightenment, pleasure and emotional enrichment!"

– HENRYK SZERYNG

"I would like to express my sincerest thanks to Henry Roth for the two lectures presented to our violin class outlining the stylistic history of virtuoso violin playing. His sense of organization and presentation captivatingly conveyed an educational message of great relevancy to each and everyone present, not the least of whom was myself. I applaud and congratulate Mr. Roth on his thoroughly inspirational and entertaining presentation and on the comprehensive research which was reflected therein. These lectures are an absolute must to any serious student and lover of the violin!"

– DAVID CERONE, President
Cleveland Institute of Music

"Henry Roth's inspiring series of lectures were a marvelous contribution to our teachers and student."

– PROFESSOR HAN LI, President
Violin Department, Central Conservatory
of Music in Beijing

VIOLIN VIRTUOSOS

From Paganini
to the
21st Century

Henry Roth

with Foreword by Josef Gingold

California CLASSICS BOOKS

LOS ANGELES, CALIFORNIA

A Lionel Menuhin Rolfe Imprint

Acknowledgements

I would like to acknowledge my gratitude to the late Josef Gingold for his invaluable advice and unswerving confidence in this volume. To my wife Esther for her myriad constructive criticisms and for her constant encouragement and assistance; to Lionel Rolfe for his editorial work; to Ken Boor and Nigey Lennon for art direction and production; to Annette Kaufman and the late Louis Kaufman for their sage counsel; to Sam Fordis for his numerous services on behalf of this enterprise; to the late Lawrence Sommers for his data pertinent to violinists of the French-Belgian School; to Nigey Lennon and my wife Esther for proof reading; to David Cerone for his wise suggestions I offer my sincerest thanks. The rare photos in this book appear through the generosity of Zino and Yolande Francescatti, Carl F. Flesch, Jr., Mrs. Gregor Piatigorsky, Yakov Soroker, Pavel Kogan, Joseph Gold, I. MonDragon, Kenway Lee, Morris Victor, Ben Berzinsky, Jill Spalding, the Carnegie Hall Archives, and *The Strad*. Contemporary photos appear through the courtesy of IMG Artists, International Artists' Management, The International Violin Competition of Indianapolis, and photographers: Christian Steiner, J. Henry Fair, Don Hunstein, Garry Chilluffo, Henry Grossman, Neal R. Keach, Ute Karen Seggelke, Jolana Kutman, Steve J. Sherman ©, Sigrídar Bachman, Yoshi ONO, Leopold Oosterlynck and particularly to David Weiss, principal oboist and official photographer of the Los Angeles Philharmonic, who went far beyond the call of duty to assist with photos. To *The Strad* for granting permission to reprint excerpts from some of my published articles; to James Creighton for his indispensable *Discopaedia of the Violin*; and to Richard Green, who provided the data on Country and Western violinists, my gratitude.

To Esther, my beloved wife —
the most sensitive, compassionate, generous
and humane person I have ever known.

FOREWORD

For the past half century I have been reading the published literature dealing with the history of violin playing and its great masters. While I found a few of these books (such as the *Memoirs* of Carl Flesch) to be highly interesting and informative, the others, for the most part, were but an encyclopedic composite of the subject matter.

Mr. Henry Roth, a professional practitioner in every sense of the word, a fine violinist, a musicologist and a splendid writer, gives us a critical analysis of the great master violinists.

In reading and re-reading the various chapters, I was captivated by the living portraits described by the author, both as to their performance and personality. His description at times is so alive that the artist under discussion seems to be playing for me. Every detail is analyzed with microscopic precision, and never for a moment does the narrative fail to convey the overall dimensions of the artist's life, the times in which he lived and his place in musical history. Roth's encyclopedic knowledge, profound powers of evaluation, uncompromising honesty and boundless enthusiasm place him among the top writers dealing with the art of violin playing.

I loved reading this extraordinary book which I am sure will be read with interest and joy by violin lovers, be they professionals or amateurs.

As a document to our beloved violin, it is *unique*!

—Josef Gingold

Josef Gingold and the author, 1986

Author's Preface

This is essentially a book of in-depth critiques—evaluations of performances by great or near-great violinists of many eras, devoted to a subject which has been, I feel, unjustly neglected and long overdue for serious examination. Although I have included a certain amount of biographical and anecdotal material, my principal endeavor is to place important violinists in historical perspective as artists and performers without gratuitous glamorization, in a manner that can readily communicate with both professional and non-professional devotees of the violin.

Since I have been a regularly published music critic for some three decades (as well as a professional violinist), I recognize the importance of widely varying esthetic tastes in matters of musical evaluations. No artist ever has been "all things to all people." And I admit that far too often critics attempt to dictate artistic tastes.

I have always disagreed with this attitude. The critic should, I believe, describe and evaluate a performance, and he has the right, also, to indicate his own esthetic preferences in details of style and interpretation if these have some direct bearing on the evaluation. But he should never assume the role of a ruthless missionary striving to superimpose his own personal tastes to a degree which becomes the dominating factor of a critique. Often, too, a critic will dislike a certain piece of music and fail to separate his feelings about the composition from his assessment of the performance, thus figuratively "throwing out the baby with the bathwater." All criticism, both negative and positive, is subjective, and this is the case irrespective of the critic's or lay observer's qualifications or dearth of them. Yet, subjectivity need not include intellectual arrogance, snobbish cultism, or mean-spiritedness. Although my opinions are

as subjective as anyone's, I strive for objectivity within the context of subjectivity. I still regard the violin primarily as an instrument of song. As the instrument closest to the human voice, beauty and individual character of tone remain among the cardinal components of violin art. Furthermore, I hold that the element of personality in performance is the principal factor that separates truly great artists from superb instrumentalists. This point of view is stressed throughout these pages.

The conditions under which an artist performs and the category of his accomplishments are vital facets in matters of evaluation. For example, a concertmaster who may appear as soloist in a concerto once a year should not be judged in the same context as a full-time concertizing artist, who performs up to 150 times a season. And one must take into consideration the disadvantages of a lesser known player who is forced to perform on an inferior instrument as opposed to an artist regularly enjoying a Stradivarius or a Guarnarius del Gesù. On the other hand, while a veteran over-the-hill artist is entitled to chivalrous treatment in recognition of his honorable past exploits, an evaluation should not degenerate into a mawkish eulogy that avoids mentioning the true status of his intonation, technical facility, vibrato, bowing, etc.. Nor need subjectivity preclude a reverent affection for the traditions of violin art on the part of the critic. Nevertheless, even with the purest of intentions, a critic is bound at some point to bend his own ground rules and inevitably risks the disapproval, if not the downright disdain, of his readers.

Violinists can be categorized in many ways: by nationality, birth date, status, national "school," pedagogical lineage, or even alphabetically, and it is certain that whichever procedure is chosen, it will be unsatisfactory to one or another commentator or reader.

Realizing that one cannot please everyone in all things, I have employed several methods of presentation, and hope the reader will find this acceptable. Each chapter is a complete entity unto itself.

From years of personal experience, the critic can never satisfy completely the artist and his uncritical venerators. He may give an artist four consecutive rave reviews, but should the fifth contain some reservations, like as not, the artist will tend to view the critic as an enemy. This is both understandable and unfortunate. Inasmuch as competition in the jungle of the concert world is so grim, even the slightest adverse comment is considered detrimental by an artist. And make no mistake, this is the case not only with younger artists still in the process of building a personal following, but also with firmly established name stars who, one might think, are far beyond and above the reach of such slings and arrows—artists who publicly boast that they "never read reviews," but privately never miss a word written about them. Consequently, the conscientious critic can scarcely be the intimate of any artist if he unqualifiedly accepts his intrinsic duty to evaluate all artists with neither undue favor nor discrimination. One must always bear in mind that the responsibility and function of the critic is in no way analogous to that of an artist's paid public relations representative!

Why, one might ask, is there so little in print that seeks to investigate honestly and knowledgeably into violin performance without sugar-coating or one-sided adulation?

An outstanding exception is the monumental Carl Flesch *Memoirs*, in which the celebrated violinist-pedagogue, for the most part, discusses his contemporaries and colleagues with erudition and an unashamed willingness to "let the chips fall where they may." However, for all his marvelous perception, Flesch's evaluations, on occasion, were influenced by his personal relationships with the artists he discussed. Conversely, we find other stellar artists gingerly avoiding the subject in their biographies or commentaries. Even those few instances in which an artist has written about the playing of a colleague (except Flesch), it is almost always done with an over-polite, cautious affability that sidesteps any candid, well-rounded exposition of the relative strengths, weaknesses, and musical idiosyncrasies of that colleague. This reluctance on the part of these violin luminaries, some of whom possess the intelligence and skill to discuss and analyze the performance of their contemporaries with invaluable insight, has left a huge vacuum

in the annals of violinistic knowledge and erudition. And more than a half-century has passed since Flesch's *Memoirs* were formulated and written.

Regardless of how the reader may feel about the comments contained herein, I can affirm that while I have had occasion over the years to meet some of the violinists discussed in this book, my relations with them have been strictly impersonal and cursory. Indeed, I have deliberately gone out of my way in this respect to preserve my status as an independent writer, beholden to no one but my readers and myself.

This volume is written by one who knows only too well how terribly difficult it is to play even the simplest piece on stage before an audience or into a merciless, all-revealing microphone. It is, in fact, one of the most demanding tasks essayed by human hands. Consider the harrowing ordeal of the soloist who stands, violin in hand, awaiting his entrance during a lengthy orchestral or piano introduction. A spate of thoughts flash through his mind. Will he be embarrassed by a recalcitrant finger before he is fully warmed up? Will the strings respond properly? Will a fleck of resin sabotage the sound? Will his memory falter? Will the press be in attendance, and if so, will the critics possess sufficient acquaintance with the distinctive characteristics of violin playing to write a reasonably knowledgeable review? And throughout this self-inquisition, with his stomach muscles knotted in apprehension if not outright nervousness, an irritating globule of perspiration slowly, but inexorably, inches its way down the back of his leg. Yes, my respect for this art and its doughty practitioners is total.

When we seek to evaluate the playing of violinists of yesteryear who lived and died before the birth of recording, we are forced to base our deductions upon the written reports available, together with the generally more valuable and reliable evidence of the compositions they left. In the area of 20th-century violinists, my personal experience includes having heard every top-ranking violinist, beginning with Kreisler, in live performance many times, with the sole exception of Grumiaux. In addition, my vast library of recordings has supplemented my acquaintance with their performance as well as that of a host of violinists of the second and third rank.

In presenting these essays, some of which have appeared in part in *The Strad* of London, I have elected to discuss violinists of the recording era rather than those of the far-distant past, with the exception of Paganini.

When making evaluations, it must be taken into consideration that some major artists are more convincing in showpieces or vignettes than heavyweight concertos; others in bravura gymnastics rather than introspective, or even patently romantic, sonatas. But there is a place for all in our wondrous pantheon of violin art.

The matter of evaluating *living* artists is a particularly sensitive undertaking—one that, if pursued with utter candor, is certain to evoke some howls of disapproval from partisans and friends of these personalities. The reader may not always agree with me, but if I am successful in stimulating constructive, penetrating thought about the past, present, and future of the glorious art of violin playing, my purpose will have been achieved.

Violin Virtuosos: From Paganini to the 21st Century does not purport to be an encyclopedia of violinists. Unfortunately, many fine violinists deserving recognition are not included for sheer lack of space. To these respected colleagues, I offer my apologies.

This edition combines re-edited versions of my original *Master Violinists in Performance* and my *Great Violinists in Performance*, plus a third volume representing a continuation of the previous two books. Thus, my goal of a trilogy has been realized.

—Henry Roth

Table of Contents

SENOR SARASATE

Pablo Sarasate, the swashbuckling Spanish virtuoso of the 19th century

Violinists--
Old Time vs. Modern

How would Pablo Sarasate have compared with Jascha Heifetz; Joseph Joachim with Yehudi Menuhin; August Wilhelmj with David Oistrakh; or Ole Bull with Ruggiero Ricci? A fascinating topic!

It is always a temptation to yield to nostalgia when one discusses ancestral heroes--in any field. The halo of long-vanished glories is prone to conflict with hard-headed reality. Conversely, a mere casual summation of brilliant new manual achievements may easily lull the superficial investigator into overlooking those vital yardsticks which represent the essential lure of music in any age--esthetic communication, spiritual sustenance, and sheer enjoyment.

Any evaluation of the art of violin playing as it existed in its infancy, 300 years ago, must be based on conjecture. We read, for example, that Corelli, the "father of violin playing," was so aggravated by his inability to execute the fifth position F on the E string (in a confrontation with a Neapolitan rival) that "his death was hastened." Of his actual sound we can know nothing, though it is possible to deduce many facts concerning comparative technical skills by studying violin works of the era. And since no one living today has ever heard Nicolò Paganini, Heinrich Wilhelm Ernst, Henri Vieuxtemps, Henryk Wieniawski, or August Wilhelmj, we are most reliant upon "ear-witness" accounts by observers and critics of the time.

How reliable are they? To quote Carl Flesch, one of the most perceptive and qualified commentators on matters violinistic: "At the outside, one of 100 music critics knows something about the technique of violin playing and its proper nomenclature. In toto — newspaper criticism is in no way a substitute for factual information. In our contemporary critical efforts, there is a tendency to conceal ignorance behind empty impressions."

All too true. Even in the writings of such renowned old-time critics as Eduard Hanslick, George Bernard Shaw, James Gibbons Huneker, and Henry T. Finck, their lack of firsthand professional knowledge of the violin is glaringly apparent, and the plethora of highly romanticized unknowledgeable gabblings by lay observers are less than worthless. However, this by no means implies that the best critics of yesteryear were not competent to make violinistic judgments. After all, a critic may not know the *hows* and *whys* of violinistics, but by sheer dint of multiple listenings, the more erudite critic ultimately gains the ability to distinguish various levels of artistry. Shaw, for instance, whose experience spanned from the 1870s to the middle of our century, contrasted the superior playing of Heifetz and the young Menuhin to that of Joachim and Sarasate.

Statements by great violinists themselves cannot always be taken at face value. Was Paganini's tone really so inferior that it was surpassed by that of his lesser rival Charles Lafont, as Paganini himself averred? Was Wilhelmj's legendary gigantic tone produced by repeated bowings on a single note, as some claim? Was not the failure of Leopold Auer to describe and compare (in his book, *My Life in Music*) the performances of Wieniawski and Sarasate as they played for him privately, back-to-back, in the same room and on the same day, a signal loss to the documentation of violin art?

One could easily fill a volume with the inconsistencies, contradictions, and questionable evaluations of violin performances — and end up actually proving little. However, there remains one invaluable source which, when double-checked with the limited number of writings by responsible observers, affords us a real-

Joseph Joachim in his prime years

factory discs for another eight years—a bit past his prime. Joachim, at 73 (some 20 years past his prime), made his few discs the following year, when his intonation was shaky and his tone bone-dry. However, to the experienced listener, the authority and virility of his playing are clearly apparent.

In the next 15 years, through 1919, some of the most exquisite and exciting violin vignette performances of all time were to be recorded by Kreisler,

August Wilhelmj, reputed to have possessed a tone of extraordinary size

istic insight into modern playing. I refer to the legacy of recordings from the first two decades of the 20th century. Here is an indelible, irrefutable testament of the art of violin playing, fully as profound, if not more so, as the impact of Paganini upon 19th-century violin technique. It is true that many of these are primitively engineered, that some of the artists were past their prime, that they were not inured to playing into a microphone (or horn) as are our modern artists, that the surface noise obscures the quality of their tone. Yet, if we listen carefully, I maintain that we can judge such essentials as intonation, pacing, tempos, musical discipline (or lack of it), musical proportion, dynamic variety, general interpretation, and even, to a certain extent, tonal quality, assuming one learns to train the ear to ignore and listen through engineering imperfections.

Sheer quantity of sound is too often mistaken for quality. Our ears have been so abused that we no longer search out the basic essence of sound timbre, but are misled by echo-chamber stentorianism and engineering dial manipulation. In this respect many violin records of the `teens and `20s offer far more fidelity of true violin tone, provided the discs are in reasonably good condition. How often in recent years have we heard a violinist in a hall sounding so inferior to his hopped-up recordings that we scarcely believe the evidence of our ears?

Let us remember that in 1904, the year of his recordings, Sarasate was only 60. Jan Kubelik was 24, in the prime of his technical powers. Fritz Kreisler was already 29, prior to the pinnacle of popularity he was to attain, but playing gloriously. Eugène Ysaÿe, at 46, was not to make his revelatory but essentially unsatis-

Mischa Elman, and the young Heifetz. The winds of change were blowing furiously. Mass interest in violin art had never been more international; its prestige never higher.

Thanks to the unique contribution of Paganini, the entire fingerboard from bottom to top had been explored and utilized. Technical feats never before considered practical had become part and parcel of the legitimate violin repertoire. After Paganini's death in 1840, such virtuosos as Ernst, Vieuxtemps, and Wieniawski incorporated that Paganini heritage into their performance and compositions. Wieniawski even popularized the rapid stiff-arm bowed staccato, a feat

Heinrich Wilhelm Ernst, who fashioned his style and composition after those of Paganini–a musician of solid worth

not accomplished by Paganini.

The French-Belgian school, except for the phenomenon of Paganini, continued to dominate the 19th century. Vieuxtemps, and later Wieniawski, introduced its principles into Russia. Though handicapped by small hands, Sarasate ultimately brought the bravura traditions of Paganini, tinctured with the flavor of his native Spain, to a new level of refinement.

By 1890 most of the finest romantic concertos had already been written. Yet, the nether side of Paganini was still casting a negative shadow in violin recital halls. Endless operatic fantasias, mazurkas, polonaises, and a redundancy of salon pieces of the most banal nature continued to clutter up programs. Everyone wanted cheap and easy success. In his American appearances, even such a giant of his time as Vieuxtemps featured his own lengthy variations on "Yankee Doodle."

In opposition to the Niagara of trivia was the Hungarian Joseph Joachim, who eventually came to head the so-called German School in Berlin. Though an eclectic in spirit who saw fit to transcribe the entire body of Brahms's Hungarian Dances for the violin and popularize them in the recital hall, Joachim was also responsible for greatly elevating the standards of violin programming. He popularized the Bach solo sonatas, the Beethoven concerto and sonatas, and a long list of masterworks which such contemporaries as Sarasate either ignored or rattled off in superficial fashion. His purification of the repertoire is still a major influence in our time, insofar as program content is concerned.

During the last half of the 19th century, a multiplicity of stylistic nuances were developed. Subtleties

of portamentos, slides, glissandos, and position changes added new elements of charm and elegance to violin art. Of course, these digital fripperies, all too often grossly exaggerated, resulted in countless examples of bad taste and emoting that would sound comical to our ears.

For all the advances, technical and musical, that had developed in the 100 or so years since Tartini, the playing of 1850-1890 was a far cry from that of our day. Bowing was comparatively rough and scratchy, violin tone dry and cool. Sensuality of sound as we know it was still in the early stages of development; intellectual discipline and musical fidelity were well below our highest contemporary standards.

The greats of the latter 19th century were giants of their day, and as such we owe them respect and reverence, but they would indeed cut a sorry figure if placed upon the modern concert stage.

Bust of Henri Vieuxtemps, stellar figure of the brilliant 19th century Belgian Violin School

How do we know this? How can we be certain? Simple enough. We know, for example, that the horse-drawn carriage was slower than our jet plane that had not yet been invented. We know that while the first Olympic sprint champion was the world's fastest human in 1891, his speed was far below the Olympian of 1996, who had at his disposal all the accumulated secrets of body training, buttressed by the availability of vitamins plus a veritable armory of modern health advantages.

Violin playing, too, was to leap forward due to an inventive device that was unknown to the ancients. It began to develop around 1880. And it was comparable in importance to such revolutionary advances in violinistic history as the raising of the violin from the relatively unstable chest or breast-bone position, to a position involving the neck, shoulder, and chin (thus permitting complete freedom for the left hand and arm movement); the reversing of the bow curvature from outward to inward, giving the bow a tension, mobility, and elasticity it had never possessed before, and endowing it with an importance essentially equal to that of the violin itself; and the monumental technical upsurge of finger dexterity in the 19th century, crowned by the daring exploits of Paganini.

Henryk Wieniawski, an immortal of the 19th century Belgian Violin School, whose challenging virtuoso compositions still delight violinists and audiences alike

The new phenomenon was the conscious development and deliberate usage of that oscillation of the left-hand fingertip known as the *vibrato*.

The origin of this concept is obscure, but it is known that Wieniawski invented special vibrato exercises which he passed on to Isadore (Gedalya Itzik) Lotto, Vieuxtemps, and others. The new gospel spread like wildfire among violinists everywhere, yet it met with stubborn opposition that required many years to overcome. (Oddly, Lotto, when confronted with Kreisler's constant use of the vibrato, said of Kreisler, "He will never amount to much.")

Previously, the use of finger oscillation was despised and forbidden by just about every "respectable" violin school. It was considered gross evidence of poor musical taste, though a few individual players may have applied some semblance of a vibrato to long, sustained tones, strictly as an unconscious kinetic emotional reflex. In any case, *this vibrato had little or nothing in common with modern romantic vibrato.*

The sensational contribution of the vibrato was to enable violinists to play with a new beauty and heightened sensuality of sound which added new dimensions of emotional communication.

Ysaÿe, who may well be considered the first violinist of modern times, burnished the extraordinary temperament of his playing with a cannily diversified usage of the vibrato. The first to introduce the *constant* use of the vibrato was Kreisler. Early in his career, this new kind of playing in which every note was alive and meaningful, even in technical passages, was indeed strange to conservative ears. In fact, in 1894, Kreisler's individuality was so startling that he was rejected for a second desk position in the Vienna Hofoper Orchestra. Kreisler's vibrato, uncommonly fast and flexible, was a cardinal factor in the charm and elegance of his playing.

With the advantage of a well developed, wisely-used vibrato, it is possible for a violinist of moderate, or even limited emotional and visceral force, to sound much superior to a player with a poor vibrato who possesses powerful inner feelings. Modern gifted teenagers, armed with knowledge of modern vibrato usage as well as many other technical advantages, can give polished performances of the Tchaikovsky and Brahms concertos, considered almost unplayable in 1880. They enjoy the command of resources and standards utterly unknown to Paganini.

The modern player is superior in many other areas besides a singular use of the vibrato. Top ranking players are now able to employ *several speeds* of vibrato which give their music multiple tonal dimensions; they now possess far more variety and subtlety of bowing shadings which further complement their arsenal for sound; they project a new sophistication of style, suavity, and fluency; they have eliminated the old-fashioned, mawkish slides and (it is to be hoped) exaggerations of tempos. Disciplined musical law and order has become the rule rather than the exception; the international-ization of violinistic know-how has broken down the narrow limitations of national schools—to everyone's advantage. The totality of modern violin art is a high-ly complex affair in which the significant extension of repertorial demands necessitates an intellectual, and even technical, development worlds above that required by 19th-century virtuosos.

Like any other mechanical device, the vibrato can be employed to disadvantage if not governed by good taste, and is often a chief contributor to the delinquen-cy of lesser players.

It was the unique impulse vibrato of Elman that accounted for his lava-like, throbbing, golden tone. (His powerful bow-arm, ideally representative of the Auer-Russian school, was responsible for the mighty sonori-ty of his tone, but not for its vibrant, sensuous quality.) Other Auer pupils, Heifetz and Toscha Seidel, possessed their own individual type of "impulse" vibrato which lent their tone a virile intensity (as separate from a one-dimensional pleasant sweetness), quite unlike the sound of a legion of their gifted contemporaries. Jacques Thibaud, and later Menuhin and Isaac Stern, have been highly individual in this area of sound production.

If the world's leading violinists were to draw their bows on an open string, one player would be quite indistinguishable from the other, but the quality of their individual finger vibrato would make each one identi-fiable to violin experts in a matter of a few bars.

No essay of old-timers versus modern violinists would be relevant without special reference to the tow-ering figure of Heifetz, the violinistic epitome of the 20th-century ethos. The preeminence of his contribu-tions is in no way dependent upon whether one does or does not prefer his musical interpretations to those of some other contemporary. Had Heifetz never lived, violin playing might never have attained the pinnacle of perfection on the instrumental level that it enjoys today—a fact freely admitted by a host of colleagues everywhere. This will be discussed in detail in the Heifetz chapter.

The old-timers were at a disadvantage in the area of career longevity. Their technical powers, trained by primitive methods, were prone to deteriorate seriously at the first onslaught of muscular decline. Because they were inconsistent, one had to hear them on a good day, whereas the technical equipment of modern players is so secure they are able to sustain their performance

Ferdinand David gave Mendelssohn advice on violinistic details during the composition of the Concerto in E-Minor, Op. 64.

through a variety of indispositions.

Life spans generally were shorter. An exception to the rule was Joachim, who lived to the ripe old age of 76. Paganini died at 58; Wieniawski at 44; Vieuxtemps (paralyzed at 53) at 61; Sarasate at 64; Ernst at 51; Maud Powell at 52. Ysaÿe lived until age 73, but was past his prime at less than 55. Wilhelmj died at 63 but ended his career in his early 40s.

Is there, then, no area in which the old-time vio-linists were superior to the moderns? This is a hypo-thetical question dependent upon individual concepts of musical taste, and we would have to make an arbitrary separation, say, between those born before and after, roughly, 1925.

Some, like myself, feel that the fascinating ele-ments of individual sound and personality are vanish-ing from violin performance—victims of the general trend toward the de-personalization of modern man. Leaving aside violinists who lived before our time, players such as Ysaÿe, Kreisler, Elman, Heifetz, Menuhin, and Oistrakh, through the uniqueness of their sound and style have been absolutely inimitable unto themselves. An interesting sidelight in this mat-ter lies in the fact that such individualist artists as

Edouard Reményi, noted Hungarian violinist, was a widely traveled Romantic virtuoso with whom Brahms once toured as a piano collaborator.

Elman, Kreisler, Bronislaw Huberman, Joseph Szigeti, and Thibaud, together with many other yesteryear players, had no official study with a teacher after the age of 12, 13, or 14, and thus were encouraged to formulate their own highly personalized styles. Today we have many great violinists who are also authoritative musicians. But do we have any true *Great Personalities of the Violin?*

As the 20th century progressed, there developed a countertrend to overt personalization in performance. Oddly, one of its leading figures was a violinist who himself played with unusual individuality, Szigeti. Some of these directions in the art of violin playing will be touched upon in the following chapters.

One of the unfortunate aspects of the violin scene in our time has been the gradual decimation of violin recitals as musical events, at least in America. The make-up of so-called "recital" programs has graduated into a

joyless, if musically erudite, affair. Three and four sonatas are often presented in a program which features a first rank violinist accompanied by a competent, experienced, but essentially lesser-rank hired pianist-accompanist. They are, in fact, essentially not violin recitals at all (even though one or two patently violinistic pieces are occasionally included) but chamber music concerts in which the piano is, or should be, a fully equal partner with the violin on the purely musical level. We seldom hear those vignettes in which a violinist is required to pour the complete reservoir of his art into a three- or four-minute span—the type of experience that countless listeners of the past often cherished for a lifetime. We are constantly warned to look askance at honest sentiment, as well as over-emoting or sentimentality. But overt honest sentiment, both in selection and contents of repertoire as well as in performance, can provide an enchanting leavening. The "Queen of Instruments," after all is said and done, is basically a lyric, emotion-oriented instrument. Today, in many quarters, any conception of violin art as entertainment has become taboo. How often do we attend "over-weight" violin events that are admirably performed, instrumentally and musically, but forget the experience even before arriving home from the concert hall? Must the mastery of such rigorous, complicated works as Hindemith's Kammermusik No. 4, the Schoenberg Violin Concerto, and the Schnittke sonatas inevitably signal the demise of the charm, poetry, and elegance that once made a Kreisler playing Dvořák's *Humoresque* or an Elman playing Drdla's *Souvenir* or a Heifetz playing Godowsky's *Alt Wien* an unforgettable experience?

With all of our modern competence and efficiency, is there a current violinist, even a Perlman, who can equal the tonal magic of the young Elman in Wagner's *Albumblatt* or Raff's *Cavatina*; Kreisler in Cadman's *From the Land of the Sky Blue Water*; or the young Heifetz in the Mendelssohn-Achron *On Wings of Song* and the Schubert-Wilhelmj *Ave Maria*? If one prefers a "heavyweight" example, which violinist under 45 (or perhaps over) can equal or surpass, with or without the artificial aid of modern electronics, the sound, sensitivity, and style of Kreisler's 1935 recording with Franz Rupp of Beethoven's ten sonatas for violin and piano?

The 20th-century revolution in violin mastery has fully matured and its benefits internationally disseminated. But is the spirit of meaningful, memorable violin art still continuing to rise, or has it begun to curve downward? For all the international proliferation of violinists possessing extraordinary violinistic equipment and studied musicianship in the final few decades of the 20th century, this writer opts for the negative point of view, at least in the collective sense.

Nicolò Paganini, the immortal revolutionary of violin technique

Was Paganini "The Greatest Violinist Who Ever Lived?"

In the annals of violin lore and tradition, one name more than any other conjures up visions of fingerboard legerdemain, a hedonistic lifestyle, and the quintessence of personal magnetism: PAGANINI!

There has been far more written about Nicolò Paganini (1782-1840) than any violinist in history. Allegations that he was 'the greatest violinist who ever lived' continue even into our era. Is this really so? How would Paganini sound to late 20th-century ears? Is it possible to make a realistic assessment of an artist who no one alive has ever heard, whose best-playing days were at least seven decades before the advent of primitive recording? And how can one go about making such an evaluation in the face of the untold thousands of words alleging so much that is contradictory, patently unknowledgeable, deliberately slanted to fantasy, and often 'pro' or 'anti' to an exorbitant degree? Thus, the sober researcher and scholar may well be both puzzled and frustrated by the excessive speculation with which he is confronted constantly. How can fact be separated from fiction?

Some may feel that any effort to solve the problem meaningfully is futile, particularly since we cannot bring Paganini back from wherever it is that violinists reside in the hereafter and ask him to play for us. However, while scientific proof is impossible, there exists sufficient material from which to draw some reasonable deductions that will lay to rest some of the more extravagant declarations concerning his performance— *so that Paganini can be seen in historical perspective according to the violinistic and musical standards of the 1990s.*

In addition to the generally reliable accounts of Paganini's contemporaries Schottky and Harrys (Fetis' are less dependable), significant contributions to the Paganini biographical bonanza are to be found in the meticulous research and detail of G.I.C. de Courcy's *Paganini, the Genoese* (1957); the polished, flowing prose of Jeffrey Pulver's *Paganini, The Romantic Virtuoso* (1936); the penetrating delvings of Arturo Codignola's *Paganini intimo* (1935); the colossal scope of the somewhat simplistic *Paganini* by Leslie Sheppard and Herbert Axelrod (1979); and even the comparatively superficial *Paganini* by Renée de Saussine (1954). Yet for all the invaluable data contained in these books, more remains to be said on the subject.

Carl Flesch, in his *Memoirs*, figuratively throws up his hands in despair at the "feuilletonistic gush from raving newspaper reporters, or...fantasies of undoubted literary value which, however, are beneath factual discussion." He adds,

> each of us has a different picture of this mysterious figure, so that our contemporary violin quacks may with impunity permit themselves to use Paganini's name as a signboard for their dubious reforms.

Then Flesch abruptly abandons the matter.

De Courcy states candidly in the preface to her comprehensive two-volume tome:

> In carrying out this task I have not attempted to appraise Paganini's influence on the world of music, preferring to leave this to the competence of the musical historian, since it is impossible to assess his place in the history of violin playing and at the same time present a full-scale narrative of his life... .

Then there is Joseph Wechsberg's *Glory of the Violin* (1972-1973), a beautifully-appointed, fluently written book which bluntly refers to Paganini as "the greatest fiddler of all times," and arbitrarily claims that

Nicolò Paganini

"he never played a wrong note." Clearly nothing can be learned from such mindless repetitions of 19th-century rodomontade. In similar vein is Alberto Bachmann's *An Encyclopedia of the Violin* (1925) which states uncritically:

> It is interesting, today, to review with all honesty the so-called evolution of the art of violin playing. Progress since Paganini died has been nil, and this is proved by the fact that no violinist who has since arisen has been his equal, for he was not alone a formidable mechanism, but a great artist who knew how to charm and touch his auditors as well.

Bachmann conveniently forgets that these "auditors" were weaned in the violinistic and, above all, musical standards existing in the 1810-1840 era. In this vein, a volume, *Paganini*, by John Sugden, written in 1980, is fancifully subtitled *Supreme Violinist or Devil's Fiddler*.

First, let us touch briefly—very briefly—on Paganini's life, since this is not intended as a comprehensive biographical survey. We could discuss Paganini's life for a week and not cover all of its inter-esting ramifications and nuances. It was a life of many triumphs, but it was also a life beset with turbulence, and ultimately, tragedy. Reading his numerous biographies can be fascinating but also frustrating because of massive contradictory information, much of which is patently unknowledgeable, unprofessional, and slanted toward fantasy. There was so much in his rich, if painful life, that is verifiable, there really is no need for fanciful embellishments such as alleging that his strings were made from the intestines of his murdered mistresses, or that when he played, the devil was at his elbow, or that he never missed a note.

Nicolò Paganini was born October 27, 1782, in Genoa. There is not too much known of his early years. His father Antonio was probably a dockworker; his mother an illiterate housewife. Both were said by Paganini to have been 'musical amateurs'. Nicolò received his first lessons from his father at age 5 1/2. It was not long before Antonio realized he had a bonafide prodigy on his hands. He was very strict with his sickly son, and the boy practiced from morning until night. Later he had 30 lessons with Giacomo Costa, which Paganini later stated were not really of any value. To all intents and purposes he was self-taught, abetted by the virtuosity he acquired on the guitar. He did spend several months studying composition with Ferdinand Paer. His early professional years were difficult, and it was not until he determined to break away from his menial position at the court of Lucca and concertize on his own, that his star began to rise.

To better understand Paganini's playing, it is necessary to investigate into the musical and performance standards of the time in which he lived and, most importantly, examine his compositions. Let us touch first upon the former.

It was an age which spawned many an eccentric instrumental virtuoso and vocalist. Among the violinists of that ilk were Giovanni Mane Giornovichi, generally called Jarnovick (1745-1804), a bizarre violinist-adventurer who was defeated twice by Viotti in fiddle-to-fiddle confrontation, but declared to be "the most elegant violinist to be heard before Paganini" by no less an authority than Domenico Dragonetti, the premier bass-viol master of his day. Anthony Boucher (1778-1861), who bore an extraordinary resemblance to Napoleon (which he exploited to the fullest), was another of the breed. Once he was received cordially by Beethoven. Celebrated as a player of acrobatic virtuosity, he often entertained by performing with his bow held the wrong way around, under the bridge, or with the violin behind his back. Franz Clement (1780-1842) premiered the Beethoven violin concerto in 1806, and on the same program played a set of variations with the violin held upside down.

A comic article could be written on the behavior of Italian orchestras in Paganini's time. Berlioz, in a relatively staid description, wrote that

> in all the theaters there is in front of the stage a black hollow filled with wretches blowing and scraping, as indifferent to what is being shouted on the stage as to what is being buzzed in the boxes and parterre, and possessed of but one thought—that of earning their supper. The assemblage of these poor creatures constitutes what is called an orchestra.

An Italian correspondent of the *Musical World* wrote in 1837:

> ...Italian orchestras are incapable of getting through even the notes of such operas as *Der Freischutz*, *Robert le Diable*, etc., not only from the difficulty of the keys in which they are written, but on account of the precision required in the performance of concert music.

Paganini encountered similar conditions in 1836 when he sought to reorganize and improve the Parma orchestra by eliminating the seniority system that sustained mediocrity and ignored ability. (The violinist was still smarting from an insult dealt him in 1806. In 1801 he had been first violinist in the *Cappella Nazionale del Potere Executivo*, an orchestra made up of Jacobinites, the democratically-minded younger musicians in Lucca. When, in 1806, this group merged with the *Cappella della Signoria*, an older organization with royalist traditions, he was put at the second desk.)

Despite the fact that he was a favorite of Princess Elise Bonaparte and, according to reports, one of a long list of her lovers, Paganini was thwarted completely by the political maneuverings of his enemies at court. Although he was one of the world's premier artists, his fee as a conductor was 1,146 francs a year. In comparison, the chef received 1,500 and his food; a professor of French or Latin, 1,200; the princess' physician, 4,000; and her personal reader, 2,000.

At that time, instrumental soloists and orchestral players were capable of ludicrous antics. An English writer in describing a performance of Angelica Catalani (1780-1849), a leading soprano of her time, states:

When she begins one of the interminable roulades up the scale, she gradually raises her body which she had before stooped to almost a level with the ground, until, having won her way with a quivering lip and chattering chin to the very topmost note, she tosses back her head and all its nodding feathers with an air of triumph; then suddenly falls to a note two octaves and a half lower with incredible aplomb, and smiles like a victorious Amazon over a conquered enemy.

As late as the 1830s, every type of affectation, gesture, and oafish gait was customary in Italy (but not abroad). In the context of such shenanigans, the specter of Paganini regaling his audiences with vaudevillian posturings and barnyard imitations does not seem abnormal. As a volatile Italian artist he knew the values of extroverted behavior. He became a master of public relations and tub-thumping hype, skillfully encouraging and 'milking' every colorful incident, far-fetched rumor, and myth concerning his private life, habits, and fictional adventures. The unvarnished phenomenon of his true personality and violinistic exploits should have been sufficient in themselves to attract mass audiences. In his defense, it should be stressed that he was painfully aware of the financial pitfalls facing the touring virtuoso. His colleague and rival Charles Philippe Lafont (1781-1839), a violinist of considerable reputation, once played a concert in Cologne netting the paltry sum of five francs. This sort of disaster could well befall any artist, no matter how celebrated. Paganini had suffered his share of economic hard knocks and utilized every device he could to avoid such catastrophe. He was not the only violinist who could run up and down the fingerboard at lightning speed, execute harmonics and left-hand pizzicatos, exaggerated finger stretches, etc.. Pietro Locatelli (1693-1746) had already paved the way in his *25* caprices and Auguste Frederick Durand (Duranowski, 1770-?) had set a living example from which the young Paganini could develop his own brand of fingerboard derring-do. (However, any violinist who can perform the Paganini *24* caprices can handle the Locatelli caprices with consummate ease, and Durand's compositions have made no impression upon violinistic history.) These two are to Paganini as talent is to genius. Thus in combining Paganini's instinctual expertise as a self-publicist with his amazing fingerboard feats, and adding to this the singular features of his appearance and dress, we have the supreme 19th-century mass-audience virtuoso—the ultimate heroic 'Knight of the Violin'.

Descriptions of Paganini abound. One, by Col. Maxwell Montgomery written in Genoa in 1814, states:

I have become acquainted with the most *outré*, most extravagant, and strangest character I ever beheld, or heard in the musical line...His long figure, long neck, long face, and long forehead, his hollow and deadly pale cheek, large black eyes, hooked nose and jet black hair, which is long and more than half hides his expressive Jewish face — all these rendered him the most extraordinary person I ever beheld. There is something scriptural in his 'tout ensemble' of the strange physiognomy of this uncouth and unearthly figure. He is very improvident, and very poor.

The *Leipzig Musikalische Zeitung* reports in 1829 what seems to be a well-considered description of both Paganini's appearance and external characteristics:

His external appearance in our eyes, exhibits nothing repellent or fearsome, but rather much that is actually attractive. He looks, it is true, pale and ill; but in no appreciable sense gloomy—and only when spiritually not excited does the least trace of the latter show in his expression. His dark eyes give evidence of something very affable in his character; in conversation he is very vivacious, though controlled by manly restraint; in manners he is courtly and polite, without concerning himself unduly about his formal outward appearance. His behavior is marked by an untroubled frankness and a certain modesty, combined with a seriousness and a consciousness of his own considerable abilities, that should belong to the constitution of every proper man. His gait, when he appeared publicly in Leipzig, was in no sense undecided, as seems to have been noticed in other places, but rather firm and rapid like that of a man anxious to avoid being late...Before commencing each of his pieces, he appears to pause for a few minutes to collect his thoughts, after which he proves himself, from the very first stroke, to be a true virtuoso...

Another report, written in 1829 by writer Friedrich von Matthieson, reads, "Paganini spent the night here and called on Goethe yesterday. I've just seen him getting into his carriage pale as a ghost, stooped, fearfully thin, with a Jewish cast of features."

According to legend, the violinist was a veritable Don Juan. Doubtless, there was some truth in this allegation. Yet, in 1829, at only 47, he wrote in a letter to his friend Germi that he had not touched a woman for more than two years—hardly the sex life of a Casanova.

But it is from Paganini's compositions that we can learn the essence of the man as a violinist. These fall into three general categories: the 24 caprices and the *Moto Perpetuo*, the six concertos (which include those that have been reconstructed), and the finger-twisting sets of variations, most of which, like the concertos, were published posthumously. I have omitted the violin-guitar duos, guitar pieces, and some extraneous chamber music and other works, since (with the possible exception of the *Barucaba* Variations) they do not represent Paganini's most basic contributions to violinistic development.

In perusing the caprices, we can see readily how Paganini, by the end of the first decade of the 19th century, far surpassed his predecessors and contemporaries in the use of *legitimate* technical devices without the addition of such spectacular embellishments as harmonics, double-harmonics, left-hand pizzicatos (save for a single variation in the 24th caprice), and passages simultaneously accompanied by left-hand finger pizzicatos. One need only compare his caprices with those of Locatelli, Gaviniès, Viotti, Fiorillo, Kreutzer, and Rode to realize immediately their superiority not only in matters of advanced technical challenges, but in sheer invention and imagination in basic musical substance. Composers such as Brahms, Liszt, Schumann, and Rachmaninoff, among others, recognized Paganini's talent as a composer and utilized some of his caprices as source material for works of their own. Schumann even wrote simplistic accompaniments for the complete 24. Later, Kreisler, Auer, and others were to provide piano accompaniments of more advanced nature to individual caprices. By his mid-20s the Genoese had contributed the monumental Opus 1 that revolutionized violin art. Future composers of wide musical latitude were enabled to employ his innovations to enhance their own technical horizons in composing violin works. There is no concrete evidence that any violinist, including Paganini, publicly performed the caprices during their composer's lifetime. However, by the mid-1840s, we learn that the ten-year-old Wieniawski played several of them for his teacher Lambert Massart, which would seem to indicate that the caprices were known and studied prior to 1845. Incidentally, how many of our finest contemporary violinists by age 25 (or for that matter, at any age) would be capable of composing a cycle of caprices comparable in creativity to those Paganini

Henri Wieniawski at age 9, with his teacher Joseph Lambert Massart

composed by his mid-20s?

The concertos, though even more technically encompassing than the caprices, generally adhere to an established pattern, as do a multitude of operas composed in that period, and are somewhat narrower in range of pure inventiveness than the caprices. Nonetheless they transcend tremendously the concertos of Kreutzer, Rode, Tartini, Viotti, and others, not only in sheer technical challenge and theatrical bravura, but in dramatic content, particularly in the operatic slow movements. And we find that, while simply constructed in violinistic vernacular, they resemble closely the major operas of Rossini, Bellini, and Donizetti. To label Paganini's concertos as "poor music" (as I was taught by some older violinists when I was a youngster) is tantamount to berating the best Italianate inspirations and style of the era. Or it may merely reveal the 'critics' to be violinists who may have been unable to handle Paganini's challenges, and were possibly envious of those who could.

The third group comprises the most difficult but most inconsequential, even banal, theme-and-variation specialties —the majority of which are based on themes by other composers, some operatic or popular airs and anthems: *I Palpiti* (Rossini), *Nel cor piu non mi sento* (Paisiello), *Carnival of Venice, God Save the King, Maestoso* Sonata, *Moses* Fantasy on the G-string (Rossini), *Sentimental* (Haydn), *St. Patrick's Day*, and many more. Though Paganini was certainly not the first to devise showy variations, it can be said that his stunning successes with such works inspired an endless stream of similar efforts by violinist-composers through the time of Sarasate (1844-1908), and even later.

Inasmuch as Paganini in his maturity avoided performing publicly any works but his own, his compositions represent not only the degree of his creative talents, but his limitations as a *violinist* and *artist*. Masterworks by Bach, Mozart, and Beethoven, as well as the notable older works of Corelli, Vivaldi, Tartini, and Locatelli, were available to him. He is reported to have enjoyed playing Beethoven quartets, including the late ones—in private for relaxation. When drawing up his organizational plan for his proposed Parma ducal orchestra (which never materialized), he suggested, among other things, that the conductor keep the string players in good form by practicing the 12 Beethoven quartets. Thus we see that Paganini, so often caviled as a superficial showman, possessed the artistic acumen to recognize the eminence of Beethoven's works, whereas his rival Ludwig Spohr (1784-1859), a pillar of respectable musicianship, did not at all appreciate or understand Beethoven's chamber music. Here we have a dichotomy between Paganini the ostentatious virtuoso and Paganini the musician of good taste.

It is logical to assume that Paganini disdained playing the music of his contemporary violinist-composers like Kreutzer, Rode, *et al*, because they were comparatively too elementary for him to display his far superior technical accomplishments. And, possibly, he shunned the existing masterworks because he sensed that he was not master of those qualities that would win him renown (and a monetary windfall) in the loftier musical spheres. But whatever the reasons, Paganini chose to confine his efforts to his own compositions, with but few exceptions. Thus, he placed artistic restrictions upon himself that precluded any possibility of his being comparable or superior to those future violinists who possessed both sheer violinistic virtuosity plus the special qualities of musical discipline, tonal suavity and

Vieuxtemps in his youth

Paganini's left hand and his constantly pure intonation were to me astonishing. But in his compositions, and his execution I found a strange mixture of the highly genial and childishly tasteless, by which one felt alternately charmed and disappointed, so that the impression left as a whole was, after frequent hearing, by no means satisfying to me.

Conversely, violinists Charles Dancla (1817-1907) and Henri Vieuxtemps were awed by Paganini's performance — but they were teenagers at the time. Heinrich Wilhelm Ernst (1815-1865), who became a disciple of Paganini and ultimately a rival in the latter's declining years and was, more than any other, his immediate violinistic heir, did not analyze Paganini's playing in writing. Nevertheless he was intimately acquainted with his performance, played for and was advised by Paganini on several occasions, and fashioned his own playing in the image of his Italian idol. Ernst did write in an 1837 letter to his brother: "I must say to you that Paganini is no longer the same man, that he has lost much." Karol Lipinski (1790-1861) greatly admired Paganini, and in 1818, early in his career, was aided by

diversity, sensitivity, expressiveness of phrasing, and stylistic panache required for elite performances of masterworks. Ignatz Moscheles, a leading piano virtuoso of the 19th century (1794-1870), who at first was astonished by Paganini's playing (and later wearied of its narrow scope), describes a rare performance of the violinist in Beethoven's *Kreutzer* Sonata as a "desecration." Aside from Moscheles's status as a highly respected professional of his day, he also had the opportunity to have heard such violinists as Joachim, Vieuxtemps, Wieniawski, and other post-Paganini luminaries in this and similar works, so that his views can be considered knowledgeable and comprehensive in the 1815-1870 era. And he was not a violinist likely to have had a personal axe to grind.

Both Liszt (1811-1886) and Schumann (1810-1856) were tremendously impressed and influenced by Paganini and regarded him as the archetypal instrumental virtuoso. Spohr, often considered Paganini's most eminent rival, was nevertheless a scrupulously honest musician and commentator. Though admittedly completely diametrical to Paganini as an artist, Spohr's evaluation merits far more consideration than the babblings of most unknowledgeable writers and observers of the time. He wrote,

Ole Bull, a theatrical violinistic personality in the sensationalist mold

Paganini's generosity in agreeing to perform publicly with him Kreutzer's Concerto for Two Violins. He tells of his amazement of Paganini's reading at sight two of Lipinski's difficult Caprices, Op. 10, playing on the Pole's violin, an instrument considerably different from his own. Incidentally, Lipinski stated that for an 1818 appearance in Padua,

> Paganini himself sold tickets, following which he locked the door with a key so that no one could enter the concert hall without paying the entrance fee; only then did he come onto the stage. During the intermission he sold tickets at half price since those who came late could hear only the second part of the concert.

Paganini could be artistically generous as he was to Lipinski, and financially generous, as with his munificent 20,000-franc gift to the needy composer Hector Berlioz (1803-1869). Throughout his life, instances of both profligate extravagance and parsimony abounded. And Paganini's exploits as a confirmed gambler are well documented in his many biographies.

Various observers of both yesteryear and modern times have sought to attribute Paganini's extraordinary technical feats to alleged physical peculiarities such as double-jointedness and abnormal flexibility of fingers, over-sized hands, an unorthodox stance, or an unusual manner of holding the violin. Several years ago Dr. Myron R. Schoenfeld wrote,

> there is good reason to believe that Paganini was afflicted with (or perhaps it would be more correct to say endowed with) Marfan's Syndrome. The long, sinuous, hyper-extensible fingers of his left hand gave his fingers an extraordinary range of motion and freedom of independent movement on the fingerboard, while the laxness of the wrist and shoulder of his right upper extremity gave him the pliancy required for masterful bowing.

Dr. Schoenfeld then cites Paganini's "cadaverous appearance" as further proof that the violinist had Marfan's Syndrome.

Apparently the good doctor made his judgments from the surfeit of the violinist's portraits, which in the main were imaginative artists' conceptions. True, Paganini was a picturesque personality who did all he could to emphasize his eerie, skeletal image in dress and carriage. And who knows, he might have had Marfan's Syndrome along with his heritage of tuberculosis, coli-

Camillo Sivori, star pupil of Paganini, virtuoso and teacher of Fortunato Francescatti, Zino's father

Courtesy Joseph Gold

tis (probably connected with emotional problems), and syphilis contracted from amorous escapades. A mercury "cure" for syphilis is said to have accounted for the loss of his teeth and his subsequent inability to eat properly, resulting in his further emaciation. But while his infirmities undoubtedly sapped his strength to a serious degree, it is not logical to believe that either these debilitations or any supposed physical advantages contributed to his technical accomplishments. Rather, it is more logical to assume that Paganini achieved supremacy despite his physical handicaps.

Paganini's son Achille testified that "Nicolò's fingers were one-half inch longer than a medium-sized hand"—a dimension scarcely to be compared to the outsized hands of Itzhak Perlman. Insofar as the factors of size and pliancy of the left hand and fingers are concerned, as emphasized so strongly by Dr. Schoenfeld and others, these factors are practically nullified inasmuch as today, petite teenage girls with comparatively small hands and fingers often perform and record Paganini's caprices, concertos, and other of his works with exceptional virtuosity. And above all, we know that in our time, and even before, a sizeable roster of bravura-type violinists whose fingers, stance, instrumental position, or muscular flexibility are and were in no way unique or aberrant, performed many or most of the published Paganini compositions. Among them have been Wilhelmj, Prihoda, Kubelik, Vecsey, Burmester, Ricci, Kogan, Menuhin, Rabin, Accardo, Francescatti, Renardy, Pikaisen, Sitkovetsky, Kremer, and Perlman. In the immediate Paganini periphery were his gifted emulators: Heinrich Wilhelm Ernst, Ole Bull, and Camillo Sivori, the last being the Italian's only pupil of note. (According to Schottky, the Neapolitan cellist Gaetano Ciandelli, sometimes called a Paganini pupil, was entrusted by Paganini with a 'secret' formula by which a mediocre player could make miraculous improvement in a few days. Despite the data gleaned from Paganini's letters and the accounts of his numerous biographers, the so-called secret has never been revealed.)

Heifetz, too, in his youth performed many Paganini pieces. Příhoda even embellished Paganini's *Nel cor piu non mi sento* Variations with extra double-harmonics and left hand finger pizzicatos. And Kreisler, in his stunning transcriptions of *Le Streghe, Non Piu Mesta,* and *I Palpiti,* furnished them with additional double-harmonics, whirlwind arpeggios of sixths, and fingered-octave scales, rendering them more difficult than the originals. These are frequently programmed by modern technicians.

There is ample evidence to prove that Paganini had his share of concerts in which he played poorly. At his first concert in Strasbourg he broke down twice and was forced to interrupt his performance until he regained his composure. His first concert in Brussels was another case in point. When in bad form he would omit some of the variations in his theme-and-variations finger-twisters. Despite his inconsistent reception in Belgium, his direct posthumous influence on subsequent Belgian star violinists (de Bériot, Léonard, Vieuxtemps, Thomson, and the Belgian-trained Wieniawski) was extremely significant. Harrys reports that when Paganini performed in provincial towns, realizing he was not in concert form, he would say, "If I were in Paris or London today, I should never play." Many of his concerts had to be postponed or canceled for reasons of illness or fatigue, and some took place that should have been canceled. It must be realized that violinistic inconsistency was a way of life before Heifetz set the standards which we take for granted today. Nineteenth-century violinists, somewhat like the old knights-errant of chivalry, roamed from country to country seeking fame and fortune. They traveled uncomfortably from town to town in horse-drawn coaches over dusty, bumpy roads;

put up their own posters and placards; hired, rehearsed, and conducted mostly sub-standard orchestras to accompany them; ate the equivalent of restaurant food for months at a time; and played in drafty or overheated halls. It is documented that Vieuxtemps once performed for an audience of 16 in one provincial town—not at all unusual, particularly for lesser-known artists. One can only imagine the vicissitudes of their social lives while on tour. Only in metropolitan centers where they would give a series of concerts could they expect satisfactory conditions.

A number of the more musically sophisticated authorities who heard Paganini, expressed amazement upon first doing so, but later lost their initial enthusiasm after the Italian's 'bag of tricks' had begun to pall through repetition. His second tour of England was dotted with reduced attendance, and his appearance as a violist, while well received on the musical level, could be no substitute for the spectacular violinistics with which his name was associated.

If Paganini were "the greatest violinist who ever lived," as claimed by so many commentators of various eras, he must, of necessity, have been superior to those who followed him. Though we can certainly fault Paganini for not performing publicly the masterworks of Bach, Mozart, and Beethoven that were available during his lifetime, we cannot berate him for not playing works in styles that had not yet been conceived. Would we consider a modern violinist who specialized *only* in Paganini pieces as a candidate for the title of *the greatest violinist who ever lived*, regardless of how impeccably he played them? I think not. We have more than a few superb players of Paganini works who definitely do not qualify for that eminence. To be "the greatest," an artist would have to be supreme in far more than the limited (if exciting) world of Paganiniana. And it stands to reason that no violinist who ever lived could or can be all things to all men in every area of violin art. As shown by the myriad of contradictory impressions of his playing, Paganini was no exception.

If one accepts the premise that the violin is an instrument of song closest to the human voice, it must follow that a violinist's tonal production and projection is one of the vital factors in making assessments. Where does Paganini stand in this area of violin art? Depending on which of his contemporaries we prefer to believe, his sound was "electrifying," "warm," or "icy cold." In his legendary head-to-head competition with Lafont, Paganini admits that Lafont probably excelled in beauty of sound. And let us remember that this judgment was made according to standards existing in the first quarter of the 19th century, long before the introduction of modern vibrato production and usage. Yet, Fétis claims that "Paganini used vibrato in melodic passages, especially on the last three strings" (whichever they are!). Chorley, in speaking of the tenor Tamberlik, attributes to him "the habit of vibration—a relic of Paganini's treatment of his strings." Nonetheless it would be the height of naiveté to assume that Paganini was a master of modern multiple-vibrato usage, or that he could produce the new intensity of sound that only developed some 40 years after his death, as introduced by Wieniawski (among the super-star violinists) and further developed by Kreisler, Elman, Heifetz, and others. Can we realistically assert that a violinist could be "the greatest of all time" without a gorgeous, sensuous sound included in his arsenal of equipment?

What about musicianship? Though Paganini was well acquainted with Beethoven's music, he never attempted to publicly perform the violin concerto, a feat which many violinists and critics consider to be the acid test for proving musicianship, as well as violin mastery. What about the elegance and sensitivity of Mozart, the majesty of concept and intellectual discipline demanded by the Bach solo sonatas and partitas—all music available in Paganini's heyday which he scrupulously avoided? How would he negotiate those complex segments of the Brahms concerto that are patently unviolinistic, the singing double-stops of Kreisler's *Caprice Viennois*, the romantic narrative of the Tchaikovsky and Sibelius concertos, the brusque, jagged Magyar imagery of the Bartók concerto and solo sonata, or the limpid impressionism of Debussy? One could go on and on in this vein. How, then, can anyone aver that he was the "greatest of all time" when common sense tells us that Paganini was not equipped to perform violinistic and musical challenges that developed long after his death?

If, by now, we can accept that fact that Paganini was a limited artist, and assuredly not the "greatest" who ever lived, how can we assess his contributions in historic perspective? Beyond doubt, *he was the most notorious and most sensational.* Accounts of his life and career will ever be a treasure trove of information and misinformation calculated to fascinate and intrigue the reader. It is sometimes said that Paganini was a violin school unto himself. While this is true in the sense that he extended left-hand technique and dazzling virtuoso

effects, and in his era was the fingerboard gymnast incarnate, his ties to his Italian roots were irrevocable and his music, Italianate to the core.

The flame of Paganini's art still burns brightly. From the reservoir of innumerable violin études and caprices, with but rare exception, it is only Paganini's that are still performed publicly. In just about every major international violin competition, one or more Paganini caprices are obligatory for the contestants. Why his caprices rather than any others? Because as a collective entity they remain a definitive violinistic challenge nearly two centuries after their composition, and the skill with which they are devised, and in many instances, the basic thematic material, is superior. In our century an increasing number of violinists have recorded the entire set: Renardy, Ricci, Rabin, Perlman, Accardo, Mintz, Zimmerman, Majeske, Midori, Pikaisen, A. Markov, Paetsch, Milanova, Vardi (on viola), and Zukovsky are among them. A veritable legion of others have recorded and/or played individual caprices on their recital programs.

In years past, the First and Second Paganini Concertos were almost always performed by violinists whose talents and musicality emphasized the gymnastic more than the masterworks (Kubelik, Vecsey, Příhoda, and a host of others). But one or more of them became an integral part of the repertoire of such violinist-musicians as Menuhin, Francescatti, Grumiaux, Szeryng, Kogan, Oistrakh, and Perlman, with Accardo having recorded all six since modern scholarship has located and reconstructed Nos. 3-6. In major competitions, often as not, Paganini's Concerto No. 1 in D is on the list of elective concertos, whereas the admirable bravura ones of Ernst, Vieuxtemps, and Wieniawski are included far less frequently. And the variations, too, are fairly familiar in contemporary recital programs.

Paganini—the young Bonapartist activist, the roué, the inveterate gambler, the vaudevillian, the confirmed adventurer, the chronically ill individual—was nevertheless a legendary artist. Perhaps his field was comparatively limited, as was Chopin's in comparison to Brahms's. But if his compositions were simplistic, they were also grandly conceived — heroic, dramatic, exciting, imaginative, and instrumentally challenging. Within the confines of his realm, the judgment of history verifies that Paganini was a musician of genius, and his heritage to his successors and, indeed, to the world of modern violin art, is unique and imperishable.

The young Eugène Ysaÿe, glory of the Belgian Violin School, who was to become one of the most individual violinistic personalities of all time

Eugène Ysaÿe

In the final quarter of the 19th century, Joseph Joachim and Pablo de Sarasate were the reigning potentates of the violinistic world—each totally unlike the other in musical attitudes, instrumental accomplishment, and repertorial preferences. To Joachim, such matters as profundity of spirit and musical integrity were paramount, superseding the more mundane considerations of mere antiseptic technical perfection and tonal luster. The elegant Sarasate, with his lightning dexterity, superficial musical inclinations, and euphony of sound, stood at the opposite pole. Neither played with the vibrant intensity of tone that was destined soon to become a vital determinant in the development of 20th-century violin art. The world of music was ready for a new king of the violin; one who could combine technical mastery with a novel beauty of sound, and furthermore, add a dimension of impassioned emotionalism previously unheard—a violinist capable of expressing the aura of a romantic age that was now in fullest maturity. Such a one was to appear in the person of the remarkable Belgian violinist Eugène Ysaÿe, who, more than any other, symbolized the violinistic bridge between the 19th and 20th centuries.

Ysaÿe was a gargantuan figure who represented, both as man and musician, the very embodiment of the uninhibited, freewheeling romantic ethos, the ideal fusion of violinistic swashbuckler and poet, a musical story-teller of inimitable skill. Carl Flesch, a master analyst of violin playing, auditor of innumerable performers, great and small, from the days of Joachim and Sarasate to the era of Heifetz, had this to say of Ysaÿe in his *Memoirs*: "The most outstanding and individual violinist I have heard in all my life." High praise, indeed, but it was echoed by many others. This from Joseph Szigeti: "My memories of Eugène Ysaÿe are particular-

ly precious and come to me with the same kind of vividness that the impact of his playing seems to have left on all who had the elating experience of hearing him."

Fritz Kreisler came under the Ysaÿe spell, and remained a close friend and admirer throughout the years. He had this to say: "It was Eugène Ysaÿe, however, and not Joseph Joachim, who was my idol among violinists... ."

In Liège, Belgium, on July 16, 1858, a child destined to become one of the world's greatest violinistic personalities, was born to Nicholas Ysaÿe and Marie-Thérèse Sottiaux (who were officially wed two years later). He was baptized Eugène-Auguste.

The boy received his first lessons from his father at age five. Then he was taught by Désiré Heynberg and Rodolphe Massart. Ysaÿe made his first public appearance at seven in a small concert, but did not win much attention. Unlike so many of the illustrious violinists, he was never a wunderkind or anything close to it. In fact, at one time, the boy was asked to leave the Liège Conservatory on the pretext that he was never likely to become a violinist.

In 1873 Ysaÿe studied privately with Wieniawski in Brussels, receiving exactly 12 lessons. (He considered Wieniawski to be the greatest violinist he had ever heard.) Then, Vieuxtemps is said to have heard the boy practicing while walking past the Ysaÿe house and, thoroughly impressed by his talents, became his sponsor. Vieuxtemps succeeded in obtaining a government subsidy for Ysaÿe which enabled him to continue his studies, highlighted by private lessons with Vieuxtemps himself.

In physical appearance Ysaÿe had become an imposing man. He was nearly six feet tall, broad-shouldered, and with smooth, handsome features. His eyes were blue and clear, and his mane of thick black hair combed well back from his broad brow further confirmed his image of the typical 19th-century artist. His tendency toward obesity began early in his career, but as he expanded his presence grew even more commanding, though this seriously affected his health.

In 1879 Ysaÿe played in Cologne where he met Ferdinand Hiller, who introduced him to Joseph Joachim. Hiller advised him to go to Frankfurt. There he made the acquaintance of Joachim Raff and Clara Schumann, the latter performing Beethoven's C-minor Sonata with him. In 1880 he was appointed concert-

Ysaÿe and his chamber music partner, pianist Raoul Pugno

master of Bilse's Orchestra in Berlin for a year.

He toured Norway in 1881 (allegedly under the management of Ole Bull's son), and in 1883 played a concert at the Paris Conservatoire under Edouard Colonne. In Paris he became a friend of César Franck and moved in a musical circle that included d'Indy, Chausson, and Debussy. Subsequently, Franck dedicated his great violin and piano sonata to Ysaÿe, who played it at his own wedding, and became its prime interpreter. In 1886 he became a professor at the

Brussels Conservatoire, a post he held until 1897.

As early as 1882 Ysaÿe began his appearances in Russia, which he visited some 15 times throughout the course of 30 years, playing in most of the large cities. Ysaÿe, like Vieuxtemps and Wieniawski before him, popularized the Belgian School in that part of the world, and their collective influence is still to be found in the repertoire and training of the so-called Soviet School. (Except for his habitual portato, a bowing stroke Ysaÿe particularly disliked, David Oistrakh's playing had far more similarities to that of Ysaÿe than does that of the outstanding Belgian virtuoso, the late Arthur Grumiaux.) Here, also, the violinist played sonatas with Anton Rubinstein, a kindred leonine spirit, and with Annette Essipova, wife of Leschetizky. His introductory recital pieces to Russia, all lifelong staples of his repertoire, included the concertos of Wieniawski (No. 2 in D-minor), Mendelssohn, Vieuxtemps (Nos. 4 & 5), the latter's *Ballade and Polonaise*, Saint-Saëns's *Introduction and Rondo Capriccioso*, and Ernst's *Hungarian Airs*, as well as some of his own short compositions.

Ysaÿe's career as a soloist was not easily attained; only after his sensational success in Vienna in 1890, when he was already 32 years old, did his reputation on the highest international level become securely established. (This was also the case with Sarasate and Kreisler, despite their youthful laurels.) He had slowly and painfully worked his way up the ladder from playing in cafes to respected concertmaster rank, to provincial concerts and occasional metropolitan appearances, to world status. This is in direct contradistinction to the overwhelming number of fine violinists whose adult careers stemmed from their child prodigy publicity and renown.

In 1894 he founded the Ysaÿe Concerts in Brussels, which he conducted. The orchestra featured many notable soloists and was an outlet for the performance of a considerable number of new works by French and Belgian composers. During this period he founded the Ysaÿe String Quartet with Mathieu Crickboom (his pupil) as second violin (later replaced by Alfred Marchot), Leon van Hout, viola, and Josef Jacob, cello. Chamber music playing became a lifelong obsession with Ysaÿe, and he participated in innumerable private chamber music soirées through the years (in which he sometimes played viola) with such stellar figures as Casals, Kreisler, Thibaud, and Pugno, in addition to the public concerts of his own quartet which in 1893 premiered Debussy's Quartet in Paris.

As a quartet player, Ysaÿe, like Joachim, Kreisler,

Elman, and more recently Heifetz, tended to dominate his colleagues with the singularity of his sound, the individual character of his style, and his expressive idiosyncrasies. The listener was always aware that he was being seduced by the sovereign-ranking artistry of Ysaÿe, and that both the composition and the other musicians were more or less an appendage to the fact. His violin-piano recitals with the formidable pianist Raoul Pugno, were also to a noticeable degree beset by this dichotomy. Ysaÿe, an elemental force, was not inherently geared to team playing. Flesch mentions that in 1902, when he heard Ysaÿe in Tchaikovsky's A-minor Trio with the celebrated pianist Busoni and the prominent cellist Hugo Becker, in the realm of sheer performance, the violinist "was still in every respect superior to his partners."

In 1894 Ysaÿe made his triumphant American debut, and in 1898 was offered the post of conductor with the New York Philharmonic to succeed Anton Seidl. This he declined. It was not until 1918 that he accepted a regular podium appointment as conductor of the Cincinnati Orchestra, a position he held until 1922.

Ysaÿe's favorite violin was a Guarnerius del Gesù, though he owned the magnificent *Hercules* Stradivarius which he customarily carried with him as a reserve instrument in the event of a broken string during a concert. The *Hercules* was stolen from his dressing room during a concert in St. Petersburg and never seen again. He also owned an excellent J.B. Guadagnini, with which he had begun his career, a Joseph Guarnerius filius Andreae, a Maggini, a superb George Chanot (a copy of his del Gesù), and several outstanding French violins. His extensive bow collection included Tourtes, Peccates, Piques, and Nurnbergers. When teaching during his later years, he used Sartory bows which were adjusted with a thick rubber grip. This undoubtedly provided a more secure bow hold to reinforce the shaky condition of his right arm. He called it the "banana."

Despite his years of foreign concertizing and his sojourn in Cincinnati, Ysaÿe lived most of his life in Belgium and was an ardent Belgian patriot. Flesch states that "his racial membership cannot be definitely established," although Ysaÿe's son, Antoine, in the biography of his father which he wrote with Bertram Ratcliffe, took great pains to assert that such names as Ysaÿe (Isaiah) and other names of biblical origin, were commonly used among people of "Christian descent." However, I have known several musicians, intimates of Ysaÿe, who vigorously echoed Flesch's not-so-subtle insinuation.

The noted American critic, James Gibbons Huneker (who was not Jewish), states in a letter to Pitts Sanborn, music critic of the New York Globe, written in 1917: "Ysaÿe—spell it Isaiah—was of Jewish origin in Belgium. Thirty years ago his brother was called Jacob Ysaÿe, a pianist. Now he is James." Apparently Huneker meant Eugène's older brother referred to as Joseph in the Ysaÿe-Ratcliffe biography, who was said to have studied the violin in his youth, rather than his younger brother, Theophile, who became an accomplished pianist. In any case, the matter would appear speculative.

Ysaÿe was wed on September 28, 1886 to Louise Bourdeau de Courtrai, by whom he had three sons and two daughters. She died in 1924, and in 1928, in his 70th year, he married a former pupil, Brooklyn-born Jeanette Dincin, who was 36 years his junior. He died on May 12, 1931, shortly before his 73rd birthday.

The life of Ysaÿe is comprehensively (though perhaps at times over-discreetly) related in the Ysaÿe-Ratcliffe biography, to which, shortly before the death of Antoine in 1979, some peripheral material was added. And the mammoth Ysaÿe exposition by the Soviet writer Lev Ginsburg, replete with a veritable galaxy of photographs, both iterates and expands the Ysaÿe-Ratcliffe version.

It is not the purpose of this comparatively short chapter to compete with those lengthy biographical accounts, but rather to investigate more closely the actual performing style of Ysaÿe, and to offer some additional comments on his role as a composer. Fortunately, my own personal experience as a violinist offers an insight into the phenomenon of Ysaÿe, the violinist.

In the mid-1930s, while in my teens, I spent two years under the tutelage of Alfred Megerlin (originally Megerlein), a turn-of-the-century pupil of Ysaÿe. Megerlin (1880-1940), listed in Alberto Bachmann's *Encyclopedia of the Violin*, had come to America in 1914, and after a limited solo career, was concertmaster of the New York Philharmonic, the Minneapolis Symphony, and the Los Angeles Philharmonic. When I began my studies with him, it was obvious that he was already suffering from the competition of Russian-trained violinists who were rapidly displacing the earlier-trained players by virtue of their superior vibrant expressiveness and more contemporary musicality.

The significance of my training with Megerlin lies in the fact that he had absorbed, and consequently transmitted to his pupils, the stylistic mannerisms, fingerings, bowings, and violinistic aura of Ysaÿe, totally unfiltered by any original ideas or alterations of his own.

Furthermore, as with many teachers of that era, his teaching involved force-feeding his pupils the fingerings and bowings he himself had been taught, with scant regard for differences in hand and finger size or other physiological considerations. Today, the more advanced pedagogues encourage pupils to think for themselves. Both systems have their positive and negative attributes. Megerlin's training helped to preserve valuable stylistic idiosyncrasies and details of phrasing at the expense of the pupil's individual enterprise and sense of revelation; the modern way spurs creative thinking on the part of the pupil, but all too often results in fingerings and bowings that may be logical and scientifically correct but not conducive to beauty of expression or stylistic eclat.

In any case, my studies with Megerlin, geared to turn-of-the-century precepts, did

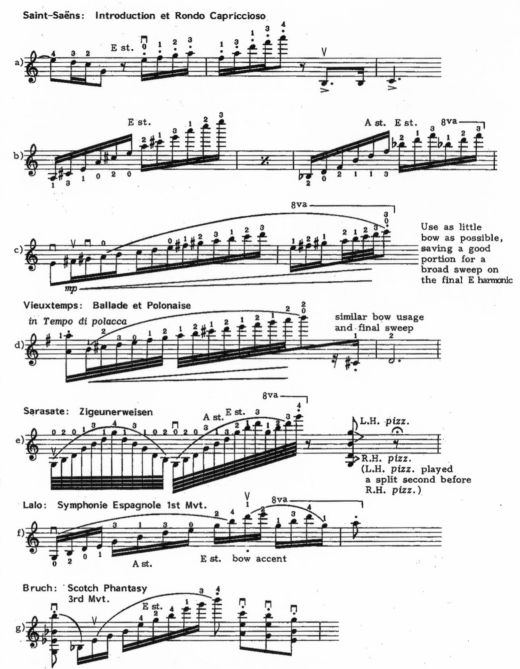

Examples of Ysaÿe's individualistic fingerings and bowings

reveal to me much of Ysaÿe's violinistic philosophy and style of execution. True, this training was probably not advantageous to my own instrumental and musical development in view of the newer standards that were inevitably coming into fashion, but my exposure to the Ysaÿe-through-Megerlin methodization was a thoroughly fascinating experience; one I have never regretted.

Megerlin paid lifelong homage to two deities:

God and Ysaÿe, though not necessarily in that order.

One day at a lesson I delicately twitted him about the comparative abilities of Ysaÿe and Heifetz. Like most of my generation I had come to believe that Heifetz represented the pinnacle of violin art. Megerlin, deadly serious, thought for a moment, then said, "Eh bien, Heifetz is like the Empire State Building" (then the world's tallest skyscraper). "But," he added with a gleam of utter conviction in his eye, "Ysaÿe was like a mountain."

Example of Ysaÿe's Bow Replenishing

Corelli-Leonard: La Folia

Bruch: Scotch Phantasy
2nd Mvt.

*Replenish Bow

Vieuxtemps: Concerto No. 5

Vieuxtemps: Concerto No. 5

Mendelssohn: Concerto in E Minor (3rd Mvt.)

Lalo: Symphonie Espagnole (Rondo)

ble on the E-string. We must remember that it was during Ysaÿe's era that the old gut E-strings, which so often broke during a concert, were replaced by the far more brilliant wire E-strings. Ysaÿe, for one, made maximum use of these new, superior strings, and devised his fingerings accordingly. I have provided some examples herein. Violinists may find these fingerings somewhat bizarre and militating against smoothness of bowing in string crossings, but Ysaÿe was comparatively unconcerned about the initial, unclimactic notes in a run, and used his bow to abet the final sweep. I can assure the reader that once a violinist gets this system in his fingers, it makes sense, and has a certain logic and practicality of its own (Examples *a* through *n*).

It is interesting to compare Ysaÿe with Heifetz in this matter of spontaneity of fingering, bowing, and interpretive changes from one performance to another. Whereas Ysaÿe was as free as a bird on the wing, Heifetz was punctiliously faithful to his own pre-set fingerings and bowings during each performance.

Ysaÿe sought to produce added brilliance through detonative up-bows in the upper part of the bow (for example, second bar of *j*), and in rapid passages would often crisply slap the up-bow notes of the group, at or near the tip of the bow (example *k*). For instance, Ysaÿe

According to Megerlin (and this has been confirmed by many observers), Ysaÿe seldom repeated the same fingerings and bowings in *lyrical passages* from one concert to the next. But this did not, of course, generally apply to rapid passage-work. In the latter he strove for a crackling, whiplash effect, often using devices that are little known or practiced today. One of his favorite ploys was playing as many notes of a passage as possi-

24

would employ this slapping (i.e., whipping) stroke (which he had learned from Wieniawski) on the first note of each rapid triplet group in the *Scherzo-Tarantelle*, with devastating effect. Like most players of his day, Ysaÿe frequently used open strings, though unlike lesser artists, his employment of open strings was not for technical convenience, but to expand his already extraordinary palette of tonal color.

Another Ysaÿe device, one often used in his day by many violinists, was replenishing the bow (almost always, for practical purposes, the down-bow). One does not often see this utilized by leading contemporary artists. In replenishing the bow, Ysaÿe would draw a full-toned down-bow on a sustained note, then near the tip, suddenly relax the pressure, deftly and silently pull the bow back to mid-bow or a bit lower, and continue the down-bow with only a quick breathing space between the two strokes (example *i*). The visual effect of bow replenishing on the audience is at least equal to its moderate value as a tone-extender.

Flautato bowing was an important implement in the Ysaÿe bowing arsenal. In this stroke the bow is drawn gently across the strings near or over the fingerboard, which, if properly executed, produces a flute-like tone. Some modern artists use flautato occasionally, but not to the degree of Ysaÿe, who was a master of this type of bowing and used it particularly in evoking imagery in French Impressionistic music. His seamless legato was a model of fluency.

Slides, portamentos, and position changes were a key element in the yesteryear lexicon of musical expressivity. But whereas even first-rate violinists of the day were prone to produce mindless meowings of every conceivable concoction, the Ysaÿe slides, while undoubtedly excessive and strange to the modern ear, were a direct, sincere projection of his emotional make-up, generally tasteful and uniquely individual. The latter does not imply that other violinists, particularly those with Belgian and French schooling, did not use many similar devices, but the totality of his expressive usage of slides was quite unlike those of any other violinist, then or now.

Some of the favorite expressive finger portamentos utilized by Ysaÿe were downward, as from a second finger E on the A-string in the third position to a third finger D on the A-string in the first position, with a pronounced (but not ridiculously so!) slide; also descending slides with one finger. (David Oistrakh, too, employed one-finger downward slides, especially with

the first finger.) And Ysaÿe made use of upward one-finger slides.

His vibrato was a direct extension of his personality, and in the matter of intensity, a far cry from either the meager, infrequent shakings of Joachim, or the emotionally-limited, one-dimensional vibrato of Sarasate. Ysaÿe, in this regard, was descended from Wieniawski, and his vibrato, never crassly extroverted, was wondrously sensitive and diversified in speed and color. He often played lyric phrases with no vibrato at all, producing his so-called *white* tone, but this practice was artfully blended with an entire range of vibrato speeds which he applied for expressive purposes. (This is not to be confused with the practice of turning the vibrato off and on like a faucet, with no consideration for sustained or varied emotional projection, as with a number of the older Soviet-trained violinists.) Albert Spalding said of Ysaÿe: "His tone was not large, but it had an expressive quality impossible to describe." Conversely, Flesch described Ysaÿe's tone as "big and noble." This dichotomy of opinion between two important violinists as to the size of Ysaÿe's tone should not be surprising. Spalding was probably correct, since some observers were prone to equate erroneously the size of Ysaÿe's tone with the massive proportions of the man himself. The tempestuous, variable nature of the Belgian's art invited a divergence of opinion even among knowledgeable listeners, almost comparable to that concerning Paganini.

A capricious Ysaÿe hallmark was his practice of changing an occasional note or rhythmic pattern to suit his fancy (examples *l* and *m*). As a practitioner of spontaneity, he would submit to his mood of the millisecond with nary a qualm. Yet his aberrations remained in accord with the spirit of the music, if not its letter.

Together with a variegated use of vibrato, Ysaÿe's bowing, suave and polished in its best days, was a key factor in his kaleidoscopic tonal palette. He controlled the bow with only three fingers and the thumb, completely excluding the fourth finger.

After 1910, though Ysaÿe was scarcely in his mid-50s, his playing began to decline. His technical deterioration grew increasingly rapid, paced by a bow arm which had begun to quiver uncontrollably. Elman, for example, possessed remarkable bow control, especially in tonal production, into his mid-70s; and Milstein, even into his 80s, still enjoyed splendid bow control. Generally, among violinists, bowing facility tends to be the first technical element to retrogress, followed by the vibrato; however, this order is sometimes reversed.

Courtesy Carl F. Flesch, Jr.

Carl Flesch, a violin pedagogue and analyst with but few peers, and a soloist of note

Flesch states:

His contemporaries were never quite clear on the reasons for Ysaÿe's early decline as a violinist...According to my close observation, the fundamental cause...was that he did not use the little finger on his right hand at the nut where he clasped the bow with only three fingers and an iron-tight grip. He seemed ignorant of the importance of the little finger as the most active agent in the supination of the forearm at the lower half of the bow.

One can agree with Flesch that "the primary cause of the trembling bow is usually of a technical nature (i.e., physiological)." But Flesch may be incorrect in citing Ysaÿe's three-finger bow grip as the agent of his increasing bowing problems after the age of 50. The master had been suffering from diabetes for some years, and diabetic neuropathy could well have been the catalyst of his troubles. As his diabetic condition worsened he experienced difficulties even in shaving, and his right hand would shake while holding a glass of water.

By the time he was 60, Ysaÿe's years as a preem-

inent international touring artist were finished. In fact, his entire career barely exceeded 25 years—not long compared to most outstanding violinists.

George Bernard Shaw, writing in 1891, refers to Ysaÿe's temperament as "prodigiously unmanageable," in a critique which excoriates an Ysaÿe London performance of the Beethoven concerto, yet holds the violinist in awe as a "prodigy." Still, this temperament was precisely the element that made him unique, the phenomenon which dominated and shaped all the other facets of his art. And it was by no means consistently "unmanageable." Ysaÿe's temperament was not a vaudevillian appendage grafted onto his performance for sensationalism; it was inherent in the man himself.

Ysaÿe was a sensualist, a hedonist, if you will, a devotee of "wine, women, and song." His appetite for food and drink was enormous, later associated with his gross obesity, chronic diabetes, and phlebitis. This eventually necessitated amputation of the lower part of his right leg in 1929.

The Ysaÿe sensuality could be both flagrant and extremely sensitized, and the range of his sheer emotional inspiration has been rivalled by few violinists of any era. His playing ran the gamut of moods: joy, tenderness, passion, bluster, bravura, poesy, fantasy, and expansive lyricism. And underlying this panorama of dispositions was a strange smoldering character, like that of a volcano about to erupt into flames. Ysaÿe could also project a rare aura of melancholy, a quality that is practically non-existent today. At times he was capable of ridiculous mawkishness, outrageously overstepping the boundary between sincere sentiment and sentimentality. He also possessed a sense of healthy vulgarity which served to infuse his playing with the human touch. If ever an artist could be characterized as playing from the heart, it was Ysaÿe. When at his best, he could move his audience as profoundly as any violinist who ever lived; and it was not uncommon in those bygone days of extravagant emotional responses for individuals among his audience to break into audible sobs.

One can write reams and deplete the thesaurus of every adjective in attempting to describe the playing of Ysaÿe—all, to a large extent, an exercise in futility. But posterity is privileged to have inherited a priceless testament: the recordings he made in 1912 at age 54. These performances of 15 short numbers, happily of varied genre, provide irrefutable evidence that validates perfectly many of the descriptions and evaluations of Flesch, Hartmann, Gingold, Megerlin, and a legion of astute Ysaÿe contemporaries and intimates. Since corrective splicing was unknown in 1912, each take was a complete entity. The original label was Columbia. All

(Left to right) Henry Rensburg (stockbroker, chairman of the Royal Philharmonic of Liverpool and of the Liverpool Art Society, introduced Kreisler and Ysaÿe to each other), Ysaÿe and Kreisler

of the discs include Camille Decreus as the pianist-collaborator.

The performances portray a manner of playing that the younger generation of today can scarcely envision. From the first bar, one is transported into another world, another age. There is, of course, a temptation for the casual listener to make an adverse snap judgment, since admittedly, Ysaÿe's style takes a bit of getting used to. That would be a grievous error. Despite the comparatively primitive engineering and anachronistic musical peculiarities, the charm and inimitable personality vested in Ysaÿe's playing almost certainly will soon bring the unbiased listener under his spell. We must remember, too, that his larger-than-life artistry was not particularly well suited to the limitations of recording—nor was he an experienced recording artist.

Beginning with the Wagner-Wilhelmj *Prize Song* from *Die Meistersinger*, the superiority of Ysaÿe to his immediate contemporaries is obvious. The playing is extremely lyrical with a beguiling air of reverie. Here is a painter of sound pictures whose inner force is strong

enough to overcome a profusion of slides and some pitch insecurity. (Incidentally, the Ysaÿe slides are sincere expressions of his esthetic needs, unlike those yesteryear players who used slides to camouflage the dullness of their intrinsic vibrato-poor sound.) The Wagner-Wilhelmj *Albumblatt*, less profligate in slides, and despite some slight finger lapses, shows Ysaÿe's intonation to be basically true and solid. Already in this second disc we can appreciate the singularity of his tone which cannot be mistaken for that of any other artist. Fauré's *Berceuse*, less intense in sound than the *Albumblatt*, is a suave, soothing example of cantilena.

The Vieuxtemps *Rondino* is one of Ysaÿe's best and most revealing recordings. Here he exhibits a real virtuosic flair, with clean, sparkling scale passagework and striking rhythmic impulse. The lyric middle section is permeated with a sense of melancholy (as marked by the composer) in the unique Ysaÿe manner, then heats up fervidly and ultimately relaxes again. The principal *Rondino* theme is wonderfully piquant. A few brief cuts are made to enable the opus to fit the 12-inch 78 disc.

Another stylistically impressive recording is Ysaÿe's own Mazurka No. 3 in B minor (*Lointaine-Passé*), a zestful vignette in which his individuality as a composer clearly separates him from a veritable horde of ambitious, but essentially unoriginal, violinist-composers. Again we encounter the Ysaÿe melancholy, though light in texture. Surprisingly, his rhythms are not overly exaggerated in this comparatively loose format. Indeed, he indulges in less license than does Igor Oistrakh in his excellent recording made in the mid-1950s—at least in the main themes—and Ysaÿe's technique, while not immaculate, is highly respectable.

Kreisler's *Caprice Viennois* is another matter. After a spotty start, he settles into a plodding tempo bereft of buoyancy. The double-stops lack sufficient vibrance and the spirit of the music is ponderous. One cannot help but feel that here is a case of miscasting, and that Ysaÿe, in paying homage to his friend Kreisler (and taking advantage of the allure of a once immensely popular vignette) made an error in selection.

Of two Wieniawski Mazurkas, the *Obertass* is marvelously whimsical; an extra frill on the second long trill is partially obscured by the engineering. The *Menetrier* runs the gamut of delicate tenderness, warm affection, exuberance, and melancholy. These miniatures display the genius of Ysaÿe— his exquisite instinct for pacing, rubatos, rhythmic thrust, modal changes, phrasing, and variety of tonal color. One can only imagine the wonders he could achieve in his prime, on a good day, in a 30- to 40-minute romantic concerto or sonata suited to his temperament.

The Brahms-Joachim *Hungarian Dance* No. 5 reflects Ysaÿe's breadth of spirit; the opening theme played on the G-string is ruggedly virile, and the peppery interpretation fairly breathes elan. Chabrier's *Scherzo-Valse* (arranged by Loeffler) is another dashing performance. Ysaÿe displays excellent digital facility, audacious passagework, and a whip-like attack. (This worthy transcription, now forgotten by violinists, was played in the original piano version as an encore for several decades by Artur Rubinstein.) He also made recordings of Dvořák's *Humoresque*, Schubert's *Ave Maria*, the Schumann-Wilhelmj *Abenlied*, and his own lovely *Rêve d'enfant* (the last two unissued).

The final recording is an outstanding rendition of the third movement of the Mendelssohn concerto. Except for a few fleeting notes, the technical passages are impeccable and the bowing crisp or fluent as required. Remarkably impressive is Ysaÿe's insistence upon instilling *feeling* on notes that are generally tossed off as mere technical adjuncts. His velocity is exceptional and, at times, pianist Decreus is hard pressed to keep up with his tempo. It is interesting to compare this tempo with the three later recordings of this movement by Heifetz. The Ysaÿe version ranges from 174-190 (♩), with the final several bars exceeding metronomic speed. This slashing, galvanic ending is matchless! The 1920 Heifetz version hovers around 200, but conveys a somewhat frenetic haste; the 1949 version, noticeably more mature, registers 184-192; the 1959 version, 182-188. The last two are with orchestra. The Ysaÿe version is marginally truncated, obviously for 78 disc time considerations.

In addition to his solo recordings with piano, Ysaÿe, as conductor, recorded the Rimsky-Korsakov *Scheherazade* and Offenbach's *Orpheus in Hades* Overture with the Cincinnati Symphony when he was its music director. The violinists in the familiar segments are not named. It has been said that Ysaÿe himself was the violin soloist in the *Scheherazade*, if not the *Orpheus* as well. This, however, does not seem logical, since Columbia Records would scarcely make a secret of something that could sell additional thousands of records.

Even as late as 1912, Ysaÿe was a technician of agile facility though he never publicly performed any Paganini finger-twisters. Many of his compositions, particularly the six solo sonatas, bristle with technical difficulties of a type wholly germane to musical communication rather than superficial variations-on-a-theme gymnastics which overly pander to sensationalism. His transcription of Saint Saëns's *Caprice, d'apres l'Etude en forme de Valse*, Op. 52, No. 6 originally for piano (*Valse Caprice*), a bravura confection employing fingered octaves, lightning-like arpeggio passages, batteries of thirds and tenths, flying staccatos, etc., verifies the brilliance of his technical resources. (The *Valse Caprice* has also been a performance favorite of David Oistrakh, Kogan, and many other violinists.) Ysaÿe never performed his six sonatas publicly since they were composed around 1924, during his retirement, but he performed the *Valse Caprice* frequently during his active career with tremendous success, and in 1911, played the arduous Elgar concerto from memory.

As a romanticist par excellence, Ysaÿe was at his best in music of overt warmth and sentiment, and was prone to play classical music with the same grandiose gesture and elasticity. In such works as the concertos of Vieuxtemps (Nos. 4 and 5), Bruch (Nos. 1, 2 and the *Scottish Fantasy*), Mendelssohn, Saint-Saëns, Lalo (Concerto in F and *Symphonie Espagnole*), Wieniawski (No. 2), and shorter works in this genre, he was supreme. Ysaÿe never essayed the concertos of Tchaikovsky (composed in 1878) and Sibelius (composed in 1905), though both were available during his prime playing years, but he did finally elect to play the Brahms concerto (composed in 1878) late in his career, with mixed results. The Franck sonata, of course, is synonymous with Ysaÿe, and he played French music, the sonatas of Debussy, Lekeu, Chausson, and Fauré, among others, with surpassing style and piquancy.

Ysaÿe was an ardent champion of new French and Belgian compositions, but his enthusiasm sometimes exceeded his aesthetic discrimination, as when he commended the inferior, now-forgotten music of Emanuel Moor. (Pablo Casals was guilty, too, of this error in judgment.)

Through the years Ysaÿe taught or coached many pupils, some of the best known being Mathieu Crickboom, Josef Gingold, Alfred Dubois, Louis Persinger, Remo Bolognini, Michael Press, the noted composer Ernest Bloch, Franz Schorg, excellent leader of the Brussels String Quartet, and Henry Verbrugghen, later a prominent conductor. Nathan Milstein is often cited as an Ysaÿe pupil, but the two never really sustained a master-pupil relationship of any significant duration. Ysaÿe loved to teach, violin in hand, playing

Ysaÿe and his young pupil, Josef Gingold (circa 1929)

written by a galaxy of undistinguished romantic violinist-composers, even allowing for those traits of his works that are in some measure derivative.

The Ysaÿe creative muse is not always consistent, but it is seldom less than interesting and, at times, engages in flights of imagination that are capable of convincing the listener he is hearing music by a composer with a highly personalized talent of superior order. Whatever the final measure of Ysaÿe's abilities as a composer, it seems reasonable to assume that violinists in ever-increasing numbers will continue to perform his compositions, and that his star as a composer of violin music is definitely on the ascendancy. Aside from such elegiac vignettes as *Rêve d'enfant*, Op. 16 and *Berceuse de l'enfant pauve*, Op. 20, Ysaÿe's violin works cater mostly to violinists with highly advanced or virtuosic techniques, and were not designed to attract mass sales. His output includes 30 instrumental works, mostly for violin (several for cello and violin duos) and an opera, *Pier'li Houyeu* ("Peter the Miner"), based on the lives of Belgian miners and sung in Walloon.

Ysaÿe characterized his early six concertos as "just imitations of Vieuxtemps." Other pieces written at age 20 bear the influence of Schumann and Mendelssohn. But Ysaÿe was serious as a composer and continued to mature in consort with the newer developments in French music. The best of his instrumental works are his six solo sonatas and eight *Poèmes*, the latter of varying lengths.

Each of the sonatas is dedicated to an outstanding violinist, in order: Szigeti, Thibaud, Enesco, Kreisler, Crickboom, and Quiroga. Oddly, none is dedicated to Mischa Elman with whom Ysaÿe often played duets in public. Ysaÿe had said of Elman . . ."He was born with a violin in his hands . . . I had intense pleasure in listening to a violin palpitating beneath the will of this young devil." Perhaps Ysaÿe felt that the solo sonata was not a preferred Elman mètier. But he did dedicate his poem, *Extase* in A-flat major, Op. 21 to Elman. The corpulent Ysaÿe fiddling away, standing alongside the diminutive Elman, must have been a platform spectacle for the ages.

Sonata No. 3 in D-minor (*Ballade*) is the most popular of Ysaÿe's solo sonatas, and has practically achieved the status of a staple in the violin repertoire. No. 2 (*Obsession*) cleverly utilizes the motive in Bach's Prelude from the Third Solo Partita; No. 4, broadly classical in form (superbly recorded by Michael Rabin), and No. 6, with a Spanish tint, are also being heard

second violin accompaniments, an art in which he was amazingly adept. Like all superstar violinists he exercised a profound influence on other players, both celebrated and humble. Colleagues like Kreisler, Szigeti, Flesch, Thibaud, Casals, Elman, and Spalding, artists of markedly different personal characteristics, affectionately acknowledged the inspiration they received from him.

In the early 1930s Carl Flesch remarked that "Ysaÿe's position as a composer is not yet finally established." Today, more than 60 years later, the same can be said. However, many violinists, disenchanted by abrasive avant-garde exercises, have been popularizing the reservoir of long-neglected Ysaÿe compositions—not only the six solo sonatas, but other lesser known works.

One is immediately aware of Ysaÿe's spiritual affinity to Franck, Chausson, and Debussy, and in his earliest compositions, Vieuxtemps and Wieniawski, but the discriminating listener will note, too, that his later violin works contain a distinctive personal flavor. They differ markedly from innumerable violin compositions

Program

1.

Suite in D minor for Violin and Piano
Geminiani (1680-1762)

I	Grave-Largo	Allegro giusto
II	Sarabande	Lento
III	Poco vivace	

M M Eugene Ysaye and Beryl Rubinstein

2.

Sonate Op 47 in A major for Violin and Piano
(Kreutzer Sonate)
Van Beethoven

I	Adagio Sostenuto	Presto
II	Andante con variazioni	
III	Finale	Presto

M M Eugene Ysaye and Beryl Rubinstein

CHICKERING PIANO USED

Program Continued

3.

Concerto in D minor No. 2 op 22
H. Wieniawski

I	Allegro moderato
II	Romance Andante non troppo
III	Allegro moderato

Mr. Eugene Ysaye.

4.

Piano soli

| A | Reflets dans l'eau | Debussy |
| B | Polonaise in A flat | Chopin |

Mr. Beryl Rubinstein

5.

A	Reve d'enfant	E. Ysaye
B	Waltz in E minor	Chopin-Ysaye
C	Havanaise	Saint-Saens
D	Polonaise	Vieuxtemps

Mr. Eugene Ysaye

CHICKERING PIANO USED

A recital program (year unknown)

more frequently. No. 1 and 5, interesting as violin studies, are performed less often. The specter of Bach hovers over the six sonatas, but Ysaÿe can be credited with creating music of considerable originality, a notable contribution to the violin repertory. Apart from the intrinsic value of the sonatas, they constitute an imperishable historical testament to the style and spirit of a violinistic giant whose musical ideas and way of life will almost certainly never again be emulated. The entire six solo sonatas have been recorded by Ruggiero Ricci, Oscar Shumsky, Hyman Bress, Gidon Kremer, Yuval Yaron, Charles Castleman, and others. Many have also been recorded by Soviet-trained violinists.

These recordings continue to proliferate everywhere. It should be noted that the late Arthur Grumiaux, who was Belgium's leading violinist, recorded only the miniature *Rêve d'enfant*, among Ysaÿe compositions. This, however, is understandable, since the musical, instrumental, stylistic, and temperamental propensities of Ysaÿe and Grumiaux could scarcely be more divergent.

Ysaÿe's *Poèmes* have been slower in attaining performances. In general, this music is imbued with reverie, restlessness, extreme moodiness, and a brooding melancholia. Since the listener is reminded often of Chausson's *Poème*, it must be pointed out that it was Ysaÿe's music, written earlier, that influenced Chausson, not vice-versa.

The 13-minute *Poème élégiaque pour violon principal et orchestre*, Op. 12, is an outstanding example of this musical resemblance, but where Ysaÿe sometimes tends to wander, Chausson's *Poème* is edited and tailored to perfection, and manifestly more powerful and direct in its musical message.

Chant d'Hiver, Op. 15, of the same length, is an agitated, yet poetically lyric ode, the type of work that demands a violinist of sovereign lyrical qualities to give it meaningful realization. (The recording by Aaron Rosand merits positive mention.)

The ten-minute *Les Neiges d'Antan* has the solo violinist weaving a meandering melodic motif which is underscored by an air of improvisation. It is fondly caressing, nostalgic in the Walloon spirit, and interspersed with short flights of whimsy, ending with single and double-harmonics; a worthy opus. All of the above have been provided with orchestrations skillfully arranged with fastidious taste by Jacques Ysaÿe, the master's grandson.

Another, even longer work in this genre is *Concerto d'après deux poèmes pour violon et orchestre*, Op. 18/19, a 21-minute melding in which *Poème*, Op. 19, (Divertimento) comprises the first and third movements of the concerto, and *Poème*, Op. 18 (*Extase*) is the middle *lento ma non troppo*. Both works were composed during the 1911-1912 period. Jacques Ysaÿe added some orchestral tuttis in order to give the whole work the traditional concerto form.

It all adds up to a major work that requires an artist of exceptional emotional thrust and intensely vibrant, opulent tonal projection. Though it contains some musically absorbing episodes, I do not believe that in its totality the concerto is a work of enduring qualities. The opening *Moderato* is dominated by an air of improvisation, music that is ever restless, probing and moody; the second movement, *Extase*, again recalls the poetic Chausson; the finale, Allegretto poco scherzando, contains many double-stop devices that are of positive violinistic interest and value.

The eight *Poèmes* bare Ysaÿe's emotional processes and sensibilities in profound perspective, and it is unfortunate that as of this writing our most illustrious violinists have not seen fit to perform them to any considerable extent. In their defense, perhaps they do not feel that these works can present them to best advantage and guarantee enthusiastic audience response as compared to tried-and-true war-horses of the repertoire.

There remains the question: How could Ysaÿe, with his towering personal magnetism and genius for violinistic and musical communication compare with contemporary stellar violinists? This must be approached from two different angles.

First, let us assume that he was taught from childhood by the most advanced modern methods, had been regularly exposed to the post-Heifetz technical standards, and thoroughly inculcated with current attitudes concerning musical discipline and fidelity to the composer's printed score. The latter would, of course, impose rigid restrictions on Ysaÿe's natural emotive capacities. However, we must remember that in the final analysis, it is the *man* who determines the degree of communication between himself and his audience. No

matter what limitations were foisted upon Ysaÿe, his seething temperament, singularity of sound, and uncommonly individualized phrasing and expressiveness would place him in the forefront among artists.

On the other hand, were we to take Ysaÿe at his peak and suddenly thrust him into the contemporary concert scene exactly as he played, certain of his qualities that so captivated the audiences of his day would appear aberrant.

Even in his loftiest moments, Ysaÿe was a musical maverick who molded the works of any and all composers to fit his personal muse. The very concept that the role of the artist is to play the music "as the composer intended" would bewilder him. When it was once pointed out that his performance of the Franck sonata, though wonderful, did not conform to the composer's directions, Franck himself replied: "This may be so, but from now on it will be impossible to play it in any other way. Don't worry, it is Ysaÿe who is right." Thus we find that an attitude toward the composer's intentions which would horrify most of our musically-computerized contemporary violinists (and critics), was part and parcel of Ysaÿe's musical dogma.

Ysaÿe was a born actor who understood perfectly the value of gestures, expressions, and posturings. When he was having a bad night, which occurred far more frequently than even with the most errant (and practice-less) among modern luminaries, he would go into his act to distract the audience from his deficiencies. He possessed a sizeable repertoire of facial grimaces, and could perform with tears streaming down his cheeks, though he warned his students against such indiscretions.

We have a number of platform eccentrics among current concert performers who are adored by their audiences, so in this instance, were Ysaÿe merely toned down a bit, he would be perfectly acceptable in this company. Another Ysaÿe shortcoming was frequent memory lapses, especially in his declining years. Today, some of our leading violinists do not hesitate to use the music in performance.

On the purely violinistic side, the slides and position changes which he employed for expressive effect might be unacceptable, in large part, to modern ears. And, in particular, the license that he took in baroque and classical music would be intolerable. Yet all of this is basically no more than incidental to the impact of his artistry, and it is conceivably possible that were we to hear Ysaÿe at his best over a period of time, even in this modern day and age, some of our concepts about what constitutes violin artistry might be altered, if only slightly.

To truly appreciate the stature of Ysaÿe's prime playing (and sadly, we can do this only through his tiny legacy of recordings), we must listen willingly, as if viewing the grandeur of a silent movie epic with all its technical anachronisms, or hearing faded discs of the peer-less tenor of Caruso with all of his controversial sobbing and musical excesses.

Only then, when all the contemporary rules of musical discipline and probity are temporarily suspended, can we realize that in the realm of sheer human communication, we are hearing one of the most gifted, intuitive, and original violinists who ever lived.

Fritz Kreisler, the personification of violinistic elegance, charm, bewitching sound and uniquely personalized style

FRITZ KREISLER

By the turn of the century, the art of violin playing had entered the flood tide of romanticism, and came to be dominated by the heightened standards of overt emotionalism as personified by the immortal Belgian Eugène Ysaÿe. The lofty academicism of Joseph Joachim (1831-1907) and the cool, glittering virtuosity of Pablo de Sarasate (1844-1908), while still held in universal esteem, were being displaced by new concepts of sound and interpretive style. Giants though they were, each in his own individual manner represented late 19th-century violinistic modes, already in decline. Vestiges of their influence could be heard among violinists in the concert halls of Europe and America for some time after their demise, but the changing tastes of audiences demanded playing that expressly emphasized sensuality of sound. In the inevitable struggle between old and new the "sensual" players of tonal opulence were destined to triumph.

If Ysaÿe can be thought of as having linked the violin art of the 19th and 20th centuries and as being the catalyst and artistic inspiration of a legion of younger hyperromantic musicians throughout the world, it was Fritz Kreisler who became his direct heir. Kreisler's hegemony spanned half a century. By the end of the second decade of the 20th century he had prevailed over Mischa Elman in contention for public favor, and not even the awesome feats of the young Heifetz could diminish Kreisler's popularity with the mass audience and with the critics. In fact, many listeners who acknowledged and revered the peerless mastery of Heifetz continued to maintain that they derived more aesthetic satisfaction from Kreisler's playing. It would be difficult to name a violinist more beloved by his public and colleagues alike. As one of the most individualistic performers in the annals of violin art, Kreisler opened up new vistas of sound, expressiveness, charm, elegance, and nobility of style. Both as composer and as instrumentalist, he expanded significantly the lexicon of violin art.

Freidrich-Max ("Fritz") Kreisler was born in Vienna on February 2, 1875 (Jascha Heifetz was born on the same date 26 years later). His father, Samuel Kreisler, was a physician and had come to Vienna from Krakow. In Kreisler's younger days his Jewish origin was common knowledge in Europe, and was often cited in print, as in *My Memories*, the autobiography of the Belgian virtuoso Ovide Musin. Later, when the Nazis came to power, his stupendous career in Germany was brought to an abrupt end. Kreisler never participated in Jewish activities, whether religious, social, or philanthropic, and like so many Austrian Jews of the period, he gravitated easily toward Catholicism, especially after his marriage to Harriet Lies, a Catholic-American. His mother, Anna, a housewife and mother of five who displayed no musical talent, played an important role in Fritz's life. Although in poor health, she accompanied Fritz to Paris for his final two years of violin study.

Kreisler was given a miniature violin at age four, and when he evinced precocity, his father, an amateur violinist, soon bought him a better instrument and proceeded to give him lessons. His first professional teacher was Jacques Aubert, a theater concertmaster. At age seven he was admitted to the Vienna Conservatory, the first student under ten ever to be accepted. Here he became the pupil of Joseph Hellmesberger, Jr., and had harmony and music theory classes with Anton Bruckner. He also studied the piano for which he had an exceptional talent. At ten, the boy won the gold medal for violinists at the conservatory, an unprecedented honor for one so young.

A group of friends presented the young Kreisler

Fritz Kreisler at 12 when he won the Conservatoire's Premier Premier Prix

(known for his pocket-size music dictionary) disagreed, writing: "young Master Kreisler is a genius who has yet something to learn . . . He is, I think, destined to become a very great artist if he does not disdain further study."

In his 1888 debut with the Boston Symphony under Walter Damrosch, the 13-year-old played the Mendelssohn Concerto in E-minor and Ernst's *Hungarian Airs*. Kreisler's biographer, Louis Lochner, states that the following year in his debut with the Chicago Symphony under Hans Balatka, the boy performed Wieniawski's *Faust Fantasy* on a program starring the pianist Rosenthal. (Actually the official Chicago Symphony was not founded until 1891.) From the *Chicago Times*: "If his bowing were as good as his left hand work, he would now be one of the most remarkable players of the day." In contradiction, the *Chicago Tribune* reported: "His performance was crude and frequently out of tune."

Returning home rich in experience but in dire economic straits, he spent the next two years studying scholastic subjects at the Piariste Gymnasium in Vienna, a school directed by Catholic laymen of the Piarist order; he then spent two years in medical school. It is said that during these years he did not touch the violin.

At 20, after joining the army, he played intermittently for the soldiers; it was about this time that he composed his monumental cadenzas for the Beethoven concerto.

Following his two years of army service, educated and ready to face life, he decided to make music his career. He spent eight weeks practicing assiduously to regain his technique. Hearing of a vacancy for the second desk in the Vienna Hofoper orchestra, he auditioned—and was turned down by no less a judge than the well-known Arnold Rosé, concertmaster and founder of the Rosé String Quartet. The verdict alleged that Kreisler was "no good at sight reading." This was a patently ridiculous statement since the young man was already a thorough musician and was known to be extraordinary at learning and mastering new scores. Doubtless Rosé was bewildered by the vivid vibrance of Kreisler's tone in contrast to his own old-fashioned, dry sound, and was possibly tainted by professional jealousy. Nevertheless, he was no different from many other observers and critics of the day who tended to look backward in performance standards. Even the great Joachim, who considered the young Franz von Vecsey

with a three-quarter size Amati and insisted he be sent to study in Paris. This represented a financial hardship for Dr. Kreisler. After auditioning before a jury of eminent professors at the Paris Conservatoire he was admitted to the class of the venerable Joseph Lambert Massart, a former teacher of Henri Wieniawski, and had lessons in composition with Leo Delibes. At twelve, the boy once again received an unprecedented honor by winning the Conservatoire's *Premier Premier Prix*.

Kreisler never received formal violin instruction after the age of 12; his further development was dependent upon his genius and keen powers of observation. Heard by the famed pianist Moritz Rosenthal, he was engaged as an assistant artist for 50 concerts, including many in America, and was paid $50 per appearance. His playing evoked contradictory evaluations. In Boston, Howard Malcolm Tichnor of the *Daily Globe* wrote: "the lad . . . accomplished his task creditably but gave no evidence of remarkable talent or remarkable training . . . He plays like a nice, studious boy who had a rather musical nature . . . but cannot be ranked among prodigies or geniuses." Louis C. Elson of the *Daily Advertiser*

a peerless prodigy, was not at all enamored of Kreisler's playing. It took many years for Kreisler's then-unorthodox sound and style to win mass audience acceptance, particularly in Central Europe. Even in his home town of Vienna, many listeners preferred the comparatively dry sound of Huberman.

Undaunted by his failure with the Hofoper orchestra, he managed to obtain various solo engagements with the assistance of influential friends who were impressed by his highly personable manner, as well as by his great talent. In Constantinople his playing delighted the Sultan, and during a Russian tour he played the Tchaikovsky concerto with much success. A second Russian tour was interrupted by a madcap decision to run off to Finland for a romantic interlude with a Finnish girl he had met in Warsaw. Later, in Paris, he pawned his violin to buy expensive presents for a girl with whom he was temporarily infatuated. It was during this profligate period that he began to compose his vignettes.

Meanwhile, his reputation as an artist was burgeoning. He won the approval of the eminent critic Eduard Hanslick for his playing of the Bruch Concerto No. 2 with Hans Richter and the Vienna Philharmonic. But it took him far longer to gain wide public favor in his own home town than in the United States and England. In December, 1899, a golden opportunity presented itself when he was invited to play the Mendelssohn concerto with the redoubtable maestro Artur Nikisch and the Berlin Philharmonic. At the conclusion of the performance, Ysaÿe, who was in the audience, stood up ostentatiously and applauded.

As early as 1901 Kreisler played trio concerts with Josef Hofmann and Jean Gerardy, often to very small audiences; before that he had given sonata concerts in a tour with Harold Bauer. It was during this period that he also barnstormed through the English provinces in joint recitals with tenor John McCormack. Often the box office receipts netted them only ten or 12 pounds, from which Kreisler's pianist was guaranteed three pounds a concert. Their largest fee was 60 pounds.

Yet for all the warmth of his growing audience and critical reception, Kreisler's solo career was in serious danger of foundering. Like Paganini, Wieniawski, Ysaÿe, and many another colossal talent before him, Kreisler was a hedonist, lacking direction and self-discipline.

Fortunately in 1902 he met, fell in love with, and married Harriet Lies (Mrs. Fred Woerz), a wealthy American woman who uncompromisingly regulated and dominated his personal, social, and professional lives, and was in effect responsible for the ultimate success of his career. Once Kreisler came under the sovereignty of this iron-willed, imperious lady, his days of wastrel frivolity were over. In late years she would declare characteristically: "I have made him," a true if not particularly modest statement. Because she was a divorcée they were married in a civil ceremony; not until 1947 were they permitted to marry in a Catholic service. Next to his wife, his closest friend and associate was his manager Charles Foley.

In 1905 Kreisler received $400 for two appearances with the New York Philharmonic; by 1910 he earned $600 per concert while touring as soloist with the Boston Symphony, and $800 for each of two recitals. By the mid-1920s he was earning $3,000 per concert, and in 1944 he received $5,000 for each of his first five broadcasts.

In the early 1900s he gradually began to overcome nearly all of his opposition, and inured the mass audience to the sound and style that were so different from those of his predecessors and contemporaries. He began to make more and more recordings: by 1914 he was among the highest paid performers in the recording field. In 1910 he accepted the preposterous sum of $1,000 for 50 of his arrangements and so-called transcriptions from the B. Schott music publishing company in Mainz, but later, of course, this was adjusted to be commensurate with his skyrocketing reputation.

During these years he greatly enlarged his repertoire. In London in 1910, Kreisler gave the premier performance of the massive Elgar concerto, which had been dedicated to him.

His success continued unabated until 1914 with the outbreak of World War I. Acting in accordance with the dictates of his conscience, Kreisler, an active reservist in the Austrian army and a devoted subject of the Austrian Kaiser, went to fight for his native land in August of that year. The Austrian government, which could have profitably employed such a world-renowned artist in any number of propaganda situations, displayed its abysmal stupidity by sending him into the trenches. After several weeks on the Russian front he was wounded in the leg and discharged as a "complete invalid." By November, 1914, he was already back in New York. The following year he wrote a small quasi-diary published in book form titled *Four Weeks in the Trenches (The War Story of a Violinist)*, a superficial if sincere account of his experiences. According to the book, it would seem that Kreisler fought strictly as a patriotic duty in "service to his fatherland" rather than for any deeply felt political or philosophical convictions. He did, however, help to support the families of some of his fallen comrades for many years, a humanitarian act typical of Kreisler.

At first, his wartime activities had no adverse effect upon his career. But as the war dragged on, stories of German atrocities became widely circulated and pro-Allied sympathies soared. When the United States entered the war, Kreisler's vast popularity, like that of other artists loyal to the German-dominated Central Powers, began to plummet. In the 1917-1918 period, many of his so-called friends deserted him, and he was forced to retire from the American concert stage. He reappeared in Carnegie Hall on October 27, 1919 amid continuing protests which forced him to cancel numerous proposed concerts. Even as late as 1924, Kreisler encountered protests in France which affected his performance schedule. However, by the 1920-1921 concert season in the United States, the public had forgiven his indiscretion and he quickly became an adored figure once again. This is the single episode in Kreisler's adult career during which he was not an idol of the mass audience. Unlike Elman, Thibaud, Kubelik, Huberman, and other stellar violinists, Kreisler's unparalleled hold on the mass audience endured, as did the esteem of his colleagues and critics—right up to his last public concert on November 1, 1947.

After 1933 Kreisler no longer appeared in Germany because of his Jewish heritage (although the 'official' Kreisler biography craftily evades the issue). In 1935 Kreisler was involved in a brouhaha with certain martinet critics concerning the spurious origin of some of his compositions, an incident which will be discussed below.

On April 27, 1941, while crossing a New York street, he was struck and seriously injured by a truck. His convalescence required several months, and he did not perform publicly until January, 1942. He became an American citizen in 1943.

In his final years Kreisler's playing suffered from the usual violinistic infirmities brought on by old age. Fritz Kreisler died on January 29, 1962, shortly before his 87th birthday.

Kreisler has been the subject of countless articles and critiques, culminated by Louis Lochner's *Fritz Kreisler*, a volume which is obviously the officially sanctioned survey of his life. Although Kreisler himself

Nathan Milstein and Kreisler in 1943

remains a beloved figure, various colleagues who knew him personally are sharply critical of the book, not only because it is written with the roseate rhetoric of an utterly compliant press agent, but also because it is marked by the customary shortcomings of an observer who has not had intimate experience with the art about which he writes. Unfortunately, the book neither offers significant details of Kreisler's violinistic training nor does it discuss the technical problems with which he had to cope during his early studies. Still, the biography contains a wealth of anecdotes, quotes, and data of importance (and a number of contradictions). If one accepts the book strictly as a meticulously orchestrated account, it is well worth reading.

Lochner tells of Kreisler's love of collecting rare books and manuscripts. He also depicts him as a philosopher, linguist, intellectual, and humanist of impeccable stature. The case for the final description is not strengthened by the violinist's warm friendship with the dictator Benito Mussolini only a few short years before the Fascists began their cruel depredations against the people of Ethiopia, Spain, and Italy. But at least Kreisler was not biased in his associations; he was also a good friend of Albert Einstein. Obviously his music-making endeared him to almost everyone. And what is even more important, he remained an exceptionally kind, benevolent man all the days of his life, ever generous to his colleagues in every respect.

Kreisler was often referred to as "The King of Violinists," a sobriquet which fits his platform image and general deportment as well as his performance. His concerts exuded a special aura, and listeners often felt like

Courtesy I. MonDragon

Fritz Kreisler in mid-career

privileged guests at a memorable royal function. Yet there was nothing pompous or affected in the man. He would walk out majestically, holding his violin by the scroll at arm's length, tune up quickly without fuss, and begin. While playing his stance was relaxed and his body gestures natural. The only sign of tension was his habit of repeatedly tensing his cheeks, a mannerism that always reminded me of a chipmunk busily munching a nut. One invariably felt about Kreisler, the artist, the same way one felt about Einstein, the scientist-humanist. His speech always retained a Teutonic accent, but the ad-lib address he gave at his 75th birthday fete was testimony to his eloquence in English. He spoke with a lisp. He had an intrinsic sense of humor which he exercised freely in his younger years, yet dignity gradually pervaded his public image as he grew older. His penchant for humor was often evident in his private relationships and, of course, in many of his compositions. But he never would play the fool at a concert in order to evoke titters from the audience. He was the king of all he surveyed, not the court jester.

There was nothing extraordinary about the size or shape of his hands: they were strong, yet pliant. His fourth finger was comparatively short, and while he used it without stint in technical passages, he almost always preferred using his third finger in vibrant lyric playing.

Kreisler's reflexes were magnificent. Though never a gymnast of the fingerboard, the sheer velocity and clarity of his filigree passage work and trills surpassed those of most specialists in Paganinian bravura. His finger articulation was almost in a class by itself; his superb penchant for trills and finger tremolos is vividly manifest in his unique cadenza for Tartini's *Devil's Trill* Sonata which, unfortunately, he never recorded. With the exception of a few sensational technicians who were infinitely inferior to him as tonalists and artists, Kreisler's technical equipment compared favorably with any of his colleagues of the pre-Heifetz era.

Much is made of the fact that Kreisler was opposed to long hours of practice; that he actually practiced little; and that he would walk onstage and perform with little or no warm-up. Because of this, the first 15 or 20 minutes of his playing could be extremely rough and untidy, and not until he was thoroughly warmed up and acclimated to his surroundings did he sound like "Kreisler." He stated: "I never practice before a concert. The reason is that practice benumbs the brain, renders the imagination less acute, and deadens the sense of alertness that every artist must possess. Before a concert I merely dip my fingers in hot water for a few seconds." He did not specify what he did when the hot water was unavailable. Of course, audiences accepted inconsistency from artists in bygone days, even from those who practiced incessantly. Perfection had yet to become a fetish. Even in Kreisler's finest playing there were apt to be minor blemishes, but when he finally reached full stride, he played so gloriously one could forgive him anything. And though his career carried over into the era of new technical standards (initiated by Heifetz), audiences tended to overlook his less elevated moments and to dote upon those that were irresistible and inimitable.

Kreisler's bowing included certain unorthodoxies. Whereas some violinists (Zimbalist, for example) took pride in their ability to negotiate the "long bow" (i.e. using a single stroke for an extreme length of time in cantilena passages), Kreisler was actually extravagant in his constant bow changes. He sought and achieved robustness and resonance of sound at all times, in every type of passage, and preferred to use strong modern bows screwed to inordinate tension. Thus, the separation of bow hair from stick was outsized; one never heard the "stick" in his playing, only the hair in full contact with the string. His bows took a beating; fortunately they were not the old, irreplaceable French masterpieces. It is safe to say that no great violinist in memory changed bows as often as Kreisler. His bowing was an integral element in one of the cornerstones of his art—the distinctive rhythmic pulse that characterized everything he played, masterwork or miniature. A key factor of his superlative rhythmic faculties was his rubato phrasing, a cardinal feature of his playing. Kreisler, like Ysaÿe before him, possessed a gift for rubato which enabled him to take rhythmic liberties without sabotaging the inherent pulse in the music. When he elected to either push or hold back in the rhythm for expressive purposes, and he did so often, he instinctively compensated for it. One of his most beguiling tricks was using the upper part of his bow to accentuate, individually, a group of notes ending with rubato.

In matters of tempo Kreisler greatly preferred deliberation to haste. He was never a player who rushed from climax to climax, leaving prosaic sections between. Every note and bar was precious to him; nothing was ever wasted and, in general, his tempos were slower than those of today's violinists; in many instances, considerably slower.

The Kreisler tone was magical in its effect, different from any other, bewitching yet virile, fragrantly sweet but never cloying. The tactile impact of his left hand fingers was amazingly articulative, yet the tonal texture was "fleshy," without a trace of lean linear sound.

Accounts of his playing, both written and "ear-witness," constantly emphasize that he was the first to use the continuous vibrato. Flesch cites his "extraordinary intensive vibrato." These statements are true, but they do not encompass the entire subject. As far back as Wieniawski (1835-1880) (who is said to have taught it to Vieuxtemps), and somewhat before, romantically inclined violinists used some degree of vibrato for expressive purposes, as opposed to the classically oriented academicians who shunned vibrato as an aberration. The latter played in a manner we would consider "dry," especially those in the German school. Kreisler sustained a semblance of vibrato even in technical passages in a manner that was far in advance of even his most romantically inclined colleagues and competitors. It is necessary to understand that other violinists, either by design or in emulation of Kreisler, could "shake their arms off" and not approximate the Kreisler sound. That is because his vibrato was not only continuous and singularly intense, but was produced differently. Where others used a wrist or arm vibrato, or even a combina-

tion of the two, or a tense fingertip vibrato (especially prevalent among French violinists) which tended to be taut and often unpleasant, Kreisler used what I have chosen to call an "impulse" vibrato. One never saw Kreisler indulge in furious hand or arm "flapping" when vibrating; rather his vibrato was generated from some point *within* the arm to the oscillating fingertip which had an extremely narrow point of contact. The result might be likened to an electric current enlivening each note he played to whatever degree he chose. Others had fast vibratos that were tense rather than intense; studied, overt appendages to their technical arsenals. Kreisler's vibrato was as natural to him as is swimming to a fish. A significant advantage offered by his unique vibrato was an ability to make lyrical passages of double-stops sound like two separate voices blended in mutual song in a manner unexcelled, and perhaps unmatched, by anyone. At no time did he indulge in the currently widespread habit of vibrating on some notes and playing others with "dead" fingers in a single lyric passage. Kreisler's tone and vibrato are all the more remarkable inasmuch as they were honed in an era that still looked askance at intense vibrato and "sound for sound's sake."

Together with the phenomenon of his vibrato, Kreisler had yet another expressive weapon of devastating import—his vast array of seductive slides, portamentos, and position changes. The scope of these devices was perhaps more extensive and diversified than that of any elite 20th-century violinists. One cannot claim that some of these devices were not also used by his colleagues, great and lesser, but the results of those who tried to imitate the entire gamut of these embellishments--who had not his prodigious vibrato, temperament, and unfailing elegance of taste (and who did?)—were usually nothing but pale mimicry. It should be recognized, however, that more than a few of the older-generation players profitably incorporated elements of Kreisler's expressive devices in their performance and even reflected a modicum of the radiance of Kreisler's elegant musicality. In his book *The Principles of Violin Fingering*, the Soviet pedagogue I.M. Yampolsky states: "The Kreisler portamento is based mainly on the *sliding of one finger*" (his italics). This is substantially incorrect. A great many of Kreisler's expressive slides and position changes involved *two* fingers—the "bridging" note and the "landing" note.

A vital component of his uniqueness in this area was his ability to articulate the "landing" note of his position changes with an instantaneous rapid vibrato that never required "getting set." Admittedly, some of Kreisler's expressive artifices may sound dated or overdone to modern ears, but whatever his excesses, they were part and parcel of his violinistic way of life, and contributed enormously to the individuality and allure of his playing.

Any attempt to make an encyclopedic survey of Kreisler's expressive contrivances could scarcely fulfill its purpose. The finger connections could be fast or slow, blatantly emphasized or exquisitely subtle. His ability to sustain "life" in position changes was transcendent. Many consisted of "bridging" effects in combination with non-primary fingers; others were employed in changes from one string to another, or were simplistic up or down one-finger slides. On occasion he even used an effect similar to the famous "Heifetz slide," gliding up the string with the "landing" finger and hitting the note with instantaneous intense vibrato. I have provided a few random examples for the interest of professionals and students, but efforts to describe them on paper can hardly be satisfactory. They must be demonstrated in the flesh. As we know, expressive slides, portamentos, and position changes of all types are now "out of style," and only Perlman (and, to a lesser extent, a few others) among contemporary violinists uses them to any considerable degree and, it might be added, with astounding success.

For all its grace, elegance, and nobility, Kreisler's playing was pure sensuality. Each note was negotiated with an ear for beauty and expressed a great *joie de vivre*. No violinist ever played more liltingly. His was a seething temperament, albeit one governed by patrician instincts. He sought consistently to charm his listeners, and every facet of his playing was oriented toward that end. But for all the sensual nuances of his art, his spiritual qualities were celestial.

Nonetheless, it would be unrealistic to say that he did not have detractors, especially in the early part of his career, and even in later years. These observers considered Kreisler a glorified salon player and a purveyor of kitsch. This was clearly nonsense. Although it was true that he was supreme as a player of inconsequential ear-tickling bagatelles, and shrewdly used this marvelous skill in the aggrandizement of his career, Kreisler was also a superlative interpreter of the masterworks within the context of his time and aesthetic priorities. True, as one of the great personalities of the violin, his sound and style were emblazoned on every

bar of his playing, in every type of work. Since the composer's text was so firmly wedded with Kreisler's unique violinistic personality, it was difficult to tell where one left off and the other began. Indeed, he freely transcribed numerous major violin works: the Tchaikovsky concerto, the first movement of the Paganini Concerto No. 1, and Corelli's *La Folia*. Many professionals, including myself, feel that far more often than not the effects of these compositions were heightened substantially. And his piano and orchestral accompaniments were invariably superior to the originals. Kreisler was seldom less than respectful, but was in no way subservient to any composer's so-called intentions. He was never a favorite of die-hard academicians. His art was dedicated to *making music* for people in every walk of life to enjoy—and to the devil with dispassionate nominal "rules." At the same time, his infallible good taste prevented him from violating the essential spirit of any composition.

Kreisler's memory was extraordinary. He rarely referred to the score on the music stand. Apart from lifelong acquaintance with his recordings, I enjoyed the privilege of hearing Kreisler in live recitals and as soloist with orchestra (as well as on radio broadcasts) over a period of many years. Each event was a memorable experience, even those in which he was flagrantly off form. His recorded legacy is comparatively limited in repertorial scope, but his live performance repertoire was broad. Among those that stand out in my mind are his Viennese-tinted interpretation of the Tchaikovsky concerto with piano accompaniment, in which a constantly whistling open E string did not disturb his unflappable poise a whit; his feisty and ineffably lyric performance of his transcribed version of Paganini's Concerto No. 1 (first movement) when he was already in his 60s; the unforgettable nobility of his Beethoven concerto when in top form; the delicious exuberance of his Mozart Concerto No. 3 (with piano); the dazzling trill-tremolo batteries in his brilliant cadenza to Tartini's *Devil's Trill* Sonata; and the magical effect of his brief transcriptions and original compositions which, despite myriad performances, always sounded fresh and vital. One could go on and on.

The Kreisler discography consists of more than 200 works, large and small (mostly the latter). Sadly, many of his prime performances of major works--the concertos of Elgar, Bach, Tchaikovsky, Mozart Nos. 3 and 5, Spohr No. 8, Vieuxtemps No. 2, Bruch No. 2, the

Courtesy I. MonDragon

Kreisler in New York, 1948

Chausson *Poème*, the sonatas of Brahms, Mozart, Franck, and Debussy, and Bach's *Chaconne*--were never recorded. Nor were such choice smaller morsels as his *Praeludium and Allegro*, or his *Recitativo and Scherzo Caprice*, ever recorded—not, at least, on accredited labels.

As far back as 1904, the primitive, pre-electric recordings he made of the Bach-Wilhelmj *Air on the G String* shows him to be tonally and stylistically in advance of his competitors (with the exception of Ysaÿe). His 1908 Brahms-Joachim *Hungarian Dance* No. 5 projects rich G-string sound and dashing spirit.

These Kreisler vignette recordings destined to enchant the world began to appear in quantity around 1910. They ranged from about two to five minutes, tailored to fit the old ten-and twelve-inch 78 r.p.m. discs, and including trifling settings of popular favorites: *The Rosary, Poor Butterfly, Old Folks at Home, Beautiful Ohio, On Miami Shore, Love Sends a Little Gift of Roses, A Kiss in the Dark, Blue Skies, The World Is Waiting for the Sunrise*, and others. Kreisler's formula for these tidbits was simple: play the melody in the lower and upper register (or both), garnish it with double-stops and, when feasible, add the embellishments of those lacy, swift filigree passages that sounded as if they were improvised. Actually, it is said that he concocted these in an hour or two, and that often he went into the recording studio and polished the rough edges shortly before the "takes." This grouping was supplemented by brief Kreisler transcriptions and originals.

What can one say about these performances, slight imperfections and all, except once again to turn to that overused word (in Kreisler's case) "inimitable." Every expressive device in his lexicon was archly instilled into these miniature gems. If one concentrates on the *core* of the sound, Kreisler's eminence is readily apparent even in weather-beaten and scratchy recordings. Each listener familiar with these has his favorites, my own being the naively sentimental *From the Land of the Sky Blue Water* by Cadman, with its ravishing tone, and imaginative passagework and rubatos; an unaccompanied version of Haydn's *God Save the Emperor*, the Austrian national anthem, set in a quasi-Bachian mode (one can almost visualize the uniformed Kreisler standing stiffly and reverently at attention as his adored Kaiser reviewed the troops). And how can one not include his early recordings of *Caprice Viennois* with its entrancing lilt and vibrant doublestops, the exhilarating *Schön Rosmarin*, and the bittersweet *Liebesleid?* These are only a few of the outstanding gems. Yes, it would be easy for a modern-day observer to question some of Kreisler's expressive ploys, as, for example, his three successive similar slides in descending triplets in Massenet's "Meditation" from *Thais*. But despite the listener's better judgment he might well find himself accepting the exaggeration because the entirety of the playing is so captivating.

Most of the Kreisler brevities and masterworks have been re-released by companies specializing in this area. Such compilations constitute an invaluable research and training bequest to the coming generations. This is not to imply that young artists should strive to imitate Kreisler. They could not do it convincingly no matter how hard they might try. The value would lie in their being able to imbibe those beauties of sound and style that enraptured millions of yesteryear listeners, and perhaps even to learn a thing or two along the way.

The post-electric recordings continue the output of stunning short-piece discs, some of them rerecordings. The 1925 through 1929 group retains all the wondrous freshness of the old acoustical discs under superior engineering conditions.

Gypsy Andante, the slow movement from Dohnanyi's *Ruralia Hungarica*, Op. 32c, is one of the magical performances of this era, though the two outer movements of the suite contain more than a permissible amount of untidiness. The Dvořák-Kreisler *Slavonic Dance* No. 3 in G is another of this caliber, with vibrant double-stop lyric passages that sound as if two violins were playing. The Dvořák-Kreisler *Indian Lament* and *Humoresque* (the latter a best-seller), Kreisler's *Chanson Louis XIII* and *Pavane*, *Gypsy Caprice*, *Tambourin Chinois*, and *Old Refrain* are but a few of the more impressive in this genre.

The quality of Kreisler recordings remained high until the latter 1930s, but it is the opinion of many observers that his playing from about 1910 to the end of the 1920s represented his peak performance. Unfortunately, many people have heard only his recordings of short numbers made near the end of his career with Charles O'Connell and the Victor Symphony Orchestra, which are considerably below his finest playing. As Kreisler approached 70, his hearing gradually deteriorated and he was increasingly subject to pitch aberrations, especially in the higher register of the E string.

Before discussing Kreisler's major work recordings, mention should be made of several collaborations with

Courtesy Yolande Francescatti

Kreisler giving an autograph

other artists. His 1915 disc of Nevin's *Mighty Lak' a Rose* with Geraldine Farrar (and a murky orchestra) demonstrates how a violin obbligato in his hands could enhance the entire character of a performance. With all due respect to Farrar, it is essentially Kreisler's record. Even more radiant are his pairings with the legendary John McCormack, one of the few artists who could participate with Kreisler on equal terms. Their 1914 recordings of Godard's "Lullaby" from *Jocelyn* (in which Kreisler plays a single incorrect note), and the 1920 Rachmaninoff *O Cease Thy Singing, Maiden Fair* and *When Night Descends* can only be described as sublime and on a par with the Elman-Caruso vignette collaborations. One can only wonder how much (or more probably, how little) preparation Kreisler made for these duos. Infinitely less balanced artistically is the 1927 recording of his transcriptions of Bizet's "Intermezzo" from *L'Arlesienne* and Corelli's *Sanctissima* played with his cellist brother Hugo and pianist Michael Raucheisen. Nine years younger than Fritz, Hugo was a solid player of orchestra section caliber but simply no match for his sibling.

An interesting pairing is the 1915 Bach Concerto for Two Violins in D-minor with Efrem Zimbalist and string quartet collaboration. As a duo effort it is not truly distinguished despite the allegation in the LP rerelease program notes by the well-known New York critic Irving Kolodin, that their "two sounds might almost be the product of the same impulse, so well are they conciliated." This is simply not the case. Kreisler's vibrant tone clearly dominates Zimbalist's cool though pure sound throughout. Each of the artists sustains his own personal style (in slides, articulation etc.), and the two are quite disparate. The disc is significant as a historic testament, and both violinists play well, individually.

Kreisler's sonata recordings with Serge Rachmaninoff (1928) and his complete cycle of Beethoven's ten sonatas for violin and piano with Franz Rupp (1935-1936) represent yet another pinnacle of his recording career. The Rachmaninoff association includes the Grieg Sonata in C-minor, a natural for the potent descriptive powers and glowing tone of Kreisler in a performance that, to my taste, has never been equalled. His novel slides and his sense of pacing and imagery are ideal for this music. Curiously, Rachmaninoff takes rhythmic liberties in the opening of the second movement ♫ ♩ instead of the printed ♫ ♩ which Kreisler plays) and elsewhere, but his third movement is boldly evocative; the melodic passages are compellingly ariose. Equally impressive is their Schubert Sonata No. 5, Op. 162, which in my opinion still remains unsurpassed in its lissome elegance, amorous tone, and infinite charm. And Beethoven's Sonata No. 8 in G, Op. 30, No. 3, is the archetype of spontaneity, silkily smooth, and refined. In these three sonatas, the

Kreisler stylistic insignia is ever the paramount ingredient of the performances.

Kreisler's complete Beethoven sonatas with Rupp, admittedly singularly personalized, are nevertheless musically valid, noble in concept, and beguiling in sound. The sympathetic, sensitive Rupp collaborations discreetly avoid stressing his own personality. The Sonata No. 5 (*Spring*) pulsates with youthful exuberance; No. 7 in C-minor is lightly dramatic, and the sound in the second movement, radiant; No. 3 in E-flat major, with its perky articulative challenges, is rhythmically superlative; in No. 10 in G-major, Op. 96, Kreisler never relaxes his expressive instincts no matter how unwieldy the passages, as in the thorny finale. The entire execution projects a disarming sense of ease. Of the ten, only No. 9 (*Kreutzer*) falls below his highest standards, with the opening a bit "wobbly." At times there is a bit of pitch flatness, and in general it is less spotless than the other sonatas, yet there is, especially in the second movement, some glorious playing. Taken collectively, had Kreisler never left us any other recordings than this Beethoven sonata cycle, his position among the immortals in the violin pantheon would be assured.

Like most of the great violinists, Kreisler played string quartets and related chamber music with his colleagues privately whenever possible. His own String Quartet in A, typically rich in string color and lustrous harmony, was recorded in 1935 by Kreisler with Thomas Petrie, William Primrose, and Laurie Kennedy. This is an unjustly neglected opus, though admittedly it requires a first violinist with a distinct flair for the effervescent Kreisler style to give it full relevance. The second movement contains echoes of *Tambourin Chinois*, the fourth reflects a rhapsodic mood akin to that of *La Gitana* and *Gypsy Caprice*. One may find the totality of the work somewhat saccharine, but its unorthodox loveliness is difficult to resist, particularly when Kreisler is presiding at first violin with such excellent collaborators. This is a seamless performance of a quartet that deserves periodic resuscitation. Those organized ensembles that regularly incorporate one work of easily listenable romanticism and instrumental opulence in their programs would do well to learn Kreisler's quartet. There is nothing quite like it in the repertoire.

Apart from the so-called Vivaldi Concerto in C-Major which is actually a Kreisler composition, he recorded only five concertos: the Beethoven, Brahms, Mendelssohn, Mozart No. 4, (recorded twice) and his own transcription of Paganini No. 1.

The Beethoven, recorded with Leo Blech and the Orchestra der Staatsoper Berlin, 1926, is more consistent in sound and technical detail than the 1936 version with Sir John Barbirolli and the London Philharmonic. The latter is still superb, and the orchestral sound is understandably superior in engineering. One can pinpoint an occasional exaggeration of slides, but the spirit of his interpretation is extraordinarily free, yet architecturally sound. And unlike so many modern violinists who smother the Beethoven first movement with constant détaché bowing, Kreisler cannily alternates détachés with spiccatos and even staccatos. The third movement cadenza comprises a lesson in remarkable bow control, and the balletic opening of the movement recalls a resonant horn-like fanfare. The Larghetto is positively celestial. In all, the performance is the very personification of nobility of spirit in the most august sense.

The Brahms concerto recording of the 1920s, also with Blech and the Berliners, is a bit superior to the

1936 disc with Barbirolli and the London Philharmonic. Kreisler does not evince the unerring technical security of the best modern players, but his expressive powers are at play in every passage; there are no uneventful "valleys" between the "peaks." The Adagio is sovereign in its tonal color and nuance, and the slashing opening thirds of the Allegro giocoso erupt with scintillating vibrance. His Brahms cadenzas may be marginally less Olympian than those for the Beethoven, but they are nonetheless grandly conceived.

Although the orchestra's sound suffers from the recording's antiquated engineering, the 1927 Mendelssohn concerto (Blech, Berlin Staatsoper) is again a smidgen technically superior to the 1936 recording with Sir Landon Ronald and the London Philharmonic. The violin sound is riveting in its winsome purity. Both discs register Kreisler's artistic propensities to an extreme degree. In the 1927 version he plays a harmonic E in the opening passage, as opposed to a solid finger E in the later disc, an unimportant detail in itself, but proof that Kreisler was amenable to changes of fingering over the years. The Andante is played like an endearing vignette; the short section connecting the Andante and Allegro molto vivace stresses poetic repose. In the earlier disc the finale is meticulously clean and buoyant.

Kreisler's temperament was intimately attuned to the Mozartean ethos. This is markedly evident in his recording of Mozart's Concerto No. 4 in D, K. 218 with Malcolm Sargent made around 1936, the second of his two recordings of this work. Ever an individualistic interpreter, this is among the most personalized of Kreisler's major-work performances. Following the so-called "military" opening, the playing is exceptionally relaxed, though a sense of buoyancy is consistently sustained. Melodic themes are more legato than is usually heard, and the cadenzas of the first two movements (his own) are highly imaginative and rich in the use of double-stops; the end of the Andante cantabile is meltingly poetic. The Rondeau is unduly slow; in the hands of a lesser player the music might be hopelessly bogged down, but Kreisler's sound and grace impart relevance to the various tempos. Surprisingly, the final cadenza is disappointing and is insufficiently related to the thematic material. In all, it is the kind of unorthodox performance that "grows" on the listener with repeated hearings.

One of Kreisler's lesser-known recordings (not issued officially) is the Bruch Concerto No. 1 in G-

FRITZ KREISLER, Violinist
CARL LAMSON, Accompanist

Wednesday, October 17

... PROGRAM ...
(SUBJECT TO CHANGE)

1.
a. SONATA, A MAJOR · · · · · · · · · · · · Handel
   Andante Allegro
   Adagio · Allegro ma non troppo
b. PARTITA IN B MINOR · · · · · · · · · · · · Bach
   (For violin alone)
   Allemande · Corrente · Double
   Sarabande · Double · Bourree

2.
CONCERTO, D MAJOR · · · · · · · · · Tchaikowski
   Allegro
   Canzonetta
   Allegro con brio
   INTERMISSION
   10 Minutes

3.
a. SUITE, FROM THE MUSIC TO "MUCH ADO ABOUT NOTHING"
   1. Maiden in Bridal Chamber
   2. March of the Watch
   3. Garden Scene
   4. Masquerade (Hornpipe)
   For violin and piano by the composer · Erich Wolfgang Korngold
b. TWO SLAVONIC DANCES · · · · · · · · Dvorak·Kreisler
   1. E Minor
   2. G Major
c. SPANISH DANCE (from La Vida Breve) · · Manuel de Falla·Kreisler

STEINWAY PIANO USED

Kreisler recital program, circa 1936

Courtesy Joseph Gold

Minor (with Eugene Goosens and the Royal Albert Hall Orchestra), made December 29 and 30, 1924, and January 2, 1925. He is in optimum form, and his opulent G-string sound sparks a sumptuously lyrical interpretation.

Although Kreisler was never included among the Paganini specialists, his arrangements of Paganini compositions verify his respect and admiration for the Genoese genius. As a young man, Kreisler refurbished *I Palpiti, Le Streghe, Non Piu Mesta,* and *La Clochette* with piano accompaniments far superior to the simplistic originals of Paganini, and added double-harmonics, finger-twisting runs of lightning-speed fingered octaves, and other intricate embellishments. I am not aware, however, of any performance of them by Kreisler in his maturity. He also renovated the *Moto Perpetuo* accompaniment, and provided accompaniments for caprices Nos. 13, 20, and 24 (as well as a few minor structural changes). Indeed, the Kreisler piano part for the opening lyric section of Caprice No. 20 is instilled with harmonic magic.

Predominant among his Paganini transcriptions is Concerto No. 1 in D-Major, Op. 6, for which he provided an original orchestration of heroic motif and lush harmonic contrivance. This comprises only the first movement, a tradition probably initiated by the German violinist August Wilhelmj (1845-1908), but constitutes a tour de force, almost 18 minutes in length, of considerably more musical substance than the Paganini original. In our time the concerto is played in its entirety in Paganini's own version except for the various individual cadenzas. It is unfortunate that the Kreisler version is scarcely ever played, since his stylistic enhancement deserves to be retained in the repertoire.

In 1936, at age 61, Kreisler recorded the concerto with Eugene Ormandy and the Philadelphia Orchestra. The performance is scrupulously clean technically, though some of the more strictly bravura passages are played at a more sober pace than is the wont of modern finger-board gymnasts. Kreisler endows the work with a special flavor, Viennese, if you will, that is quite irresistible. The sheen of his tone, his lyric phrasing, and the uniqueness of his expressive devices add up to a memorable performance. (Alfredo Campoli has an admirable recording of this transcribed version.)

For many years Kreisler refused to perform in radio broadcasts, but he ultimately yielded to the lure of tremendous fees, and possibly to a desire to keep abreast of his younger colleagues. In addition to his record-

ings there are undoubtedly air-checks of some of his broadcasts. I once heard an air-check of a portion of Viotti's Concerto No. 22.

A key element in the success of Kreisler's compositions was his exceptional gifts as a pianist. In 1925 he recorded piano transcriptions of eight of his popular violin vignettes for Ampico player-piano reproduction, all executed in a manner closely akin to his violin playing.

His compositions and transcriptions were direct extensions of his musical personality and performance. How does Kreisler rank as a composer? He was a significant composer, albeit a minor one. It is true that except for his string quartet, operettas, and a few individual songs, Kreisler was strictly a composer of violin music, and in that respect was extremely limited. But compared to the thousands of violin vignettes written by violinists of all categories, Kreisler's works were a landmark of novelty in construction, harmonic invention, and inspiration. They represent a genre of music quite different from any other efforts in the field. Those who tried to imitate or emulate these compositions could not produce pieces of equal caliber, although certain transcriptions, in particular those of Heifetz, do contain exceptional elements of harmonic novelty, inventiveness, and genuine talent. Kreisler, however, was not only a composer of charm and originality, and transcription stylist supreme, but was also an important influence in elevating piano accompaniments for violin vignettes from the old, basic chordal patterns to a much higher level of harmonic diversity, color, nuance, and imagination.

For the better part of a century Kreisler originals and transcriptions dominated those sections of violin programs devoted to short pieces and encores. Their popularity and universality were further ensured in that many of them could be negotiated by lesser violinists or capable amateurs. When changing standards and critical snobbery rendered them out of fashion for modern recitals that had been transformed into chamber music sonata concerts, they lay idle for a couple of decades and were not often included in major recitals. But recently we have been witnessing a Kreisler renaissance. Most of the best younger-generation violinists have produced all-Kreisler albums, and are including some of these pieces in their live programs. Frankly, in terms of sound and style, these performances, except in a few instances, are sorely lacking the kind of magic that can raise this type of music to its fullest potential. Nor can all of the echo chamber amplification and engineering artifices this side of heaven equate their individual sound with that of Kreisler. But at least the pieces are now approached more and more seriously and conscientiously, and less often with the sort of condescending attitude that "we play this trivia to please audiences whose artistic tastes are shallow." The fact of the matter is that Kreisler's works are very difficult to play even with top-level artistry. They demand tonal and interpretive powers considerably in advance of the more technical show-pieces of Paganini, Vieuxtemps, Wieniawski, Sarasate, and their lesser counterparts. Many a facile finger-board practitioner who can sail brilliantly through Wieniawski's *Scherzo Tarantelle* or the Original Variations, Op. 15 will founder badly when faced with the prospect of playing the double-stops of *Caprice Viennois* with vibrant beauty and lilting musicality.

In 1935, the origin of 14 of Kreisler's so-called classical manuscripts was the subject of a heated exchange between the violinist and various music critics, specifically Ernest Newman, the noted British musicologist. For over 30 years Kreisler had been playing and publishing these pieces. Printed on the sheet music was the statement: "They are, moreover, so freely treated that they constitute, in fact, original works." This cue should have prompted any alert critic to view them as Kreisler originals, a fact that had long been known to such musicians as Zimbalist, Spalding, Heifetz, Enesco, Persinger, Rupp, and Lamson, among others. After all, if *both* the violin and piano parts of the piece have been completely rewritten, what is left, save possibly a theme, or remnants of a theme?

But these compositions contained absolutely no thematic material from old classical masters (except for the first eight bars of *Chanson Louis XIII and Pavane*), and no one ever said they did. Instead, they were individually subtitled "in the style of" individual old masters, some of whom were not necessarily "masters" at all. Yet, even this modest allegation is specious. Why? Because each of these compositions: *Praeludium and Allegro* (Pugnani), *Allegretto in G Minor* (Porpora), *La Chasse* (Cartier), *Menuet* (Porpora), *La Precieuse* (Couperin), *Scherzo* (Dittersdorf), *Sicilienne et Rigaudon* (Francoeur), *Study on a Chorale* (Stamitz), *Tempo di Minuetto* (Pugnani), *Chanson Louis XIII and Pavane* (Couperin) and Concerto in C-Major (Vivaldi), is *pure Kreisler* in style from *first note to last*, except for the eight bars mentioned above. Any first-class critic should have noted this. At no time did Kreisler say or imply that

Courtesy Zino and Yolande Francescatti

Zino Francescatti and Kreisler in the former's New York home, 1954

these pieces were based on themes of these old masters, as he did, for example, with his transcription of Tartini's "Variation on a Theme of Corelli." Had Newman's ego been less pontifical, he would have taken the mild hoax in good humor, as did Olin Downes, the American critic. But even the latter erred in this friendly statement:

> It was undoubtedly to the great advantage of the compositions that they did not bear his name as a composer. Neither the public, nor the press, nor Mr. Kreisler's colleagues would have taken as kindly to these compositions had they been designated as being merely the creation of a living violinist.

Nonsense. His principal colleagues already knew of the innocent masquerade. The public would have adored these pieces regardless of who wrote them, especially as played by Kreisler. (Did they not continue to love them even after Kreisler admitted his authorship?) And had not Kreisler been a beloved international figure for more than three decades before the controversy, except for the World War I incident? And can anyone truly believe that had the words "in the style of" been deleted the critics would have attacked the pieces because they were "the creations of a living violinist"? More likely, many of them might have highly commended Kreisler for his obvious genius in this field.

A half-century has passed and the "scandal" has long since been forgotten. The protagonists are no longer living. But Kreisler's delightful compositions still are published widely wherever the violin is played. One cannot say that all of these vignettes are of highest quality. *Syncopation, Marche Miniature Viennoise, Aloha Oe, The Volga Boatman* paraphrase, and others are eminently forgettable, even in the capacity of miniatures. But such gems as *Praeludium and Allegro, Recitativo and Scherzo Caprice, Liebesleid, Caprice Viennois, Liebesfreud, La Gitana, Gypsy Caprice,* the Mozart *Rondo, Tambourin Chinois,* the Tartini-Kreisler Variations, *Schön Rosmarin,* the three Dvořák *Slavonic Dances,* and a host of other Kreisler originals and transcriptions seem destined to outlive us all.

Another important facet of Kreisler's inventiveness was his cadenzas. Although they are far from being technically simple they are devised with such canny understanding of the violin that they tend to sound much more difficult than they are. Certainly his cadenzas for the Beethoven and Brahms concertos, and Tartini's *Devil's Trill* Sonata, rank among the finest ever composed. In listening to post-Kreisler cadenzas, one can often feel his influence, even in cello concerto cadenzas.

Kreisler began at age four with a toy violin; at eight he was given a half-size Thir; at ten, a three-quarter size Amati; and for his Paris Conservatoire victory, won a gleaming red Gand-Bernadel, a gift from his father. He played on a Grancino for eight years, then a Nicolò Gagliano. During his Gagliano period he bought a Stradivarius he subsequently disliked, and then graduated to the 1727 "Hart" Stradivarius. Later he purchased his favorite, a 1733 Guarnerius del Gesù. He bought and sold many instruments: a 1733 Strad, ultimately acquired by Huberman; the 1734 "Lord Amherst of Hackney" Strad; the "Greville" Strad; the "Earl of Plymouth" Strad; a Petrus Guarnerius of Mantua; a Carlo Bergonzi; a 1732 Guarnerius (from Tivadar Nachez); a 1720 Daniel Parker; and a magnificent Vuillaume copy of a Guarnerius.

No doubt his finest violins played an important role in the quality of his sound, as with any other violinist. But blessed with a natural tone and vibrato of such seductive beauty, Kreisler would have sounded phenomenal even if he had played on the proverbial "cigar-box."

Kreisler owned a Tourte bow, but usually played with one of his several Hill bows or a Pfretschner, with the hair inordinately tightened. He shunned the use of shoulder pads, feeling that such appendages vitiated an instrument's tone.

In his "wunderkind" and early adult years, Kreisler's piano accompanist-collaborator was Dr. Bernhard Pollak and, in the early 1900s, Andre Benoist. Later, his European pianists included Michael Raucheisen, Franz Rupp, Erno Balogh, Hubert Geisen, Arpad Sandor, and Otto Schulhoff. For concerts in the British Isles his pianists were Sir Hamilton Harty, Haddon Squire, Charleton Keith, and Jorge Zulueta, though the British-recorded Beethoven sonata cycle was performed with Rupp. His North American and Australian collaborator was Carl Lamson from 1912 to the end of his career, possibly a record for such a partnership. Kreisler was reportedly exceptionally kind and generous to his pianists (which cannot be said for all of the great violinists), and his relationship with Lamson was one of utter benevolence.

As a man of his time, serial music and avant-garde experimentation were an anathema to Kreisler's sense of musical form and beauty. The aesthetic and spiritual qualities of his playing embody values and standards vastly different from those of our day. He produced tonal, expressive, and stylistic effects that are no longer heard or even sought after, and in his time he exerted a tremendous influence upon the performance of violinists everywhere. In that respect he taught untold numbers of violinists, though he had only two official pupils, Samuel Dushkin, noted for introducing works of Stravinsky, and Louis Edlin, concertmaster of the Cleveland Symphony in the early 1920s.

The depersonalization of the computer age has somewhat dimmed the lustre of Kreislerian romanticism, but his spirit lives on through his infectious compositions. As an artist he was a molder of phrases from which dreams are made, revered by audiences and critics alike; a true monarch of his realm who brought an incomparable state of grace to violin art that endured for half a century.

Fritz Kreisler

Courtesy Joseph Gold

Jacques Thibaud, purveyor of Gallic charm par excellence

Jacques Thibaud

Those who insist that the element of charm is a vital component in the realm of violinistic communication, will always cherish the artistry of one of its foremost purveyors—Jacques Thibaud. And precisely what is the literal definition of charm? According to Webster it means: "To attract irresistibly; to delight exceedingly; to enchant, fascinate, bewitch; as sounds that charm the ear." Though many observers may hold that charm in violin playing is fast becoming an anachronism in our time, more than any other single word it describes the cardinal feature of Thibaud's muse.

Thibaud was for 40 years the pride of the French violin school. Born in Bordeaux, September 27, 1880, he first studied with his father, a violin teacher, until the age of 13. He was then accepted as a student at the Paris Conservatoire, where he became a pupil of Martin Marsick. In 1894, at only 14, he competed in the annual Conservatoire competition which was won by the 21-year-old Carl Flesch, another Marsick pupil. Although the boy Thibaud was soundly defeated in this first attempt at glory, the following year he won third prize, and in 1896 the 16-year-old lad was awarded first prize.

Like Brahms, Ysaÿe, Kreisler, and many another luminary who started on the lowest rung of the ladder playing in nightclubs, cafes, and even brothels, Thibaud fiddled at the Café Rouge in the Paris Latin Quarter. He was heard there by Edouard Colonne, who invited him to join his celebrated orchestra. When the concertmaster was indisposed young Thibaud stepped into the breach and scored a sensational success playing the solo in Saint-Saëns's Prelude to *Le Déluge*. He became concertmaster and consequently appeared as soloist with that orchestra 54 times during the winter season of 1898, thus establishing himself in Paris.

Thibaud toured Europe, winning excellent critical response, and in 1903 toured the United States for the first time. In 1916, following a year's service in the French army during World War I, he again returned to the United States where he rapidly gained recognition as a violinist of international stature. Thibaud was also noted as a chamber music artist through his association, for three decades, with the renowned trio which included Pablo Casals and Alfred Cortot. He appeared in many sonata recitals with such keyboard notables as Harold Bauer and Artur Rubinstein, as well as in trio concerts with his two brothers. The violinist, together with Casals and Cortot, helped to found the École Normale de Musique in Paris, and with the pianist Marguerite Long founded the school and international competition which bears their names. Jacques Thibaud died tragically in a plane crash, September 1, 1953, on Mount Cemet near Barcelonette, France.

Aside from his compelling talents as a violinist and musician, Thibaud's charm extended to his person, and he became the intimate of many of the supreme artists of his day. The perceptive pen of Albert Spalding in his autobiography, *Rise to Follow*, provides a revealing thumbnail sketch of his close friend, Thibaud:

Thibaud exemplified the adventurous spirit of Gascony; the sun-shot warmth of Southern France illuminated his smile. He could tell tales with enthralling zest. The same grace and charm that individualized his violin playing was evident in everything else he undertook. He was irresistible to women, young and old, and was as proud of this power as he was modest about his musical genius. He cannot have been unaware of the spell which his inimitable playing could evoke; only a fool or an insensitive man could fail to

Thibaud with pianist Harold Bauer

know it, and Thibaud was neither. His wife adored him and accepted his frequent infidelities as the price of his companionship.

Mrs. Thibaud, Marguerite, nicknamed "Didi," who was quite wealthy, had been described as resembling and speaking like "a smaller Sarah Bernhardt"; the Thibauds had two sons, Roger and Philippe.

Thibaud was an incurable prankster who once secretly saturated his fastidious manager's hairbrush with butter. One can readily surmise the degree of his personal magnetism, inasmuch as the frivolous Frenchman was able to gain the bountiful affection of the conservative, utterly strait-laced Spalding, so much his antithesis in personality and character. Thibaud played at Spalding's wedding with André Benoist (who at different times served as piano accompanist-collaborator for both) presiding at the organ.

The stature of Thibaud's art can be assessed through comments by eminent colleagues. Auer, a pedagogue of a violinistic school diametrically different from that of Thibaud, states in his reminiscences: "The beginning of the 20th century heralded the appearance of two master violinists, Fritz Kreisler, who grew up artistically in Vienna and Paris, and Jacques Thibaud, a Frenchman by birth, who may be said to represent the school of his own country as Albert Spalding does the American and Jan Kubelik that of Prague."

Artur Rubinstein cites the first time he heard Thibaud in 1899. "His performance of the G-minor Concerto by Bruch I shall never forget. He managed to turn this pretty, unpretentious piece into a master-

piece, playing the second theme of the first movement with such tenderness that it brought tears to my eyes." Thibaud was 19 and Rubinstein 12 at the time. They remained cordial friends until Thibaud's fatal accident. During the World War I period, they gave numerous sonata recitals together. The pianist states: ". . . the concerts with Thibaud were sheer joy. We were musically in complete harmony and enjoyed our rehearsals almost more than the concerts."

Szigeti recalls "the great violin performances heard in my early years of Ysaÿe, Kreisler, Elman, and Thibaud," and places Thibaud with the moderns of that era, as opposed to such yesteryear players as Burmester, Marteau, Kubelik, Thompson, Serato, and Manen.

Casals characterizes Thibaud as "a consummate instrumentalist. He played the violin with incomparable elegance. Thibaud hated work, rarely practiced and had no sense of responsibility. He often behaved like a child, a naughty child. But he was wonderfully witty and gay, and kept his trio partners constantly entertained when on tour. He loved practical jokes and had a remarkable inventiveness for them."

Benoist, a struggling 23-year-old pianist in 1903, earning a living playing in a French café in New York, describes his first meeting with Thibaud as a candidate for the position of accompanist for the violinist.

Thibaud was fairly tall and graceful in his bearing. He wore his hair almost shoulder length, as was the mode for any artist worthy of the name, and a rather flowing moustache. He received me with true French courtesy, more in the manner of greeting a colleague than a flowering accompanist. He put me at ease immediately and quieted the budding nervousness I felt. After a few moments of conversation in which he asked several diplomatically put questions as to my background, we found we had many acquaintances in common, a fact that created an immediate bond. Then we began to play. I felt there would be no difficulty in assimilating myself to so musical an artist. Though his tone was not large, he never forced an issue. There were no temperamental exaggerations. It was the loveliest quality imaginable—velvety, warm and pure.

Benoist was accepted and became Thibaud's pianist for his debut 1903-4 American tour which opened with a Carnegie Hall recital, November 20,

Carl Flesch and his students

1903 at 3 P.M., offering the following program:

1. **Sonata - Franck**
2. **Prelude & Fugue from the G-minor Solo Sonata - Bach**
3. **Piano Solo: Polonaise in E Major - Liszt**
4. **(a) Rondo Capriccioso - Saint-Saëns**
   (b) Serenité - Vieuxtemps
   (c) Scherzando - Marsick
   (d) Melodrame - Guiraud
   (e) Polonaise (no number given)
   **   - Wieniawski**

(Reserved seats were 75 cents to $2.00.)

Carl Flesch was a Thibaud admirer, and included him with Kreisler, Elman, and Heifetz as players who were great at age 12, though he felt that Thibaud was a lesser spirit than Kreisler. He stated that "at age 22, Thibaud was the youngest violinist of great stature . . . his tone fascinated audiences with its uniquely sweet and seductive color, literally unheard of at that time." Flesch also refers to Thibaud's "habitual nervousness," and points out that "Thibaud, together with Elman, Busch and many others, must be heard in the flesh (i.e. rather than recordings) in order to be fully appreciated." Speaking of Thibaud in the 1923-28 period when the violinist was already over 40, Flesch was of the opinion that "Thibaud's musical character was of a young, rather than a mature man."

Flesch, who acknowledged the superiority of Thibaud without envy, remained a lifelong friend—another instance of the blithe Frenchman's ability to win and keep the favor of a stern, critical personality completely contrary to his own.

Further comments by Flesch include:

However unconsciously, his (i.e. Thibaud's) art

as well as his thoughts and actions, were dominated by the eternal feminine. His playing was imbued with his yearning for sensual pleasure, with an unchastity that was all the more seductive for its refinement. What a difference from the ideals pursued by Joachim and even by Ysaÿe in their youth! . . . He could not be compared to any other violinist . . . His left-hand technique was sufficiently accomplished to do justice to the exigencies of the repertoire (when he was on form), and his right hand, too, showed a high degree of mastery, both in its diverse bowings and in its modulation of tones...he even seemed to be considered heir presumptive to Ysaÿe.

The rigid immutability of his artistic attitude, at the age of 50 and beyond, still made him regard the erotic side of mental life as the center of musical experience. Not that I think that emotion should take second place in an aging artist, but it must be a different kind of emotion, more spiritualized and sublimated. Old men giving themselves youthful airs are among the stock comic figures, on the stage as in life.

This approach remained Thibaud's musical *raison d'etre* throughout his entire life. It still permeated his playing when I heard him for the last time, shortly before his death. The recital itself was embarrassingly ragged on the technical level. As so often happened with yesteryear violinists in their period of decline, Thibaud's interpretations were geared to his stylistic idiosyncrasies and waning technical resources, which turned the performance into a self-caricature. However, Thibaud's *Spanish Dance* by Granados was still sensuous, and an encore, Rameau's *Tambourin*, as elfin as ever.

Despite Flesch's favorable testimony regarding Thibaud's basic technical equipment, he does point out that "His art was in fact rooted in his innate talent, rather than in the acquisition of a solid technical ability. He lacked the manual routine which will step into the breach on days of physical or mental indisposition." This observation, of course, can be more or less applied to all the master violinists trained before or around the turn of the century, with the possible exception of Sarasate. For a realistic appraisal of their playing, they had to be heard on a good day, which might occur in Kalamazoo or Bombay, rather than New York or London. It is known, though, that Thibaud made repeated attempts toward drastic improvements in stabilizing his technical resources. When Flesch heard Thibaud in Berlin, in 1931, he said: "I found him surer of himself technically than eight years previously."

Thibaud's desire to solidify his technical equipment would appeared to be verified by a taped live performance of Lalo's *Symphonie Espagnole* (*Intermezzo* omitted), with Stokowski and an unnamed orchestra in 1947, when the violinist was 67, despite the constant assertions that Thibaud practiced little. This unlisted recording was released in disc form in 1974. It is a far-from-perfect performance, but most of the intonation in the passagework is right on target and pristine in clarity. Thibaud, with enviable audacity, rips off the sparkling Rondo finale with the speed worthy of almost any bravura specialist. The awkward broken-octave passage is truly brilliant, but the final high D of the Andante is woefully off pitch, almost as if his hearing were impaired. Stylistically, the Latin-oriented interpretation is totally engaging, honeyed in sound, with many individual subtleties in phrasing, albeit occasionally vitiated by unseemly slides.

Kreisler, Enesco, and Thibaud

Winsome, popular, and respected for his art by his colleagues, Thibaud enjoyed the intimate friendship of some of the world's greatest artists, including Ysaÿe, Kreisler, Casals, Enesco, Cortot, and a sizeable roster of other notables. Throughout the years he made music with them in chamber music groups of all types, both professionally and privately. Countless chamber music soirées by these artists, together with such colleagues as Harold Bauer, Artur Rubinstein, Pierre Monteux, Lionel Tertis, and Paul Kochanski took place at Muriel Draper's home in London, the Thibaud home in Paris, and that of the instrument collector, Reifenberg, in Paris, among others. Alas, none of these spontaneous sessions were recorded.

Thibaud's relationship with Ysaÿe was especially

From left, Eugène Ysaÿe and Jacques Thibaud

profitable, not only on the personal level, but in the development of his art. As a rising young star he learned much from the master, 22 years his senior. The influence of so powerful a violinistic personality might have been harmful to the younger man, but Thibaud's own musical individuality was so marked and indomitable, nothing could impair its character.

Together with Kreisler, Ysaÿe was Thibaud's idol (by his own statement) and he played certain of Ysaÿe's works, particularly the *Chant d'Hiver*, even before 1920. The Solo Sonata No. 2 in A Minor was dedicated to Thibaud.

The trio of Thibaud, Casals, and Cortot, fortunately, has left several recordings of major works to posterity. From the early years of the century they performed whenever time and commitments would permit. At the outset, Casals underwrote the trio's expenses and consciously lent his personal prestige to its formation. As the years passed, from modest beginnings the group went on to become a sell-out attraction at the box office. But the warm camaraderie was shattered by World War II, when Casals, the dedicated anti-fascist, went from Franco Spain into self-imposed exile. Cortot accommodated his talents to the Vichy French collaborationists, and Thibaud, who remained in France, though he reportedly never played for the Nazis (his son Roger was killed in battle by the Germans, and his son Philippe was a prisoner of war), was shunned by Casals. The cellist complained bitterly that when he was in exile in Prades, neither Cortot nor Thibaud ever sent much-needed food or inquired about him, though they knew very well where he was. After the war, Cortot begged Casals's pardon, admitted his wartime collaboration, and received Casals's forgiveness. But Thibaud never sought the latter's pardon, and the last time they met, Casals ordered the violinist out of his sight. A sad ending!

In violinistic ethos, Thibaud belongs in the company of Ysaÿe, Kreisler, and Elman, though admittedly, he never achieved their supremacy. All were inimitable violinistic personalities. Thibaud was limited by the smallness of his repertoire, which was possibly the least prolific of any leading 20th-century violinist (even including Erica Morini). He excelled in works of French composers, was an exquisite performer of Mozart, and, in general, a rather small-scaled player. Yet, audiences so relished the singularity of his style, they came again and again to hear him play the same compositions. It is said that one evening in the green room after a concert, an admirer asked him to write a few lines in his autograph book. The noted pianist Moritz Rosenthal, known as a wag, happened to be standing nearby. "What shall I write?" asked Thibaud of the pianist. Rosenthal quipped: "Just write your repertoire, Jacques."

In regard to his repertorial inclinations, Thibaud once remarked: "I would not exchange the first ten measures of Vieuxtemps's Fourth Concerto for the whole of Tchaikovsky's. I consider the Tchaikovsky Violin Concerto to be the worst thing the composer has written."

Like all of the romantic-oriented violinists of the recording era, at least since Ysaÿe, Thibaud had an individualized vibrato that together with his rare style, rendered his playing unlike any other. And like them, his vibrato was a natural extension of his personality, and uncontrived in contrast to some of the well-known French violinists who produced an excessively rapid vibrato, mostly from the finger-tip, with highly-arched fingers. The latter usage resulted in a stiff, constricted, somewhat nervous, whinnying sound which some observers came to associate with French players. (Renée Chemet is a prime example.)

The Thibaud vibrato was exactly on the core of the note, narrow in oscillation, and he knew instinctively when to vary its speed. At times his first finger sound recalled that of Elman, but any similarity ended at that point. Whereas Elman's tone was voluptuous, that of Thibaud was sweetly modulated and delicately glittering, far better suited to small-scale music of subtlety than heavyweight blockbusters. His intonation was excellent, and if a finger strayed occasionally, his tone remained pure and pellucid. However, his G-string sound was neither potent nor opulent. In tonal timbre Thibaud was essentially a soprano.

He possessed a fine trill—not of the electric type, but crisp and fast. Nor was his facility of bravura proportions, but it was ample to handle the challenges of the standard repertoire, or at least those works that he preferred. Even though he shunned works like the Tchaikovsky and Sibelius concertos, he often played both the Brahms violin concerto and the Double Concerto for Violin and Cello, however not with optimum power and breadth. His bowing was smooth and flexible, his spiccatos light and airy, his staccato adequate, although not of the ultra-rapid stiff-arm variety.

An important element in the personalization of his playing were his slides and position changes, patently sensual and distinctively Gallic. Thibaud was prone to use and overuse these effects indiscriminately in all types of music, but while individual slides might be considered *outré* by modern standards, they were never ugly or palpably unpleasant. Often they added a delightful tincture of piquance to his interpretations, particularly in French and Spanish music. There was always a touch of the French café fiddler in Thibaud, though it was artfully tempered by an air of nobility. Never really serious in character, profound, or intellectual, his playing exuded buoyancy of spirit and spontaneity, and he possessed a good measure of Kreisler's rare ability to phrase with rubato without victimizing the rhythm.

In the early part of his career Thibaud played a Bergonzi, but later acquired the beautiful Strad that once belonged to Baillot.

Thibaud, Leo Strokov, and Ysaÿe

It is undoubtedly true that Thibaud was more impressive when heard live than in recordings. Yet, he did leave a legacy of discs incorporating 86 listed works of various types and dimensions (plus 21 re-recordings), of which only six are solo or duo-solo concertos: No. 3 in G-Major, No. 5 in A-Major, and No. 6 in E-flat Major by Mozart, the No. 2 in E-Major by Bach, the Brahms Double for Violin and Cello with Casals, and the Chausson in D-Major with Cortot.

Perhaps the most memorable of Thibaud recordings is the Mozart Concerto No. 6 in E-flat Major, K.268 (sometimes called No. 7), whose authenticity is disputed, but is nevertheless a radiant creation. The work was popular with French and Belgian violinists, and Auer, in Russia, invariably taught it to his pupils. Unhappily, the engineering sorely lacks brilliance, but the uniquely individual Thibaud interpretation, made in the 1930s, ineffably sensitive and delicately etched, is one of the all-time significant Mozart violin recordings.

His Mozart Concerto No. 5, with Charles Munch and an Orchestre Symphonique (no date given; a French Pathé recording) is less outstanding but still a worthy performance. It was probably recorded in the latter part of Thibaud's career. His tone is gleaming, though there are inconsistencies both in sound and technique.

The outer movements are played at a fairly fast tempo; the Adagio contains less subtlety than one might expect, but is still admirably lyric. The finale is graced by feathery spiccatos and staccatos; some repeats are omitted. Cadenzas are by Joachim.

The Mozart No. 3 with Paul Paray and the Lamoreaux Orchestra (no date given), is a bit less effective; his artistry is best vested in the Andante, despite some glassy tones. The opening Allegro is taken at a fast pace and the difficult unidentified cadenzas are negotiated reasonably well.

Thibaud made some discs as early as 1905. These acoustically primitive efforts include Vieuxtemps's *Serenité* (for all its fogginess, his style is apparent) and *Gavotte* from Bach's E-major Solo Partita (clean, bright, and dancy).

A Thibaud favorite was Saint-Saëns's *Havanaise*, and a 1933 recording with piano reveals an aurally fragrant interpretation, exceptionally personalized with many expressive slides (some in questionable taste). Though technically neat, there are occasional blemishes; tape splicing was unheard of at the time. Although the recording has interesting features, it would seem reasonable to believe that his *Havanaise* performance in the concert hall was much more effective.

Another perennial Thibaud chestnut was the Debussy sonata, recorded with Cortot in 1929. It is an interpretation that projects the essence of French Impressionism with highly perfumed sound and extraordinary rapport between violinist and pianist. The aura is small-scaled; for example, on the first page, where modern players go up high on the E-string for a solid D and B, Thibaud plays the notes in simple fingered harmonics with striking effect. Slight imperfections give the disc the feeling of a live performance. A further brief sampling of this genre is Debussy's *Minstrels*, which Thibaud tosses off with delicious whimsy.

Chausson's *Poème*, another of Thibaud's preferential vehicles, with Eugene Bigot and the Lamoreaux Orchestra, probably recorded later in his career, contains many personalized slides, along with technical weaknesses not heard in recordings by current artists. It is the kind of performance that can offer the well-disposed listener nostalgic gratification through its individualized phrasing and stylistic nuances.

More satisfying is Chausson's Concerto for Violin, Piano and String Quartet, with Cortot and a French quartet, 1931. Apart from minor digital violin lapses and some over-ripe slides (particularly in the opening theme), this interpretation, distinctively French, has much to offer that is different from later high-powered recordings. Its mercurial impulsiveness and almost exotic flavor are calculated to give the modern listener an unusual experience. Surprisingly, the accompanying Fauré *Berceuse* is disappointing, tonally and otherwise.

Shorter pieces with piano include the Vitali-Charlier *Chaconne* (1936), with slides more appropriate to spicy Granados than baroque music, even considering the opus has been transcribed with romantic overtones. The prickly passages of thirds and octaves shortly before the final section have been omitted. To modern ears this must be considered a case of musical miscasting. Conversely, the Granados-Kreisler *Danse Espagnole* (1927) is played with Kreisler-like allure, but without the tonal intensity of the peerless Viennese. The de Falla-Kreisler *Danza Espagnola* (1929) is stylishly attractive, though soft-grained in sound, as are the Vivaldi-Pochon *Adagio*, one of Thibaud's more serious characterizations, and the Eccles-Salmon sonata (both 1930).

The Franck sonata, one of Thibaud's prime items, recorded in 1928 with Alfred Cortot, seems to represent

Thibaud with his longtime musical partner, Alfred Cortot

an off day for the violinist. Except for a few episodes in the second and third movements, his performance is arid, lacking in beauty and variety of tonal color, and often unstable technically. Unfortunately, the totality represents an example of his weakest playing. Conversely, Fauré's Sonata No. 2, recorded in 1927 with Cortot, another Thibaud favorite, though harried by surface noise in the Odeon disc, contains some of his best lyric work. The rapid passages of the third and fourth movements are exceptionally nimble and clean.

The Thibaud-Casals recording of the Brahms Double Concerto in 1929, conducted by Cortot, with the Casals Orchestra of Barcelona (a variable ensemble), is the earliest recording, in my recollection, of this massive work by artists of international stature. Many play this opus with more muscularity, digital surety, and essential power than Thibaud, but few offer comparable sensitivity and lustre of E-string tone in lyric passages. The Casals cello sound, more weighty and solid, is better suited to Brahms, though Thibaud's lighter-grained tonal projection has more sheen, as it does in all of their chamber music recordings. The Andante lacks sufficient tonal intensity by both instruments, but at least a portion of this may possibly be due to the period of the recording and the Spanish engineering of the time.

In the Thibaud-Cortot version of Beethoven's *Kreutzer Sonata* (1929), the violinist, after a somewhat tentative start, warms up to a well-ordered performance, though it is small-scaled. Thibaud seems to have occasional problems in regulating his vibrato, but in general, his dulcet tone dominates the less caressing Cortot piano sound. Despite a glaring piano blunder midway through the final movement, it is a fluent interpretation, if not a memorable one.

The trios with Casals and Cortot represent a major segment of Thibaud's recordings. All of the group's recordings have exceptional spontaneity of performance and are technically sound. There are, however, certain discrepancies between the bright Thibaud sound, the more solid, less vibrant Casals tone, and the somewhat sinewy piano sound of Cortot. This is more than compensated for by the felicity of their ensemble and the overall polish and suavity of their playing. In all of the recorded trios a natural musical flow prevails, and unless one insists on pinpointing some of Thibaud's slides, the group's music-making avoids mannered effects or affectation.

The Haydn Trio No. 1 in G-Major, Op. 73, No.

Pablo Casals, Thibaud, and Alfred Cortot

2 (1927) is beautifully articulated and subtly phrased, and the *Gypsy Rondo* finale contains some provocative alterations of tempos. Beethoven's *Archduke* Trio (1928) is perhaps the least impressive of the trio recordings, with intermittent dryness of sound and flickers of slightly off-target cello intonation in the opening movement. Mendelssohn's Trio No. 1 (1927) is a sprightly, neatly-balanced reading, vitiated to some degree by lackluster cello sound. In the Schubert Trio No. 1, Op. 99 (1926), the playing is warm and exuberant. Again the cello sound is rather tubby, especially in the finale. Thibaud employs his own personalized slides (much like Heifetz in his trio recordings of later years), yet his sound does much to add overall sparkle to the performance.

A 1940 recording of Fauré's Piano Quartet No. 2, Op. 45, with Marguerite Long, Maurice Vieux, and Pierre Fournier, displays Thibaud still in reasonably good form at 60. (The unhappy man had no way of knowing that his elder son was to die in battle the following day.)

In view of the current pervading presence of decathlon-type instrumental contests, there may never be another violinist quite like Thibaud. The era which produced and applauded his manner of individualized violinistics has passed into history. A good number of modern violinists, including some of French derivation, have surpassed him in many respects. Even in his heyday, for all his successes, he was never quite able to cross the threshold into true greatness. Yet he was the premier French violinist of the early 20th century, and eminently deserving of his niche in the violinistic Hall of Fame.

Jacques Thibaud

Jan Kubelik at the turn of the century

Jan Kubelık

Paganini's wizardry, nurtured in the atmosphere of operatic classicism, made a revolutionary impact that left its imprint, to a greater or lesser degree, upon all of the succeeding schools and trends of violin art. The fingerboard explorations and innovations that he introduced directly influenced the performance and compositions of Vieuxtemps, Wieniawski, and a legion of lesser lights who applied various elements of the Paganini swashbuckling bravura to the new, rapidly-maturing romanticism. Even the stern, often austere German School, as eventually represented and epitomized by Joseph Joachim, could not help but be affected, at least in terms of purely technical accomplishments of the left hand.

The phenomenon of a violinist performing his own compositions almost exclusively, died with Paganini. But there was still a breed of player whose performance and compositions, to a major extent, continued in the image of Paganini; limited artists, but of some importance in the violinist pantheon. Among the most prominent in this category was the Moravian, Heinrich Ernst, who had followed Paganini throughout Europe, fashioning his own playing and compositions perhaps more closely after the Genoese than did any other—a musician of solid worth. The Norwegian Ole Bull, too, was a Paganini imitator, a quasi-vaudevillian whose personal aura was blatantly more colorful than that of Ernst, but a feeble composer, even in the context of superficial theme-and-variation and vignette violin concoctions. Then there was the Italian, Ernesto Camillo Sivori, the sole legitimate pupil of Paganini; the German, August Wilhelmj, editor of sundry Paganini compositions and initiator of a Paganini resurgence in the 1870s, whose playing was brilliant but brief; and the Belgian, César Thomson, noted for his octave feats, a

cool, respectable mechanic who suffered the fate of being greatly overshadowed and downgraded by his countryman, Ysaÿe. One need only note the diverse nationalities of these violinists to comprehend the geographical scope of the Paganini fertilization.

By the turn of the 20th century, however, advances in stylistic subtlety, tonal beauty, security of intonation, and breadth of repertoire had almost rendered the pure technician (i.e. gymnast of the fingerboard) anachronistic. Both audiences and critics had begun to seek violinistic satisfaction in more musically significant provinces. Compared to our era, there was still considerable instrumental primitivism, questionable taste, and shallow musicality to be found. Within two decades, a new revolution was destined to shake the very foundation of violin-dom. But in 1900, Ysaÿe was "king," Kreisler the "heir-apparent," and Elman a "princeling of the blood," soon to vie with the peerless Viennese for the Belgian's crown.

Nevertheless, the spectacle of an intrepid man walking a tightrope without a safety net exercises a compelling fascination, whether it be in a circus aerial act, or figuratively speaking, on a violin fingerboard. This was as true in 1900 as it was in Paganini's time, or, for that matter, today. And in 1900, the era of Paganini was no more distant than were the early careers of Kreisler and Elman, and the European debut of Heifetz, from this writing. For all its progress, the world of violin performance was ripe for the spiritual revival of the Paganini legend. It materialized in the person of a 20-year-old Czech, Jan Kubelik, who, aided by a tremendous publicity barrage, took his audiences by storm and, incidentally, probably amassed more money from his concerts than had any violinist except Paganini (and perhaps Ole Bull) up to that time.

The appearance of Kubelik brought the ever-flickering Paganini syndrome to a new plateau. It represented a retrogressive diversion in the burgeoning advancement of violinistic progress, but one that had enormous appeal for the less musically sophisticated mass audience.

Kubelik was born in Michle, near Prague, July 5, 1880, of Czech parents. He began study of the violin at age five with his father, a gardener by profession and an amateur musician. At eight he made his first public appearance in Prague, playing a Vieuxtemps concerto and some Wieniawski pieces. He next had lessons with K. Webera, K.J. Ondricka, and F. Srsne, each for one year. His real teacher was Ottokar Sevčik, with whom he studied for six years at the Prague Conservatory. Sevčik pupils are said to have totalled in the thousands during his exceptionally long teaching career in Europe and America, among them: Erica Morini, Efrem Zimbalist (after Auer), Franz Ondřiček, Jaroslav Kocian, Marie Hall, and Leonora Jackson.

Noted for his technical exercises which are still universally in use, Sevčik's teachings were centered around the development of finger and bow dexterity to an incredible degree. Such matters as beauty of tone, grandeur of style, and subtlety of detail were not part of the Sevčik lexicon. His most diligent pupils practiced upwards of eight hours a day, attaining an extraordinary instrumental agility that was employed in the service of lackluster, backward-looking interpretations.

If a pupil possessed an inherent penchant for musical expressiveness, overmuch exposure to the Sevčik methods (which were beneficial when used in moderation) could, and in many instances did, transform him into a player of juiceless mechanical rote. Kubelik was the prime example. Yet Flesch, for all his criticism of Kubelik, called him ". . . a talent of the highest calibre," and Thibaud labelled him ". . . a genuinely talented violinist . . . if he had had another teacher he would have been great . . . I consider him one of Sevčik's victims." Thibaud, describing the Czech's preparations for a performance of the Beethoven concerto, ". . . he spent the livelong day before the concert practicing Sevčik exercises." Kubelik, with aching fingers, often practiced incessantly even on the day of a concert. Naturally such stupefying toil served to deaden the sensitivity of his fingertips, and militated against musical spontaneity.

Kubelik represented the ideal of Sevčik pedagogical achievement. At 18 he played the Brahms concerto with his own cadenzas and the Paganini Concerto No. 1. Although his repertoire embraced most of the standard favorites of the time, it was with the music of Paganini and kindred ilk that he made his reputation. In the course of two years, his gymnastic feats conquered audiences (if not all of the critics) of Vienna, Budapest, Paris, and London. These successes included an Italian tour during which he received the Order of St. Gregory from Pope Leo XIII at Rome. Honors and decorations from the crowned heads of Europe proliferated rapidly. In 1902 Kubelik made his first of many tours of the United States, causing a veritable sensation. He was dubbed "The Heir to Paganini," and in the tradition of Paganini, shop windows displayed hats, boots, scarves, and other items "a la Kubelik." At one point, his box office receipts exceeded even those of Paderewski in Chicago. Society girls deluged him with offers of marriage. Within a few years he amassed more than a half-million dollars from his American concerts, a gigantic sum for that era. (Kreisler received $400 for two concerts as soloist with the New York Philharmonic in 1905!)

Kubelik's piano accompanist in his early American concerts was Rudolph Friml, later to become famous for his delectable operettas.

All, however, was not unalloyed triumph. Germany, with its comparatively more conservative and sober musical standards, responded to the Kubelik invasion with moderation. And the well-known American critic Henry Finck, writing in 1909, was positively disenchanted by the Czech's performance. Finck correctly compared the Paganini concertos to the operas of Rossini and Donizetti, but he was overly subjective when he referred to these operas as "antiquated . . . . . in which the ornamental style is rampant." Apparently Finck's musical sensibilities were not in consonance with the magic of classical Italian opera. Nevertheless, his firsthand comments on Kubelik's early performances deserve scrutiny.

Finck wrote, in part:

. . . such sensational reports had come across the ocean that when he made his first appearance in New York the audience had evidently made up its mind beforehand (as in the case of Tetrazzini) to be enthusiastic; he was received with such applause as is usually bestowed only on old favorites. And after the first pause of the solo instrument in the Paganini concerto he was playing, the audience burst out into a perfect tornado of approval, although up to that point, the young Bohemian violinist had done nothing whatsoever to justify such a demonstration. His playing, so far, might have been easily duplicated by any one of the violinists in the orchestra.

As the concerto proceeded he performed feats which the orchestral players could not have imitated. Runs, skips, trills, double-stops, simultaneous pizzicato and arco, and all the other tricks of the fiddler's trade were at his command to astonish the natives. Most amazing of all were his 'flageolet-tone' or harmonics. These were flawless. A New York audience probably had never heard anything quite equal to this display of fireworks. The artistic value of a melody or staccato run in harmonics is, to be sure, not much above that of a tune blown on one of the bird whistles sold by street peddlers.

Certainly Mr. Kubelik did not succeed in restoring life to the Paganini concerto. While his playing was comparatively free from the exaggeration of the grandiose style, he lacked the exotic charm and magnetism of Sarasate, Remenyi, and Ole Bull, and as an artist he could not be placed on the same high level as Ysaÿe, Kreisler, Kneisel, or Maud Powell. The only piece of good music on his first program was Schumann's hackneyed *Traumerei*, and this he played in the lackadaisical salon manner.

Finck continues at length in this vein, concluding with,

But where there is so much to suggest the circus, would it not be well, for the sake of consistency, to have sawdust on the floor and peanuts for sale in the lobby?

However, Finck does acknowledge that when Kubelik returned to America four years later, he had made significant artistic progress.

There was a deeper comprehension of good music in Kubelik's playing, as well as the spirit, abandon and enthusiasm that go by the comprehensive name of temperament. He now gave pleasure to those who expect a violinist to do more than dazzle them. Still, the bulk of his fortune—a big fortune it was—was made by dazzling . . . Obviously there are various ways of winning success, due to the fact that there are various kinds of audiences.

While Finck's remarks are certainly valid on the

Jan Kubelik and his wife, the former Countess Czaky Szell

musical and aesthetic levels, he obviously had general, rather than intimate knowledge of violin art (like most all-purpose music critics in every era), and obviously no genuine affection for violinistic bravura traditions. Violin circuses, like any other, provide delightful entertainment to masses of people, and the stupendously laborious process of acquiring Paganini-like agility should be given neither smart-alecky maltreatment nor cavalier dismissal. It is certainly more equitable to accept Kubelik for the type of player he was, in the repertoire of his own choice, and conduct our evaluation of his performances from that point.

In 1903 Kubelik married the Countess Czaky Szell in Hungary, becoming a citizen of that country;

their eight children (five daughters and three sons) include the well-known contemporary conductor, Rafael. In 1915 he retired from the concert stage, ostensibly to devote his time to compositions. This produced six violin concertos, many small pieces, transcriptions, concerto cadenzas, and a symphony, none of which is currently performed. In 1921 he resumed concertizing, but his playing no longer provoked any of the excited response that was accorded him in the naive turn-of-the-century era. Kubelik made his final comeback appearances in 1935, one of which will be described in detail later. He died December 5, 1940, in Prague.

Another firsthand report of Kubelik's initial American concert states:

> Whether he played well or ill, salvos of tremendous applause were his invariable reward . . . The seeker of sensations who had been repressing his emotions for several years has found a long desired idol in this young Czech, and is going to make hay while the sun shines.

Kubelik was fortunate in appearance, manner and style. He gave an impression of suffering sensitivity, which went well with the ladies who could make or break a concert artist at the box office.

He was described as

> . . . small for his years . . . slender, narrow-shouldered with the stoop of an old man. He walks with a step which suggests the lisp of speech, holding his arms angularly. His face is rugged, with colorless skin, absolutely expressionless. His hair is thick and falls over his head like the mane of a horse.

The New York *Tribune* found it necessary to criticize the publicity as much as the artist, saying

> It is a pretty appreciation of the notion that the world of today, in spite of all that is seen, said, and written of its sordid commercialism, is still fond of a hero and needs only to be told with sufficient assiduity and emphasis that the hero is arrived, to believe the statement and adopt the attitude of adoration.

To give an example of the fierce competition among artists, it is said in Louis Lochner's Kreisler biography that Kubelik (whose deportment was generally amiable, reasonable, and unassuming, as opposed to the bombast of his publicity) tore down a poster of Paderewski in a Chicago hotel elevator, angrily declaring, "That's what you do for another artist when I'm the man who made your hotel famous!" This imprudent action is said to have cost Kubelik some of the goodwill that he had created by his technical wizardry.

It is all too easy to dismiss Kubelik as a meteoric phenomenon of interpretive, tonal, and musical anachronism, who flashed across the scene and filled his purse at the expense of mass audience naiveté. This would not be true essentially. Although Kubelik used sensationalist effects to overwhelm his listeners, these effects were perfectly legitimate violinistically, not to be compared with the stagy folderol of Bull, or Franz Clement, who played a sonata for a one-stringed violin with the instrument held upside-down, on the same program in which he premiered the Beethoven Violin Concerto. In Kubelik's day there were numerous second- and third-rate technicians who rattled off difficult show pieces in a slovenly manner. Such matters as intonation, fidelity to the notes in rapid passagework, and any semblance of musical probity were abominably victimized by these Paganini caricatures.

By contrast, Kubelik was a technician of honorable and thorough integrity, who stressed the value of slow practice and the importance of rhythmic precision. In his own way, he was a perfectionist, and as the years elapsed, he strove to develop musically. Unfortunately his gains were minimal, inasmuch as his violinistic priorities, muscular habit patterns, and stylistic inclinations were too deeply rooted in the past. However, for all the automatism of his performance, he remained a respectable figure in the evolution of that segment of violin art (and an honorable, if limited one it is!) which lays primary stress on digital derring-do.

Kubelik has left some 60 recordings of pieces (several were recorded more than once) which are either short in their original form, or tailored to fit the old pre-electric ten- and 12-inch platters. For all the aboriginal drawbacks of their engineering and manufacture, they provide a reliable barometer of his strengths and weaknesses. Some were made possibly as early as 1906 in Milan for Fonotipia; probably none later than 1915.

Although Kubelik was invariably likened to Paganini, his playing, cool in temperament, calculated, metronomically measured in technical passagework, and comparatively slow in digital velocity compared with modern virtuosos, was quite the opposite of that attributed to Paganini, whose playing was described by his adulators and detractors alike as being audacious, explosive, and impassioned in musicality.

When one compares his recordings of Bazzini's *Ronde des lutins* and Sarasate's *Zapateado* with the first Heifetz discs of the same pieces, the revolution that took place in a mere ten or twelve years (in virtuosity as well as in sound and polish) becomes apparent immediately.

As one listens to the tonally-oriented works on the Kubelik recordings (if we can manage to overlook the tasteless slides and slender tone), it becomes clear that any allegation that Kubelik had no musical feeling

The young Jan Kubelik

at all is not quite true. He does exhibit a sort of chaste emotion, but it is rather rustic, incredibly unsophisticated in style, and almost bereft of intensity.

The best of his slow performances is the Gluck-Wilhelmj "Melodie" (*Dance of the Blessed Spirits*), a version considerably longer than Kreisler's. It has more emotional projection comparatively than the others, is warmer in sound and has more finger vibrance. On the HMV label, it is probably one of his later discs, and one gets the impression that he has been somewhat influenced, beneficially, by more modern players.

Drdla's *Souvenir*, its opening theme partially embellished with double-stops, is also reasonably expressive, but sabotaged by many inept slides. Drdla's *Serenade*, for all its digital clarity, is paper-thin in tone

and riddled with ludicrous slides. Kubelik's innate lack of musical buoyancy is an anathema to the piece. A theatrical fingerboard-length back-sliding E-string trill-chromatic scale and a frisky little left hand open E-string pizzicato have been added for spice.

Canzonetta, the slow movement of the Tchaikovsky concerto, is about a quarter-tone flat in pitch (in the engineering), and exceedingly bland, though again, Kubelik seems to be trying to update his playing. The slides are prolific, but less so than in the most anachronistic of his discs, and a simple ending is appended to provide a static finish to the movement.

Drdla's *Visions* is poor, and some of the double-stops are not clean. The piano introduction is particularly brittle. A Kubelik arrangement of a "Romance" attributed to Mozart is hopelessly dull, exceptionally one-dimensional in sound, and endowed with an over-simplistic piano part. (Was this arrangement perhaps Kubelik's own composition, à la Kreisler?) The opening "Adagio" from Handel's Sonata No. 15 in E is disjointed in lyric flow and detached in spirit, but the ensuing Allegro second movement, a bit hectic in pace, registers a degree of verve. George Falkenstein, who accompanied many top violinists of the pre-1920 era, collaborates at the piano. Most of the Kubelik disc accompanists remain unnamed.

One of the most enjoyable vignettes, but appallingly naive, is Alberto Randegger Jr.'s (1880-1918) *Pierrot's Serenade*, which, to me, ideally epitomizes Kubelik's expressive ethos. Its thematic material may be lugubrious but it is also charming, and the listener can fairly visualize the hands of the clock flying backward. Randegger was also one of several accompanists used by Kubelik.

Of the bravura works, Ries's *Perpetuum Mobile*, with no melodic lines, is clean, even-tempered, and even displays some impulsive zip—a good performance. Hubay's *Der Zephir* has much pesky surface noise, is clean-cut but heavy-handed, and permeated with tasteless backward slides in the melodic theme. Wieniawski's *Scherzo-Tarantelle* is moderately brilliant in the outer sections, but the lyric middle segment clearly indicates Kubelik's difficulty in sustaining tone quality in position changes. As in several of the virtuoso numbers, there has been some cutting to conform with 78 recording time requirements.

An abridged version of Wieniawski's *Faust Fantasy* has more than usual surface noise, but scampers along exuberantly, and is one of Kubelik's most brash and fiery (for him) interpretations. Wieniawski's *Dudziarz Mazurka* to modern ears is droll in style, and the sinuous melodic episode abounds in absurd finger slides, yet a measure of Kubelik's inherent sincerity filters through. There is some open-string pitch deviation, probably brought about by string-pullings of the left hand finger pizzicatos. The surface noise is distracting.

Fiorillo's *Caprice* No. 28, which was a favorite of many old-time violin teachers for ensemble performance by their entire class, is tastefully played, with piano support. Of course, it is a technical exercise for crossing strings, sans melody.

Some of the poorest playing is in Sarasate's *Zigeunerweisen* and Nachez's *Danse Hongrois* (wrongly attributed to Lizst on the original American Fonotipia disc). Kubelik simply had no gypsy blood in him, and the rudimentary nature of his vibrato is cruelly exposed. Even many of the rapid passages are played heavily detaché rather than crisply spiccato. Both are a case of gross miscasting, though they are clean in intonation.

Bazzini's *Ronde des lutins* and Sarasate's *Zapateado*, noticeably slower than played by later virtuosos, are metronomic and very weak in the few lyric passages. Oddly, the left hand finger pizzicato batteries, spectacular in the "Goblins," are either poor or eliminated in the *Zapateado*. The latter may be a later disc.

Conversely, in Paganini's *Nel cor piu non mi sento* variations (unfortunately only the first two variations are played), Kubelik's left hand finger pizzicatos are exceptionally clean, though very measured. In a four-minute cadenza to the first movement of Paganini's Concerto No. 1, composed by himself (fairly well conceived, but without the inspired cadenza-writing subtleties of Kreisler, Joachim, Ysaÿe, Auer, or even Sauret), Kubelik, after a slightly tentative start, negotiates passages of thirds, tenths, fingered octaves, and glissando octaves with admirable virtuosity.

The finale of Sarasate's *Carmen Fantasy* is played at an unduly slow pace, carefully and very cleanly, but with no vestige of audacity or excitement. On the other hand, Leon Saint-Lubin's *Sextette from Lucia* paraphrase for violin alone (the disc includes several episodes starting with the beginning, but only part of the complete opus) is an extraordinary performance. His left hand pizzicatos accompanying the thematic line are stunning and one can only assume that Kubelik's playing of this finger-twister at the turn of the century must have left his audiences with mouths agape.

Despite all the criticisms of these recorded per-

formances, it is a thoroughly fascinating experience to hear them in continuity—one every violin enthusiast should cherish. Most of the above can be heard on James Creighton's *Masters of the Bow*, MB 1001; *Rococo*, 2001, and Biddulph Records.

Flesch has said of Kubelik,

> Even before he was 30 there were clear indications of a decline. The astringency of his tone developed into dryness, the absolute reliability of his technique began to break down, his chastity turned into coldness, and the unpolished quality of his execution, which had been attributed to his youth, proved to be a lack of musical culture.

But let us also recall that several American metropolitan critics had noted musical progress in Kubelik's interpretations in the years following his American debut.

The Flesch remarks undoubtedly have some validity, since the later Kubelik discs of the 'teen years display a certain though not really marked digression. But applied to the entire Kubelik concert career which carried over until the latter 1930s, I think Flesch's evaluation is over-simplistic and not cast in historic perspective. Regardless of the degree of Kubelik's alleged technical decline (my own listening experience, both of discs and Kubelik 'live,' does not confirm this decline), I believe that the answer to his career demise lies elsewhere.

If Kubelik, at the turn of the century, already represented a backward-looking musicality, he was fated to view nearly 40 more years of tremendous violinistic development. The world of violin art simply passed him by, and the state of his playing had nothing to do with the near-oblivion of his career. New technicians with equal dexterity, far better sound and interpretive styles, had developed. By 1925, Kubelik could be likened to a Cro-Magnon artist.

He retired in 1915, but made several comebacks. His final return to the stage was in 1935 at age 55. I vividly recall his Los Angeles concert, and can testify that his playing of a tremendously difficult program was as clean and agile as that of his best early discs; more mature musically, and divested of many of the old-time ludicrous slides. However, even at its technical best, it retained the basic deficiencies of his prime years. His admirable digital facility, utterly without brilliance of sound, was "typewriter-like," and his tone almost bereft of vibrato.

At the time I was still a highly impressionable teenager and to me, the reappearance of Kubelik, this long vanished titan from out of the distant past, was indeed a memorable occasion. When the concert was announced, I immediately bought a ringside ticket (which I could ill afford) and awaited the event with bated breath.

The large Los Angeles Philharmonic Auditorium was not quite filled to capacity but the local Czech community was out in full force to greet its hero, even though only a handful of professional violinists and students deigned to attend. For some reason the lights remained at maximum brightness throughout the evening (a rare occurrence for an instrumental recital in that era), encouraging complete visual contact between audience and artists. This also lent a rather festive air to the proceedings.

Kubelik came onstage followed by his rather gangling young pianist-son Rafael. He was a short man with bushy hair that crowned his bald pate like a laurel wreath. His expression was benign and smiling, and from the very first moment I was entranced by his charming, old world personality. I noticed that his feet were large, somewhat flat, and his playing stance struck me as being slightly Chaplinesque.

The program opened with the Goldmark concerto, a work of about 33 minutes, after which he performed one of his own equally long concertos which, in general, reflected a musicality similar to that of the Goldmark. This comprised the first half. Scarcely a note was off pitch in this arduous workout, but neither was there any perceptible degree of emotional projection or communication.

After intermission, Kubelik started with an étude-like interpretation of the Bach *Chaconne*, followed by a lengthy group of shorter pieces beginning with Paganini's Caprice No. 6, the trill-tremolo étude, and ending with Paganini's *La Clochette* (*La Campanella*). Kubelik had a fabulous up-and-down movement finger facility, and since then I have never heard the trill-tremolo caprice negotiated with more pristine clarity—not even by the most brilliant modern technicians. This assessment has been reinforced by my recent hearing of Kubelik's early recording of the opus, though admittedly, the disc performance contains some gauche emotive slides and a few wrong notes.

After every composition, long or short, fast or slow, Kubelik, for a brief moment, would indulge in the quaint idiosyncrasy of holding his bow absolutely still at

Jan Kubelik

the tip. Then he would extend his arms full length, one holding the violin, the other the bow, in the manner of an Olympic athletic champion accepting his deserved plaudits from an adoring public. And as to be expected, the audience applauded wildly. In a modern artist such 'ham' would be unacceptable, even obnoxious, but the gesture was such an inherent element of Kubelik's entire aura and image, that I actually found it endearing.

At the conclusion of the printed program, the applause continued vociferously. Kubelik obligingly responded with two encores. The friendly audience, insatiable, cheered even louder. At this juncture, beaming from ear-to-ear in the certainty of having achieved a triumph, he strode onstage carrying a bulky armful of music, prepared to play on into the wee hours if need be.

Eventually he reached his eighth encore, the Schubert-Wilhelmj *Ave Maria*, with its oh-so-difficult sostenuto G-string theme, octaves, and double-stops. At this point I was greatly saddened. Kubelik, unwisely, had seriously overstepped the limitations of his equipment and was in obvious distress. One could easily count the slow, mechanical oscillations of his inflexible, primitive vibrato. As a performance it was both embarrassing and disastrous. The unknowledgeable lay audience, too, seemed to sense that something was amiss. The marathon affair had sputtered to a halt.

My fascinating visit to the violinistic world of yesteryear was over. For all of Kubelik's picturesque blandishments, I realized that his art was totally anachronistic to contemporary values and standards, but nevertheless, I have always cherished my recollections of the experience.

The question arises: How did Kubelik compare, *strictly on the virtuoso gymnast level*, with Paganini specialists of recent and current times? With all the best will one can muster toward a respected ancestor, the answer would have to be that Kubelik could *not* compare with our contemporary technicians, except possibly in an isolated instance, such as the Paganini trill-tremolo Caprice No. 6, an unadulterated finger exercise.

Apart from his inferiority in sheer brilliance and warmth of sound, and comparative blandness of attack, Kubelik could never compete in bravura works with the diabolical, kamikaze explosiveness of a Ricci in his prime years. Nor could he play Paganini caprices with the speed, precision and finesse of a Heifetz, Kogan, Rabin, Perlman, Renardy, Accardo, Pikaisen, Příhoda, Gulli, or numerous lesser-known modern players. Today the per-

formances of Paganini concertos are more than mere technical feats. We have the grippingly dramatic interpretations of the young Menuhin, the tempestuous gymnastics of Ricci, the technical brilliance and luxuriant tone of Kogan, Perlman, and Rabin, the elegant expositions of Francescatti, Grumiaux, and Szeryng, and the feisty expoundings of Shmuel Ashkenasi. Each of these players has performed or recorded one or more of the concertos; Accardo has recorded all six, including those that have been reconstructed recently and were unknown to Kubelik. Excellent renditions of Paganini abound, even among women players whose comparative smallness of the left hand was once thought to militate against such music. In the area of repertoire, players like Ricci, Accardo, and Pikaisen, among others, play (collectively) obscure Paganini pieces--*Maestosa Sonata Sentimentale, Sonata Appassionata, Variations on a Theme of Joseph Weigl, La Primavera Sonata, Sonata Napoleon for the G-String*, and *Duo Merveille*, all little played in Kubelik's day, along with the familiar theme-and-variation works, plus other bravura conflagrations by Ernst, Wieniawski, and Vecsey.

Nevertheless, Kubelik was a key figure in the sustenance of our glorious bravura traditions, and as such, deserves his special niche in the history of violin art.

Jan Kubelik

Bronislaw Huberman, a controversial artist of heightened social conscience and humanistic purpose

Bronislaw Huberman

One of the most provocative and controversial violinists of the past century was Bronislaw Huberman, whose extraordinary individualism was as remarkable in matters of political and humanistic endeavor as in his instrumental characteristics and musical philosophy.

Huberman, in his prime, enjoyed colossal prestige in Central Europe, Poland, and several other countries in that general periphery, though his success on the international scene was varied. At one time, Viennese audiences accorded him homage equal to, or even surpassing, that given Kreisler.

Born in Czestochowa, Poland, December 19, 1882, son of a Warsaw barrister, he began study of the violin at age six with Michalowicz, and at seven performed Spohr's Violin Concerto No. 2 and played first violin in a quartet by Rode. He also studied for a few months with Isador Lotto at the Warsaw Conservatory. In 1892 his father brought him to Berlin where the boy's playing was highly praised by Joachim, who referred him to Markees (Joachim's assistant) for further study. At this juncture Huberman remained in Berlin for only eight months, and during the period of his lessons with Markees, he studied secretly with the noted virtuoso Charles Gregorowitsch. In later years Huberman credited Gregorowitsch with teaching him "all that could be learned from a teacher." Subsequently he had a few lessons with Hugo Heerman in Frankfurt and Martin Marsick in Paris, but by 1893, he was already acclaimed a violin prodigy in Belgium and Holland, and the following year, in Paris and London. By the age of about 12, Huberman unfortunately had concluded his formal violin training (such as it was) and entered the concert field under the supervision of his father, who retired from his own career as a barrister to tend to the affairs of his precocious son. Thus, Huberman may be considered, for the most part, a self-trained violinist.

The celebrated soprano Adelina Patti heard the lad in London and engaged him to participate in her farewell concert in Vienna in January, 1895, where he created a sensation playing the Mendelssohn E-minor Concerto. This resulted in a series of ten sold-out concerts in Vienna. In January, 1896, the scarcely-tutored boy played the Brahms concerto before an audience that included the composer who, amazed at the impressive performance by one so young, presented him with an autographed photo.

In Huberman's youth he was given a valuable old Italian instrument by a patron, Count Jan Zamoyski. His Stradivarius, "The Gibson" (1713), was stolen from his hotel room in Vienna in 1919, but was quickly recovered from the thief, who served a three-year term in prison. Again, in 1936, it was stolen from his Carnegie Hall dressing room, but was not found until it surfaced in the hands of a salon violinist during the 1980s. Even at that time, the era of the Great Depression, the violin was insured for $30,000, which Huberman eventually collected. His beautiful Guarnerius del Gesù subsequently became the property of Ruggiero Ricci.

During the 1896-97 season Huberman appeared in Carnegie Hall as a boy prodigy, winning acclaim for his performance of the first movement of the Mendelssohn concerto with the New York Philharmonic. Huberman's striking individuality was noted in a review which stated in part:

If a musical hearer, unacquainted with the nature of the occasion, had turned his back to the stage...his conclusion would have been that some hitherto unknown but very individual violinist was

*Martin Marsick, prominent Belgian violinist
and teacher*

giving his own interpretation, at many points, of
the familiar classic.

According to the critic, he never would have
believed that such mature musicianship could be
demonstrated by a boy of 13. However, in his debut
recital which took place shortly after, the *New York
Times* rather uncharitably remarked:

> ...Bronislaw Huberman suffers from overadver-
> tising and underdressing. There is really no good
> reason why Huberman should be advertised as a
> mature artist, nor is there good reason for dress-
> ing him in knee trousers, loose silk shirts and
> long hair.

Some 25 years later during the 1921-1922 season,
the violinist returned to Carnegie Hall as a fully
matured artist.

After this first American tour Huberman retired from
the concert scene for about five years, one of several
career hiatuses taken either for reasons of personal
choice (for musical development, political study, and
activity) or because of the serious plane accident he
experienced in 1937. He reappeared in 1902, playing
in Europe and the United States, and in 1903 was invited by the city of Genoa to play on the Paganini
Guarnerius, the instrument reposing in the city museum which is occasionally performed upon by invited
eminent violinists.

His career burgeoned rapidly. He gave 14 concerts in Paris in 1920, ten in Vienna in 1924, and eight
in Berlin in 1926. The city of Vienna put the
Hetzendorf Palace at his permanent disposal in 1926.
Huberman's hold on the public was unique; important
people among the nobility, political figures, and indus-
trial moguls were staunch Huberman supporters and
intimate friends. His personal magnetism, despite his
unprepossessing physical appearance, was enormous.

In the 1920s Huberman became involved in the
Pan Europa movement sparked by Count Coudenhove-
Kalerghi, lecturing and giving unstintingly of his time
and energy to the cause of a United States of Europe.
Though this project was destined for failure, his political discernment was sharply intensified. Fortified by his
extraordinary personal integrity, he gradually became
known as a fearless spokesman for democratic ideals.

When the Nazis came to power in Germany in
1933, at a time when certain other noted Jewish musicians were either trying to gloss over their Jewish extraction, or treading water, hoping they would be permitted to continue performing in Germany, Huberman
boldly and selflessly refused to perform in that country. Invited by Wilhelm Furtwangler to play in Berlin,
Huberman responded with an open letter to the conductor titled *J'Accuse*, proclaiming the individual's right
to physical, intellectual, and spiritual freedom, and
pointing out the direct relationship between the flourishing of great art and culture, and these inalienable
rights. He understood perfectly the aims and ramifications of fascism in their entirety, not only in regard to
the Jewish question; as a humanistic citizen of the world
and a Jewish artist, he spurned the Nazi offer. His letter made front-page news, but he never swerved an iota
in his principles. Others less knowledgeable politically,
or less confirmed in their Jewish heritage, or already
converted to another religion, shakily bided their time
until Hitler informed them that they were persona non
grata. A few years later the Nazis consigned to concentration camps, enslavement, and death those rank-
and-file professional Jewish musicians who were unable
to flee the country.

One of the most sincere tributes to Huberman was
written by the noted maestro, Bruno Walter, who said:

I found within him a well co-ordinated combination of utter devotion to his art and an active participation in the events of the day...In both his personal and his public life he gave utterance by clever words and a courageous attitude to what he considered his duty as a democratically thinking man and as one who felt a responsibility for world happenings.

Then Walter humbly adds:

I admit, with deep regret I have never attained to that happy balance between artistic and human duties.

Huberman taught intermittently at the Vienna State Academy of Music and continued his concertizing outside of Germany. Meanwhile, in 1936 he undertook the massive task of organizing the Palestine Symphony Orchestra in Tel Aviv, an aggregation composed of displaced Jewish musicians who had managed somehow to escape the Nazi terror. The conductor William Steinberg was also active in this undertaking. Toscanini, at his own expense, traveled to Palestine to conduct the inaugural concert. In 1948 this orchestra became the Israel Philharmonic. Huberman is still revered in Israel, and a Tel Aviv street bears his name. After his death, his library and papers were ensconced in the Tel Aviv Music Library.

Sensing the approach of fascism in Austria in 1938, Huberman left prior to the Nazi takeover. In 1937 while on tour in the Orient, his plane crashed in Sumatra. Apart from being badly shaken up, he suffered a broken left wrist and two smashed fingers, and it was thought that his playing career might be at an end. Describing the accident, he said:

It was a chain of miracles. My secretary had refused a seat for me at the front of the plane, and had taken one at the rear, even though the airline representative considered it not as good. The man in the front seat was killed. Had my right wrist been broken and my left hand crushed, I would never have been able to play again, but just the reverse happened. Also, we crashed within a half hour's distance from an excellent hospital which had just been opened in the Dutch East Indies. All these events were my salvation. Perhaps the experience was good for my soul. It has served to deepen my outlook on existing values in life and beyond life. Once you have looked in the face of death like that, you are a different man.

With indefatigable perseverance, Huberman succeeded in regaining his instrumental skills.

He revisited Palestine in 1940 and then returned to the United States where he applied for citizenship. In 1941 he appeared with the New York Philharmonic for the first time in five years, and continued his concert career. Just as he had previously given innumerable concerts to raise money for support of the Palestine Orchestra, he played many concerts in the United States for war relief. He died June 15, 1947 at Corsier-sur-Vevey, Switzerland.

Huberman had always been generous with money on behalf of his fellow musicians, and went out of his way to encourage and assist young gifted violinists. Whenever he could, he used his connections in high places to help musicians and non-musicians alike to escape the Nazi conquest. This benevolence was not always reciprocated. Seymour W. Itzkoff cites a striking example of such ingratitude in his most excellent book, *Emanuel Feuermann, Virtuoso*, a biography of the late celebrated cellist.

Out of admiration for the cellist's superlative gifts, Huberman had used all of his good offices to give considerable impetus to Feuermann's career. He played public chamber music concerts with him in Europe, helped him with contacts, and gave him invaluable advice. But more than that, as the Nazis came to power in Austria, when Feuermann's parents and his violinist brother Sigmund were about to be exterminated in the terror (Sigmund had already been brutalized in the streets), Huberman, in response to Emanuel Feuermann's desperate pleas, used his influence with important personages to obtain visas for the Feuermann family enabling them to escape the country at the last moment and flee to Palestine. This action certainly saved their lives. Later, in the United States, when Feuermann's star as an artist was in the ascendancy and Huberman's on the wane, the latter asked Feuermann's participation in some proposed joint chamber music concerts. The cellist studiously avoided making a commitment to his old benefactor, and except for a 1936 trio concert in Town Hall, never performed with Huberman again. Characteristically, the magnanimous violinist did not bear any ill will toward Feuermann and later, at the cellist's request, used his influence in having a close Feuermann friend admitted from Cuba to the United States. There was, of course, a tremendous disparity between the styles and musical outlooks of Feuermann (who ultimately per-

Publicity for a Huberman recital

formed with Heifetz, and rightly so) and Huberman, and by 1939, the cellist had nothing to gain by playing with the comparatively old-fashioned violinist. Some may consider this factor a valid excuse for Feuermann's crass ungratefulness.

All people of goodwill and democratic precepts have good reason to admire and respect Huberman, the man. But Huberman, the violinist, has aroused a wide diversity of reactions. Many cannot understand whence he derived his tremendous reputation. Others, who perhaps examined his performance more realistically, at least in terms of its time and place, are able to perceive in it elements of provocative interest, and even positive attraction. And a sizeable coterie of listeners was absolutely thrilled by his art.

Huberman was of the same generation as Kreisler, who was born in 1875, Thibaud, 1880, and Enesco, 1881. But whereas they came to represent a forward trend in interpretation and particularly, in vibrant quality of sound, Huberman's playing, in contrast to his progressive social ideas, remained rooted in late 19th-century concepts. Like the aforenamed colleagues,

his technical training reflected pre-turn-of-the-century practices. Unlike the others, however, Huberman seemed perfectly content to reside in this anachronistic violinistic clime, relying strictly upon the innate fire of his temperament and individuality of style and delivery to shape and communicate his interpretations. In the manner typical of yesteryear violinists, these interpretations were formulated to a large degree in accordance with the strengths and weaknesses of his equipment. Like a host of other violinists of his time, and even later, the new, developing standards (and means of production) of violin sound, and comparatively greater musical discipline, culminating in the historic 20th-century revolution epitomized by Heifetz, completely passed him by. Other intellectually inclined violinists like Flesch, born in 1873, and Szigeti, 1892, though trained in anachronistic methods in their youth, readily recognized the direction of violinistic and musical progress, and willingly yielded to its influence within the contexts and limitations of their own physical endowments. While they wisely moved ever forward in matters of repertoire and musical circumspection, Huberman steadfastly

William Primrose

remained his *own* man, ignoring the swirl of violinistic achievement evolving around him. It was perhaps this dichotomy of outlook between Huberman and Flesch that induced the latter to so roundly criticize Huberman. It may well be that Flesch simply could not understand how Huberman could be so oblivious to the modern trends in violinistic performance while he, Flesch, so acutely grasped them. Yet, seemingly in direct contradiction to his dated violinistic way of life, Huberman enthusiastically endorsed and pioneered such novel items as aluminum bow hair and all-steel strings.

Huberman was an assiduous worker. The noted violist Lionel Tertis tells this anecdote about the violinist's habits while touring the United States by train in a Pullman car with the Harold Bauer Piano Quartet (Bauer, Tertis, cellist Felix Salmond, and Huberman):

> He would be found in the men's wash-house playing his violin from morning till night, mealtimes excepted. He never stopped, no matter how many passengers were performing their ablutions, and how it came about that he was not forcibly restrained from turning the wash-house into a practice room I shall never understand.

Another supreme violist (and violinist), William Primrose, wrote of Huberman:

> He was greatly esteemed by a host of admirers but I never could enjoy his playing. As I recall, it was unlovely playing. To my ears he scratched abominably. He was one of the great violinists that I would never go out of my way to hear.

This opinion of Huberman's performance is only to be expected from one who was accustomed to hear-

ing and playing with such historic giants of string playing as Heifetz, Feuermann, and Piatigorsky, with their glittering, luscious, vibrant sound and sophisticated phrasing. I believe it can be said with but little fear of contradiction that most violinists who were taught in the Auer concepts, or were influenced by them, or have been indoctrinated by any of the current violinistic ideologies, would agree with Primrose about Huberman's playing.

Conversely, as late as January, 1944, the New York critic Olin Downes wrote of a Huberman performance of the Brahms concerto:

> Mr. Huberman, with some stridency of tone and roughness of style, played in a great spirit, with a splendid grasp of the music's essence and a virile spirit that inspired his audience...Some might prefer more polish, maybe more of Olympian balance and suavity in the playing of the noble, rugged music of Brahms. We would rather hear the dramatic fire of Mr. Huberman, feel the exaltation of his sentiment, hear him scratch in his excitement or ask more than one stringed instrument can readily give in the course of some grand pronouncement.

This judgment emanates from a superior musical mind and observer whose experience at the time of this writing included hearing a host of assorted violinists, from the young Elman in the first decade of the 20th century to Isaac Stern.

Carl Flesch's *Memoirs* analyzes and takes to task many a prominent violinist, among them Huberman. His various criticisms of Huberman even incited a response from the book's editor and translator Hans Keller, who rose to Huberman's defense in a brief but sharply contradictory rebuttal in the appendix—an odd function indeed for an editor. The latter elicited an even shorter counter-rebuttal from the author's son, C.F. Flesch. This unusual imbroglio merely points up the kind of contrary opinions Huberman's playing could arouse. Since I heard Huberman in several live performances and have carefully studied many of his recordings, it is only natural that I compare my own impressions with those of Flesch.

At the outset, in reviewing my recollections of Huberman's playing and more importantly, evaluating Huberman in historic perspective as a violinist, I must confess that in most particulars I agree with Flesch's appraisal of his technical equipment, sound production, interpretive attitudes, and violinistic idiosyncrasies.

However, in the crucial matter of sheer performer-to-auditor musical communication, leaving violinistic and musical criticisms aside for the moment, elements of Huberman's playing in certain compositions (or even in individual sections of these compositions) perhaps impressed me more favorably than they did Flesch, and might be said to represent a certain triumph of the human spirit.

As one of the most analytical and progressive violinists and pedagogues of record, Flesch sought to apply every desirable new facet of violinistic knowledge and practice to his own playing. Dissatisfied with the vibrato of his early training, he utilized all of his analytical powers to develop his vibrato in a more modern image. Not so Huberman, who used an anachronistic finger vibrato (when he used vibrato at all), and with all due respect to Hans Keller, there is no evidence in his late recordings or live performances that he ever significantly updated his vibrato. Yet, in his best lyric moments, this antiquated vibrato could be quite engaging, even effective, though generally it was inconsistently employed. There was no juice in his higher position G-string sound. What vibrato he had was a natural extension of his sentiment rather than a cultivated appendage.

Huberman is the product of an age in which a violinist's personality patently dominated his interpretation, and his musicianship in the literal or scholastic sense was subjugated to the dictates of that personality. At times he could charm the listener, but it was a charm that evolved not from any external splendor of violin tone or polished refinement of nuance, but from the inner grace and self-conviction of the man himself!

Nor did Huberman's bow arm elicit a sustained tone of rich flowing sonority. Like his vibrato, it belonged to a bygone era, and often produced choppy, uneven, eccentrically-articulated sounds and strokes. The dull detonation of his chordal passages could be abysmally primitive. In contrast, his rough, percussive impacts could be remarkably exciting in propulsive barrages of spiccato and marcato bowings.

Huberman's runs and passagework were fast, clean, and of sparkling clarity when he was in good form. But as with most late 19th-century violinists, particularly those of Central Europe, these runs and technical passages ended perfunctorily with dull, dead-finger dispatch, devoid of any semblance of brilliant climactic vibrance.

In view of Huberman's shortcomings, how was it possible for him to achieve the fame, fortune, and sustained success that he did? I believe the reasons for his hegemony in Central Europe and Poland, where his acceptance and prosperity were so pronounced, were twofold. First, at the time Huberman attained maturity, the old traditions of dry-toned but sincere, conscientious musicality established by Joachim, were still strongly prevalent. Large numbers of conservative listeners not only preferred the old dry sound, but were actually repelled by the new tonal glitter and opulence, and slick stylistic innovations.

The second factor impelling his success was vested in the sheer talent and dynamic force of the man himself. Huberman was a person of passionate ideals, fiery temperament, and indomitable conviction, qualities which were as conspicuous in his music-making as in his non-musical proclivities. His violinistic rivals of conservative stripe were simply not as gifted in audience communication. The very unpredictability of his playing and its ever-latent coiled-spring tension which constantly threatened to erupt, served to whet the anticipation of listeners who were willing to overlook mundane musical considerations and technical crudities. And let us remember that Huberman's facility and finger-bow coordination, when in top form, were extraordinary, even though they projected neither the brilliant tonal edge or awesome perfection of a Heifetz. His trill was incredibly fast. As a violinistic evangelist of singular persuasive powers, he possessed the rare ability to turn many of his listeners into true believers.

The question arises: Why was Huberman less successful in the United States, England, and, to a degree, France and the Latin countries? Flesch suggests that it was because

...to the Anglo-Saxons, (his) ecstasy was immoderation, (his) exaltation, a lack of understatement.

This view may contain some element of fact in individual instances. Flesch fails to take into account that violin audiences in predominantly Anglo-Saxon countries are not at all necessarily of Anglo-Saxon descent, and this sizeable bloc of non-Anglo-Saxon listeners certainly included many who were relatively unmoved by the "ecstasy" and "exaltation" in Huberman's playing. What, then, of a violinist such as Menuhin, whose best playing was so often strikingly marked by ecstatic emotional flights of fancy and exaltation, who was triumphant in both Anglo-Saxon and Latin countries as well as Central and Eastern Europe?

I believe the answer to this seeming contradiction

is clear. The elements of ecstatic, exalted sentiments embodied in Menuhin's playing were swathed in vibrant modern sound, sheen, sophisticated slides and position changes, and piquant stylistic devices. Even before the end of World War II, the old Joachim traditions and standards were becoming extinct; exposure to the newer developments in violin art had greatly altered audience tastes and demands. Huberman was already an anachronistic artist and large numbers of his most vociferous admirers had passed on. As a top-notch soloist he was essentially in eclipse, and only a relatively small body of listeners still responded to those personalized characteristics of his art that had once hypnotized audiences and rendered him a heroic figure among violinists.

The first time I heard Huberman live was in March, 1936, in a performance of the Beethoven concerto with Klemperer and the Los Angeles Philharmonic. I had looked forward to the occasion with keen anticipation, anxious to form my own impressions of this violinist with so august a reputation, who evoked such a miscellany of opinions from my older violinist colleagues. It proved to be a memorable evening in more ways than one. I wondered how he would compare in this epic work with my idols: Kreisler, Heifetz, the young Menuhin, Elman, or even Spalding,

Musikalien-Handlung R. PIRNGRUBER
FÜRSTLICH SCHAUMBURG-LIPPESCHE
HOF-BUCH- UND KUNST-HANDLUNG
Landstraße Nr. 34 LINZ a. D. Landstraße Nr. 34.

Festsaal des Kaufmännischen Vereinshauses, Linz.
Dienstag den 20. November 1917, abends ½8 Uhr.

VIOLIN-KONZERT

Bronislav HUBERMANN | unter Mitwirkung des Pianisten **Paul FRENKEL.**

VORTRAGS-FOLGE:

1. J. S. Bach:	Sonate E-dur für Violine und Pianoforte.	
	Adagio.	
	Allegro.	
	Adagio ma non tanto.	
	Allegro.	
2. Hermann Goetz:	Konzert in einem Satze op. 22.	
	Allegro vivace. — Andante.	
	Tempo des ersten Satzes. — Lebhaft.	
3. a) Dvořak:	Zwei romantische Stücke:	
	Allegro maestoso.	
	Larghetto.	
b) Suk:	Zwei Stücke:	
	Un poco triste.	
	Burleske.	
c) Krzyzanowski:	Ballade.	
4. Wieniawski:	Faust-Fantasie.	

Kartenvorverkauf in der
Hofbuchhandlung R. PIRNGRUBER (vorm. E. Mareis), dahier,
Landstraße 34. Telephon 1016/VI.

Wenden!

Courtesy Joseph Gold

A 1917 Huberman recital program

who played this particular opus in such a pellucid, stately fashion.

The capacity audience waited intently for Huberman to appear. After an unseemly delay, the diminutive violinist slowly sauntered on stage in company with the towering, austere conductor; an odd pairing, visually, to say the least.

His bow was strung with aluminum fibers which he proceeded to rosin with exasperating deliberation. Then he began to tune loudly and re-tune each string with circumspect care. This process continued for several minutes. Some in the audience started to titter and

fidget at the peculiar rite, thus sorely ruffling the serene atmosphere that should rightfully precede the Beethoven. Huberman continued imperturbably. It appeared as if he were almost reluctant to start. At long last he concluded his fussy preparations, planted his feet to his satisfaction, and stood uncomfortably awaiting his entrance as the tympani announced the opening of the orchestral introduction.

His initial broken octave passage was dry and methodical, and indeed, the first two-thirds of the movement was admittedly dull and uneventful except for some trills of electric speed and clarity, magnificent in

Courtesy Joseph Gold

Bronislaw Huberman

themselves, but rather out of character for this contemplative music. The Joachim cadenza, too, had little lustre, though it was negotiated with admirable digital authority. But, in the majestic theme immediately following, Huberman seemed to enter into a transcendental state, into a world of his own. The notes were not vibrant in sound, but the entirety of the phrase was compelling in a way difficult to describe, and the ensuing scale passages built to a wondrous culmination of the movement.

The Adagio was dotted with similar breathtaking phrase-making, but also vitiated by dry tone and unpolished continuity. It was both aggravating and inspirational. The Rondo bounded along brightly and brusquely, rough-edged, but utterly convincing in spirit. It could not be said that Huberman had conquered all, but his playing definitely stirred up a storm of conflicting emotions exceeding anything of its kind concerning any violinist I had heard before or since.

I was taken backstage and given a perfunctory introduction to the violinist by a mutual friend. At close range I was somewhat startled by his appearance. He was even smaller than I had thought and his shoulders sloped wearily. His bald head topped a capacious, noble brow that bespoke the intellectual; his lower lip protruded prominently. I was riveted and momentarily flustered by his eyes which were not only crossed, but more extremely than any I had ever seen. His response to our brief meeting was warm and friendly, but somehow I felt that he was still under the influence of his self-mes-

merization. Huberman spoke with a lisp that prompted a flush of sympathy on my part, since at the time I was afflicted by the same problem (long since overcome). It is said, too, that he was a chronic insomniac.

I also heard Huberman in several sonata concerts with Artur Schnabel, but the disparity of temperamental and musical priorities between violinist and pianist was so marked, the collective results could only be viewed as an unfortunate example of miscasting. Somewhat more impressive were broadcasts of the Brahms concerto, rugged, rough-hewn, and impassioned, and (to a lesser degree) the Bach E-major Concerto. An airing of Lalo's *Symphonie Espagnole* revealed a gross absence of Latin suavity and sensuous sound in the lyric episodes, and much propulsiveness and daring in bristly negotiations of the rapid passage-work.

Huberman taught intermittently in Vienna, but pedagogy was not an integral part of his career. It seems unlikely that even with his unusual intellectual capacity, he could be effective in that role, and his unbridled individuality must certainly have been a disconcerting factor to his students. In any case, he is not known for having produced any pupils of prominence. His repertoire was not especially far-reaching; rather he concentrated mostly on the familiar standards. In his younger years he performed the Karlowicz concerto, a Polish favorite.

The violinist was married but later divorced. Ironically, his ex-wife married his one-time friend, the pianist-composer Ernst Von Dohnanyi, who in later years became a darling of the fascists.

The Huberman discography is not large, consisting of only 37 recordings plus 14 repeat discs: eight are concertos; one, a major sonata. The remainder are short concert- and encore-type pieces.

Two additional performances are air checks, one of the Tchaikovsky concerto, the other the Mendelssohn, both with the Berlin Philharmonic, in which the violinist was listed under the pseudonym Fritz Malachowsky. Several air checks of concerto excerpts were also issued. In all, it is a surprisingly small output for a violinist who had so notable a reputation. Perhaps it is just as well, since Huberman's genre of playing was best heard live, where one could directly imbibe the radiant glow of his intense inner spirit.

Yet, some of the recordings are not only revealing but gratifying, either in toto or in part. Let us examine a cross-section of these 78 relics, all of which, I believe, were made before his 1937 plane accident.

I recall vividly how, some time before I first heard Huberman in public, I found an old 78 recording he had made of Elgar's *La Capricieuse*. As a youngster and fanatical Heifetz partisan, I immediately began to make back-to-back comparisons between the epoch-making 1917 Heifetz recording of the piece and my newly found Huberman acquisition. After the first few listenings, as a brash youth will, I began to ridicule the Huberman performance. The opening theme was slow and dreamy rather than buoyant. He possessed no rapid, crackling stiff arm staccato à la Heifetz; his staccato was slow and deliberate. Unlike the Heifetz high G-string vibrance, singing double-stops, and suave slides and position changes, Huberman's sound was dry and his tempo wayward. Heifetz played the final ascending passage with purly staccato incisiveness; Huberman played it much faster, with blazing speed, but with spiccato rather than staccato. Then, as I continued listening to the two versions, something happened. It was not that I began to relish Heifetz less, but that I started to appreciate Huberman more. The crusty individuality of his conception and the ingenuousness of his exposition ultimately won my respect, even affection. His *La Capricieuse*, I realized, was truly capricious.

Two Sarasate gems point up Huberman's strengths and weaknesses in vivid relief. *Jota Navarra* suited his temperament ideally. The pacing between the sharp rhythmic batteries and the sultry double-stop melodic themes are instinctively and imaginatively integrated. The crisp, bouncing bowings are highly charged, the finger pizzicatos explosive. Intonation is very good, if not absolutely perfect; the tone in lyric utterances vacillates between moderately sweet and dry. It all adds up to an exciting, individual interpretation. However, the *Romanza Andaluza* (slightly truncated) fails in all departments. The pacing lacks ebb and flow, the tone is thin and arid, the mood somnolent, rather than indolently voluptuous. Here and there the innate Huberman ferment asserts itself, but is unable to compensate for the overall shortcomings of the performance. Siegfried Schultze is at the piano.

One of the most enjoyable of his disc performances is a ten-minute version of Vieuxtemps's *Ballade and Polonaise*. The "Ballade" is played with a reverie that brings to mind Ysaÿe; the dashing opening theme of the "Polonaise" is actually more convincing and characteristic than in the Heifetz air check (surprising!) and the Grumiaux recording, though the tone, as usual, does not

sparkle sufficiently. The style reflects flickers of the old Belgian School. The same can generally be said for Wieniawski's *La Menetrier* Mazurka in a spirited reading. The playing in both may be dated, but not in the sense that it is totally archaic. In Tchaikovsky's *Melodie*, Huberman gives a solid, gutsy performance, mildly sweet-toned and with a fair measure of subtle phrasing—some of his better lyric playing. The last three pieces have Paul Frenkel at the piano.

Four widely-varied major works include Mozart's Concerto No. 3, recorded in the mid-1930s, and Bach's Concerto in E-major, with Dobrowen and the Vienna Philharmonic; the Tchaikovsky Concerto with Steinberg and the Berlin State Orchestra, recorded about 1930; and the Beethoven *Kreutzer* Sonata, made in 1930, with Ignatz Friedman as piano collaborator. The Mozart is charmless and ponderous—a performance oriented to the ultra-conservative tastes of yesteryear Middle-European listeners. The Bach is marginally better, but the slow movement is beset by some ungainly slides.

The Tchaikovsky, in the original pre-Auer version (with none of the customary small cuts in the finale) is a prime exemple of un-Russian early 20th-century playing. The opening is without any vibrance to speak of; the exquisite theme that starts in bar 69 is temperately warmed with finger vibrato; the triplet double-stop salvos rage percussively with marvelous brio, as do all the spiccato passages throughout. The opening chords of the cadenza are slashed off with fossilized non-vibrance, and the cadenza itself is crudely etched. The Canzonetta, containing some dubious slides, is laden with an underlying fervor which is not realized in the tonal timbre. The finale epitomizes the Russian peasant ethos, wild and vehement, with a good measure of the vulgarity inherent in the movement; the tempo is exceptionally fast. The performance would be quite unacceptable today; indeed, it was already outmoded in 1930. Even then, many a listener was captivated by the super-charged Huberman drive and propulsion.

The *Kreutzer* Sonata is a happy partnership with Friedman, who conjures up a dynamic style and delivery compatible in most particulars with that of the subjective violinist. The initial violin statement is completely without vibrance. Once in tempo, the music proceeds at a rapid pace, spurning any vestige of introspection or repose in the second movement variations. The sheer drive, power, and clarity of the finale may well thrill the auditor, and all is very clean for what is probably a one-take unspliced performance. Here, in general, Huberman displays his significant superiority as an artist and music-maker to violinists of the Kubelik-Vecsey-Burmester-Marteau ilk.

It cannot be said that Bronislaw Huberman was part of the mainstream or a positive contributor to the development of violin art. He was a loner, stylistically speaking, whose immense sincerity of purpose endeared him to many—a violinist of meaningful, if not ear-titillating, musicality. And as a man of integrity, he represents an illustrious criterion for all violinists who would fashion their lives and activities in accordance with the profound humanistic dictates inherent in the ennobling art of music.

Mischa Elman, a unique bard of the violin

Mischa Elman

In the wake of the turn of the century's new wave of violinist-bards headed by Ysaÿe, Kreisler, and Thibaud, whose vibrant sound, subtlety, and scintillating emotional thrust were inexorably ousting the dry-toned, old-fashioned players from the top echelon, came yet another. His name was Mischa Elman, and he was an inimitable personality of the violin.

Even more, Elman, historically, was the initial catalyst of a phenomenon still very much in evidence—the incredible proliferation on the international violin scene of Jewish violinists from Eastern Europe. Elman (1891-1967) was the first Jewish violinist to emerge from the Pale of Settlement area of Tsarist Russia and win fame on the highest level.

The 19th century had witnessed a number of leading violinists of Jewish extraction (not necessarily religion), among them: Ferdinand David, Heinrich Ernst, Miska Hauser, Ferdinand Laub, Isador Lotto, Edouardo Remenyi, Leopold Auer, and the immortals, Joseph Joachim and Henri Wieniawski. Others born in the 19th century who reached maturity before the end of the century, include Jakob Gruen, Adolf Brodsky, Arnold Rosé, Alexander Petschnikoff, Charles Gregorowitsch, Michael Press, Tividar Nachez and, of course, Fritz Kreisler and Carl Flesch.

However, these artists and pedagogues were essentially products of long-established Western European violin schools. And while Wieniawski had seconded Vieuxtemps in carrying the French-Belgian School into Russia, the Russian School that developed from it through Auer and others, had characteristics distinctly different from both preceding and contemporary schools. Beauty, sonority, and opulence of sound, fiery temperamental projection, and glittering technique gradually became emblematic of the new Russian vio-

linistic way of life, and were embodied in the playing of many of its most prominent representatives.

It is, I believe, germane to the discussion of Elman's impact on the art of violin playing to describe briefly the roots from which he sprung. The Pale of Settlement was the proscribed territory in which the Jews were permitted to live in the tsarist empire. Only by religious conversion or special permission could a Jewish person live in St. Petersburg. Other good-sized cities and villages, each with its own Jewish ghetto area, were located within the Pale. Without conversion it was practically impossible for a Jew to enter fully into the artistic and cultural life of the nation. Thus it was no wonder that Jews aspiring to fame and fortune (or even participation and acceptance) in the gentile world converted in sizeable numbers.

The question is often raised as to why Jews have become so closely identified with the violin, and indeed, music in general. The reasons are part and parcel of Jewish history and tradition, a subject far too lengthy and complex for this volume.

Insofar as the Jewish people of Eastern Europe are concerned, their inherent love for and affinity with music was enormously stimulated by the emergence of Chassidism in the mid-18th century. This was a religious movement that challenged the conservative religious establishment which, by custom, vested its power and authority in scholars and learned ecclesiastical functionaries. In opposition, Chassidism brought religion directly to the Jewish masses, offering the poor, the uneducated, and the downtrodden a new type of religious participation in which music, songs, and dance were important elements. This provided an invaluable additional outlet for a sorely oppressed people. The violin, with its direct appeal to sentiment and heart-felt emotion, together with its accessibility, compared to, say, an expensive piano or organ, became immensely popular.

Elman's grandfather was a "klezmer" violinist, one of numerous untrained country musicians who entertained at fairs, parties, social gatherings of all types, and even in the streets. Mischa's father Saul, placed a violin in the boy's hands when he was only four years of age.

In later years Elman became a symbolic folk hero to Jewish people everywhere—a sort of knight in shining armor who slew dragons wielding violin and bow rather than sword and lance. This wee man, whose height hovered around the five-foot mark, was acclaimed by kings and princes the world over. Half-starved needle workers slaving 16 hours a day in sweatshops, racked by consumption, saw their talented little boys as future Mischa Elmans. Bedraggled pushcart peddlers in teeming big-city ghettos hoarded their pennies to obtain lessons for their young hopefuls. After Elman's success, new Mischas, Jaschas, Toschas, Saschas, Grischas, and Abraschas multiplied like mushrooms after a storm. Only a rare few reached the topmost echelon, but in the process, thousands of fine Jewish violinists were spawned in Western Europe, the Americas, the U.S.S.R., and now, Israel. Their presence and violinistic influence is to be found wherever the violin is played.

Elman was born in Talnoi, Russia, near Kiev, January 20, 1891. His father, a Hebrew teacher, gave Mischa his first elementary violin lessons, was the boy's guardian and companion during his early career, and took him to Odessa where he entered the Imperial Music School. Here, from age six, he studied with Alexander Fidelman, a pupil of Auer and Brodsky. Elman's progress was astounding; at eight he played De Bériot's Concerto No. 7 in public with orchestra.

Auer heard the lad in Odessa. Though racked by nervousness at the audition, Elman proceeded to amaze Auer with his performance of the Wieniawski Concerto No. 2 and Paganini's Caprice No. 24, and was immediately urged to study with the master in St. Petersburg. With a capital of three rubles, Mischa and his father set out for Nikolayev where he played for cheering audiences, earning 400 rubles for the continuation of his studies. After several more such successes, the pair ultimately arrived in St. Petersburg. Mischa was given permission, as a Jew, to study there, but his father was persona non grata, even though the ten-year-old boy was

alone. Only after Auer personally pleaded for mercy from the arrogant Minister of the Interior, de Plehve (later assassinated), was Saul Elman permitted to remain after having led a ragtag fugitive existence in the city for weeks.

At this point it is necessary to examine a phenomenon which I believe is of historic moment. When Auer was asked to hear the young Mischa Elman in Odessa, he agreed with scant enthusiasm, inasmuch as he had long since been sated with alleged infant prodigies. However, after the audition and during his early stewardship of Elman's comparatively brief period of training (Elman stated that he studied with Auer "in Petrograd for a year and four months"), there is much reason to believe that the precocity and uniqueness of Elman's talent and playing influenced Auer to change some of his own fundamental violinistic values and priorities.

Auer's principal teachers had been Jacob Dont and Joseph Joachim. Thus his own technical and tonal resources had been honed in a violinistic milieu worlds apart from that which Mischa Elman came to represent.

Auer's distinctive ability to inspire his pupils to their highest potential has been amply demonstrated in numerous instances, and on the instrumental level he was most certainly a first-class pedagogue. However, it would be naive to believe that the peerless Elman bow arm, his absolutely unique vibrato, and his novel lyric propensities were acquired as the result of Auer's teaching. It is only logical to assume that when Auer first heard the boy and was literally astounded, the fabled Elman sound was already a hallmark of his playing, perhaps not fully matured, but strikingly in evidence. Nor can the Elman exceptionality be attributed to Fidelman, though Fidelman deserves to be credited with guiding Elman's elemental studies correctly while at the same time preserving his rare individuality. There can be little doubt that the penchant for vibrant beauty and lushness of tone accredited to Auer and his new Russian School dates from the appearance of Elman on the scene.

Elman's success had a marked bearing upon the stylistic evolution in the area of lyrical expressiveness of those Auer pupils who were his immediate successors: Piastro, Poliakin, Seidel, and Heifetz. For example, the playing of Elman and Heifetz may be radically diverse in the overall sense, but a careful examination of lyric-oriented pieces such as the Chopin nocturne transcriptions performed by Heifetz in his earliest recordings, will clearly indicate the Elman influence. Insofar as the Auer-Elman relationship is concerned, it is a moot question as to whether the master or the pupil was the more influenced by the other.

When Auer introduced Elman to St. Petersburg musical circles, the 13-year-old boy scored a tremendous success in the Mendelssohn concerto, Paganini's *Moto Perpetuo*, and a Chopin nocturne. Shortly after, accom-

The youthful Ferenc von Vecsey

panied by his father, he went to Berlin where the young Ferenc von Vecsey (1893-1935) had recently created a sensation.

Violinistic jousts have been traditional (Paganini-Lafont, Vieuxtemps-Bull and more), and the Elman-Vecsey imbroglio, though not exactly face-to-face, aroused great interest. Auer had already heard Vecsey (who had been proclaimed by Joachim to be the greatest living violin genius), and canny professional that he was, realized that for all of Vecsey's fabulous facility, Elman's irresistible lyricism was far more impressive than mere flashy finger gymnastics. It was another confrontation between the new and the old. In fact, after

the inevitable Elman triumph, Vecsey's manager left him to represent Elman, and a few months later arranged the boy's London debut. Elman proceeded to make London his headquarters until the outbreak of World War I. (In 1923 he became an American citizen.)

Meanwhile, following his German concerts, Elman appeared in the Scandinavian countries and Austria. At 13 years of age, his career had already started on a full-time basis. It would seem that Elman's father had been primarily responsible for the Berlin debut (October 14, 1904), since Auer states: "I would have preferred to have him mature under my own eye." Elman never did return to St. Petersburg for further study, though Auer went to London where, following Elman's London debut, he worked daily with the lad on repertoire "for a period of several weeks."

Thus we find that at barely 14, Elman's days of formal training were over. This undoubtedly had a serious effect on his future musical development. No 14-year-old, even a talent of genius proportions, should discontinue supervised study, particularly in the 20th century, with its proliferating musical and repertorial demands. In later years Elman probably sensed his deficiencies in matters of musical discipline and probity when he elected to organize the Elman String Quartet. But interpretive idiosyncrasies deeply ingrained in youth are almost impossible to eradicate, and no amount of chamber music playing could alter his fundamental manner of performance, with both its strengths and shortcomings. His string quartet, like its name, was predicated upon and shaped in the image of the Elman sound and ethos, and like all quartets with an elite solo violinist as leader, was essentially top-heavy, even though it was accorded a certain degree of critical approbation.

After his initial European successes, Elman continued to concertize, and in December 1908 made his New York debut. At first the opinions of the critics were divided. Aldrich praised his technical equipment and proclaimed him an extraordinary talent, but cited "serious" defects in the musical aspects of his playing. De Koven stated that Elman was the finest violinist since Ysaÿe, and believed that he would shortly take his place among the handful of great violinists. Both, of course, were correct. Elman, at that time, was just a youngster of 17. The next year he played the Beethoven concerto to a packed house, and his American acceptance was firmly established. At 18, Elman was now an international violin celebrity, and in the span of another five

The young Mischa Elman

the printed score. Not Elman! He played directly from the heart. If need be, rhythmic exactitude or the architectural structure of a work could always be forfeited to the Elman mania for ear titillation. He had no scruples about such matters. In the days before musical discipline became a dominating factor in performance, Elman not only had his way, but made believers out of most of his critics. "Do not sacrifice real sentiment," he would exclaim, and in his own playing, sentiment was his lodestar. If a particular work or passage thereof was not basically oriented to sentiment, Elman, fortified by his mighty tone, would manufacture the sentiment.

Elman lamented:

> In the past an artist showed his true greatness by the way he played slow movements. Today, we have no slow movements, for even adagios are played twice as fast as they should be, and even at these speeds the performers are bored, ever rushing faster and faster. Beauty can take any tempo, but they do not recognize it because they play so mechanically.

Elman had no love for mindless speed, and his own tempos, as to be expected, were carefully (sometimes gingerly) restricted to the realities of his technical facility. Moreover, Elman habitually instilled as much lyric feeling as he could in technical passages which are customarily played rapidly and brilliantly.

In discussing the subject of tone, Elman said:

> A great deal of damage has been done to younger players' conception of tone by the microphone. So much of the music one hears today has passed through the mike which filters out most of the beautiful quality. A tone should be an expression of a player's personality. One player may have a larger tone than the next; one player may have a sweeter tone; still another may have a generous supply of both qualities; but all should express the player. The color, the finer nuances that make a beautiful tone, these are disappearing because most young players concentrate on acquiring a big tone such as they hear on the radio and records. They completely forget that the mike can transform a thin, squeaky tone into one that sounds enormous from the loudspeaker. The result of trying to imitate this big tone is that they produce a harsh, loud tone to which their ears become accustomed. Let us not even discuss their quality of tone in a pianissimo. While I am up-to-date in most things, my background is a preventative in this case,

years surpassed even Kreisler as a box office attraction in the United States. In 1913 Elman received $35,000 as the annual commission for his recordings, a considerable sum for that era. His disc of Massenet's *Elegie* in consort with his friend, the matchless tenor Enrico Caruso, was practically a household item, and Elman's beguiling segment, if anything, somewhat overmatches that of the marvelous Italian. It is significant that Szigeti, an artist so totally different in every respect, held the young Elman in highest esteem.

Elman's own statements provide a certain degree of insight into his musical philosophies and violinistic theories. "The true test of all interpretations is—how does it sound?" This was his credo. He was, of course, referring to communication with the audience in terms of sheer aural beauty. Others might find beauty in musical introspection, intellectualism, or exact fidelity to

enabling me to cling to my traditional conception.

Elman, ever true to his own violinistic way of life, was not at all in sympathy with the direction violin art was taking. In 1952, when asked to compare masters of the past with young contemporary players, he asserted:

The old masters such as Ysaÿe, Kreisler and De Pachmann...gave great pleasure to their audiences. They moved people with their messages, and to attend one of their recitals was an experience never to be forgotten. Most of the younger generation play exceedingly well, technically, but lack individuality, color and imagination. It is as if they were mass-produced at a factory.

In art one needs leisure and contemplation in order to discover and reveal the beauty of music. Today we turn out musicians by the thousands, like automobiles and, it seems, for the main purpose of playing as many notes as possible.

Elman, while performing, had a habit of moving his head and body, swaying along with the music, but this was a natural movement, and in no way to be associated with ego-trip shenanigans. He would stride onstage, erect as a dwarf pine, moonface smiling, bald pate gleaming, with a cock-of-the-walk hauteur and a glint in his eye that seemed to proclaim, I am Mischa Elman, and there is no other violinist quite like me in the whole world.

His intonation was absolutely impeccable. When asked to pinpoint the single fundamental element of violin technique, he replied:

Absolute pitch, first of all...Many a player has the facility, but without perfect intonation he can never attain the highest perfection. On the other hand, anyone who can play a single phrase in absolute pitch has the first and great essential. Few artists, not barring some of the greatest, play with perfect intonation. Its control depends, first of all, on the ear. And a sensitive ear finds differences and shading; it bids the violinist to play a trifle sharper, a trifle flatter, according to the general harmonic color of the accompaniment; it leads him to observe a difference, when the harmonic atmosphere demands it, between a C-sharp in the key of E major and a D-flat in the same key.

Elman claimed that he had no difficulty in acquiring the varied facets of tonal production, or spiccato and harmonics, but admitted that mastering double-stops cost him much effort. Accordingly, he concentrated on producing scales in double-stops, as well as the double-stop passages in the Paganini caprices and the Ernst concerto. In details of fingering he was a complete individualist, utilizing finger selection in total conformity with beauty of sound, even in technical passages.

His ideas on shifting (i.e., position changes in expressive lyric passages) are typical of his playing style and, I believe, logical.

This feeling of young players to eliminate as many shifts as possible can do much harm. Remember that the violin is a singing instrument and that the tones must be connected. When a singer slides beautifully from one note to another it is permissible. Why then object when a violinist does it?

Although Elman was not celebrated as a technician, it would be a mistake to assume that his facility was stunted. He had sufficient dexterity to play practically all of the basic repertoire, with perhaps the exception of some of the Paganini gymnastic specialties. His tempos were not fast, even in his best years, but his facility was clean and bow arm sagaciously articulated. Except for the A-minor and E-major concertos, his repertoire of Bach, at least in public performances, was limited. He said of Bach: "His music is so gigantic that the violin often seems inadequate to express him. That is one reason why I do not play more Bach in public." Frankly, the immensely introspective profundities of Bach sonatas and partitas were scarcely conducive to emphasizing either the singular Elman tone or his quasi-Levantine temperament.

The voluptuous Elman sound was produced by an utterly individual synthesis of his bow arm and his vibrato. Despite his comparatively short arms, Elman, often bowing exceptionally close to the bridge and using a maximum amount of bow hair, drew a tone that was extraordinarily sonorous, even for the Auer-Elman Russian School, which later bred so many master players with voluminous tones. This bow arm remained consistently powerful throughout his career, in contradistinction to those of leading violinists whose sovereign bow control had begun to wane sometime during their 60s or even before. At 75 (in the last of the numerous concerts in which I heard Elman), though his left hand and his playing in general were no more than a caricature of his prime years, his bow arm was incredibly steady and productive.

His inimitable vibrato was something peculiar to Elman alone. It was what I have come to call an impulse vibrato, as differentiated from the slower wrist-or-arm motivated vibratos. The latter, controlled essentially by muscular manipulation, can produce a tone that is beautiful and sweet, but not thrillingly sensuous. (Kreisler, Heifetz, and Seidel also had impulse vibratos, which accounted for the spellbinding virility of their sound, though each of the three was patently dissimilar from the others.) The impulse vibrato, centering on the very core of the note, is exceedingly narrow in oscillation and emanates from *within* the arm to the fingertip with an impulse charge that might be likened to an electric current. It generates intensity without tenseness and tension without tautness. At times it is not overtly visible to the eye of the beholder. Elman was a wizard in the art of employing a diversity of finger pressures on the string which was an invaluable asset in evolving his wide palette of tonal colors and nuances. He used the meat of his fingertips to maximal advantage, and often would play very close to the fingernail, especially with the first and second fingers, eliciting a throbbing, almost lascivious sound. His application of vibrato was cleverly varied, thus his tone was multi-dimensional, never satiating the listener. In addition he possessed an uncommon ability to sustain tonal intensity from finger-to-finger and position-to-position; there were no dead spots in this area of his lyric expressiveness. It is important, however, to point out that the Elman vibrato, so instinctual in production, sometimes lost intensity in the very highest registers. Whether this problem was physical due to arm and finger structure, or a matter of ear conditioning, is not possible to deduce absolutely. Yet this shortcoming did not constitute a deformity in his playing since the lion's share of melodic episodes in his repertoire were not in the ultra-high positions. The small pieces which for many years were a cardinal element of his mass popularity, were cast mainly in the lower half of the fingerboard.

Whereas Heifetz can be characterized as the "tenore assoluto" of the violin in tonal timbre, Elman was a "baritone grandioso," perhaps somewhat limited in vocal range, but within that range, unequalled in burnished richness of sound. His fleshy, soft-grained tone was a natural for lyric eloquence and conversely, not well suited to brilliant, bombastic, high-position eruptions in rapid and bravura passagework. Thus his technical sorties were always couched in mellow textures.

Though he was a thorough-going romantic in style and temperament, Elman loved to play music by baroque and classical composers. One of his specialties was the Handel sonatas, which he played leisurely and with compelling charm. Each movement was interpreted as a gorgeous vignette, and every note was an integral part of the whole. Naturally they reflected a romantic aura that would undoubtedly offend modern classical purists, but he succeeded in transforming these glowing sonatas into consummately entertaining vehicles, whereas in our time they are being heard less and less, since they are admittedly not programmatic blockbusters.

Elman believed that romantic music should be played romantically, and his conception of such works might be likened to the florid, grandiloquent rhetoric of some of the better 19th-century novelists. In this respect he recalls Ysaÿe. Elastic tempos and exaggerated phrasing were integral parts of this approach, and Elman did not consider at all that he was in violation of any sacred musical tenets. He once declared that Ysaÿe's tempos in the Franck sonata were even slower than his own.

He asked: "Should we play the great romantic works in present day (i.e., mid-20th-century) style?" In commenting on the Tchaikovsky concerto, he said:

> Today we hear it played much differently (i.e., than in former years), and I feel that much of its romantic beauty is lost. It has become too mechanical.
>
> Let us take the opening passage. It is an introduction to the concerto and yet it has nothing to do with the work itself. The theme of the introduction is not heard again. There is no reminiscence of it during the entire concerto. Tchaikovsky wanted to create an atmosphere, and the particular atmosphere he wanted cannot be evoked by mechanical playing. It is an improvisation. Completely so!

Before the appearance of Heifetz, the Tchaikovsky concerto was synonymous with the name Elman. In the first decade of the century the work was considered to be tremendously difficult, and only a limited number of artists performed it in public, unlike today, when it is a repertorial standard played by innumerable violinists of all nationalities. In those years one did not go to hear the Tchaikovsky concerto as such. One went to hear an *Elman* or a *Huberman* or a *Zimbalist* play the Tchaikovsky concerto. Each interpretation was vastly different from the other, and when the votes on the Tchaikovsky were counted, Elman, at that time, *owned* the concerto.

In the matter of interpretation, it is necessary to

understand that Elman, in consonance with all the great violinists of the pre-Heifetz era, formulated his interpretations not only according to his esthetic and musical philosophies, but equally important, in keeping with his violinistic strengths and deficiencies. Today, when all accomplished violinists can negotiate the technical challenges of the Tchaikovsky with comparative ease, their interpretations are generally adapted to coincide scrupulously with markings in the score and thus, collectively, are infinitely less diversified.

A typical Elman recital might consist of the following:

1. **A Handel sonata**
2. **Choice of the Franck, Beethoven "Kreutzer" or "Spring," a Fauré, a Brahms or a Grieg sonata**
3. **Bach "Chaconne"**

INTERMISSION

4. **Choice of the Conus, Spohr "Gesangsscene," Glazunov, Vieuxtemps No. 4 or 5 Concerto, Lalo's "Symphonie Espagnole" (four movements)**
5. **Saint-Saens "Introduction and Rondo Capriccioso" or Vieuxtemps "Ballade and Polonaise"**

In a program of this type, he might omit the Bach and precede the finale showpiece with a group of four or five shorter pieces, including, possibly, Sarasate's *Romanza Andaluza*, *Caprice Basque*, or *Malaguena*, Wieniawski's *Souvenir de Moscou*, Espejo's *Airs Tziganes*, or some Kreisler compositions, many of which he played exquisitely. Elman considered the interpretation of a miniature to be as serious a task as that of a giant canvas. He asserted: "To play *Hejre Kati* in the right style is as subtle as interpreting Bach in the manner his music demands."

Apart from the violin, Elman was a sociable man known for his occasional tart or unpredictable comments and observations. His self-confidence and self-esteem were conspicuous facets of his personality. Elman stories are legion, and although this volume deliberately limits anecdotal material, it would be almost sacrilegious to discuss Elman without referring to at least a few.

Most famous, by far, is the one emanating from the Heifetz American debut recital in which Elman allegedly complained during intermission that "It's a hot night," to which Leopold Godowsky quipped: "Only for violinists."

Another, cited by Howard Taubman, concerns an Elman birthday dinner to which he invited the pianist Mischa Levitzki. Afterward the pair decided to attend the Ziegfield Follies. They were seated in a box close to the stage, being regaled by a bevy of beauties who were generously exhibiting their charms. Suddenly the ever-so-practical Elman tapped Levitzki on the shoulder and said: "Tell me, Mischa, what has happened to John McCormack's drawing power?"

Perhaps the drollest is one that I have on reliable authority. It seems that Elman was persuaded to attend the American debut recital of David Oistrakh. After sitting noncommittally through the program, he was asked to express his opinion of Oistrakh's playing. He thought for a moment, then shrugged his shoulders and replied: "He's all right, but even Jascha's better!"

The early vignette recordings of Elman made during the pre-electric 1910-1925 era are among the most enchanting treasures in the violin disc legacy. Like Kreisler, he was a supreme master in this metier, and it is a sad fact indeed, that RCA, the continuer of the old Victor label on which Elman made most of his early recordings, has not seen fit to refurbish 50 or 60 of these gems and re-release them, as has been done with early recordings of Caruso, Heifetz, McCormack, and many others. James Creighton's Discopaedia: *Masters of the Bow* series, Edition I, contains 17 Elman pieces, but many of the finest could not be included on a single disc. Young musicians (and the mass lay audience) who have not had the opportunity to hear these brief odes have been deprived of one of the most wondrous listening experiences violin art can offer. I recall the time I presented the first of my "Violin Virtuosi" radio programs consisting of records by yesteryear violinists together with prepared commentary; it contained a couple of Elman's early recordings. Subsequently, more than a few young listeners who had heard Elman only in some of the unfortunate discs made in his final decade, were dumbfounded, never dreaming that Elman could play "like that." Thankfully, Biddulph Records has more recently released five compact discs containing nearly all of Elman's vignette treasury--motivated by Eric Wen.

Among the most delectable are the luscious Saenger *Scotch Pastorale*, Schindler's paraphrase of Fibich's syrupy *Poème*, Dvořák's *Humoresque* (embellished

Mischa Elman at the zenith of his career

with Elman's own innocent species of double-stops), Raff's ariose *Cavatina*, Sarasate's languorous *Romanza Andaluza*, Drdla's limpid *Souvenir*, Bruch's poignant *Kol Nidre*, Schumann's bittersweet *Traumerei*, and the haunting Wagner-Wilhelmj *Album Leaf*. Also memorable are the peppery Hubay *Hejre Kati*, Espejo's *Airs Tzigane*, and the ebullient Haydn-Burmester *Minuet*. In two surprising technique-oriented peregrinations, Elman negotiates the dexterous middle passages of Vogrich's *Dans le Bois*, a setting of Paganini's Caprice No. 9, agilely and smoothly (though he substitutes harmonics for occasional high E-string notes) and handles the nimble variations of Sarasate's *Caprice Basque* (a slightly abbreviated version) with perspicuous clarity, albeit relaxed tempos. One could easily name an additional 25 to 30 titles for inclusion in this preferential early Elman inventory, for example: the scintillating Kreisler *Sicilienne et Rigaudon* and the *Chanson Louis XIII et Pavane*, the latter which is even more fragrantly lyric than the per-

formance by Kreisler himself, although not as gracefully buoyant. He also composed and transcribed a roster of simplistic short works.

Despite Elman's versatility in short pieces, it would be fallacious to conclude that he could not play the major works with first-class authority. For all his tempo-bending and stylistic idiosyncrasies, I heard him give polished, stimulating, entertaining live performances of the Tchaikovsky, Beethoven, Brahms, Glazunov, Vieuxtemps No. 5, Spohr *Gesangsszene*, Mendelssohn, and Saint-Saëns concertos, plus several more standard concertos of the repertoire, and at least a dozen major violin-piano sonatas, all from memory. In the mid-1930s he performed some 15 major concertos, including the Paganini-Wilhelmj Concerto No. 1, on five consecutive Saturday afternoons, with Leon Barzin and the American Orchestral Society Symphony. In contrast to some violinists whose playing is enhanced in recordings, Elman, like Milstein and Morini, sounded better in live performance. (I served as page-turner for his pianist on two occasions, and nearly came to grief as a result of my concentrating on the violinist instead of the piano music.)

He was quite unadventurous in repertoire though he commissioned the Second Violin Concerto by Boleslav Martinu, and successfully premiered it during the 1943-44 season with Koussevitsky and the Boston Symphony. In his 70s he learned and recorded the Khachaturian concerto, woefully slow in tempo, but invested with some glowing lyric passages.

The total number of Elman recordings approximates that of Kreisler (about 200, not counting re-recordings and Elman String Quartet discs) and similarly, the number of major works is in the minority. Unfortunately, most of the major works were recorded in his declining years, but the early Tchaikovsky concerto disc is a historic milestone in the evolution of that work, and the Mendelssohn concerto with Désiré Defauw and the Chicago Symphony, recorded on the old 78 platters, is a sparkling, beautiful performance by any standards. His Debussy sonata, recorded around the mid-1940s with Leopold Mittman, makes no pretense of mirroring misty French Impressionism, but the plush, suave performance is convincing in its own right. The major-composition recordings made in his later years range from acceptable to curious to disastrous, although his commendable recordings of the Nardini E-minor and Vivaldi G-minor (Op. 12, No. 1) concertos are welcome exceptions.

Elman's active concertizing career was one of the longest in violinistic history, more than 60 years, but unlike those of Joachim, Kreisler, and Heifetz, did not gain momentum as the years passed, or bring ever-increasing, or even sustained, glory. His 50th anniversary on the concert platform in 1954 was feted with a modest degree of publicity when he played his old favorite, the Tchaikovsky concerto, in Carnegie Hall. In 1959, again with no more than meager fanfare, he celebrated the 50th anniversary of his American debut.

It is important, I think, to trace briefly the course of Elman's career and examine those violinistic events which influenced it. The initial impact of Elman on the world of violin playing was powerful, and as we know, from around 1909-1917, his box-office success outstripped that of Kreisler, who required many more years to solidify his career on the highest echelon, even though his playing had attained peak performance shortly after the turn of the century. Ysaÿe was now on the decline, with Elman and Kreisler battling for supremacy, the latter ultimately gaining the upper hand.

The phenomenon of Heifetz in 1917 swiftly downgraded all violinists with the exception of Kreisler, particularly those of the Russian School, including Elman, who was the second most renowned of the Auer progeny. Kreisler survived, and even increased his hold on the hearts of the public due to his unique sound and style and the magnetism of his personality. His art represented a complete, and to many, welcome antithesis to Heifetz. By the mid-20s Elman was significantly superseded by these two rivals in the struggle for public favor. Subsequently, with the meteoric rise of the young Menuhin, plus the lesser but potent successes of Milstein, Szigeti, Ricci, and Francescatti in the 1930s and, in the early 1940s, Stern, Elman found himself to be a near-anachronism before he was scarcely 50 years old. The number and importance of his engagements, and the size of his fees steadily dwindled, yet he retained a small but intensely loyal audience right up to his 75th year.

The new standards were not propitious for the Elman blandishments: tempos accelerated and general technical virtuosity had proliferated, even among those stellar violinists who did not stress virtuosity for virtuosity's sake. The pliable musical concepts of the recent past were out of favor, and the individualistic violinist-poet who lovingly caressed every note was inundated by the new perfectionism and heightened discipline.

Elman retained most of his powers until he was about 50, when the tonal fires gradually began to flicker; his tempos waxed even slower, and as his left hand facility slackened, his interpretations grew more shapeless and unorthodox. The recordings of his last two decades caused irreparable harm to the historic Elman reputation, and consequently, most of the younger generation, knowing little or nothing about his prime playing, assume that Elman was some sort of near-comic figure.

I recall a 1963 Hollywood Bowl performance in which Elman required 47 minutes to inch his way through the Beethoven concerto (which I thought was a record until I heard the recorded disc version of over 48 minutes by Anne-Sophie Mutter with von Karajan). About two years later, in a Los Angeles Music Center Pavilion recital, the venerable violinist at 74 put it all together. It was a monumental performance which completely confounded and delighted the professional violinists in attendance, who had long since come to regard Elman as a nostalgic relic of the past. That evening he was a veritable potentate of his instrument.

Historically, Elman has not had a lasting or profound influence on the art of violin playing. Aside from the existence of the *Elman Chair* at the Manhattan School of Music in New York, all that remains of Elman is a diminishing number of unbelievably beautiful discs of the 'teen years, a few salubrious recordings of his middle years, and some embarrassingly poor ones of his final period. There are, too, the reminiscences of older people who heard him in his prime, and will always cherish the memory of the *Arabian Nights* quality of his sound, and the legerdemain and fantasy of his narrative. It stands to reason that with the continually changing violinistic concepts and criteria, and the ever-lessening importance of sheer tonal lavishness as a dominating factor in violin art, his like will probably never be heard again.

Joska Szigeti

Joseph Szigeti: No violinist ever served his art with more integrity.

Joseph Szigeti

By the mid-1920s it seemed as if the zenith in bewitching sound, charm, elegance, suavity, and virtuosity, as variously vested in Kreisler, Elman, and Heifetz, had been attained. There was, of course, always room at the top for another phenomenally gifted personality of comparable esthetic persuasion—the young Menuhin being the subsequent example of the breed; their lesser next-of-kin in this syndrome of hyper-romantic violinistic endeavor were proliferating everywhere.

Yet there were two top-echelon artists who remained outside the broad confines of this category. Each was strikingly different from the other, and in maturity, essentially unrelated to any specific violinistic school; players whose personal styles and musical eloquence were of a magnitude sufficient to overcome certain antiquated features of their technical training. This pair appealed to audiences that refused to accept the Kreisler-Elman-Heifetz criteria as the ultimate experience in violinistic art.

One was the Polish-Jewish Bronislaw Huberman, an unorthodox player of stunning gut communication (though inclined to roughness of delivery and not possessing opulent vibrance of sound), the idol of Vienna, and a special favorite in middle Europe, who also enjoyed an international reputation and following. The other was the Hungarian-Jewish Joseph Szigeti (1892-1973), an artist whose career, temporarily restricted by World War I, had already begun to blossom into international renown.

Szigeti (whose original name was Singer) was born in Budapest, Hungary, September 5, 1892. During his childhood he lived with his grandparents in Máramaros-Sziget, a small Carpathian town in the general area which had produced Joachim, Auer, and Flesch. The family included several musicians who played at weddings and similar local functions. It was his uncle Bernat who started the boy on the violin at age seven. His father was a leader of café bands and a teacher in Budapest; another uncle, Dezsö, who had studied with Jenö Hubay in the 1890s, was the first classical violinist to emerge from the family, and eventually became a member of the Metropolitan Opera Orchestra in New York.

Later, young Joseph was taken to Budapest by his father and enrolled in a small private conservatory, where he studied for several months with an unnamed teacher who doubled as a backstand member of the opera orchestra. Here he was taught the "book-under-the-arm" method, an archaic position of the right arm, vestiges of which remained throughout his career. (Erica Morini was schooled in a similar fashion.) Despite this mediocre training, when he auditioned several months later for admission into a class preparatory to Hubay's at the State Music Academy, Hubay took him directly into his own class.

The Szigeti story is recounted in his autobiography, *With Strings Attached—Reminiscences and Reflections*, first published in 1947 and provided with a brief insignificant addenda in 1967. For all the interest contained in its notes and anecdotes, the book is woefully disorganized and its rambling style can be most frustrating to the exacting researcher. Szigeti tells little about his study with Hubay, his practice regimen and habits, his problems, or specifics about his student colleagues. He does state that "there prevailed an atmosphere of such puerile sibling rivalry, we were so completely absorbed by the externals of our craft, that I have difficulty in conveying this satisfactorily, still more in explaining it." Oddly, no mention is made of his Jewish

Jenö Hubay

derivation or any difficulties he might have encountered in this aspect, or precisely why his concerts in Germany ceased from May, 1933 until the post-World War II period.

Szigeti also wrote *A Violinist's Notebook*, 1964, and *Szigeti on the Violin*, 1969. In the latter, a provocative book, he discusses the pros and cons of violin competitions in considerable depth, and enunciates the scarcity of accomplished young orchestra violinists as opposed to the prolific number of would-be soloists who are perennial contest entries. He bemoans the shortcomings of "the present crop of brilliant violinists" in the matter of violinistic individuality, and decries the current practice of young violinists who, for economic considerations, record works which have not had sufficient time to ripen interpretively. The volume emphasizes the supreme importance of perfect intonation and contains valuable commentary on repertorial and interpretive matters. A slim volume, *The Ten Beethoven Sonatas for Piano and Violin*, edited by Paul Rolland, appeared in 1965, in which Szigeti contributes helpful material pertaining to the masterwork cycle.

Hubay, though purportedly a pupil of Joachim, had been powerfully influenced by Vieuxtemps whom he revered, and for a time was a professor at the Brussels Conservatory. His musical inclinations followed the precepts of the Romantic Belgian School virtuosity, and it was in this milieu that the young Szigeti's musicality was formed. At 13, following in the footsteps of his contemporaries Ferenc von Vecsey and Mischa Elman, he made his Berlin debut. The program included: Ernst's Concerto in F-sharp Minor, Bach's *Chaconne* and Paganini's *Witches Dance*. His repertoire, at this time, consisted of only the Wieniawski No. 2, Ernst, Mendelssohn, and Viotti (unspecified) concertos, the Bach *Chaconne* and E-major *Preludio*, Tartini's *Devil's Trill* Sonata, and sundry bravura showpieces by Paganini, Sarasate, Hubay, Wieniawski, and Saint-Saëns. He had never heard the Brahms or a Bach concerto, Chausson's *Poème*, or sonatas of Beethoven, Mozart, Handel, or Franck played in Hubay's class.

Although Szigeti scored some successes as a prodigy, he was not destined for meteoric youthful fame as were Vecsey, Elman, Heifetz, and Menuhin. His road to international renown was to be long and laborious. Szigeti's was the art of full maturity. Like Elman, Szigeti had no formal training after his early teen years.

As a product of Hubay, whose school numbered many superior talents such as Vecsey, Emil Telmanyi, Steffi Geyer, Stephan Partos (who died young), Duci de Kerekjarto, Erna Rubinstein, Jelly d'Aranyi and her sister Adila Fachiri, Eddy Brown (before he went to Auer), Eugene Ormandy (the conductor) and, in later years, the brilliant Robert Virovai, Szigeti could easily have slipped into obscurity. Even the best of the older Hubay pupils were doomed to be inundated by the new wave of brilliant players from the so-called Russian School. As a prodigy he could not compete with the phenomenal successes of Vecsey or Elman. He might have continued on the path of superficial, backward-looking virtuosity, as did Vecsey, or he might have gone to Auer, as did so many others, and been eclipsed in a violinistic environment which was essentially alien to his natural equipment and temperament. At any rate, those lofty qualities in Szigeti's playing that eventually won him international renown in later years, can scarcely be attributed to his two years of training (plus two brief summer sessions in 1908) with Hubay.

93

Flesch remarks:

At 16, Szigeti was supposed to become my pupil . . . I have always regretted that he did not spend two years of his youth under my supervision. I could have normalized his bowing within the shortest space of time, broken him of the habit of his head-accents, and taught him methods of study which would have reduced his excessive working time to a minimum.

However, Szigeti elected to adhere to his own devices. If ever there was a self-made artist, it was he! He turned aside from his early musical predilections and around 1906, influenced by Ferruccio Busoni, a superlative all-round musician, began the slow, arduous maturing process that in later decades was to induce many observers to consider him "the greatest musician among violinists." At about this time he played for the aged Joachim, who proposed that Szigeti complete his repertorial studies with him, and even offered to provide the boy a wealthy patron. But after attending a Joachim class at the Berlin Hochschule and viewing the uninspired coaching of a pedagogue no longer able to demonstrate on his instrument, Szigeti decided not to accept the opportunity. This was undoubtedly a wise decision, since the strait-jacket teaching of Joachim, for all his vast eminence and erudition, had never produced a single violinist of elite international stature.

Meanwhile, to advance his general education which, like his musical training, had been prematurely discontinued, he started a program of prolific, if random, reading of books in English. As a result, his newly formulated astute observations in the area of culture and esthetics served to separate him from the spate of superbly gifted but basically uncultured and unintellectual young virtuosos who ultimately could not quite make it to the top rung.

Tended and accompanied by his father, and managed by a London impresario, Szigeti played with or for such musicians as Myra Hess, Vincent D'Indy, and Karl Goldmark, among others, and was an assisting artist on programs with Nellie Melba, John McCormack, and sundry singers, constantly, as he put it, "grinding out the same obsolete salon pieces by Sarasate, Hubay and Wieniawski in musicales and provincial tours." Fortunately, his invaluable friendship with Busoni was renewed and intensified. The violinist refers to this period as these "aimless, happy-go-lucky years." They were also years that exposed him to the stringent realities of

Joseph Szigeti in a pose epitomizing the thoughtful musician that he was

life. As a teenager, the pressure of having to support himself and his father was constant.

It is indicative of his deficient early training that Szigeti publicly performed the Goldmark concerto before he had studied any of the concertos by Mozart. He first performed the Beethoven concerto with an amateur orchestra when he was 18. Aside from some sonata playing, he had practically no experience with string quartets or chamber music. A vivid instance of his musical immaturity is his 1908 recording of the Preludio from Bach's Solo Partita in E-Major, which he rattles off cleanly but perfunctorily in two minutes and 58 seconds, as compared to the recorded performance of his maturity made in the 1950s that requires three minutes and 53 seconds—an arrant disparity.

He now had the opportunity to hear violinists like Ysaÿe, Kreisler, Elman, and Thibaud, and immediately recognized what was then the new trend of violin art. These concerts were revelatory to the youngster. Unlike a host of violinists schooled in a comparable anachro-

94

nistic manner who, unable to comprehend the new concepts of sound, style, and musicality, clung doggedly and obstinately to dated violinistic precepts, Szigeti fairly basked in the wondrous glow kindled by the aforementioned four masters. In later years he called Ysaÿe, Kreisler, Elman, Busoni, and the conductors Arthur Nikisch, Sir Hamilton Harty, and Sir Henry Wood "my real teachers."

He describes the eleven- or twelve-year-old Heifetz playing the Bruch Concerto No. 1 in Berlin before World War I as "touchingly beautiful."

However, he was sufficiently shrewd to understand and reject those facets of contemporary playing that stressed technically flawless, vibrant-but-arid performance, devoid of inner spirituality. He realized that sheer beauty of tone, in itself, could be potentially dull if not tempered with introspection, stylistic fidelity, and sincerity of purpose.

Szigeti's concert appearances continued to grow in number and expand geographically throughout Europe until the beginning of World War I, although in 1913 he was forced to undergo a cure for tuberculosis in Davos, Switzerland, during which period he was able to practice only 30 to 40 minutes a day. This deprivation served further to orient his methods of technical practice toward achieving maximal results in the least amount of time.

During the war his appearances were confined to Switzerland and Germany, and in those years he devoted much of his time and energies to "reading and playing through vast quantities of music not destined for public consumption." In 1917 he settled in Geneva and assumed the pedagogical duties of the "classes de virtuosite" at the Geneva Conservatory, and in 1919 married his wife Wanda. He retained the Geneva position until 1924, and in this period combined his teaching with 35 to 45 concerts a year in Switzerland and Holland, most of which were self-managed and of second-level importance. These aided in financing the resumption of his concertizing in the inflation-ridden countries across the borders.

Szigeti was highly respected by his violinistic peers in Europe, including Ysaÿe. In a surprisingly candid statement, he says of Ysaÿe:

> His solo sonatas, the first of which, the one in G-minor, he dedicated to me, probably are more important as a violinistic testament than as a creative effort that can stand critical evaluation in cold blood. What gives them signifi-

cance is that they are a repository of the ingredients of the playing style of this incomparable interpreter.

Joseph Szigeti

Kreisler, always generous to his colleagues, helped pave Szigeti's way in the United States by praising him to American journalists who, as yet, had little or no acquaintance with the Hungarian's art.

The maestro Stokowski, after hearing Szigeti play the Bach *Chaconne* in Zurich in 1925, promised him an American appearance, and unlike so many conductors and managers who make high-flown pledges that are promptly forgotten, he kept his word. Consequently, Szigeti's Philadelphia debut in the Beethoven concerto, which was shortly after repeated in New York, followed by a recital, triumphantly launched his career in the New World. He had already appeared in the Soviet Union in 1924, and later, when he toured the Orient in the 1930s, his reputation became fully internationalized.

In the face of his awesome competition, it would have seemed almost impossible that Szigeti could carve out a top-flight career for himself.

But he did!

There were many factors involved in the realization of this phenomenon. Firstly, Szigeti knew who and what he was. Wisely, he did not attempt to compete on the so-called home ground of Kreisler, Elman, Heifetz, Menuhin, or Milstein, as did so many other gifted players who subsequently failed. Szigeti's strength lay in the fact that he was different, and a sizeable potential audience was waiting for just such a violinist to appear on the scene.

Like Joachim before him, Szigeti fought the battle for artistic survival and success on his own turf, so to speak. He shunned, in his maturity, the immensely popular romantic concertos of Tchaikovsky, Bruch, Wieniawski, Vieuxtemps, Lalo, Paganini, Sibelius, Glazunov, Elgar, Walton, and Saint-Saëns; or show-pieces such as Sarasate's *Zigeunerweisen* and *Carmen Fantasy*, Ravel's *Tzigane*, and Saint-Saëns's *Introduction and Rondo Capriccioso* and *Havanaise*. One may be certain that he had carefully studied all or nearly all of these works since in his interesting and comprehensive *A Violinist's Notebook*, he provides fingerings, bowings, and commentary for selected difficult passages from most of them. For all his championing of works by Bartók and Prokofiev, neither the two concertos nor solo sonata by the former, nor the latter's lyric Concerto No. 2 in G-Minor were part of Szigeti's active repertoire.

He knew well his repertorial strengths and weaknesses, and concentrated on those masterworks of Bach, Mozart, Beethoven, and Brahms in which he felt, rightly, that he could offer interpretive insights that were both individual and musically provocative. He became known as a champion of contemporary music, not all of which was worthy of his efforts, though some of the better works attained permanent repertorial status. As early as 1912, at the age of 20, Szigeti performed the Busoni concerto.

I vividly recall one particular Szigeti recital that fell directly on the heels of the disastrous 1933 earthquake in the Los Angeles area. The program included sonatas by Bach, Brahms, and Debussy, an audacious choice for that day. There he stood, handsome and aristocratic of bearing (yet never aloof), the consummate, cosmopolitan sophisticate seemingly unruffled by a series of unnerving after-quakes, while his intrepid listeners, who had left the comparative safety of their homes to attend, cheered lustily.

Szigeti recitals (in his maturity) were always designed for the adventurous auditor. However, even in the latter part of the 1940s and perhaps a few years later, he included short encore-type pieces such as the Dvořák-Kreisler E-minor and G-minor *Slavonic Dances*, Bartók's *Roumanian Folk Dances*, Kreisler originals, and his own difficult setting of Scriabin's *Study in Thirds*. I remember his daredevil upbow flying staccato in the Rigaudon of Kreisler's *Sicilienne and Rigaudon* and the pristine, honest intonation of Rimsky-Korsakov's *Flight of the Bumble Bee*. Five of the 24 Paganini caprices were in his performing repertoire, and at his best, he played them with unerring accuracy. Caprice No. 9, *La Chasse*, was one of his favorites.

The finest qualities of Szigeti were not vested in dessert music. He was not a violinist of the Kreisler type who was, as Flesch aptly put it, "always ready", one who could pick up the instrument any time of the day or night and with little or no warm-up period, play beautifully. In the United States during the late 1930s and for several years into the 1940s, a popular commercial radio show would periodically invite a noted violinist for a spot of about five to eight minutes in a nationwide broadcast. Whereas a Kreisler, Heifetz, or Menuhin appearance was almost always crowned with success, Szigeti, by comparison, sounded ill at ease and out of his element.

In assessing the instrumental equipment of Szigeti, it is necessary to understand that while he was not generally categorized as a virtuoso violinist in the sense of Heifetz, Milstein, or Kogan, his technique was formidable and comprehensive, no doubt the result of his bravura repertoire background as a youngster. His tone was soft-grained in texture, and his vibrato, even at its most rapid oscillation, was no more than medium in speed, often tending to become slow, and on occasion, a bit wobbly. Its communication, however, was sweet, though not patently so (as is the sound of Francescatti), and at its best, was thoroughly ingratiating.

His was not a resplendently personalized, ear-titillating sound, nor could he climax or conclude his runs and passagework with high-voltage vibrance as do many current violinists. But in his prime he negotiated the most unviolinistic, awkward passages, as in the Brahms concerto, with seeming ease and superb precision. As a pioneer in contemporary music, he developed a penchant for polished delivery of many works that had not been tailored for violinistic fingerboard comfort. The Szigeti intonation, even in his declining years, was almost always impeccable. He used many slides and position changes in lyric passages, but always as an inte-

Szigeti enjoying a respite during an arduous rehearsal

ing. He had the ingrained habits of waggling his head on accented beats and breathing heavily, but overall, his deportment while playing was visually engaging.

Observations about Szigeti's art are invariably centered around his superior musicianship. Such remarks, while well-intentioned and true, merely skim the surface of the matter. What is important, I feel, is the level of musicianship he represented, since we know that many music commentators equate musicianship with literal academicism. Szigeti was the ideal personification of the master musician who was *not* an academician. Although he consistently sought out the musical message and intents of a composition, he was at the same time a powerful individualist. Numerous contemporary violinists follow (or claim to follow) the *Urtext* of the Bach solo sonatas, and strive with might and main to avoid any vestige of personalization by employing little or no vibrato, eliminating all slides or audible position changes, using finger extensions wherever possible, and shunning any original bowings or dynamics. But Szigeti, in the spirit of such celebrated Bach exponents as Pablo Casals and Wanda Landowska, was an enterprising and individual interpreter, quite unlike the pedants of so-called authenticity.

In studying these Bach masterworks, he not only consulted the *Urtext*, but also the greatly varied editions of Joachim, David, Hellmsberger, Busch, Hubay, Capet, Champeil, and Flesch, as well as the ideas of Enesco. He supplemented his investigations into Bach's music by reading the Bach commentaries of Dr. Albert Schweitzer and Professor Ernst Kurth.

At no time did Szigeti sacrifice his own musical ideas to some amorphous philosophy of carrying out punctiliously the composer's alleged intentions. What he did was to create an often wondrous fusion of the style, spirit, and rhythmic pulse of a composer's era and ethos with his own considerable temperament and intelligence. He was a master of both musical propulsion (as graphically demonstrated in his performance of the opening movement of the Beethoven concerto) and celestial repose. His was a genuine spiritual repose, not to be confused with the pretentiousness of certain current string artists whose repose consists of stopping their vibrato, playing with bone-dry, barely audible sound, and rolling their eyes heavenward as if in private communion with The Deity.

Szigeti's playing exuded a positive aura of virility and sensuousness. This sensuousness, however, was not communicated through any rare beauty of tone or

gral part of the expressive function and never for superficial emotive effect.

Hampered by a bow arm that had been originally schooled in the antiquated close-to-the-body, book-under-the-arm method, he nevertheless drew a tone that was large and resonant. His right-arm technique was generally secure though somewhat unorthodox, and his détaché bowing often tended to be on top of the string and distractingly glossy in sound. At times his fortes could be scratchy, and his spiccato, bowed exceedingly close to the bridge, was inclined to lose some clarity, especially in climactic passages. As if compensating for this shortcoming, Szigeti could produce delicate staccato passages and a variety of piquant, crisp bow impacts that added marvelous diversity to his music-making, as in segments of the first movement of the Beethoven concerto. All too often in these episodes, elite violinists resort to a plethora of conservative and correct, but unimaginative détachés.

Physically, Szigeti was one of the most attractive and charismatic of the prime violinists; a man who looked as if he would be at ease in the most sophisticated and erudite company. Comparatively tall, balding in his maturity, he radiated the aura of a serious-minded yet affable scholar, worldly, but modest of bear-

memorable stylistic mannerisms as with Kreisler, Elman, or Heifetz, but rather through the visceral intensity of his interpretations. In contrast to the aforementioned trio, Szigeti's sound never dominated or got in the way of these interpretations. Each phrase had been meticulously thought out in advance, although in the execution there was no sacrifice of spontaneity. Szigeti's Bach solo sonatas, as I heard them live in his prime, were superlative examples. His Bach bristled with individual nuances and personalized detail, and yes, he even used a few tasteful, expressive slides in the slower lyrical movements. Add to this Szigeti's rare ability to divine the architecture of masterworks, refined through the years by his meticulous analysis of these compositions, and we have Bach solo sonata performances of Olympian stature. Thus it can be said that Szigeti served the music, but served it in his own way. I am referring to his performances of the most exalted major compositions.

Though Szigeti was not opposed to transcriptions of short pieces and often performed them, he was not the kind of artist who could take almost any piece of superficial music and endow it with a beauty and distinction far above its intrinsic worth, as could many of his colleagues. Instead, the greater the music, the more likely that Szigeti would impress the discriminating listener—provided he was in top violinistic form.

Born nine years before Heifetz, and trained in an entirely different violinistic milieu, Szigeti remained untouched by the revolutionary Heifetz influence. His art appealed in particular to the musical connoisseur, and while he gradually amassed a large following, many of whom were fanatical Szigeti devotées, his financial rewards were never in the topmost bracket. We find that in the 1949-50 period, Szigeti received $2,800 for a three-concert series as soloist with the New York Philharmonic, as compared to $3,600 for Francescatti, $3,800 for Milstein, about $5,000 to $6,000 for Menuhin, and $9,500 for Heifetz.

He performed or recorded sonatas with numerous piano collaborators: Ferruccio Busoni, Myra Hess, and Wilhelm Backhaus in his youth and later, Artur Schnabel, Walter Gieseking, Claudio Arrau, George Szell, Bela Bartók, Igor Stravinsky, Mieczyslaw Horszowski, and Roy Bogas. His recital partners included Andor Foldes (Farkas), Kurt Ruhrseitz, Ignaz Strasfogel, Carlos Busotti, Henry Byrd, Leonid Hambro, and Nikita Magaloff, his son-in-law.

As to be expected, due to the type of repertoire he favored, Szigeti is not among the leading violinists in number of recordings, but he has bequeathed a sizeable collection, about 138 compositions of all dimensions and styles, plus some 51 second and third recordings, which compares generally with the output of Stern, Szeryng, Francescatti, and Grumiaux. It is an exceptionally large number considering that his recorded repertory does not include a great many of the standard romantic compositions, and only a few chamber music works for three or more featured artists.

Flesch states that Szigeti sounded better in recordings than live. In the final analysis this may be so, but several of his live concerts which I heard during the 1930-46 period were magnificent, equal or superior to any of his recordings. Some of his most definitive and satisfying discs were made in the late 1920s and early 1930s; others, including a number of exceptional musical significance, date from after 1950, when both his recorded and live performances had already begun to decline in quality.

Among the most eminent of his recordings are the Prokofiev Concerto No. 1 in D-Major (Beecham, London Philharmonic, 1935), the Beethoven concerto (Walter, British Symphony Orchestra, 1932), the Mozart Concerto No. 4 in D-Major K.218, (Beecham, London Philharmonic, 1934), the Brahms concerto (Harty, Hallé Orchestra, 1928), the Handel Sonata in D-Major Op. 1, No. 13 (Magaloff, piano, 1937), and the cycle of Bach's solo sonatas and partitas made during the 1950s.

When Szigeti popularized the Prokofiev No. 1 in the mid-'30s, it was considered to be cacophonous and far out by most concertgoers, and no other major violinist performed it. Columbia Records was indeed courageous in recording and releasing the work. This may seem strange today, since the concerto has almost become a standard of the repertoire and has been recorded numerous times.

In spite of splendid modern recordings by David Oistrakh, Stern, and others, the one by Szigeti remains a memorable performance, with its kaleidoscopic range of moods, dynamics, and tonal colors. The intensity of the brusque bowing batteries, the lacy flights of misterioso lyricism, and the biting satire that pervades the entire interpretation mark it as an all-time great recording.

The Beethoven, with the Joachim cadenza, is one of three Szigeti recordings of the work. It is a noble performance in which the usual détaché bowings are artfully interspersed with light staccato and spiccato sorties that militate against any vestige of tedium. The outer movements are briskly paced, with conductor Bruno Walter guilty of some rushing in one of the finale tuttis. One can pinpoint occasional tubby or airy sounds, faults that are endemic to Szigeti's playing, but the overall reading is of historic stature. Again we see in glaring perspective the rare Szigeti ability to infuse his playing with compelling inner vitality without the asset of a tone that is of singular beauty in itself. He sustains the utmost tension in the great principal themes of the Larghetto, wonderfully abetted by some prominent slides and position changes that add extraordinary flavor to the celestial passages. His recording of this movement should be required listening for all the violinists of this generation, not for the purpose of imitation, but to illustrate the magical potential inherent in the music.

The Mozart No. 4 in D-Major, with the Joachim cadenzas, which Szigeti often played in recital with piano, is one of the very finest interpretations of a work that is quite difficult to communicate to an audience — perhaps more so than the Mozart No. 3 in G-Major or No. 5 in A-Major.

In hearing it played by nearly every important violinist from Kreisler to Perlman, these ears have heard no interpretation more elegant and stately than that of Szigeti's though many, naturally, have performed it with much grace, charm, and beauty of sound. Somehow, the concerto's demands seem to meld perfectly with Szigeti's temperament and equipment. His tempos are bright, his spiccato, flexible; the Andante, pensive and heartfelt, is enhanced by some savory, expressive backward position changes; the Rondo is permeated with surprising joie de vivre. All is ineffably polished.

The Brahms concerto (Joachim cadenza), recorded in 1928 with a rather mediocre orchestra, and long before modern editing, is dramatic, yet introspective and tough of basic fibre. The tone does not glitter, but the Adagio is steeped in what might be described as masculine tenderness; the Allegro giocoso throbs vigorously and joyously.

The Handel sonatas are not often programmed these days, and when they are, seldom constitute more than finger-warming opening works. In the hands of an Elman or Szigeti, each vastly different from the other, these comparatively small-scaled sonatas are potential gems. But when tossed off immaculately but perfunctorily by pedants (including those with a beautiful sound), they are relegated into wallpaper music of

Szigeti in rehearsal at the Hollywood Bowl in Los Angeles

superficial interest. Szigeti's recording of the Sonata in D-major has all the color, drive, and subtlety of phrasing one may hope for in the performance of the greatest masterworks. Above all, its sense of style is consistent in every bar.

It is unfortunate that Szigeti's Bach solo sonatas and partitas were recorded so late in his career, though the interpretations are still unique. The old 1931 recording of Sonata No. 1 in G-minor has always been considered a model performance by most violin devotées, and is somewhat better than its counterpart made over three decades later. In the latter—and this is true of the entire cycle—the Szigeti technical mechanism has begun to wane, not to a critical extent, but noticeably. His moderate-speed vibrato has become even slower. Intonation-wise, his left hand is immaculate. The chordal bowing thrusts are majestic and resonant. He often takes bowing risks in defiance of smoothness of execution in order to achieve unusual effect, as in the finale Double of the Partita No. 1 in B minor, which he plays spiccato (a very unusual ploy) for most of the first section, then breaks it up with détachés and legatos. His airy détaché is now more pronounced. On the purely musical level, this version is fully equal to the earlier live performances previously described. As in many other movements, the variety of shadings and the general excitement Szigeti generates in the *Chaconne* has seldom been paralleled. Unhappily, his live Bach playing deteriorated badly in his twilight years.

The Concerto in A-minor by Ernest Bloch, composed for Szigeti, is a work powerfully cast in the *Schelomo* Old Testament idiom, an opus of exceptional strength of conviction, clothed in a voluptuous instrumental accompaniment. Strangely, it has thus far been ignored by some violinists who make a public fetish of their affection for Israel and matters Hebraic, often in favor of less satisfying and less moving compositions. The 1939 Szigeti recording with Munch and the Paris Conservatory Orchestra, the first recording of the concerto, is an earnest, deeply-felt performance that lacks the essential plush vibrance of sound to endow the fervent declamations with maximal biblical intensity.

His recording of the Mendelssohn Concerto in E-minor with the London Philharmonic, conducted by Beecham in 1933, is an affectionate, if not really beautiful performance. The Andante contains more than the average number of emotive slides and position changes. The final movement is robust and very clean. A few minor imperfections can be noted in the opening movement, and the triplet octave passage on the last page is patently sullied. Despite many an effective nicety of phrasing, Szigeti's Mendelssohn does not have the brilliant lustre of sound projected by the best of the tonally-oriented artists. The latter can also be applied to the recordings of Schubert's Sonatina No. 1 with Foldes, and the Schubert-Friedberg Rondo Op. 53, with Magaloff, both undated 78 discs.

The vaunted Szigeti musical profundity is ever present and persuasive in the ten Beethoven sonatas with Arrau (1944), especially the Sonata in A major (*Kreutzer*), which is played with reflective expressiveness, but never dryly. Those sections of the sonatas that are intellectually oriented are more convincing than, for example, the consistently lyric No. 5 in F-major (*Spring*). A 1948 recording of the latter with Schnabel indicates a perceptible slowing down of his vibrato.

Among his post-1950 discs are Henry Cowell's Sonata No. 1, a simply-contrived work based on British-Irish-American folk tunes (with Bussotti); Arthur Honegger's Sonata No. 1, the chief feature being a sportive, spirited Presto; Webern's forgettable Four Pieces Op. 7; Debussy's Sonata in G-minor; Ives' Sonata No. 4 (the last four works with Bogas); Hindemith's Sonata No. 3; the Ravel Sonata, in which the Perpetual Motion is exceedingly clean, but the jazzy effects in the Blues have a Hungarian tint (with Bussotti); and 15 Mozart sonatas with Horszowski.

In the above group Szigeti's superior musical qualities remain consistently in evidence, and his intonation is still true, but his vibrato continues to languish, enervating all of his lyric episodes. This is a bit less obvious in Prokofiev's Solo Sonata Op. 115, since it contains only minimal melodic material—another late recording.

A 1940 recording of the Debussy sonata taken from a live performance, is much more stable in sound than the post-1950 version. Bartók, as the piano collaborator, plays with solid competence and sensitivity, though in the later disc, Arrau registers more plausibly as a full-fledged partner. Two other 1940 items with Bartók at the piano are the latter's Rhapsody No. 1, a rough-hewn goulash of Magyar themes that Szigeti often performed, and Sonata No. 2. The former, stylistically scrupulous, is vitiated by intermittent vaporous tone. (One can only wonder why Szigeti, as a Bartók partisan, favored this mediocre work and neglected the Concerto No. 2 and the epochal Solo Sonata.) The Sonata No. 2, also rich in Hungarian flavor, is played with marked attention to detail—a decisive, modish interpretation.

Several early discs of short numbers made probably around 1908 under the name of Joska Szigeti, include *Ungarische Weisen* Op. 5 by Laszlo, a superficial salon piece in the "Hejre Kati" style, and Hubay's *Unter ihrem Fenster from Two Pieces* Op. 38, No. 2, with pianist Henry Byrd, a similar entertainment bauble. They are of interest in that they display Szigeti as a young, aspiring virtuoso before he developed into a musician of stature. The performances are clean-cut and buoyant, with none of the distasteful exaggerated slides and elastic phrasing that were still rampant among many violinists in those years. But for all the probity of the playing, one can see why "Joska" was no serious rival of the young Elman or Heifetz in pieces belonging to the underside of the repertoire.

Szigeti, a man of culture, was very well liked. He frequently played chamber music with rank-and-file professional musicians, maintained correspondence with them, and was known as a person of democratic ideals and disposition. His chamber music parts were meticulously marked with fingerings and bowings which he practiced carefully in private (he was not a facile sight-reader).

Gerald Moore, in his memoirs, *Am I Too Loud*, chides Szigeti for not mentioning the musical contributions of his longtime piano collaborator Nikita Magaloff in *With Strings Attached*, an oversight that Szigeti amended in the 1967 re-issue of the book. Menuhin writes of Szigeti's "persnicketiness" and the "perversity of his opinions" as a juror at the City of London Carl Flesch Concours, but also states that "he was a violinist whom I much admired and a man of whom I was fond." Szigeti's reputation, both in public and private, as musician and man, in life and in death, remains exemplary.

Szigeti was one of the first classical violin luminaries to join musical forces with a leading jazz musician. In a 1939 Carnegie Hall recital, he and Benny Goodman gave the premiere of Bartók's *Contrasts* for clarinet, violin, and piano. It was later recorded with the composer at the piano.

Not only was Szigeti a paladin in the cause of contemporary compositions, but he delved into the archives of baroque and classical music resuscitating and, in some instances, re-editing scores such as Bach's Concerto in D-minor for Violin and Orchestra, Tartini's Concerto in D-minor, and Weber's Sonata in D (*Air

Russe and Rondo*). I seem to recall that he once began a major concert playing Corelli's *La Folia* with orchestral accompaniment.

Szigeti devoted much time to teaching in his later years. Those who studied with him include: Arnold Steinhardt, Kyung-Wha Chung, Yoshio Unno, Masuko Ushioda, Nell Gotkovsky, Elaine Weldon, and Yoshio Takebe.

In the tradition of Joachim, Szigeti has helped to refurbish purity of concept, scholarship, and spaciousness of musical architecture in violin art. His has been a crusading intellect constantly in pursuit of the highest musical values. The success of his honorable career proved beyond doubt that character and intelligence in violin playing can win the hearts and minds of audiences as separate from mere beauty of sound, technical gymnastics, and bravura flair. Admittedly, Szigeti's select audience was not equivalent to the mass audiences of Kreisler and Heifetz, but as often as not, knowledgeable violin devotees who adored either or both of the latter two giants, immensely admired and respected Szigeti.

Historically, Szigeti must be credited with exerting a powerful influence on the type of violin programs that are prevalent today. As an artist, however, he cannot be included among those current violinists or musicians who insist upon the subjugation of an instrumentalist's personality to the dictates of the so-called "composer's intentions." His art radiated his own humanism, and no violinist ever played with more integrity!

Joseph Szigeti

Heifetz was publicized as "the violinist without a peer," a claim which few of his colleagues would dispute.

Jascha Heifetz

Why is it that so many of his eminent colleagues and a veritable legion of violinists the world over freely admit that Heifetz is the greatest among them? Oistrakh once said: "There are violinists and then there is Heifetz." Stern has said: "When the history of violin playing in our time is written, it will be known as the Heifetz era." From Perlman: "Heifetz is the greatest violinist who ever lived." Szeryng always referred to Heifetz as "The Emperor." Zukerman has stated: "I consider Heifetz the King of Virtuosos." Kogan revered Heifetz, and his playing and violinistic priorities were greatly influenced by Heifetz. For practically three generations, the expression "to play like a Heifetz" has been used to represent the closest thing to perfection in violin playing. Each of these star violinists, each with the powerful ego and massive self-confidence it takes to be a world-class violinist, had the artistic humility to admit Heifetz's supremacy.

In the 'teen years of the 20th century, while Kreisler and Elman were vying for supremacy in the world of violin art, players such as Kubelik, Vecsey, Willy Burmester, and Henri Marteau, representing a level of playing that was already anachronistic, no longer were in top contention. Mighty Ysaÿe was in the process of phasing out his career as a soloist; Zimbalist, Enesco, Huberman, Thibaud, Paul Kochanski, Powell, Spalding, and Szigeti, violinists of vastly diversified talents, were engaged in careers of distinction. The new playing of sensuous tonal vibrance and sophistication had, for the most part, ousted the dry academicians from the scene. Even in Berlin, once a bastion of performance conservatism, audiences preferred, for the most part, the emotion-oriented violin stars trained in Eastern and Western Europe to the lesser talented legatees of the prosaic, intellectualized Joachim school. Considering the mass popularity of Kreisler and Elman, scarcely anyone realized that violin art was on the threshold of yet another revolution, one comparable to that generated by Paganini a century earlier. However, rumors had already begun to circulate about a young boy in Russia who threatened to dwarf all competitors.

In 1913 the 12-year-old Jascha Heifetz made his first incursion into the Western world playing the Tchaikovsky concerto with Arthur Nikisch and the Berlin Philharmonic. Nikisch then invited him to appear in Leipzig, after which the lad performed in various cities of Central Europe. The outbreak of World War I in 1914 interrupted his burgeoning career, and he returned to Russia to resume his studies with Leopold Auer.

After a series of concerts in Norway in 1916, an American impresario offered to present the young violinist in America, and the entire Heifetz family: father, mother, and two sisters, together with the prodigy, emigrated to the United States. Heifetz became an American citizen in 1925.

On October 27, 1917, at the age of 16, he continued his world conquest in an epoch-making New York recital at Carnegie Hall. The revolution had been triggered into motion!

Heifetz was born February 2, 1901 (though certain compendiums list his birth a year or two earlier), in Vilna, Lithuania, a part of Tsarist Russia in the Jewish Pale of Settlement. He was given a tiny violin at the early age of three, and received his first lessons from father Ruvin, a violinist with the Vilna Symphony. At five the boy entered Vilna's Royal School of Music where he studied with Ilya Davidovitch Malkin, a pupil of Auer; a year later he played the Mendelssohn concerto in public and was graduated from the conserva-

Members of the Heifetz family in Russia, circa 1916: Jascha, the prodigy, with sisters Pauline (left) and Elza

tory before he was eight years old.

Through Malkin's influence, the lad secured an audition with Auer when the latter was visiting Vilna, and the celebrated professor, as was to be expected, marveled at the boy's talents and agreed to admit him to his class in St. Petersburg. As with Zimbalist and Elman before him, the Tsarist laws forbidding Jews to live in St. Petersburg (even after the gifted child had received permission to study at the conservatory) plagued the Heifetzes. This was eventually circumvented with the connivance of Auer and Glazunov (who was director of the conservatory), when Ruvin Heifetz, already in his 40s, was accepted as a violin student. The subterfuge enabled father and son to remain together in the capital. Meanwhile, since Auer's class was filled, Jascha was enrolled temporarily in the class of Professor Ioannes Nalbondyan, Auer's assistant.

In 1911 the boy played three open-air recitals in Odessa before audiences of 5,000, 14,000, and 28,000,

respectively, the final performance exciting the crowds to a state of near-riot. During the next few years Jascha often played solo or duet concerts with Toscha Seidel, his contemporary and closest rival in the Auer class. One critic dubbed Jascha "the angel of the violin" and Toscha, "the devil of the violin," in an attempt to characterize their individual playing styles. However, Jascha's clear-cut supremacy was not long in manifesting itself. In 1917 the cream of the world's violin talents were associated with Auer, and more than a few were of uppermost rank. But once Heifetz had made his New York debut, the other Auer disciples who appeared during this general period were downgraded, even though the best of them engaged in a certain amount of concertizing before they were dispersed to other musical spheres. Seidel, who possessed one of the most powerful and luscious sounds of any violinist I have ever heard, live or recorded, ultimately ended up in the Hollywood recording industry. Efrem Zimbalist succeeded Josef Hofmann as head of the Curtis Institute in Philadelphia. Eddy Brown, a masterful technician, and a Hubay pupil before he went to Auer, became a musical director in radio. Michel Piastro was concertmaster of the San Francisco Symphony and the New York Philharmonic, and noted for his numerous solo appearances with the orchestras; later he was conductor of the Longines Sinfonietta. Richard Burgin became concertmaster of

The celebrated Professor Leopold Auer with four of his star pupils, 1915. Standing left to right: Eddy Brown, Jascha Heifetz, Max Rosen, Toscha Seidel (young lady is unknown)

the Boston Symphony. The legendary Miron Poliakin, who is credited with having been superlatively brilliant but inconsistent, and tending to be overly-nervous in public concerts, settled for some time in the United States then returned to the Soviet Union where he died in 1941. Russian recordings reveal him to have been a formidable violinist, but scarcely a serious competitor of Heifetz. The career of Max Rosen, a violinist of admirable lyric qualities, gradually evaporated. Mischa Elman succeeded in sustaining his solo career for almost fifty years after the 1917 Heifetz debut, but in his last four decades he no longer commanded the highest fees and the most desirable engagements.

The leading pupils of Hubay, Sevčik, and Kneisel also had to settle for less, and the list of excellent violinists born in the 1890-1905 era who can be added to it is legion. Symphony orchestras and conservatories everywhere were the ultimate beneficiaries of the Heifetz suzerainty. It is reasonable to assume that without him, violinistic instrumental standards would be appreciably lower.

It may be that no one will ever know the exact detail of Heifetz's early training: his practice regime, his problems, if any, or how he managed to evolve the wondrous equipment which surpassed that of the foremost violinists before and after him. Heifetz himself has never publicly discussed these matters except in the broadest generalities. His father placed the violin in Jascha's hand; Malkin continued the process, and by the time Heifetz reached Auer, he was already a superb instrumentalist. According to Heifetz, during the six years (age ten to 16) he was with Auer, he played no exercises or technical works for his master, only important compositions of the performance repertoire and shorter concert pieces. In those days there were no practice tapes of recordings of major works by great artists. The incredible Heifetz ear was honed with no mechanical assistance whatsoever. He was, of course, intimately familiar with the Auer concepts as reflected through the art of Elman, and with the playing of the other gifted pupils in Auer's class, but the fact of the matter is, those facets of Heifetz's mastery that none of his colleagues or rivals could match are not qualities that were teachable by Auer or anyone else.

To begin with, like a super-athlete, the Heifetz reflexes and muscular coordination in both hands were unparalleled, as was his dead-center accuracy of intonation and clarity of articulation. Using a high-wrist bow position and the Auer bow grip that stresses pres-

sure of the index finger, and a close-to-the-bridge bowing line (which opts for maximal tonal sonority), his right arm was at once a tower of strength and a marvel of suppleness.

The Heifetz left hand fingers were of ideal length, breadth, and proportion. He was a complete master of both vertical and horizontal movement, not only in feats of fingerboard facility, but in those subtle horizontal devices which involve exquisite expressive slides and position changes (an art rapidly disappearing from the violinist's lexicon). His vibrato was of the uncommon fingertip impulse type which produced a virile sound (as did the vibratos of Kreisler, Elman, and Seidel), as opposed to the sweet, mellow sound of those artists who employ one of the various types of more widely-oscillated wrist- and arm-impelled vibrato. He was able to produce it with each finger and combination of fingers in every position of the fingerboard in accordance with his esthetic desires. Even more significant was his ability to diversify his vibrato from a speed of incredible intensity (albeit always free of tenseness) to

The young Heifetz

the opposite pole, together with all degrees of velocity between. The palette of sound at his disposal superseded that of any other violinist; there was never a one-dimensional quality to his playing.

Any knowledgeable listener can easily single out the Heifetz sound from that of a hundred fine violinists. He has often been characterized as the greatest technician. In the fundamental sense this is true because of his matchless overall command and control, even though there are fingerboard gymnasts who specialize in Paganini showpieces that had not been in the Heifetz repertoire since his youth. Most importantly, in addition to his technical resources, he raised the singing capacity of the violin to its highest level! His fusion of dexterity and lyricism, of tension and flexibility, represent the ultimate in violin and bow technique to this day.

The art of bowing is a cardinal element in violin performance. Apart from the satiny sheen, coloristic variety, and seamless fluency of the Heifetz bow arm, his spiccato was ever crisp and incisive, with no vestige of the flapping or semi-détaché one sometimes hears from other virtuosos; his up-and-down staccato, even though it may be equaled in speed, had superior bite, and the crackling impact of his assertive bow in instantaneous unity with his left hand finger intensity, generated an attack that was climactic and inimitable.

Another Heifetz propensity was his kamikaze audacity, an inherent element of his violinistic character, not only in diabolical technical flights at breakneck speed, but in buoyant medium-speed phrases of elegance or slow cantilena. Where others would opt for a fingering or bowing that is adequate, reliable, or safe, Heifetz would dare any hazard to produce a special effect that he felt would add an extra fillip of brilliance or expressivity. Taken collectively, these added immeasurably to the suavity and sophistication of his playing—imparting to it an aura that bespoke the glitter, drive, and spirit of the 20th century, setting him apart from even the greatest of his predecessors. In addition, the man's violinistic stamina was monumental.

All of these virtues are immediately evident in the earliest Heifetz recordings dating from 1917. Among the pre-electric discs we can hear the 1917 Paganini *Moto Perpetuo* with its stunning fluidity, breathless pace, and unerring bull's-eye intonation. A few violinists have subsequently equaled his speed on the stop-watch, but never the staggering perfection of the entire performance. The same can be said of such dazzlers as the 1917 Bazzini *Ronde des lutins*, the 1918 Sarasate

Heifetz in the 1930s with his first wife, actress Florence Vidor, his eldest son Robert and daughter Josepha

Introduction and Tarantelle, the 1917 Wieniawski *Scherzo Tarantelle*, and others of this genre. Even when the Heifetz speed is matched by others in rapid episodes, his balance of digital facility with the polish of the briefer melodic segments is unapproachable, as is his wondrous pellucidity of sound.

Just as significant is his penchant for glowing ariosity as heard in the 1917 Schubert-Wilhelmj *Ave Maria* with its consistently lush vibrant G-string theme, ticklish, pulsating octaves, and perilous singing double-stops, together with similar tonal opulence in the 1918 Mendelssohn-Achron *On Wings of Song*.

The bonanza of the Heifetz salad years also includes numerous charming vignettes: the 1917 Elgar *La Capricieuse* with its glittering staccato and flowing song, the 1919 d'Ambrosio "Serenade," an endearing salon morsel, the 1919 Mozart "Minuet" from *Divertimento No. 17*, angelically graceful and embellished with purl-like staccato scale passages, and the scintillating 1924 Achron *Hebrew Dance*, which bewitchingly reflects the Chassidic essence. All of the foregoing are but a small fraction of the glorious early recordings which were tailored to fit the old ten- and 12-inch 78 platters. Collectively, these performances of the teenage Heifetz have not been equaled by any other violinist in the more than seventy years that have elapsed (at this writing), save by Heifetz himself. It is true that these discs consist, in the main, of music that is not profound and is often downright superficial. It is important to realize, however, that from a purely instrumental point of view, they embody the principal technical and tonal production challenges in the violinistic gamut, as well as a tremendous stylistic perspective.

One can also note occasional juvenile shortcomings in several of these recordings, exemplified by the grotesque speed of the Mozart-Kreisler "Rondo" and the finale of the Mendelssohn Concerto in E-minor, both from 1920, and the overwhelming drive and detachment of the Schubert-Friedberg "Rondo," 1926. A few of the emotion-oriented pieces, including Achron's *Hebrew Melody* and Tchaikovsky's *Serenade Melancholique* derive their feeling more from the finger than the heart.

It is not surprising that Heifetz, like all superstars, had his detractors. Practically from his debut appearance, he was charged by some observers with being cold. Whether this charge was motivated by his stoic visual image, his actual music-making, or both, remains a moot question. Violinists both before and after Heifetz have been prone to exhibit all manner of platform idiosyncrasies: body contortions, heavy breathing, and facial grimaces. The erect figure of Heifetz, his violin held proudly at shoulder level disdaining any vestige of sag, his features chiseled and dispassionate, his torso immobile, demonstrated how the violin and bow could be ideally manipulated without the vitiation of physical folderol. Yet somehow this very flawlessness in consort with his seeming personal aloofness served to militate against the human warmth that is a necessary component in affectionate artist-audience communication. On the audible level, Heifetz's playing does not gush or sentimentalize; rather it epitomizes the cool, yet blazing, adamantine brilliance of a priceless diamond—the utterances of a powerful, implacable personality; the most self-disciplined violinist either in living memory or violinistic annals. Those who sincerely feel that Heifetz was cold, should beware, lest like so many who have felt this way, they may find themselves deeply moved by one or another Heifetz interpretation.

Heifetz was punctiliously faithful to his own preset fingerings, bowings, and musical game plan during each performance. I recall vividly the filming of *They Shall Have Music* in 1938. Sitting on the first stand of the adult orchestra, virtually at Heifetz's elbow, I heard him perform repeatedly, over a period of five days, Saint-Saëns's *Introduction and Rondo Capriccioso*, Wieniawski's Polonaise No. 1, and Tchaikovsky's *Andante Cantabile*, while he played along with the prerecorded sound track at performance level dynamics.

Heifetz during the filming of "They Shall Have Music"

Every note, even in the most dexterous passages, every lyrical phrase and bowing stroke, was impeccably attuned to the amplified sound track performance. And both the Saint-Saëns and Wieniawski pieces were practically indistinguishable from his previous phonograph recording performances in every detail! (He did not commercially record the *Andante Cantabile*.)

Although Heifetz established the revolutionary 20th-century standards of violin instrumentalism as early as 1917, it would be incorrect to infer that his development had reached its zenith at that juncture of his career. During the ensuing 15 years, perhaps to some extent goaded by the accusation of coldness, Heifetz continued to intensify his vibrato, and further sharpen and sensitize his stylistic individuality. If anything, his playing became even more disciplined, though it must be noted that this discipline, as always, was inexorably linked to the exaggerated speed that is a part of his musical character. And the provocative, if sometimes over-utilized Heifetz slide, became synonymous with his interpretations. One of the traits for which he was criticized was his manner of applying slides and position changes to the same alluring effect in all of his playing, whether or not this interfered with the structure or ethos of the composition.

It cannot be claimed that he never had an occasional off-night, but it can be said without fear of contradiction that Heifetz had far fewer off-nights than any other violinist. Because his basic standards were so high, even below par he was closer to perfection than any of his colleagues in live unedited performance. Once

Heifetz had reached his maturity in his mid-30s, his interpretations evinced little change during the following three-and-a-half decades. This can be readily verified by listening to those of the major concertos that he recorded two or three times in that period.

What about Heifetz as an interpreter? In order to assess his interpretive powers, one must recognize and accept the fact that his esthetic concepts were formulated in an era which admired highly personalized artistry. Consequently, this credo, plus his inimitable sound and style, marked him as a Great Personality of the Violin at a very early age. Everything Heifetz played was stamped indelibly with his personal brand. However, certain masterworks, particularly those of Bach, do not profit from over-personalization. It is in such music that Heifetz has been dealt his harshest criticism. It is obvious that he approached his recorded performances of the Bach solo sonatas and partitas with genuine deference to the composer, and negotiated the music with care, consideration, and exactness. Yet for all that, his overpowering violinistic personality, as vested in his sound and stylistic devices (although he seemed to make an honest attempt to curb excesses), endowed the music with a personal aura, particularly in the slower movements, which is an anathema to those who demand that these masterworks be completely free from even the slightest personalization by the performer. It is not difficult to respect this point of view, provided it is not itself exaggerated.

More than a few of these same critics accepted, yes, even extolled the personalized Bach of a Casals, Kreisler, or Landowska, but abhored the glittering musicality of Heifetz when it was applied to Bach. They accused him of serving himself rather than serving the music. If one listens without bias to the *Chaconne* as recorded by Heifetz in 1935, there is much to admire, as there is in various single movements of the complete Bach solo works (1952). The root of the Heifetz-Bach dichotomy lies in the matter of spiritual repose, which happens to be a quality not in keeping with the aggressive, urgent, imperious Heifetz temperament. Bach's solo works, perhaps to a greater degree than any music in the violin repertoire, demand this spiritual repose. Despite his magnificent instrumentalism, Bach's works are not among those for which the violinist is most celebrated. Those who insist that Bach's solo works be uncontaminated by the performer's personality must seek elsewhere.

Other Heifetz recordings of Bach, namely the prettified transcribed excerpts from the "English Suites" with piano (1934 and 1946), the intemperate "Minuets 1 and 2" from Partita No. 3 (1925), and the mechanical Double Concerto in which he unwisely played both parts without the balancing factor of a competent live partner (1946), have certainly not abetted his reputation as a Bach interpreter. Yet Heifetz's transcendental lyricism in the slow movements of Bach's E-major and A-minor concertos are scarcely matched by anyone.

The Bach solo works are one of the keystones of a violinist's repertoire, yet it might be well to remember that Paganini, who many deified as "the greatest violinist that ever lived" for more than a century, never performed them at all. Closer to our own time, Fritz Kreisler never recorded the complete works (though he did record ten Beethoven sonatas), and neither have such stars as David Oistrakh and, at this writing, Isaac Stern and Pinchas Zukerman, though the number of recorded offerings by them is prodigious; nor has this lapse dimmed their lustre as artists.

If one sits, music in hand, listening to Heifetz's recordings of masterworks, it is soon apparent that he plays with exceptional fidelity to the composer's markings even though the auditor may validly complain that some of his tempos are faster than the innate pulse of the music. It was as if Heifetz were born with a built-in time clock that ran at a hyper-rapid pace. This, at times, impairs segments of his performances of the major Beethoven compositions; for example, the opening movement of the concerto with Toscanini and the NBC Symphony (1940), which, because of undue haste, forfeits a measure of the introspection that can elevate this music to Olympian heights. However, the beatific purity of the Larghetto and the sleek ebullience of the finale are apt to make one forget any initial shortcomings.

The concerto-like *Kreutzer* Sonata assumes heroic proportions in Heifetz's hands, specifically as played with the sturdy, resolute collaboration of Brooks Smith (1960), which is better balanced, artistically, than the 1951 recording with Benno Moiseiwitsch; the Sonata No. 7 in C-minor, Op. 30, No. 2, with Emanuel Bay (1950), is remarkably symmetrical and restrained. The complex, inward-looking Sonata No. 10 in G-Major, Op. 96, is treated with consummate delicacy and sensitivity, and the multifaceted Heifetz sound instills the Adagio expressivo with ravishing vibrance. Less salubrious are the *Spring* Sonata, No. 5 in F-Major Op. 24, and the Allegro assai and Tempo di Menuetto of

Sonata No. 8 in G-Major, Op. 30, No. 3, which all too often project an air of impatience and muscularity. The Romances in F and G with Steinberg and the RCA Symphony, 1951, are models of cool, chastely-limned grace.

Heifetz attains the pinnacle of elegance in a highly unorthodox interpretation of Mozart's Concerto in A-Major, No. 5, K. 219, with Barbirolli and the London Philharmonic, 1934, perhaps the choicest among his three recordings of the work. Though the pace is somewhat propulsive, the performance is punctuated with inventive, personalized touches which bend many a rule of classical tradition, but result in a reading of refreshing originality. The Concerto No. 4 in D-minor, K. 218, with Beecham and the Royal Philharmonic, 1947 (a second version was recorded in 1962), is airily invigorating, projecting the so-called "military" opening theme with lissome transparence, the Andante cantabile with guileless euphony, and the finale, though briskly paced, is nonetheless stately. Of two Mozart sonatas, both with the well-tempered collaboration of Brooks Smith (1954), the No. 10, K. 378 is delightfully coy and feathery, whereas the No. 15, K. 454 is not as consistently ingenuous as it might be, and the Andante is overstylized.

The Heifetz muscle is ideal for Brahms, and the concerto (Reiner and the Chicago Symphony, 1955), with the violinist's own explosive cadenza is a spellbinding interpretation, a prodigy of sheer virtuosity. And his live performance of this titanic work in the concert hall is likely not ever to be forgotten by those fortunate enough to have heard it. Here were power, tension, and polish personified. Equally thrilling is the Sonata in D-minor, No. 3, Op. 108, with the superlative partnership of William Kapell (1950), a heroic reading bristling with imaginative nuances. The Sonata in A-Major, No. 2, Op. 100, occasionally unduly mannered, nevertheless communicates the cordial lyricism of the opus with surpassing warmth (Emanuel Bay, 1936).

Heifetz recorded the Mendelssohn Concerto in E-minor with Beecham and the Royal Philharmonic, 1949, and with Munch and the Boston Symphony, 1959; the latter version may be an iota mellower than the former, but there is little difference in the two. The playing is disputably propulsive in the outer movements, but the Andante glows beautifully, and the finale, for all its haste, sparkles with pixie-ish charm.

Other popular concertos of the repertoire are exalted by stunning Heifetz performances. The three

Heifetz in rehearsal with piano collaborator Emanuel Bay

recordings of the Tchaikovsky concerto (1937, 1950, 1957) are much the same, except for the advancement of engineering techniques and the souping-up of two first movement section endings with additional technical fripperies by Auer and Heifetz in the 1950 and 1957 versions. There are many ranking recordings of this opus, but none is graced with the peerless diversified tonal beauty offered by Heifetz. And no one has so captured the icy, yet impassioned ruggedness of the Finnish ethos as has Heifetz in the twice-recorded (1935, 1959) Sibelius concerto. His performances of the 1930s are to a great extent responsible for the enormous popularity the work has attained in the past several decades.

Heard less often but equally convincing is his Lalo *Symphonie Espagnole* (1951, Steinberg, RCA Symphony, without the Intermezzo movement, which was customarily omitted by the Auer pupils); a delivery brimming with suave, sophisticated Latin inflections swathed in a mantle of highly-charged sound. If one compares the Heifetz Scherzando (an exceptionally challenging movement for achieving maximum subtlety) with even the most lustrous of recordings, it will be evident quickly that his contains the ultimate distinction.

A staggering feat is his disc of the Elgar concerto (Sargent, London Symphony, 1949). Some may prefer the Edwardian inclinations of the early Menuhin interpretation, but as purely magnificent violin playing, Heifetz has set the criterion for all of his colleagues.

There is a sizable body of works that belongs to Heifetz in the sense that few observers would dispute his supremacy: the concertos of Glazunov, Vieuxtemps

No. 4 and 5, Conus, Spohr No. 8 (*Gesangscene*), Bruch No. 2 and *Scottish Fantasy*, the sonatas of Saint-Saëns, Richard Strauss, Bloch Nos. 1 and 2 (*Poème Mystique*), the Saint-Saëns *Introduction and Rondo Capriccioso* and *Havanaise*, Sarasate's *Zigeunerweisen*, and the Sinding Suite in A-minor. The Bruch No. 1 and Wieniawski No. 2 Concertos, Ravel's *Tzigane* and the Debussy, Fauré, Op. 13, and Franck sonatas might well be included in this category. The Franck, as recorded in 1937 with Artur Rubinstein, is an historic performance, with each artist conspicuous in his own right and successfully integrated as a duo. This recording is patently superior to the Heifetz-Smith live concert recording of 1972. The most memorable Franck I have heard by any violinist was a live performance (from memory, of course, in the early 1940s) by Heifetz in prime form. Among other bounties he played the second ascending theme of the last movement in slashing fingered octaves with such vibrance and climactic effect it seemed as if his mighty Guarnerius del Gesù might collapse under the onslaught!

Another area in this rarefied province comprises contemporary concertos, either expressly composed for, or popularized by, Heifetz. There is the Prokofiev Concerto No. 2, its blend of saucy badinage and ethereal melody seemingly created for Heifetz; Gruenberg's concerto, a jazz-tinted panorama of Americana, fashioned specifically for the Heifetz style and stupendous technical arsenal (no other violinist has yet attempted its performance); the quasi-biblical rhetoric of Mario Castelnuovo-Tedesco's Concerto No. 2 (*The Prophets*); Erich Wolfgang Korngold's concerto with its sweeping cinematic declamations, the high-spirited rhapsody of William Walton's concerto, and the lusty vigor of Miklos Rosza's concerto. Shorter standouts of contemporary vintage are Tedesco's marvelously idiomatic *Figaro*: Paraphrase on *Largo al Factotum* from Rossini's *Barber of Seville* (however, a Russian recording by Leonid Kogan just about matches the great Jascha), and *The Lark*, a bouncing rondo, along with Franz Waxman's fiery *Carmen Fantasy*.

Heifetz easily led the violinistic procession in the performance of virtuoso jazz-oriented delicacies by virtue of his rhythmic exactitude, sound, and infallible ear for intricate syncopation. And in French music, though he did not instill it with the Gallic perfumery of such French artists as Thibaud, Francescatti, Merckel, and company, Heifetz's cool incandescence and glistening sophistication conjured up an aromatic bouquet

Heifetz playing for the troops during World War II

of sound inimitably his own, as in Debussy's *La plus que lent* and *Beau Soir*. His most controversial interpretation in the Gallic repertory is probably that of Chausson's *Poème* with Solomon and the RCA Symphony, 1952. Despite occasional gleaming phrases that might be accepted as poetic by Heifetz partisans, the drive and constant aggressiveness of his playing can be onerous to those who conceive this work as exuding reverie.

The history of violin art is rife with examples of great violinists who avoided pieces they deemed unsuited to their temperament or technical equipment. Paganini, who scarcely played anything other than his own compositions, was the prototype for that syndrome. Heifetz, too, exerted his prerogative in this regard. Apparently such concertos as Bartók Nos. 1 and 2, Prokofiev No. 1, Stravinsky, Schoenberg, Berg, Hindemith (1939), and *Kammermusik* No. 4, did not appeal to him. But can anyone seriously doubt that Heifetz could not have performed them masterfully if he so desired? It is easy to perceive how the abrasiveness or limited melodic content of some of these works would not be tempting to the Heifetz musical palate.

In view of his peerless technical equipment, it might seem odd that Heifetz did not exploit the bulk of Paganini's music. While he was never loath to emphasize his technical superiority, he didn't make a fetish of circus gymnastics as have other super-technicians. He didn't have to, since his technique-tone supremacy extended infinitely beyond the confines of simplistic one-dimensional Paganiniana. For all that, no one has yet equaled his *Moto Perpetuo*, the suave stylings

Heifetz, Artur Rubinstein, and Gregor Piatigorsky, a legendary trio, 1949

of Caprices No. 13 and 20, or the spine-tingling bravura of the Auer violin-with-piano setting of Caprice No. 24. In his early career Heifetz performed the single-movement Paganini-Wilhelmj transcription of Concerto No. 1, the Kreisler versions of Paganini's *I Palpiti, Non Piu Mesta*, and *Le Streghe*, and Ernst's concerto and *Othello Fantasie*. On the set of *They Shall Have Music* in 1938, I heard him quietly practicing the *I Palpiti* double-harmonics during a lull in the filming.

Though Heifetz's career overlapped into the current era in which all-sonata programs have come to replace the former combination of concerto-with-piano, sonata, showpiece-vignette recitals, the roster of the latter that he performed (even in his final concerts) is tremendous in size and scope. In showpieces, vignettes, and transcriptions he transformed the most innocuous musical trivia into minor miracles of ear titillation. Because of his scarcely-disputed supremacy in this metier, he was criticized by a number of commentators who regarded the performance of such purely violinistic entertainment as a musical felony. However, the all-embracing violin mastery and artistry required to play these admittedly slender and often frivolous pieces on a truly exalted level, is no longer an attribute of a host of excellent contemporary violinist-musicians, who can perform sonata masterworks with creditable, even admirable competence. Since audiences have always loved these sparkling brevities, and still do, it would be well for all violin observers, irrespective of musical attitudes, to realize the extraordinary instrumental authority and stylistic acumen that are involved in top-bracket performances of such pieces.

Through the years Heifetz became progressively more involved in chamber music collaborations, and at his retirement, the number of chamber work recordings in which he participated well exceeded, to date, the output of any celebrated solo violinist since the dawn of recorded musical performance. In this role he encountered the same problems of all the *Great Personalities* whose singular sound and style set them apart from lesser mortals.

When assessing his art in this medium, it is necessary to separate the violin-piano sonatas and other instrumental duos from forms embracing three or more players. In two-artist vehicles it is possible for two striking musical personalities to exercise their individual identities (within reasonable limits) to gain advantage. Although such Heifetz pianists as Emanuel Bay and Brooks Smith are masters of their craft (indeed, I have heard Smith wax exceedingly feisty), intrinsically, their musical relationship with him as hired collaborators is different from those duos in which Heifetz is paired with Artur Rubinstein, William Kapell, William Primrose, or Emanuel Feuermann. As cited previously, the Heifetz sonata discs with Rubinstein and Kapell are of historic stature.

Numerous testaments exist as to the difficulties of working with Heifetz, the lordly perfectionist. Rubinstein, for one, publicly excoriated his onetime musical associate as being personally incompatible (to put it politely). Primrose, too, indicated problems in this regard, though in more gentlemanly fashion. Piatigorsky apparently worked out his own method of coping with the Heifetz phenomenon. In the best of their collaborations, among them the rhapsodic Kodaly Duo for Violin and Cello, Op. 7, and Martinu's Duo for Violin and Cello with its madcap Rondo finale, he sturdily asserts his own massive personality, yet scrupulously avoids any instrumental slugging matches. His attitude seems to be one of gentle, affectionate, permissive forbearance toward an esteemed, precocious, willful brother.

Feuermann, too, stood his own ground with Heifetz, though in the 1939 record of the Brahms Concerto for Violin and Cello with Ormandy and the Philadelphia Orchestra, the general aggressiveness and vibrance of Heifetz, particularly in the opening G-string theme of the violin, invariably precipitates that instrument into the forefront. This is an outstanding performance by any standards. Nevertheless, the 1960 recording with Piatigorsky is perhaps superior, in that Heifetz has somewhat mellowed; he listens to his partner more intently, the ensemble is integrated meticulously, and the engineering is improved. In addition, the basic timbre of the Piatigorsky tone is somewhat more in affinity with that of Heifetz than is the tone of Feuermann.

Primrose is an especially convincing collaborator of Heifetz, and their ensemble recordings are usually strong in instrumental balance. His tone is exceptionally sumptuous in Arthur Benjamin's *Romantic Fantasy* for Violin, Viola and Orchestra (Solomon conducting the RCA Symphony, 1956), a fetching contemporary opus of resplendent instrumental interplay and lush textures aptly titled. The balance of the orchestra with the solo instruments is sometimes less than ideal, but the Heifetz-Primrose matchup is dashing and ornate in sound.

Another fine performance is of Mozart's *Sinfonia Concertante*, also with Solomon and the RCA Symphony, 1956. The interpretation is elfin, the playing, ineffably silken, vitiated only by an occasional lash into a climactic note. The Adagio exudes seraphic transparency rather than the bittersweet sentiment implied in the music; but for all that, it is effervescent music-making.

A superlative Heifetz performance is the 1941 disc of Chausson's Concerto for Violin, Piano and Quartet in D (Op. 21), with Jesus Maria Sanroma and the Musical Art Quartet. The Heifetz style, with its ever-insinuating nuances, is made to order for this work. There is, however, a certain instrumental imbalance as Sanroma, a sensitive, conscientious stylist, is too small-scaled an artist to be matched one-on-one with Heifetz, and tends to become part of the background with the quartet.

Four of his choice chamber music collaborations were recorded in 1941, three with Rubinstein and one with Feuermann. The Heifetz mannerisms are in low profile in an uncommonly relaxed (for him) version of Beethoven's Trio in B-flat, Op. 97 (*Archduke*), a robust Brahms Trio in B, Op. 8, and a glistening, seductively dulcet reading of Schubert's grateful Trio in B-flat, Op. 99, D.898. The piano and cello are beautifully balanced with the violin, both in performance and engineering. The fourth of this vintage is a trenchant performance of Dohnanyi's Serenade in C, Op. 10, with Primrose and Feuermann, in which Primrose, his tone fervidly vibrant and sonorous, amply demonstrates once again that he was the premier violist of his time.

A 1950 recording of Tchaikovsky's Trio in A-minor, Op. 50, with Rubinstein and Piatigorsky, has the violin and piano vying heroically for primacy—neither paladin inclined to give an inch, with the cello decidedly under-miked. Yet it contains some epic playing from all three in the grand Slavic manner.

Even in Heifetz's moments of most affable concurrence with his partners, the listener is hard put to forget throughout every bar and phrase that he is being wooed by a peerless virtuoso. It is not only the incur-

l to r Max Rosen, Heifetz, Auer, and Seidel

siveness of his attack, the singularity of his sound, and his liberal usage of personalized slides and position changes, but the fact that he indiscriminately uses these Heifetz-y devices in repetitive and interchanging phrases while his partners do not. In various types of music—and according to the degree of such misapplication—the overall group performance is impaired. Those listeners who are inclined to resent these intrusions will find them particularly overt in the recordings of Boccherini's Sonata in D for Violin and Cello (with Piatigorsky, 1964), Beethoven's Serenade, Op. 8, Trio in D (with Primrose and Piatigorsky, 1960), and Mozart's Quintette in G-minor, K. 516, (with Primrose, Piatigorsky, Baker, and Majewski, 1961). All are works of comparative transparency. Brahms's Piano Quartette in C-minor, though thicker in instrumental texture, also contains more than the norm of these indispositions albeit the piano performance of Jacob Lateiner, bountiful in color and shadings, deserves special mention (Piatigorsky, Lateiner, Schonbach, 1965).

Three more Heifetz disc ensemble performances merit singling out: the scintillating Mendelssohn Octette in E-flat Major, in which his personal virtuosity, plus the vigorous, strongly etched collaboration of his partners, add up to a performance of surpassing brilliance (with Piatigorsky, Primrose, Baker, Belnick, Stepansky, Majewski, Rejto, 1961); Dvořák Piano Quintette in A (Piatigorsky, Lateiner, Baker, De Pasquale, 1964), a reading of thrilling lyricism; and Mendelssohn's Trio No. 2 in C-minor, Op. 66, (with Piatigorsky, Pennario, 1963), a buoyantly felicitous romp. These memorable recordings may well set the standard for these works for a long time to come.

A number of additional ensemble performances featuring Heifetz, Piatigorsky, and "Guests" reflect similar positive and negative features to one degree or other. Thanks to recordings, future generations will have the privilege of hearing these interpretations and placing them under microscopic examination. While they may note that Heifetz, the supreme virtuoso, was not the ultimate team player, time and time again he created stunning effects that all the finest team players in existence, if rolled up in one, could never achieve. Criticism aside, had these records never been made, the world of chamber music would be considerably the poorer.

Heifetz scored extraordinary achievements in yet another area—as a transcriber of short encore pieces from other musical mediums. An able pianist, Heifetz has been the logical successor to Kreisler in this province and is said to have made in excess of 150 violin-piano settings, of which he recorded 62. His transcriptions are imaginatively conceived, bold in instrumental contrivance, and harmonically ingenious. Unfortunately, changing fashions in the make-up of violin recitals have reduced drastically the potential of his success in this field since confection pieces are seldom programmed today.

The Heifetz transcriptions came into prominence shortly before this new trend became widespread—a trend which has been an important factor in public interest in bonafide violin recitals plummeting to a low ebb. Recently, Perlman and a few of the younger artists have programmed some of the old showpieces and transcriptions. It is to be hoped that the best of the Heifetz arrangements will eventually receive their share of play.

Most of his transcriptions cannot be readily bandied about by students and non-professionals as can, for example, Kreisler's *Old Refrain*. They are too violinistically demanding, and collectively are not calculated to equal those of Kreisler in mass saleability.

Historically, violin transcriptions have reflected strongly the violinistic idiosyncrasies of their creators. In order to creditably perform Heifetz transcriptions, a violinist must have some affinity with the Heifetz violinistic vocabulary: controlled intensity of tone, a knack for negotiating suave and vibrant finger slides and position changes, the ability to sing in double-stop combinations of every type, and a commanding facility. The artfulness and variety of the Heifetz transcription double-stops and harmonic embellishments rival, and, in some instances, even transcend those of Kreisler, and are markedly contemporary in concept—an irrefutable testament to the age in which Heifetz lived and performed.

Among the most popular are his settings of Godowsky's *Alt Wien*, a Viennese strudel in which Heifetz concocts his own brand of *gemueltlichkeit*, and the Dinicu *Hora Staccato*, that in its days of prime popularity, raised the staccato consciousness of violinists everywhere to an acute pitch. Both have been favorites of mass audiences. Also highly favored are the six transcriptions of songs from Gershwin's *Porgy and Bess*, topped by the luscious *Bess, You Is My Woman Now* and the sultry, whimsical *It Ain't Necessarily So*, both striking Heifetz recordings. The Gershwin "Three Preludes" settings are also widely played, and many of these jazzy transcriptions have been featured in recordings of Soviet players (Kogan, Bezrodny, Goldstein, Gutnikov, and others), demonstrating the geographical extent of the Heifetz influence.

Two Prokofiev transcription recordings, *Masques* (from *Romeo and Juliet*) and March in F-minor, are a smidgeon below the Heifetz standard. But the traditional spiritual *Deep River*, with its searing G-string and double-stop vibrance, constitutes legendary violin playing, and Albeniz's *Sevillianas* is saucy and sinuous. The Ponce *Estrellita* may not exactly smile when it twinkles, but the glowing performance reflects an urbane, sophisticated charm. And the Dvořák *Humoresque* again points up the brash Heifetz audacity, as among other ornamental devices, he chooses to incorporate a wide open double-stop fifth in a delicate melodic phrase ending.

If a general revival of violin recital encore type numbers should come to pass, the Heifetz transcriptions offer a rich potential to enterprising violinists, and in historical perspective, they merit an esteemed niche in their metier.

As far back as the early 1940s, if not before, Heifetz began to teach. He later expanded his teaching activities at the University of California at Los Angeles and then at the University of Southern California, where he taught on a regular basis, sometimes to as few as two students twice a week. One might think that upon the announcement of his availability as a teacher, the finest violin talents in the world would immediately beat a path to his doorstep, but this never materialized to any significant degree. Over the years many students came and went, complaining about either musical or personal incompatibility. The most successful of his pupils, Erick Friedman, Eugene Fodor, and Pierre Amoyal, held him in reverence as a violinist, but had little, if any personal relationship with him. In discussing Heifetz as a teacher with a representative number of his pupils, privately, of course, it is their consensus that much could have been learned from him in close-hand observation as he demonstrated passages at lessons. His explanatory person-to-person pedagogy, they reluctantly admitted, engendered little of importance. It was indeed a sad note to see paid advertisements by the university soliciting applicants for the classes of this 81-year-old paragon of the violin, when gifted pupils should, at least ostensibly, have been breaking down the door for acceptance. Instead, these pupils gravitated to others.

The paradoxical element in this situation is the fact that Heifetz has been the greatest teaching influence of the era, since violinists and pedagogues the world over have profited immensely from listening to, and watching him, all the while striving to analyze the working of his violinistic equipment. He has shown us the ultimate achievement in the handling of the instrument, a feat which far supersedes any incapacity he may have had for gainful personal communication in the teaching studio.

Heifetz was often characterized as grim, unapproachable, caustic, and irascible, especially in his later years. Yet some, admittedly a minority, found him possessed of a variety of personal virtues. In his younger days he is reported to have had an active sense of humor. One of his outlets for amusement was that of imitating an excruciatingly bad violinist. According to his colleague Primrose, a recording exists (undoubedly now a collector's item), played by Heifetz and issued by Medina Records (pressed by RCA). The jacket has a photo of an innocuous-looking violinist labeled "Joseph Hague" (initials J.H.), with "Floyd E. Sharp" at the piano. The contents consist of side-splitting parodies of Saint-Saëns's *Introduction and Rondo Capriccioso*, Paganini's Caprice No. 13, Sarasate's *Habanera*, Schubert's Sonata No. 1 (actually, the Sonatina), and drollest of all, the complete *Canary*, attributed to Poliakin (of which a portion was used as *The Hot Canary*, a pop violin favorite some years back). The playing embodies every cliché of miserable violin playing conceivable—the total antithesis of Heifetz's art. Many professionals, including this writer, believe the disc to be a Heifetz prank. He also has a side-splitting video of the first movement of Vieuxtemps's Concerto No. 4, in which he deliberately plays like the archetype "bad" student.

Unlike Stern and Menuhin who are astute, aggressive, and experienced in the field of public relations, Heifetz was not. After his ill-starred interview in Life Magazine, which was, in the main, a malicious collection of his alleged misdeeds in his relationships with his family and sundry other individuals, he withdrew gradually from public life. Instead of receiving continual accolades from a public all too willing to confer them, he seemed to prefer semi-isolation.

Heifetz's playing remained spectacular even into his early 70s, though it would be unrealistic to claim that it equalled the super-brilliance of his period from 35 to 50. His fanatical devotion to the instrument and his mania for perfection preserved his enormous capabilities longer than any violinist of the past, with the exception of Milstein, who was able to surpass this violinistic longevity without drastic deterioration of performance.

In this era of the de-personalization of violin playing, the Heifetz influence is receding. Indeed, some young violinists hold his playing to be out of style, though not one of these can even remotely compare with a Heifetz. Others, like Perlman, have the good sense to realize they have much to learn from him.

No violinist who ever lived has been "all things to all men" in every type of music—not Paganini, Joachim, Sarasate, Ysaÿe, Kreisler, Elman, Oistrakh, Szigeti, Francescatti, Szeryng, Menuhin, Stern, Grumiaux, or any other. No one ever expected it of them. Only Heifetz has been criticized for not being the embodiment of the "impossible dream." The very demands made upon him by certain critics and observers are in effect a sort of reverse tribute to the man—an admission of his special stature as a violinist. People came to expect perfection from Heifetz, and where the foibles of other violinists are often overlooked or excused, his tended to be emphasized—another reverse tribute. Expecting Heifetz never to have misused his prodigious gifts is like asking the world's richest man never to exploit the power vested in his wealth; it is too much to ask of any human being.

Does Heifetz serve the music or does the music serve him? The totality of his recordings indicates time and time again that the answer to the question is—both. His violinistic and musical style reflects the spirit of his time and place as vividly as any artist who ever lived, in any medium. He dared to seek out new violinistic effects, and if they were not successful in every instance, they were eminently provocative and unique unto themselves. His commanding position in the pantheon of violin art is assured. The violinist died December 12, 1987, in Los Angeles.

Meanwhile, let us correct those who sometimes refer to Heifetz as "The Paganini of the 20th Century." More properly, he is "The Heifetz of the 20th Century," and controversies notwithstanding, he is a nonpareil.

Zino Francescatti, *a truly noble artist, a scintillating technician, and an elite representative of piquant, cultivated music-making*

Zino Francescatti

During the late 1930s the Great Depression was still raging. Kreisler, Heifetz, the young Menuhin, Szigeti, and Milstein represented the topmost echelon of violinists in box office draw, followed by Elman, Huberman, Spalding, the young Ricci, and Morini. Enesco had become deeply involved in composition and teaching, and Thibaud, though still concertizing, was no longer in significant contention. The young Stern had already made his youthful debut, but was not yet ensconced among the leading mature artists or those ex-prodigies who had built mass followings in their childhood. Severe economic retrenchment represented an almost insurmountable barrier to new artists seeking to scale the heights, and in this period many outstanding talents were forced to enter the symphonic or commercial fields in order to earn a livelihood.

Many a European violinistic luminary had made an American debut during the Depression years, hoping for success. Despite everything, the United States was still the mecca for musical artists in terms of financial reward. But a good many of those who won critical acclaim here were forced to return eventually to their places of origin; some remained as political refugees. Gifted Americans, too, sought gold and glory with scant results. Among the aspirants were new young artists like Ossy Renardy (1920-1953), first to record all 24 Paganini caprices (with piano accompaniment), and Guila Bustabo (b. 1919), an intense, propulsive player with extraordinary facility and the first woman to record the Paganini-Wilhelmj Concerto No. 1, with the Sauret cadenza. Their bids for recognition were initially successful, but neither was destined to enter the "charmed circle." Only a violinist of the very highest qualifications—and one whose musical personality and character were in some measure different from those of the reigning stars—could hope to launch a top-level concertizing career.

Such an artist was René Charles (Zino) Francescatti. At 37 he was already a fully seasoned player when he made his American debut in November, 1939, playing the Paganini Concerto No. 1 (complete version) with the New York Philharmonic. His rise to stardom had been long and arduous, but he was recognized eventually not only as the heir to Thibaud, once the "greatest French violinist," but also as one of the world's leading violinists.

Francescatti's date of birth has often been given as 1905 or 1903, but he himself stated that he was born on August 9, 1902, in Marseilles. As the name suggests, his father Fortunato Francescatti, originally from Verona, was of Italian lineage; his French mother, Ernesta Feraud, was from Marseilles. Both were trained violinists and teachers. Before their marriage she had been his pupil. They were wed when he was 46 and she was 17. Zino had one younger brother, Raymond, who did not become a violinist. In Milan, his father had been a pupil of two noted virtuosos, Antonio Bazzini, composer of *Ronde des lutins* and other bravura dazzlers, and Camillo Sivori, the only important pupil of the legendary Paganini. From Sivori he learned Paganini's unique methods of fingering.

At age five Zino was given a tiny violin, more a toy than a legitimate instrument, and in the first lesson he clearly negotiated a G-major scale. He is the only sovereign 20th-century soloist to have been taught exclusively by his parents. His father gave him lessons "from time to time" (as Francescatti stated), and his mother supervised his daily practice. With the three of them and their pupils, there was violin playing in progress in all parts of their large home, day and night.

Francescatti, his wife Yolande, and his mother Mrs. Ernesta Francescatti, in Monterey, Massachusetts

The elder Francescatti, concertmaster of the Marseilles Symphony, was a stern, sometimes harsh taskmaster, who once kept his son working on a single scale for over an hour until it was absolutely perfect. The boy's mother, a violin soloist in her own right, was his champion and, at times, his protector. In her 80s she was still playing well. She died at age 98.

Zino was a willing pupil, and as a child practiced one hour before and one hour after school. In his early years he worked diligently at the various exercises of Sevčík and the études of Kreutzer and Gaviniès. He stated that he relished every type of technical challenge: double-stops, trills, and harmonics; that he had a natural vibrato ("My vibrato developed by itself, naturally") and staccato, and encountered no particular difficulty in developing facility in either hand. From his tenth to his 15th year he was enrolled in a private school to enable him to practice at least four hours daily. During this period his working day often approximated 16 hours; his practice began at 6:30 a.m. Like

Fortunato Francescatti, Zino's father

most boys there was a time when he preferred playing ball to practicing, but this soon passed. At ten he performed the Beethoven concerto. Ysaÿe, Thibaud, and Kreisler became his idols.

At 15 he made his formal debut on a Marseilles *Concerts Classiques* program with the organist Marcel Dupré; the recital included the Wieniawski Concerto in D-minor and Bach's *Chaconne*. Francescatti was never touted as a child prodigy and never participated in a competition. His rise to renown progressed slowly, with illness disturbing the early part of his career.

Since Francescatti's father did not want him to play publicly, he continued to work intensely until he was 20, at which time he went to Paris to make his way in the world. There he played the first movement of the Paganini concerto. Later he learned the entire concerto, and it became one of his musical hallmarks, though he was never limited to the role of a violinistic gymnast. At 22 he was granted an audition with Thibaud, who greatly encouraged the young man. Shortly afterward he was engaged to accompany Maurice Ravel and the singer Maggie Teyte on a concert tour of England. As late as 1928 he worked for a living in the Straram Orchestra, at that time a leading orchestra in Paris. He was also presented as a duo soloist with that ensemble in Mozart's *Symphonie Concertante*. Over the years he doggedly climbed the ladder of success in Europe, and in 1938 made a triumphant Western Hemisphere debut in Buenos Aires, playing the Paganini Concerto No. 1 under José Iturbi. After each of several performances at the Teatro Colon in Buenos Aires, the police had to escort him from the audience to protect him from the congratulatory crowds. Once in Detroit, after a performance of Paganini's *I Palpiti*, the audience cheered for 17 minutes.

Francescatti gave first performances in Paris of Szymanowski's Concerto No. 2, Respighi's *Concerto Gregoriano*, and Witowski's *Dances*; in Philadelphia, of Milhaud's *Suite*; in New York, the Casadesus sonata. His repertoire of contemporary works included major compositions by Prokofiev, Walton, Ben-Haim, Hindemith, Stravinsky, and Leonard Bernstein.

Francescatti married another violinist, Yolande Potel de la Briere of Paris, whom he met when he was concertmaster and she was a member of the Gaston Poulet Orchestra. They had one child who did not survive.

In 1975 after a brilliant career, he decided to retire at age 73. He stated: "I had enough of this life of travel. It was becoming tiring, and I wanted to enjoy the last part of my life quietly, doing what I enjoy. I finished my concert career in fine form, and no one can say that I retired because I was playing poorly."

Zino Francescatti had never sought the limelight by means of extra-musical exploits or publicity feats. He was a quiet, modest person whose deportment and social graces were as polished and refined as his playing. Though universally celebrated as a French violinist, he was a direct violinistic descendant of Paganini through his father and Sivori. "Sivori initiated my father into the secrets of the violin, and father later imparted to me the knowledge gained from the virtuoso," said the violinist. His playing possesses the purity of line and statement attributed to the pre-Paganini Italian school and not an iota of Paganini's sensationalist excesses. But it also reflects an aura which is ineffably French. It has been said that if Paris is "The City of Light," the art of Francescatti is its embodiment—radiant, lustrous, perfumed, graceful, utterly felicitous and, at times, cloyingly sweet. His sound is striking in its brightness and clarity. It is 20th-century playing, smartly disciplined, free of interpretive exaggerations.

Whereas Thibaud was essentially a stylist with perhaps the most limited repertoire among international-level violinists, Francescatti expanded tremendously the so-called French violinistic horizons as represented by his predecessor, not only in repertorial scope, but also in technical achievement. Former French violinists such as Emile Sauret (1852-1919) and Henri Marteau (1874-1934) were credited with having more sheer fingerboard facility than Thibaud, but he surpassed them by far in tonal beauty, sophistication of style, and overall artistry. In turn, Francescatti, though listed as only a year younger than Heifetz (whose birth date of 1901 is generally accepted), came to maturity after the awesome new Heifetz standards of instrumental command had already been established. Although he had been greatly impressed and, to a sizeable degree, influenced, by Ysaÿe, Kreisler, and Thibaud, he belongs to a later generation of artists.

In the following article from *LISTEN* magazine, April, 1945, Francescatti described his musical priorities and approach, and touched upon the differences between himself and the players preceding him.

It is self-evident that quite different demands are made today upon the violin virtuoso. When I stand on the concert stage in front of a large audience I am fully aware that I have to give not only my best all through the evening, but that I have to transmit the spirit of the composition as faithfully to the public as I possibly can, without any distortion or interpretative conditions beyond the scope of the work.

The great Belgian master of the violin, Eugene Ysaÿe, once gave a concert in Bordeaux. He was not feeling too secure as a result of excessive drinking on the previous night. The audience jeered at first, but later in the evening the virtuoso collected his wits and delivered one of his inimitable performances that carried the public to the limits of frenzy and enthusiasm. In one evening he brought forth the gamut of emotions from jeers to delirious applause. But today an artist must be at the top of his form from the first note to the last; the level can never fluctuate. ... The honest and sincere artist of today is a professional man who loves his profession but does not endow it with any mysterious qualities in order to attract people eager for out-of-the-way sensations. How ludicrous it would be today to influence an audience by telling it that the virtuoso is in league with the devil or is a secret Casanova. And while it may have been more glamorous to be touched by people on the street who wanted to see whether one is made of flesh and blood (as happened to Paganini in London), it is certainly more satisfying to see the thousands of grateful people to whom the modern artist has opened the true world of genuine music.

One cannot assert that Francescatti's musical aura was as striking or explicit as that of Ysaÿe, Kreisler, Elman, Heifetz, or the young Menuhin. Nonetheless there was a special character, a vitality, and a *savoir faire* to his playing that set him apart from a host of gifted virtuosos who possessed vibrant sound and creditable musicianship. In hearing Francescatti at his best, the first adjective that may come to mind is—*enchanté*. Indeed, one can become so mesmerized by the total effusiveness of his musicality and the charm of his tone that such matters as spiritual sublimity and musical introspection are temporarily banished from the mind. He is never less than the impeccable gentleman of the violin.

As a bravura technician Francescatti belongs in the first rank. In addition to his splendid performances of the first Paganini Concerto No. 1 in D-major, he played and recorded Paganini's *God Save the King, The Carnival of Venice Variations, I Palpiti* (with his own original, brilliant finale) and eight of the Paganini caprices. And what is more important—he never sacrificed beauty of sound or sincerity of purpose in the interest of technical exhibitionism. He constantly sought out and stressed the Italianate lyricism and musical blandishments of these works, as opposed to single-mindedly executing fingerboard gymnastics. His coordination between right and left hands was of the highest order. His immaculately manicured fingers were of no more than average length, and the span of his hands and breadth of his fingertips were not at all unusual in comparison with, for example, the massive hands of Perlman. But his fingerboard facility was superbly flexible.

The Francescatti tone, though ever ear-titillating, was quite soft-grained and tended to be rather single-dimensional; a quality which placed certain limitations on his art, lending a veneer of "sameness," a lack of diversity to his sound. The root cause of this lay in his vibrato, which was produced by the wrist and arm and had a widish oscillation. True, he produced degrees of variance in its speed, but not to any great extent. Its speed approached rapidity but not the ultimate in intensity; it reflected no vestige whatsoever of the stiff, tense fingertip vibrato once widely associated with French-trained violinists. His interpretations were piquant, amiable, infectious, sleek, and elegant, rather than probing or emotionally profound. Thus his most convincing performances were of works that are bright, buoyant, and brilliant. Somber or cerebral music was not really his forte, though he played it with commanding instrumental authority and provocative sound.

The Francescatti bow arm was honed in the general manner of the so-called French-Belgian school (though I prefer to consider the Belgian school as related to, but separate from, the French). His crisp spiccatos were neatly controlled, his flying staccatos scintillated, and his on-the-string staccato was sturdy, though he did not employ the extremely rapid stiff-arm variety. And his sustained, cantilena bowings, seamless in delivery, were mellow in texture.

In the area of expressive finger slides and position changes, Francescatti stood somewhere between artists such as Kreisler and Heifetz who were lavish in their use, and current violinists who employ them little or not at all (although Perlman employs them liberally). Strong in the influence of Kreisler, Francescatti's slides occasionally recalled those of his older colleague, but were in no way imitative; most were distinctly his own, and he used them sparingly and with patrician discrimination. Generally he favored the use of "bridging" fingers in expressive position changes rather than direct

"fleshy" slides to a climactic lyric note. And the selection of this expressive device was tastefully governed by the style of music he was performing. His music-making sang constantly, and tenderness, an element in serious decline in current playing, was one of his most endearing qualities. Some observers feel that this tenderness had a feminine tinge, in the positive sense, but this should by no means imply that there was either physical weakness or effeminate frailty in Francescatti's playing. His tone could become almost hypnotic in its uniformity and, at times, the "perfume" could become too intoxicating. However, it was a decidedly masculine perfume, calculated to seduce the listener.

Francescatti's musical temperament was ever ardent and lightly sensuous, but not intensely voluptuous. Nor were dramatic utterance and tension hallmarks of his art. Yet his playing possessed a constant glow even when his vibrato was minimal or not being used; he was one of the few whose music-making "smiled."

According to his own statement, he never practiced an "enormous" amount during the mature years of his career, nor did he ever use a tape recorder when practicing. Overpractice, he felt, could be harmful and detracted from the freshness and spontaneity of playing, though he was definitely opposed to the theory of little or no practice as ascribed to Kreisler. He did suffer from pre-concert nervousness, but once onstage kept matters under firm control. Before a concert he warmed up with scales and Sevčik exercises rather than passages from the works he was to perform. He ate little before a concert, perhaps only buttered bread, and drank coffee, which he also drank at intermission.

Francescatti vigorously recommended stronger finger pressure on the strings, especially in soft passages: "That is what gives it a beautiful tone." He strove continuously to improve his fingerings. "After each public performance you analyze those passages that have been awkward, and proceed to make changes." Stressing the need for different bowings when concertos are played with orchestra as opposed to concerto performances with piano, he stated: "Twice as much power is required when one is being accompanied by an orchestra. Orchestral sound resounds far more than that of the piano. In many passages I use two bow strokes with orchestra as opposed to one with piano."

He derived much pleasure from playing chamber music privately. Publicly he performed trios with pianist Cutner Solomon and cellist Pierre Fournier at the Edinburgh Festival, and his longtime partnership with pianist Robert Casadesus produced some of the more felicitous live and recorded sonata playing of their era.

The recordings of Francescatti number about 110 compositions, large and small, including the multiple recordings, comparable to the 120 of Milstein. From the mid-1940s to the mid-1950s many of his finest major-work recordings were made in mono and early stereo. His sound was especially well-suited for the microphone, and it can be said that his recorded art was at least equal to that of his live performance, if not actually superior in sonority and projection. In *The Way They Play*, Volume 1, p. 35, by Samuel and Sada Applebaum, Francescatti states:

> The nuance problems are solved in a different manner when making recordings than when playing in public. The dynamic markings must be handled in a different way. When making a crescendo from piano to forte, the range must not be so great, or rather let me put it this way, play forte most of the time. If you wish to get softer, become only marginally softer. If you wish to make a crescendo, get only slightly louder, since there must not be a wide range of dynamic expression. . . In a concert hall, of course, there are no such limitations. When making recordings, it is very easy to overdo. While playing in the manner I prescribe for recordings, it may sound dull to the human ear,a but the microphone picks up the subtle, tiny nuances.

One of the most impressive and widely known of his recordings is that of the Paganini Concerto No. 1 in D-major (with Eugene Ormandy and the Philadelphia Orchestra). At the time, the Francescatti version represented the antithesis of the heaven-storming drama and operatic thrust of the 1934 recording by Menuhin at 18 which was the only recording of the entire version for quite a few years. Francescatti's interpretation, less sensuous, but nonetheless charged with bravado, is exquisitely lyric and technically impeccable. It compares to the Menuhin performance as does a superlative lyric soprano to an equally great dramatic soprano. His flying-staccatos sparkle. A section of the last movement is omitted, perhaps in the interest of record space limitations prevalent at that time. Through the years this recording still ranks among the finest in style and individuality. (Francescatti stated that he used both his own cadenza and that of Carl Flesch in his performances; the one used in the recording is that of Flesch.)

Another of his most renowned recordings is the Saint-Saëns Concerto No. 3 in B-minor (Mitropoulos, New York Philharmonic), an ideally polished interpretation that embodies the Gallic spirit of the music with unsurpassed lustre. His expressive portamentos are never overdone. The opening movement is taken at a propulsive rate, but not so fast as to distort the lyric flow. The *Andantino*, though lovely, would perhaps have benefitted from a bit more repose; the finale is played *Allegro non troppo* as indicated, and avoids undue haste. In subtlety, color and nuance, it remains a model for works of its kind.

Lalo's *Symphony Espagnole*, without the *Intermezzo* (Mitropoulos, New York Philharmonic), is as dashing as D'Artagnan and suavely etched, perhaps the most desirable of Francescatti's three recordings of the work. The *Scherzando* is enriched by many intelligently placed expressive slides; the languorous triplet theme midway through the finale represents some of his most sensuous playing. The charm of this performance recalls Thibaud; somewhat less individualized, but far more disciplined musically, and digitally perfect.

In this category belongs the Vieuxtemps Concerto No. 4 (Ormandy, Philadelphia Orchestra), a recording that, together with those of Perlman and Menuhin, is just a notch below the peerless Heifetz recording; technically cleaner than that of Menuhin, if a bit less forceful and spontaneous. Overall it is superlative bravura playing.

Bruch's Concerto No. 1 in G-minor (Schippers, New York Philharmonic) is warm and affectionate rather than dramatic, and does not project the ultimate tension, but in the Mendelssohn Concerto Op. 64, Francescatti's penchant for lightly amorous, vivacious utterance is at its zenith. Mozart's Concerto No. 5 in A-major and No. 2 in D-major (de Stoutz, Zurich Chamber Orchestra), Tartini's Concerto in D-minor (deftly orchestrated and conducted by Francescatti, Zurich Chamber Orchestra), and the Bach Concerto in E-major (Szell, Columbia Symphony), mirror the multiple virtues of the Mendelssohn. The Mozart No. 3 in G-major and No. 4 in D-major (Walter, Columbia Symphony) are pure and straightforward performances, although in the latter there are glimmers of airy sound in the *Andante*. Chausson's Concerto for Piano, Violin and String Quartet, Op. 21 (with Casadesus, Guilet Quartet), commemorating the 1955 centenary of the composer's birth, is ineffably polished in the traditional French manner; the *Sicilienne* in particular is exquisitely wrought.

Francescatti (far right) with Mr. and Mrs. Robert Casadesus and Mr. and Mrs. Albert Spalding

Among more contemporary major works, his Walton concerto recording (Ormandy, Philadelphia Orchestra) is eloquently lyric, as is his superbly expressive rendition of Prokofiev's Concerto No. 2 in G-minor (Mitropoulos, New York Philharmonic), which is climaxed by a finale of exciting articulation and drive. The recording of Leonard Bernstein's Serenade for Violin, String Orchestra, Harp and Percussion (Bernstein, New York Philharmonic), compares favorably with Stern's.

Francescatti handles the stratospheric challenges of the Beethoven concerto with noble artistry (Walter, Columbia Symphony). It is not an interpretation that digs consistently below the surface of the music, but his sound is always beautiful, and his phrasing, lovingly expressed. Walter's relaxed, reflective accompaniment adds much to the whole. Kreisler's cadenzas are tossed off with lithe virtuosity, and only a fleck or two of spotty intonation at the close of the *Adagio* mars an otherwise immaculate performance. Such a blemish would be summarily edited out in a current recording.

Although Francescatti played the heavier-textured Romantic concertos with complete authority, the inherent incandescence of his tone and his harmonious temperament were less than ideally suited to their performance. His recording of the Brahms concerto, for example (Ormandy, Philadelphia Orchestra), while containing a sensitive *Adagio* and a brash, gutsy finale, and while seemingly larger-scaled than his live performance, does not convey the requisite darkness of sound and spirit in the most expressive and introspective passages. The same dichotomy marks his spirited recordings of the Tchaikovsky concerto (in which he surprisingly

inserts the Auer-inspired D-major scale in thirds like a rapier thrust into the cadenza); effulgence rather than impassioned utterance is the distinctive feature of this interpretation. The Sibelius concerto (Bernstein, New York Philharmonic) also possesses strengths and shortcomings similar to those of the Brahms and Tchaikovsky.

In Brahms's Concerto for Violin and Cello, with Pierre Fournier (Walter, Columbia Symphony), the violin dominates, as the cellist plays rather placidly and reticently; the entire performance registers insufficient tonal intensity for this weighty music, and there are minor lapses of ensemble detail between the solo instruments.

One of Francescatti's important virtues was his ability to play violin-piano sonatas meaningfully, an accomplishment that is by no means shared by all eminent violinists, especially those who emphasize works of bravura gymnastics. In their chosen repertoire, his collaboration with Robert Casadesus constitutes one of the best-integrated violin-piano duos recorded for posterity. Aside from the instrumental and musical factors involved, their performance reflects a kindred artistic ethos and a singleness of purpose that are encountered only rarely.

Prominent among their sonata recordings are those of Gallic origin: the Franck, Debussy, Fauré No. 1 in A-major, and the lesser-known No. 2 in E-minor, the last an intensely songful but rambling work that requires a team of the Francescatti-Casadesus caliber to give it relevance.

Their recording of the complete Beethoven sonatas unfailingly communicates a sense of exhilaration and spirit. In No. 5 *(Spring)*, Francescatti's radiant tone is ideally suited for the season. The ticklish passages from the *Allegro con spirito* of No. 3 in E-flat major are gracefully negotiated; the *Adagio*, alert to climactic surges, misses a bit of dark quality in the more wistful passages; the *Rondo* finale scampers merrily. The No. 7 in C-minor, sometimes dubbed *Winter*, mirrors a glistening snowy landscape more than a gusty hiemal tempest; the *Allegro* finale is exceptionally zestful. The sharp changes of mood in the knotty No. 10 in G-major are deftly delineated in a sensitively etched interpretation; the last sections of the *Poco allegretto* finale are articulated adroitly. The introduction and opening movement of No. 9 in A-major (*Kreutzer*) enjoy optimum clarity of line; in the *Andante con variazioni*, Francescatti sustains interest even in those variations in which the piano is dominant. There is never a feeling of prosaic academicism; the *Presto* finale is propulsive without mindless haste, and the few lyric passages receive their full due. The remaining sonatas of their Beethoven cycle are comparable in blithe artistry.

In his recording of the Ravel sonata, with Artur Balsam at the piano, their approach to the opening *Allegretto* is rather aggressive. The *Blues* movement, unexpectedly schmaltzy for a player of Francescatti's gentility, undulates impudently; the *Perpetuum mobile*, a technical tour de force, noticeably faster than Oistrakh's recording, is spotlessly clean. The violinist joins pianist Eugenio Bagnoli in Schubert's Sonatinas No. 1 and 3, Op. 137, and the massive *Grand Fantasy*, Op. 159. The ungainly passages of the latter are handled with a sense of ease, and all is superbly polished, though the violin's presence is slightly undercut in the engineering. It is among the few best recordings of this thorny work.

Francescatti's recordings of the Bach Solo Partita No. 2 in D-minor and No. 3 in E-major accentuate songfulness. Although a sense of baroque refinement is ever present, he does not patently minimize his vibrato, and if a "meaty" position change suits his musical purpose, he utilizes it.

Obviously he is neither dominated nor hampered by any of the various current theories about Bach performance. It would seem that his aim is to render it pleasing to the ear. Except for *Menuetto No. 2* of Partita No. 3, in which he deliberately stops his vibrato in the opening bars and then turns it on (to no apparent musical advantage), his playing is never mannered or arty. The *Chaconne* is organ-like. In four-string chords he will lash back from the higher strings to emphasize a lower thematic note, but not in every instance. Those movements that are ancient dance forms are played very rhythmically; his *Gigue* is joyous, his *Saraband*, stately, his *Courante*, a straightforward Italian dance. Studied overintellectualization is not a component of Francescatti's art.

Medium-length works of stylish bravura are among his most superb performances. Saint-Saëns's *Introduction and Rondo Capriccioso* exudes a typically French bonhomie; the *Havanaise* is lightly amorous and languorous. Ravel's *Tzigane*, recorded with pianist Artur Balsam and again with Bernstein and the New York

Philharmonic, is both gloriously rich in sound and crystal-clear, more French in spirit than rhapsodically Magyar. The composer, his longtime friend, preferred it played in that context. Chausson's *Poème* is another of his choice renditions, lustrous in tone and sophisticated. Sarasate's *Zigeunerweisen*, the historic predecessor of Ravel's *Tzigane*, is spicy and colorful both in the piano version with M. Fauré and with the orchestra (Smith, Columbia Symphony). Two versions of the Vitali-Charlier *Chaconne*, one with pianist Balsam, the other with de Stoutz and the Zurich Chamber Orchestra (somewhat thickly orchestrated by Francescatti), finds the variations admirably diverse in mood and elegantly stated, with the heroic thematic octaves of the final section vibrantly alive. One can appreciate all the more the stature of Francescatti's playing by comparing these performances with the mediocre recording of Viktor Tretyakov, gold medalist of the Tchaikovsky Competition. In Paganini's *I Palpiti*, tastefully orchestrated by Francescatti, he captures the work's pure Italian flavor while disposing of the devilish technical challenges with complete aplomb; the double-harmonic passages are pellucid (de Stoutz, Zurich Chamber Orchestra).

Like his great colleagues, Francescatti was a master of the art of the vignette. A partial survey of these disc performances, all with pianist Balsam, finds Ravel's *Pièce en forme d'Habanera* as exquisite as a fragment of the finest Castilian lace, and the Poulenc-Heifetz *Presto* in B-flat major, an outstanding transcription, is stunningly facile. Villa-Lobos's *Black Swan* is visually allusive; Massenet's "Meditation" from *Thais* artfully captures the anguish of the repentant courtesan. Eight of Paganini's Caprices, No. 9, 13, 14, 15, 20, 21, 22, and 24, with piano accompaniments composed by Pilati, patently accentuate the lyric, but are technically superb. Ravel's *Kaddish*, underplayed, with scant vibrato, is quite "un-Jewish;" only the final bars register some of the poignance of a "mourner's" prayer.

His recordings of a group of Kreisler originals and transcriptions recall the impeccable taste of their creator, though of course Francescatti's comparatively slow vibrato fails to approximate the magical tonal vibrance of Kreisler. Nor does he strive to imitate the unique expressive slides and position changes of Kreisler. But the nobility of his style and his infallible finesse render the interpretations compelling, although one may wish to debate minor details of the performances. *Allegretto* and *Minuet*, both purportedly "in the style of

Casadesus (left) and Francescatti, 1965

Courtesy Yolande Francescatti

Porpora," *Caprice Viennois, Tambourin Chinois,* and *Schön Rosmarin* are among the most winning. In *Praeludium and Allegro,* the speed of the prelude dissipates a measure of the segment's grandeur, but the *Allegro* portion is delightfully expressive and not at all played like a technical exercise. *Londonderry Air* is heartfelt and poignant, but the high E string repetition of the theme, unaccountably played in harmonics, lessens the intensity of the climax. *Liebesleid* sings tenderly, but just misses the bittersweet essence of the music. *Rondino on a Theme of Beethoven* is a bit too slow for optimum charm, and *Liebesfreud* begins with brio, but surprisingly, some of the variations are omitted. Deserving positive mention is Tartini's *Variations on a Theme of Corelli* (from *L'arte del arco*), played with cultured virtuosity, supported by de Stoutz and the Zurich Chamber Orchestra, in a fastidious Francescatti orchestra setting of his own sparkling arrangement.

Most of the Francescatti recordings should be reissued. Such new exposure could provide many a valuable lesson to our younger generation of violinists, as well as immense listening pleasure to all. It is but rarely that one hears a French violinist (or one of any nationality) playing in a manner so expressive of the Gallic ethos.

Francescatti was a competent pianist, spoke French, English, and "very little Italian", and was an inveterate chain smoker. He believed that "Violin contests are good. They develop interest for the instrument and give opportunities to young violinists." In keeping with this conviction, he served as a juror in the Queen Elisabeth, Thibaud, Flesch, Geneva, and other competitions. Among the current generation of violinists, he was particularly partial to Perlman, which is easily understandable since Perlman so definitively carries on the direct traditions of the romantic, post-Ysaÿe era in which Francescatti himself was a leading figure.

The violinist possessed a magnificent "Hart" Stradivarius and the Sanctus Serafin on which he played his historic performances of the Paganini Concerto No. 1. He also had an Andreas Guarnerius and a Scarampella which he presented to pupils, and several modern instruments were donated to the Galamian Foundation. Among his collection of a dozen bows, his favorites were those by Peccatte, Lamy, and Voirin. He preferred lightweight bows and used different bows for different works. For Brahms and Sibelius he used the Lamy.

Francescatti made a major contribution to violin pedagogy by editing a considerable portion of the standard violin repertoire for the International Music Company, which has also issued two of his original compositions: *Aria* and *Polka.* He had several transcriptions published by Mills, and wrote various other violin pieces and some preludes for piano, all as yet unpublished.

In 1928 and 1929 Francescatti taught pupils at the École Normale de Paris, but did not teach during his long career as a touring soloist. Later he conducted some master classes in Montreux. After his retirement many young violinists came to him for advice and coaching, among whom he named Ayla Erduran, Regis Pasquier, Marie-Annick Nicholas, a Tchaikovsky Competition laureate, Nina Bodnar, a winner of the Thibaud Competition, and William Preucel, first violinist of the Cleveland String Quartet. Francescatti coached only those young people he felt were uncommonly gifted, and once accepted, he gave of his time and energy without stint. He advised pupils to listen to recordings of the works they are studying, but vehemently warned against any tendency to imitate the interpretations. Live concerts, he felt, can be immensely helpful to those students who are wise enough to treat each violin concert as an invaluable lesson from a master rather than an occasion for superficial criticism. He never (except in his impecunious youth) accepted payment for his lessons, which ran a minimum of two hours. And he did not speak kindly of "prestige" teachers whose outrageous prices for lessons are out of reach of many deserving students.

Because he chose to keep a low profile, Francescatti did not always receive the approbation he deserved, yet professional violinists hold him in very high esteem. Kreisler considered him "one of the finest representatives of violin playing that we have." Francescatti has been cited as a *Commandeur de la Legion d'Honneur, a Commandeur de l'ordre de Leopold de Belgique*, and in August, 1985, a *Grand Officier de l'ordre National du Merite*.

Among his many touring experiences was a trip to Israel at the time of the 1956 military campaign. When other artists might have fled the country to avoid the dangers of war (as did the Jewish Erich Leinsdorf in 1973, deserting the Israel Philharmonic without notice), the non-Jewish Francescatti insisted upon remaining and continuing his numerous concerts under any and all performance conditions. At one point he played in a Jerusalem hall that was only a few hundred yards from the Arab gun emplacements. In appreciation, the Israeli government presented him with *The Sword of Solomon* Award.

Intimates of Francescatti speak glowingly of his philanthropic assistance to deserving pupils which was always conferred privately, as he sought no recognition for such gestures.

Concerning the status of current violin performance, Francescatti stated in the March 1986 issue of *Strad* magazine:

> The art of violin playing is progressing in *quantity* not in quality. It is a good thing that more young people are studying the violin. But we no longer produce great musical personalities. The training of young musicians today is much more rounded than in my day. Pupils are immersed in study of solfeggio, harmony, theory, chamber music playing, orchestral rehearsals

The Francescattis in their former New York home

etc.. This is excellent for producing teachers, career orchestra players, and "team" players in general, but not necessarily for solo artists. Virtuoso command of the violin must be acquired while one is still young, and the hand and finger muscles are at their most supple, that is, if the violinist has aspirations of becoming a soloist. After about 20 it is too late to acquire this degree of technical prowess. Mastery of the great concertos and showpieces must come early in life, the sooner, the better. Once this is accomplished, the young musician has an entire lifetime to read about music history and take pleasure in playing chamber music. I am referring, of course, only to the most *gifted* youngsters who realistically have a potential for a solo career. With this approach, the young violinist's musical personality, assuming he or she has some latent measure of individuality, can best be encouraged and developed. We have many young players today who play marvelously, but one is not very much different from the other in terms of personalized musicality.

Another problem is the emphasis on "competition" repertoire. One hears of students who wander from one competition to another slaving away at the same compositions year after year.

The 83-year-old violinist continued:

At last I can do exactly what I want. I am privileged to live in a quiet little town, La Ciotat, near Marseilles where the climate is exceptionally good. I look at my garden and receive my friends at lunch or in the afternoon. I enjoy good food. I listen to young violinists when they come to play for me. From time to time I attend concerts, listen regularly to recordings and radio broadcasts and watch television. My hobbies are chess and my stamp collection.

Francescatti, after recovering from a serious 1983 illness, no longer touched the violin. In 1987 a Francescatti International Violin Competition was inaugurated in Aix-en-Provence. The late violinist, who passed away September 16, 1991, is honored in Aix-en-Provence annually by a significant violin festival dedicated to him, and organized by Madame Francescatti.

A truly noble artist, Francescatti was a fount of tasteful, cultivated musicality, who has long since won the right to be included among the foremost violinists of the 20th century.

Courtesy Yolande Francescatti

Francescatti and a young Michael Rabin

Francescatti

Nathan Milstein, a shining symbol of stunning virtuosity, dashing, ever-vital musicality, and incredible career longevity

Nathan Milstein

When Nathan Milstein made his American debut on October 17, 1929, Kreisler was still charming his adoring international audiences. Heifetz had long since vanquished a legion of outstanding players and established his awesome new violinistic standards. The boy Menuhin was the phenomenal prodigy of the time, packing concert halls everywhere. Szigeti, with his crusading intellect, continued to attract listeners who sought lofty, unpretentious musicianship. Such top-ranking artists as Elman, Seidel, and Zimbalist had already been comparatively downgraded. It seemed impossible that another Russian-Jewish violinist whose formal training had been attributed mainly to Stolyarsky and Auer, could launch a major career, particularly in the colossal shadow of Heifetz. However, a virtuoso of Milstein's caliber was simply not to be denied. He succeeded in surviving all of his former competitors, and his brilliant career became the longest in the annals of violin art. Indeed, if anyone ever discovered the violinistic equivalent of the legendary "Fountain of Youth," it was he.

Milstein was born in Odessa, Russia, on December 31, 1903, one of seven children. (Odessa colleagues allege that he was born two years earlier.) Neither of his parents was a musician and he stated: "I started to play the violin not because I was drawn to it, but because my mother forced me to. She sensed my affinity for music. But only when I progressed far enough to feel the music itself did I practice willingly and eagerly."

At age seven, after a brief unsatisfactory period with a local teacher, he went to the renowned Odessa pedagogue Pyotr Stolyarsky, who was David Oistrakh's only teacher. Milstein remarked, "I studied with Stolyarsky at the Odessa Music School for about three years. We were with him twice a week, and eight or ten pupils would come to the lesson. We would learn from each other." Stolyarsky never played for his pupils at lessons; all his teaching was done by explanation. In 1915 the boy went to St. Petersburg and studied with Auer until the master left for the United States in 1917. It is not clear who brought him to the capital, or how and under what circumstances he was accepted into Auer's class.

Milstein was not at all charitable toward his teachers. Among other derogatory statements, he has said, "Some of what you hear about the great teachers amount to no more than myths. Stolyarsky used to eat an egg when we played for him in Odessa, and Auer was no teacher at all—he picked only pupils who didn't need him." In another interview he said, "I don't feel that Professor Auer had a great influence on me. It was the surroundings and the atmosphere in the class where we worked, because there were so many very gifted young people playing from whom you learned more than from the teacher. In the class of 50 to 60 pupils, only two or three played." Milstein is not specifically mentioned in Auer's autobiography, nor even, oddly enough, in the comprehensive Flesch memoirs.

Taken at face value these remarks might lead one to conclude that the child Milstein learned the rudiments of violin playing strictly on his own. And there can be no doubt that on the whole, Milstein was Milstein's teacher—but someone somewhere must have shown him how to hold the violin and bow properly, how to place his fingers on the strings correctly, how to draw a bow tone resonantly, how to vibrate, and the many other purely technical details that every serious violinist must master. Even the young Heifetz had his father, a competent violinist, to help him in daily practice. Elman's father, too, assisted his son. Milstein, however, in the years during which he was still too young to navigate violinistically by himself, claimed that he had no one but his mother, who was not a musician, and his teachers, whom he censures. All this makes no sense. Was it perhaps Stolyarsky, well known for his ability to teach the rudiments of violin playing, who was actually responsible?

Unlike many of the finest violinists, Milstein was never a child prodigy. In any event, like Huberman, Elman, and Szigeti, Milstein was on his own as a violinist at a ridiculously young age (in his instance, at 13). Nor does he appear to have had a mature artist of any type as his overall musical and artistic mentor. His general scholastic education was sacrificed in behalf of incessant violin practice, and it was only in later years that he "filled in the gap and did a great deal of studying."

When next we hear of Milstein, in 1921, he is not yet 17 and is giving four concerts at the Kiev Conservatory with the pianist Sergei Tarnowsky (in later years the noted pedagogue). Here he was heard by Vladimir Horowitz, his senior by one year, and they became fast friends. In fact, the violinist moved into the Horowitz menage where he was treated like a member of the family for three years. During this period he performed in numerous concerts with Vladimir as co-soloist on a single program, usually with Genya, the pianist's sister, serving as Milstein's accompanist.

Sponsored by the new Soviet government and publicized as "children of the Soviet revolution," they were presented throughout the country in clubs, factories, political gatherings, and concert halls, and before every conceivable type of audience. They were soon joined by the even younger cellist Raya Garbousova. It was the post-revolutionary period of

Milstein at age seven

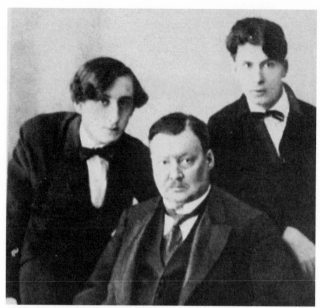

Left to right: Vladimir Horowitz, Alexander Glazunov, and Milstein in Leningrad circa 1920

near-famine. Often they received chocolate for payment when they would have preferred "bread and salami." Touring conditions were abominable. In 1924 Szigeti heard Milstein at the home of Nadine Auer, daughter of Leopold, in the USSR, and described him as "a fabulously gifted young man who seemed diffident about his impending first trip across the borders to Berlin."

It was their manager Alexander Merovitch who sparked the emigration of Milstein and Horowitz from the beleaguered Soviet Union in 1925. Sent abroad officially to represent and herald the cultural status of the new state, they never returned. Merovitch proceeded to introduce them to European audiences and to build their careers. That of Horowitz burgeoned rapidly, whereas the rise of Milstein progressed at a much slower pace.

In 1926 Milstein went to Eugène Ysaÿe as a prospective pupil, but the Belgian master remarked: "Go, there is nothing I can teach you." Their association was very brief, and Milstein can in no way be considered either a bona fide pupil or disciple of Ysaÿe. Yet despite his Russian origin and background, one can perceive strong influences of both the old Russian school and the Belgian school in his playing.

About this time he met the cellist Gregor Piatigorsky, and the pair, taking an instant liking to each other, subsequently teamed up with Horowitz to form a trio though each was primarily interested in furthering his solo career.

From the left: Alexander Merovitch, manager of the trio, Milstein, Gregor Piatigorsky, Vladimir Horowitz, and unidentified man arriving in New York on the S.S. Leviathan for their 1932-1933 American tour

Piatigorsky, in his book *Cellist*, describes Milstein as he was then:

His quick movements, lively eyes and shiny black hair, and his strong medium-sized frame suggested youth that would stay with him forever. It didn't take long to realize that he stood squarely on the ground and was equal to any situation he might encounter...So spontaneous and harmless was he that one hated to be critical of anything he said...His violin belonged to his body no less than his arms and legs...Nathan could be only what he was, a marvelous violinist...He was self-sufficient, unperturbed and always neat; his friends, his surroundings, his violin, his exquisite cashmere sweaters, all existed to augment his pleasures.

Of Milstein's playing habits, Piatigorsky adds:

I never caught him practicing scales or any other exercises. In fact, he did not give an impression of practicing at all. He just played on the fiddle and with the fiddle. I only rarely found him without the violin in his hands. As long as he had his violin, no one could disturb him...Occasionally he imitated other violinists, but when I asked him to impersonate one he particularly admired, he said: "It's dangerous, for if I succeed in playing like him, I would not want to play like myself ever again."

The cellist once told me privately that even when

Milstein shaved, the violin was perched on a nearby chair should he think of a new fingering or bowing to try out. It is said that an important part of his technical development resulted from practicing difficult passages from Chopin's piano music.

He became an American citizen after his first American tour in 1929. In 1931 the illustrious trio, sometimes referred to as "The Three Musketeers," gave some concerts with but limited success. Of the three, only Piatigorsky had had any comprehensive chamber music experience, and apparently while each played his own part impressively, the "musketeers" were often prone to shoot at different musical targets in terms of ensemble, and their individual sounds did not blend. They did not make a single chamber music recording as a group.

Milstein was one of the least publicized of the 20th-century elite virtuosos. Yet for the past five decades most observers have consistently included him among the first half-dozen leading violinists. The sheer brilliance of his playing sustained his career with no assistance whatsoever from notoriety garnered through extracurricular social, political, or philanthropic activities, such as involved certain of his famed colleagues.

Like the few most illustrious violinists, his tone had several different facets of color as opposed to those outstanding players who possess only a one-dimensional wrist vibrato sweetness of sound. His tone could be

Milstein and Piatigorsky

132

fervent, but was never quite voluptuous. Its quality might best be described as "silvery." Its power of penetration was superb, and it possessed extraordinary solidity and toughness of fiber without becoming hard-edged. His intonation vied with that of Heifetz in accuracy.

Family photo, 1950; rear: Milstein; front left: Jill Spalding (Milstein's step-daughter), daughter Maria and wife Thérèse

Milstein's vibrato was that of a "classicist." His style ranged from no vibrato to a sweetly lyric "medium" and thence to a fast, ardent, closely-knit vibrato in which the top joint of the finger played a significant role. He used his vibrato as a "coloring" agent rather than as a device to titillate the ear, and the fact that he was often sparing in his use of vibrato tended to make his climaxes all the more intense when he "turned it on." This use of vibrato also had its negative side, in that his subdued lyric passages were at times comparatively understated. Throughout most of his career Milstein manifested a vibrato idiosyncrasy by often beginning a lyric note without vibrato and starting vibration at some point during the note. But in his late years this habit was eliminated to a large extent. Though Milstein frequently alternated non-vibrato notes with vibrant ones, he did not approximate the irritating and vitiating practice of "hot and cold" vibrato in a single singing phrase that has become so prevalent among violinists in the last two or three decades.

Milstein's playing encompassed many moods. He could intone with chaste, almost detached sobriety, or generate the propulsion of a jungle cat. The spirit of his art is eternally youthful, as was the aura of the man himself. It was perhaps his *intensity of spirit* that was the dominating characteristic of his performance. His playing was ignited by an impellent drive that could border on fury. Conversely, it did not reflect an exceptional degree of poetic imagery. Purity of line and refinement of taste, rather than graceful elegance, were important components of his musicality. A single, short work could reflect both brashness and modesty.

Milstein's interpretations were deeply felt and always well-ordered, though not profoundly cerebral. His art eschewed heart-on-sleeve emotionalism, and while he often played with abandon, it was not a wayward abandon. He was adept in the use of subtle, suave slides, and position changes for expressive purposes, but in a manner less pronounced than that of Ysaÿe, Kreisler, Heifetz, Menuhin, or even David Oistrakh.

There was nothing unusual in the physical structure of Milstein's hands; they were remarkably supple and flexible. The coordination between his hands was astounding, and accounts not only for the speed and clarity of his rapid passagework, but also for its inordinate smoothness and fluency. One may attend a Menuhin, Stern, or Ricci concert that is well below their highest standard, but Milstein's consistency seldom faltered. A "live" Milstein recital was almost always a memorable event. Although many of his recordings are superb, the ebullient Milstein vitality, thrust, and propulsion were at their communicative best in the concert hall. Milstein's audiences, like those of Heifetz, instinctively felt as if the artist were in complete control. Hence they were relaxed and at ease, subject only to the music itself. His instrumental control was phenomenal; his knowledge of the instrument, encyclopedic.

Milstein stated: "The shoulder should play an important part in the equalization of the (bow) tone. I object to too much wrist and lower forearm. Most times I use very little wrist. I change bow from the shoulder rather than the wrist." This somewhat unorthodox shoulder application could be noted easily; he used no pad or cushion.

It is often pointed out that having a good staccato is not essential, and that a violinist can enjoy a brilliant career without ever using stacca-

Thérèse Milstein playing Liszt's piano in Count Cini's palace with adoring husband looking on, circa 1954

to. Milstein was the living example of this view. For all his marvelous technical skill in both hands, he apparently did not possess a reliable staccato, or if he did, he chose not to use it in public. Even such passages as the scales in the first page of the *Rondo Capriccioso* section of Saint-

Nathan Milstein in 1956

Saëns's *Introduction and Rondo Capricciso*, traditionally played in staccato, were negotiated in spiccato by Milstein. As if in compensation for his avoidance of staccato, he had a spiccato in which the crispness, articulation, and control were breathtaking. And in detonative bowing passages, his explosive yet crystal-clear impact has rarely been equalled.

The late celebrated violist William Primrose, in his book *Walk on the North Side* (1978), said of Milstein: "Once he starts playing (in private) he is difficult to stop, I am happy to relate...His pragmatic knowledge of violin playing is vast, and I hope he will teach regularly someday...It is well known that since this writing he has established himself as one of the violin's most outstanding teachers...He believes in taking a common sense approach to everything, doesn't make anything mysterious."

In discussing Milstein, Piatigorsky told me: "Nathan is at his very best when he plays by himself, as in the Bach solo sonatas or Paganini caprices. Here he is in entire command without the need to deal with another personality. He is next best when in collaboration with a pianist, though he is very hard on and demanding of his piano accompanists. With conductors he is generally uncomfortable, and tends to regard them as the enemy, sometimes with good cause."

I had occasion to verify this last statement, and described such an incident in a 1965 review:

In more than 40 years of concertizing, Nathan Milstein has earned and sustained a reputation

as a paragon of violin consistency in addition to his status as an invariably brilliant technician. Indeed, in these areas he has but few peers. Thus, it came as a rude shock to hear Mr. Milstein hack and race his way through the Brahms D Major Concerto with a disdain for clarity and phrasing that bordered on the flippant. What should have been a masterful performance turned out to be a hollow caricature of the celebrated Milstein art at his Friday afternoon Music Center appearance with Zubin Mehta and the Los Angeles Philharmonic Orchestra. And if Messrs. Milstein and Mehta were on speaking terms it was not particularly evidenced in their musical rapport. In fact, at one point in the third movement the gentlemen were perilously close to musical fisticuffs. The entire affair had best be forgotten.

Yet two days later, on Sunday, at a UCLA recital with pianist Leon Pommers, I was able to write, "Nathan Milstein came to town. He is now 60 years of age and looks 15 years younger—and he combined the ebullient enthusiasm of a youth making a debut with a seasoned artistry that was, if possible, greater than ever. He was, in a word, magnificent!"

The Milstein public performance repertoire was neither as broad in scope nor as large in size as that of Heifetz, David Oistrakh, Menuhin, Stern, Szeryng, o r Ricci. Szymanowski and Prokofiev represented the limits of his contemporary music, though on occasion he played the Stravinsky concerto, and he spoke of his desire to one day play the Berg concerto, which he called "glorious." He insisted upon playing only those works for which he had affinity and

Jill Spalding, Nathan and Thérèse Milstein, circa 1958

affection, and was decidedly not a pioneer of new music. However, the continued repetition of his chosen repertory never resulted in a loss of freshness or inspiration, as he invariably sought and found new musical insights in those works, constantly modifying fingerings and bowings to suit his changing ideas. Even in the standard repertoire one could compile a long list of familiar works he did not play in public and did not record, including the concertos of Sibelius, Elgar (he is purported to have studied it in Russia), Paganini, Bruch (Concerto No. 2 and the *Scottish Fantasy*), Bartók, Walton, and Vieuxtemps, along with numerous sonatas and concert showpieces. But by and large, most of the important masterworks were part of his active repertoire.

The Milstein discography consists of some 120 different works, large and small, several of which have been recorded as many as three or four times. The Tchaikovsky concerto has always represented some of Milstein's most effective playing, and he recorded it four times. All are dashing performances, but my favorite is the version made around 1948 with Frederick Stock and the Chicago Symphony, because it is the most personalized. Milstein uses some, but not all, of the Auer alterations, though his interpretation, freely limned, is not particularly of the so-called Russian school. It is intense in character yet not conspicuously emotive; the *Canzonetta* is played simply and unaffectedly, and the final section of the third movement is propelled at an astonishing rate that is decidedly faster than the 1937 Heifetz recording.

His Brahms concerto, although lacking intellectual profundity, is violinistically superb and viscerally impressive, particularly in the section following the first movement cadenza, and in the Adagio, where he is generous in the use of suave slides and position changes. The finale is a typical Milstein tour de force. The cadenza, written by him, is exceedingly brilliant and not overtly imitative. Of his three recordings I prefer the vigor and unassuming musicality of the one with Anatole Fistoulari and the Philharmonia Orchestra.

The straightforward, respectful Milstein approach to the Beethoven concerto is not conducive to sensitive introspection, although his performance is instrumentally impeccable. For example, there is no variety in the repetition of phrases, especially in the Larghetto. All is crystalline in sound and earnestly wrought, but the phrasing is scarcely Olympian. Nor does he take many risks in pursuit of personalized nuances. His three original cadenzas sparkle, but again, their merits are more

technical than creative. Recordings with Erich Leinsdorf and the Philharmonia Orchestra, and with William Steinberg and the Pittsburgh Symphony, are about on a par.

Milstein's Mendelssohn concerto with Steinberg and the Pittsburgh Orchestra is the best engineered of his three recordings, but the old mono version (Bruno Walter, New York Philharmonic) is perhaps a bit superior in terms of spontaneity. It is one of the most personalized of his performances: propulsive, ardent, and immaculate.

His Bruch Concerto No. 1 contains much dramatic intensity; the final G-minor scale at the end of the first movement (in the recording with Steinberg and the Pittsburgh Symphony) is reinforced with octaves in the top notes. The opening of the Adagio is somewhat reticent, but the climaxes soar, and the finale is highly charged. This is perhaps the most buoyant of his three Bruch discs.

Milstein chose to be his own conductor in recordings with the Philharmonia Orchestra of Mozart Concertos No. 4 and 5, resulting in readings that are more metronomic than they should be. As violin playing, they scintillate, but lack the ultimate in charm and amiability. Somehow the music does not seem to be in complete rapport with his temperament, though many a passage is rendered piquant by his remarkable spiccato. He composed all the cadenzas, of which the one for the first movement of Concerto No. 4 is, while rather predictable, the most inventive.

Two of his finest discs are the Dvořák concerto (Fruhbeck, New Philharmonia Orchestra), a perennial favorite among professional violinists, and the Saint-Saëns Concerto No. 3 (Fistoulari, Philharmonia Orchestra), a stylish, spirited performance, if not a tonally opulent one. The Glazunov concerto, his United States debut vehicle with the Philadelphia Orchestra under Stokowski, is neatly lyric and ineffably polished, but lacking in tonal richness, at least in comparison to the peerless Heifetz performance.

The dashing Iberian motifs of Lalo's *Symphonie Espagnole* (Ormandy, Philadelphia Orchestra), without the third movement (habitually omitted by the Auer pupils), contain some of Milstein's most sensuous playing. Several of the more songful episodes could profit from a heightened sense of languor, but on the whole this is a debonair, electrically charged interpretation, and the tension he generates in the Andante is extraordinary.

The Prokofiev Concerto No. 1 (Carlo Maria

Giulini, Philharmonia Orchestra) is played with consummate agility and silky smoothness, but lacks the acerbic attack of the memorable Szigeti disc. Concerto No. 2 (Fruhbeck, Philharmonia Orchestra) is a dutiful performance somewhat wanting in affection; the lovely second movement is rather pallid.

Beethoven's two *Romances* (Harry Blech, Philharmonia Orchestra) are played purely and literally without inspiration, as are the Bach A-minor and E-major Concertos which he performs with an unnamed string and cembalo troupe. The celestial slow movements project little subtlety. In two albums comprising eight of Vivaldi's nondescript concertos with a small baroque ensemble of American musicians, poor engineering diminishes Milstein's solo role. The results are dullish both in sound and style. However, the Vivaldi Concertos Nos. 28 (P. 258) and 39 (P. 229), recorded with the Bach concertos and realistically engineered, offer batteries of détaché bowings that are glitteringly executed, and show the violinist to his best advantage.

One of Milstein's recorded gems is the Goldmark concerto (Blech, Philharmonia Orchestra), a stunning exhibition of virtuosity that once again demonstrates why Milstein ranks among the greatest violinists of this era. This recording of the Goldmark was unchallenged for many years until the appearance of the Perlman recording (Bronislav Gimpel also made an excellent recording).

Milstein's collaborations with artists other than his piano partners or orchestras are few in number. A two-violin album with Erica Morini comprising Bach's familiar Concerto in D-Minor, BWV 1043 and Sonata in C-Major, BWV 1037, and Vivaldi's Concerto in D-Minor for Two Violins, Cello and Strings, Op. 3 *L'estro armonico*, No. 11, is quite unconvincing. Though Milstein appears to be striving for musical camaraderie with Morini, his more robust tone and articulation clearly dominate her thinner sound and comparatively fragile violinistic presence. The chaste performances are lackluster.

Recordings with his old comrades, one with Piatigorsky, the other with Horowitz, are outstanding. In the Brahms concerto in A-minor, Op. 102 (Fritz Reiner, Robin Hood Dell Orchestra, 1951), the Milstein tone, possibly inspired by the sumptuous Piatigorsky cello sound, is at its most intense. Their ensemble is excellent, and the overall performance is rugged and invigorating.

The 1950 recording with Horowitz of the Brahms Sonata No. 3 in D-Minor, Op. 108, is surprisingly well-disciplined considering the propensity for individualism of each artist. Horowitz succeeds in projecting his famed "orchestral" sound without overpowering the violinist, and the duo's general restraint provides leeway for many subtleties.

Three Mozart sonatas, C-major, K. 296, E-minor, K. 304, and G-major, K. 301, with pianist Leon Pommers, are performed with propriety and brio, but somehow Milstein does not "get under the skin" of the music. The same might be said of Beethoven's Sonata in G-major, Op. 30, No. 3, and Sonata No. 9 in A-major (*Kreutzer*), Op. 47 with pianist Artur Balsam. The outer movements are sprightly, though oddly, Milstein does not generate the excitement in the *Kreutzer* finale that he did in his live performances. The slow movements tend to be cool and fastidious, with but little probing. Truly transcendental interpretations of such movements require a greater degree of spiritual repose than Milstein seems to possess. Balsam's role is more that of an accompanist than that of an equal participant, although he plays with thorough efficiency.

The list of recorded Milstein showpieces and vignettes is extensive, and many of the performances are memorable. Heading the roster is his own *Paganiniana*, a hair-raising concoction of virtuosity for violin alone (about seven minutes in length), featuring refashioned themes from Paganini's caprices Nos. 6, 14, 21, and 24, *Witches Dance*, and the first movement of Concerto No. 1. Although the opus contains no double-harmonics or melodies accompanied by left-handed pizzicato, it is extremely difficult and demands the utmost in manual coordination. In his latter years Milstein composed another dazzler of the same genre based on Liszt's *Mephisto Waltz*, and playing it at age 78, he still scampered up and down the fingerboard with wonderful agility.

Milstein's other superlative recordings include Szymanowski's *Nocturne and Tarantella*, Op. 28, in which the glacial misterioso of the *Nocturne* and the meteoric propulsion of the *Tarantella* are equally compelling; the impetuous dexterity of the Paganini-Kreisler *La Campanella* (the only Paganini opus aside of his own derivative *Paganiniana* that Milstein has recorded); the amazing speed and articulation of Suk's *Burleska*, though the haste of the middle section slightly militates against the work's innate "rollick"; the sustained excitement of Wieniawski's *Polonaise* No. 1 in D-major; the lissome gracefulness of Tchaikovsky's *Valse-Scherzo*; the Rimsky-

Korsakoff-Hartmann *Flight of the Bumble Bee*, unhurried, with buzzing ponticello effects and an artful usage of open A- and E-strings to simulate "bee-stings"; the heady abandon of Wieniawski's *Scherzo Tarantelle* (the version with Balsam); the zesty, fervent, but not quite sensuous recording of Sarasate's *Romanza Andaluza* (with Balsam); and the striking nimbleness and "dead-shot" intonation of the *Perpetuum Mobiles* by Ries and Nováček.

Among his best lyric-oriented recordings are his own tasteful transcriptions of Chopin's Nocturne in C-sharp minor, the Larghetto in A-major from Nardini's Sonata in D-major, Massenet's "Meditation" from *Thais*, and the Brahms Waltz in A-Major, all reflecting a cool, gem-like luster and inner tension, but not calculated to bring a tear to the eye. In terms of charm, Milstein's most convincing vignette disc is perhaps the Leclair-Kreisler *Tambourin*.

Not all of his short piece recordings are impressive. The Bach-Wilhelmj *Air on the G-String* has insufficient richness of sound; Kreisler's *Rondino* and *Sicilienne et Rigaudon*, though seamlessly fluent, is neither very subtle nor elegant; Handel's *Larghetto* is uneven in vibrato and quite colorless; his Debussy *La Fille aux cheveux de lin* personates a bland, rather unaffectionate young lady.

In concert Milstein frequently included a Bach solo sonata or partita, or a movement from one; the last was often presented as an encore, even after he had played a concerto with orchestra. He recorded the entire cycle twice; once in 1957 and again in 1975. Milstein's solo Bach recordings are immensely respected by most professionals and critics. The clarity of his sound and phrasing, his obvious sincerity of purpose, and the aura of virtuosity that pervades his playing are compelling. Some listeners may prefer their Bach more intellectualized, but both sets of Milstein's recordings of Bach rank high in competition with those of other artists, and are widely preferred to the extremely personalized set of Heifetz.

It is interesting to compare the solo Bach playing of Milstein at age 53 with that at age 71. The 1957 performances are more vibrant and propulsive, the engineering more candid. The 1975 version is broader in concept, contains more minor rhythmic liberties, and reveals certain changes in phrasing and choice of bow strokes. The expressive portamentos are fewer and less prominent in the later recordings. Milstein's tempos are in no way metronomic, but, for example, the basic tempo in the 1957 G-minor Presto hovers around 170

as against 148 in the 1975 version; the Double (Presto) in Partita No. 1, 152 as against 132; the C-major Allegro assai is 136 as opposed to 126 in 1975; and the same tempo variance occurs in the E-major *Preludio*. All of the 1975 fugues are slower and more staid in character. Milstein said: "In my Bach playing I stress the bass and middle voices separately, with particular emphasis on the bass almost as a separate entity." To an extent, Milstein mellowed with age; his later interpretations are more relaxed, and in some instances slower in tempo, owing perhaps to his desire for deeper musical introspection, or to the encroachment of age, or both.

The question is raised sometimes as to why Milstein's career, for all its eminence, did not attain the international success of the Heifetz phenomenon. One can pinpoint similarities in their masterful platform poise and ease of execution. But leaving aside their respective qualities of acquired musicianship and technical achievement, they are utterly unlike in temperament and musical perspective. True, Heifetz was established earlier, but this alone cannot account for his supremacy, since the history of violin art contains many instances in which well-known artists, still in their prime, have been superseded by newcomers. The number of Heifetz recordings is at least triple that of Milstein's. And the fact that impresarios regulate the fees of artists on their ability to fill halls and sell records (for example, in 1950 the New York Philharmonic management paid Heifetz $9,500 for three concerts as against $3,800 for three Milstein concerts), is as good a barometer as any to judge their comparative mass audience popularity and box office draw.

The essence of the matter is that Milstein, for all his wonderful elan and boldness of thrust, was a classical violinist in the tradition of the old masters, whereas the unique Heifetz style, which is more readily identifiable, somehow epitomized the sophistication and immediacy of the 20th century. Heifetz's playing is, as Kreisler's was, decidedly "commercial"—Milstein's was not. Milstein's instrumental powers were prodigious, but those of Heifetz were even more so, particularly in the realm of tonal production and expressive nuances. This merely means that Heifetz's playing was more readily accessible to the mass public, just as those great violinists of the 20th century with the most sensuality of sound (Kreisler, Elman, Heifetz, Menuhin, Stern, Perlman) have reaped larger monetary rewards than their colleagues.

Although Milstein was a strong violinistic personality, his individuality was not nearly as overpowering as that of Heifetz. And while his tone was appealing, it was nowhere near as recognizable as the singular Heifetz sound. One can hardly imagine Milstein playing *Bess, You is My Woman Now, Alt Wien, Hora Staccato,* or *White Christmas,* or for that matter the concertos of Gruenberg, Walton, Korngold, and Elgar. The ability to play these compositions ravishingly may not be of marked significance to musical aesthetics, but these are the pieces that "sell." Thus it is much more than just a strange "quirk of fate" (as Boris Schwartz stated in his recent book on violinists) that has determined the comparative magnitude of these two careers.

The very absence of such "commercial" qualities endears Milstein to a sizeable segment of violin enthusiasts. He enjoys the utmost respect of professional violinists because he never upsets their sense of propriety, while at the same time offering artistry of virility, vigor, and virtuosity of the highest order. Professionals understand and appreciate the subtle mechanics involved in Milstein's fabulous instrumental mastery. Yet if they were given the choice, it is a fair wager that most would prefer to play like Heifetz.

Milstein's career did not attain the renown of either Menuhin or Stern. One reason was that he did not generate publicity by indulging in extramusical activities, nor did his playing reflect Menuhin's profundity of spirit or Stern's intellectual authority and earthiness. But Milstein is superior on a purely instrumental level.

Milstein's transcriptions are not numerous. His *Paganiniana* and *Mephisto Waltz* arrangements are artfully conceived in the violinistic sense, as are the best of his cadenzas and encore type pieces. His knowledge of the instrument is rivalled by few. However, his cadenzas are not likely to be taken up by other violinists as were those of Kreisler and Joachim.

At one time he played on the 1710 "Dancla" Stradivarius, but since 1945 he performed on the 1716 "Goldman" Strad which he renamed the "Marie-Thérèse," after his wife and daughter.

Little has been published about his personal life. His hobbies were painting and tennis ("when one plays correctly from the shoulder, it is the same as bowing"). For many years he refused to fly, but he finally reversed this policy. Milstein received the Cross of Honor, First Class in 1966 from the Austrian Ministry of Culture. He held decorations from Italy and Belgium, and was an officer of the French Legion of Honor.

On teaching, he said: "What I feel I can offer these young musicians is simply what I have learned myself through experience. I try...not to impose my way on them, not to teach them to play, even, but to help teach them how to think." (From "A Conversation with Nathan Milstein," Richard D. Freed, Bach Sonata album [1975], program notes booklet.)

In 1990, with the ghosting of writer Solomon Volkov, Milstein offered a volume titled *Musical Memoirs and Reminiscenes, From Russia to the West,* an autobiography that is prolific in entertaining anecdotes. However, it is rather impoverished in material that can impart violinistic knowledge on a level that offers practical advice to students and teachers. Nor does it really tell the story of how Milstein dealt with the complex task of becoming a great violinist; how he acquired his massive technique (particularly since he was far from enthusiastic about what he learned from his nominal teachers); whether he encountered any instrumental problems in becoming "Milstein", and if so, what were they and how he overcame them.

Nathan Milstein, who passed away in December 1992, shortly before his 89th birthday, achieved a distinction unique in the history of modern violin art. At well past 80 he still concertized, performing the great concertos and masterworks as well as such technical feats as his *Mephisto Waltz* and *Paganiniana* transcriptions. Even Heifetz was forced to retire at about 73 due to arm problems, and the playing of most of the stellar violinists began to fray in their late 60s, if not before. Joachim and Elman played publicly until their mid-70s, but their performances were more nostalgic than impressive. It would be unrealistic to assert that Milstein's violinistic equipment in his mid-80s was as formidable as it once was. The intensity of his vibrato and his general tone were clearly less consistent, as was the overall fluency of his playing. But the caliber of his performance was still incredibly high on his best days, establishing a new standard for violinists everywhere. Those who begin to find excuses for waning powers at 65 can look to Milstein. Such violinistic longevity can doubtless be attributed to a selfless dedication to his art which shunned potentially debilitating distractions, to the lofty status of his basic technical powers, and to his excellent physical condition.

In the lexicon of violin art, the name of Milstein will be forever a shining symbol of violinistic virtuosity and mastery.

David Oistrakh, an embodiment of impeccable instrumental authority, lofty musicianship and heartwarming expressiveness

David Oistrakh

The emigration from Russia of Leopold Auer and his star pupils during and after the 1917 revolution was followed by numerous important violinists and pedagogues from Eastern and Central Europe. After the Nazi persecutions the main centers of violin art were located in Western Europe and the United States. Little was known in the West about violinistic developments in the USSR, which was beset by widespread famine, counterrevolution and, during the 1930s, sanguinary political strife.

But in 1935, at the Wieniawski Competition in Warsaw, it became apparent from the strong showing of the two Russian contestants that violin art was still flourishing in that country. And in 1937 the Western world was astounded and shaken by the sensational success of Soviet violinists, who won five of the first six prizes in the prestigious International Ysaÿe Competition in Brussels. The gold medalist in that unprecedented triumph was David Oistrakh, not yet 29 and a seasoned concertizing artist destined to become one of the top-ranking instrumentalists of the century. Since that time Soviet violinists have played a significant, sometimes dominant role in every major competition in which they have appeared.

The Soviet phenomenon, temporarily isolated by World War II and the hardships of the immediate post-war period, did not fully establish international status until the mid-1950s. Yet Oistrakh's reputation, based on European performances and his early recordings, had burgeoned through the years. His debuts in London, 1954 and in New York, 1955, merely served to validate what the international grapevine had been insisting—that Oistrakh was an artist on the highest level, both as violinist and as musician.

David Fedorovich Oistrakh was born on September 30, 1908, in Odessa. It is said that his biological father's name was Kolker, but the violinist always considered his stepfather as his real father. His mother sang professionally in the Odessa opera chorus; his stepfather, a shopkeeper, was devoted to music and played several instruments semiprofessionally. Captured by the Germans during World War I, he became a member of the Russian prisoners orchestra.

At age three and a half David was given a toy violin, and at five, a real one-eighth size instrument. He was one of the few eminent violinists who studied with only one teacher, Pyotr Stolyarsky, whose roster of pupils included many of the finest violinists in the USSR. Stolyarsky possessed an unusual ability to recognize those children who had extraordinary gifts.

In early childhood little "Dodi" was anything but an incessantly toiling prodigy. On the contrary, according to his son Igor, "he would make incisions on his violin strings and bow hair to avoid having to practice on Saturday and Sunday," a heavy burden for a family that could ill afford to replace them. However, he soon responded favorably to the excellent Stolyarsky system which, while taking great care to emphasize fundamentals, abstained from boring young pupils with dry exercises. The pedagogue won their good will and interest by introducing them to group and orchestral playing as quickly as possible. Though never exploited as a prodigy, Oistrakh began to thrive under this regimen.

In 1914, the child, not yet six, appeared in his first concert on a program which concluded with the graduation performance of Nathan Milstein. At 15 he played Bach's A-minor Concerto with the Odessa Conservatory String Orchestra, and the next year in his first solo recital, the same concerto was included, together with several virtuoso-type pieces. In 1926 he

Oistrakh at age five and a half

Oistrakh at age eleven

was graduated from the conservatory in viola as well as violin. Anton Rubinstein's Sonata for Viola and Piano was incorporated into his valedictory program that also comprised Prokofiev's Concert Concerto No. 1, the *Devil's Trill* Sonata and Handel's *Passacaglia* (the last two with string accompaniment). For all his skill as a violist, Oistrakh once stated: "The instrument didn't sit well in my hands." His graduation concluded his formal violin training.

In the following year he had occasion to play the *Scherzo* of the Prokofiev Concerto No. 1 for the composer, who reprimanded him publicly for performing it incorrectly. It was a disaster for the 18-year-old. Years later, after having attained world recognition, Oistrakh reminded Prokofiev, who had become a close friend, of the incident. The composer was visibly embarrassed.

A few months after the Prokofiev setback, he was invited to play the Glazunov concerto in Kiev under the composer's direction, after which they performed it in Odessa. At the behest of the conductor Nicolai Malko, Oistrakh made his Leningrad debut on October 10, 1928, with the Tchaikovsky concerto. Despite being forced to play on a poor instrument, the violinist deemed his performance a success. But he was treated shabbily after having the misfortune of being ten minutes late to the first rehearsal. The orchestra musicians

seemed to resent the appearance of this young upstart from the provinces.

By 1928 he had moved from Odessa to Moscow, where he was little known and unaffiliated with the Moscow Conservatory. It was suggested that he go to work as first violinist in the Bolshoi ballet orchestra, a dreary, unacceptable way of life for one of Oistrakh's temperament. The concert functionaries ignored him, and he earned his daily bread by playing in popular entertainment "concert brigades."

During these years Oistrakh performed in open-air concerts in freezing weather, played background music for popular singers and dancers, and traveled from town to town in horsecabs, spending the nights in railway stations.

In 1930 he was married to Tamara Ivanovna Rotareva, an Odessa girl of Bulgarian descent who had graduated from the Conservatory as a pianist. The same year he took first prize at the All-Ukrainian Violin Competition in Kharkov, a victory that added to his slowly rising prominence. In 1933 a break came when he was engaged to play solos for the film *The Petersburg Night*, in which the main character was a violinist. The highly emotional score was by Kabalevsky. Oistrakh dubbed the violin playing offscreen, thereby contributing significantly to the film's success. In the same year he performed the concertos of Mozart, Mendelssohn,

David and Tamara Oistrakh

and Tchaikovsky on a single program. He was appointed assistant violin professor at the Moscow Conservatory in 1934.

Standing head and shoulders above all the other contestants, he won the first prize at the 1935 Second National Competition of Instrumentalists in Leningrad. Soon after, he was designated to compete in the First International Wieniawski Competition in Poland, an event that proved to be his first step toward international renown.

The demands of the Warsaw competition were lower than those of present-day major international contests: a maximum of 12 minutes of Bach, three Wieniawski pieces, one romantic or contemporary work no longer than ten minutes and, if one reached the finals, two movements from a Wieniawski concerto.

It is well known that the atmosphere in Poland was virulently anti-Soviet and anti-Semitic. The awards were presented by none other than Jozef Beck, the Polish Foreign Minister who was a consort of Hitler. Yet despite this handicap, five of the first nine laureates were Jewish, a fact viciously excoriated by a writer in the *Warsaw Gazette*, who even assailed the Jewish ancestry of Wieniawski. Oistrakh was awarded second place. Ginette Neveu, a blazing talent of only 15 or 16 at the time, took first prize. For all Neveu's admitted gifts, one must wonder how, as teenager, she could be declared superior to the seasoned 26-year-old Oistrakh in prime form, one of the supreme violinistic talents of the 20th century. One can only conjecture as to the competence of a jury which placed the talented seven-year-old (or 11, according to the Grove Dictionary)

Ida Haendel ahead of the 24-year-old Bronislav Gimpel, another considerable talent who had a substantial amount of concertizing behind him. Were they awarding current accomplishment, or what they thought was potential? For insight into Oistrakh's mental processes and depth of character, one can do no better than to read his touching letters to his wife written during the 1935 and 1937 competitions, as presented in Yakov Soroker's stimulating book *David Oistrakh*.

The Soviet establishment was extremely gratified by Oistrakh's Warsaw success. Following several concerts in Poland, the violinist was permitted to tour Vienna, Budapest, and Istanbul. After winning the gold medal in the 1937 Ysaÿe Competition in Brussels, his career skyrocketed. He was now the acknowledged leader among Soviet violinists, respected all over Europe, and in a position to obtain the most attractive assignments. Though he was not able to make his London debut for another 17 years, he did visit the city in 1937 and heard a concert by the 62-year-old Kreisler, a revelatory experience that made a lifelong impression. In 1955 Kreisler attended Oistrakh's American debut, which the older master praised unstintingly.

Oistrakh's son Igor was born in Odessa on April 27, 1931, and David became the first world-class violinist whose son was to become an internationally known violinist in his own right. Later, Leonid Kogan and his son Pavel shared this distinction, and still later, Dmitri Sitkovetsky, son of Julian, became an international violin competition winner.

Although it was Stolyarsky who, with the assistance of Valeria Merenblum, set Igor on the right path, his father contributed immensely to his training and

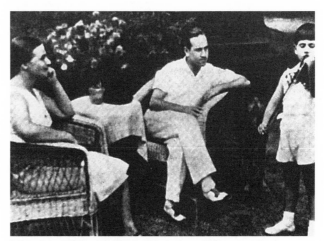

The Oistrakhs: Tamara, David, and Igor at their summer dacha in 1938

Laureates of the 1937 International Ysaÿe Competition: Standing, from left: David Oistrakh, Boris Goldstein. Seated, from left: Elizabeth Gilels, Professor Pyotr Stolyarsky, Mikhail Fikhtengolts

Courtesy Yakov Soroker

career development and strongly influenced his playing style. One can only imagine the psychological problems that Igor encountered as the son of the great David Oistrakh. The elder was a conscientious and caring parent, but rumors concerning tension between the adult Igor and his mother, and eventually his father, were rife in Soviet music circles. Father and son, however, began to play duets publicly while Igor was still in his teens in 1947, and their fruitful musical collaboration continued until David's death.

As his fame soared and his influence in the Soviet music establishment increased, it was only natural that Oistrakh became a Communist party member in 1942. Now a ranking artist and public figure, he was often "on the spot" between government policy and personal feelings. On many issues he was compelled to bob and weave artfully against the fluctuations of the official political line, though he was ever a staunchly patriotic Soviet citizen. He supported his friend Shostakovich courageously throughout the composer's vicissitudes with the powers that be, while managing to maintain his own artistic and personal integrity.

Oistrakh was a vociferous champion of Shostakovich's works, several of which were dedicated to him. It is interesting to note the firmness of his artistic views in the case of Prokofiev's Solo Sonata for Violin. Despite his intimate friendship with the composer, despite the fact that he was renowned as an interpreter of Prokofiev's music, he steadfastly refused to perform the work because he felt it to be inferior. Even more difficult and sensitive was his position in relation

to the growing anti-Israel and anti-Semitic sentiment in the USSR. Irrespective of his beliefs (and they were certainly pro-Jewish), he carefully avoided public martyrdom on the issue, even taking an occasional small step backward in the interest of survival. Yet after the 1967 "Six-Day" war, he bravely refused to sign the anti-Zionist, anti-Israel document circulated by the government on the breaking of relations between the USSR and Israel. When I stayed at the Israel Philharmonic's artists' guest house in Tel Aviv in 1974, Oistrakh's photograph was hanging on the wall in the office, the only musician so represented there at that time. He also refused to sign a document attacking the "formalism" of Shostakovich and Prokofiev.

In 1939 he was made a full professor at the Moscow Conservatory, and in 1941 he formed his trio with pianist Lev Oborin and cellist Svyatoslav Knushevitsky. Following the outbreak of World War II he played innumerable concerts at the front, behind the lines, and during the siege of Leningrad.

Oistrakh's life after his rise to eminence was one of constant work, as a performing artist, teacher, and public figure. He contributed many cogent articles on a wide variety of musical subjects. His schedule left scarcely a moment for any significant relaxation; nonetheless, he always managed to keep abreast of cultural, political, and social happenings. Unlike many excellent musicians whose interests are mostly limited to their art, he was an extremely intelligent man with an intensely humanistic spirit and outlook. No violinist since Kreisler has been so universally idolized as a person. Whether the state of relations between the USSR and the West was one of brinkmanship or détente, peo-

David Oistrakh, Queen Elisabeth of Belgium at the Casals Festival in Prades, 1961

David Oistrakh conducting Igor in the Big Hall at the Moscow Conservatory

ple readily sensed the special qualities of Oistrakh as they did of Kreisler during the anti-German atmosphere of World War I. For the most part they tended to exempt him from anti-Soviet prejudice. He never required a public relations network to keep his name in the news, as have at least two of his noted colleagues.

As he sped from triumph to triumph, his almost constant fatigue, later aggravated by obesity, continued to take its physical toll. In 1964 he had his first heart attack during a performance of Prokofiev's Concerto No. 2 in Leningrad. After a comparatively brief respite he was once more immersed in work. Again in 1973 he spent many months in the hospital. One is tempted to blame the arbiters of the Soviet establishment for not taking direct measures to preserve so invaluable a national resource, since they closely policed the work and activities of their artists. Had they ordered him to curtail his schedule by half, they would have been justified. But it is perhaps unfair to censure them since Oistrakh's life-style was one he preferred, thrived upon, and refused to mitigate. In 1960 he had assumed yet another responsibility, that of conductor, making his podium debut in Moscow; his heart must have failed under the cumulative strain.

On October 24, 1974, David Oistrakh died in

Amsterdam. His widow Tamara, unable to overcome her deep depression after his death, took her life in 1978.

Oistrakh's merits as an artist are myriad; he was one of the most all-embracing violinist-musicians of the century. His British and American debuts were made in an era of comparative détente between East and West. However, even as the leading violinistic emissary of the Soviet Union, his career could easily not have taken off were he not so supreme an artist. There was always a plethora of observers and commentators ready to denounce the "Soviet School" as being old-fashioned and retrogressive. As is the case with all artists, there were some who were genuinely dissatisfied with certain aspects of his performance. But no one could deny that Oistrakh's emergence from Russia heralded something different in violin art, as did the appearance on the scene of Auer's pupils several decades earlier.

The key element in Oistrakh's artistry was his marvelous ability to move his listeners. This power enabled him to surpass many superb violinists and place him at the forefront as the chief rival of Heifetz, his violinistic and musical antithesis. His natural expressive abilities were incredible, and he represented a style of personalized playing that was different from that of any other artist. Many fine violinists mold phrases; Oistrakh caressed them lovingly. He was a wonderful storyteller. Though always controlled and in exquisite taste, sentiment was an essential component of his playing. He was a visceral player of sensuality; one of those elite violinists who can truly be called a poet. Few players are able, as Oistrakh was, to transform a mood of tenderness into

Zino Francescatti and David Oistrakh in the former's New York home

144

dramatic intensity in a single bar. In addition to his finesse, precision, and intelligent, meticulously disciplined musicianship, there was always an aura of mystical Hasidic charm pervading his playing; a unique synthesis of bittersweet atavistic yearnings, with the intense love of life so typical of the Jewish people.

His short, stout figure radiated a glow of healthy simplicity and rugged inner strength. Onstage he avoided all physical mannerisms. The texture of his tone was soft-grained. Occasionally in relaxed passages it was even airy, quite the opposite of the electrically charged sound of Heifetz. Oistrakh's technical command was prodigious. He could read and play at sight many of the most complex compositions such as Shostakovich's Concerto No. 2 and his violin-piano sonatas, unlike, for example, Szigeti, who required incessant toil in mastering any unfamiliar work. And probably as a legacy from his difficult early days in Russia playing under a variety of adverse conditions, his hands required little warm-up. Like Kreisler, his digital reflexes were the epitome of suppleness. His playing gained considerably in warmth, introspection, and discipline through the years.

Oistrakh's vibrato was never extremely fast, and especially in his later years often ranged from medium speed to slow. But his fingertips were well padded and his basic sound was always rounded, even when his vibrato was at its slowest. Surprisingly, the comparative slowing down of his vibrato did not notably effect his emotional impact. In contrast to players like Kreisler, Elman, and Heifetz, the intensity of his vibrato was not a prime factor in his tonal communication. Nonetheless, in impassioned passages, his double-stops sang uninhibitedly. His trill, too, was not of the greatest velocity, but he employed it so cleverly that in the trill-laden Kreisler cadenza for Tartini's *Devil's Trill* Sonata, it is impressive.

On the purely technical level he could play as fast as anyone, but he never made speed a preoccupation, or substituted sheer brilliance of execution for musical probity and insight. Clarity of statement was ever a priority. His sense of rhythm was unwavering, and the bowing articulation of his passagework, of great incisiveness. The Oistrakh bow arm was smooth, molded more in the Belgian tradition than in the old Russian manner of Auer. As a colorist of the highest order (in contrast to many superb violinists whose playing is essentially one-dimensional), his artful bowing and the canny variance of his vibrato played key roles in the spectrum of his sound. His bow strokes ranged from near the bridge

to the area near the fingerboard, investing his playing with a diversity and subtlety rarely equalled.

Like Ysaÿe, Kreisler, and Heifetz (though perhaps to a slightly lesser degree), Oistrakh had a highly individualized system of expressive slides and position changes that enabled knowledgeable observers to readily identify his playing. To a large extent these were based on one-finger slides, and especially down the fingerboard usually with the first or second finger. This he was able to negotiate with hypersensitive grace. For portamento effect he employed "bridging notes," some fairly overt, others barely perceptible. His use of these devices in the playing of his middle period, roughly from 1945 to 1960, was prolific, and in certain instances a bit overdone. However, in his later period he employed them less often, possibly as a result of his continued exposure to Western playing which had begun to frown upon such embellishments.

In discussing Oistrakh's equipment and style of delivery, it is necessary to stress one of his idiosyncrasies, a tendency that had a deleterious influence upon many violinists, some of outstanding achievement. I refer to the habit of using vibrato in lyrical phrases in an "on-and-off" manner which has no relationship to the development or expressivity of the phrase. Among violinists this digression is often resorted to either as an aid for intonation or general technical security, thoughtless indulgence, or an acquired mannerism. For many violinists it has become a musical way of life which blatantly detracts from the singing propensities of an interpretation. It is so prevalent that critics and commentators who would mercilessly lambast a singer were he or she to do this, seem not to notice the distortion in a violin performance.

One could not rightly blame Oistrakh for this epidemic, although many Soviet (and now other) violinists who consciously or unconsciously strove to imitate his style, succumbed to the infection. Curiously, the overall performance of Oistrakh himself was not seriously undermined even if the listener, on occasion, wished he would do it less frequently. His expressiveness was so natural that he surmounted the aberration. Unfortunately, his emulators are not endowed with such prodigious gifts. The special character of Oistrakh's sound came from within the man.

His repertoire was very extensive. There were but few works of substance he did not play. Oddly, he never stressed the solo works of Bach in his programs or recordings as did, for example, Milstein, though he often performed the Bach sonatas for violin and piano (originally harpsichord), and recorded them all with harpsichord. Beginning with the compositions of Locatelli, Leclair, and Tartini, his repertoire extended through the great classical and romantic masterpieces to the concertos of Stravinsky, Hindemith (but not the *Kammermusik* No. 4), Bartók No. 1, Prokofiev and Shostakovich, and many Soviet concertos not often played in the West, such as those of Miaskovsky and Rakov, and Taneyev's *Concert Suite*, Op. 28. It is said that he also performed the concertos of Elgar and Walton in the USSR. He did not publicly perform much of Paganini's music aside from the *Moses Fantasy* and a few of the caprices, but he valued his music highly, particularly the caprices. Oistrakh wrote:

Paganini's music is a handbook for every violinist; it is wonderfully expressive and reaches any audience; filled with passion, it evokes ardent response in the listener's heart . . . the caprices are as fresh harmonically as if they were written yesterday ... I believe that had Paganini created nothing but these caprices he could have entered the history of music just because of them. (Yakov Soroker, *David Oistrakh*, p. 59).

But as a balancing factor he also stated to young people:

Strive to know more. Narrow-mindedness, limited range of interests may cripple any talent no matter how strong. Avoid prejudice in your repertoire. Do not let the brilliance of virtuoso pieces blind you to the many measures of musical thought, often less spectacularly attired. (Soroker, *Oistrakh*, p. 105)

And on interpretation, he never regarded the printed score as inviolate gospel, and often said: "Don't be afraid to argue with the composer, and you will find what is your own" (Soroker, *Oistrakh*, p. 110). Only a few of Kreisler's bonbons were incorporated into his programs, but he often played such bravura pieces as Sarasate's *Carmen Fantasy*, the Saint-Saëns-Ysaÿe *Valse-Caprice*, Zarzycki's *Mazurka*, and Tchaikovsky's *Valse-Scherzo*. One need only hear his recordings of Wieniawski's Three Études, Caprice Nos. 2, 4 and 5 (with Igor playing the simplistic second violin role), to appreciate the scintillating virtuosity and digital surety of his basic violinistic equip-

ment. A recording of Sarasate's *Zapateado* made around 1937 compares with those of Heifetz and Kogan in sheer propulsion and brilliance.

He considered sound production to be an instrumentalist's goal, and wrote: "Technique is not only fluency, it is also intonation, rhythm and, of course, as an ultimate expression, sound."

On the subject of fingering, the violinist stated in the preface of *The Principles of Violin Fingering* by I.M. Yampolsky:

Ease of execution is not necessarily the most important criterion in the choice of fingering, for this should always be subordinate to the musical content of the work. Often, the "rational" fingering proves to be not better, but positively worse in not producing the tone color needed, nor giving sufficient clarity to the musical phrase. In this sense one can talk of the aesthetics of fingering, for the failure to understand the "style" of fingering at times destroys the musical conception of the work.

Oistrakh was not immune to nervousness, saying: "If one plays less than twice a month, it could crack anyone's nerves," and he recommended constant public playing as the only sure antidote. He admitted: "In most cases I feel a tremendous inner tension," but warned against the danger of being "too calm." He always used a shoulder pad to relax his left shoulder, and was convinced that the amount of tone sacrificed was negligible.

Oistrakh frequently berated the flagrant competition mania in the USSR, though he served perennially as juror and functionary:

We cannot accept as correct a situation where the whole artistic career of a beginning musician is tied up with his results at an international competition. It must be remembered that winning a prize at a contest does not always define the real worth of an artist. Cases are known of international competition winners who, returning to their day studies at the conservatory, could not live up to their previous success and became mediocre students. We know also of unfortunate mistakes that have been made at times in the choice of candidates for this or that contest, not all and not always the most deserving were included (Soroker, *Oistrakh*, p. 111).

Obviously Oistrakh felt deeply about the injustices inherent in the entire international competition syndrome, including those perpetrated in his own country.

His recordings, numbering some 350 compositions, rank him as one of the top three recording artists together with Heifetz and Menuhin. Perlman is probably next in line. This total is all the more remarkable since he did not make commercial recordings in his youth as did the boy prodigies Heifetz and Menuhin. More than a few works were recorded several times. It is unfortunate that some of the finest performances of his prime period (1945-1954) were on poorly produced Soviet discs, many of which were (together with tapes of live concerts and radio air checks) either reproduced on license or pirated in the West. One particularly inferior recording of the Beethoven concerto on the British Egmont label lists him as Marcus Belayeff with Vassili Shiveski and the Odessa Philharmonic. Close scrutiny identifies the record as definitely played by Oistrakh early in his career. He never recorded the complete Bach solo works; his single disc effort is the Sonata No. 1 in G-minor. In terms of engineered sound, it must be borne in mind that those of his discs originally made in Western Europe and the USA are far superior to those recorded prior to about the mid-1960s in the USSR.

Among his concerto recordings, the Mendelssohn (with Eugene Ormandy and the Philadelphia Orchestra, 1955) is wonderfully spontaneous, fresh and sparkling, indelibly stamped with Oistrakh's personalization. His powers are at their zenith. As in all his playing there are vestiges of "on-and-off" vibrato, but overall his vibrato is beautiful and freely applied.

The Dvořák concerto (Kondrashin, State Orchestra of the USSR) is another gem. Oistrakh begins in a comparatively relaxed mood, ending the opening phrase with a soft high E harmonic. But the modulated repetition is climaxed by the topmost A on the E string hit solidly with dazzling vibrance. The entire interpretation is graced with a sort of home-spun Czech charm. The orchestra is competent, but not in the upper strata.

The Glazunov concerto, played with the same group, is a highly individualized performance. One can pinpoint an over-abundance of slides, but its sheer expressivity ranks the interpretation among the most compelling two or three Glazunov recordings. However, the hair-raising 1934 Heifetz recording is still the front-runner.

An off-beat work, Taneyev's five-movement *Suite de Concert*, Op. 28, the equivalent of a concerto (Malko, the Philharmonia Orchestra, all five movements), again from the mid-1950s, is among the most stylish. Not only brilliant violinistically, it contains an abundance of subtleties not found in most of the other fine recordings of the work. His vibrato is at its fastest and the performance is permeated with fervor.

One of Oistrakh's exceptional accomplishments was his ability to create a mood and sound of *misterioso*, which was to a large degree produced by artful bowing near the fingerboard. This is employed to great advantage in the opening and final sections of the first movement of Prokofiev's Concerto No. 1, as well as the filigree passagework of the composer's Sonata No. 1 and the third movement of Sonata No. 2. The biting satire of this disc of the mid-1950s (von Matacic, London Symphony) compares favorably with that of the splendid Szigeti recording of the mid-1930s. The same combination performs Bruch's Concerto No. 1 with surpassing affection; the Adagio is especially heartfelt.

Two recordings of Khachaturian's concerto, one with Gauk and the USSR State Symphony, the other (in stereo) with the composer and the Moscow Radio Orchestra, are about equal in performance; the violinist lovingly communicates the Armenian folkishness of the work.

The 1962 Bruch's *Scottish Fantasy* (Horenstein, the London Symphony) is played with winsome tenderness, in contrast to Heifetz's burning intensity. Oistrakh's vibrato idiosyncrasies are evident; nevertheless, it is a graphic interpretation, infinitely more sentient and poetic than the recordings of Grumiaux and Chung, and far superior in tonal color to that of Campoli. Nor has the excellent Rabin recording (clearly influenced by Heifetz), or that by Perlman, the individuality of Oistrakh's.

Four versions of the Brahms concerto reveal it as one of Oistrakh's most exalted interpretations. The first, from the mid-1950s (Konwitschny, the Saxon State Orchestra), with the Joachim cadenza, is perhaps the most masterful and brilliant, though a 1961 version (Klemperer, French National Radio Orchestra) runs it a close second. A later recording (Szell, Cleveland Orchestra) is easily the best engineered, though the performance, while still formidable, is less alive in sound and marginally less than perfect in execution. There is also an early recording with Kondrashin and the USSR State Symphony. In this work Oistrakh's introspective powers elevate his performance above those of his colleagues whose playing is limited to virtuosity and visceral application without intellectual force.

A similar mastery is evinced in his Beethoven concerto, especially in a mid-1950s recording (Ehrling, Stockholm Festival Orchestra) in which he plays all of Kreisler's brief second movement cadenza. Here he imbues the work with a celestial glow, and yet it is ineffably human, marked with elegant classical sentiment without excessive emoting. The third movement, played rather slowly, emphasizes lyricism. Overall, the performance is one of the most moving of this immortal opus. A version with Cluytens and the French National Radio Orchestra (with a truncated second movement cadenza) is comparable. The "Belayeff" Odessa recording is, as indicated earlier, inferior in every respect. A Russian recording with Gauk and the USSR State Symphony is good but the engineering is inferior.

Oistrakh's Tchaikovsky concerto is an infinitely personalized interpretation. Who else could play the turn embellishment in the first phrase of the *Canzonetta* with such grace? He instills in it a Russian character that differs from performances of both Western performers and the old Auer pupils. Even in medium-speed passages he projects a lyric aura where others play these as purely technical progressions. He recorded the work six times. The recording with Konwitschny and the Saxon State Orchestra of the mid-1950s is especially strong in emotional impact, although the Moscow Philharmonic in the 1968 version under Rozhdestvensky is instrumentally superior, as is the engineered sound. On the violinistic level there is not an appreciable difference among the six; however, the 1968 live recording, commemorating his 60th birthday, displays occasional flickers of fatigue.

Ordinarily, the Sibelius concerto is not a preferred work for violinists with soft-grained sound. But Oistrakh's exceptional virility and verve, along with his penchant for wistful expressiveness, add up to a superb performance at the opposite end of the spectrum from the sovereign, icily rugged, yet heroically impassioned Heifetz interpretation. Of his four recordings a mid-1950s version (Ehrling, Stockholm Festival Orchestra) is the most alive in sound, closely followed by the one with Ormandy and the Philadelphia Orchestra.

For all of Oistrakh's disciplined, tasteful musicianship, his Mozart was romantically inclined in keeping with his innate style and personalization. Many listeners, including myself, enjoy his warm, buoyant

Mozart performances. Others, such as the late American critic B.H. Haggin, prefer Mozart to sound more classical and strait-laced. Haggin roundly criticized both Oistrakh's Mozart, No. 4 in D, and his Mendelssohn concerto recordings. The most satisfying of his Mozart discs are the 1955 No. 4 in D-major, K. 218 (Ormandy, Philadelphia Orchestra) and No. 7 in D-major, K. 271, of disputed origin (Kondrashin, National Philharmonic — probably a Soviet orchestra). The No. 7 Colosseum label recording from the early 1950s begins with the third movement and ends with the first! Concerto No. 3 in G-major, K. 216 (Barshai, Moscow Chamber Orchestra) is surprisingly lacking in subtlety. A 1972 set consists of Mozart's five authenticated concertos and related shorter works, plus an admirably integrated performance as violist with Igor on violin of the *Symphonie Concertante* with the Berlin Philharmonic. The concertos, with Oistrakh as violinist and conductor, are vitiated by that metronomic feeling which nearly always ensues when there is no independent conductor, and the artist and orchestra are not year-round collaborators. Oistrakh's mastery is always in evidence but it is not his most spontaneous playing.

Other concerto recordings of special merit are the two by Shostakovich: the sprawling, emotion-laden 47-minute No. 1 (Mitropoulos, New York Philharmonic, 1956), a work now being widely accepted into the standard repertoire; the darker, intensely dramatic 29-minute No. 2 (Kondrashin, Moscow Philharmonic), less popular but eminently worthy; the hauntingly beautiful Szymanowski No. 1 radiating imagery and instrumental colors (Sonderling, Leningrad Philharmonic); the eloquent Prokofiev No. 2 (Galliera, Philharmonia Orchestra, 1959); the impassioned 21-minute Bartók No. 1 (Rozhdestvensky, USSR State Symphony) in a performance noticeably more expressive than the Stern recording (he never did record the popular No. 2); and the stately, charming Viotti No. 22 (Kondrashin, USSR State Orchestra), dully reproduced on a German tape from a 1948 Soviet performance. Also of interest is the intricate, at times unviolinistic concerto by the East German Ernst Hermann Meyer (Suitner, Staatskapelle Berlin, 1965), a grim, agitated, heavily-orchestrated 35-minute work of wide rhythmic diversity, not calculated to win a mass audience. In a Stravinsky concerto recording (Haitink, Lamoureux Orchestra), Oistrakh sounds fatigued, and seems to be searching for a profundity that is not inherent in the work.

Oistrakh was a master sonata player, and unlike

several of his eminent colleagues, never made mere "accompanists" of his piano collaborators. If he dominated the duo, musically, it was always out of sheer talent, never by royal command. He handled many styles equally well, from the gay, rollicking Leclair Sonata No. 3 in D and the austerely poetic Locatelli-Ysaÿe Sonata in F-minor (with pianist Vladimir Yampolsky), through Mozart, Beethoven, and the romantics, to Prokofiev and Shostakovich.

Among his most memorable sonata recordings are Prokofiev's No. 1 (with Yampolsky), which constituted a model for Soviet players and others, including Perlman; Schubert's *Grand Fantasy* in C (with pianist Frieda Bauer), in which his amazing ability for coloristic variety makes a delightful experience of a work that in lesser hands can be dull; Szymanowski's Sonata No. 1 in D-minor, Op. 9 (with Yampolsky), a work of impassioned lyricism; Grieg's No. 1 in F-major, Op. 8 (with pianist Lev Oborin), light-hearted, intensely Nordic in mood, is somewhat superficial music played with the meticulous care, respect, and affection of a truly great artist.

Other outstanding sonata recordings are those of Karen Khachaturian, No. 3 in G-minor (marked Op. 1 in the Heifetz recording) and Prokofiev No. 2 (Yampolsky), with the third movement properly played *misterioso*, an uncommon occurrence among other artists, and a finale that is not rushed; Tartini's *Devil's Trill* (with Bauer) is a bit breathy in the opening lyric section, but Oistrakh daringly takes the final notes of the first two phrases of the ensuing section on the G-string, unlike many of his colleagues who opt for the easy low positions. He also imitates Kreisler's four grace note endings, played poetically, at the tip of the bow in the second bars of the second and third *Grave* sections.

Several of his later sonata recordings project a sense of fatigue. Tempos are slower, and so is his vibrato. Many of the Franck tempos are so slow that the pulse of the music is affected, and to a lesser degree this is the case with his Brahms No. 3 (both with Sviatoslav Richter, 1968). An earlier version with Yampolsky is marginally better in this respect. Brahms's No. 1 (Bauer) is also tinged with fatigue, but Oistrakh's sheer talent surmounts this shortcoming. Notably superior are the Brahms No. 2 (Richter, 1972) and Schubert, Op. 162 (Bauer). Although the latter work "belongs" to Kreisler, Oistrakh's performance, much less intense in sound, is thoroughly charming and exceptionally attentive to detail.

In Mozart's No. 15 in B-flat (Yampolsky) from the mid-1950s, the slow movement is approached with marked romanticism and has quite a few slides, but the overall interpretation is gracious and compelling. And in Mozart's Twelve Variations on the theme *La Bergère Célimène* and Six Variations on the theme *Hélas, j'ai perdu mon amant*, Oistrakh imparts an extraordinary relevance to the slight, convivial music (with Paul Badura-Skoda).

His complete recordings of Beethoven sonatas, with the superb performance of Oborin on piano, is one of the few most intriguing cycles. The sonatas are pervaded by a spirit of intimacy and ingenuousness. All is leisurely in tempo and cogently proportioned. The lighter, bright works such as Nos. 1, 2, 5 and 8 are limned with affection. In introspective passages, as in Sonata No. 10 and the second movement variation of the *Kreutzer*, Oistrakh transforms passages that sometimes can be uninteresting into endearing musicality. The deceptively difficult No. 3 is archly delivered with ease. Collectively speaking, one can pinpoint an occasional trace of tonal blandness or "airy" sound, but Oistrakh's Beethoven has few rivals in subtlety of nuance and range of color.

Oistrakh also recorded the complete cycle of six Bach duo sonatas with harpsichordist Hans Pischner. This is solid, tasteful playing sparked by Sonatas No. 3 in E-major and No. 4 in C-minor.

Two other sonatas merit special mention. One is Shostakovich's Op. 134 (Richter, 1969), an arduous work that has yet to be discovered by most Western players. Like so many sonatas of the era, it lacks compelling lyric themes which may deter its popularization. Oistrakh sounds somewhat tired but negotiates the brusque, fast movements with his customary incisive flair. The other is the now popular Ysaÿe *Ballade*, No. 3 (solo, 1953). Here he is at his peak, capturing the work's poetic spirit, as opposed to so many (including Igor) who approach it as a purely technical tour de force.

Among medium-length concert pieces with orchestras are three from the early 1950s transcribed from Russian tapes; a stunning imaginative recording of Chausson's *Poème*, in which the high octave passages soar with expansive grandeur; Ravel's *Tzigane*, in a dynamic interpretation that is diversified in mood; and Glazunov's *Mazurka-Oberek*, a trifle that he could only have recorded out of his deep affection for the composer. All are with the USSR State Orchestra (instrumentally mediocre); the first two with Kondrashin, the third with Yudin.

In those short pieces with piano that he favored, Oistrakh could conjure up a magical spell comparable to that of the most notable vignette players. He respected such brevities and imbued them with every facet of his art. His early recording of the Chopin-Sarasate Nocturne in E-flat major (with Makarov), may well bring a tear to the eye, along with Suk's sensuous *Song of Love*, Sarasate's languorous *Zortzico*, Wagner's sentimental *Albumblatt*, and Tchaikovsky's *Meditation*, an old meandering Russian favorite. One can particularly appreciate Oistrakh's expressive powers by comparing his version of the *Meditation* with that of Milstein in the Glazunov arrangement with orchestra.

One might add to this prime list Szymanowski's shimmering *Fountain of Arethusa*, the exquisite reverie of Debussy's *Clair de Lune*, the captivating narrative of Wieniawski's *Legende*, the almost Hebraic lilt of Vladigerov's *Song from the Bulgarian Suite*, the folkish high spirits of Kodaly's *Dances from the Village of Kallo*, the superb virtuosity of Zarzycki's slight but sparkling *Mazurka*, and the glittering Saint-Saëns-Ysaÿe *Valse-Caprice*. All except the Chopin are with Yampolsky. Many more deserve mention.

In his duo discs with Igor, David invariably plays first violin, and as with his duos with Stern, David Oistrakh's special sound and style can be readily detected. As a chamber music player he was a generous partner, and while he tended to dominate his collaborators by virtue of his talent (as have all the greats), his willingness to blend with them in sincere unity is easy to ascertain in recordings. His roster of worthy trio recordings with Oborin and Knushevitsky include those of Haydn, Beethoven, Chopin, Glinka, Dvořák, Mendelssohn, Schubert, Smetana, Rimsky-Korsakov, and Rachmaninoff, among other chamber works.

Many of the brightest violin talents in the USSR were assigned to study with Oistrakh as a finishing course after their preparation with other leading professors. As was to be expected, practically all became laureates of major competitions. Among the best known, in addition to his son Igor, are Valeri Klimov, Viktor Pikaisen, Gidon Kremer, Nina Beilina, Rosa Fain, Stefan Gheorgiu, Eduard Grach, Oleg Kagan, Mark Lubotsky, Victor Danchenko, Stoika Milanova, Ion Voicu, and Oleh Krysa.

Oistrakh devoted much thought and care to his responsibilities as a teacher. Not only did he demonstrate his ideas with his violin, but as a man of superior intellect he was able to write about pedagogical details with clear, penetrating thought. He did not have his pupils play scales at the lessons; rather he instructed them how to practice scales at home. Pyotr Bondarenko was his chief aide, who helped prepare the students. Other assistants were Igor, Viktor Pikaisen, Olga Kaverzneva, and Solomon Snitkovsky. Often Oistrakh would ask a pupil to relate what he thought were his shortcomings, thus transforming him into his own critic. He strongly reprimanded pupils who played in a dull, over-careful manner, and would urge them sometimes to "lose their heads" or to play as they would act in a scene of anger. Beauty and distinctiveness of sound were all-important goals towards which he constantly exhorted his students. Concerning practice, he recommended that they "live with the violin all day, everyday." However, he thought that four hours of work in the morning was too much, and advised shorter sessions throughout the day and night, so that the mind could remain alert during practice.

He wrote:

Youth is very sensitive. It watches carefully the work of its teachers, and one has to strive forward intensely and unremittingly not to be left behind. I believe that the growing of my performance since 1934 is due in a large extent to my teaching activities as well. . .The level of our young violinists is so high that one feels somehow elevated just by associating with them . . . The evolution of my creative art and my teaching activity merge together. Both the positive qualities of the pupil's performance and its weaknesses, and the difficulties encountered, leave a useful imprint on an attentive teacher; one notices in a pupil what one misses in himself. Students' mistakes are an important warning, pupils' achievements make imagination work (Soroker, *Oistrakh*, p. 101).

Oistrakh showed great appreciation of and consideration for his piano collaborators: chief among them were Abram Makarov, Lev Oborin, Vladimir Yampolsky, Frieda Bauer, Sviatoslav Richter, and Paul Badura-Skoda.

His main instruments were a Stradivarius 1705, once the property of the French violinist Martin Marsick, which he seemed to prefer in his later years, and another Stradivarius 1714, formerly owned by Jacques Thibaud. Queen Elisabeth of Belgium, herself a violinist and longtime friend of Oistrakh's, willed him her own Stradivarius, a family heirloom. The viola Oistrakh played over a long period was an Andreas

Guarnerius. His bows, oddly, were neither Tourtes nor prime French bows but of German make. A biographer, Ernst Krause, states that his main bow for a good part of his career was a Nurnberger; the violinist himself affirmed that he owned German bows by Dolling and Hermann. Whether this was merely a gesture of goodwill to the East German makers or whether he actually used them in concert is not clear.

Oistrakh was not immune to the "conducting fever," and as so many instrumentalists have done, he turned to the podium for an extension of his artistic sensibilities in his early 50s. Like his ambitious colleagues, he had extensive musical knowledge and razor-sharp instincts, but precious little practice of the conducting technique that takes so many years of study and experience to master. He was wise enough to realize his deficiencies in this respect, and strove to learn all he could of his new venture. His recordings as a conductor, which are reasonably good, include several major works from the symphonic repertoire and collaborations with soloists. But he never reached the point where he could be regarded as a professional maestro. Had he lived longer, he might have attained this goal.

The honors bestowed upon Oistrakh were numerous. In the USSR he was awarded a Stalin prize, first degree in 1943, was given the title of "People's Artist" in 1953, and won a Lenin prize in 1960. Abroad, he received an *Honoris Causa* degree from Oxford University and citations from the London Royal Academy of Music, Santa Cecilia in Rome, and the USA Academy of Arts and Sciences, among others.

I recall vividly my own meeting with Oistrakh. He had played six concerts in the previous seven days. Following the sixth concert, I was introduced to him backstage. After the long, arduous recital, he was obviously exhausted. However, he insisted on "talking violin" for the better part of an hour. I was embarrassed, feeling that I was keeping this great artist from his deserved rest, but his zest and enthusiasm were all-consuming. Finally, and regretfully, he departed from his dressing room, and stepped into his waiting limousine and left for his hotel.

Oistrakh's characteristic generosity and kindness are widely known and documented. Menuhin offers an example of this in his *Unfinished Journey* in relating how Oistrakh, in 1955, gave him a facsimile score of the then unperformed Shostakovich Concerto No. 1, so that both could introduce the work at the same time. Numerous testimonials from his colleagues corroborate his rare stature as a human being as well as that of an artist.

In the hierarchy of 20th-century violinists and, indeed, in the history of violin art, Oistrakh sits on the topmost level. His superlative expressiveness, sensitivity, lofty musicianship, and technical authority have seldom been equalled. All great violinists have their adulators and admirers, but David Oistrakh, truly beloved by so many, was a transcendental artist and human being.

Yehudi Menuhin, an incredible violin prodigy who developed into a multi-faceted man and musician of comprehensive scope

Yehudi Menuhin

As the decade of the 1920s began, the awesome young Jascha Heifetz was en route to the dominance of the violin world he was destined to attain. The aging Eugene Ysaÿe, in virtual retirement as a soloist, was engaged in conducting, composing, and teaching. Fritz Kreisler, in fullest maturity, was still the most beloved of living violinists, and to a wide mass audience, the most aesthetically satisfying. Szigeti, greatly respected in Europe, had yet to introduce his special brand of lofty musicianship and adventurous repertoire to the United States. The scintillating virtuosity of Milstein, too, had not yet appeared in the New World. The career of Elman, though still potent, was beginning to recede from its once stratospheric position, while other leading violinistic talents vied among themselves for the remaining lower-fee concert engagements and tours.

Suddenly, in 1927, a new meteor flashed across the violinistic skies in the person of an amazing 11-year-old *wunderkind*, Yehudi Menuhin, born in New York, April 22, 1916.

Violin prodigies have always been plentiful and indeed, the lion's share of notable violinists (and many not so notable), historically, have been child prodigies. Most so-called child prodigies are merely precocious youngsters, who, in response to parental and pedagogical domination and guidance, willingly (or unwillingly) practice incessantly, gobbling up notes and compositions like voracious mini-computers, attaining instrumental proficiency in their early teens or even before. But for all that, the quality of their playing is patently immature. One who hears this type of prodigy is apt to marvel at the youngster's instrumental facility and remark, "He should really be great by the time he's 25" or, "He will learn to play with feeling when he's older

and has experienced more of life." The latter, of course, is wishful thinking. The feelings of a young person may intensify as he matures and his musical perception may deepen, but if he displays nothing other than a penchant for rattling off more notes faster and cleaner than his contemporaries without a powerful, persuasive degree of emotional communication, the youngster is only a pseudo-prodigy, not to be confused with the rare, real commodity.

The true prodigy or *wunderkind* is one who has the sound and musical communication of an adult while still a child in years. Such a one was Menuhin. By the time he was 15 or 16, he played like a man (i.e., a great artist) of 35 or 40, and had already been concertizing on the top international level for several years. His transitional stage from child to adult took place while he studied and concertized simultaneously.

Menuhin's first major appearance was at eight, performing Lalo's *Symphonie Espagnole* in San Francisco, his home town. During the next four years his progress was incredible, resulting in a sensational Carnegie Hall debut playing the Beethoven concerto with Fritz Busch and the New York Symphony Orchestra. The boy had already played his New York debut recital at ten, and even before the Beethoven with Busch, had performed the Lalo and the Tchaikovsky concertos with Paul Paray and the Lamoreaux Orchestra in Paris.

My first acquaintance with Menuhin was at a recital I attended in the vast 6,600-seat Los Angeles Shrine Auditorium in 1928, when he was 12 years old. The impact of that event still remains with me. Standing in the middle of one of the largest indoor stages in the world, the tiny, chubby lad, clad in knee pants and blouse, with his teacher Louis Persinger serving as piano collaborator, proceeded to play a monumental program:

The Menuhin family

Corelli's *La Folia* (in the David edition), Mendelssohn's Concerto in E-minor, Bach's Solo Partita in E Major, No. 3, and a lengthy group of shorter pieces. These included Monasterio's *Sierra Morena*, a Bloch Hebrew vignette, *La Capricciosa* by Ries, the Moskowski-Sarasate *Guitarre*, the Beethoven-Auer "Turkish March" from the *Ruins of Athens*, and Bazzini's *Ronde des lutins*. Each of the last three pieces was repeated by audience demand, and during the second round of the "Goblins," the weary boy at long last had a memory lapse, but concluded in fine style. After that, I believe he played Paganini's *La Campanella* plus encores.

It was one of the most memorable events of the thousands I have heard, and transformed me into a lifelong "Menuhin-watcher," motivating me to follow his career through fabulous triumphs, agonizing vicissitudes, growth, retrogression, acclamations, and disparagements. Meanwhile, Menuhin has become a *Great Personality of the Violin*. He has received countless awards and honors. Yet he is, without doubt, the most paradoxical and controversial violinist among the most significant players of his era; a man whose illustrious accomplishments far supersede his failures, but whose failures are part and parcel of his unique story.

The Menuhin career has been amply chronicled in detail, first in a remarkably frank biography, *Yehudi*

Menuhin by Robert Magidoff (1955), and again in *Unfinished Journey* (1976), which generally reiterates its predecessor, adding another 20 years of narrative, with authorship credited to Menuhin in joint copyright with Patrick Seale and Associates Limited. The violinist has also written several other books, including *Theme and Variations*, a compendium of his esthetic, social, and philosophical theories. Another volume, *The Menuhins: A Family Odyssey* by his nephew Lionel Menuhin Rolfe, presents the entire Menuhin menage in fascinating relief, in a manner which is respectful of family affiliation but less idealized in character delineation than the two biographies which are obviously officially sanctioned accounts.

It is interesting to note that in the Magidoff book, Menuhin's technical problems in early maturity are given major emphasis. *Unfinished Journey*, though it mentions these difficulties, discreetly veers away from the subject, tending to leave the reader with the impression that these problems have been overcome, and subsequently, were neither non-existent, nor at least presented no serious obstacle to his performance.

Among other things, it is the intent of this essay to examine the subject and discuss the various violinistic and musical phases of Menuhin's career, beginning with his 11th year. This is possible not only by virtue of the fact that I have heard Menuhin live (and on radio and television broadcasts) countless times through half a century, but by means of his huge recording roster of well over 400 separate listings, which place him in scroll-to-scroll competition with Heifetz and David Oistrakh for top honors in number of recordings. Obviously we cannot discuss each disc individually,

Menuhin at about age 12, already capable of rare musical expressivity and memorable communication with his audience

155

but a broad cross section of them will be cited.

How wonderful it would be to hear a recording of the 13-year-old Paganini as he played his audition for Rolla; the 14-year-old Vieuxtemps, described by Ignace Moscheles as "a wonderful boy who attracted great attention by his fine violin playing"; the 13-year-old Joachim as he played the Beethoven concerto under the baton of Mendelssohn; the ten-year-old Wieniawski as he played the first ten Paganini caprices for his teacher, Massart; the 12-year-old Kreisler when he won first prize at the Paris Conservatoire; the 11-year-old Vecsey in his London debut; the 12-year-old Elman as he made his Berlin debut in the Tchaikovsky concerto. But only in our time do we enjoy the privilege of hearing sensational performances as they really were and are, thanks to the treasure-trove of recordings. Happily, in the case of the boy Menuhin, we need not depend upon the reports of contemporary critics who avidly poured forth superlatives in describing the overwhelming effect of the youngster on his listeners and the precocity of his inherent esthetic endowments, but seldom, if ever, offered any serious clinical evaluation of his instrumental resources.

The first recordings of Menuhin in 1928 postdate his memorable Carnegie Hall appearance in the Beethoven concerto with Fritz Busch and the New York Symphony. Thus, even though the initial discs contained only short pieces, we can get a reasonably accurate purview of the essentials of his playing at that time: the status of his intonation, the comparative development of his vibrato, the tonal production of his bow arm (and, of course, its resiliency), the level of his budding musicianship, the idiosyncrasies of his evolving style, and the degree of his musical communication. The very first pieces represent, after all, the playing of a little boy. Yet, they provide definite clues to the later evolution of his playing—not only the positive facets, but the negative as well.

Immediately one can perceive why the boy, who was not yet 12 years old, was labelled a genius by so many observers. His instinctive ability to express a phrase—to tell a story with his violin—is astonishing. It is ineffably sweet, child-like expressiveness, but it is already tinged with a certain quality of maturity which defies any age categorization. His musical personality is already definitive, though far from fully formed.

His intonation is generally clean, but not without defects, and his digital facility is extremely flexible, although it is a technique that is rather soft and not

set in the rigid exactitude that results from long, arduous, and careful scale and arpeggio practice. His vibrato is wide and tends toward slow oscillation, yet his tone already projects an individual character. A number of slides intrude, many of which are tasteful but overdone. His bow arm draws the resonance of sound that is vital to big-scale playing, and his détachés articulate clearly but are not crisply incisive. Musically, his playing is disciplined in the broad sense, but reflects the free-wheeling, sometimes quasi-Gypsy spirit of the later Menuhin. His style represents none of the traditional schools. Self-expression is the hallmark of his musical manner. All of his 12 early 1928 and 1929 disc performances have as piano collaborator the first of his renowned teachers, Louis Persinger.

La Romanesca, an anonymous, plaintive 16th-century air, transcribed by Joseph Achron, is listed as Menuhin's first recording, one of three made on March 15, 1928. The others are the lilting Monasterio *Sierra Morena* and Ries's *La Capricciosa*. The latter two are among the very best of the early Menuhin discs; the Monasterio, its ardent songfulness welling out from inside the boy, and the Ries, with its marvelous "chute-the-chutes" buoyancy. The Fiocco "Allegro," made two weeks later, is brisk and sunny with the wide vibrato on the phrase-ending notes betraying the soloist's immaturity.

Seven pieces are dated February 12, 1929. The status of the boy's vibrato and stylistic application have not changed appreciably, but it was a period in which his repertoire was growing by leaps and bounds, most of the works to be recorded later. Bloch's *Nigun* is played with juvenile warmth, and the lad's difficulty in vibrating on octaves and in the G and E-string highs demonstrates that his left hand is still unevenly developed, though it was a year in which he had regularly performed such fireworks as Bazzini's *Ronde des lutins* and Paganini's *La Campanella*. The Handel-Flesch *Prayer* is slide-ridden and not perfectly clean, but the tonal timbre is quite individual. In Leclair's *Sarabande* and *Tambourin*, the slow episode is over-romantic and the fast movement rushed, but the seeds of the future Menuhin nobility of style in baroque and classical works are beginning to sprout.

The Mozart Adagio from Concerto No. 3 in G (K. 216) (with piano) provides a revealing insight into the magnitude of the boy's talent. True, the performance approach is again over-romantic and contains too many slides, mostly of the one-finger variety, but every violinist knows how difficult it is to communicate a Mozart slow movement with beauty of sound and spirit, and the youngster projects these qualities with moving sentiment. Saenger's *Scotch Pastorale* is played in the original complete form rather than the truncated version of the old Elman disc, and conveys a charming, cherubic innocence; however, Elman's rendition, with its exquisite tone, remains supreme. Serrano's *Cancion del Olvido*, a Persinger setting, and Samazeuilh's *Chant d'Espagne* are both excellent examples of the boy's instinctive feeling for sensual melody; the brief Spohr-Persinger *Rondo* romps airily.

Significant in this period was Menuhin's first recording of a major work—the monumental Bach Sonata No. 3 in C-major, November 13, 1929. The Beethoven Sonata No. 1 (Op. 12) was recorded the same day. This must be considered a premature, if well-meaning, effort. We hear a little boy with a wide finger oscillation and no particular musical acumen cumbersomely wending his way through the thorny challenges of these masterworks. His shortcomings are especially evident in the Bach. This is not to denigrate an endeavor which was in itself a grand feat for a 12-year-old, but to stress the fact that despite the mass of hosannas from adoring critics, Menuhin, at that point, was essentially unfledged, and some three years away from the initial stage of his most spectacular period.

Progress was swift. By December 11, 1930, in the Corelli *La Folia* disc, his vibrato is noticeably tighter and stronger in an indulgently ardent reading embellished with some untoward slides. The intonation is good, though not consistently on the mark, but despite his stylistic excesses, it is engaging playing. Paganini's *La Campanella*, recorded the same day, still reflects a youthful aura, but it is a stunning tour-de-force performance. The version includes most of the finale of the composer's Concerto No. 2, and Menuhin plays the lyric double-harmonics with vibrato and abandon, a feat that few virtuosos of any age have been able to accomplish. By November 6, 1931, in the first of his five recordings of the Bruch Concerto No. 1 in G-minor (with Sir Landon Ronald and the London Symphony), his sound has become distinctly more virile, his style more impassioned. Menuhin was on the threshold of changing from a boy wonder to a teenage phenomenon whose expressive faculties were blossoming into full flower. During these early years he often played three-concerto performances with orchestra, perhaps incorporating a Bach concerto with those of Brahms and Beethoven, or a Mozart concerto, all five movements of Lalo's *Symphonie Espagnole*, plus the Beethoven concerto. I recall a concert including the last three in which the first two works were superlative, but in the Beethoven, gradually overcome by fatigue, his performance wilted. As expected, the audience cheers were deafening. When Menuhin was only 16, his publicity material asserted that the boy could perform the Beethoven concerto "with a warmth that Heifetz could never instill." His concerts were packed.

At this juncture, let us look into the matter of Menuhin's teachers and training. The lad was taken at age five to Sigmund Anker, with whom he spent about a year learning his violinistic abc's. Then in 1922 he started to study with Louis Persinger, a Ysaÿe pupil, who had been for two years concertmaster of the San Francisco Symphony. In his charming, valuable booklet, *Why the Violin?*, Persinger states: "I don't believe that anyone would dare argue against the fact that in the beginning the violin was intended to be a singing instrument." And the core of Persinger's musicality was to sing, sing, sing on the violin, a credo he immediately inculcated into his brilliant pupil.

It would seem that Persinger, himself a well-grounded player, was so overwhelmed by the unlimited capacity of the boy to absorb the repertoire, that he permitted him to indulge his fabulous intuitive powers at the expense of developing his analytical faculties. Then, when Menuhin went to Georges Enesco (whom he considers to be "the greatest all-round musician I ever met in my entire life"), this was not only compounded, but applied to the most august areas of the repertoire. In fact, for a number of years the boy worked alternately with both teachers in accordance with the time and commitments of each. This system proved successful since the background of Persinger as an Ysaÿe disciple and that of Enesco, who was essentially a product of the French-Belgian Violin School, were not in conflict. Moreover, the Persinger mania for violinistic expressiveness above all, and the quasi-Gypsy ethos of Enesco, particularly in his concept of violin sound (though it must be stressed that the latter was tempered with aristocratic musical tastes), were in concurrence.

Oddly, it was Enesco who recommended that Menuhin work with Adolf Busch, the German violinist, brother of the conductor Fritz Busch, and later, father-in-law and performance partner of pianist Rudolf Serkin. Menuhin suggests that "Enesco saw his great German colleague as a corrective influence." (Did

Menuhin actually mean a balancing influence?)

Busch was apparently a man of highest moral and humanistic standards who, as a Gentile, had the integrity and intestinal fortitude to refuse to perform in Hitler's Third Reich after the Nazis forbade him to give concerts with Serkin, a Jew. This was in contradistinction to the celebrated maestro, Furtwangler, so passionately extolled by certain Jewish artists (including Menuhin) for allegedly helping a few Jewish musicians. However, Furtwangler blithely continued to perform for the Nazis while the overwhelming body of rank-and-file Jewish musicians and music educators, conveniently forgotten, were rounded up and, like cattle, slaughtered by one means or another, among them members of his own orchestra.

I have used the word oddly in reference to Enesco's recommendation of Busch, because while Menuhin may have learned something from Busch about German cultural and musical traditions, he could have acquired this from many other sources. And I think it is necessary to separate Busch's admirable qualities of personal character from his attainments as a violinist. Menuhin makes a point of discussing his two summers of study with Busch in the kindliest terms. Yet the fact remains that Busch represented a school of violin playing that was woefully anachronistic and antipathetic to all of the new and intriguing violin advances that had thus far taken place in the 20th century.

My point is this—a few months of contact with the arid, retrogressive violinistic propensities of Busch could certainly do no serious harm to so irrepressible a violinistic talent as Menuhin. But what Menuhin sorely needed at the time was the influence of an eminently analytical violinistic mind, one capable of ferreting out and correcting technical weaknesses with discursive intellectualism in the most progressive manner of the era. That description is applicable not to Adolf Busch but to Carl Flesch, and it is amazing that so experienced and sensitive a musician as Enesco did not see this. Also inexplicable is Persinger's similar error in not insisting upon the early solidification of the lad's technique. Persinger's teacher, Ysaÿe, immediately spotted Menuhin's deficiencies, when, following the boy's audition for him, he asked to hear a four-octave A-major arpeggio. Menuhin writes: "I groped all over the fingerboard like a blind mouse," whereupon Ysaÿe laconically advised him to practice scales and arpeggios.

In the ensuing years Menuhin negotiated every type of scale and arpeggio in performing technical

Yehudi Menuhin

works, if only by virtue of his astonishing innate talent, but this could be no compensation for the failure of his mentors to indoctrinate this boy (who had a mind like a sponge) with an intellectual, analytical grasp of what he was doing on the violin. One cannot help but wonder whether the skyrocketing career of Menuhin, with its attendant publicity and huge monetary rewards, did not unduly influence both Persinger and Enesco away from this all-important phase of their pedagogical responsibility.

Irrespective of where the responsibility lies, this failure to deal with Menuhin's incipient technical problems eventually resulted in many long years of torturous self-appraisal and frustrating experimentation for him, and indeed, may well have altered the entire perspective of his career.

Meanwhile, the boy continued to amass triumph upon triumph. On July 15, 1932, Menuhin achieved what may well be the most notable feat ever for a 16-year-old in his recording of the Elgar concerto with the composer conducting the London Symphony. His vibrato was still not quite as fast as it was to become in another two years, but his communicative and expressive powers were wondrous. In the intervening decades there have been many recordings of this work (which despite Albert Sammons' earlier recording, owes much of its renewed popularity to Menuhin), but none, in my opinion, captures the Edwardian flavor of the concerto to a comparable degree, although the Heifetz version is more immaculate. (Menuhin's 1966 version is less clean, and both his spontaneity and sound are less consistent.) Also in this year is the outstanding recording of the Paganini-Kreisler Caprice No. 24, unaccompanied, with the scale variation of thirds and tenths, generally negotiated rapidly, played slowly and songfully. In the finale section some Auer variations are thrown in for good measure. The octave variation, too, sings uninhibitedly.

Wieniawski's *Scherzo Tarantelle* is dated May 23, 1932, just a month and a day before Menuhin's historic Elgar concerto recording. He had become a brilliant virtuoso in the adult sense and tossed off the "Scherzo" with expert agility of fingers and bow. This tour-de-force has been recorded by more than 40 violinists. All play it cleanly, but it is the degree of suavity and tonal richness in the melodic part of the middle section that separates the men from the boys, and in this respect, the version of the 16-year-old Menuhin ranks among the four or five best.

On June 20, 1932, with Enesco and the Paris Symphony, Menuhin made his first recording of Lalo's *Symphonie Espagnole*, a spicy, fervent reading that included the sultry, most Spanish portion of the work, the third movement Intermezzo which had been habitually neglected (allegedly for reason of overall length) by the Auer disciples. Menuhin was the catalyst of the Intermezzo's resurgence to fashion, and today it is seldom omitted. A 1947 recording with Fournet and the Colonne Concerts Orchestra has more intensity of vibrato but is less tidy.

The same year Menuhin recorded the first of his numerous Mozart concertos (which ultimately included all eight: the five authenticated ones, plus the *Adelaide*, the elfin E-flat major, usually labelled No. 6, and the stately D-major, or No. 7). Menuhin's special affinity for Mozart is evident in his June 4, 1932 interpretation of the No. 7. This might be described as youthful, innocent buoyancy without any vestige of affectation or pretentiousness. His Mozart invariably *smiles* in the outer movements and sings effervescently in the slow ones. These qualities are masterfully imbued in the May 19, 1934 *Adelaide* recording.

The year 1934 (May 19th) was emblazoned with Menuhin's recording of Paganini's Concerto No. 1 which included Sauret's lengthy, spectacular cadenza, with Pierre Monteux conducting the Paris Symphony.

It was he who re-introduced the concerto in its three-movement entirety, supplanting a tradition, especially among the Auer students, who favored Wilhelmj's edition that incorporated only the first movement and cadenza. Many exciting recordings of the complete work have since appeared, but this, the first of the three Menuhin recordings, made when he was 18, is still among the most distinctive of all. The concerto, inherently strongly operatic, bears the Italianate influence of Rossini, Bellini, and Donizetti. In the theatrical second movement, Menuhin's dramatic flair equals or surpasses that of any violinist in this work. A second recording in 1950, with Fistoulari and the London Symphony, and a third, around 1960, with Erede and the London Symphony, are well played, but neither has the consistency of spontaneity, technical perfection of detail, beauty of sound, and sheer freshness of spirit, to the degree of the 1934 version.

One might ask if there is not a tendency to exaggerate the blandishments of the first Elgar and Paganini concertos recordings because of Menuhin's youth? Absolutely not! These represent his cleanest, most inspired playing, with no inhibitions, neither physical nor psychological.

Also in 1934 Menuhin recorded Paganini's *Moto Perpetuo*, in which his speed exceeds that of the teenage Heifetz by a few seconds, but without the riveting core-of-the-note intonation spotlessness of Heifetz. And again, in the Bazzini *Ronde des lutins* record, he seems to be vying deliberately with Heifetz in bravura virtuosity, but though the performance is dazzling, it is not as scrupulously clean as Heifetz's.

In this banner year he made his second recording of Bach's Sonata No. 3 in C Major. Over a five-year period his vision and musicianship grew immensely. The sound became powerful, the pacing admirable, and the technique, outstanding. Later versions evinced even greater maturity of concept, but violinistically (particularly in his final recording of this work during the 1970s), his bowing is softer-grained, less steady, and has become mannered in stroke, especially in the middle-to-tip area.

It is important to categorize Menuhin's solo Bach playing as compared to those among his colleagues who perform the six masterworks in recording with crystalline clarity, jewel-like neatness of detail, and studied elimination of romantic gesture.

These assets may be very impressive, but in live performance, the discriminating listener would soon realize that for all the highly polished violinistic and musical perspicacity involved, this playing is somewhat small-scaled, and in certain instances, somewhat anemic. Not Menuhin's. In his youthful prime, and even for several decades after, his live solo Bach was massive, full-blooded, organ-like in bowed chordal resonance—playing worthy of the feisty spirit who sired 20 children and was once thrown into jail for defying his employer. Menuhin projects the rugged essence of Bach, not merely the prim niceties. His Bach is never dull or academic.

A 1935 recording of the B-minor Solo Partita is technically superb, though the Allemande and Bourrée are somewhat hectic and, on occasion, his vibrato is overdone. In his version of the 1970s, with some echo chamber fortification, the Allemande is notably slower; the Bourrée still brisk in pace, but more relaxed; the overall delivery is not as clean.

In making comparisons between Menuhin's pre-1940 performances and later ones of the same works, it should be emphasized that in Bach, Beethoven, Brahms, and other masterworks in which the need for intellectual force and studied musicianship are at least equal to that of instinctual expressiveness, his playing definitely matured and mellowed with the years. I am not referring, of course, to purely violinistic considerations.

During December 1935, and the years of 1936 and 1938 (no 1937 recordings are listed), Menuhin recorded a host of popular violin vignettes by Kreisler, Sarasate, Wieniawski, Paganini, and similar entertainment fare.

Four pieces recorded January 21, 1936 are prime examples of the Menuhin magic. His vibrato, at 19, has become fiery in its intensity, his incredible spontaneity is at its zenith, as is his audacious penchant for "taking the great leap into space" to achieve singular effects (rather than the comparatively safe, sane, scrupulous virtuosity of most other artists)—a quality limited to the chosen few. Sarasate, Ysaÿe, and Heifetz were among these swashbucklers, and Paganini, too, must certainly have been in this company. Menuhin habitually hits the uppermost stratospheric notes on the G and E-strings with solid-finger electric vibrance instead of resorting to old-fashioned *safer* harmonics.

The three Brahms-Joachim *Hungarian Dances*, No. 7, 17, and 1, are ablaze with Gypsy-like fervor. The optional whip-like arpeggios in No. 1 have some intonation deviation, but the sheer communication of the

Yehudi and Hephzibah Menuhin

music is phenomenal, particularly in No. 7. Sarasate's *Zapateado* scampers and sparkles with crackling left hand finger pizzicatos, crisp staccatos, and sinuous phrasing. *Caprice Basque*, too, is racily stylish in a slightly abbreviated version; the final variation, exceptionally rapid, is not of Heifetz-like perfection. In tonal-oriented discs of this era, Ravel's *Kaddisch* is wonderfully impassioned, though a few intonation blemishes intrude; Wieniawski's *Legende* is dramatically expressive; the Schumann-Kreisler *Romance* in A is provocatively restless in mood, and Granados' *Spanish Dance* No. 5 pulsates with voluptuous gusto.

Among important works, he continued recording his first cycle of Bach solo sonatas and partitas, along with violin-piano sonatas of Bach, Beethoven, Franck, Brahms, Mozart, Enesco, Lekeu, and Pizzetti with Hephzibah, the elder of his two younger sisters. Menuhin has performed and recorded with many pianists during his long career (though seldom with his talented sister, Yaltah), but the Yehudi-Hephzibah duo always represented a special chapter in the collective Menuhin documentation until her lamented premature passing in 1980. Their recording collaboration began in

1933 with Mozart's Sonata (K. 526), and continued in the following year with sonatas by Schumann and Beethoven.

Hephzibah was a splendid pianist, never self-effacing, but fastidiously attuned to her brother's esthetic ethos. It may be true that Yehudi was the guiding spirit of their partnership, but this tends to be the case whenever a divinely gifted, extremely individualistic instrumentalist is paired with another musician. The duo not only projected a handsome physical image, but performed with a mutual rapport of extraordinary polish and poise.

In 1937 Menuhin became involved in a tempest-in-a-teapot fracas over which of three violinists, he, Jelly d'Aranyi, or Georg Kulenkampff (whom Hitler had adopted as his "favorite Aryan violinist") would be the first to re-introduce the long-forgotten Schumann concerto. Kulenkampff, backed by the Nazi government who owned the rights, played it first by a matter of days; Menuhin was next, performing it in Carnegie Hall with piano and shortly after, with the St. Louis Symphony. D'Aranyi, grandniece of Joachim (who claimed she had learned of the work from a seance involving the spirit of Schumann), was third. For all intents and purposes, it was Menuhin who is responsible for giving this Brahmsian, darkly brooding, repetitious, inconsistent, and often beautiful work whatever moderate popularity it attained at the time. He was, after all, on an infinitely higher plateau of artistry than the other two violinists, and his 1938 recording with Barbirolli and the New York Philharmonic exploits nobly the concerto's salubrious points and, to a considerable extent, strengthens the weak ones.

Thus, the golden age of Menuhin's youth began to draw to a close somewhere around the end of the 1930s and the early 1940s. Many professional observers insist that he never again played as well, and that like Elman, after about the first 15 years of his public career, his playing began to deteriorate. If we are speaking solely on the limited level of instrumental expertise, this writer would tend to agree. But then, one can no more write off a man and artist of Menuhin's stature than ignore an elemental force of nature. Let us investigate closely the violinistic and aesthetic attributes of Menuhin as denoted in his prime playing.

The Menuhin sound and style are permeated with sensuality. It has been said that this was a result of his association with the Gypsy-tinged musicality of Enesco, a claim which may have some validity. But if

Menuhin had not possessed a powerful natural predilection for sensuous communication, no one could have taught it to him. The highly individual Menuhin slides and position changes are, at times, especially in romantic music, downright lascivious. Since his early youth he has never been averse to dragging a finger (or fingers) up or down a string in pursuit of febrile expressiveness, and in his best playing, as an integral element of his style, he does this with marvelous effect.

Lord Yehudi is also a distinctively Jewish player in that his ethos is in close communication with the intensely emotive heritage of his ancestors. Individual violinists of Jewish racial lineage have always run the entire gamut from extreme emotionalism to bone-dry academicism. Such violinists as Elman, David Oistrakh and now, Perlman, are also palpably "Jewish" in their musical expressivity, but in a different manner. This trio, each in his own fashion, reflects the popular Chassidic spirit historically associated with Eastern European Yiddish culture. But Menuhin's Jewishness, with its highly-charged, expansive dramatization, mirrors a certain Old Testament, biblical mode of declamation, whether in Bloch, Bartók, Brahms, or Elgar, or for that matter (though to a lesser degree), if he is in complete control, Beethoven, Mozart, and Bach.

For all its sensuality, the Menuhin tone has an ineffably human quality in a strikingly personal way. It is an inimitable sound that places him among the tiny elite company of violinists whose playing cannot be mistaken for that of any other. And, too, there is a conspicuous air of nobility in his interpretations that imparts a patrician aspect to his music-making. This exotic blend of the earthily rhapsodic with the urbanely cultivated has produced a singular artist.

As a child, Menuhin was a sentimental favorite with his audiences who "oo-ed and ah-ed" delightedly at the incongruous spectacle of his tiny physical presence combined

Menuhin, his wife Nola and their children

with his astounding talents. Grown to manhood, his listeners unfailingly sense that he is a magnanimous spirit, a man of many virtues who transcends the limitations of mere violin playing, and are immediately sympathetic to him. Thus he has successfully sustained the Menuhin legend by the force of his personality, if not always by the caliber of his performance.

Reared and trained in the era of Heifetz, and thus irrevocably influenced by the technical standards established by Heifetz, Menuhin, for all his virtuosity, is essentially a stylist in the tradition of Ysaÿe, Kreisler, and Enesco, a big-scaled graphic depictor of musical moods and descriptive narration. Even in his best playing, antiseptic perfection has never been a fetish. Rather, he aims for the heart of the music as he feels it, and is willing to make sacrifices toward that end.

If one were compelled to select the single quality that dominated the playing of his prime early years, it would be spontaneity, which was inexorably linked with the intuitiveness of his interpretations. The failure of his illustrious teachers to drill him properly in technical fundamentals exacerbated the tremendous disparity between his exquisite musical instincts and his impoverished ability to analyze and understand what he was doing, mechanically. Although Menuhin is apparently too charitable to lay the blame where it belongs, he does candidly acknowledge that the time came when "he had to pay the piper." Magidoff, in *Yehudi Menuhin*, refers to this crisis as a period of "retooling." Here we perceive a bona fide genius of international fame on the most exalted level, going through the agonies of purgatory seeking to discover, intellectually, how to play the violin.

During this period he was further bedeviled by the adversities and dissolution of his first marriage. A lesser spirit could easily have foundered in this maelstrom of tribulations, but Menuhin doggedly fought back, though many of his performances courted disaster. I can recall the World War II years in the 1940s when he started his recitals with a grandiose version of "The Star Spangled Banner"; his playing was distressingly beset with technical infirmities and memory lapses.

Menuhin sought help everywhere, but despite all well-intentioned advice, he essentially ended up relying upon his own intelligence and devices. His recordings during the first six or seven years of the 1940s also indicate instrumental retrogression.

Kreisler discussed Menuhin's problems with paternal solicitude, saying: "I foresaw he would have great difficulties. Some of them, fortunately, proved to be rooted not so much within the process of his own development as within those of his listeners who tended to ignore the laws of nature. They expected Yehudi to grow and mature after adolescence at a rate comparable to that of the period preceding it...he has achieved the artist's most difficult goal; he remains himself, he is Yehudi no matter what he plays or however faithfully."

I fear that Kreisler, in his zeal to be generous to a respected colleague, missed the point. Of course Yehudi remained Yehudi "no matter what he plays or how faithfully." This would apply to any powerfully individualistic personality, whether battening on the flow of artistic prosperity or wallowing in the slough of despair. But the fact of the matter is that Menuhin had a critical breakdown—one from which, despite his most prodigious efforts, he has never fully recovered! And this catastrophe had nothing whatsoever to do with what his listeners expected of him; nor was Kreisler really helping him by politely avoiding the reality of the situation.

Menuhin has had to cope with another colossal obstacle; not only has he had to survive the competition of other supreme performers, but he has had to contend with the most onerous rival of all—Yehudi Menuhin and his early reputation. He did survive the pressure of his violinistic competitors if audience attendance, size of fees, and box office clout are any barometer, though his violinistic potential, in the opinion of many firsthand observers, has never been completely fulfilled. He has had to learn to live with the undercurrent of such statements as "What ever happened to Menuhin? He was great, but Enesco ruined him."

Thus far we have perceived Menuhin in three general phases: a pre-teen prodigy, a phenomenal adolescent, and a young adult in the throes of disintegration. Had his incredible instincts been the only assets he possessed, he might have been consigned to oblivion like so many fallen prodigies of lesser eminence. But being, in addition, blessed with a fine intellect with which he began to analyze his technique, he made a recovery that, if not total, was sufficient to ensure a respectable and successful career after a disordered period lasting several years. Now grown out of the prodigal personal naiveté which had blighted his youth (a result of his hothouse upbringing), invigorated by a new stabilizing force in his marriage to Diana Gould, and fortified with philosophies dealing with diet and relaxation, he entered another phase of his development.

Menuhin and his pianist sisters, the late Hephzibah and Yaltah, in the 1950s

Despite his comparative recovery, Menuhin was still harried by problems of instrumental control. Indeed, at times one got the feeling that he was not entirely certain what would come out once he put his finger and bow to the string. Yet, in spite of whatever trepidations he may have had in the ensuing dozen years, he played innumerable concerts that were edifying and provocative. And I think the tendency of many professional violinists to insist upon judging Menuhin in terms of technical consistency, or lack of it, rather than musical communication, was a matter of misplaced emphasis during this period. Yes, there were violinists who played more nearly perfectly, but for all the brilliance and probity of their performance, many among them were never really capable of moving the listener. Even when the surge of Menuhin's spontaneity is unduly repressed by the counteraction of his thinking apparatus, or his inspirational facilities are in temporary eclipse, the listener can always expect an occasional transcendental phrase to breach the cerebral barrier.

In the period from 1947 to the end of the 1950s, Menuhin produced many admirable recordings. Among them are the fiery virtuoso performances of the Vieuxtemps Concertos No. 4 and No. 5; the Brahms concerto with Furtwangler, a virile, expansive interpretation; the intricate Bartók solo sonata which he had commissioned (1959, his second recording) and Concerto No. 2 (1953, his second recording) with Furtwangler, both played with surpassing rhapsodic imagery; a hauntingly beautiful reading of Prokofiev's Sonata No. 1; an elegant, noble rendition of the Beethoven concerto in which he encountered difficulties in the Kreisler third movement cadenza (in a later recording with Klemperer, he omits the offending section); and an exceedingly emotive, almost sybaritic read-

ing of the Lekeu sonata with Gerald Moore. And in the realm of the ludicrous, a recording of Nin's racy *Granadina* which well might be described as orgasmic. Again it must be pointed out that for all their many merits, most of these recordings contain minor technical blemishes.

It is not possible to pinpoint the exact date, but in his early '50s, Menuhin's bow arm began to waver perceptibly in the lower half, a problem which has had a deleterious impact upon other facets of his playing. His early difficulties had involved the evolution of his youthful intuitive performance to that in which his intellect became a decisive factor, a situation that embraced both the psychological and the physical. Menuhin elects not to discuss these problems of his later years in *Unfinished Journey*, though it would appear that the cause is physical. Whether this is the case or not must remain conjecture. If he has a problem of that nature, he prefers to keep it private. In addition to his bowing

Otto Klemperer and Menuhin

insecurities, his intonation has developed an intermittent tendency to be slightly sharp (seldom flat), suggesting some measure of aural disorientation.

These aberrations are infinitely more apparent in Menuhin's live or televised appearances than in recordings. Here it is readily obvious that he is making a Herculean effort to sustain control, but the trembling in the lower half of the bow has become disastrous to a degree where Menuhin's well-wishers are embarrassed. On the positive side, if he happens to play détachés in the upper portion of the bow, such as in Bach's Preludio from the E-major Solo Partita, he is

Menuhin, Ravi Shankar and David Oistrakh are shown together at a United Nations Day concert in 1958

able to negotiate quite well. However, his détaché often projects a sort of abrasive rubbing character. There are times when his live performances are so riddled with imperfections in both hands, that retirement seems the only honorable solution. In any case, listeners who wish to enjoy those remnants of the dwindling Menuhin resources must be prepared to make considerable allowances for the defects of his live concerts.

Oddly, and possibly thanks to the wonders of modern recording engineering, Menuhin has produced some commendable records during this approximate two decades of regression. His Bloch concerto is a model of Hebraic apocalyptic fervor, far more tonally convincing and satisfying than the meritorious pioneering effort of Szigeti. And his Walton, Sibelius, and Delius concertos contain many a glint of the wondrous, deeply felt emotion of his youthful Elgar concerto. His cycle of the complete Mozart concertos, Mendelssohn D-minor, Viotti Nos. 22 and 16 concertos, and Vivaldi's *The Four Seasons* still possess flickers of the surpassing Menuhin buoyancy. The singular timbre of his sound lends eclat to the Neilsen and Bruch No. 2 Concertos, as well as the interesting contemporary concertos of Malcolm Williamson and Lennox Berkeley. The fires of yesteryear have indubitably simmered down; here and there the tone is patently dry, but his mighty expressive capacities are still recurrent. It is painful to hear him in travail, attempting to compensate for his inability to negotiate a phrase properly by indulging in an utterly misplaced and poorly executed emotive slide, especially in a work of immaculate classicism like the Beethoven concerto.

Through the years Menuhin's interests and activities have continued to proliferate; an example is his viola playing. As a violist, in addition to a competent recording of Berlioz's *Harold in Italy*, he has recorded the Walton and Bartók viola concertos. The latter feat has not yet been duplicated at this writing by any of his colleagues, including Zukerman, who has incorporated viola playing as an integral part of his career. The performances, rich in sound and expansively etched, are praiseworthy.

His incursions into Indian music in consort with Ravi Shankar represent another experiment which, if not really establishing a new, permanent violinistic dimension, are both engrossing and entertaining. The jazz duos, with the marvelous "hot fiddler" Stephane Grappelli, in which Menuhin plays *straight* man to Grappelli's *noodlings* in several discs of delicious pop tune arrangements, are tasteful and eminently refreshing. Like Heifetz, Menuhin has the sound and style necessary to play these delightful baubles convincingly.

The Menuhin repertoire is extremely wide and embraces all types of music except the sensationalist avant-garde. Surprisingly, he has never recorded the concertos of Glazunov, the two by Prokofiev, the two by Wieniawski (I heard him play the Wieniawski No. 1 in F-sharp minor with formidable virtuosity in his younger years), or Bruch's *Scottish Fantasy*.

He has had several recital pianists, principal among them Marcel Gazelle and, in addition to Hephzibah, has performed chamber music, recorded and live, with at least a score of artists: pianists Louis Kentner (his brother-in-law), Gerald Moore, Wilhelm Kempff, and Adolf Baller, to mention a few; cellists Maurice Eisenberg, Maurice Gendron, Paul Tortelier, and Gaspar Cassado; violist Rudolf Barshai, flutist Elaine Shaffer, French hornist Alan Civil, and violinists Georges Enesco, Gioconda de Vito, Alberto Lysy, and Nell Gotkovsky.

Menuhin has become a man of many parts: an inveterate cosmopolitan citizen-of-the-world, a knight-errant in the cause of World Peace, a philanthropic altruist who gives generously, often privately, without self-serving fanfare, a staunch advocate of Hatha Yoga for physical health, an investigator into scantily documented cultures (as manifested by his book with Curtis W. Davis, *The Music of Man*), and an outspoken human being, never loath to support his opinions, popular or not, with indefatigable action. At times he has been labeled an unrealistic visionary.

The violinist continues to engage in conducting with certain limited success, and has expended much time and effort in behalf of the younger generation through the Yehudi Menuhin School, a boarding institution for young musical talent in Surrey, England, and the International Menuhin Music Academy in Gstaad, Switzerland.

He has written a volume, *Violin—Six Lessons with Yehudi Menuhin*, a verbose treatise containing some original ideas. He assigns several pages to such matters as breathing, posture, stretching, balancing, and yoga exercises, but only 162 words to so important a subject as vibrato. Essentially, for all of the author's obvious sincerity, it suffers from an intellectualized approach that fails to offer any definitive daily practice regimen from which a student can apply the conflux of Menuhin's precepts in a practical, organized manner. Thus, it remains one of the curiosities of violin pedagogy.

Menuhin, a classic example of the new 20th century breed of violinist-citizen, is rivalled only by Isaac Stern in the articulation of his statements and participation in social and humanitarian projects. True, time-consuming involvement in social, philosophical, and political pursuits often runs counter to a violinist's indispensable need for constant and sufficient practice and undiluted concentration and has, on innumerable occasions, undermined the performances of such activists.

One may wish to applaud many of his non-violinistic exploits, or single out some of them as being naive, non-productive, self-defeating, or even insensitive. However, in the final analysis, Menuhin has proved himself a man of resolution, courage, impeccable intentions, and imagination. And as a violinist he must be reckoned a colossal talent of his time—an artist quite unlike any other, whose best playing has had a devastating appeal to those who *feel* music as well as hear it.

Yehudi Menuhin

Courtesy Lionel Rolfe

Ruggiero Ricci, a spectacular swashbuckler of the fingerboard whose repertoire and recording roster are remarkable in size and scope

Ruggiero Ricci

Around the turn of the 20th century, Jan Kubelik was dubbed "The Heir to Paganini." Later, in our own time, during a career that has spanned more than six decades, Ruggiero Ricci has been called "The Reincarnation of Paganini." When one compares the accurate, but rather stodgy tonally drab playing of Kubelik's Paganini recordings and live concerts, with the explosive character of Ricci's Paganini, it is clear that the Ricci musical muse and often astounding technical facility are far closer to descriptions of the spectacular playing ascribed to the legendary Genoese necromancer than are those of the "Heir."

Yet for all his accomplishments in the performance of Paganini's music, it would be grossly unfair to label Ricci a mere purveyor of fingerboard gymnastics. His vast repertoire and recording repository, as well as his catalogue of air-checks, is as extensive as those of any other stellar violinist, and surpasses most.

Ricci was born July 24, 1918 in San Bruno, California, the third in a poor family of seven children. In a flush of patriotism his trombonist father Pietro named him Woodrow Wilson Rich, though he was actually baptized Roger. Later, persuaded that an Italian-sounding name would be more suitable for a musical career, his father changed the boy's name to Ruggiero Ricci.

Pietro gave Ruggiero his first violin lessons, and though handicapped by a lamentable home environment, the lad by virtue of incessant practice progressed rapidly, and at age eight was taken to play for Louis Persinger. It is said that his audition piece was *The Bluebells of Scotland*. He was immediately accepted as a pupil, and Persinger placed him in the charge of his assistant Elizabeth Lackey. Her kind guidance, together with Persinger's pedagogical expertise, plus

a gruelling regimen of five to six hours of practice a day, worked wonders for the gifted youngster. Concurrently he spent several more hours a day with a private tutor for general education purposes.

In 1928 Pietro appointed Miss Lackey the boy's legal guardian. That same year the ten-year-old made his debut at San Francisco's Scottish Rite Hall with Persinger at the piano, playing a $30 three-quarter size violin. His program featured the Mendelssohn concerto and difficult pieces by Vieuxtemps, Wieniawski, and Saint-Saëns. The audience and critical response was sensational. Only about two years after the phenomenal success of Persinger's other star pupil Menuhin, lightning struck again. Here was yet another bona fide world-class prodigy.

I first heard Ricci in 1931, a Lilliputian figure on the massive stage of the Hollywood Bowl, playing with the Hollywood Bowl Orchestra. At 13 he appeared to be no more than ten. I vividly recall, after breezing through the arduous Vieuxtemps Concerto No. 5, he returned to play several encores with piano accompaniment, among them the Tchaikovsky-Auer Waltz No. 2 from *Serenade* in C, Sarasate's *Introduction and Tarantelle*, and, I believe, *Zapateado*. No doubt about it — here was a blazing violin talent. His tone was large and penetrating, with the intense vibrance necessary for a modern soloist's career, and his technique was already of virtuoso proportions. Purity of line, clarity of phrasing, and neatness of detail characterized his musical approach, and all was delivered with audacious flair. Perhaps there was not the imaginative expressiveness and nobility of spirit of the boy Menuhin, but little Ricci's playing exuded a distinctive aura of its own, rich in the promise of blossoming into extraordinary artistic stature. At that time the boy Ricci already projected, in adolescent form, the best elements that would subsequently characterize the adult Ricci.

Two years previously Ricci had already made his New York debut and was en route to a lucrative career. Consequently, in 1930, his father petitioned to regain custody of the child. His appeal was denied in a California court, but after many legal wranglings Pietro eventually was given custody by the New York Supreme Court. The bitter controversy was extremely upsetting to the boy and his performance was temporarily adversely affected. His older brother Giorgio, who was to become a prominent cellist, was also enmeshed in the imbroglio.

Louis Persinger, teacher of Menuhin, Ricci and a sizeable roster of fine American violinists

During the ensuing years he studied for a while with Mishel Piastro and Paul Stassevich, and in Europe with Georg Kulenkampff, the latter an odd choice after his previous teaching. Later he returned to Persinger. However, as a musician, Ricci is essentially his own man, and his playing contains scant influence by any teacher or national 'school.' He spent several years in intense study, limiting his concerts to European engagements. Returning to the U.S. he appeared in a so-called 'comeback' recital on November 24, 1934, re-igniting a triumphant international concert career that continued until his three years of service in the U.S. Army Air

Force that began in 1942. Stationed at Santa Ana, California, he appeared frequently at army camps as soloist with the top-notch Air Force orchestra which included many of America's finest draft-age musicians.

Ricci had gradually been mastering the solo violin repertoire to an extent scarcely rivalled by any of his colleagues. His postwar debut took place in New York's Town Hall in 1946, presenting an unaccompanied recital featuring Bach's A-minor Partita, Ysaÿe's Sonata, Op. 27, No. 4, Hindemith's Solo Sonata, Op. 31, No. 2, and solo pieces by Paganini, Kreisler, and Wieniawski. The unorthodox concert, splendidly performed, re-established his career. The first to record Paganini's 24 caprices in the original solo version (Renardy's earlier recording contained some abridgements and piano accompaniment), Ricci, at this writing, is the only important violinist to have recorded the entire cycle of the Paganini caprices, the Ysaÿe six solo sonatas, the Bach solo sonatas and partitas, plus the Bartók, Hindemith, and Prokofiev solo sonatas, and just about every important solo work for violin--an achievement of historic import. Like Milstein, Ricci has sometimes practiced difficult passages from piano works to aid in extending his technical skills.

Not long after his first post-war appearance, I heard Ricci in Bruch's *Scottish Fantasy* with the Los Angeles Philharmonic. At that time its regular conductor was Alfred Wallenstein, once a cellist of some note, who was adept at striking terror into the hearts of his orchestra members. In those days symphonic musicians had little or no job security. Wallenstein was capable of giving a creditable accompaniment, and during the 1950s even conducted some recordings with Heifetz. But woe to any young artist whom he did not consider to be among the foremost established soloists. He seemed to enjoy pushing tempos to the extreme in order to bedevil these lesser-known soloists. Apparently Ricci's enforced absence from the stage tempted Wallenstein to pull his usual mean-spirited shenanigans. But no matter how much he pushed the tempo, Ricci stood seemingly unperturbed, his stupendous instrumental agility meeting every challenge, each note crystal clear. Of course the poor *Scottish Fantasy* was savagely victimized, but in my eyes, at least, Ricci had won an edifying moral victory, if not an artistic one.

Ricci plays the magnificent 1713 Stradivarius known as the "ex-Gibson," once owned by Bronislaw Huberman. Though his art bears no tonal or stylistic resemblance whatsoever to that of Huberman, both are short, sturdy men, both communicate exceptional virility in their music-making and persona, both reflect something of the maverick in the independence of their aesthetic priorities, and both have never been loath to indulge in rough, percussive bowing in seeking a desired effect. Through the years I have heard Ricci in live concerts many, many times under a variety of performance conditions. His individual concerts can be incredibly exciting or quite disappointing. At its best, his facility is awesome, his large hands negotiating such intricacies as double-harmonics, fingered octaves, and left-hand pizzicatos with a sovereignty most of his colleagues must sincerely envy. And his up- and down-bow stiff-arm staccatos are remarkable in speed and clarity. But it is his kamikaze attack and propulsion, his willingness to 'go for broke,' that sets his playing of bravura-type music apart from that of violinists who play this genre of composition with comparatively careful circumspection. If Ricci is not in top form, his gymnastic peregrinations can be inexcusably blemished.

It is in the areas of tone production and details of expressivity that Ricci's playing is most controversial. His sonorous and pervasive tone is almost always one of sinewy brilliance in all types of music, though he is ever sensitively alert to dynamic variance. This is dominated by an exceedingly fast vibrato which, in lyricism of emotional bent, often becomes taut to the point of tremulousness and stridency. Thus his playing in songful segments can be brittle and limited in coloristic range, even though his essential emotive thrust is invariably impassioned. Nevertheless, as we can note in more than a few of his recordings, his playing can be tonally compelling in individual melodic statements. But while these statements may be warmly etched, they are not really calculated to touch the listener's heart.

Ricci does not regularly employ expressive slides and position changes as do such overtly sensuous violinists as Kreisler, Heifetz, Menuhin, and Perlman. He does use them sparingly, though not always convincingly. One might characterize his general musical approach as fervent but not patently amorous. Nor do charm and tenderness play a significant role in his interpretive palette. Rather, he can win his audience with the sheer onslaught of his visceral force and demonic virtuosity. His energy and stamina are astounding.

The prodigious Ricci repertoire runs the entire gamut of styles and is wider than those of Milstein, Stern, and Zukerman, among others. In addition to the entire standard repertory, he has performed 20th-century concertos by Ginastera, Jacques Dalcroze, Menotti, Lees, Respighi, Schumann, Goehr, Veerhof, Zimmermann, and von Einem, as well as little-known compositions of Weber, Spohr, Bull, Pizetti, Vecsey, Sibelius, Paganini, Saint-Lubin, and Arnold.

Ricci's complete recordings and air-check performances exceed 500, featuring compositions of every length, quite a few recorded more than once, spanning from 1938 into the 1990s. Naturally an individual survey of them all is not practical.

Among the concertos, his Tchaikovsky is outstanding (London Records; Sir Malcolm Sargent, London Symphony, 1961). Robust and vigorous, it is fortified by Sargent's tuttis in the 'grand manner,' and is cannily paced. The cadenza includes the slashing D-major scale in thirds *á la* the Auer pupils, and several of the other Auer embellishments. Paired with the Tchaikovsky (same conductor and orchestra), Ricci's Dvořák concerto enjoys boldly incisive articulation in the opening movement. The Adagio ma non troppo (complete version) has some instances of tremulous tone; the finale is sportive and firmly disciplined—in all, it is a strong performance, but is marginally inferior to the Tchaikovsky.

The Mendelssohn and Bruch concertos, both with Pierino Gamba and the London Symphony rank with Ricci's best concerto interpretations. His tone production is adequately controlled, and the spirited performances are perceptive and affectionate.

The Goldmark concerto is admirably facile throughout, and the Air (Andante) contains some of his warmest lyric playing (Louis de Fromet, Orchestra of Radio Luxembourg). Lalo's *Symphonie Espagnole* is an interpretation of brilliance and muscularity with a fair measure of Iberian flavor; the first section of the Andante is particularly moving and the finale, agile and playful—paired with a dashing, tonally intense Ravel *Tzigane* in which the left-hand pizzicatos crackle superbly.

Ricci's Glazunov concerto may not be among the most suavely expressive, and one can perceive some G-string forcing (Reinhard Peters, Philharmonia Hungarica, 1975), but, for the most part, his tone is unusually bright and sonorous; the overall delivery is invigorating and well worth hearing despite an orchestra that is a bit raucous. The accompanying Glazunov *Meditation* is imbued with considerable sentiment.

Prokofiev's Concerto No. 2, despite a rather monochromatic beginning and some tonal unevenness in the slow movement, is a genial performance superior to his Concerto No. 1 in which the *misterioso* opening suffers from tremulous sound—the totality is not equal to Ricci's highest standards (Ernest Ansermet, L'Orchestre de la Suisse Romande, London Records). One of his more satisfying recordings is the Brahms Double Concerto partnered by his cellist brother Giorgio. Both Riccis play with strong conviction and excellent instrumental balance (Kurt Masur, New Philharmonia Orchestra). On the flip side Ricci joins Masur and the Leipzig Gewandhaus Orchestra in a sturdy performance of Schumann's dullish *Fantasy*.

The concerto by Benjamin Lees, composed in 1958 and premiered in 1963 by Henryk Szeryng with Erich Leinsdorf and the Boston Symphony, is a worthy, if not memorable, work; the first movement reflects glimmers of Prokofiev's Concerto No. 2. Ricci plays it with surety and dispatch, and handles the occasionally complex rhythmic patterns with incisive articulation (Kazuyoshi Akiyama, American Symphony Orchestra, 1976), as he does the Khachaturian concerto, though one can perceive slight tonal disparities in its exotic slow movement (Anatole Fistoulari, London Philharmonic).

Ricci collaborates with virtuoso bassist Francesco Petracchi in Bottesini's "Grand Duo," a forgettable funfest of cliches written by a composer of questionable talent, well played by two artists who might have spent their time and energy more profitably. Paganini's *Le Streghe* (Witches' Dance) is vintage Ricci, bold and propulsive (original version; even more overwhelming is his Kreisler version with Persinger at the piano [*A Paganini Recital*]). And he 'goes for broke' in Paganini's Concerto No. 4, utilizing an extremely difficult (unnamed) cadenza. His inordinate speed suggests that he might have been striving to outdo Grumiaux's more temperate, thoroughly elegant disc performance (all with Pier Bellugi, Royal Philharmonic).

Paganini's familiar Concerto No. 1, Sauret cadenza, with cogent abridgements of the overlong, simplistic tuttis by Anthony Collins, is a typical Ricci tour-de-force sparked by incredibly rapid stiff-arm staccatos and marvelous propulsion, but lacks the diversity of tonal color and lyric subtleties of several of the best competing recordings. Concerto No. 2 proceeds brilliantly, highlighted by the eruptive finale *La Campanella* (which he also recorded as impressively with piano earlier in his career; all with Collins, London Symphony, London Records). However, his recording of Concerto No. 2 with Max Rudolf and the Cincinnati Symphony

(cadenza by pianist Artur Balsam) is even more exciting, with its hair-rising pristine double-harmonics, percussive left-hand finger pizzicatos, sleek chromatic octaves, and overall satanic thrust. This is the most stunning performance of *La Campanella* (original version) these ears have ever heard. The Decca disc also includes the rather dull Saint-Saëns *Konzertstucke* (Concerto No. 1 in A-major, Op. 20), a work popular in Ysaÿe's era. The performance is acceptable but below Ricci's best playing.

His most recent concerto recording, the Brahms D-major, a work he never recorded until 1991 at age 73, may well be considered an historical landmark inasmuch as it contains 16 different cadenzas, most written by eminent violinists. The basic performance, except for some roughness of bowing in the finale, is thoughtfully phrased and well-ordered; the cadenzas are tossed off immaculately. They include not only the more familiar ones by Joachim, Kreisler, and Heifetz, but provocative free-wheeling inventions by Ysaÿe, Auer, Milstein, Marteau, and Donald Francis Tovey, plus interesting concoctions by Ondriček, Busoni, Busch, Kubelik, Heermann, Kneisel, Singer, and Ricci himself.

Ricci is masterful in most works of the solo repertoire, especially those in which fingerboard heroics play a greater role than lyricism. Notable among them are the Ysaÿe sonatas. It is big-scaled playing throughout, and music made to order for the Ricci drive, facility, and temperament; and he captures convincingly such segments as the pensive mood of Sonata No. 5 opening movement. Particularly exciting is Sonata No. 2 with its masterful use of the "Preludio" from Bach's Solo Partita No. 3 and the "Dies Irae" motif. Sonata No. 6 may be a bit 'breathless' but it contains some astonishing technical flights. Sonatas No. 1, 3, and 4, too, offer extraordinary digital feats.

In Bartók's exceptionally arduous solo sonata, Ricci handles every challenge with aplomb and seeming ease, as he does in Stravinsky's muted, dolorous, dour *Elegie*. In the opinion of David Oistrakh, Prokofiev's solo sonata is an inferior work, and he informed the composer, his good friend, that he would not perform it. Nevertheless, Ricci's incessant verve almost renders it worthwhile. The two short, skilfully-wrought but rather academic Hindemith solo sonatas also fare well in Ricci's hands (London Records).

A group of gymnastic-type solo pieces show him at the zenith of his technical prowess. Some of the most hair-raising are Wieniawski's *La Cadenza* Étude and "Variations on the Austrian National Anthem,"

Paganini's *God Save the Queen* with several variation omissions (which he recorded even more stunningly in a longer version earlier in his career, Persinger at the piano), the *Nel cor piu non mi sento* Variations, with two variations omitted, and Locatelli's *Labyrinth* Caprice (*Bravura*, 1970).

Virtuoso Music for Solo Violin (1979) includes Ernst's horrendously difficult *Last Rose of Summer* Étude, the Ricci arrangements of Tarrega's *Recuerdos de la Alhambra*, a piquant Spanish theme replete with furious string crossings a la Locatelli's *Labyrinth* Caprice, and "Traditional Spanish Ballad," a clever, zestful *oeuvre* familiar to guitar enthusiasts.

His ingenious setting of the Presto from Bach's G-minor Solo Sonata No. 1, combined with the Brahms right and left hand piano transcription, preserves scrupulously the spirit and sanctity of the original. Also outstanding is Saint-Lubin's "Fantasy on Sextet from Lucia," a superficial piece abounding in 'fingerbusting' stretches and string crossings popular in the 19th century, and Vito's *La Cumparsita* tango, a cheeky confection clothed in irksome digital hazards. Ricci also joins the prominent New York violinist David Nadien in Prokofiev's provocative Solo Sonata for Two Violins, a well-tempered, tonally amicable association ("Violin Plus One," 1970).

He has won much-deserved renown for his many live recitals featuring the entire 24 Paganini caprices and for being the first to record the cycle in the 1940s and again in 1969 (with the so-called #25, the *Farewell* caprice, a quasi-march brevity). His recorded versions are brash and eruptive, but in the intervening and later years have been equalled or surpassed in sound quality and spotlessness by younger colleagues.

Early in his career Ricci recorded the Bach Solo Sonata No. 2 and later, the entire cycle. Violinistically the playing is impeccable, though his musical approach, laden with fast 'romantic'-oriented vibrato, is not calculated to appeal to purists. Rhythmically, all is circumspect, and Ricci is attentive to dynamics. The *Chaconne* is, in particular, quite overwhelmed with vibrato, some of it over-taut. Overall the performances lack a sense of spiritual repose and communicate an unidiomatic aura of muscularity. Tempos are thoroughly disciplined, and the dance movements, generally felicitous. The Adagio from the Sonata No. 3 in C-major contains some of his most satisfying playing of the cycle (Decca Records).

In 1978 Ricci recorded 14 Kreisler pieces (*Liebesfreud* and *Liebesleid*, Intercord Records, with pianist Bernhard Kontarsky, in Germany). Lengthy program notes by a Dr. Udo Unger proclaim, among other sweeping generalizations, that Ricci possesses "Kreisler's temperament" and that he has "the same sense as Kreisler for dramatic effects and sentiment." Quite ridiculous! Ricci's playing and that of Kreisler could scarcely be more dissimilar in every area: tonal timbre, use of expressive slides and position changes, bowing techniques, stylistic nuances, personal mannerisms, vibrato usage, etc.. However, Ricci's *Praeludium* and *Allegro* is one of the best on record, and *Liebesfreud* is a clean-cut performance, as is *Menuet* (after Porpora). But in matters of grace, elegance, and sensuousness, Ricci is essentially miscast. Nor could Kreisler ever negotiate many of the bravura pieces played so spellbindingly by Ricci.

He has always had a penchant for seeking out unusual or forgotten works (not all of which deserve exposure or revival), such as the Villa-Lobos "Suite for Voice and Violin" with soprano Lee Venora, in which the violin both parallels the voice and provides rhythmic accompaniment. Others of this ilk are Saint-Saëns's *Fantasy* for Violin and Harpsichord, with harpsichordist Gloria Agostini, one of the French composer's less-inspired works, given in this instance a tonally routine performance (*Violin Plus One*); and Spohr's pleasant but inconsequential "Concertante in G-major for Harp, Violin and Orchestra" (Orchestra of Radio Luxembourg, Louis de Froment, with harpist Susan Mildonia, 1977).

Another unique Ricci contribution is the Sibelius *Complete Works for Violin and Piano* with pianist Sylvia Rabinof, consisting of pieces all under five minutes in length, with the exception of the 10-minute "Sonatina, Op. 80." Written between 1912 and 1929, they make no pretense at profundity. Rather, they embody a wide spectrum of moods, and bear such titles as "Berceuse," "Mazurka," "Valse," "Souvenir," "Minuetto," "Ballade," "Rondino," "Rigaudon," etc. . Several contain knotty technical challenges and radiate the psyche of the North. They are definitely worth knowing, and Ricci and Rabinof perform them with panache. In style, this music has one foot in the late 19th century and one foot in the 20th. ("Masters of the Bow" Studio Series, Discopaedia Records, 1979.)

Least imposing of Ricci's interpretations are his forays into the violin-piano chamber music repertoire. Violinistically, of course, his playing is formidable. But, as can be noted in his Strauss and Dohnanyi sonatas with pianist Ferenc Rados (Hungary, 1963), his Beethoven sonatas with pianist Friedrich Gulda lack the ultimate suavity and sensitivity necessary for this genre of music (London Records).

One of Ricci's most intriguing enterprises is *The Glory of Cremona*, in which he plays 15 melodic-oriented short pieces on 15 exquisite Cremonese violins by Antonio Stradivari, Joseph Guarnerius del Gesù, Andrea and Nicola Amati, Carlo Bergonzi, and Gasparo da Salo (MCA Records, 1964, Leon Pommers, piano). The Strads include the "Spanish," 1677; the "Monasterio," 1719; the "Lafont," 1735; the "Madrileno," 1720; the "Joachim," 1714; the "Rode," 1733; and the "Ernst," 1709. The del Gesùs are the "Plowden," 1735, the "de Bériot," 1744, the "Ex-Vieuxtemps," 1739; and the "Gibson," 1734, the last, Ricci's own instrument. Others are the undated Andrea Amati and da Salo; the 1656 Nicola Amati, and the gorgeous "Constable" of Bergonzi, 1713. This recording, later re-released on CD by *The Strad*, the violin journal, contains some of Ricci's most expressive lyric playing. Noteworthy are Hubay's *Violin Maker of Cremona* (the de Bériot); Tchaikovsky's "Melodie" (the Lafont); the Brahms-Joachim "Hungarian Dance No. 20" (the Joachim); Kabalevsky's "Improvisation" (the Spanish); the Mozart-Friedberg "Adagio" (the Plowden); the Brahms-Joachim "Hungarian Dance No. 19" (the Gibson); and Handel's "Larghetto" (the Madrileno). Of course, while this compendium may be thoroughly entertaining, it cannot deal with one factor extremely important to the violinist— what is the response of each instrument to the player, and to what extent does each instrument help the player to achieve his maximal performance in comparison not only to other supreme Cremonese violins, but to well-made violins of lesser pedigree and age?

The Ricci cornucopia of stylistic bravura music delves deeply into the Sarasate legacy. Perhaps such rarities as *El Canto del Ruisenor* ("Song of the Nightingale"), *Jota de Pablo*, *Jota Aragonesa*, *Adios Montanas Mias*, *Peteneras*, *Canciones Rusas*, and *Zortzico del Iparaguirre* (1978, re-released by EMI Records titled *Sarasate Obras* with pianist Miguel Zanetti) are rather flimsy compositions, even by comparatively simplistic Sarasate standards. But they are part of a noble tradition that should certainly provoke the interest of all violin fanciers. And Ricci plays them with uncommon zest and deference. *Danzas Espanolas*, with Persinger at the piano, incorporates all of the familiar Sarasate pieces. Outstanding among them are *Playera*, warm and sensitively phrased; *Jota Navarra*, vehement; *Spanish Dances* Nos. 7 and 8, spicy and idiomatic; *Caprice Basque*, with the Elman cuts and a breathtaking final page; and *Zigeunerweisen*, one of Ricci's most stylish and satisfying.

Virtuoso Showpieces, with pianist Ernest Lush, includes Achron's *Hebrew Melody*, respectful but not very 'Hebraic'; Wieniawski's *Scherzo-Tarantelle*, one of the best recorded versions of the ubiquitous piece; Vecsey's *Le Vent*, a whirlwind bagatelle; Suk's *Burleska*, scintillating, with discriminating dynamic shadings; Elgar's *La Capricieuse*, a wondrous exhibition of staccato; Hubay's *Le Zephir*, a sparkling trifle; and Bazzini's *Ronde des lutins*, crackling left-hand pizzicatos and flute-like double-harmonics equal or superior to any other recorded version.

Any Ricci recording round-up would be heresy without mention of his Paganini *Moto Perpetuo*, as fast as Heifetz, though not quite as 'dead-center' in intonation; and the absolutely electrifying *I Palpiti* in the finger-twisting Kreisler transcription! (*A Paganini Recital*, Persinger, piano, London Records.)

Ricci is a delightful personality who fairly lives and breathes the violin. The multi-married virtuoso has five children, two sons and three daughters. He has taught at the Juilliard School, Indiana University, the University of Michigan, and is currently a professor at the Mozarteum in Salzburg. Even at age 77 he enjoys an active international concert career, and is highly sought after as a juror for major international competitions.

His art has ever been bounteous in instrumental derring-do and adventurous repertoire. And his championing and performances both of nearly-forgotten 19th-century bravura pieces and of major contemporary works has constituted a significant contribution to our violin heritage.

Henryk Szeryng, a crusading artist of rare musicianship, a virtuoso of Olympian stature, and an illustrious cosmopolitan personality

Henryk Szeryng

It was 1950 in Mexico City when purely by chance I ran into Elias Breeskin, once a star Kneisel pupil whose gambling peccadillos had resulted in his virtual banishment as a professional musician from the United States. "What are the violinistic standards here in Mexico? Are there any really fine players here?" I asked.

"The collective standards are not very high; there is just one violinist who is absolutely first rate, Henryk Szeryng," he replied. I asked him to spell the unfamiliar name.

"How good is he?" I inquired, knowing that Breeskin was not one to confer undeserved kudos on another violinist. "He plays in a different style, but he is generally in the Milstein class," was the surprising answer. How strange, I thought, that such a world-class artist was marooned in the comparatively limited musical climes of Mexico. Fourteen years later I was to become familiar with the Szeryng story, and despite the fact that any long-term artist-critic relationship might be likened to walking through a mine field, we somehow succeeded in maintaining an amicable, if not intimate association for more than 20 years.

Szerying (whose original family name was Serek) was born on September 22, 1918, of Jewish parentage in Zelazowa Wola, a Warsaw suburb which had also been the birthplace of Chopin. His father was a wealthy industrialist, a man of uncommon enterprise. But it was his mother, an accomplished pianist who was responsible for the boy's introduction to music study. At age five she gave him lessons in piano and harmony. His older brother George played the violin, and fascinated by the sound, young Henryk switched to that instrument at seven-and-a-half. However, he retained his love for the piano, which he played competently and, in later years,

relaxed frequently by playing the piano.

His first violin teacher was Maurice Frenkel, once an assistant to Leopold Auer. It was Frenkel who instilled in him a lifelong penchant for purity of intonation and the practicing of double-stops for building and maintaining technical proficiency. The youth's progress was very rapid. Shortly before he was ten he played the Mendelssohn concerto for Bronislaw Huberman, who urged that he be brought to Berlin and Paris for top-level teaching and study in counterpoint and composition. The Polish virtuoso suggested he go to Willy Hess, Carl Flesch, or Jacques Thibaud, in that order. Although he made some progress during the year with Hess, the boy realized that the Hess approach represented an obsolete German methodology, and asked to be taken to Flesch, who had long since established himself as a violin pedagogue with scarcely a peer. He remained with Flesch from 1928 to 1932, receiving two lessons a week, and attending his summer master classes in Baden-Baden. Flesch always sought to preserve the individuality of his pupils, and Szeryng later described Flesch's pedagogy as 'a wonderful science of teaching'. Among the internationally-known violinists who studied with him were Szymon Goldberg, Ida Haendel, Bronislaw Gimpel, Ricardo Odnoposoff, Max Rostal, Henri Temianka, Roman Totenberg, Alma Moodie, and the ill-starred Josef Wolfstahl, Joseph Hassid, and Ginette Neveu who died prematurely. And as we know, it was Szeryng who was destined to become the superstar among the formidable Flesch violin progeny.

Upon his graduation from the Flesch class, Szeryng was soloist with the Warsaw Philharmonic in the Brahms concerto and made his debut in Paris before he was 15. Yet he was not satisfied with his playing, either interpretively or, for that matter, even violinistically. In the course of a single week he heard Thibaud and Kreisler and became entranced with the tonal and emotional impact of their playing. He determined to become inculcated in the French style of playing which they represented, particularly in the area of tonal production and the subtle communication of such elements as charm, elegance, and tenderness. His intent was to study with Thibaud in Paris, but Thibaud's extensive touring schedule made that impossible, so he went to Gabriel Bouillon, a violinist in the Thibaud mold, at the Paris Conservatoire. He remained with Bouillon for only nine months, and in 1937 won the Conservatoire's 'premier prix' for violin. During this period he met and performed with Mlle. Berthelier, daughter of the noted blind violinist Henri Berthelier, a pedagogue much admired by Kreisler around the turn of the century. She introduced him to the then contemporary French sonata repertoire, and Szerying stated "I learned even more about the French musical spirit from her than I did from Bouillon."

With war clouds hovering over Europe, his budding career was suspended, and in 1939 Szeryng went to London. According to the violinist's account he volunteered his services to the Polish government-in-exile and was appointed a liaison officer, serving until 1945. During that time he gave over 300 concerts for allied troops in Europe, Africa, and the Americas. He said that in 1941 he accompanied the exiled Polish premier to Latin America in search of a home for 4,000 Polish refugees displaced by the war; ultimately they were accepted by Mexico. This generosity influenced Szeryng to return to Mexico in 1945, where he was appointed head of the string department at the National University of Mexico. He reorganized its operation, and the following year was granted Mexican citizenship in recognition of his services. However, according to William McDermott, a ballet conductor and pianist who served as his accompanist in Chile and Brazil during the 1942-1946 period, Szeryng's wartime appearances were regularly scheduled concerts in Spain and throughout Latin America under the auspices of Don Ernesto de Quesada, president and founder of Conciertos Daniel. McDermott (who considered Szeryng "the finest violinist of his day") also cites a 1946 Szeryng American debut with Rodzinski and the New York Philharmonic in the Wieniawski Concerto No. 2, which unfortunately received virtually no notice. Irrespective of the conflicting versions, Szeryng came to be regarded as practically a national treasure in Mexico by virtue of his

Szerying with Ernest Ansermet, 1952

superb performances, teaching contributions, and his championing of the music of Mexican composers such as Chavez and Ponce, among others. In 1956 he was accorded the title of Mexico's Cultural Ambassador of Good Will, with the privilege of traveling on a diplomatic passport, an honor in which he took great pride throughout his life. At times, depending on his mood of the moment, he might testily chide an individual for not addressing him as "Ambassador Szeryng."

In 1954 Szeryng's life and career were suddenly altered. Following a concert by Artur Rubinstein in Mexico City, he went to congratulate his compatriot. The next day, after being invited by the celebrated pianist to play for him at his hotel, Szeryng played Bach's solo Partita No. 3 and then several sonata masterworks with the pianist. Rubinstein noted quickly that the violinist was a world-class artist and telephoned five of his managers in various parts of the world, including the formidable impresario Sol Hurok, in order to recommend him. Szeryng's big break had arrived, and he was more than equal to the task. He ultimately established himself as one of the world's top-ranking violinists, plying the international concert circuits ten months of the year. Even with the assistance of Rubinstein his ascent to fame was not easy. Szeryng was already 36 when he met Rubinstein, older even than Ysaÿe (who was 32) when he attained true international recognition. Szeryng strove incessantly to make contacts among cultural activists everywhere and his utter devotion to the violin was never subjugated to non-musical pursuits. In later years he admitted, "there were certain inimical forces which militated against me (he intimated that these 'forces' were generated by a very powerful figure in the American violin world) but I chose to ignore them. This attitude eventually proved to be wise." When speaking about living colleagues he was always kind and generous, and even though his ultimate unassailable international status would have permitted him to say whatever he wished, he studiously avoided critical personal remarks.

His New York debut in 1956 (the debut cited in 'official' accounts) established him as one of the great violinists of the 20th century. He performed in some 65 countries to universal acclaim. The Szeryng repertoire was huge, encompassing an entire range of works from the Baroque composers to those of the present day. Numerous major works were dedicated to him by contemporary composers such as Benjamin Lees, Jean Martinon, Carlos Chavez, Rodolfo Halffter, Xavier Montsalvatge, Ramon Haubenstock-Ramati, Manuel Ponce, Julian Carillo, Peter Frick, Comargo Guarnieri, and Jose Sabre Marraquin. And he played many other 20th century compositions, among them the concertos of Reynaldo Hahn and Stan Golestani, as well as the works of Szymanowski, Bartók, Berg, Prokofiev, and Khachaturian.

In scrutinizing Szeryng's art, one cannot help but marvel at his sovereign instrumental mastery and the depth and perception of his musicianship. Every bar has obviously been penetratingly analyzed, yet there is no vestige whatsoever of academic rigidity. It is playing of iron control and prodigious self-discipline. His interpretations are formulated with the balance and proportion of a master sculptor. Thus the listener need not concentrate merely on the attractiveness of his sound or the technical perfection of his execution, or both, but can revel in the totality of the composition's musical impact. The exactitude of his rhythm and the consistency of his patrician good taste and phrase-making are ever in evidence. His was a cultured art in every sense

of the term, and spiritual repose as well as drive, played a prominent role in his musical communication.

The Szeryng sound could be fervent, if not quite opulent. It was a violin tone that, at its best, radiated a sort of inner warmth calculated to seduce the listener, a compelling sound that marked his special talent. His vibrato was generally of medium speed, though he was capable of generating a surprising degree of intensity in climactic lyric passages—particularly in high notes on the E and G strings. On occasion he used 'on-and-off' vibrato in a single lyric phrase, recalling Oistrakh, but not to any patently annoying extent. The crowning quality of his tonal production was an ability to vary the speed of his vibrato within the framework of his natural physical range of finger oscillation. This enabled him to produce an exceptionally broad palette of colors and shadings. Szeryng was a master of the use of expressive devices (i.e. slides and position changes) and although he employed them far more sparingly than Kreisler, Heifetz, Menuhin, and even Oistrakh in his earlier years, he used them more frequently than, say, Grumiaux, Stern, or Francescatti in Romantic music. His sound was never one-dimensional. On the technical level, the purity of his intonation, the clarity of his passagework, his fanatical devotion to detail, and his sheer finger agility rivaled those of his most eminent colleagues, and surpassed some whose talent for engendering publicity were demonstratively greater than his. In fact, it was rather incredible that Szeryng was able to attain the lengthy top-level career that he did, even with Rubinstein's assistance, considering the lateness of his arrival on the international concert scene, though admittedly he strove valiantly to compensate for this handicap. Most of his leading competitors had already achieved fame either as child prodigies or in their youthful years.

Various observers have charged Szeryng's playing with a certain lack of passion. There is some truth in this allegation as it applies to some of his individual performances, especially in live concerts (albeit seldom in his recordings). Szeryng was not one to exhibit spontaneous outbursts of unbridled passion and, on occasion, his remarkable intellectual powers could dominate a specific interpretation. Nevertheless it would be a serious error to mark him as a 'cool' dispassionate artist. One need only hear his recordings of the "Andante" from Lalo's *Symphonie Espagnole*, with his sultry songfulness, his glowing sound in the Schumann and Khachaturian concertos, and the fervid sentiment of his de Falla *Suite*

Populaire Espagnole, Debussy *La plus que lente*, and Kreisler *Liebesleid*, as well as numerous other performances to realize that in his most emotion-oriented moments Szeryng could display extraordinary intensity of spirit.

Like Heifetz he was completely consecrated to the violin, above all, as the motivating force of his life, and practiced incessantly. Often he would practice the entire morning by himself, rehearse a concerto with an orchestra in the afternoon, perform it in the evening, and then play non-stop at a reception well into the wee hours of the morning until everyone else was exhausted. Frequently, particularly in European concerts, he would perform a Bach concerto, together with the Beethoven and Brahms concertos in a single program. And among other distinctive achievements, it was his ability to play such masterworks with an exalted artistry that placed him above many a formidable tonalist and fingerboard gymnast whose performances in these supreme challenges were less than memorable.

Szeryng did not believe in using a tape recorder in practice. He said, "If by now I cannot detect those things that require improvement without resorting to a tape, I might as well take up another profession." He sought constantly to pinpoint any unsatisfactory spots in his execution and worked at them persistently, and advised students to concentrate on improving their weaknesses rather than continually emphasizing their strengths. He recommended to them, "When it is not possible to practice with violin in hand, for example, when on a plane or train, or just sitting around a pool, use the time to practice mentally."

Fluent in seven languages, his memory was prodigious. In contrast to many famous soloists who have only a cursory knowledge of what goes on in the orchestra, Szeryng knew virtually every note played by every instrument. He regarded spiccato as a rapid, flying détaché. "The closer to the string and the shorter the stroke, the better its quality will be...Staccato is no more or less than a quick series of martelé strokes in one bow. I suggest the student master a crisp martellato. The bites should be very even, first-upbow, then down, reversing the hair. As for the stiff-arm variety, I think one must come by it naturally."

Although Szeryng's hands were of no more than average size and his fourth finger comparatively short, he trained himself to play tenths and double-harmonics with amazing dexterity and accuracy.

In addition to my early problems with stretches, my vibrato, initially, was far from satisfactory. It was gradually improved by learning from the example of my older brother, George. He was a multi-faceted person, who was practically a self-taught violinist.

George studied voice and engineering, and ultimately became an internationally-known lawyer. His time for violin practice was limited, but he had a gift for violin pedagogy. George had a perfect vibrato, a combination of finger, wrist, and forearm which served as a living model for me. He supervised my practice of Flesch's vibrato exercises. My wrist was too stiff, among other things. The remedy proved to be simple. I worked at long notes, starting in the fourth position with my hand anchored against the violin. That helps to increase the flexibility of the wrist. At certain times my vibrato was too slow. This was corrected by placing my first finger on the G-string firmly, and then quickly relaxing to a very light, harmonic touch, up and down like a vertical 'one-finger' trill. The process was repeated with all fingers in all positions. One must start very slowly and gradually, increase the speed of the trill, taking care to keep the thumb from interfering with the process. Also, the thumb must not be pressed against the neck of the violin. In general, I use only moderate finger pressure on the fingerboard. And in long leaps, such as in the first movement of the Brahms concerto, I advocate very little finger pressure. There are times when one finger must help another. In vibrant, lyric playing I prefer using the fourth finger, but if I feel the sound will not be sufficiently rich, I will, like Kreisler and Flesch, use my third finger and even give it some help with my 'loose' second finger. I do not believe in hitting the fingerboard with the left hand. This merely desensitizes the fingertips.

Szeryng never competed in the type of international and regional competitions that have become an integral part of career building. Nevertheless, he was in favor of competitions.

It is good for young players to have to face the music. The exchange of ideas and musical conceptions among contestants is very fruitful. It gratifies me to see the friendships blossoming after a competition. Statesmen and diplomats would do well to catch some of the wonderful spirit that imbues people who consider themselves implacable rivals only a day or two earlier. In itself, winning a competition is not of paramount importance. As we have seen so often, a fourth or fifth prize winner can eventually carve out a career equal to or even surpassing that of the first prize winner.

He thought very highly of the current state of violin art (circa 1987), though he revered the far more personalized playing of the older 20th century generations. In the post-Heifetz generation he had special admiration for Kogan and Perlman.

Thanks to the influx of oriental violinists, violin art has taken another giant leap forward. Our art is also flourishing in those European countries which historically have produced violinists of every calibre. And let us not forget Israel. If one compares the number, quality, and internationalization of orchestral and chamber music string players with those of 80 years ago, the superiority of our era is staggering. A most significant element in modern violinistic life is the proliferation of women competing on equal terms with men in every facet of our art. However, if we compare the soloist superstars of yesteryear with those of our time we must generally separate the pre-Heifetz from post-Heifetz playing. Heifetz raised the instrumental standards enormously. With his advent, such things as faulty intonation, slovenly playing, erratic rhythms, and erroneous textual readings were rendered archaic and no longer tolerated by the critics and public. He established such a high standard that modern players with even moderate ability owe it to themselves to play in tune and, in rhythm, and to observe the composer's dynamic markings.

Szeryng was very sensitive to the modern syndrome of violin-piano sonata (i.e. chamber music) concerts masquerading as violin "recitals." He realized acutely that the concert-going public adored the wonderful stylistic short pieces that in past years had been such a beloved ingredient of the old all-embracing recital programs, and he had his own method of dealing with this problem. He would perform his printed program of three or four varied sonatas. Then, instead of fleeing the audience as is often done by violinists after an arduous sonata outing, or grudgingly offer a single vignette encore, he would play as many as six or seven,

Henryk Szeryng

Courtesy Waltraud Szeryng

cannily taking care that he returned onstage before the enthusiastic audience was exhausted applauding after each number. He performed such works with surpassing stylistic acumen and panache. They could include Locatelli's *Labyrinth Caprice*, the Brahms-Joachim *Hungarian Dance* No. 17, the Bartók *Rumanian Dances*, a Paganini caprice, Kreisler, Sarasate, and Wieniawski pieces, Heifetz transcriptions and others of this genre. In this way he sought to stamp a Szeryng recital as an event that would offer his audience complete musical satisfaction.

Szeryng always allotted as much time to teaching as his concert schedule would permit. Through the years, the number of students who attended his master classes is legion. The science of pedagogy was dear to his heart. However notwithstanding his profound respect for productive teaching, he believed that "truly great violinists are not made, but born with a divine spark." He also believed that every student should receive a complete secular education. "Musical knowledge comprises much more than mere mastery of the instrument."

180

The Szeryng recording roster, begun on Argentine labels in the early 1940s, graduated to the major internationally circulated labels in the middle 1950s, and is equivalent roughly to those of Francescatti, Milstein, and Stern. It numbers about 150 works, large and small, including a number of re-recordings. In quality, they are consistently impressive. Listening to this superlative collection is an exciting violinistic and musical experience, from masterworks to entertaining baubles. They reflect musicality that is definitely individual without being strikingly personalized.

In surveying a sampling of his recordings, Szeryng's early Beethoven concertos with Jacques Thibaud and the Orchestre de la Societé des Concerts du Conservatoire (Monitor Records) is a typical example of his gift for introspection despite a first movement that is a bit urgent. His Joachim cadenza is exceptionally brilliant. The nobility of his style, the sincerity of his phrasing, and his meticulous devotion to minutiae result in an outstanding interpretation, and the variety of his bowings evokes special violinistic interest. A later version with Hans Schmitt-Isserstedt and the London Symphony (Mercury) is marginally more leisurely in the first movement, but the engineering has less violin presence.

The Brahms concerto with Pierre Monteux (RCA Victor, London Symphony, 1959) is another Szeryng triumph validating his position among the violinistic elect. And the awkward bars of the Joachim cadenza are tossed off with a perfection one seldom hears. His Mozart Concerto No. 5, K-219 (Alexander Gibson, New Philharmonia Orchestra, Philips Records) conveys an intensely human aura, over and above mere purity of sound and musical line. It is paired with the Concerto No. 7, K-271a, with excellent cadenzas by Enesco; a superb performance of a controversial work which Szeryng felt was definitely by Mozart except for 16 or 18 bars that were altered by the violinist Eugene Sauzay. Oddly, the engineering is somewhat below par. The Mendelssohn Op. 64 (Antal Dorati, London Symphony, Mercury Records) is crisply articulated and fluently rendered, vitiated by a bit of on-and-off vibrato in the opening movement, and graced by a pixie-ish finale of uncommon agility.

Szeryng's Tchaikovsky concerto may not be the most impassioned on record (Munch, Boston Symphony, RCA-Victrola), but it is consistently warmhearted, technically impeccable, and masterful in nuance. The first movement cadenza incorporates the slashing scale in thirds favored by the Auer pupils plus a dazzling passage in fingered octaves, probably of Szeryng's own device. The finale is laced with subtle effects and is invariably exciting. In all, the interpretation represents disciplined, thoughtful, tasteful musicianship on the highest level. The accompanying Tartini's *Devil's Trill* Sonata with pianist Charles Reiner (Kreisler cadenza), offers superb variety of sound and mood; an elegant delivery. Another Tchaikovsky recording with Dorati (London Symphony, Mercury) approximates the Munch version.

His Sibelius concerto with Gennady Rozhdestvensky (London Symphony, Mercury), is different from most. Though it is a strong, big-scaled interpretation, Szeryng strives for intimacy, clarity, and tenderness rather than melodrama and bombast, and disdains any of the quirky discourse or hysteria occasionally evidenced in the Sibelius of younger generation players. Interesting.

In sheer perfection of passagework and celerity, Szeryng's Lalo *Symphonie Espagnole* compares with those of Heifetz, Oistrakh, and Kogan; the Andante seethes, and though he patiently sustains discipline, his interpretation is imbued with more Iberian sensuousness than many of the other stellar recordings (Walter Hendl, Chicago Symphony, RCA-Victrola, 1964). The Schumann concerto, potentially a dullish work in lesser hands, becomes an exciting vehicle as Szeryng invests its sometimes Brahmsian declamations with razor-sharp insight and tonal allure.

Paganini's Concerto No. 3, resuscitated by Szeryng with the accommodation of Paganini's descendants, is a tuneful, buoyant slice of Paganiniana à la early Rossini, bristling with technical devices recalling Concertos No. 1 and 2. Its inspiration as a composition is not as marked as Concerto No. 1, but it abounds in captivating violinistic derring-do, and is enhanced by a rousing Szeryng cadenza in the spirit of the thorny Sauret cadenza for Concerto No. 1. Szeryng masters its double-harmonics and other hazards with ease, and plays it consistently with aristocratic Italian style. His cadenza for Concerto No. 4 is a bit less brilliant than that for No. 3, but the totality of the performance is outstanding, sparked by an exquisitely lyric slow movement. Concerto No. 1, with the lesser Wilhelmj cadenza, contains many passages infused with ardent songfulness and, of course, is technically immaculate. (The section beginning with the G-string horn-like motif in the finale is omitted.) Szeryng does not incorporate glittering stiff-arm staccatos or emphasize 'kamikaze' flourishes as heard in certain other recordings, but his overall artistry is irresistible. All these works are with Alexander Gibson (London Symphony, Philips; Concerto No. 3, 1971, Nos. 1 and 4, 1976).

Szeryng's recording roster of 20th century works is lengthy and diversified. Among the more popular concertos is the Bartók No. 2. Again he presents an interpretation that differs from the norm by infusing the music with dulcet rather than fiery sound, and probes deeply into its essence without sacrificing its inherent rhapsodic character. The passagework is flawless and never blurred or rushed. It is paired with Rhapsody No. 1 in which he succeeds in conferring an unusual degree of scrupulous order on an opus that so often degenerates into a superficial "Magyar mulligan." (Haitink, Concertgebouw of Amsterdam, Philips.) And he enunciates the hyper-Romantic yearnings of the Berg concerto with graphic euphony. It is accompanied by Jean Martinon's 31-minute Concerto No. 2, a massive work of symphonic scope, dedicated to Szeryng and premiered by him in 1961 with the composer conducting. Skillfully wrought in an eclectic style and superbly orchestrated, it offers many pages of interesting, provocative effects. Yet it lacks the ultimate inspiration that ensures repertorial permanence. The first movement cadenza contains some of Szeryng's most inspired virtuosity. (Kubelik, Symphonie-Orchester des Bayerischen Rundfunks, Deutsche Grammophone.) His Prokofiev Concerto No. 2 is striking in digital clarity and cogently-diversified tonal lustre, and thankfully he does not strive to emulate the Heifetz style as do various other formidable violinists (Rozhdestvensky, London Symphony, Mercury). In the Khatchurian concerto Szeryng is at his zenith in a recording that rivals that of Oistrakh. The intensity of his sound, his boundless energy, his stylistic acumen and exceptional instrumentalism combine to convey stunningly the work's exotic Armenian flavor (Dorati, London Symphony, Mercury).

As a tribute to his Mexican colleagues, he recorded three major concertos: Manuel Ponce's, 31 minutes in length, dedicated to Szeryng in 1942, displays the violinist in 1984 at age 66, with vibrato a bit slackened but virtuosity undiminished. Following a rather uninspired, eclectic opening movement, the Andante cleverly echoes the composer's beguiling *Estrellita* in impressionistic style abetted by an astute usage of double-stops, and the boisterous finale draws heavily upon Mexican

Courtesy Waltraud Szeryng

Szeryng with Paul Paray, 1960

folk music. The 22-minute concerto by Rudolfo Halffter, like Szeryng a European emigré to Mexico, was premiered by Samuel Dushkin in 1942, and revised by Szeryng in 1952. It opens with swift, saucy scales in fifths and is replete with swashes of Iberian motifs, but in toto is not a particularly inspired work (both are with Enrique Batiz and the Royal Philharmonic, EMI-Angel). Best of the trio is Carlos Chavez's massive 37-minute concerto, alive with exciting syncopated rhythms and orchestral flair, intersected by two intensely dramatic different violin soliloquies played magnificently by Szeryng. Surprisingly there is little that is patently Mexican about the work (Chavez, Orquestra Sinfonica Nacional de Mexico, CBS Records).

Szeryng joins cellist Janos Starker in the Brahms Double Concerto with seamless ensemble and meticulously accommodates his bright sound to his partner's light-grained silken tone (Haitink, Concertgebouw of Amsterdam, Philips). He coalesces with Artur Rubinstein and cellist Pierre Fournier in an elegant fellowship featuring the three Brahms trios and the

Schumann Trio in D-minor. Overall this is historic chamber music playing, though one can pinpoint some blandness of cello sound and, occasionally, the engineering has the piano's sonority dominating the strings in densely textured passages.

It is unfortunate that Szeryng and Rubinstein did not record more violin-piano sonatas since their musical and spiritual rapport is so ideally attuned. In fact their unity ranks with the topmost partnerships of the genre. Among these treasures are an exquisite Beethoven *Spring* sonata coupled with a superb *Kreutzer* sonata in which the outer movements sustain a sense of propulsion without regressing into a sprinting 'perpetuum mobile,' and the slow movement variations are super-sensitive (1958, re-released on CD in 1994). A second recording pairs a zestful Beethoven Sonata No. 8 in G (1958) with a bold reading of the Brahms Sonata Op. 78, No. 1 (1961; all are for RCA-Victor). Szeryng is at his most discriminating, and Rubinstein sounds as if he is relishing every bar of the performances. Several Mozart sonatas with pianist Ingrid Haebler are further examples of Szeryng's penchant for the Mozartean muse.

Ever since his cycle of Bach solo sonatas and partitas received France's Grand Prix du Disque in 1954, Szeryng has become increasingly identified with those works. Numerous observers consider his Bach solo performances to be among the most satisfying on record. In listening to more than 15 cycles by leading violinists, I know of none that is more fastidious in detail, discriminating in execution, or reverent in spirit. And violinistically they are equal or superior to any. Like Szigeti, he probes exhaustively into every bar of the music, yet his playing is never dry or over-intellectualized.

His vibrato is always scrupulously moderated and his organ-like triple-stops and chordal playing sound almost as if he were performing with a Baroque bow. His ability to emphasize the melodic note in a chordal pattern whether it is a top, middle, or bass note is awesome. Thus the great Fugues in the G-minor, A-minor, and C-major Sonatas are both jewel-like and sonorous, prodigies of the art of bowing. One may find the G-minor Adagio, the A-minor Grave, and the Largo in the E-major Partitas slightly pale in sound, particularly in the 1954 cycle (less so in his later version). But this is more than compensated for by his verve and buoyancy in the numerous dance segments. One could cite each movement and find provocative nuances deserving of mention. And the Szeryng détachés convey a marked lilt

of individual disposition. (Odyssey, Deutsche Grammophon.) Eminently augmenting the recordings is Szeryng's edition of these solo works which include comprehensive fingerings, bowings, and dynamic markings, plus abundant suggestions on execution—an invaluable contribution to Bach study and performance.

Like his most eminent colleagues, Szeryng was a master stylist in a cornucopia of lyric and technical short pieces. Two collections on the Everest label with pianist Jasso Janopoulo offer generous helpings of these vignettes. Outstanding in *Henryk Szeryng Plays Music of Spain and Mexico* are Ramon Serratos's *Etude en Octaves*, a hair-raising octave exercise; Ponce's *Estrellita*, which rivals that of Grumiaux in delectable sound; Ponce's three-part *Sonata Breve*, a well-crafted modern vehicle with a particularly interesting piano part, deserving of frequent performance; Sarasate's *Romanza Andaluza,* rich in G-string sound and languorous statement; an audacious tossing off of the Spaniard's *Zapateado*; Jose Sabre Marroquin's *Berceuse*, a lovely Mexican melody with lilting triplets; and Halffter's *Pastorale*, a challenging, worthwhile contemporary piece. Szeryng's superb de Falla-Kochanski *Suite Populaire Espagnole* is also included.

His *The Virtuoso Violin* contains (in part) a Wieniawski *Scherzo Tarantelle*, which rivals that of Heifetz in speed and "dead-center" intonation; an elegant delivery of Francescatti's *Variation on a Theme of Corelli by Tartini*; a sparkling performance of Auer's excellent setting of Paganini's Caprice No. 24; and Vitali's *Chaconne* handled with a distinctive classical approach.

Continuing the dessert delicacies is *Treasures for the Violin* with pianist Charles Reiner, sparked by a galvanic performance of Locatelli's *Labyrinth Caprice*, piano part by Ferdinand David; the Brahms-Joachim *Hungarian Dance* No. 17, liberally sprinkled with paprika; a melting Gluck-Kreisler *Mélodie*; an absolutely luscious Debussy, *La plus que lente*; and whirlwind stints of Nováček's *Perpetuum Mobile* and Rimsky-Korsakov's *Flight of the Bumblebee*, the latter highly charged with some spectacular spiccatos (Mercury Records).

Quite a few fine violinists (and others "not so fine") have made recordings consisting of all-Kreisler compositions and transcriptions. *Henryk Szeryng Plays Kreisler* (pianist Reiner, Mercury) is one of the most stimulating among them. Szeryng is conversant with all the Kreisler expressive devices (slides, position changes, etc.) and employs just enough of them to imbue the music with Kreislerian tintings, yet he stubbornly remains "his own man" in interpretations that are quite individual. Among them are a movingly tender *Liebesleid*, a *Recitative* and *Scherzo Caprice* in which the *Recitative* has extraordinary introspection as well as tonal beauty, a *Caprice Viennois* that exudes a broad gamut of color and shadings, an endearing *Schön Rosmarin*, a noble *Rondino on a Theme of Beethoven* and *Allegretto in the Style of Boccherini*, a highly personalized *Chanson Louis XIII et Pavane*, an amorous *Old Refrain*, and oddly, a *Liebesfreud* that is somewhat square-cut and heavy-handed.

In historic perspective, it would be a signal loss to the treasure-trove of violin art if the bulk of Szeryng recordings were not re-released on CD and made available to the present and upcoming generations.

I first met Szeryng in 1964 and maintained intermittent contact with him until his untimely death on March 3, 1988 in Kassel (then West Germany), prior to a scheduled concert in Brussels, after which he was to begin another American tour. He was an enigmatic man; much about his private life was secretive, even to his colleagues. Yet in company he was a larger-than-life figure; he could be generous, overbearing, eccentric, high-spirited, impassive, courtly, pretentious, amiable, or crusty, often depending more on his mood of the moment than the objective situation. A confirmed imbiber, he also drank wine with nearly every meal in the French tradition, but this never affected his performance. After he married Waltraud von Neviges, a lady of Continental elegance and warm disposition, in 1984, he seemed comparatively more at peace with himself and the world. I always felt that his Herculean uphill struggle to gain the recognition he so richly deserved played a significant role in fashioning his many-sided personality. Although Szeryng ultimately attained a top-level international career, he never quite achieved the public acclamation that his artistry merited, particularly in the United States.

He had been a pupil of Nadia Boulanger in composition and produced a violin-piano sonata, a *Prelude in the Old Style*, and several other pieces which he described as "not too bad."

Szeryng owned many instruments through the years; two Stradivari, one Andrea Guarneri, a fine Gofriller, two Vuillaumes (one of which is a copy of the 'Messiah' Strad) and, of course, the magnificent 1743 "Le duc" Guarnerius del Gesù. Except for the Gesù, Szeryng gave all of his instruments away. Two of his violins went to younger colleagues—Shlomo Mintz, who studied with him for two summers in Geneva, and Espin Yepez of Ecuador, a former teaching assistant. Another was presented to the city of Warsaw, and the 'Messiah" Vuillaume was given to the Prince Sovereign of Monaco. The Andrea Guarneri was given to Mexico City and, in an event which received international news coverage, Szeryng donated his 1734 'Hercules' Strad to Mayor Teddy Kollek of Jerusalem in 1972, as a special token of friendship to that nation. The 'Hercules' is presently used alternately by the co-concertmasters of the Israel Philharmonic. Szeryng's generosity in this respect was monumental. During his final period, in addition to the "Le duc," he played on two French violins, one by Pierre Hel made in 1922 and the other by Jean Bauer, a contemporary maker.

Fortunately for posterity, Szeryng left a legacy of more than 25 video tapes filmed in the United States, Eastern and Western Europe, Japan, Australia, and Mexico, encompassing both recitals and solo appearances with orchestra. His honors include six *Grand Prix du Disque* awards, the Officer's Cross of France's Legion of Honor (1984), the Polania Restitute Order (1956), the Golden Medals of Paris and Jerusalem, the Gran Premio of Mexico (1979), the Commander's Cross of St. Charles from the Prince Sovereign of Monaco, plus a host of decorations from other countries around the world, including an honorary Doctorate from Georgetown University in Washington D.C. In recognition of his contributions to young people, he was named Honorary President of the World's *Jeunesses Musicales*.

When asked about what he would do after he was 70, Szeryng replied,

> I plan to curtail my heavy concert schedule. Naturally I would not want to 'apply the brakes' too suddenly, but when the time comes for each of us, we should be prepared to leave. I believe destiny helps determine the proper time. I am eagerly awaiting the day when I shall have the leisure time to play more and more chamber music on the concert stages. One of the greatest joys of my life was playing chamber music with Rubinstein and Fournier. There is so much fine music waiting to be discovered, one could not possibly exhaust this wealth in a lifetime. I also hope to have more time for teaching, visiting museums, being with my wife and children, even walking the dog.

Unfortunately his 70th birthday never came to pass.

One of Szeryng's greatest satisfactions and pleasures was tracking down lost compositions. It was in such research that he discovered and resuscitated Paganini's Concerto No. 3 in E major. When he spoke of this planned future research, his eyes lit up. In recalling the most memorable concerts of his life, he said: "There were so many that were truly memorable. But offhand I can think of two that were particularly inspirational—one which I performed in 1967 with Wolfgang Sawallisch and the Vienna symphony on United Nations Day at the U.N., and the other when I played in *The Garden of Prayers* on the Mount of Olives in Jerusalem." Mme. Szeryng has dedicated herself to keeping her husband's memory alive by creating the Henryk Szeryng Career Award, based in Monaco. The event, supported by a panel of noted international musicians and impresarios, takes place every three years, and the single award consists of two years of concert appearances procured and sponsored by the organization. There is also a competition in Toluca, Mexico, dedicated to Szeryng.

Throughout his career Szeryng consistently expressed his concern for the welfare of humanity, and contributed his art to that end whenever and wherever he could. Perhaps the most fitting conclusion to this account of the eminent violinist would be to quote his sentiments as printed in the announcement of his interment in Monaco: "I consider music as the noblest language, bringing comfort, joy, inspiration and peace to mankind. I think that it's vital that peace be preserved, and if music can help—then let's have music!"

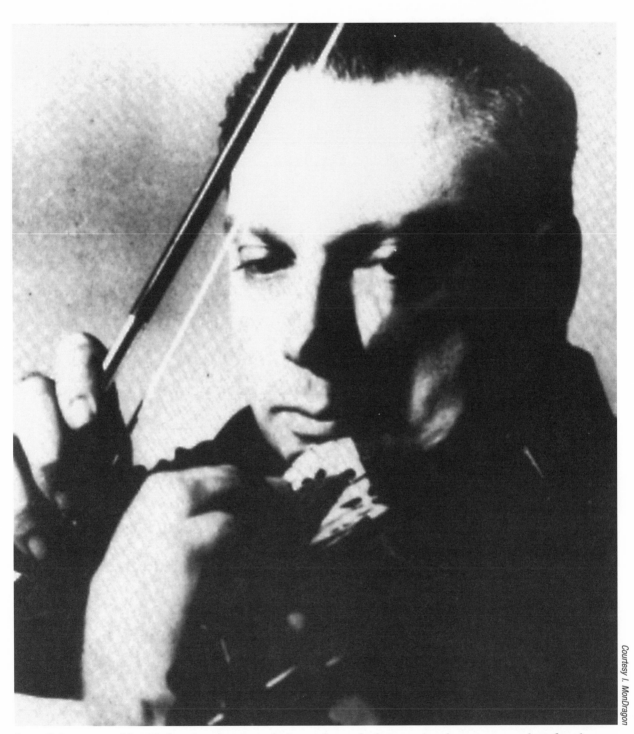

Isaac Stern, a superbly gifted artist whose best playing embraces both impassioned utterances and profound musical introspection

Isaac Stern

The decade of the 1930s was graced by some of the best violin playing in the history of the art. It was nearly impossible for a new young artist to break into the hierarchy represented by Kreisler, Elman, Heifetz, Menuhin, Milstein, Szigeti, Ricci and, by 1939, Francescatti. Yet as always, dauntless young hopefuls sought to try their wings in an effort to join the ranks of the masters.

One of these was Isaac Stern. His first bid for an international career took place in 1937 in New York. I recall his nationwide broadcast which featured the final movement of Bruch's G-minor Concerto, played with heroic thrust and tonal opulence. At the time I felt that this young man possessed qualities of a top-level violinist and artist. But he was not destined to be a world-acclaimed boy prodigy as was Menuhin, or even Ricci. His brilliant Carnegie Hall recital in 1943 sparked what eventually blossomed into one of the most significant and widely publicized instrumental careers of the 20th century.

Stern's official birthdate is given as July 21, 1920; the place, Kriminiecz, in the Soviet Ukraine, a town about 350 miles northwest of Odessa. However, his early teacher Robert Pollak, in his article published in the *Tokyo Evening News*, September 1953, stated: "One day in the fall of 1926, a short time after I had been appointed head of the violin department at the San Francisco Conservatory of Music, a husky little boy of eight came to my class for an audition. Technically he was not very advanced, but I recognized immediately his outstanding talent." I knew Pollak to be a highly intelligent, honorable person, a man not likely to forget the year he received a respectable conservatory position. Nor does it appear probable that Stern's parents would represent him as being eight if he were only six. Gdal

Saleski cites Stern as having taken piano lessons at age six, then switching to the violin at eight. Perhaps a Stern autobiography will one day settle the point.

Stern's father was a painter and his mother studied singing at the Imperial Conservatory in St. Petersburg. They emigrated to San Francisco before Isaac was one year old. For about four years the boy studied with Pollak, whose roots and musical background originated in Vienna. From ages 12 to 16 he studied with Naoum Blinder, a former concertmaster of the San Francisco Symphony, and himself a pupil of Alexander Fidelman and Adolf Brodsky in Russia. Stern credits Blinder as his principal teacher who taught him, among other things, to teach himself. At 15 he played the Bach Double Concerto with Blinder and the San Francisco Symphony. Veteran San Franciscans, however, report that he had appeared as soloist with this orchestra under Willy Vandenburg several years earlier. He also studied for a brief period with Louis Persinger.

Through the years Stern has become a leading figure of violin art, a superlative instrumentalist and musician, sponsor and mentor of such younger talents as Perlman, Zukerman, Mintz, and others, and a most provocative personality who has evoked both mass adoration and, in certain quarters, bitter animosity. As one of the most influential forces on the international music scene, he is a fiery, immensely convincing speaker and proponent of humanitarian and cultural causes, celebrated as the savior of Carnegie Hall in 1960 and for his efforts toward establishing the National Endowment for the Arts in 1964. An intimate friend of many prominent political, social, and economic leaders, Stern is an indefatigable champion of the welfare of Israel and is intensely proud of his Jewish heritage. He still refuses to play in Germany as a protest against the Holocaust. Together with his activities in support of many Israeli musical organizations, he has been the prime force behind the America-Israel Foundation which continues to provide scholarships for talented young Israelis. In addition to his eminence as a soloist, Stern is a chamber music artist of prodigious stature, whose trio with pianist Eugene Istomin and cellist Leonard Rose performed with distinction for many years, both in concerts and recordings. He also participates often in chamber music events with his younger colleagues.

Stern appeared in the film *Tonight We Sing* (playing the role of Ysaÿe), based on the life of the impresario Sol Hurok, his longtime manager, and was heard as the soundtrack violinist in *Humoresque*, starring John Garfield and Joan Crawford, and in the *Fiddler on the Roof* film. The 1981 film *From Mao to Mozart*, a report of Stern's 1979 sojourn in China, won an Oscar for best documentary.

Once married to the ballerina Nora Kaye, Stern was married for over 40 years to his second wife Vera, who was intimately involved in her husband's activities. They have three children, Shira, Michael, and David. They are now divorced. He played alternately on a magnificent 1740 Guarnarius del Gesù, which once belonged to Ysaÿe, and on the 1737 "Vicomte de Panette" del Gesù. (He sold the latter in 1994.)

Stern's playing, at its best, combines the traditions of the pre-Soviet Russian School, with its emphasis on beauty of tone and fervent individuality of interpretation, with the lofty ideals of musical integrity as inherited from Joachim through Szigeti. His hands, while not comparable in immensity to those of Perlman, are large and fleshy, and the character of his sound is as solid and robust as his presence. It is a sound that hearkens back to the rapturous outpourings of Kreisler and Heifetz, but is not as voluptuous and vibrant. However, in his younger years Stern could "turn on the heat" through his impulse-type vibrato to an extent that few of his colleagues could equal or surpass. It is a sound impelled genuinely by the fingertip, as opposed to the current prevalence of slower, wrist-motivated oscillations which tend to produce tone that is sweet and lovely, but not eminently vital. Stern's tone, while powerful and rich, is not as highly personalized as that of Kreisler, Heifetz, Menuhin, or Oistrakh. But by means of his masterful use and control of vibrato, Stern's range of tonal color surpasses that of all but a few of his colleagues. He uses vibrato not merely as a device to

bewitch the ear, but as a means of instilling maximal diversity in his interpretations. Thus he is able to project the darker hues of Brahms and Bartók as readily as the lighter textures of Mendelssohn and Mozart. Even when his vibrato is not in force, his tone retains a sense of life, and is never subject to the "on-and-off" aberrations of Oistrakh's imitators. He takes scrupulous care to adjust the type and speed of his vibrato to whatever style of music he is performing.

Though Stern has more digital facility than some may think, he was never a bravura technician who publicly featured or specialized in the finger-twisting escapades of Paganini, Ernst, or even Vieuxtemps. Nevertheless, in his rise to eminence he vanquished a long list of gifted young musicians, some of them far more accomplished in fingerboard gymnastics. None, however, had the overall intellectual force, perseverance, and sheer willpower of Stern; the authoritative virility of sound that is the hallmark of the truly sovereign violinists; or the mastery of the most musically significant styles which distinguishes the violinist-musician from the more limited violinist-virtuoso. Nor for that matter did they possess, as Stern does, those elusive ingredients of inherent musicality and spiritual elevation that separate a great violinist from a great artist. Throughout his adult career he has refused to force his hand into unnatural positions for the sake of performing gymnastic feats, choosing rather to develop into an interpretive artist. Consequently his handling of sonatas and music stressing introspection is decidedly more profound and satisfying than that of most violinists whose playing gravitates toward superficial tour de force exploits. Stern, if he wished, could play with a lush, heightened romanticism that Szigeti could never produce tonally, and yet could accommodate himself to the most exacting demands of musical and stylistic rectitude. But he became so enamored of "turning off the emotion", that many of his concerts, especially from 1960 to 1970, began to approximate cerebral musical seminars. This never failed to delight those of his listeners who equate dull, lusterless playing with good musicianship.

Stern's brawny, yet utterly flexible bow arm is one of the most dependable components of his violinistic arsenal, and functions sturdily even into his later years, producing large-scaled sonority. He possesses a crisp spiccato and both the normal and stiff-arm staccato. The latter enabled him, in his younger years, to play Dinicu's *Hora Staccato* (which Heifetz had transcribed and popularized), and although his rapid-fire staccato

The young Stern

was lighter and had less bite than that of Heifetz (or, for that matter, the late Michael Rabin), it was nonetheless impressive.

In sostenuto strokes Stern uses as much of the bow hair as possible, whether playing forte or pianissimo. His bow grip is centered on a circle of the middle finger and thumb, and is not dominated by the pressure and extension of the forefinger in the manner of the Russian Auer pupils. He describes his own bow arm as "rather heavy," and does not keep it inordinately high.

Stern advocates strong finger pressure in the left hand for optimum tone production. His fingers can be heard hitting the finger board in many recordings. But his trill, though rapid, is soft in texture and neither hard in impact nor electric in speed. And while more than a few fine violinists are ill at ease in lyric octaves of first and fourth finger combination, Stern plays them easily, cleanly, and resonantly. He uses a shoulder pad, which is unusual, considering the shortness of his neck. In memorizing, he has stated that he prefers to rely on a mental picture of the score, rather than on finger patterns learned by rote.

Expressive slides and position changes do not play as major a role in his performance as they do with Kreisler, Heifetz, Menuhin, or Perlman, but he does employ them frequently in his most ardent playing in the romantic repertoire, and almost always with mastery. One may hear him deliver a Mozart or Bach concerto with scarcely a finger portamento and then be nonplussed when he plays the final bars of the Franck sonata *Recitativo-Fantasia* movement with two rather gross downward slides. However, his innate good taste has but rarely yielded to such abuses, and his use of expressive slides has generally declined in his later years.

Stern has been a prime force in the changes that have taken place in program building since the Kreisler-Elman-Heifetz era. In carrying on a trend toward "good" music as emphasized by Szigeti, his influence has helped to transform the all-embracing violin recital of yesteryear into violin-piano chamber music concerts. Whether he did this out of a musical conviction, for technical convenience (to avoid the drudgery of constant practice demanded by difficult showpieces), or for both reasons, the modern violin recital has lost a great deal of its luster, charm, and sheer entertainment. Unfortunately, in order to conform to this trend, we hear many violin virtuosos programming sonata masterworks for which they are intellectually and musically unsuited. And all too often in these chamber music affairs (including Stern's), the duo sonatas are played one-sidely as violin solos, with a hired pianist who subjugates his own musical personality to that of his employer. Like most of the supreme violinists, Stern candidly defers to the supremacy of Heifetz and has stated that the present time will be known historically as the Heifetz era. Yet he was never loathe to compete with Heifetz in many of the choice Heifetz masterworks, and even in such showpieces as Sarasate's *Zigeunerweisen* and the Bizet-Waxman *Carmen Fantasy*.

Many listeners have preferred Stern's well-ordered, sagacious interpretations to the extreme individuality of the Heifetz sound and style, his super-speed, and the aloofness of his personality. Or for that matter, they have preferred Stern's playing to the technical waywardness of the mature Menuhin; the mellifluous but rather restricted tonal palette of Francescatti; the scintillating but scarcely introspective virtuosity of Milstein; or the intellectual emphasis of Szigeti. To them, Stern has represented the consummate violinist-musician who possesses some of the finest characteristics of each plus a definitive personality of his own. On the other hand, it has been frequently pointed out that Stern does not achieve the thrilling vibrance, hair-raising articulation, and perfection of Heifetz; the daring imagination and spontaneity of Menuhin (at his best); the heartfelt expressiveness of Oistrakh; the tonal seductiveness of Kreisler and Elman; or the amazing agility and manual coordination of Milstein. Be that as it may, Stern has fully earned his place among the hierarchy. With the appearance of Oistrakh in the Western world, Stern's position as the leading competitor to Heifetz (after 1955) in mass popular acclaim was marginally sidetracked by the Soviet star's immense success, although the two became intimate friends and recorded duos together. The increasing inconsistency of Stern's concert playing due to his aversion to daily practice (as opposed to Oistrakh's meticulous preparation), did not abet his critical reputation. Many, particularly knowledgeable professionals, resented Stern's instrumental laxity and felt it was unfair, or even dishonest, for a modern artist to misuse his public by offering an inferior performance at top box office prices.

With the passing of the years Stern's playing took on some new characteristics, some say as a result of his association with the aged Pablo Casals. The hot-blooded scion of the Russian-Jewish tradition, while always a disciplined artist, began to intellectualize to such a degree that his performances took on an aura of preciousness (i.e. underplaying), especially in music of the classical repertoire. In fact, at times one would think that he was hoarding his energy for the next concert, afraid of exhausting all his resources in a single appearance, a single work, or even a single movement of a work. This was tantamount to a form of sophistication bordering on the blasé. One of the deleterious side effects of this musical way of life has been its effect upon impressionable young players who do not possess Stern's strengths but are prone to emulate his musical mannerisms. For a violinist who probably was beset by instrumental or musical idiosyncrasies to a lesser extent than any of his colleagues, this trend represented a major turning point in his art. And when, following his tremendously publicized Carnegie Hall exploits, Stern, the *violinist*, became Stern, the *institution*, the instrumental consistency of his performances began to decline.

Stern's career as a public figure and spokesman expanded enormously. An anecdote widely circulated runs as follows: A man meets a friend and says: "I heard Isaac Stern last night." "Yeah?" quips the friend, "What did he have to say?" But more seriously, during the last couple of decades when Stern comes to town for a concert, invariably the first thing a professional will ask is: "Has Isaac been practicing?" Professionals greatly respect Stern's best playing, but many no longer buy tickets to his performances. This is unfortunate, for it may be that Stern *did* take time to practice and played impressively. Of course, irrespective of what professionals do or think, a Stern appearance practically guarantees a capacity audience and a tumultuous ovation whether he plays well or is shamefully off-form.

Unlike Menuhin, whose instrumental vicissitudes in his later years seem due to a complex of problems, Stern's basic instrumentalism, while not equal to that of his earlier years, is still potent in his best playing. His technical vagaries are generally the result of insufficient practice. In his younger years he prepared conscientiously for each appearance. But his lifestyle now precludes his being a slave to the instrument as were Heifetz and Milstein. Stern's extramusical activities have doubtless prevented him from realizing the fullest potential of his talent.

In contrast to nearly all of his colleagues and competitors who, at once time or another, have performed works for which they are technically, musically, or temperamentally unsuited, Stern is careful to play only those compositions for which he has complete musical affinity and instrumental equipment. He has deviated rarely from this principle, hence he success-

Stern at the Hollywood Bowl

fully has avoided criticism in this regard. This reperto-rial discrimination naturally extends to his recordings. The low-keyed oversophistication that regularly vitiates, at least in part, even the best of his latter-day concerts, is only minimally evident in his meticulously edited recordings. And unlike Oistrakh's recordings, many of which were produced under inferior Soviet engineer-ing conditions (i.e. those early recordings of works that were never rerecorded in the West), the body of Stern's

recordings, including the early 78 RPM and mono 33 RPM efforts, are well produced.

In the totally uncritical section on Stern in Boris Schwartz's *Great Masters of the Violin*, it is asserted that "His recorded repertoire is immense; there is hardly a piece in the violin literature that he has not put on a disc." This is clearly incorrect: Stern's disc inventory comprises about 160 works, large and small, including rerecordings and chamber music, considerably fewer than that of Heifetz, Menuhin, Oistrakh and, by now, Perlman and Ricci. Admittedly, his colleagues have recorded far more short and medium-length pieces to inflate the total. But what is really significant in rebutting Schwartz's claim is the fact that Stern had never (at the time of Schwartz's publication) recorded any of the Bach solo sonatas and partitas, or a single Paganini caprice, which are essential components of basic violinistics, whether or not Stern finds them amenable to his tastes or technical convenience. Stern has recorded only one of the ten Beethoven violin-piano sonatas, and none of the Mozart sonatas. (Stern has never recorded the Bach solo sonatas or the complete Beethoven sonata cycles. If now, in his mid-70s, he elects to do so, it will scarcely represent his playing at its peak.) Nor has he recorded the concertos of Elgar, Walton, Vieuxtemps, Spohr (*Gesangsszene*), Bruch's *Scottish Fantasy* and Concerto No. 2, Glazunov, Bartók's solo sonata, Tartini's *Devil's Trill* Sonata, or many other short and medium-length items considered part and parcel of the standard repertoire. He has recorded only two Kreisler brevities, none of the sparkling showpieces by Wieniawski or Vieuxtemps, and only two by Sarasate. Stern's latter-day programs, generally overweighted with sonatas, do not often include Bach solo works, although I once heard him play a satisfactory large-scaled performance of the *Chaconne*, and recently, a spotty rendition of the Solo Sonata No. 1 in G-minor. Whereas Heifetz chose to record the Bach solo cycle and incurred much criticism for what many observers feel is an over-personalized performance of music alien to his temperament, Stern avoided interpretive controversy or competition with his peers in these monumental works by simply choosing not to record them at all when he was in his prime, technically.

Stern did not have the opportunity to record many short pieces in his youth, as did the boy prodigies Heifetz and Menuhin. But the best of those he recorded in maturity (which total about 40), are played with subtlety, sincerity, and affection, in the tradition of earlier artists. And when he chooses to include as encores such vignettes as the Wagner-Wilhelmj *Albumblatt* or Kriesler's *Liebesleid* and *Schön Rosmarin*, even in his veteran years, he played them with a tonal lustre and a charm unheard in the younger generation, except perhaps by Perlman. Some of his choice efforts in this genre were recorded fairly early in his career with pianist Alexander Žakin, and focus upon pieces he played habitually in his concerts. In addition to those

named above, Sarasate's *Caprice Basque* (omitting the double-stop theme repetition we hear, as on the old Elman disc) is both stylish and audacious; Nováček's *Perpetuum Mobile* is spotless; the Dvořák-Kreisler *Slavonic Dance* No. 2 in E-minor is relaxed in tonal intensity but amiably expressive; Milhaud's *Tijuca* from *Saudades do Brazil* lilts idiomatically; the Prokofiev-Grunes *Danse des jeunes Antillaises* is compellingly bittersweet, and *Masques*, grandiloquently sprightly. In Bloch's *Nigun* from the *Baal Shem* Suite, the climactic passages are fiery, dramatic, and soulfully "Jewish."

Less successful is a 1963 vignette collection with Milton Katims and the Columbia Symphony, orchestral arrangements by Arthur Harris. The title piece, Tchaikovsky's *None But the Lonely Heart*, is tonally inconsistent; the Brahms *Hungarian Dance* No. 5 finds the violin line cluttered by the orchestral setting, as are Copland's *Hoedown* from *Rodeo*, Benjamin's *Jamaican Rumba*, and Dvořák's *Humoresque*, though the last is graced with some exceptional double-stop playing. His Rimsky-Korsakov *Flight of the Bumble Bee* is appreciably less clean than those of Heifetz and Milstein, Gershwin's *Bess, You is My Woman Now*, Foster's *Jeannie With the Light Brown Hair* (much like the Heifetz transcription), and a somewhat simplistic arrangement of Schubert's *Ave Maria* are all played with warmth and affection, but these pieces essentially belong to Heifetz and are best passed over by other violinists. The choice item of the group is a personalized interpretation of Kreisler's *Liebesleid*.

A 1973 brevity compilation with Frank Brieff and the Columbia Symphony, also with orchestral arrangements by Arthur Harris, finds most, but not all of the settings less overblown than on the 1963 disc, and more amenable to the nature of the material. Tchaikovsky's *Serenade Melancholique* is heartfelt, with a sumptuous G string sound not equalled by the more sweet-toned, wrist-vibrato artists. Borodin's *Nocturne* from his String Quartet No. 2, in an admirable setting, is also outstanding in tonal richness. A long-winded version of Schubert's *Serenade* benefits greatly from some singing high-position double-stops. Debussy's *La Fille aux cheveux de lin*, its inherent delicacy vitiated by a busy orchestration, is nonetheless played beautifully, and Wieniawski's *Romance* from Concerto No. 2, underplayed at the beginning, gradually takes on an impassioned air. An arrangement of Mendelssohn's *On Wings of Song* is merely a pale impersonation of the splendid Joseph Achron transcription. In Rachmaninoff's *Vocalise*,

Stern plays with polished lyricism, but somehow fails to get under the skin of the music. Rubinstein's *Romance* is rather dry in sound and at times underplayed; the Chopin-Sarasate Nocturne in E-flat (with the ticklish, agile cadenza, just before the ending, omitted; Sarasate's name is not mentioned) is well phrased and tonally robust, but lacks the magic of the Heifetz, Elman, and Oistrakh recordings. In retrospect, it is clear that Stern is potentially a superb vignette practitioner. But although in the 20- to 40-minute masterworks emotional restraint can be an integral part of the music, deliberate underplaying in short emotion-oriented pieces, even in minimal dosage, can detract significantly from the total impact of the performance.

On the technical level there is not a great deal of difference between the earlier and later Stern concerto and sonata recordings, though this is not necessarily the case in comparing his earlier and later concerts. It is impossible, of course, to know the exact extent of editing in the later recordings. Technical considerations aside, the differences are mostly revealed in musical approach. At some point in his maturity, Stern apparently came to believe that slowing down or even stopping his vibrato in certain passages expanded the range of his expressive powers and could add what might be termed a celestial element to his interpretations. (This has nothing whatsoever to do with the widespread habit of "on-and-off" vibrato within a single lyric phrase discussed above.) This change was coupled with a lowering of his softer dynamic shadings to the point of whispering. Many, including myself, feel that this attitude has weakened rather than improved his music-making. His most convincing playing occurs when he lets his emotions speak, or at least plays with sustained warmth. Musical effeteness is essentially unnatural to Stern's temperament.

Although the majority of Stern's recordings of major works reflect his highest standards, some are particularly outstanding. Among these is the Brahms D-major Concerto, with the Joachim cadenza, recorded three times (Ormandy, Philadelphia Orchestra; Beecham, Royal Philharmonic; Mehta, New York Philharmonic). The Ormandy version is perhaps the best of the three, with engineering superior to the earlier Beecham recording, but some may prefer the marginally superior tonal intensity and individuality of the latter. The 1979 Mehta recording, less consistently intense in sound and exhibiting a few mannerisms, is still formidable. The dramatic thrust and virility of Stern's

Brahms easily place it among the best half-dozen performances of the work ever recorded, and in terms of introspection and profundity, it decidedly outranks that of any of his younger colleagues to date.

The thrice-recorded Tchaikovsky concerto (Hilsberg, Philadelphia Orchestra; Ormandy, Philadelphia Orchestra; Rostropovich, National Symphony) is also most satisfactory in the Ormandy version. The opening is played leisurely, as it should be, but too often is not. Solidity of tone (with no vestige of airiness) and lyricism mark the interpretation. In the finale Stern captures the rustic peasant essence of the melodic phrases, a characteristic of the music that is seldom understood by many modern players who all too often race through it rather mindlessly.

The Mendelssohn Op. 64 concerto has always been among Stern's finest interpretations. There is little difference in performance caliber among his four recordings (two with Ormandy, Philadelphia Orchestra; one with Bernstein, Israel Philharmonic, and a 1976 version with Barenboim, New York Philharmonic), though my own favorite is the earlier Ormandy recording. Stern's fairyland is clearly terrestrial; his *Andante* favors serenity more than intensity of spirit, and there is a sense of strength even in the finale's impishness. Yet it sustains an aura of lightheartedness that unfailingly illuminates the fey music.

The Mozart Concerto No. 5 in A-major (Szell, Columbia Symphony) is among his most buoyant and sunny Mozart recordings. Concerto No. 2 in D-major is occasionally too low-keyed, while No. 4 in D-major, strengthened by a brilliant rendering of the first movement Joachim cadenza, is more consistent in lyric statement (both with A. Schneider, English Chamber Orchestra, 1979).

In the realm of fiery romanticism, Stern's early recording of Wieniawski's Concerto No. 2 in D-minor is second only to that of Heifetz. The sound is positively opulent, and he employs expressive slides to grand effect. The Ormandy, Philadelphia Orchestra recording is better engineered than the one with Kurtz and the New York Philharmonic. Another great success is Lalo's *Symphonie Espagnole* (Ormandy, Philadelphia Orchestra) in the complete version. The Scherzando is more subtle and languorous than piquant, but the opening of the Rondo lacks the optimum lilt; the Intermezzo is dashing and impassioned. The G-string climaxes in the Andante are rich in sound, and the lyric triplet section of the finale is compellingly suave. In all, it is larger-

From left, Nathan Milstein, David Oistrakh, Stern, Eugene Ormandy, and Sol Hurok

scaled than many excellent competitive recordings. The Dvořák concerto (Ormandy, Philadelphia Orchestra) is also among the three or four finest recordings of the work. All is muscular, and Stern hits the climactic high E string notes of the opening with brash attack. The final movement may be less devilishly brilliant than that of Milstein, but the eloquent *Adagio* is more glowing in sound and spirit.

Bartók's Concerto No. 2 (Bernstein, New York Philharmonic) is an ideal vehicle for the rugged propensities of Stern's temperament. Some may feel that the Menuhin recording projects more pure feeling, but Stern's performance excels it in neatness of detail, and is equally large-scaled and stylistically alert. The Concerto No. 1 (Bernstein, New York Philharmonic, circa 1960) is less consistent violinistically and tonally, but offers many moments of fervent sound and incisive passagework. In Bartók Rhapsodies No. 1 and No. 2 (Bernstein, New York Philharmonic), works rendered more relevant by their exotic orchestrations than by the blustery, rather banal violin material, Stern actually raises the level of the music by virtue of his ability to project the quixotic Magyar spirit.

Stern's intellectual capacities and unerring instinct

for order and cohesiveness are especially effective in the outer movements of the Beethoven D-major Concerto (Bernstein, New York Philharmonic; Barenboim, New York Philharmonic, 1976). The two performances are about equal, though the later disc, surprisingly, shows more life in the *Larghetto*. There are moments in this movement when Stern plays with such relaxation that it is almost musically noncommittal, yet the lyric portions of the *Rondo* are exceptionally expressive. Kreisler's cadenza, freely played, is used for the first movement only; the second cadenza consists merely of the Kreisler trill and a connecting passage; the third, not identified in either recording, is idiomatic and brief.

Any performance differences in the two Sibelius recordings (Beecham, Royal Philharmonic; Ormandy, Philadelphia Orchestra) are minor. The first movements are stalwart and ardent but not particularly imaginative, and the Adagios are somewhat underplayed, though the Ormandy version is a bit more intense. The finales are outstanding; Stern's marcatos crackle marvelously, and he does not insert any slurred bowings in the tempestuous opening passages, as does Heifetz. His staccatos, too, are exceptional. This movement contains some of Stern's most audacious playing.

His recording of the Prokofiev Concerto No. 1 is superb, quite different in sound and approach from those of Szigeti and Oistrakh, but comparable to either in flamboyance and satiric bite. Concerto No. 2, also a fine performance, ranks among the three or four best in the category, just below the peerless Heifetz recording (both Ormandy, Philadelphia Orchestra).

Stern's Bruch Concerto No. 1 lacks dramatic tension in the opening; the first two movements meander between rich expressiveness and underplaying; the finale is wonderfully vigorous, crowned by stunning G-string opulence. In the Viotti Concerto No. 22, played with Joachim's cadenzas (with some cuts) and adhering fairly close to the Joachim alterations in the Adagio, Stern's performance is musically authoritative but scarcely exciting (both with Ormandy, Philadelphia Orchestra). Stravinsky's Concerto in D is played robustly, but is not the type of music that displays Stern's talents to their best advantage (Stravinsky, Columbia Symphony, 1962). The hyperromantic Berg concerto, with its highly charged lyricism, is considerably better suited to Stern, and he imbues it with acute tension (Ormandy, Philadelphia Orchestra).

Saint-Saëns's Concerto No. 3 is fairly stylish but inconsistent in tonal lustre, especially in the slow movement, and at times the orchestra overpowers the violin in the second and third movements (Barenboim, Orchestre de Paris). The Bach Concertos No. 1 and 2 are pure in sound and concept, but the slow movements are vitiated by too much repose, and remain earthbound. Samuel Barber's infectious concerto is affectionately played and consistent in lyric utterance. Ebullience and dynamic thrust mark the recording of the Hindemith concerto. All four works are with Bernstein and the New York Philharmonic.

One must admire and respect Stern for choosing to tackle, in his late 50s, such formidable challenges as the contemporary concertos of George Rochberg (Previn, Pittsburgh Symphony) and Krzysztof Penderecki (Skrowaczewski, Minnesota Orchestra), especially since his career was perfectly secure and there was no need for such exertion. Obviously he had to practice assiduously to master these arduous, complex works. Both recordings are decisive interpretations. The much more lyric Rochberg is a prime example of the mellowing of Stern's playing in his later years.

In the area of recorded medium-length showpieces, the early Waxman *Carmen Fantasy* (Waxman, unidentified orchestra) is a tremendously brilliant performance, comparable to the Kogan recording, both just below that of Heifetz. Saint-Saëns's *Introduction and Rondo Capriccioso* (Ormandy, Philadelphia Orchestra) displays Stern's consummate understanding of the jaunty Gallic essence of the *Rondo*, playing it at a much slower tempo than the bravura of the overwhelming majority of younger violinists. Yet he tosses off the final page as dexterously and rapidly as the best of the technicians. The *Introduction*, too, is suave, though not graced with the exquisite Heifetz sound.

Ravel's *Tzigane*, which so often has been performed excellently on recordings, is endowed by Stern with sensuous tone throughout, and easily takes a place among the finest half-dozen renderings (Ormandy, Philadelphia Orchestra). His impetuous approach is, of course, quite different from the less Gypsy-like French styling of Francescatti. Chausson's *Poème* finds the violinist not in top form (Barenboim, Orchestre de Paris). The opening orchestral introduction is conducted so slowly that it threatens to grind to a halt, sabotaging the inherent pulse of the music. Technically, some of the difficult solo passages are insufficiently polished, and the playing is tonally inconsistent.

The individual listener may disagree with a Stern sonata interpretation, or may decry the frequent vacillations of his inspiration or tonal intensity. But the fact remains that he was, at his best, a superlative sonata performer. Despite the fact he is still insistent upon performing publicly in his mid-70s, not even Stern's patrician musianship, frankly, can compensate adequately for the serious deterioration of his technical powers.

Nearly all of his sonatas were recorded with his longtime collaborator Alexander Zakin, an impeccable instrumentalist who, like the pianists of most great violinists, scrupulously avoids emphasizing his own personality. Even in the most complex sonatas, one always knows for certain who is the soloist and who is the faithful retainer.

Among the most compelling of his sonata recordings with Zakin are the Bloch Sonata No. 1, transcendentally opulent in sound, communicating the vehement passion of an Old Testament pronunciamento, the two versions of Bartók's brusque, craggy Sonata No. 1, and the marvelously Magyar (not Gypsy) convolutions of Sonata No. 2. The exotic Enesco Sonata No. 3 in the Rumanian style is another commanding Stern interpretation.

Prokofiev's Sonata No. 2 in D-major, Op. 94A is an outstanding recording, lyrical and dashingly spirited, though (as is so often the case) the third movement misses the mood of reverie implicit in the music. Sonata No. 1 in F-minor, Op. 80, is solidly etched, but does not capture the subtle air of mystery in the subdued episodes that marks Oistrakh's matchless performance. Hindemith's uncharacteristically blithe Sonata in C stands high among Stern's lyric interpretations, and Beethoven's Sonata No. 7 in C, an early recording, is consistently alive in sound, large-scaled, and sinewy in articulation, and is one of the finest performances of that work.

The earlier of two Franck Sonata in A-major recordings is the more vibrant and buoyant in a deeply felt interpretation. The Debussy sonata of the late 1950s, musically unimpeachable, contains underplaying and dullish tone, and does not sustain the French disposition of the work. Brahms's four sonatas, No. 1 Op. 78 (mid-1970s), No. 2, Op. 100 (1973), No. 3, Op. 108 (1963), and the Clarinet Sonata in E-flat, Op. 120, No. 2, transcribed for violin by the composer, are all examples of astute musicianship, but intermittently suffer from loss of tension and understatement.

Stern has recorded all of the Beethoven, Brahms, and Schubert trios, the Mendelssohn No. 1, Op. 49, and several other chamber music masterworks with his perennial partners Leonard Rose and Eugene Istomin. Each of these recordings is a model of prime musicianship, instrumental authority, and faultless ensemble playing. Stern's sound and musical inclinations, less individualistic than those of Heifetz, do not unduly dominate his colleagues, but his soloistic instincts color the overall musicality of the group. Two recordings of Brahms's Double Concerto for Violin and Cello with Rose (Walter, New York Philharmonic; Ormandy, Philadelphia Orchestra) are about equal in performance, though the violin presence is stronger in the latter's stereo engineering, and the instrumental relationship is similar to that of the trios. Overall it is one of the four or five most satisfying recordings of the work. Mozart's *Symphonie Concertante*, K. 364 for Violin and Viola, one with William Primrose (Casals, Perpignan Festival Orchestra), another with Walter Trampler (Stern, London Symphony), a third with Pinchas Zukerman (Barenboim, English Chamber Orchestra), are played affectionately and with meticulous detail. Fortified by superior engineering (1972), the Zukerman recording's rich viola tone marks it as perhaps even more impressive than the one with Primrose, although both performances are exceptional. The Trampler version, lacking an independent conductor, reveals a distinct dichotomy of tonal intensity between violin and viola. Stern recorded duos with Oistrakh, trios with Myra Hess and Casals, and quartets with Jean-Pierre Rampal, Alexander Schneider, and Rose, and his chamber music recordings will no doubt continue. For all the high level of his recordings, Stern, like Milstein, is even more impressive in live performance where the force of his personality adds an extra dimension to his art.

Stern, the musician, cannot be separated from Stern the enterprising, aggressive personality and concerned world citizen. Whereas Heifetz's lifestyle grew progressively more private and almost austere, Stern has relished his status as a public figure, and thrives on publicity. He has been known to refer openly to music critics as "howling dogs," yet in our single meeting, when I was introduced to him as a music critic he was most cordial and affable, and at his own initiative discussed musical matters with me at length.

Regardless of one's assessment of Stern as artist and man, his willingness to express publicly his opinions about himself is a rare and admirable quality. The following quotation from the *New York Times* (October 14, 1979, Stephen E. Rubin) is a revealing, refreshing case in point:

I am honestly very doubtful of my primacy. That I can do certain things differently—I don't say better—that I accept, too. But I look at the enormous accomplishments of some of my older colleagues and the incredible talent of some of my younger ones, who gobble up the literature, and I cannot honestly put myself in a class apart and say I know more than all of them collectively. I don't think I am really the kind of complete success musically that I'd like to be. There are many things I don't do well. I couldn't play a Paganini étude the way Milstein does today—no way! And there are other things that I have not done enough of.

I just hope that God will grant me time, in the next 15, 20 years of work, now that I have made my mistakes, and done my experimentation, to concentrate on the areas I think are important musically, which would be, let us say, my final musical statement.

That means that out of many years of trying, I found the things which I think are right and are wrong, for better or for worse. They're my way. In the same sense, I have learned in life what I think is right and wrong, and therefore I must do what I think is right. Yes, there have been people I've hurt, people I've overlooked, moments I would rather not think about when I have been foolish, stupid, excessive, arrogant. Arrogant. Sometimes I have walked over a colleague in a rehearsal without waiting for him to have the opportunity to say something.

I would do better if I lived more healthily, exercised more, ate less. I'm a hog. I love food and drink. I love tastes and textures. I think I could be called a sensualist. But that is the power source of my playing. When I'm caressing music, it is very sensual. I love feelings and I love gratifying the sense. I would find it difficult to be abstemious. What I am, I think, more than anything else, is a willing and capable catalyst. You see, I have ambivalence. I'll be approaching my 60th year—45 years of playing on stage. That's a helluva long time. The trouble is, I don't feel 60. I feel as if I'm about to launch on the major part of my career.

When Stern is not in form and having difficulties, he uses his vast experience and the utmost force of his imperial personality to distract his audience from the realities of the situation. For example, on one occasion, during a ragged performance of the Beethoven concerto, while awaiting the solo violin entrance in a long orchestral tutti, he surveyed the musicians and conductor with patriarchal hauteur, and perhaps even disapproval, as if they were somehow playing with insufficient expertise. Then he gazed at the audience with a "stern" look that seemed to say, "How lucky you are. Isn't this the greatest Beethoven you ever heard?" All this was but a prelude to the climatic moment when Stern tossed his head wildly, jowls quivering, stamped his foot furiously, and made his solo entrance a split second before the orchestra, a ploy calculated to establish himself as the undisputed ruler of the domain. It was one of the more comical charades of the season, and except for a few musical misanthropes, the crowd of worshipful listeners savored the scene with uninhibited relish, thoroughly convinced of their idol's infallibility. On the other hand, when Stern has sufficiently prepared himself and is in full command of his violinistic resources, he is capable of giving a performance of the Beethoven that possesses a majesty and mature masculinity that only a few of his colleagues could or can approximate.

The late George Szell, a sometimes irascible maestro of impeccable musical credentials, once publicly berated Stern and refused to record the Tchaikovsky concerto with him unless he "got into shape." But even Szell was no match for the wiles of Stern, and they finally developed a modus vivendi. If it so happens that Stern finds himself at odds with a conductor, he merely turns his back to the podium and fiddles away, leaving the conductor to follow him. Stern, with his reputation and box office magic, can, of course, get away with much. But woe to any young or less eminent violinist who dares imitate him; the conductor could, and very likely would, maliciously sabotage the performance.

The story of Stern's indomitable leadership in saving Carnegie Hall from the wrecking crew in 1960 is now legendary. He cannot be praised too highly for his organizational efforts in this behalf. He was consequently named president of the nonprofit corporation which directs and controls the hall's musical and financial destiny. Vera Stern was at his side in many of the pursuits connected to its affairs and welfare. In fact, they were once accused by James Wolfensohn, the executive board chairman, of running it "like a mom and pop store." A public brouhaha involving a large block of tickets for a Vladimir Horowitz recital caused more than a little embarrassment for the Sterns, though it was never clear exactly who was responsible for the discrepancies; former executive director Julius Bloom took the official blame.

Stern is hardly one not to take advantage of power once it is in his hands. His enormous influence in Carnegie Hall's musical scheduling, his former unlimited access to the managerial clout of the late Sol Hurok, the eminence of his violinistic reputation, and the perpetual thrust of his dynamic personality have been utilized in the service of many a positive cause. Conversely, his detractors, some of whom bear him implacable animosity, if not downright hatred, are of a different opinion.

In a world in which only a handful of violinists, historically, have been able to attain full-time, lifelong careers as soloists, the competition is incredibly fierce. Today, even most of the major competition winners who succeed in obtaining a certain number of concerts cannot generate topmost careers. The young aspirant must possess a God-given talent clearly superior to his competitors. Even with such talent and a pocketful of medals, his success is not assured. But given this talent, plus the sponsorship of Isaac Stern, a young violinist is well on the way to stardom. Unlike Heifetz, who was never known to use his stupendous reputation to assist a pupil or protégé gain a concert career, Stern will move mountains to assist a talent whom he recognizes as extraordinary.

As a rare violinistic talent himself, Stern is eminently qualified to evaluate the degrees of talent among younger generation hopefuls. And his intimate ties with Israel, a nation peopled with a race that has produced violinists of genius since the days of Ernst, Wieniawski, and Joachim, have enabled Stern to guide the careers of the phenomenal Itzhak Perlman and Pinchas Zukerman. Without doubt, in these two instances, Stern has selected the utmost in current violinistic talent, and his efforts in behalf of other promising talents continue. In light of the ascendancy of Perlman and Zukerman, certain other violinists of solo caliber have had to settle for lesser careers, just as the phenomenal success of the young Heifetz downgraded a host of excellent violinists.

Stern has made some comments from which aspiring violinists can profit greatly—"The violin is a continuation of the voice," he asserts. "You sing in your head and play what you hear." This is invaluable advice in an era in which the essential lyric qualities of the violin are being diminished in favor of such things as the depersonalization of sound and style, correct but sterile and colorless interpretations, and unmelodious percussive and sensationalist effects, or both. He also points out that it is the milliseconds between notes; it is *how a violinist goes from one note to the other*, that makes great music. Actually, it is the lack of this instinctive ability which transforms the concerts of many an outstanding contemporary violinist into highly respectable, but easily forgettable events.

Stern is steadfastly devoted to the welfare of Israel. In addition to being of great assistance in bring-

ing Israeli talent to the world, he has played innumerable concerts in its desert army camps as well as its cities; engaged in endless fund-raising; persuaded other artists to donate their services there; and even organized a musicians' boycott of UNESCO in protest of its 1974 cultural aid ban against Israel. This boycott, along with other organized protests, eventually ended the ban. He has been (and still is) in effect Israel's cultural ambassador. But never one to follow blindly, Stern, a profoundly political entity, has publicly criticized individual policies of the Israeli government.

Stern either speaks or understands six languages, plays tennis with a gusto quite in contradiction to his portly physique, and loves to play chamber music even when he is at the point of exhaustion.

In the *New York Times* interview with Stephen Rubin cited above, Stern remarks:

Whether I'm capable of the same uncaring, unworried pyrotechnics of thirty years ago doesn't make any difference. What has happened is that my music-making has deepened and that cannot be touched. That can only get bigger. So that as long as I can hold a fiddle decently and make a good sound, I will always be able to make music.

Criticisms notwithstanding, when future histories of violin art are written, Stern will certainly be honored as a supremely gifted, impulsive, invigorating, productive, driving, insuppressible, caring, silver-tongued, dauntless, and sometimes ruthless musician-activist, who was also one of the most important violinists of his era.

Arthur Grumiaux, heir to the glorious traditions of the celebrated Belgian School of violin art — an artist of immaculate musicality

Arthur Grumiaux

One of the most fascinating chapters in the history of violin art is the astonishing ascendancy of super-violinists born in the 19th century in tiny Belgium in an area centering around Liège. Beginning with Charles de Bériot (1802-1870), the trend continued with such historic figures as Henri Vieuxtemps, Lambert Massart (1811-1892), Francois Prume (1816-1849), Hubert Léonard (1819-1890), Ovide Musin (1854-1929), César Thomson (1857-1931), and Eugène Ysaÿe, together with a legion of fine pedagogues and lesser-known players. Very often this school of playing has been called the French-Belgian School. However, I prefer to view the two separately even though there are many similarities between them. I believe that the Belgian School, which developed from the French School, possessed an original stylistic concept, and a more robust and expressive manner of music-making. Through the impact of its touring virtuosos and their brilliant, extremely violinistic compositions as well as their pedagogic ideas, the Belgian School has had a tremendous influence on other national schools and, indeed, wherever the violin is played.

The undisputed heir to this noble tradition on the highest levels was the late Arthur Grumiaux (born March 21, 1921 in Villiers-Perwin, in the Walloon province of Brabant in Belgium; died October 16, 1986 in Brussels). Despite his violinistic heritage, Grumiaux was in every respect an artist of the 20th century whose musical and stylistic philosophies were as different from those of Ysaÿe as Ysaÿe's were from those of his countryman, Thomson. And he completely divorced his art from any vestige of the hyper-personalization and eccentricities that marked the playing of many of the yesteryear Belgian virtuosos. In fact, if the appellation "Mr. Purity" could be applied to any violinist, it would be

Arthur Grumiaux. His was a purity that embodied not only total commitment to the dictates of musical probity, but communicated a rare nobility of spirit, tasteful musicality, and sincerity of purpose that was consistently swathed in vibrant tonal beauty and delivered with impeccable technique. The patently sensual and the erotic were not a part of his aesthetic muse, yet his playing was ever warm-hearted and affectionate.

Reared by his grandparents from infancy, the boy Arthur was introduced to music by his grandfather, who ran a small sheet music store and was the local bandmaster in Fleurus, a small town near Villiers-Perwin. He displayed perfect pitch at about age three-and-a-half and was given a tiny violin. Taught by his grandfather, he made his first public appearance at five; at the conclusion of the concert the youngster brashly bade the audience to stand while he played the national anthem. The following year he was taken to Charleroi for admittance to the Conservatory. Initially refused entrance because of his tender age, he was accepted after an audition.

Arthur spent the next five years commuting by train to Charleroi accompanied by his grandmother, who knitted in the great hall while the boy practiced. Unfortunately his teacher had only limited interest in music, and the fact that the boy managed to manipulate the violin and bow more or less correctly was purely instinctive. Nevertheless he was able to leave the Conservatory at 11 with a *premier prix* in both violin and piano. (Like Kreisler, Heifetz, and Enesco before him, Grumiaux became a proficient pianist, and in 1957 recorded both the Brahms Sonata No. 2 and Mozart Sonata K.481 in a 'self-duo,' playing both instruments.)

Recommended by the director of the Charleroi Conservatory, he was taken to Alfred Dubois in Brussels. Dubois (1898-1949) had been a pupil of Ysaÿe,

The young Arthur Grumiaux,
age three-and-a-half

and was himself an excellent violinist who left praiseworthy recordings of the Franck, Debussy, Beethoven No. 7, and Ysaÿe (solo, No. 3) sonatas, and the Vieuxtemps No. 5 and Mozart No. 6 in E-flat concertos. He was also a good teacher and a kind man.

At this point Arthur was forced to make a choice between violin and piano. He wished to continue with both, but the Conservatory director, M. Henry, convinced him to choose the violin. During this period Grumiaux led an arduous life; twice a week he had to rise at 5 a.m. to travel to Brussels for lessons, and return at 6 p.m. to go to evening classes in Charleroi. Dubois often took the boy to his home for additional lessons. At 11 Arthur won the *premier prix* with distinction at the Brussels Royal Conservatory, and by the time he was 18 Dubois said there was nothing more he could teach Arthur; he suggested that he go to Paris to study with Enesco.

According to Madame Grumiaux, her husband spent "one season" with Enesco. It is not clear whether this season was restricted to the study of composition, or included violin coaching as well. In any case, whereas Menuhin's playing was decidedly influenced by the Enesco violin style, Grumiaux's playing in no way mirrored that of Enesco. He then returned to Brussels and was appointed assistant to Dubois. Years later, upon Dubois' death in 1949, he was invited to replace his teacher as professor in the Conservatory.

He made his debut in Brussels with Charles Munch, was awarded the "Special Prize for Virtuosity" conferred by the Belgian government, and prepared to inaugurate an international career. These plans were interrupted by the war. As assistant to Dubois, the occupation forces exempted him from enforced labor in a factory, and the Nazis offered him a position as concertmaster of a leading German symphony orchestra. Not wishing to serve them, Grumiaux went into hiding and managed to avoid detection until the war ended. Fortunately he was able to keep his skills intact.

At last young Grumiaux received the opportunity he deserved. Heard by Walter Legge, the director of HMV Records, he was immediately offered a major tour encompassing England, Belgium, and the Netherlands, and a series of five recordings. His career blossomed rapidly throughout Europe and the Soviet Union and he made a triumphant American debut in 1952. Unfortunately, the number of his concerts in the United States and England were insufficient to win the degree of public recognition enjoyed by some of his stellar colleagues, though wherever he performed he won enthusiastic acclaim as a violinist and artist of the first rank. I recall a period when some of his concerts were canceled, ostensibly for reasons of health. Reports from various respected violinist commentators suggest that Grumiaux's live concerts could be inconsistent. But violin fanciers the world over became familiar with his art by means of his prolific record catalogue embracing more than 150 recordings of both major and minor compositions, plus a score of trio and other chamber works. Many of the masterworks were recorded by him more than once. His vast repertoire ranged from sonatas of Vivaldi and Nardini to the concertos of Berg, Stravinsky, and Bartók, while his roster of shorter numbers ran the gamut from finger-twisters by Paganini to charming transcription gems by Kreisler and Heifetz.

In assessing Grumiaux's playing it must be stressed that he viewed the violin as an instrument of song, and as a tonalist he ranks among the topmost bards of his era. Once, in a discussion of Grumiaux, Henryk Szeryng told me how he admired tremendously the Belgian's vibrato production and usage. It was a vibrato capable of exceptionally rapid velocity and evenness, but Grumiaux, ever an artist of the most discriminating instincts, meticulously controlled it to the dictates of the music's style and mood. There was never a hint of the on-and-off vibrato on individual notes in a single lyric phrase. Like the greatest tonalists of all time,

Yehudi Menuhin, Arthur Grumiaux, and David Oistrakh in the early 1960s

he never 'wastes' a note. This is a significant factor in the consummate polish of his playing. Nor does one ever hear an obvious 'changing of gears' as he varies his vibrato speeds. His tone is neither passionately sensuous nor cloyingly sweet, but neither is it ever blandly cool or uninspired. His tone flows like a refreshing mountain stream, perhaps with a certain sameness of timbre, but always gratifying to the ear. In character, it is a ravishing soprano.

It is interesting to note that along with his admiration for Nathan Milstein, Mischa Elman, a tonal immortal, was one of the violinists Grumiaux most esteemed. Elegance played a major role in his music-making; however, it was not the erotic elegance of Kreisler, but the more circumspect elegance of a consummate gentleman whose interpretive inclinations shunned capriciousness and fantasy in favor of pellucid clarity of line and consistently captivating, scintillating sound. Grumiaux employed expressive slides and position changes only sparingly, but when he elected to use them, they were executed unobtrusively, with great subtlety and regal taste. His expressivity is vested in his innate musicality rather than in the use of expressive manual devices.

In surveying the totality of his recordings, one cannot help but be struck by the uniformity of their excellence. Only a comparative few merit any degree of serious criticism, and that mostly involves questions pertaining to Grumiaux's temperament in relation to the inherent spirit of the music. Of course, as with any other artist, the listener may prefer individual interpretations

that stress more sheer opulence of sound and earthiness of character in works of supreme romanticism. Realizing that the preference resides in the specific tastes of each listener (and their individual temperament), I decided several years ago to test the matter. In presenting one of my lectures on violin art, I play two taped versions of Paganini's Andante and Allegro vivo e spiritoso from Sonata No. 12, Op. 3 No. 6, a piece with a slow segment of sparkling Italianate lyricism and a bumptious Allegro of medium difficulty. Without telling the audience the names of the performers, I refer to them as "Mr. Purity" and "Mr. Sensuality" after alerting them to listen carefully in preparation for an open vote upon conclusion of the two performances. The unnamed artists are Arthur Grumiaux and Itzhak Perlman. As to be expected, "Mr. Purity" is crystalline in sound, angelic in style, and technically precise—a delivery of utter refinement. However, "Mr. Sensuality," Perlman, with his patently lush sound and ultra-propulsive daredevil style, has been invariably the overwhelming choice in more than 50 such confrontations. Yet the minority who vote for the Grumiaux performance are vociferously adamant in their preference. Does this vote imply that the Perlman version is superior? Not necessarily! It is merely a vivid comparison of two violinistic philosophies that represent the two extremes of the wondrous rainbow of violin art, and a barometer of the personal sensibilities of the listeners. Some feel that overt sensuality in violin playing is vulgar. Others consider playing that does not communicate overt sensuality to be cool and unmoving.

Mini-assessments of Grumiaux's sizable recording roster might well begin with his jewel-like renditions of Leclair's Sonata Op. 9, No. 3, Vivaldi's Sonata Op. 2, No. 2, and Nardini's Sonata in D (a fine sonata with wider range and more substance than many in its genre), all with pianist Istvan Hajdu. Oistrakh's Leclair may be more subtle in phrasing, but the gleaming Grumiaux sound and simply-etched lines impart a courtly aura to the music. Milstein's version of the Vivaldi exhibits more drive and propulsion, while Grumiaux's is more dulcet and relaxed.

He plays Bach's solo sonatas and partitas in the modern manner, with vibrato live and brilliant, making no attempt to camouflage the fact that he is a violinist of the 20th century by deliberately altering his vibrato and personal style to conform to an amorphous authenticity. In that context it ranks with the most impressive recordings of the cycle, though he employs fewer subtleties than Szeryng or Szigeti. Grumiaux pays great attention to changes of dynamics, and his chordal playing, sonorous and spotless, is superb. He scrupulously avoids over-intellectualization. These performances have been recently re-released on CD by Philips.

The Grumiaux-Clara Haskil collaboration is one of the truly superlative violin-piano partnerships. They veritably 'breathe' together in the Beethoven sonata cycle. The outer movements of the *Kreutzer* may not possess the ultimate drive, but all ten are ineffably polished and their instrumental balance is like exquisite lace. Though his later Beethoven cycle with Claudio Arrau is also excellent, the version with Haskil is even more impressive as a duo. His lustrous Mozart sonatas with Haskil also deserve similar praise.

The name Grumiaux is practically synonymous with the music of Mozart; large numbers of violin lovers consider his Mozart playing to be the *ne plus ultra* of the genre. They prefer the simplicity of his phrasing, the glorious pristine beauty of his vibrant sound; his is the expressivity of sovereign clarity rather than personalized subtlety through the use of left-hand devices. This syndrome can readily be imbibed in Concerto No. 4, K.219, with brilliant cadenzas by Grumiaux, and Concerto No. 3, K.216, the latter with superb cadenzas by Ysaÿe (a valuable find for those who might relish a change from the ubiquitous Franko cadenzas), and the less inspired Concerto No. 1, K.207; all are with the sensitive support of Colin Davis and the London Symphony. There is, of course, a body of listeners who feel that performances of Mozart should reflect at least a modicum of the earthiness attributed to Mozart himself, but this school of thought is an anathema to those who revere Grumiaux's 'unadorned' Mozart.

The Beethoven concerto, with Alceo Galliera and the New Philharmonia Orchestra, is much the same in quality and musical approach—a glistening performance; the Larghetto is delicately wrought, the Rondo finale sparkles. Its superficial cadenza is not by Kreisler, albeit the opening cadenza is Kreisler's. A version with Edward van Beinum and the Concertgebouw of Amsterdam is similar, if marginally less effective in the engineering. A release of the Brahms concerto with the same collaborators contains some of Grumiaux's most dramatic playing (Joachim cadenza). Technically it is immaculate, and if his tone is less than the ultimate in coloristic variety, it is uniformly beautiful. In keeping with his general style, expressive position changes in the Adagio are minimal.

Viotti's delightful Concerto No. 22, garnished with a skillfully concocted cadenza by Grumiaux, is a model of clean-cut elegance; it is paired with a more or less derivative concerto by Michael Haydn which is mostly distinguished by a jolly third movement that offers some glints of originality; cadenzas by Grumiaux (Edo de Waart, Concertgebouw Orchestra).

Since Grumiaux is such an outstanding classicist, it is perhaps a bit surprising that in the ultra-Romantic repertoire his Tchaikovsky concerto, with Bogo Lescovich and the Vienna Symphony, is so imposing. Using the original version with none of the Auer accoutrements, his playing is bold and big-scaled, though always scrupulously refined. His Canzonetta does not convey the uniquely Russian character of Oistrakh, but it is lovingly stated, and the lyric sections of the brash finale are exceptionally stylish. It certainly merits inclusion among the more significant of the work's myriad recordings. Coupled with a compelling performance of Bruch's Concerto No. 1, the engineering does not quite measure up to his later recordings of the concerto.

One of the few really disappointing Grumiaux recordings is Bruch's *Scottish Fantasy* with Heinz Wallberg and the New Philharmonia Orchestra. Compared to his best playing, one can note some vibrato inconsistency in the lyric sections, even some slight pitch aberrations; the Allegro Guerriero is ponderous and lacks ultimate power. Somehow the work is not wholly in consonance with his temperament, and the totality is inferior to the discs of Heifetz, Oistrakh, Rabin, Perlman, and a few more recent versions. Conversely, the Mendelssohn Concerto Op. 64 (paired with the buoyant though inconsequential D-minor concerto written when the composer was only 13) is accorded a bright, sparkling performance, elfin in spirit; Grumiaux employs batteries of spiccatos in certain phrases in which slurs are traditionally used. Interesting. Here the Philharmonia is under the sturdy leadership of Jan Krenz.

In two recordings of Lalo's *Symphonie Espagnole*, both with the Orchestre des Concerts Lamoreux, the five-movement presentation with conductor Manuel Rosenthal is superior both in engineering and performance to the four-movement version with Jean Fournet. Both are luminous in sound and meticulously tidy—the Intermezzo in the Rosenthal version is particularly effective. Yet for all its merits, it fails to fully convey the intense degree of sensuousness and suavity inherent in the music.

The Saint-Saëns Concerto No. 3 is somewhat more satisfying stylistically (with Fournet and the Lamoreux Orchestra); the third movement is a bit slower and more deliberate than in the most propulsive recordings of the concerto. His approach is amorous but never gushing; the slow movement sings winsomely. In the version with Rosenthal and the Lamoreaux Orchestra, the outer movements are marginally more expressive.

Despite the increasing number of performances and growing popularity of the Berg Concerto, there is a fair-sized body of listeners who still do not care for the work. I would heartily recommend the Grumiaux recording to this audience (Igor Markevitch, Concertgebouw of Amsterdam). The violin-orchestra balance is superb, and his vibrant, ever-polished sound and even-tempered style is ideal for the Berg's hyper-romantic, yet movingly plaintive essence. Another Grumiaux conquest is the Stravinsky Concerto with Ernest Bour and the Concertgebouw. His wondrous clarity of line and phrasing and his immaculate, unlabored instrumentalism add up to an illustrious performance.

In four bravura concertos Grumiaux is ever the cultivated virtuoso rather than an advocate of devil-may-care exhibitionism. As an entity, the most impressive is Paganini's Concerto No. 4, featuring Grumiaux's own skillfully-wrought cadenza, with Franco Gallini and the Lamoreux orchestra. His stunning sound production is at its vibrant best, and he handles the batteries of tenths with ease; the double-harmonics in the finale project with delicate sparkle. The lyric movement, one of Paganini's most poetic gems, sings gloriously, and all is rendered with a sort of aristocratic flair. Scarcely less gratifying is Paganini's Concerto No. 1, utilizing Wilhelmj's first movement cadenza, with Piero Bellugi and the Orchestre de L'Opera de Monte Carlo. His flying staccatos articulate crisply. Once again his sound dazzles the ear as he plays the operatic slow movement with tender affection, as a lyric soprano (as opposed to Menuhin's dramatic soprano). Grumiaux chooses to omit the heroic, trumpetlike G-string theme midway through the third movement. Both are technically inviolate.

The Vieuxtemps Concertos No. 4 and 5 are also played with supreme technical command yet communicate an aura of affable gentility rather than highly-charged visceral intensity in the lyric segments (both with Rosenthal and the Lamoreux orchestra). Nevertheless the vibrant tone never fails to ingratiate.

In Concerto No. 4 the ticklish third movement is a marvelous display of whirlwind facility, and the stormy triple-stop barrages in the finale represent Grumiaux at his most exciting. In Concerto No. 5 he does not emphasize sufficiently the up-bow accents in those passages indicated by Vieuxtemps, but the tranquil episodes of serenity are honed with simple elegance. He elects to use the seldom played cadenza No. 1 and concludes it with the nimble passages of cadenza No. 2. His sound in itself exudes intensity, although his basic expressiveness stresses lucidity more than outright fervor.

Seven of Grumiaux's medium-length pieces further accentuate the essentials of his art. Highlighting them is his graceful handling of the Saint-Saëns *Introduction and Rondo Capriccioso*, in which the Introduction flows amiably; the Rondo, jauntily deliberate in pace, is provocatively piquant; the final page is as rapid as any and cleaner in intonation than some. The *Havanaise* is properly languorous and relaxed, quite unlike the suave, highly personalized Heifetz version; the Allegro sections are exceedingly fast, and the final coda is delectably charming. (Both with Rosenthal, Lamoreux Orchestra.) In Ravel's *Tzigane* Grumiaux rather oddly divides his interpretation between ultra-refinement and Gypsy abandon, with the latter the more effective of the two. As in the *Introduction and Rondo Capriccioso*, the final page is a prodigy of ultra-speed and exact intonation. Chausson's *Poème* is delivered with a sense of repose and poetry; his tone sings clearly and fluently, though some listeners may feel that the overall interpretation is comparatively low-keyed. (Both with Fournet, Lamoreux.) Paganini's original versions of *I Palpiti* and *Le Streghe*, with pianist Riccardo Castagnone, except for a bit of discomfort in the singing octave section of *Le Streghe*, are regal performances, tonally rich and technically meritorious, graciously styled in the Italianate spirit of the Paganini lyric muse. Surprisingly, Vieuxtemps's *Ballade et Polonaise*, though cleanly etched and tonally warm, is a lackluster performance. All the details are properly in place, but the interpretation is wanting in tension and excitement. (With pianist Dinorah Varsi.) Without the advantage of Grumiaux's beautiful sound, and vitiated by quite a few dated, ludicrous slides, the old Huberman recording is actually more exciting.

Grumiaux's tonal beauty and patrician sense of style is conducive to first-class violin-piano sonata playing in Romantic works as well as those of the classic era. Schubert's delicious Sonata Op. 162, which straddles both eras, is a striking example (with pianist Riccardo Castagnone). Thanks to his gleaming sound and exceptionally captivating phrasing, this recording is perhaps second only to the legendary Kreisler-Rachmaninoff version. In an extremely thoughtful reading, the Brahms Sonata No. 2, Op. 100, with pianist Gyorgy Sebok, is as relaxed and mellow as fine aged wine. And in a pensive, unusually introspective performance of Sonata No. 3, Op. 108, only the main theme of the finale is overtly aggressive. Grumiaux makes no attempt to compete with the propulsion and thrust of a Heifetz or Milstein. Lekeu's meandering sonata, with the somewhat self-effacing pianism of Dinorah Varsi, is performed genially and sensitively.

Grumiaux is an outstanding purveyor of short vignettes, and in expressive lyric pieces is capable of conjuring up a quality of tenderness that more than a few violinists, particularly among those of the later generation, do not possess. Deserving special mention is his moving Ponce-Heifetz *Estrellita*, von Vecsey's nostalgic *Valse Triste*, the angelic Bach-Gounod *Ave Maria*, the warm-hearted Dvořák-Kreisler *Songs My Mother Taught Me*, the songful Veracini *Largo*, Massenet's *Meditation* from *Thais*, and the Kreisler pieces *Liebesleid*, *Schön Rosmarin*, *Rondino on a Theme of Beethoven*, and *Andantino in the style of Martini* (with Hajdu, piano, Philips). Unaccountably, his Kreisler *Caprice Viennois* is rather stodgy and lacks *joie de vivre* (with pianist Castagnone).

With Edo de Waart and the New Philharmonia,

Grumiaux succeeds in touching the heart with John Svensen's sentimental ode, the Romance in G, a work once extremely popular, and deserving of revival. His Tchaikovsky *Serenade Melancolique* is only marginally melancholy and not calculated to bring a tear to the eye. Wieniawski's *Romance* from Concerto No. 2 is warmly rendered, but Grumiaux does not quite "get under the skin" of the music. Many of Grumiaux's other vignette performances are outstanding, and it is to be hoped will one day be made available to the new generation.

Like his preeminent colleagues, Grumiaux delved into chamber music. One of his finest in this genre is Beethoven's String Trios, Op. 9, No. 1 and 3, with violist Georges Janzer and cellist Eva Czako. Of course, as with all great violinists who team up with "lesser mortals," the gorgeous Grumiaux tone tends to dominate his partners, but the trio has admirable spiritual rapport, and its ensemble is first class.

Grumiaux had a lengthy list of major recording awards to his credit, and in 1973 was honored with the title of Baron by King Baudouin of Belgium. During his career he performed on two Stradivari violins, one of which was the *Titan*, but he preferred the sonority of a del Gesù. After he obtained his marvelous 1744 Guarnerius del Gesù, he played on it until his death. Of his many bows he favored his Peccatte.

Arthur Grumiaux ranks among the most distinguished string artists of the 20th century, and upon his passing the world lost a true nobleman of the violin.

Leonid Kogan, a dazzling artist who tinctured his rigorous Soviet training with the Heifetz influence while retaining his own individuality

Leonid Kogan

When David Oistrakh took first prize at the Brussels Ysaÿe Competition in 1937, the Soviet music establishment was already well advanced in the process of unearthing the nation's finest violinists and developing them in that arduous, rigid crucible that came to be called the Soviet School. All of Auer's most famous pupils had long since emigrated, with the exception of Poliakin who, returning from a nine-year stay abroad, was not destined to attain international stardom. However, lesser-known pupils of Auer, some of them leading professors at the Moscow, Leningrad, and other Soviet conservatories, carried on his teaching and traditions.

But Auer's approach was by no means dominant. Oistrakh, a pupil of Piotr Stolyarsky, the singularly gifted pedagogue from Odessa, was to lead and influence violinistic and musical attitudes far removed from those of Auer. The USSR was rich in violin pedagogues such as Konstantin Mostras, Boris Sibor (Livshits), Abraham Yankelevich, Oistrakh, and a host of assistants, many of whom were outstanding teachers. Collectively they produced a continuous stream of fine instrumentalists who generally lacked marked musical personality but often have dominated violin competitions, at times overwhelmingly. Oistrakh was always above such criticism, and to his final days remained the Soviet Union's most revered violinist. In the more than four decades since his initial success, only one Soviet-trained violinist ever emerged who could seriously challenge Oistrakh's supremacy despite the plethora of Russian gold medalists and laureates of major international competitions—and that was Leonid Borisovich Kogan.

Apart from the unchallenged dominance of Oistrakh, Kogan had to triumph over many superb violinists in his own country even before being permitted to compete abroad. For example, from 1922 to 1933, at least a dozen outstanding rivals had been born. There was Boris (Busya) Goldstein (b. 1922), who as a teenager was singled out by Heifetz as being the USSR's most brilliant violin talent. Others were Julian Sitkovetsky, Mikhail Vaiman, Nellie Shkolnikova, Rosa Fain, Igor Oistrakh, Valery Klimov, Boris Gutnikov, Mark Lubotsky, Viktor Pikaizen, and Albert Markov. Later we will discuss many of these individually, as well as the better-known of the younger Soviet luminaries.

Kogan was born in 1924 in Dnepropetrovsk (formerly Ekaterinoslav) in the Ukraine during a period of extreme economic hardship. His parents were both photographers; his father, a nonprofessional violinist. By the age of three he was already fascinated by the sound of the violin, and he states that he began musical study at age six. His first teacher was Philip Yampolsky, a former Auer pupil, with whom he studied through his ninth year. At ten, following a successful public recital in Kharkov, his parents decided to take him to Moscow, where he was accepted as a pupil in a special children's group connected with the Moscow Conservatory. His teacher was Abraham Yampolsky (neither related to Philip nor a pupil of Auer), with whom he continued study at the Central Children's Music School, and subsequently at the Moscow Conservatory, from which he graduated in 1948. As a youngster he practiced about three hours a day while carrying a full course of academic subjects for general education. His violin training included mastery of all the standard études: Kreutzer, Fiorillo, Rode, Gaviniès, Dont, and Paganini, as well as those by his teacher, A. Yampolsky (unknown in the West). In 1941 he made his orchestral debut as soloist with the Moscow Philharmonic in the Brahms concerto. At 22 he played his first foreign concert in Prague.

Following World War II, the Soviet authorities were extremely eager once again to gain top honors in the Brussels Ysaÿe Competition (now called the Queen Elisabeth Competition), suspended since 1937, when the Russians had their historic success. Oistrakh's advice was to send Kogan as a guarantee of victory. Kogan promptly won the gold medal, with Vaiman garnering second prize. He married Elizabeth Gilels (sister of the celebrated pianist Emil Gilels), one of the country's leading violinists, who had taken third place honors at Brussels in 1937 after Oistrakh and Flesch's pupil Riccardo Odnoposoff.

Like the Oistrakhs, the Kogans became parents of a boy, Pavel, who developed into a concert-caliber violinist, and is now forging a major career as a conductor. They also have a daughter, Nina, who toured as a piano collaborator with her father in sonata masterworks during the final phase of his career. Though Elizabeth Kogan continued to play and perform, her concertizing career was subordinated to her husband's.

Kogan made his debut in London in 1955, in Vienna in 1956, and in the United States with Monteux and the Boston Symphony in 1958. His violin, a 1707 Stradivarius, was owned by the state. At the height of his career in 1958 he received 2,000 rubles per performance in the USSR. He eventually became chairman of the violin department at the Moscow Conservatory. His hobby was collecting and tinkering with automobiles.

In appearance Kogan was a slim, wiry man a bit under medium height, with a high forehead, deep set eyes shaded by thick, prominent eyebrows, and a generous sprinkling of gold teeth. Despite his immense violinistic stamina developed through a Herculean practice regime, one could detect a hint of pain in his face which grew more pronounced as the years passed, as if he were suffering from an illness. It is said that his ailment was chronic ulcers, and for all his great instrumental command, he was often prey to nervousness before performances. His stage presence was unusually sober, almost reticent, devoid of body or facial mannerisms, though he was capable of an occasional smile and could be warm and affable to those he favored. He had good-sized hands with long, powerful fingers, and there was no digital challenge or expressive subtlety he could not negotiate with ease. He used a bow grip recalling that of the Auer pupils, with the index finger, highly placed, regulating the pressure and strokes, although his right wrist and elbow were held comparatively low for that school of playing. In sostenuto bowings, and for that

Leonid, Elizabeth, and Pavel Kogan

matter every type of stroke, his control was immaculate; his staccato, although exceedingly brilliant and fast, was not of the "stiff-arm" variety. Another striking feature of his bowing was its wondrous Heifetz-like articulation.

Toward his mid-40s Kogan's tonal consistency and emotional projection clearly began to decline, although his technical powers were only marginally below his highest standards.

During what was to be his final tour, Kogan had performed the Beethoven concerto on five successive days in Vienna. He then left for the Russian city of Yaroslavl where he was to have given two performances of Bach's E-major Concerto, Shostakovich's Concerto No. 1, Saint-Saëns's *Havanaise*, Chausson's *Poème*, and the Castelnuovo-Tedesco setting of "Largo al Factotum" from Rossini's *Barber of Seville*, with Pavel conducting the Yaroslavl Symphony. The programs never took place.

In 1982 Kogan succumbed quietly to a massive heart attack while en route by train from Vienna to Yaroslavl. And so died a violinist of exceptional modesty and scarcely rivalled instrumental mastery. Elizabeth had been scheduled to travel with him, but feeling unwell, did not make the trip. Sadly, Leonid Kogan passed away alone, among strangers, at 58, the same age as Paganini whose music he played so superlatively.

In evaluating the artistry of Kogan, it is necessary to refer constantly to Heifetz, whose playing during a 1934 tour of the Soviet Union had utterly entranced the ten-year-old boy. In contrast to Oistrakh's manner of playing, Kogan can be considered the perpetuator of the Auer heritage as influenced by his idol. Whereas Oistrakh was a heartwarming poet of the violin, essen-

Kogan with his conductor-son Pavel

tially descended from the line of Ysaÿe, Kogan's glittering blend of crystalline yet impassioned lyricism with hair-raising virtuosity emanates from the Heifetz tradition. He performed Paganini and other bravura works that Oistrakh, for all his vast technical prowess, preferred not to perform in public. Kogan was certainly no crass Heifetz imitator, but eventually his technical equipment, sound, and style came to resemble more closely that of Heifetz than of any official Heifetz pupils except, perhaps, Erick Friedman in his youth. Indeed there are certain compositions in which their violinistic effects are remarkably similar. In any case it can be said that Kogan was the preeminent disciple of Heifetz, in the loftiest sense. He was, however, trained in an atmosphere quite different from that of Heifetz, and traces of this could frequently be noted in his vibrato production and general musical ethos.

Kogan's finger-bow coordination and muscular reflexes came closer to Heifetz's than did those of any other violinist. He could play with unsurpassed speed, but unlike Heifetz, he never permitted his marvelous facility to dominate an interpretation. His scintillating exactitude of intonation also recalled Heifetz. One of the most stunning of his digital assets was his ability to connect smoothly vibrant lower-position singing notes with those at the topmost reaches of the fingerboard without losing an iota of tonal intensity, comparable to the standard Heifetz had previously introduced. And Kogan well understood and mastered not only the gamut of tasteful expressive slide intricacies, but also the even more subtle art of one-finger horizontal position changes that sustain a sense of legato expressivity with-

out any vestige of overt sliding. This, too, was a Heifetz specialty which Piatigorsky also employed and taught. He was expert in negotiating the familiar Heifetz expressive slide, but generally reserved its use for passages of extreme intensity.

Boris Schwartz states in *Great Masters of the Violin* (p. 471) that Kogan's "tone was lean, with a tight and sparse vibrato." This description might be applicable to Kogan's final years, when his playing had deteriorated tonally and emotionally to an infirm state that was little more than a caricature of his glorious playing. But Kogan possessed one of the most effective vibratos in memory, impeccably controlled, with reflex fingertip intensity of the Heifetz type, capable of all speeds, absolutely thrilling in the high stretches of the G and E strings. This can be easily corroborated by his recordings prior to the mid-1960s. Among other superb recordings, his playing in Wieniawski's *Original Theme and Variations*, Op. 15, apart from its dazzling pyrotechnics, is one of the most incredible exhibitions of lush tonal vibrance anyone could ever hope to hear. Like Heifetz's 1918 recording of Paganini's *Moto Perpetuo*, this recording of Wieniawski's work represents the ultimate performance in its genre. I recall an incident backstage after one of Kogan's solo appearances with the Los Angeles Philharmonic around 1960. He was demonstrating a few passages to some of the orchestra violinists. At one point he scampered up the G-string, ending his runs with an electric vibrance, without the need to "get set" manually, in a way that had the musicians shaking their heads in disbelief and admiration. The strength in his fingers was awesome. Nevertheless, his application of vibrato was wisely eclectic, and he would never think of using a sensuous Tchaikovsky vibrato in

A close-up of Kogan's hands and powerful fingers

212

music of Bach or Mozart. Kogan's basic tone, while not exceptionally large, had pronounced penetrative power and was uncommonly compact in texture. There was no 'air' in the sound. For all his ability to produce stunning intensity, his tone, like that of Heifetz, could be ineffably pure.

There was, however, one important difference between Heifetz's use of vibrato and Kogan's. Heifetz had an almost magical ability to sustain a sense of vibrance at all times, even in non-vibrato passing tones. Kogan, probably as a result of his Soviet background, was not entirely immune to the employment of "on-and-off" vibrato in a single lyric phrase to no musical purpose (as discussed in the Oistrakh chapter). Unlike many fine violinists who have fallen prey to this misuse and who do it as a sort of technical crutch, Kogan's left hand possessed both the flexibility and sharpness of reflex needed to abstain from it completely had he thought of it as a negative factor. The best playing of his earlier years contained only intermittent traces of this habit, so slight that only a hard-nosed critic would call it to account. In fact, I had never heard criticism of his playing on this point. Admittedly, it was not a vitiating factor in his finest performances. As he grew older his inner fires began to cool and his physical capacities waned. His playing became more stolid, impersonal, and aloof, and the "on-and-off" vibrato syndrome increasingly became an integral element in his interpretations. It was distressing to hear him perform this way, knowing what a magnificent and communicative violinist he had been in his prime.

For technical development, Kogan, like Heifetz, emphasized daily scale practice. He criticized the Flesch scale system for its noninclusion of four-octave scales and arpeggios, being convinced that the three-octave method was insufficient for developing complete fingerboard mastery. In daily practice he advocated devoting at lest 50 percent of the time to scales, exercises, and études, and the rest to pieces. One of the many rewards of such a regime was a fourth finger of immense strength that he used regularly in vibrant lyric passages, as well as in purely technical flights.

Kogan, a musician of utmost integrity and intelligence, sought to play each style of composition in its proper context without misusing his vast violinistic equipment in the service of interpretive exaggeration or personal whim. In this regard he is considerably less vulnerable to adverse criticism than is Heifetz. In compositions of overt violinistic persuasion (as differentiated

The informal Kogan

from the most profound masterworks), Kogan was among the foremost stylists of the 20th century. This is not meant mean to imply that he was incapable of musical introspection, but he was first and foremost a spectacular virtuoso. And while his interpretations of the so-called heavyweight works were thoughtful and well-ordered, they tended to reflect good taste and suavity of execution rather than heightened spirituality or graphic imagination. His comprehensive repertoire ranged from Corelli, Bach, and Rameau to Berg, Bartók, Stravinsky, Jolivet, and Mannino. I heard him play the Berg concerto with grandly intense romanticism and an insight into the knotty music equal to anyone's. Among contemporary Soviet works he performed not only those by Shostakovich, Prokofiev, Khachaturian, and Khrennikov, but also lesser-known major works of Vainberg, Barsukov, and Karaev. Numerous compositions were dedicated to him.

Kogan's violinistic personality was well defined, but lacked the striking individuality of Ysaÿe, Kreisler, Elman, Heifetz, Menuhin, and Oistrakh. Thus Heifetz does not recall Kogan—rather, it is Kogan who conjures up the Heifetz image. Heifetz, once fully matured, never recalled any pre-Heifetz violinist either in living or recorded memory. It is no reflection on Kogan's stature as an artist to say that in terms of individualized personality, he belongs in the category just below that of "The Great Personalities of the Violin," while purely as an executant he was perhaps closest to Heifetz.

Taking his bows in the Big Hall of the Moscow Conservatory

Kogan's recordings number about 160 compositions, masterworks and miniatures, plus some 40 rerecordings, comparable to the discographies of Stern, Milstein, and Francescatti. Only a minority were originally recorded in England, France, and the USA, though many were officially rerecorded or pirated from Soviet discs and tapes. Some of the Soviet performances were reasonably well engineered. Unfortunately, the overall body of Kogan recordings are less known to listeners in the West than those of his noted colleagues. A partial survey of his more important discs in all categories reveals many that are staggering performances with which dedicated violin fanciers should be acquainted. Only a minority of these are less than extraordinary. Kogan's sound, like that of Heifetz, was wonderfully adapted to the recording process.

There are at least a dozen exceptional recordings of the Paganini Concerto No. 1 in D-major. None, however, excels the Kogan rendition, with Charles Bruck and the somewhat tinny sounding Orchestre de la Société des Concerts du Conservatoire, in electric tonal tension and technical perfection. It compares with that of the boy Menuhin in dramatic force, although perhaps projecting less sheer spontaneity. The brilliance of his scale and arpeggio endings are practically without peer. Each phrase is exquisitely polished.

He recorded the Tchaikovsky Concerto in D-major three times. My favorite, with Vassili Nebolsin

and the (Soviet) State Radio Orchestra, contains all of the Auer embellishments, including the two climactic endings in the first movement composed of rapid triplet batteries of thirds and tenths. The variation section, just before the cadenza, is especially sensitive. It is a warmly expressive, personalized interpretation with emphasis on lyric values. The tempos are quite deliberate, never rushed, an approach which benefits the first two movements, but deprives the finale of the ultimate sense of abandon and excitement. Overall it has a decided Russian flavor, as does the performance of Oistrakh. They differ in style from that of non-Soviet players and, of course, from each other. A later recording with Constantin Silvestri and the Paris Conservatoire Orchestra, without the Auer first movement climactic endings, is the version best known in the West, and is marginally less fresh and ardent. The third is also with the Paris ensemble.

His Lalo *Symphonie Espagnole*, including the *Intermezzo* (Bruck, Paris Conservatoire Orchestra), easily ranks among the very finest recordings of this work. The G string sound is invariably opulent and the high E string notes scintillate. All is subtle, crisp, and graceful. One can detect some "on-and-off" vibrato in the *Andante*, but generally Kogan's tone sustains intensity of the Heifetz type. The orchestral sound, unfortunately, does not emulate the quality of the soloist. Overall it is a memorable, stylish violin performance.

A 1961 recording of Mendelssohn's Concerto in E-minor (Silvestri, Paris Conservatoire Orchestra) features both glittering finger intensity and "on-and-off" vibrato in the first movement. The *Andante* is songful, and the finale offers superb bowing articulation that emphasizes phrases often sloughed over even by great violinists in the interest of speed. Yet Kogan takes care not to rush the final sections of the outer movements, and heightens the effect of the lyric passages with tasteful, cannily selected slides and position changes. The other side of the disc presents Mozart's Concerto No. 3, with the cadenza by Sam Franko. Here Kogan is eminently relaxed, combining sweetness of sound with a sense of virility, but never projecting a feeling of haste. This recording is somewhat more elegant than a better-engineered one with Otto Ackerman and the Philharmonia Orchestra which features the idiomatic, smartly crafted Oistrakh cadenzas. A noteworthy factor is Kogan's adaption of his vibrato to the classical Mozart style. These performances, together with a charming rendition of Concerto No. 5 in A-major

Kogan in performance stance—note the length of the fourth finger

Courtesy Pavel Kogan

(Rudolf Barshai, Moscow Chamber Orchestra, Joachim cadenzas), establish Kogan as a prime Mozart interpreter.

Vieuxtemps's Concerto No. 5 (Kondrashin, State Radio Orchestra), like the Paganini, is a miraculous tour de force of finger and bow articulation, and stylistic panache. In my opinion it is second only to the Heifetz recording, with those of Perlman, Zukerman, Menuhin, and Chung providing strong competition. Also in the Heifetz image is Kogan's cool, jewel-like recording of Prokofiev's Concerto No. 2 (Basil Cameron, Philharmonia Orchestra). The Khachaturian concerto, with extraordinary collaboration from Monteux and the Boston Symphony (1958), technically immaculate in the outer movements and voluptuously exotic in the Andante sostenuto, vies with that of Oistrakh in idiomatic descriptiveness.

In the two greatest musical challenges of the concerto repertoire, those of Beethoven (recorded four times) and Brahms (three times), Kogan falls somewhat short of the topmost sphere. This, of course, has nothing to do with instrumental factors, but rather with such ephemeral elements as spiritual force and inner grace. The Beethoven (Kondrashin, USSR State Symphony, early 1950s, Joachim cadenzas) is a perfectly beautiful performance, exactly as I heard him in concert. All is pure in sound, buoyant, and musically well-ordered. The trills scintillate; the high E string notes resound

superbly. Only a couple of minor soloist-conductor loose ends slightly detract from a vigorous, exuberant *Rondo*. It is difficult to find fault with such a performance, yet one cannot say that it is as strikingly personal and individual as those of Kreisler, Oistrakh, Szigeti, Heifetz, Menuhin, or Stern. The Brahms (Kondrashin, Philharmonia Orchestra, mid-1950s, Joachim cadenzas) is also an outstanding rendition, though its inspiration is not fully consistent; some climactic phrases soar, others are neatly polished, but almost matter-of-fact.

One of his most masterful concerto performances is of the Shostakovich No. 1, Op. 99 (Eugene Mravinsky, Leningrad Philharmonic), a vehicle ideal in every respect for Kogan's temperament and violinistic attributes. The disc is taken from a live concert. At the opposite end of the stylistic spectrum are Vivaldi's Concerto in G-minor, Op. 12, No. 1, and Rameau's Concert No. 6 in G-minor, a work much like a *concerto grosso*, replete with quaint ornamental devices. Both are played with chaste spirit and delicacy (Barshai, Moscow Chamber Orchestra). Also with the same ensemble is Bach's Concerto in E-major, with some unwisely selected slides and "on-and-off" vibrato—not actually a poor performance, but decidedly earthbound. This is paired with the Bach Double Concerto, an efficient but routine reading in which Kogan gallantly relaxes his sound to coincide with the slower vibrato of his partner, wife Elizabeth.

Other Soviet concerto recordings include the Khrennikov No. 1, Op. 14, a readily listenable work standing somewhere between the simplistic Kabalevsky concerto and the popular Khachaturian; quasi-oriental lyricism and brilliant passagework add up to what is essentially superficial, ingenuous fare (Kondrashin, USSR Radio Symphony). This work and the composer's second violin concerto, written 15 years later, are both dedicated to Kogan. The 1959 concerto of Moishe Vainberg, dedicated to Kogan, recorded in 1971 (Kondrashin, Moscow Philharmonic Symphony) is strongly influenced by Shostakovich, and colorfully orchestrated. Some of the basic material is rather banal, but the concerto contains much that is festive and exciting. Essentially it is in a category above the Khrennikov No. 1 and easily assimilable at first hearing. Kogan's performance is superlative. A much less palatable item is the Barsukov Concerto No. 2, written in 1962, a fragmented hodgepodge of difficult passagework with many trite fortissimo effects that lead nowhere. Barsukov seems to be a better orchestrator than composer, and

Kogan with his pianist-daughter Nina

only the Lento, quasi Berceuse, reminiscent of Szymanowski, offers a flicker of talent. Why Kogan chose to spend the time and energy necessary to learn it is anybody's guess (Rozhdestvensky, Great Symphony Orchestra of Moscow Radio, inferior orchestral sound).

An interesting work in the contemporary idiom is the Triple Concerto by Franco Mannino, written in 1966 and recorded by Leonid, Elizabeth, and Pavel in 1974. The opus is weakened by excessive repetition, but Mannino weaves the busy, three-violin tapestry with admirable skill, fortified by a variety of powerful percussion devices. A successful, adventurous family project (Mannino, State Academy Symphony of the USSR).

Kogan ranks among the chosen few in showpieces and short numbers demanding digital virtuosity, tonal beauty, and stylistic flair. In addition to the previously mentioned fabulous Wieniawski *Original Variations*, the mercurial Castelnuovo-Tedesco setting of Rossini's *Largo al factotum* easily equals the Heifetz recording, and possibly even communicates a bit more humor. Professional violinists hearing Kogan's record simply marvel at his overwhelming blend of agility and sound. Saint-Saëns's *Introduction and Rondo Capriccioso* (Alexander Gauk, State Radio Orchestra), the *Havanaise*

(Monteux, Boston Symphony, 1958) and Ravel's *Tzigane*, all spotlessly clean, vividly recall Heifetz but are not imitative; Kogan's playing is a little less sleek and sophisticated, but masterful in all phases. His Sarasate *Carmen Fantasy* (Nebolsin, State Radio Orchestra) is not quite as spectacular as the truncated, precipitous 1924 Heifetz version, but is musically superior. Among contemporary recordings, Perlman's dulcet-toned performance is perhaps the closest competitor, though Oistrakh, Rabin, Ricci, Spivakovsky, and Rosand also have outstanding *Carmen* recordings. The Paganini *Nel cor piu non mi sento* Variations and *I Palpiti* are tossed off brilliantly in pellucid Italian style.

Wieniawski's *Faust Fantasy*, once considered by many to be the finest of the innumerable 19th-century violin operatic transcriptions, is not often played outside of the USSR these days. It is one of the most demanding and delightful medium-length works of its genre, and Kogan's recording is delectable from first note to last. How unfortunate that the recording is not re-engineered and circulated in the West! This *Faust* version, while certainly not devoid of occasional superficiality, represents the very heart-beat of late 19th century bravura and sentiment, and the orchestral accompaniment is considerably more varied and colorful than any by Paganini or Sarasate (V. Degtiarenko, USSR State Symphony). Another of Kogan's triumphs is Wieniawski's little-known *Adagio Elegiaque*, containing vibrant singing octaves unsurpassed by anyone (A. Kaplan, piano). And although there are several excellent recordings of Polonaise No. 2 in A-major, Kogan's cogent, unhurried interpretation more fully captures the polonaise spirit than any I have heard (A. Mitnik, piano).

In his prime years Kogan possessed a high degree of the stylistic subtlety and discipline necessary to play violin-piano sonatas with meaningful musicality. Later I heard him perform a charmless "on-and-off" vibrato Handel sonata, and about two years before his death, a Beethoven four-sonata program with his daughter Nina that was dry sounding, almost cerebral, and unimaginative. In fact, Nina's playing was the more communicative of the two. But he left several sonata recordings of outstanding merit, including the Strauss Sonata in E-flat major, Op. 18, strongly influenced by Heifetz, and Brahms's Sonata No. 1 in G-major, Op. 78, which after a somewhat over-relaxed first movement, is delivered with admirable thoughtfulness and serenity, building to intense climaxes. Both are with the expert partnering of his principal piano collaborator Andrei Mitnik.

Prokofiev's Sonata in D-major, Op. 94, recorded in the mid-1960s, is one of the few best of the many recordings of the work; highly charged, though varied in tonal texture, technically immaculate, and tremendously muscular in articulation. The single vitiating element is the underplayed pianism of Ephraim Koenig, which may or may not be the fault of the Soviet engineering.

Bach's Solo Sonata No. 3 in C-major, violinistically impeccable, exudes a sense of power, and makes no pretense of trying to achieve academic authenticity, although it never stoops to patent romanticism. The disc sounds exactly like Kogan's performance of the work in concert as I heard it. Yet for all its instrumental impressiveness, there are instances where one gets a feeling that he is still in the process of formulating his interpretation.

More than a few of the Soviet-born violinists, both citizens and émigrés, criticize the Soviet School for giving insufficient training in chamber music. But both Oistrakh and Kogan were excellent players in this area. Beethoven's String Trio in E-flat major, Op. 3, with Kogan, Barshai, and Rostropovich is performed with meticulous phrasing, purity of tone, and elegant classicism. And the polished recording of Tchaikovsky's *Souvenir of Florence*, in which Kogan is joined by Elizabeth, Barshai, Heinrich Talalian, Knushevitsky, and Rostropovich, compares with the finest performances on record. His sound is commanding but not utterly dominating as is Heifetz's in much of his group playing.

It is clear that Kogan made an exhaustive study of Heifetz's manual production and performance style. Nowhere is this more apparent than in his playing of short pieces of all types, and glaringly so in Heifetz transcriptions. One cannot fault Kogan for performing Heifetz vignette settings in the Heifetz style any more than those supreme players who try to emulate Kreisler tidbits in the Kreisler manner. Let us remember that if one hundred of the world's finest violinists were to spend years trying to recreate Heifetz's sound, articulation, and expressive subtleties, just about all of them would fail. For example, although Perlman plays many choice pieces of the Heifetz repertoire in the Heifetz style (the Conus concerto, Saint-Saëns' sonata, etc.), the softer-grained texture of his tone clearly differentiates his performance from that of Heifetz. And this is apart from such Heifetz-influenced players as Erick Friedman, Pierre Amoyal, Joseph Silverstein, Eugene Fodor, and David Nadien. Frankly, how effective can performances of such pieces as Gershwin's "Tempo di Blues" from

Kogan—a study in rapt concentration

Courtesy Pavel Kogan

Porgy and Bess and Prelude No. 1 be in any style other than Heifetz's? Suffice it to say that Kogan plays them smashingly, as he does the Godowsky *Alt Wien*; Dvořák's *Humoresque* (brimming with sophisticated contemporary harmonies); Prokofiev's *March*, Op. 12, No. 1; Albeniz's *Sevillanas*; Poulenc's *Presto*, another dexterous tour de force; and Prokofiev's "Masques" from *Romeo and Juliet*. Less consistent are the Debussy-Heifetz *Beau Soir* and Krein's forgettable Dance No. 4.

Other choice renditions are the Vieuxtemps *Rondino*, which does not reflect the inimitable swagger or modal variety of the Ysaÿe recording but is nonetheless glistening and captivating; Bloch's *Nigun*, heartfelt, and perhaps the most tonally ravishing of all the *Nigun* recordings; the Shostakovich-Tziganov Four Preludes, played with whimsy, gaiety, and acute rhythmic pulse; Sarasate's *Zapateado*, with the staccato passage executed in thirds, after Oistrakh, and the swift harmonic scale passages all on the A string, a memorable performance; Khachaturian's *Folk Bards*, an intensely lyric piece strong in Armenian motifs; Achron's *Hebrew Melody*, at times a bit aggressive, but in the category just below Heifetz, comparable to the discs of Elman and Josef Hassid in tonal opulence. The Mendelssohn-Kreisler *Song Without Words*, Op. 62, No. 1 (*May Breezes*), is played with neatly disciplined lyric splendor; Kreisler's *Caprice Viennois* begins with surpassing rhapsodic imagery, but the double-stop waltz theme misses the requisite Kreislerian lilt. And suprisingly, Sarasate's *Caprice Basque*, powerful and dashing in the double-stop repetition of the opening theme, falls slightly below Kogan's standards in the whirlwind final variation.

Kogan, a stern taskmaster, had taught as many as seventeen pupils and postgraduate students from the USSR and abroad in his Moscow Conservatory class. Oddly, neither Viktoria Mullova or Ilya Grubert, his prize-winning pupils, registers even a modicum of Kogan's tonal beauty or stylistic acumen and breath, though both are well-trained, technically formidable instrumentalists. Talents of Leonid Kogan's caliber are indeed rare, and no amount of drilling and practice can produce playing of his instinctive artistry.

Apparently Kogan, though Jewish, was not liked by many of the Jewish émigré violinists, who charge that Kogan's authority over Soviet string players was similar to that of Khrennikov among Soviet composers. Practically all of the leading Soviet musicians were either active or nominal members of the Communist party. Naturally, the competition for concert bookings, especially those of importance, was just as fierce in the USSR as in the United States.

The dissatisfaction with Kogan's alleged misuse of power somewhat coincides with accusations against Stern, except of course that Stern's authority had no connection whatsoever with government political maneuverings. Few, however, will dispute Kogan's stature as the single authentic Soviet competitor to Oistrakh, and there are those who even preferred Kogan.

With Kogan's untimely death, there remains, at this writing, no Soviet-trained violinists living either in Russia or abroad who can approximate the splendor of his finest years. Indubitably, he deserves to be ranked high among the sovereign violinists in the 20th century.

Itzhak Perlman, an elite violinist of the latter decades of the 20th century renowned for his sensuous tone, prodigious instrumental mastery, and heartfelt expressivity

Itzhak Perlman

It is sometimes said of a violinist, "He was born with a fiddle in his hand." This expression, of course, can be applied to an extraordinarily gifted violinist of any nationality, including an untutored Gypsy player. But perhaps it has been most often associated with Jewish violinists of Eastern European heritage whose forebears were identified with the social and religious ghetto, or *shtetl*, life-style and traditions. It also implies musicality that is fraught with heightened emotionalism, cloaked in impassioned, deeply-felt sentiment and sensuous sound. In recent years the musical *Fiddler on the Roof* has popularized this style of music as well as its origins. However, in the development of serious violin art, it coincides in particular with the emergence of Mischa Elman at the pinnacle of the international violin scene, followed by the most talented of his Eastern European colleagues. Although many of them developed into eminent violinists, collectively, representing every facet and characteristic of violin art, only a rare few have merited the "born with a fiddle in his hand" appellation. In the post-Heifetz-Oistrakh-Menuhin-Stern era, perhaps the violinist most symbolizing this description is Itzhak Perlman.

Born in Tel Aviv, Israel, in 1945 to parents who had emigrated from Eastern Europe, Perlman was attracted to the violin at age three-and-a-half and began lessons at age five. However, he was stricken with polio at age four, which left his legs paralyzed. Thus he has always played the violin sitting down, possibly the only supreme violinist to do so in solo works since Wieniawski who, when severely ill, played concerts seated. Initially Perlman had lessons for a few weeks from a cafe violinist, then went to the Tel Aviv Academy of Music where he studied with Rivka Goldgart for eight years. Russian-trained Goldgart was obviously a com-

mendable teacher; when Perlman was brought to the United States in 1958 at age 13 to appear on the Ed Sullivan television show, playing the finale of the Mendelssohn concerto and the *Flight of the Bumble Bee* impressively, it was apparent that he had been well-taught. Barred by his physical handicap from participating in many of the normal childhood activities, he became devoted to music; even at the age of seven he practiced three hours a day. In his youthful training he worked on Kreutzer, Rode, Gaviniès, and Casorti études and Sevčik, Flesch, and Dounis scales and exercises.

His television success led to a two-month American tour with Sullivan's *Caravan of Stars*, after which the Perlman family settled in New York so that the boy could continue his study and broaden a repertoire that was still comparatively limited. At Juilliard he had lessons with the celebrated Ivan Galamian and on alternate weeks with Dorothy DeLay. Later, at Galamian's Meadowmount School for Strings, he worked on chamber music with the renowned Josef Gingold. Stern, too, exerted considerable influence on his development. However, if one analyzes Perlman's playing in the areas of subtle expressivity and general interpretive approach, particularly in Romantic music, it is easy to note that as with Rabin and Kogan, the Heifetz influence is tremendously strong. Though Perlman is no Heifetz imitator or clone, he employs many of the expressive slides and finger 'glides' readily identifiable in Heifetz's playing. In fact, Perlman so venerates Heifetz, he has referred to Heifetz (in the violinistic sense) as *God*. Of course the character of Perlman's beautiful soft-grained, sweetly-etched tone is quite different from the gorgeous, intense glitter of the Heifetz sound. In Perlman's best playing, his visceral commitment can be astonishing.

of the violinistic and musical qualities that characterize his artistry and contribute importantly to his eminence?

His repertoire runs the gamut from the most exalted masterworks to dazzling virtuoso showpieces, to sonatas and chamber music, to ear-titillating vignettes representing a kaleidoscope of moods and characters. He is both a master technician and a superior tonalist, with a consistently dulcet sound that is ever thoroughly appealing and ingratiating. Moreover, he plays with that superbly communicative element often referred to as 'heart', and is in general a supremely sensual player. The Perlman sound and style may not be as identifiable as that of certain preeminent violinists of the past, but he is decidedly a player of individual inclinations.

Perlman has been, and is, making two significant contributions to violin art. With such massive hands, Perlman could easily span the entire fingerboard and change positions merely by stretching his fingers, as do many contemporary violinists. However he obviously realizes the vital role that horizontal position changes (i.e. slides and glides) play in producing expressive phrasing and sensuous effects, and uses his left hand accordingly. He has played a leading role in reintroducing the use of slides and position changes for expressive purposes in lyric playing. As is widely known, for the past several decades many respected pedagogues have held the view that such devices are archaic, even vulgar, and they have accordingly constrained their pupils from employing them. Thus it is not an exaggeration to state that the majority of players under 50 have not learned (i.e. been taught) to negotiate readily and convincingly these specific horizontal fingerboard movements. Without a doubt, this has reduced the element of manifest sensuality in playing. Today we find that Perlman, together with cellists Lynn Harrell and Yo Yo Ma, among others, uses them quite uninhibitedly, and with great success, though he wisely refrains from overuse in Baroque and Classical music. It would seem that he has studied carefully the playing of Kreisler, Heifetz, and Oistrakh in this regard, and has utilized some of their devices for his own expressive purposes in accordance with his temperament, but never in blatant imitation. Thanks to Perlman and his like-minded cellist colleagues, a trend is developing that in time may well influence considerably players of the upcoming generations.

Secondly, he is exerting an important influence in recital programming by specifically catering not only to critics and connoisseurs but to the lay concert-going

Perlman at a tender age

Courtesy The Strad

At Meadowmount he met Toby Lynn Friedlander, his future wife, and they are now the parents of five children.

After winning the prestigious Leventritt Award in 1964, his career as an international-level artist proliferated rapidly. At this writing he has long since attained the pinnacle of his profession with scarcely any worlds left to conquer. His mass audience is enormous, thanks, in part, to consistent television exposure. His fees are equal to, or possibly exceed, those of any other currently performing violinist. Although his career is only in midstream, the number of his recordings on major labels is rapidly approaching that of Heifetz, Oistrakh, and Menuhin. He has won international acclaim from critics, colleagues, and lay listeners alike. What are some

audience as well. For approximately the first half of the 20th century, recital programs were all-embracing, possibly beginning with a Baroque sonata, progressing to one of the violin concertos that can be played well with piano accompaniment, then continuing with a Bach solo or Romantic violin-piano sonata, and finishing with a group of lyric and stylistic vignettes culminating with a medium-length bravura piece. However, this type of program gradually gave way to so-called recital programs that are in reality chamber music concerts consisting in the main of three or four sonatas in which compositionally the violin and piano are equal partners. In fact, the old-fashioned violin recital has gone into a state of limbo—that is, until recent years in which Perlman initiated a reverse trend. Although he does not incorporate concertos with piano accompaniment in his recitals, he now devotes most or at least part of the second half of his programs to short, encore-type pieces calculated to delight audiences, while devoting the major portion to more substantial longer works. Unfortunately he does not list the shorter pieces on the printed program, choosing instead to have his pianist appear carrying an armload of music from which he makes oral selections as he jokingly elicits guffaws from the more naive of his listeners. He then plays them with a zest, affection, and panache that is seldom equaled by any of his colleagues. He is to be lauded for transforming recital events into more enjoyable affairs. There are those however, including myself, who resent Perlman's omission of such violinistic giants as Kreisler, Wieniawski, Sarasate, Vieuxtemps, Paganini, and others on the printed program. They, who have made such immortal contributions to the traditions and glory of violin art, deserve popular audience recognition no less than the composers of major works. Should one omit Chopin's name from the program merely because a pianist elects to play his short nocturnes, preludes, mazurkas, or études?

There is yet another area in which young violinists could profit by studying Perlman's playing—*vibrato usage*. More than a few observers feel there is a crisis in current violin performance that is characterized by vibrato inconsistencies. This is vested in a mannerism of epidemic proportions which is sabotaging lyric playing among a tremendous number of violinists of all nationalities. The mannerism consists of turning the vibrato on and off in a single melodic line or phrase to no expressive purpose. Violinists will use vibrato on several notes of the 'singing' phrase, generally the climactic

notes, then play the other notes with no vibrato whatsoever, rather than employ a lesser intensity of vibrato that will sustain the singing essence of the phrase. While Perlman may be guilty occasionally of this malfeasance, in his best playing he uses his vibrato in the manner of a skilled vocalist, cannily varying its speed and intensity in emulation of the most illustrious violin tonalists of the past. His production of lyric lines is to be admired. In an era in which strong emotionalism and overt sentiment play no more than minor roles in violin performance (if they play any role at all), emotional projection remains a salient feature of Perlman's playing, and the mass audience adores him for it. Unlike his idol, the stoic-faced Heifetz, Perlman unhappily reveals the intensity of his feeling by indulging in a variety of unsightly facial grimaces. In the area of interpretation, admittedly, there are those who prefer a more objective, more impersonal approach. Such listeners must, of course, seek their aesthetic satisfaction elsewhere.

Another praiseworthy factor in his career so far is that he has not yielded to the temptation of transmuting himself into an 'instant' conductor as have so many instrumentalists and even singers, to Lilliputian effect. And there can be no doubt that considering his massive, infinitely pliable hands, he could easily star as a virtuoso violist if he so desired.

Apart from his dominance as a violinist, Perlman is a compelling personality. Yet, for all the adulation he receives, he seems to crave even more public exposure and acclaim. His efforts in other ventures have engendered both pluses and minuses. He is a fluent speaker who can articulate his thoughts convincingly. And he possesses a rich basso voice which he utilized to fine advantage in a brief role of the Jailer in the 1981 Angel recording of Puccini's *Tosca*, starring Placido Domingo and Renata Scotto. Perlman's bubbling sense of humor is almost constantly in evidence, and his appearances on the delightful children's television show, *Sesame Street*, have always charmed viewers. But as a would-be comic, he is less satisfying.

I have seen him gawk deliberately at some naive ladies in the front row at a concert in which he played the Beethoven concerto, evoking some inane titters during the celestial tutti just before his entrance to the heavenly slow movement. And in consort with fellow prankster, conductor Zubin Mehta, he once repeated the mini-cadenza in the Tchaikovsky concerto finale at least a dozen times, jokingly challenging Mehta to see if either would 'muff' the following entrance (with the Los

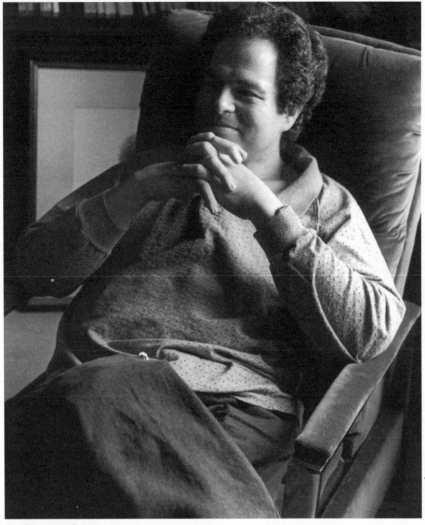

Perlman at leisure

for his activities as a champion and spokesman in behalf of issues affecting handicapped persons.

Perlman has recorded practically all of his extremely broad repertoire. His sound registers superbly, and his recorded performances project almost as much spontaneity as his live concerts. In number, his recordings decidedly exceed those of Kreisler, Milstein, Francescatti, Szigeti, and Stern, as well as any of his contemporaries, and is still increasing by leaps and bounds. With the recent release of his Bach solo sonatas and partitas, together with his previous recording of Paganini's 24 caprices, he has completed a titanic recording twosome equaled only by a few players.

Like so many 20th century violinists, Perlman's performances of both the 'live' and recorded Bach solo sonatas and partitas are romantic-oriented in his sound production and vibrato usage. Though he applies his vibrato carefully and tastefully in tribute to the character of the music, he makes no attempt to masquerade as a so-called 'authentic' instrumentalist.

His opinions on vibrato usage are strongly articulated in a *Strad* interview with R.D. Lawrence (April, 1989):

Angeles Philharmonic). Hardly tasteful public behavior for one who many consider to be the greatest violinist of his era. It is true that Heifetz, too, had a sense of humor (albeit a rather sardonic one) which he loved to exercise by artfully and hilariously imitating an excruciatingly bad violinist (which he did in one of his masterclass videos, and comic routines that he consigned to an incognito recording). But onstage Heifetz assumed an image of royalty, monarch of all he surveyed, and the audiences revered and respected him as such.

As the official commentator for the circus-oriented Encore Television spectacular of the *Three Tenors*, Domingo, Pavarotti, and Carreras, Perlman was miscast badly and obviously ill at ease. Too, as a violinist he is capable of an 'off-night' as evinced in a patently inelegant televised performance of the Beethoven concerto. He does, however, deserve cheers

I feel that vibrato is probably the most underrated element in violin playing. Its importance is too minimized. I'm afraid that people don't really think of it as an expressive musical tool. It is a very, very serious musical tool that's being ignored. Perhaps this is because it's not always easy to control, leading some players to be satisfied with a vibrato that's just there. It may be a good vibrato—not too wide, narrow, fast or slow—but they don't do anything with it. Vibrato is extremely important in producing colors, in producing a relaxed quality as opposed to an intense quality. It is also a very dangerous element because it can cause boredom or irritation in the listener. It can create an overall impression of a player that is annoying. I just feel it's not used enough. Vibrato is not being ignored as far as the basic approach to teaching goes: for example, vibrato exercises—speeding it up, slowing it down. In the final analysis, it is just not used properly. It's almost as if people are drawing a landscape and using just one color. Imagine a painter doing a very intricate, beautiful picture and slathering blue all over it. For me, tone is the quality of sound that you produce. Not so much the quality, perhaps, as the *character*. Tone is something that is in your ear that you either hear or you don't. I always had a very nice tone. When I arrived in the United States my tone was beautiful, but it may not have had the quality or solidity that it later acquired with a different bow arm which better enabled me to sustain it. Obviously, vibrato is a part of it—for sure. If the vibrato is monotonous, one's tone can only be pleasing for about three or four minutes, after which a listener can go out of his mind. *Varying* the vibrato is being ignored. I'm talking about very subtle things. I *don't* mean vibrating like mad and then not at all, and thinking, 'Ah there's a musical expression!' Everything I'm talking about is very subtle. Perhaps vibrato can be considered the 'final frontier', but sometimes that frontier never gets explored, and it's a shame.

When asked his views on the authentic performance movement, he replied:

I can't stand it. I feel that the performances are often devoid of any expression; they sound very sterile, without any warmth. The people involved say "Well, that's the way they played then". Well, I prefer the way we play today. I feel that there is a weakness to this movement; everytime I complain about something in a particular performance, I'm told "Oh, well that's a bad performance; you should hear so-and-so playing it and it sounds very modern—much closer to the way we play anyway!"

Regarding this whole 'vibrato versus non-vibrato' business, I'm sure that Mozart and Haydn would loved to have heard a 'blood and guts' kind of performance of their music. I'm *sure* of that. There are letters of Mozart in which he says that he wanted more warmth and 'real stuff' in performances of his music. I'm sure he would have been a great fan of our concept of vibrato. But, as far as the movement's popularity goes—everything these days is related to how well something sells, and there are a lot of these recordings which are obviously quite successful. One thing leads to another, and a lot of people jump on the band wagon. I hope that it's a phase that will finally settle in its proper place, that is, listening to music from an historical point of view. But when I listen to radio stations and it's all I can hear, I go berserk.

I think there can be an *incredible* purity in the way we play today: it doesn't have to be all one approach or the other. You can still have a wonderfully pure performance with a controlled, varied vibrato without calling it the Early Music type of performance. It shouldn't be all fat and soup, nor should it be just lean. You can have a nice combination.

Collectively his recordings incorporate the most exalted masterworks along with such salon-type miniatures as Raff's *Cavatina*. It would require many thousands of words to comment comprehensively on the individual works of Perlman's vast recording output. Technically they are impeccable, and his romantic-oriented tone pervades his music-making in all styles. One could pinpoint a bit of overwrought enthusiasm in the rapid passagework of the variations in Paganini's Sonata in E minor (Op.3, No. 6) among his occasional lapses from tasteful musicianship, or one may prefer a less tender, less amorous sound and approach to Baroque and Classical works, or indeed, even some of the overly Romantic works. Irrespective of differences in taste, in terms of overall quality, Perlman's recordings are rivaled by few, if any, violinists of his era.

In deserved tribute to his 50th birthday, EMI Records released a set of 20 CDs encompassing a comprehensive overview of the violin repertoire, a generous helping of Perlman's vast catalogue—surpassed in number in this category only by the enormous RCA set of Heifetz's re-releases and Sony's 44 CD set of Stern re-releases.

In scanning his recording bonanza, let us start with the explicitly Romantic works. In Bruch's G-major Concerto No. 1, Perlman's expressive powers are at their peak, especially in the ariose slow movement: his *Scottish Fantasy* is comparable to the Rabin recording and second only to that of Heifetz (Haitink, Concertgebouw of Amsterdam). And, if anything, Bruch's D-minor Concerto No. 2 eclipses both of the aforementioned in sheer gut communication—a searing performance rife with Old Testament flavor-playing that distinctly emphasizes Perlman's ancestral heritage (Mehta, Israel Philharmonic).

The Dvořák concerto, too, is another superb delivery fully equal to the best on record; the captivating Adagio literally pulsates with feeling. The finale of his Glazunov concerto, 'live', suggests that it might have been more immaculate in an edited studio recording, but the surpassing spontaneity of the whole equates the recording with those of Oistrakh, Milstein, and Rabin (Mehta, Israel Philharmonic).

Perlman's Khachaturian concerto revels in crackling bow articulations and ravishing sound, which in the Andante sostenuto recalls the exotic tonal eclat of the Oistrakh, Kogan, and Kaufman recordings (Mehta, Israel Philharmonic). His Conus concerto is absolutely hair-raising in its virtuosity and daring, only a dollop under the supreme Heifetz version, and equal, if not superior, to the exciting recording of the late Soviet violinist Boris Goldstein. In the Sinding Suite, Perlman's whirlwind speed and exactness of intonation in the opening Presto are simply breathtaking (both are with Previn and the Pittsburgh Symphony).

The affectionate cinematic motifs of the Korngold concerto are made to order for Perlman's sweet sound and aggressive musicality. I do not know of any living violinist who can perform this work as effectively as heard on this CD (Previn, Pittsburgh Symphony).

In the bravura metier, the Vieuxtemps Concerto No. 4, a grandly conceived work (conveniently overlooked these days, possibly because of its devilish Scherzo), finds Perlman in his element, handling its technical challenges with valiant derring-do and instilling the angelic Andante Religioso with impassioned yet reverential decorum. The composer's shorter Concerto No. 5 receives fiery treatment in swashbuckling style. One must commend Perlman for his superb recording of Paganini's 24 caprices, a challenge avoided by Stern and Zukerman (who have not deigned to record a single one of them). His performance almost, but not quite, equals the supreme Rabin version; No. 17 with its immaculate fingered octaves, and the dextrous 19 are particularly exciting. He does not play the finger-twisting Paganini "Variation" pieces, but he does play the Concerto No. 1 with the Sauret cadenza. His tremendous virtuosity together with his sweet tone in the Italianate lyrical segments adds up to a performance that rates inclusion among the supreme five or six on record.

His Wieniawski Concerto No. 1 bristles with awesome finger and bow command; only Rabin's is comparable. Concerto No. 2 is richly lyric and recalls the early Stern recording (Ozawa, London Philharmonic). Polonaises No. 1 and 2 are tossed off in true polonaise style; No. 1 concludes with flawless fingered octaves and tenths; the staccatos in No. 2 erupt insolently. And in his own way, Perlman's charm in the feisty *Obertass Mazurka* equates with that of the 1912 Ysaÿe recording (Samuel Sanders, piano).

Like such illustrious colleagues as Szeryng, Grumiaux, Milstein, Menuhin, and Francescatti, Perlman plays Bach as an unashamed romantic-oriented 20th-century violinist. Shunning the role of an 'authentic ancient', he plays with varying degrees of vibrato. His *Chaconne* is richly organ-like and tempered as necessary with leaner sound in subdued variations; his rhythmic impulses are exceptionally strong—a tasteful, hearty performance. The slow movements of the Bach E-major and G-minor Concertos are beautifully, if somewhat romantically, etched (Barenboim, English Chamber Orchestra). The Double Concerto with Zukerman is admirably matched and energetically played; the Perlman vibrato is more pronounced.

Perlman's Beethoven concerto is thoughtful and attentive-to-detail in a 'live' recording; only an over-propulsive Wieniawski-type scale midway through the Larghetto ruffles its serenity. All is astutely phrased, yet it is not quite memorable. The Kreisler cadenzas are brilliant; the finale cadenza is un-cut (Barenboim, Berlin Philharmonic). His Mendelssohn Concerto, Op. 64 revels in a glorious dulcet sound, and the final Allegro is elfishly facile (Haitink, Amsterdam Concertgebouw). The opening movement of the Brahms concerto is played leisurely; the Joachim cadenza dazzles. Perlman imparts a tinge of sentiment to this rugged music that differentiates this performance from most interpretations (Giulini, Chicago Symphony).

He plays the original version of the Tchaikovsky concerto (except for the repetition of the Canzonetta theme reprise and the flashy mini-cadenza of the finale, both by Auer). It is warm-blooded, deeply-felt playing throughout (Ormandy, Philadelphia Orchestra). After the first page of the Sibelius concerto in which he seems indecisive about how much vibrato to apply, the impassioned exposition is equivalent to his Tchaikovsky (Previn, Pittsburgh Symphony).

A man of his time, Perlman's repertory is prolific in 20th-century works. (Worthy, if not memorable concertos by Earl Kim and Robert Starer have been dedicated to him.) Included are Bartók's Concerto No. 2: tempestuous, though avoiding the hysteria sometimes injected, vigorous, seasoned with ample paprika, but without toughness or vulgarity (Previn, London Symphony.) The Shostakovich Concerto No. 1 is rapidly earning a place in the modern repertoire. Perlman communicates its multiple moods: bittersweet, sad, reflective, and boisterous with a sculptor's hand, in a performance vying with that of Oistrakh (Mehta, Israel Philharmonic). I have yet to hear anyone play the opening segment of Prokofiev's Concerto No. 1 with the transparent serenity of Szigeti, but Perlman performs the remainder with explosive bite, uncommon daring, and some luminous quiescence in the thematic 'embroidery' (Rozhdestvensky, BBC Symphony).

Castelnuovo-Tedesco's Concerto No. 2, *The Prophets* (commissioned by Heifetz), is a superior contemporary work with a strong violinistic affinity. Replete with biblical declamations, it merits more exposure than it receives. Perlman's recorded 'live' performance probes its essence with graphic idiomatic utterances (Mehta, Israel Philharmonic). Enhanced by the superb, supersensitive pianism of Bruno Canino, Perlman's Stravinsky-Dushkin 'troika'—the saucy, whimsical *Divertimento*, the *Suite Italienne* with its occasional Kreislerian overtones, and the thornier *Duo Concertante*—are endowed with optimum stylishness and virtuosity, and in lyric statements, with uncommon sweetness of tone. And meriting special mention is Perlman's Goldmark concerto which rivals the long supreme Milstein recording—the Andante is perhaps even warmer in sound.

High in contention among his chamber music CDs are the three Brahms Sonatas, Op. 178, 100, and 108, with Vladimir Ashkenazi's stunning collaboration. As in the D-major Concerto, Perlman's rendition is tonally opulent, intensely romantic, but meticulous in rhythmic impulse. Also exceptional is the Tchaikovsky trio with cellist Harrell and pianist Ashkenazi, despite intermittent 'under-miking' of the cello and several over-percussive piano sorties (apparently an engineering gaffe); the fugue of Variation 8 is marked by superlative instrumental interplay. In Tchaikovsky's often played, but seldom 'melancholy' *Serenade Melancolique*, Perlman delves deeply 'under the skin' of the music (Ormandy, Philadelphia Orchestra). And among the plethora of Vivaldi's *The Seasons* recordings, more than a few of which are quite impressive, Perlman's rhythmic precision and distinctive tone place his performance in the topmost bracket. He conducts himself, abetted nobly by the exceptionally bright strings of the Israel Philharmonic. Beethoven's *Archduke Trio*, with Harrell

and Ashkenazi, plus a flashy, romantic-oriented Spohr Duo, Op. 67 with Zukerman providing the underpinnings, and a warm-blooded, yet elegant Mozart Oboe Quartet (K. 368b), with Harrell, violist Zukerman, and oboist Ray Still, all noteworthy performances, flesh out the chamber music presentations.

The wealth of Kreisler originals and transcriptions, and other brevities display Perlman as the wondrous stylist he is. To cite just a·few among them that are memorable: Dvořák's *Slavonic Dance* No. 3 and *Caprice Viennois* with their their lush double-stops, the delicate fragrance of Chaminade's *Serenade Espagnole*, the Iberian tang of Granados's *Spanish Dance* No. 5 and Albeniz's *Tango*, the buoyant lilt of *Schön Rosmarin*, *Liebesleid*, *Frasquita Serenade*, and *Tambourin Chinois*, the bold *Recitativo* of *Recitativo and Scherzo Caprice*, the lilting Chopin A-minor Mazurka, and the ragtime rhythmic flair of *Syncopation*. Raff's *Cavatina* still belongs to Elman, but the mellifluous Perlman account runs him a close second. The Rachmaninoff *Vocalise*, the Ponce-Heifetz *Estrellita*, and the Paradis-Dushkin *Sicilienne* all touch the heart. And a trio of Sarasate favorites: the languorous *Romanza Andaluza* and *Malaguena*, and the spirited *Caprice Basque*, are the equal of any recorded version. Sanders handles all the piano accompaniments with neat dispatch. For sheer finger and bow frolickings, Nováček's *Perpetuum Mobile*, Sarasate's *Zapateado*, Elgar's *La Capricieuse*, and the Poulenc-Heifetz *Presto* glitter.

Together, a CD of songs with Placido Domingo, finds the violin essentially relegated to a supporting role. The best of the selections is Massenet's *Elegie*, in the spirit of the 1913 Elman-Caruso collaboration, but not as awesome (Jonathan Tunick, New York Studio Orchestra).

Perlman has always been immensely proud of his Jewish heritage and has sought ways and means to emphasize this in his musical endeavors. Accordingly he has become a passionate devotee and performer of klezmer music, which reflects Yiddish life as it existed in Eastern Europe in the ghettos and shtetls, proscribed areas where the Jewish people were forced to live. Klezmer musicians were mostly professionals who played at weddings, at social and religious affairs of all types, and even in the streets. It is strongly influenced by Rumanian, Polish, Gypsy, and Hungarian folk music.

For his CD *In the Fiddler's House*, Perlman joins forces with several superb klezmer groups in a heartfelt outpouring of 15 pieces representing a kaleidoscopic insight into the Jewish heart and soul. Led by Perlman's eloquent violin, it is a treat for listeners of every denomination who delight in moving ethnic idioms. Interesting, but somewhat less effective, is *Tradition*, a collection of special arrangements of Jewish songs played by Perlman. *Yiddish Mamme* is overlong (Israel Zohar's clarinet doodlings are delicious); an anonymous bumptious *Donya*, with Rumanian roots, and the imaginative *Oif'n Weygstenyt a Boim* are far more convincing (Seltzer, Israel Philharmonic). Among two CDs of jazz confections by, and with, André Previn and a small combo, *A Different Kind of Blues* is a standout, and Previn's keyboard peregrinations are remarkable. Yet, one cannot help feeling that Perlman is not really comfortable in this genre. In the limited medium of Joplin Rags, *The Entertainer* in the *The Easy Winners* is most edifying. A special virtuoso treat is Vieuxtemps's swaggering, tumultuous *Yankee Doodle* Variations (Souvenir d'Amerique).

In listening to his recordings in their entirety, it is difficult not to concede that Perlman has contributed more to *expressive*, moving, sentiment-tinctured violin art than any violinist in the post-Kreisler, Heifetz, Elman, Menuhin, and Oistrakh era. And in the scope and style of his playing, he, more than any other contemporary violinist, represents and continues the historic traditions of violin art. This set is a veritable "Feast for the Ears." Indeed, in the opinion of this writer, Itzhak Perlman ranks among the half-dozen violinists of the 20th century.

BoRis

Pinchas Zukerman, one of the most gifted instrumentalists of his era, distinguished as both a violinist and violist

Pinchas Zukerman

In all deference to the many formidable violinists currently concertizing, it is the opinion of many, including myself, that the last two decades of the 20th century have been dominated by two players, Itzhak Perlman and Pinchas Zukerman. At first glance the similarities between them are vividly marked. Both were born in Tel Aviv, Israel, only three years apart (Zukerman in 1948 on July 16th, the same month and day as Ysaÿe). The forebears of both came from Eastern Europe. Both had many years of study with Ivan Galamian. And whether in a duo of two violins or violin and viola, their artistic rapport and ensemble are equal or superior to those of any analogous pairing in memory. But as individual artists they are significantly divergent in career priorities and, of course, musical and personality inclinations. Their long intimate association as violinists and friends has been brilliant and successful, yet it is only natural that violin fanciers and critics comment upon a certain competitiveness, perhaps even healthy rivalry, that can scarcely fail to exist between them on the purely artistic level. In terms of mass audience appeal, Perlman has gained the advantage. However, in assessing their prodigious intrinsic talents, one is approximately equal to the other. Each camp has its adherents.

As pointed out in the previous essay, Perlman represents a cultural continuity of the most heartfelt Eastern European Jewish ethos in musical communication even though he was born in Israel. Zukerman, on the other hand, is the personification of a *sabra* (the prickly fruit of a native Israeli cactus), an appellation commonly applied to native-born Israelis. This character is obvious in Zukerman's bearing, his attitudes, and the pungent impact of his vigorous musicality. He has elected to take a different path from that of Perlman,

specifically in his emphasis on the viola, his choice and preference of repertoire, and his efforts at conducting. Zukerman is certainly not the first violinist to perform on the viola in a serious manner. But he is a pioneer (at least on the topmost level) in regularly presenting concerts combining works for both instruments on a single program. He possesses an almost uncanny ability to switch instruments immediately without sacrificing purity of intonation. His viola sound is invariably rich and sonorous; indeed, some observers hold that his viola playing is superior to that of the violin. I do not agree with this evaluation. When Zukerman is at his violinistic best and fully committed viscerally (which is not always the case in his public appearances), he is a dazzling violinist in that range of the repertoire which he has elected to perform. Later we will further discuss other cardinal differences between Perlman and Zukerman.

Zukerman began his musical training with his father. At age eight he began study with the late Ilona Feher at the Israel Conservatory and the Tel Aviv Academy of Music. Feher was a Hungarian, a pupil of Hubay, who miraculously escaped from the Hitler terror. (She was also the teacher of Shlomo Mintz and Shmuel Ashkenasi in their youth.) Heard by Stern and Casals, Zukerman was brought to the United States with the support of the America-Israel Cultural Foundation in 1961. Receiving scholarships from the Helena Rubinstein Foundation and the Juillard School of Music, he began study with Galamian at Juilliard in 1962. In 1967 he shared first prize with Kyung-Wha Chung in the Leventritt Competition. A video tape of the finals reveals Zukerman somewhat below his best in a spotty Wieniawski Polonaise No. 1. However, it is said that due to Stern's influence, the boy was spared what would have been a humiliating loss, the kind of humiliation other contestants have suffered who did not have an Isaac Stern to use his 'muscle' in their behalf.

I first heard Zukerman in 'live' recital early in 1970 in an event that was abysmally under-publicized, attended by an audience of about 110. Though obviously he was not a fully matured artist, I was tremendously impressed by most of his performance (with pianist Gerald Robbins). My review categorized him as "an exciting talent of rare capacity... Zukerman already possesses the instrumental equipment of a great violinist. The program included Mozart's B-flat major Sonata, K.454 (smooth, sensitively-nuanced lyricism... sustained interest in every step of the way). Schumann's A-minor Sonata came to life in Zukerman's hands with ardent glowing sound and incisive drive. Bach's D-minor Solo Partita was the least successful ... as mere violin playing, the extrovertish performance was above reproach. But it wanted a sense of repose and serenity—and if Mr. Zukerman has any artistic humility in his make-up, it was not evinced in his Bach where it was sorely needed."

Zukerman's career proliferated by leaps and bounds. As a chamber music performer he has performed and recorded not only duets with Perlman, but in consort with Stern, cellist Jacqueline du Pré, pianist Daniel Barenboim, flutist Jean-Pierre Rampal, and other eminent musicians.

He was attracted to conducting as early as 1970, and in 1980 was named Music Director-Conductor of the St. Paul Chamber Orchestra. In assessing his stature as a conductor, it is necessary to separate his artistry as a soloist-conductor (performing violin and viola works without an independent conductor) and his efforts as a symphonic conductor of orchestral masterworks. Whereas all too many performances by soloist-conductors lack the sensitivity of dynamics, phrasing, and instrumental rapport that can be elicited by a truly first-class independent conductor, Zukerman is generally superb in the dual role, especially when he is performing with a familiar ensemble such as the excellent St. Paul group. However, as a big-scaled symphonic conductor with baton in hand, he has been the target of considerable criticism, and even described derisively as "ursine." It will be interesting to see what the future holds for him in the latter role.

While at Juilliard, Zukerman met and later married flutist Eugenia Rich, with whom he had two daughters. They subsequently separated. It was a troubled time for the violinist, who sought help from psycho-analysis (interview with John Von Rhein, *Ovation* magazine, December, 1985). At this writing he is married to actress Tuesday Weld, former wife of actor-musician Dudley Moore.

In sheer violin (and viola) command, Zukerman's facility is remarkable. Nevertheless, like Stern, he has steered clear of the great gymnastic violin challenges such as represented by Paganini, Ernst, et al, though Perlman has recorded the 24 Paganini caprices, the Concerto No. 1 with the Sauret cadenza, and the thorny Wieniawski Concerto No. 1 in F-sharp minor, and has often performed many of the caprices and the two Wieniawski concertos 'live'. Zukerman's sole concession to Paganini is his recording of the ariose *Cantabile*. Then, too, Perlman has played and recorded a huge assortment of the technical, lyric, and stylistic short pieces that have traditionally played a significant role in the violin repertoire; pieces that have endeared violin art to mass audiences (and violinists) for well over a century. Zukerman's principal effort in this metier has been an album of Kreisler pieces made early in his career. Perlman, with his mastery of horizontal digital devices for expressive purposes, distinctly orients his playing toward overt sentiment and sensuality. Zukerman, though he obviously can produce such effects (and, on occasion, does), generally keeps expressive slides and position changes to a minimum. While Zukerman's playing, like Perlman's, is less personalized than that of the most eminent violinists of yesteryear and not as overtly sensuous as that of Perlman, it communicates a certain 'toughness" of fiber and spirit that is particularly compelling in big-scaled music such as that of Brahms. Zukerman's violin-viola concerts almost always consist of Brahms sonatas and music of kindred spirit. And his performances of Mozart, Beethoven, Schubert, and Schumann, though perhaps not as intimately nuanced as those of Perlman, possess an authoritative, straightforward strength of purpose, purity of line, and lustrous sound that have tremendous appeal for many listeners. Zukerman has also helped to popularize the small existing viola repertoire and extend it by encouraging the composing of new works. He has but few rivals as a violist.

Several years ago I had an assignment to interview Zukerman in San Francisco. It was a task I looked forward to with some trepidation since he had, and still has, a reputation as a figure whose statements, ideas, and manner of presenting them often evoke controversy, as in his *Fanfare* magazine interview with David K. Nelson, a piece bristling with belligerent declamations. After decades of interviewing musicians, I have found that most prefer to express themselves with a sort of cultivated veneer sprinkled with aesthetic niceties. Indeed, some actually respond gratefully to having words put in their mouths. But on occasion, there is one who, like Zukerman, seems to relish "shooting from the hip." This can present a problem to the interviewer inasmuch as the artist, upon sober reflection, may deny having made the contentious statement. My own system for coping with this contingency is to repeat the remark and ask the artist pointedly if he wants that remark attributed to him (or her) in print. Nonetheless in our association, spread over a three-day period in the Golden Gate city, I found Zukerman to be affable ("call me Pinky", he insisted), generous in giving of his time, voluble to the point of loquaciousness, exceedingly frank, and resolute in defense of his artistic tenets. The arrogance for which he has sometimes been censured was not patently in evidence. Yet, one could still sense the sharp edge of the *sabra* lurking just beneath the surface. At one point the subject of reading books was touched upon. "I never read a book from cover to cover," he stated blithely and unblushingly. "I just leaf through it."

I examined his left hand. It is large but not outsized; his fingers are powerful, yet the flesh pads on the tips, while 'fleshy', are no more than average for his hand structure. His fourth finger (the 'pinky') is unusually shaped—sturdy to the second joint, then swiftly tapers to the tip. "When I use my fourth finger I support it with my third." The muscle on the side of his palm is of iron toughness. He has a large, reddish protuberance on his neck from the friction of the violin. "Isn't there any way to avoid this?" I asked. "Sure, don't play," he quipped.

"In view of your heavy schedule, how long do you practice generally?"

"I don't need to practice much to keep in shape. The performance itself serves as a practice period for me. I play scales but not routinely, and I have certain exercises of my own invention that I use. At least 85 percent of my practice time, such as it is, is devoted to the bow arm. The right arm plays a significant role in producing variety of tone color and is a vital factor in matters of coordination. In learning to play Mozart, I practiced with a pre-Tourte bow though it was a bow arched in the Tourte fashion.

"When I was a youngster I practiced two to three hours a day. However when I was with Galamian, I adhered strictly to his practice regimen which demanded four hours from 8 a.m. to noon and another hour from 5 p.m. to 6 p.m. every day. During our summer sessions at Meadowmount he often made a practice of checking on his pupils in the afternoon, poking his nose in the doorway to make certain the pupil wasn't idling. Of course, if I'm preparing to perform an arduous work like the Elgar concerto or the Bartók Concerto No. 2, I increase my practice in order to build up my stamina. In this respect a violinist can be likened to a long distance runner."

I noticed that he used a slightly curved shoulder pad. "Yes, I need it. Generally I recommend foam rubber for the average player who feels he requires a pad. But I prefer this one because it's much firmer. Believe it or not, it was once a door stop in Galamian's studio. One day after a lesson I picked it up and stuck it in my pocket. It has been re-covered many times, and I always use it.

"My lessons with Galamian were one hour usually, but in the summer when he had any extra time, he would spend it working with individual pupils. Galamian was dogmatic about his pupils adhering exactly to his teaching system. 'I teach you how to walk,' he would say; 'after that you go on your own if you wish'. He was particularly effective in teaching students what *not* to do, ridding them of instrumental bad habits and avoiding exaggeration or musical indulgence. Exact adherence to the printed score was one of his most rigid rules. His method was multilayered but essentially simple. 'Let the bow be your friend', he would keep repeating. The more gifted the pupil, the more he demanded. Every so often I would play for Stern."

Zukerman enjoyed expounding on the fundamentals of violin and viola playing. "First of all, the solidity of the stance is very important. At times I beat my foot or even go into a deep kneebend, but my weight is always properly distributed for exerting maximum power in communication with my instrument. Every would-be violinist must find the correct angle for holding violin and bow in relation to each other. Even among more advanced pupils there are all too many flaws in this regard. Another common error is the 'locked-in' left thumb. This interferes with the necessary flow and control of the vibrato."

I sought his opinion on the reasons for the widely prevalent habit of playing with 'hot-and-cold' vibra-

Pinchas Zukerman

Photo David Weiss

to in a single lyric phrase. "There can be several reasons, but I think that those violinists whose vibrato is impelled basically by the arm are the most likely to be victimized by this habit. In fact, it is a technical flaw as much as a bad habit, since an arm vibrato actually forces the player to stop his vibrato for an instant between notes and position shifts.

"I had a problem with over-tenseness in my vibrato, but when I was about 15 Stern taught me how to relax my wrist and fingers by tensing the biceps in my left arm. I used to use what was mainly an arm vibrato and applied too much pressure and muscle. Let me show you something." He rolled up both shirtsleeves. His left bicep was noticeably more developed than his right. "Naturally one must be careful not to over-tense the bicep, or it can be painful, but the proper degree of bicep tenseness can free the forearms, wrist, and fingers. Viola vibrato is particularly easy for me. I soften my vibrato for the viola and apply more tension for

the violin. When I play pianissimo I tense my fingers and bicep. When I play louder I relax them. This may all sound a bit complicated, though it's not, really. It is merely a matter of learning the correct allocation of relaxation and tension. I don't have a heavy bow arm. In bowing, the wrist should be the equilibrium, and the finger motion, the culmination of the wrist movement."

"Do you not have differences in intonation and bowing when you change from violin to viola? You don't seem to require any readjustment or warm-up period in switching instruments."

"I grant that there is a slight difference between the two instruments in spacing the intonation, but somehow this has never bothered me. I make a practice of listening to myself objectively, and I'm hypercritical in striving for perfect intonation. As for bowing, in viola playing, the bow arm is more extended. I use more shoulder in the stroke and less concentrated bow pressure. To me, the viola is the more natural instrument. Awhile back I gave the premiere of Miklos Rosza's viola concerto."

I wondered why he had not recorded any or all of the Bach solo sonatas and partitas, particularly in view of his long-established emphasis on lengthy, substantive works in his recital program. "I used to play most of them except for the C-major Sonata, but as time went on I became dissatisfied with my performances. If I am to play them again in public, it must be at a time when I feel I can really do justice to them. Meanwhile I play some of them for myself, and hope to perform them again one day." As of 1995, he has not yet chosen to do so.

In his more recent recitals I had noticed that Zukerman invariably played from the music, or at least had it perched on a lowered music stand close at hand. I decided to ask about it.

"Memorizing has become a problem for me ever since I had several memory lapses during a performance of Chausson's *Poème* around 1969. And since I've become a conductor I've had to put so much music into my mental computer, I just decided that I wasn't going to beat myself to death anymore. One of my worst bugbears is the fear of memory lapses. I still play many works from memory, but they are works I have played continuously from early youth. In the process of trying to grow artistically, while I still love and play these basic works, I have determined to find new ways to express myself through learning and presenting new compositions. But I do hope one day to record several concertos of the standard repertoire that I have missed." The last includes the concertos of Paganini, Dvořák, Goldmark, Saint-Saëns, Glazunov, Spohr No. 8, Bruch No. 2, Wieniawski No. 1, and Vieuxtemps No. 4. Other standard works besides the Bach solo sonatas and Paganini caprice cycle not heard in Zukerman's repertoire are the Bartók solo sonata, the Ysaÿe solo sonatas, Tartini's *Devil's Trill* Sonata, Sarasate's *Carmen Fantasy*, and Saint-Saëns *Havanaise*, all performed and recorded by Perlman. However, Zukerman has recorded well over 100 works representing all lengths and styles: major concertos such as Tchaikovsky, Sibelius, Beethoven, Mozart, Wieniawski No. 2, Vieuxtemps No. 5, Bartók No. 2, Lalo, Bruch No.2, Mendelssohn, and two outstanding recordings of the Elgar concerto, all the Beethoven and Brahms sonatas and sundry full-length sonatas, medium-length compositions such as Chausson's *Poème* and Saint-Saëns's *Introduction and Rondo Capriccioso*, a Kreisler album, and quite a few viola

and various chamber music works. His recordings are invariably among the most impressive of his era.

"How about Bruch's *Scottish Fantasy*?"

Zukerman laughed heartily. "No way. That one belongs to Jascha Heifetz, along with the Sinding Suite, Ravel's *Tzigane*, and many other works. I consider him the *King of Violinists* even though I never had any intimate or personal relationship with him."

In some of his more recent recitals with his close friend and piano collaborator, Mark Neikrug, Zukerman has included works by Lutoslawski, Takemitsu, and other contemporary composers. "What criterion do you use for selecting modern compositions?"

"Music without form and substance, or music that seeks to use the violin as a percussion instrument is where I draw the line. The violin was never meant to exploit percussive sounds. I don't like sensationalism for the sake of sensationalism in music, and especially, for the violin. I will play anything that I believe reflects talent, and if it provokes controversy, so much the better. Anyone who doesn't like my programming a Bartók sonata, doesn't have to listen. That is the way I feel about it."

"In general, do you think the level of string playing is going up or down?"

"It varies. In the case of cellists, I believe the standards have risen considerably. The effect of such great playing and teaching of Casals, Feuermann, and Piatigorsky, not to mention Leonard Rose and others, has brought cello playing to its highest peak in history. But apart from sheer technical mastery I think the standard of violin playing on the top-most level has definitely retrogressed in terms of real artistry. And I think that nowadays really great violin pedagogy and teaching are in short supply. However, let me hasten to say that on the level of orchestral players, the standard of violin candidates for symphony orchestra positions has risen sharply. Lagging behind is the collective standard of viola playing." I certainly could *not* agree with Zukerman in his appraisal of modern viola playing. Since my own student days in the 1930s, I have seen an immense collective improvement in the standard of viola performance.

Zukerman has two Guarnerius del Gesù violins, one of which was formerly owned by Samuel Dushkin, and an Andreas Guarnerius viola. In 1976 he became an American citizen. He now holds dual American-Israeli citizenship which is accepted by both nations.

I remarked: "I've heard you can be quite brusque

with students in your master classes."

That is true. I don't think a master class should be an occasion for an artist to breeze through the session, show off his playing, take the money and run. Rather, I consider it an opportunity to express truth and honesty as regards the realities of a young player's performance. To me, a master class is a very serious business. Often I have someone's pupil playing for me who has been slaving away for ten or 12 years, is already of mature age, and still plays miserably. I think the kindest thing I can do for that pupil is to indicate he must obtain better training immediately or quit because he is merely wasting his time. If I have to step on the toes of some incompetent teachers—so be it.

I read the statement back to him. "Sounds a little rough, doesn't it?" he said smilingly. "Do you want me to delete it?" I asked. Zukerman thought for a moment. "No, leave it in. That's what I think and that's what I'll say." In essence, Zukerman makes a valid point. But the question remains, is public humiliation of a youngster in the best interest of either propriety or art, even if some master class auditors take pleasure in guffawing at the discomfiture of a fellow student such as I witnessed when attending a Zukerman master class?

According to his angry statements quoted profusely in *Fanfare*, Zukerman has (among other complaints) two special peeves. One is against the North American Musicians Union. He deeply resents having to pay the orchestra musicians overtime pay even if it involves only 15 minutes. He cries: "We need to really try in the next century, very soon, to try to change some of that unionized thinking in music, in the arts." Zukerman is incensed because he is not allowed to cancel a recording session at the last minute in the United States as is permitted in England. It probably never occurred to him that some musicians may have had to turn down work scheduled at a conflicting time, and by canceling his session at the last minute it is possible that these musicians could lose both dates. That is only one of a myriad of instances in which the American union protects its members.

Perhaps even more vehement is his 1,500-word *Fanfare* diatribe (of which the following quotes are a mere fraction) against the purveyors of so-called 'authentic' instrumental performances, in particular, those concocted by Roger Norrington and Christopher Hogwood. About Norrington's recording of the 'original' *Fantastique*, Zukerman remarks: "Ha-ha! It's like an impregnated cow that's gone wrong ... Ah, God, and people unfortunately are going to buy it, and the critics are going to say, 'isn't this incredible!'" Playing a few notes on the E-string of an 'authentic' orchestra player's violin, he said: "sounds like a cat trying to puke." He further states,

But all this Norrington-Hogwood nonsense. That is absolute and complete asinine *STUFF*. I mean it has nothing to do with music, it has nothing to do with historical performance. Zero. It's nothing. It means nothing. Companies and the damn reviewers like Rockwell have made this into some incredible, symbolic 20th-century discovery ... You go to a live performance and you can't believe what it sounds like ... There's no question that there are players that have gone way out with all kinds of portamentos and vibratos and slides, but you know what? It still sounds better than what they do! I mean, Jascha Heifetz; I don't exactly agree with his exact way of playing Mozart but it's still Jascha Heifetz, and I dare say that in 75 years people will listen to his rendition of a Mozart concerto rather than to some idiot that played it with an authentic instrument, you know? There's no question about that.

In all fairness, there are many competent professional instrumentalists who agree with Zukerman, including some who participate in the 'authentic' recordings for the purpose of earning a few extra dollars. And there are also many who hold that live 'period' orchestras are an ideal (and profitable) refuge in which inferior string players can hide, making abrasive, ugly sounds and still receive critical acclaim. The point is—would not Zukerman, as one of the world's most celebrated instrumentalists, be much more effective in presenting his opinions by expressing them with more dignity and intellectual maturity?

To the arsenal of his musical chores, he has added teaching at the New York Manhattan School of Music. Doubtless his reputation will enable him to obtain some of the finest talents who, trained by less prominent teachers, are already young artists.

It is to be hoped that the results of these pedagogical efforts will approximate the level of his stature as an instrumentalist. Meanwhile, Zukerman's powers as a leading violinist and violist add distinction to the collective art of his time.

Albert Spalding—outstanding American violinist, cultured gentleman and author

AMERICAN VIOLINISTS IN HISTORICAL PERSPECTIVE

Who, precisely, can be designated an American violinist? Certainly one who was born in the United States and received all or most of his or her training in that country from teachers who were themselves taught in the United States. What then of such yesteryear players as Maude Powell, Leonora Jackson, Nettie Carpenter, Albert Spalding, and others born in the United States, but whose principal training was in Europe? Would anyone deny them the right to be called American violinists? What of a long list of artists including Zimbalist, Seidel, and Piastro, born and trained in Russia, who arrived in America as young men, became American citizens, and had many decades of career activity in the United States? And what of Isaac Stern, born in Russia, taught in the United States by the foreign-born, foreign-trained pedagogues Naoum Blinder and Robert Pollak; or Josef Gingold, born in Russia, trained by Ysaÿe in Belgium, yet who, like Stern, was as American as apple pie? Are not any naturalized citizens in any field considered American, even though their training was obtained in the land of their birth? One could conjure up several more variations on this theme to no constructive purpose or definitive answer.

Rather than become mired in chauvinistic contradictions, I prefer to touch all the bases and to discuss American citizens who have made significant contributions to American violin art irrespective of their national origin or training.

All 18th- and 19th-century American classical music has European roots. Data concerning the violin in the colonial era is sketchy. We are told that Thomas Jefferson had regular lessons with an Italian violin teacher (in America), practiced three hours a day for at least 12 years, and played music by Purcell, Handel, Corelli, Boccherini, and Haydn. In his bachelor days he performed duets with Martha Wayles, his future wife, who had some skill on the harpsichord. And in his latter days he played for his grandchildren despite being impaired by a wrist that had been broken. Patrick Henry fiddled by ear at parties. In the early 19th century Mark Beaubien fiddled for an audience of 600 on a river bank.

One of the first European virtuosos of some significance to tour America was the Hungarian-Jewish Miska Hauser (1822-1887), an adventurous world traveler and freewheeling personality whose name was linked with the notorious Lola Montez. Hauser trekked as far as the California mining camps in the early 1850s, and was equally at home whether playing on the concert stage or in a mercantile store display window. The Norwegian Ole Bull (1810-1880), whose brash American projects and peregrinations have been comprehensively documented in two biographies (one by his widow, the other by Mortimer Smith), made a striking impact upon the American scene in the middle decades of the 19th century. Naive early American audiences were quite enchanted by his superficial vaudevillian tricks and handsome blond image. Bull's rivalry with the Belgian Henri Vieuxtemps in New York created quite a stir. For all his great success with the unknowledgeable American audiences of the time, playing mostly light-minded music, Bull's London appearance with Franz Liszt in Beethoven's *Kreutzer* Sonata was a fiasco for the violinist. Bull, like Heinrich Ernst, represented the afterglow of the splendid Paganini tradition (though he was not nearly as schooled a musician as Ernst), and left no influence whatsoever on the gradually developing native American participation in European-oriented classical violin music.

Other noted 19th-century continental visitors to America were the Italian Camillo Sivori, Hungarian-

Jewish Edouard Reményi, Polish-Jewish Wieniawski, Wilma Norman-Neruda (Lady Hallé) (1839-1911), the French Camilla Urso (1842-1902), the Spanish Pablo de Sarasate, the German August Wilhelmj, and the Belgians César Thomson and Eugene Ysaÿe.

THEODORE THOMAS

German émigré musicians played a leading role in the salad days of American symphonic and instrumental performance. Only a minority of conductors have musical backgrounds as violinists, but oddly, the two men most responsible for early American symphonic development, Theodore Thomas (1835-1905), who arrived in America in 1845, and his arch-rival Leopold Damrosch (1832-1885), were transplanted German violinists. An 1862 *New York Times* review of Thomas playing the Mendelssohn concerto states... "Mr. Thomas produced a firm tone and stops absolutely in time, and plays without any affection of sentiment. He was completely successful." Another, in 1868, says: "His performance of Beethoven's *Kreutzer* Sonata, Op. 47 did not compare unfavorably with that of Joachim in the same sonata." In his book *Memoirs of a Musical Life*, William Mason points out that "he had a large tone, the tone of a player of the highest rank. He lacked the perfect finish of a great violinist, but he played in a large, quiet, reposeful manner." Thomas's violin repertoire in his active playing years ranged from Ernst's *Otello Fantasy* and Lipinski's *Concerto Militaire* to Bach's *Chaconne* and the Beethoven concerto. He performed the latter in 1868, well into his conducting years, and Beethoven's Quartet Op. 59 as early as 1855. In 1855 Thomas, Mason, and a cellist gave the world premiere of Brahms's Trio, Op. 8, possibly the first publicizing of Brahms's name in America. Ultimately, of course, his fame as a maestro far overshadowed his reputation as a violinist.

LEOPOLD DAMROSCH

Damrosch, of Jewish parentage, came to America in 1871 and shortly thereafter performed the Beethoven concerto with the New York Philharmonic, featuring his own cadenza. He is described as having a tone that was not large, though pure and consistent. Damrosch prac-

ticed the violin dutifully two hours a day for many years despite his ever-mounting responsibilities as conductor, teacher, and entrepreneur. He also wrote and performed a violin concerto.

It was common practice for American-born violinists of the 19th century to go abroad to receive the finishing touches of their training from world-renowned teachers. Thus they could boast that they were pupils of Joachim, Vieuxtemps, Wieniawski, Dancla, and other notables. Later generations were to travel to Europe for study with Auer, Flesch, Sevčik, Ysaÿe, Thomson, Rémy, Schradieck, and other famous teachers. In some instances, it was done as much for the sake of status as for knowledge. By the time Auer, Flesch, and Sevčik came to reside and teach in America, there were already many highly qualified teachers in this country.

SAM FRANKO & NAHAN FRANKO

Sam Franko (1857-1937), born in New Orleans, a pupil of Joachim and Vieuxtemps, was among the first noteworthy American-born violinists. He edited and performed many compositions that he unearthed in European libraries, and founded and conducted the 65-member American Symphony Orchestra in 1894. Franko's cadenzas to Mozart's Concerto in G-major, No. 3, are still widely played. His brother Nahan Franko (1861-1930) was also a violinist of prominence, whose teachers included Wilhelmj and Joachim. As a boy of eight he toured with Adelina Patti. In 1883 Nahan Franko became concertmaster of the Metropolitan Opera Orchestra, and in 1889, organized the Franko Symphony Orchestra of which he was the conductor.

LEOPOLD LICHTENBERG

Leopold Lichtenberg (1861-1935), a native of San Francisco, studied with Wieniawski for three years after touring with him in the United States at the age of 12. At 14 he won first prize in Brussels, playing Vieuxtemps's Concerto No. 5, with Vieuxtemps a member of the jury. He edited many major violin works and was soloist with Theodore Thomas and the New York Philharmonic. Detroit-born Max Bendix (1866- ?) was concertmaster of the Germania and Thomas orchestras with which he often appeared as soloist. He also founded his well-known string quartet in 1900.

DAVID MANNES

David Mannes (1866-1959), born in New York, included Karl Halir (1859-1909) and Ysaÿe among his teachers. He was concertmaster of the New York Symphony under his brother-in-law Walter Damrosch, organized the "Music Settlement for Colored People," played many major sonata recitals with Clara, his

David Mannes

pianist-wife, and in 1916 founded the prominent Mannes School of Music in New York. As a music educator Mannes occupied a distinguished position in the development of American music.

THEODORE SPIERING

St. Louis-born Theodore Spiering (1871-1925) studied with Joachim and Schradieck (1846-1918), making his debut in 1893 with the Thomas orchestra. He was also a member of the Chicago Symphony. For 12 years he toured widely as leader of the Spiering String Quartet, then, in 1905, he relocated in Berlin. In 1909 he accepted Gustav Mahler's invitation to become concertmaster of the New York Philharmonic. He gained renown as an editor of violin works for the Carl Fischer publishing firm.

During the dawning of native American violin art, women began to play an important role. Armah Senkrah (née Harkness, 1864-1900), born in New York, pupil of Wieniawski, Vieuxtemps, Massart, and Arno Hilf (1858-1909), won first prize at the Paris Conservatoire and toured Europe and England. New York-born Nettie Carpenter (1865- ?) also studied at the Paris Conservatoire and toured Europe and the United States after winning first prize. Geraldine Morgan (1868-1918), born in New York, worked with Leopold Damrosch, Schradieck, and Joachim, and was the first American to win the coveted Mendelssohn prize in Germany. Her American debut in 1892 featured the premiere of the Bruch Concerto No. 3 with Walter Damrosch and the New York Symphony. Morgan also toured Europe and England and once performed the Bach Double Concerto with Joachim. Olive Meade (1874 -?), born in Cambridge, Massachusetts, studied with Franz Kneisel (1865-1926). She appeared as soloist with the Boston Symphony in 1898, toured the United States, and formed her own concertizing string quartet. A Joachim pupil, Boston-born Leonora Jackson (1879 -?), won the Mendelssohn prize in Germany, toured with Paderewski and Adelina Patti, was soloist with the Boston Symphony and appeared in more than 150 concerts in 1901. Jackson's reputation was second only to that of Maude Powell. She gave up concertizing after marrying a man named McKim, and ultimately left a fortune to the Library of Congress to establish the McKim Fund.

Except for three negligible vignettes by Lichtenberg, none of these American pioneer violinists left behind any commercially made recordings. Though all were respectable artists of their time, one cannot assert that any one of them was of topmost international caliber. American violin art was still in its infancy.

We now enter the era when it is no longer necessary to rely upon antiquated performance evaluations. The best of these may be reasonably accurate by the standards of their time, but they lack the vast knowledge of violinistic and musical advances made during the 20th century to which we have access today—thanks to the marvel of recordings.

MAUD POWELL

Maud Powell (1867-1920) represented a sizeable step forward. At the turn of the century she was the leading American violinist and the first violinist to record for the Victor Company. Powell's playing is an excellent example of a first-class violinist whose basic training was completed before 1890. Her teachers included William Lewis of Chicago, Schradieck, and Joachim, but while having high praise for Lewis, she considered Charles Dancla (1818-1907) to be her most inspiring teacher. Her repertoire was large, and she introduced many works, both major and minor, to American audiences, including the Tchaikovsky, Sibelius, and Dvořák concertos. Her 71 recordings, apart from de Bériot's Concerto No. 7 with piano and single movements from sonatas by Bach and Leclair, are all of short numbers, since she died before the era of complete masterwork recordings. These recordings were made in the 1905-1919 period, but a rather dull-sounding Vieuxtemps *Ballade and Polonaise* possibly dates even earlier.

Her playing, of course, sounds quite old-fashioned to modern ears. On the purely technical level, her recordings reveal her ability to handle the Sarasate pieces with assurance and considerable facility. Her intonation is clean and her bowing fluent. Her innate temperament and expressive phrasing would seem to indicate that had she been trained with modern expertise; she would have been a first-class player even today. She plays with drive, boldness, and a keen sense for pacing.

In assessing a cross-section of these discs, we can note that Powell's tone is not voluminous. In the manner of her time, her vibrato (of slow to medium speed) is only partially developed and inconsistently applied. She used it more as a reflex emotional adjunct than as a consciously controlled element of a tonal range that, in her case, was rather limited. Yet her native talent often renders her playing surprisingly communicative. Her slides and position changes are frequently gauche, but her playing is quite well disciplined, if one allows for the romanticized standards of her time.

Powell also played many concerts as leader of her own string quartet (with three male colleagues), and her musical horizons were by no means narrow. She was constantly alert to those special difficulties confronting women artists, and could be outspoken on the subject without sacrificing awareness and pride in her own femininity.

The Grieg-Kreisler *To Spring* has purity of line, and is cannily paced and clean in intonation. Her vibrato fluctuates in intensity and the slides are "dated." Cadman's *Little Firefly* is bland in sound. Bruch's *Kol Nidrei*, however, has warm G-string tone and much

Maud Powell

inner feeling. If some questionable slides and position changes were to be removed, it could be a viable modern performance.

Boisdeffre's *Serenata Champetre*, an inconsequential genre piece with harp support, helps to display her nicely controlled trill. Ogarew's Caprice in A, in part a deft spiccato showpiece, reveals her impressive one-finger glissando, dryness of tone, and agile but not immaculate facility, while it builds to an exciting finish.

Elgar's ubiquitous *Salut d'amour* is delivered with charming sentiment. Moszkowski's *Serenata* shows neat attention to interpretive detail and warmth of sound, except for some rather lifeless double-stops, and is played with sober purpose. The Thomas-Sarasate Gavotte from *Mignon*, a weak transcription, exhibits dexterous bowing in the variations and is brightly styled. The de Bériot concerto is a dashing performance, one of her best, with biting articulation and ardent temperament.

The Massenet-Hubay *Crepuscule*, arranged for violin and harp by Powell and retitled *Twilight*, is a brief, forgettable bagatelle, as is the Sibelius-Powell *Musette*, in which the piano support is too loud for the violin. Franz Xavier Neruda's *Berceuse slave d'après un chant polonais* projects some vibrant sounds, but the piece is naive in conception and fails to live up to the promise of its florid title.

Sauret's *Will-O-The-Wisp*, a showpiece of medium difficulty with an uninspired melodic middle, is dry in tone and has many tasteless slides, but is admirably aggressive in style. The Schubert-Kreisler "Entracte III" from *Rosamunde* is nicely lyric, but strongly invites comparison between the yesteryear playing of Powell and the far more modern performance of Kreisler—to her considerable disadvantage.

Sarasate's *Spanish Dance* No. 8 recalls the dry tonal world of Kubelik, but Powell projects much more Iberian flair and shows adroit digital command. Raff's *Cavatina* has good G-string tone and clean double-stops, and avoids over-sentimentality, but is not consistent in vibrance. Leybach's *Nocturne*, an inferior piece with orchestral support, has unusually bad surface noise. Hubay's *Hejre Kati* is clean, conscientiously phrased, and fervent in motivation.

Maud Powell's record legacy offers a rare insight into the early era of recorded violin playing, and is invaluable to the connoisseur of violinistic lore and highly entertaining, too. At one time she toured as soloist with the famed Sousa band, playing Saint-Saëns's *Introduction and Rondo Capriccioso* twice a day for 30 weeks.

Her husband was H. Godfrey Turner, son of a famous English journalist. He became her manager and chauffeur, driving their Franklin car from town to town, concert to concert, in Gypsy fashion. Inevitably this rigorous life ruined her health. Her doctor advised her to drink two quarts of milk a day, and when told this disagreed with her, he ordered an increase to three quarts. She complied, but collapsed during a recital and died before her 53rd birthday.

During the first two decades of the 20th century, the influx of émigrés from all parts of Europe, representing the many varied schools, raised immensely the stature of American violin art. It became less and less necessary for American-born players to travel abroad for top-level training. Eastern European violinists, most of them Jewish, fleeing czarist oppression and the rigors of the Russian revolution, played a leading role in the American leap forward. Foremost among them were the pupils of Leopold Auer (1845-1930) who, as the ranking professor at the St. Petersburg Conservatory in the capital city, was in a position to procure as pupils all the stupendous Jewish talents from the Russian Pale of Settlement where the Jewish people were incarcerated. It is interesting to note that Auer had taught for many years, but it was not until he gained access to these pupils around the turn of the century that his reputation and production as a teacher became in any way exceptional. And Heifetz, originally taught by his father and Ilya Malkin; Elman by Alexander Fidelman; Seidel by Max Fidelman; Zimbalist by his father; and Eddy

Brown by Jenö Hubay, were all extraordinary violinists before coming to Auer for "finishing."

ALBERT SPALDING

Meanwhile the title of greatest American-born violinist had passed from Powell to Albert Spalding, ostensibly born in Chicago, who probably deserved that distinction until the rise of Menuhin. Spalding (1888-1953), a scion of the famous sporting goods family, enjoyed personal affluence. Most renowned violinists have come from families of moderate or impoverished economic circumstances. But Spalding's struggles to attain violinistic eminence and his unswerving artistic integrity were in no way less pronounced than those of his colleagues.

According to his written account, the Spalding family spent their winters abroad, and young Albert's first teacher was Ulpiano Chiti, in Florence. In fact, rumors persisted that Spalding was actually an Italian child adopted by the Spalding family, a claim the violinist never took the trouble to deny. Later, Spalding studied with Jean Buitrago in New Jersey and with Narcisse-Augustin Lefort as a private pupil in Paris. Spalding did not study at the National Conservatoire in Paris. In 1903 he passed a rigorous examination at the Bologna University (accompanied at the piano by the then-unknown Ottorino Respighi), with a mark of 48 out of 50, a feat equalled only by Mozart at a similar age.

Spalding's Paris debut at 16 included the Bach *Chaconne* and Saint-Saëns's Concerto No. 3 in B-minor. This was followed by concerts throughout Europe. In 1908 he made his New York debut with the New York Symphony under Walter Damrosch playing the Saint-Saëns concerto, a Spalding favorite. An older-generation violinist who was present, told me of Spalding's extreme nervousness in a performance that was a near-disaster. Inexplicably, Spalding was free from that affliction after his service in the American army in World War I, during which he served as adjutant to Fiorello La Guardia, who was to become mayor of New York. Greatly inspired and influenced by the art of Ysaÿe, Kreisler, Elman, and Heifetz, Spalding continued to forge ahead, gradually building his own audience. Ultimately he recorded about 155 different works, large and small; his best date from the 1920s and 1930s, though a few, like Spohr's Concerto No. 8 (*Gesangszene*) with Ormandy

Albert Spalding

and the Philadelphia Orchestra, were recorded later. André Benoist was his piano collaborator in most of the shorter works. His compositions include two violin concertos, a violin-piano sonata, a solo violin sonata, a suite for violin and piano, the delightful *Etchings*, Op. 5 (first performed by Elman), and a number of short violin pieces, transcriptions, piano pieces, songs, and an orchestral suite.

I heard Spalding on numerous occasions in his mature years and was invariably attracted by his person and impressed by the sincerity of purpose vested in his musicality. It was unfortunate that certain people misused Spalding's deserved reputation as the greatest "American" violinist to insinuate, snidely, that he was not Jewish. This continued long after Spalding had been surpassed by more than a few American-born players. A man of highest ethical principles, he numbered many Jewish artists among his close friends.

Spalding was the proverbial "gentleman and scholar." Onstage he possessed the appearance, poise, and presence of a distinguished diplomat. He spoke in an educated, cultivated manner. As a writer of considerable literary style, he wrote, in addition to his autobiography, an interesting, meticulously researched novel based on the life of Tartini, *A Fiddle, a Sword and a Lady*—all without a ghostwriter.

Spalding must be considered part of the "new wave" of violinists, even though his birth year predates that of quite a few widely known players whose antiquated training and musical horizons relegated them to an anachronistic category. Surprisingly, he did not study with any of the eminent "name" teachers, and represented no particular school, but he obviously had the intelligence to shape his playing along progressive lines. His vibrato was highly developed and extremely rapid, contributing to a tone of striking beauty. In music of linear construction and mood, such as the Beethoven and Mozart concertos and the old classical sonatas (*Devil's Trill*, etc.), the extraordinary clarity of his articulation, combined with his compelling tone, produced playing of distinction. His trill was of "electric" speed. Generally, Spalding's musical inclinations were an extension of his refined personality, and his interpretations were respectful of whatever musical idiom he performed.

Yet for all its tonal vitality, his playing had a decided element of reserve. In overtly romantic music his style could be stiff, inflexible, and too tense. His aesthetic muse lacked innate sensuality, and his crystalline phrasing somehow precluded subtlety of nuance and diversity of color, thus imparting a somewhat one-dimensional cast to his art. His technique was not of spectacular virtuosity, but was entirely adequate to handle the exigencies of the masterworks.

Spalding's artistic generosity was uncommon. He wrote of the New York Symphony of 1920: "The orchestra itself was composed of virtuosos; many of the men in the string section, I reflected, could and should take over my (soloist) role." Here was a man to respect!

Spohr's *Gesangsszene* is easily his most impressive recording. The opus, uniquely conceived, is constructed to showcase the finest elements in Spalding's playing, and he responds with an honest, clean-cut performance that is both elegant and pellucid.

In a brief cross section of his recordings of shorter works, we find Lily Boulanger's *Cortege* cleanly wrought but occasionally too tense. Suk's *Burleska* is nimble, though not impeccable in intonation. Chopin's Waltz No. 10, a Spalding transcription, lacks both pliancy and poetic subtlety, and is strangely alien to his temperament. Spalding's own *Dragonfly*, a cleverly contrived unaccompanied technical study of arpeggios, is deft, neat, and conscientious in delivery.

Cassado's *Danse du diable vert* is clean and agile, but has only moderate resilience. The Moszkowski-Sarasate *Guitarre* is much more modern in style and sound than the Vecsey disc version, and reveals some sparkling trills. Clarence Cameron White's setting of the spiritual *Nobody Knows the Trouble I've Seen* exudes honest, deeply felt sentiment. The Mendelssohn-Achron *On Wings of Song* has fervent G-string tone, tenseness on the E string, some galvanic trill-tremolos, and glints of imperfection in the double-stops.

The Schubert-Wilhelmj *Ave Maria* has rich G-string sound and admirably vibrant octaves and double-stops, though occasionally one gets the feeling that Spalding is concerned more with execution than with the essence of the music. Sarasate's *Introduction and Tarantelle* (with a brief cut in the introduction) is a dexterous, brilliant performance, among the very best of Spalding's recorded virtuoso-type stints.

Wagner's *Prize Song* suffers from a too-rapid vibrato, and a "stiffish" Chopin-Sarasate Nocturne in E-flat that is about one-quarter of a tone flat in the basic engineered pitch. The Schumann-Wilhelmj *Abenlied*, sparse in tenderness, has some exciting trills. Schumann's *Traumerei* is one of Spalding's most satisfying vignettes, and better balanced in sound production than most.

Albert Spalding may not have been a dangerous competitor to the likes of his colleagues Kreisler, Elman, Heifetz, Szigeti, and Francescatti, or the young Menuhin, but he was an exceptional, multitalented man who, on his own terms, could always be relied upon to charm an audience with his violin and personality.

FRANCIS MACMILLEN

American-born violinists continued to make their mark. Francis Macmillen, born in 1885 in Marietta, Ohio, included Joachim, Thomson, Flesch, and Auer among his teachers. Auer cites him as one of the best American pupils to study with him in Russia. Macmillen toured in Europe and the United States with a degree of success, and at one time was known for his short violin pieces and transcriptions. An assessment of his vignette recordings reveals him as a neat, conscientious, small-scaled player, stylistically aware, but no more than a moderate talent.

FREDERIC FRADKIN

Frederic Fradkin (1892-1963), born in Troy, New York, was taught by Schradieck, Rémy, and Ysaÿe, among others. He won first prize at the Paris Conservatoire in 1909, winning a splendid Caressa violin which he later willed to Josef Gingold. Fradkin was

Francis Macmillen

concertmaster of many orchestras, both symphonic and commercial, among them Diaghilev's Russian Ballet in 1915 and the Boston Symphony (1918-1919). In 1911 he performed the Mendelssohn concerto with Mahler. He commanded much respect from professionals, and deservedly so. Some 75 vignette recordings exist, a few in consort with such noted singers as Elisabeth Rethberg and Mario Chamlee. In them his playing reflects the influence of the French and Belgian schools; his sound is smallish, sweet, and of medium vibrance; his delivery, quite polished.

EDDY BROWN

Eddy Brown (1895-1974), born in Chicago, studied in Europe from an early age, was a prodigy who studied with Hubay, and performed the Beethoven concerto at the Budapest Royal Conservatory at age 13. Upon meeting Auer in London, he decided to return to Russia with him for further study. Brown ultimately was regarded as one of Auer's finest pupils. Following successful recital tours in Europe, he made his American debut with Walter Damrosch and the New York Symphony, playing the Beethoven concerto and later that same year performed the Tchaikovsky concerto with Josef Stransky and the New York Philharmonic.

It was Brown's misfortune to be one of that group of major players who were inundated by the Heifetz phenomenon. An outstanding technician in his prime, Brown was engaged for lucrative vaudeville appearances, performing such showpieces as Bazzini's *Ronde des lutins*.

Eddy Brown

In 1933 he became musical director of radio station WOR, and with pianist Clarence Adler, was probably the first to perform the cycle of Beethoven sonatas on radio. He recorded some 65 pieces including the Mendelssohn and Tchaikovsky concertos, and in later years, when his powers had waned, the concerto by the American woman composer, Mana-Zucca (originally Zuckerman).

Brown's most impressive recording was undoubtedly the Tchaikovsky concerto with the Berlin Philharmonic, made in the mid-1920s, now a collector's item, which I have heard. It is a brilliant technical performance by any standards, somewhat small-scaled but warm in temperament. At its best, his tone is pleasantly vibrant, though not thoroughly consistent; at times one can sense Elman's influence in the projection of his lyric playing, but of course, without Elman's sumptuous timbre. His trill is extraordinary. Brown's musical personality and expressive powers are considerably less definitive than the topmost Auer pupils, but he was undoubtedly one of the premier American-born violinists of the pre-1925 period.

FRANK GITTELSON

Frank Gittelson (1896-197?), born in Philadelphia, was Flesch's student for three years. In *The Memoirs of Carl Flesch*, Flesch states:

Few Americans realize that (Gittelson) is the most talented violinist (not excepting Spalding) that America has so far produced, and that he was only prevented by a combination of adverse circumstances, by extreme bad luck, from taking the place he deserves in the musical life of America...Not only I but many others, among them Nikisch and Godowsky, regarded him as a possible successor to Ysaÿe. Forced by Walter Damrosch to play the Bach E-major Concerto, which was quite unsuitable for an American debut and which, to make matters worse, he did not know too well, he suffered a sensational failure which caused a grave depression, paralyzed his willpower, and for years gave him a distaste for the concert platform.

Later he became the head violin teacher at the Peabody Institute in Baltimore, and ultimately concertmaster of the American Ballet Theatre orchestra. In the late 1940s I had occasion to play in that orchestra during one of its Los Angeles sojourns. Gittelson, an enormously stout, bald, unprepossessing figure, played the Tchaikovsky ballet solos with a voluminous, vibrant sound, a striking sense of style, and granite solidity. I cannot recall having heard them performed so beautifully. Gittelson left only about ten recordings, all vignettes. But even in these it is obvious that his gifts were bountiful.

JOHN CORIGLIANO

John Corigliano (1901-1975), born in New York, was one of Auer's pupils in America. Succeeding Mishel Piastro in 1935, he served as concertmaster of the New York Philharmonic for 31 years and performed both staple and contemporary works as soloist with that organization. Corigliano's concerto stints, often broadcast nationally on radio, were always engaging and of admirable stature. His tone was extremely vibrant and penetrating, though at times slightly taut—not sensual in character, but coolly beautiful, somewhat reminiscent of Spalding's clean-cut sound. One can note Heifetz's influence in his subtle position changes. His listed recordings both as soloist and concertmaster number about 15 works, including Beethoven's Triple Concerto with Leonard Rose and Walter Hendel, Bruno Walter

John Corigliano

conducting; the *Scheherazade* solos and Vivaldi's *The Four Seasons* with Leonard Bernstein; and several more Vivaldi concertos with Guido Cantelli, all with his New York colleagues. Perhaps the most impressive of his records is the colorful sonata (1963) by his son John Jr., one of America's significant composers, with pianist Ralph Votapek. The work itself deserves much more exposure than it has received. The elder Corigliano performs it with brilliant articulation and bravura flair. He ranks among the more important 20th-century American concertmasters.

BENNO RABINOF

Benno Rabinof (originally Rabinowitz, 1908-1975) was the archetypal poor Jewish boy in New York's Lower East Side in an era when Elman's magical tone inspired Russian-born parents to make every economic sacrifice to rear their sons in his image. His early teachers included Kneisel and Victor Kuzdo, and it is said that in later life he studied with Thibaud and Enesco. It was Auer, however, already 73, newly emigrated from Russia, who became his teacher around 1919, and taught him for a period of nine years. In his playing, Rabinof represented the continuation in America of Auer's most brilliant pupils from Russia, perhaps more so than any of the numerous violin hopefuls who flocked to the Auer banner after his American arrival. Auer conducted the 19-year-old Rabinof's 1927

Carnegie Hall debut in the Tchaikovsky and Elgar concertos, with a 60-member orchestra chosen from the New York Philharmonic. But like so many others in the Heifetz shadow, Rabinof was unable to generate a top-level career despite encouraging reviews. In the early 1930s he played a 28-week concert cycle of nationwide radio broadcasts with Alfred Wallenstein conducting. I recall being thoroughly impressed.

Rabinof was a fervent admirer of Heifetz, though his own sound and temperament more resembled that of Seidel. His tone, dominated by a rapid fingertip impulse vibrato rather than by the slower wrist and arm vibratos currently in vogue, was sumptuous and intensely virile in the tradition of the great tonalists. And he thoroughly understood and employed the expressive devices in position changes of both Heifetz and Kreisler with good taste. Technically he could handle any genre of music in the staple repertoire with ease. In the hierarchy of ear-titillating violinists, Rabinof ranks among the elite. It was essentially instinctual, spontaneous, visceral playing. His violinistic personality was strong but not as overpowering as those of the already entrenched superstars. His bad luck was to have reached his prime around the onset of the Great Depression, with its deflated box office returns, plus the established competition. And as was the case with Seidel, there was no more room at the top for another violinist of his stature. Rabinof concertized successfully with his pianist-wife, the former Sylvia Smith, in sonata recitals, often performing the complete Beethoven sonata cycle. In 1955 they commissioned a Double Concerto from Boleslav Martinu, which they played with Ormandy and the Philadelphia Orchestra.

He continued to develop his musicianship through the years, but it was the violin-oriented works of ardent lyricism and virtuosity that best suited his gifts,

Sylvia and Benno Rabinof

rather than works demanding intellectual profundity. Only a dozen on phonograph recordings represent his available legacy, most of which are on the Decca release, *Gypsy Violin Classics*. The best of his volcanic, supremely romanticized art is illuminated in Sarasate's *Introduction and Tarantelle* and *Zigeunerweisen*, Kreisler's *La Gitana* and *Gypsy Caprice*, Brahms's *Hungarian Dance, No. 20*, the Kreisler arrangements of Dvořák's *Slavonic Dance, No. 1*, Albeniz's *Tango*, Granados's *Spanish Dance No. 5*, and the de Falla-Kochanski *Jota*. The listener who can come into possession of this disc is in for a treat of beguiling aural splendor and colorful stylization.

Rabinof died unexpectedly of a heart attack shortly before he was to have played a concert in North Carolina.

KNEISEL AND HIS PUPILS

Franz Kneisel (1865-1926), born in Bucharest of German parents, was destined to play an important role in the coming-of-age American violin art. A pupil of Grün and Hellmesberger at the Vienna Conservatory, he possessed a violinistic aura typical of the vibrato-poor, dry-sounding 19th-century playing of middle Europe, as exemplified by Joachim. But while his tone would probably sound dull and dry to modern ears, Kneisel was a master musician who possessed a comprehensive knowledge of musical architecture, aesthetics, and stylistic probity. After his arrival in America in 1885, it was no longer necessary for American-born pupils to travel abroad for instruction in high-minded, intelligent musicianship.

At 17 Kneisel performed the arduous Joachim Hungarian Concerto, and at 19 became concertmaster of the Bilse Orchestra (later the Berlin Philharmonic), a chair once occupied by Ysaÿe. Upon emigrating to America, he was appointed concertmaster of the Boston Symphony and made his debut in the Beethoven concerto. He held this position until 1903. However, it was as a chamber music player and teacher that Kneisel was most successful. The Kneisel Quartet helped to popularize and win acceptance for chamber music throughout the United States. They played the American premieres of quartets by Brahms and Dvořák, and on their programs gave special emphasis to the late Beethoven quartets. As a forward-looking musician, Kneisel championed such "modern" works as the Debussy quartet when many colleagues still considered

The Franz Kneisel String Quartet

it hopelessly avant-garde.

As was to be expected, the group adhered to the late 19th-century, cool, often "whitish" tone of the old German school, and as far as he could, Kneisel influenced his quartet colleagues to play in this vein. Yet their musical standards were unusually high for their time. The quartet performed until 1917. Such Kneisel pupils as Sascha Jacobsen, Jacques Gordon, and William Kroll eventually became leaders of prestigious string quartets.

As a teacher, Kneisel was a typically Prussian, tyrannical disciplinarian. On the one hand he molded a number of exceptionally talented pupils, who were originally raw and uncultivated, into fine musicians at the Institute of Musical Art in New York. But he also broke the spirits and crippled the playing of certain gifted pupils who were too sensitive to resist those of his demands that produced negative results. More than a few left Kneisel and went abroad to study with Auer, Flesch, or Sevčik. His own son and daughter, Frank and Marianne, were never more than mediocre violinists. The best of Kneisel's students were Jewish, and their hot-blooded musicality and vibrant tonal production (which they had acquired before they came to Kneisel) were an anathema to his unaffectionate methodology and latent anti-Semitism. Yet somehow this teacher-pupil dichotomy was productive, and Kneisel merits recognition as a significant pedagogue of his era.

SAMUEL GARDNER

At least eight of Kneisel's pupils made their mark upon the American scene and deserve mention. Samuel Gardner (1892-1982), born in Russia, came to America as a child and, before becoming Kneisel's pupil, studied with the violinist-composer Charles Martin Loeffler and Felix Winternitz. His teacher in composition was Percy Goetchius at the Institute of Musical Art. In 1918 his String Quartet in D-minor won a Pulitzer Prize, and his Symphonic Poem for Orchestra was awarded the Loeb Prize. However, as a composer Gardner is best known for a catchy syncopated trifle, *From the Canebrake*, a fillip of Americana which has continued to delight young violinists for more than six decades. During the 1924-1925 season he was soloist in the Mendelssohn concerto with the New York Philharmonic under Mengelberg, and shortly after in a concerto of his own. Gardner's recording output lists about a dozen vignettes which reveal his playing as well-ordered, sensitive, and free of exaggerated expressive devices. His tone and musical ethos register a bit cool but are quite congenial. He devoted many decades to teaching, and was a venerable figure in the New York violin world.

ELIAS BREESKIN

Elias Breeskin (1895-1969), born in Russia, possessed a discriminating musicianship and controlled temperament that made him a Kneisel favorite. Unfortunately, as one of the most freewheeling personalities among American violinists, he became well-known to his colleagues for his practice of borrowing instruments and money that were seldom returned. Married to a wealthy woman and much sought-after for lucrative jobs as concertmaster, he nevertheless found himself in embarrassing predicaments owing to his compulsive gambling. As a result he moved from city to city, ultimately landing in Hollywood in the 1940s. His introductory recital in Los Angeles, crowned by a scintillating technical display in the Saint-Saëns-Ysaÿe *Caprice in the Form of a Waltz*, ensured a huge success, even in this ferociously competitive jungle. But again his peccadilloes destroyed the goodwill that his playing had created. He retreated to Mexico, where he succeeded in escaping the Mexican version of Devil's Island by the skin of his teeth. In 1950 I found him playing salon music as a strolling musician in a Mexico City restaurant. His performance had begun to deteriorate, but the remnants of his formidable equipment and disciplined musicianship were still impressive. His recordings, numbering 13 vignettes, are marked by a purity of tone and

style somewhat recalling Zimbalist; the sound is only moderately vibrant, although the scope of his playing is large-scaled. In his final years he returned to the United States, but by this time his performance was no more than a hollow shell of his prime. Had Breeskin been more stable, he might have enjoyed a sustained career as a top concertmaster and soloist, and as a conductor of respectable ability.

SASCHA JACOBSEN

Sascha Jacobsen (1895-1971), born of Russian-Jewish parents in what is now called Helsinki, arrived in America at age 11. Considered a star pupil of Kneisel (though Flesch refers to him as "a former pupil"), he won the 1915 Loeb prize at the Institute of Musical Art in New York, and made a successful debut later that year. But Jacobsen, for all his superior ability, became yet another casualty of the 1917 Heifetz phenomenon. As a soloist he was not quite equal to the best of the Auer pupils, who were tremendously in vogue at the time. At Kneisel's death in 1926, he succeeded him as a teacher at the Institute and then formed the Musical Art Quartet with violinist Paul Bernard, violist Louis Kaufman (later renowned as a violinist), and cellist Marie Roemat-Rosanoff. The quartet performed for nearly 20 years, though there were a few changes in the second violin and viola positions. Around 1945 the group disbanded and Jacobsen resigned his teaching post at Juilliard, moved west, and became concertmaster of the Los Angeles Philharmonic in 1946. Jacobsen's exceedingly warm, meticulously controlled if smallish sound was superbly suited for quartet playing, and in the areas of subtlety and stylistic grace, he merits ranking with the finest quartet violinists. He received wide publicity when, as a result of a driving mishap in which he nearly drowned, his "Red Diamond" Strad was lost in the Pacific Ocean. As luck would have it, someone found the badly soaked, practically ruined instrument and returned it to the violinist. Thanks to an incredible job of restoration by violin maker Hans Weisshaar, the violin was saved. Jacobsen left recordings of over 50 works, the most important of which is Saint-Saëns's *Introduction and Rondo Capriccioso*. They indicate basic talent of a high order; his tone is consistently vibrant, and he employs expressive devices with invariably good taste.

MICHAEL GUSIKOFF

Michael Gusikoff (1895-1978), born in New York City, was among the most intrinsically talented of the Kneisel pupils. Like Gardner, he studied composition with Percy Goetchius, but the acme of his works is *The American Concerto* (co-written with Benjamin Machan), an entertaining potpourri of quasi-jazz lyricism and lightly syncopated rhythms in the popular mood of the 1920s and 1930s. Gusikoff made his debut in 1920, subsequently becoming the concertmaster of the St. Louis Symphony, the old New York Symphony, and concertmaster of the Philadelphia Orchestra under Stokowski. He also held the same position with the NBC Orchestra and was for a time associate conductor of the Pittsburgh Symphony. Gusikoff's recording legacy consists of about seven bits of trivia, such as *I'll See You Home Again Kathleen*, the type of piece demanded of important violinists for mass consumption in the days of ten- and 12-inch acoustical discs. Nevertheless, these performances reveal Gusikoff as possessing a beautiful, intensely vibrant sound of first-class timbre in the tradition of the Auer tonalists. He had the courage to dress up the simple themes with double-stops of more than average difficulty, in sharp contrast to the simplistic way many of his competitors treated vignettes of this type. However, one cannot say that he exhibits exalted aesthetic motivation in his playing.

JACQUES GORDON

Jacques Gordon (1899-1948), born in Odessa, studied there with Franz Stupka at the Imperial Conservatory, and at age 13 was already a prize-winning pupil. Emigrating to America, he continued his studies with Kneisel at the Institute of Musical Art. He became a member of the Berkshire Quartet in 1917, a post he held for three years. In 1921 Gordon was selected by conductor Frederick Stock to be concertmaster of the Chicago Symphony, where he remained for nine years. As a soloist it is said that he was the first to perform Respighi's *Concerto Gregoriano* in America. Also in 1921 he formed the noted Gordon String Quartet whose members at one time included violinist Henry Sellinger, violist Clarence Evans, and cellist Naum Benditsky.

Jacques Gordon

Once as a publicity stunt, Gordon, dressed as an itinerant fiddler, performed on a street corner with his 1732 Stradivarius (claimed to have been played by Paganini, Spohr, and Joachim) to prove that passersby would toss money into a hat for good violin playing as readily as for any other kind of fiddling. He substantiated his point and received newspaper publicity throughout the country.

Gordon was conductor of the Hartford, Connecticut Works Progress Administration (WPA) Symphony from 1936 to 1939, and in 1942 became head of the violin department at the Eastman School in Rochester in conjunction with his quartet duties. Following a stroke in 1947, he resigned from the quartet, and died in 1948 of a cerebral hemorrhage after a musical soirée at the home of Albert Spalding, at which Kreisler had been present. Gordon's recordings are few, but a disc of his quartet in several light music arrangements shows him as a player of extraordinary polish and sophistication, with a suave, pure, somewhat small tone ideally suited to quartet playing.

JOSEPH FUCHS

Joseph Fuchs (b. 1901), born in New York, was the eldest of five children. His sister Lillian became a noted violist, and brother Harry was at one time first cellist of the Cleveland Orchestra. At an early age Fuchs began his study with Kneisel at the Institute of Musical Art, made his debut in 1920, toured for a time in Europe, and became concertmaster of the Cleveland Orchestra in 1929. In 1941 he resigned this post to pursue a solo career. He became director of the New York Musicians Guild, a group dedicated to chamber music. Often joining musical forces with his sister Lillian, he toured abroad extensively. In 1960 he commissioned the

Joseph Fuchs

of the Hindemith concerto, live and recorded. Yet, rather surprisingly, he produces more than a few stylistic subtleties in Grieg's Sonata No. 3 with the splendid piano collaboration of Frank Sheridan. Though Fuchs's prowess as an instrumentalist exceeds his impact as an artistic personality, he merits ranking with the finest concertmaster-soloists America has produced. He still played well in his mid-80s, and I heard him give a commendable master class in his early 90s.

WILLIAM KROLL

William Kroll (1901-1980) was born in New York, and as a youngster studied at the Berlin Hochschule with Henri Marteau from 1911 to 1914. After returning to New York in 1915, he became Kneisel's pupil at the Institute of Musical Art, where he also studied composition with Goetchius. Kroll's playing was ideally scaled for chamber music. He served as leader of the Elshuco Trio, 1922-1929, Coolidge Quartet, 1936-1944, and the Kroll Quartet, 1944-1969. In 1942 he received the Coolidge medal at the Library of Congress. He held teaching posts at the Institute of Musical Art (1922-1938) and the Mannes College of Music as well as at the Berkshire Tanglewood Festival, the Peabody Conservatory, the Cleveland Institute, and Queen's College. Kroll played a Guadagnini violin until 1950, then came into possession of the 1709 Strad once owned by Ernst.

Like Gardner, his fellow Kneisel pupil, Kroll as a composer is best known for a violinistic trifle, the showpiece *Banjo and Fiddle*, popularized by Heifetz and at one

Walter Piston concerto (through the Ford Foundation), and gave first performances of concertos by Nikolai Lopatnikoff and Ben Weber. Boleslav Martinu dedicated his *Madrigals* to the Fuchs brother-sister duo. Obviously an outspoken person of strong convictions, Fuchs once appeared on a nationwide television special in the role of pedagogue. Evincing neither prudence nor artistic humility, he unrealistically predicted that his pupil Christine Edinger, who played a portion of the Brahms concerto not very impressively, would defeat Pinchas Zukerman and Kyung-Wha Chung in a forthcoming competition. She did not, of course (but has since achieved a measure of success as a soloist in contemporary and avant-garde compositions). Fuchs is a formidable virtuoso with considerable temperament. His instrument is the 1722 "Cadiz" Stradivarius.

The Fuchs recordings number about 65 compositions, including the Beethoven sonata cycle, sonatas by Debussy, Fauré, Copland, Piston, Franck, Grieg, Schubert, and Strauss, the Stravinsky *Duo Concertante* and the Hindemith and Mozart (No. 3 in G) concertos. These recorded performances match closely his live playing that I have heard. Fuchs's musical approach is one of consistent drive and tremendous energy, and his articulation is invariably powerful. His tone, brilliant if somewhat hard-edged and muscular, is dominated by a very fast vibrato that often reflects tenseness rather than intensity, and is limited in variety. In general his playing projects visceral force and fervor, while lacking a sense of poetry, particularly in the sonatas of Franck, Fauré, and Debussy. His playing seldom smiles. Nor do tenderness, elegance, or affection play a prominent role in his music-making. All of the above-mentioned qualities and faults can be readily noted in his performances

William Kroll

time widely played. As a violinist Kroll was greatly influenced by Kreisler. His playing, meticulous though at times a bit over-refined, was not without glints of temperament. His sweet, clear, comparatively small tone never dominated his colleagues, and the chamber music performances he led were always marked by the suppleness, fluency, and polish of his playing.

LOUIS KAUFMAN

In terms of violinistic posterity, Louis Kaufman (1905-1994), born in Portland, Oregon, may well turn out to be foremost among Kneisel's pupils by virtue of some 125 recorded works, most of them major, plus featured solos in hundreds of film scores. Among the latter are such immortals as *Gone With the Wind, Modern Times,* and *The Diary of Anne Frank.* He studied in Portland with Albert Kreitz, Frank Eichenlaub, and Henry Bettmann, and at 13 he went to New York to study with Kneisel. After six months of preparation with Hugo Kortshak, he entered the Kneisel class where he had two half-hour lessons a week plus the privilege of hearing the lessons of other students, an opportunity he seized eagerly. Kaufman recalled, "Kneisel never told me what works to play. I selected my own music and brought it to him for instruction" (*Strad* magazine, June 1983). Tired of playing second violin to the older pupils in quartet playing, he took up the viola, "though," he states, "at the conclusion of the quartet session I immediately stashed my viola case under the bed and spent all my time with the violin."

Word soon circulated that Kaufman was a fine quartet violist, and eventually he was called upon to play privately on numerous occasions with such stars as Kreisler, Elman, Casals, and Zimbalist. "The musical understanding and discipline I received from Kneisel were vital to my education, but my opportunity to learn from the great masters with whom I played quartets significantly influenced my artistic development."

In 1927 Kaufman won the Loeb prize at the Institute of Musical Art and, in 1928, the prestigious Naumberg Award, both on violin. He accepted the post of violist in the Musical Art Quartet, a position he held until 1933. Meanwhile, he acquired Zimbalist's Guadagnini. In 1932 he married pianist Annette Leibole, a pupil of David Saperton. Deciding to seek a major career as a violinist, Kaufman resigned from the

Louis Kaufman

quartet. The Kaufmans traveled west, ultimately settling in Los Angeles, where they were soon playing three recitals a week on radio. Heard by film director Ernst Lubitsch, he was engaged to record the violin solos for *The Merry Widow.* Before long he was sought after by all the Hollywood studios.

Kaufman had a rare gift in the commercial realm for endowing a prosaic four-bar phrase with compelling beauty, and in lyric solo segments he had few serious rivals. But he never forgot his principal goal, and after 14 lucrative years made the fateful decision to desert the Hollywood "fleshpots" and to seek recognition in the jungle of the international concert world. Even while fully committed to film work, he had produced successful recordings of the Saint-Saëns No. 3 and Khachaturian concertos, the Smetana trio with pianist Rudolf Firkusny, and the Ernst Toch Quartet with the composer at the piano.

Kaufman's first post-Hollywood recording, Vivaldi's *Four Seasons* with conductor Henry Svoboda and members of the New York Philharmonic, was awarded the French Grand Prix du Disque. He gave premiere performances of concertos by Boleslav Martinu (Concerto de Camera), Anthony Collins, Lars-Eric Larsson, Henri Sauguet, Dag Wiren, and Leighton Lucas, plus performances of major works by Milhaud, Poulenc, Copland, and Robert Russell Bennett. Many of the above grace his list of recordings, together with concertos of Chausson, Vaughan Williams, and Giuseppe Torelli. More than a few violin authorities place Kaufman's discs of the Barber, Saint-Saëns,

Mendelssohn, Khachaturian, and Chausson concertos among the finest recorded versions of these works.

After eight years of touring and recording (with Paris as their base), the Kaufmans returned to their home in Los Angeles. In his mid-70s, following a detached-retina operation, he decided to retire. "I didn't want to decay in public," he remarked wisely.

While Kaufman was a thoroughly well-rounded, disciplined musician, the dominant characteristic of his playing is a bewitching, vibrant tone. His impulse-type vibrato is exceedingly fast, and is applied in all compositions from "portal-to-portal." Thus, as a hyper-romantic artist, the character of his sound is naturally more suited to romanticism than to classical or baroque music, although he gained much critical acclaim for his classical and baroque interpretations. His style incorporates many of the artful slides and position changes introduced by Kreisler (particularly those involving string crossings), as well as emotive position changes recalling those of Heifetz.

Among those outstanding violinists who have endeavored to recreate Kreisler's sound and style, Kaufman, with his entrancing fast vibrato and versatile emulation of many of Kreisler's expressive finger devices, can be counted among the few most convincing. In support of this contention, a comparison of Kaufman's recordings of *Londonderry Air* and *Hymn to the Sun* with those of any other violinist save Kreisler himself, is recommended. And in short confections of popular and jazz-tinted Americana widely performed in the 1930s and 1940s, and even later, Kaufman's stunning sound, sophisticated style, and rhythmic verve are of the highest order.

With his comparatively small hands, Kaufman did not specialize in the more gymnastic areas of the repertoire, but had a solid, secure technique which readily conquered the many difficulties and hazards posed by the contemporary compositions of his era. His playing, unusually consistent in quality, can scarcely fail to captivate the ear, and he deserves ranking among the top American-born violinists.

THE COMMERCIAL PHENOMENON

The role of the violin purely as a vehicle of entertainment in dance halls, saloons, theaters, restaurants, and even bordellos, is one of long standing. In their youth, such luminaries as Ysaÿe, Kreisler, Casals, Thibaud and, of course, the Strausses in Vienna, to mention but a few, played in one or another of these institutions to earn a living. The quality of so-called commercial playing has ranged from the sleaziest pseudo-Gypsy *shmeerings* to stylish vignette performances, in many instances reflecting polished artistry even in music of admitted banality. As the 20th century progressed, the historic development of the American musical theatre and light opera, and the tremendous proliferation of various types of Tin Pan Alley popular music and jazz, drove many exceptional violinists to the comparatively lucrative theatre pits and movie house orchestras. As phonograph recordings, radio, and talking pictures attracted vast audiences, commercial playing escalated to a new, more sophisticated level, demanding violinists capable of playing into an all-revealing microphone with genuine eclat. Film moguls, who invested huge sums to produce movies of quality, insisted on the finest orchestras money could buy. Excellent musicians from the Eastern theatre pits, as well as graduates of the leading American conservatories, flocked to Hollywood to reap the potential bonanza. Others quit comparatively low-paying jobs in symphony orchestras and rushed to the new Klondike. This influx has continued for over 60 years and now includes violinists born in Israel, Japan, the USSR, England, Hungary, and other countries. New York, and to a lesser degree, Chicago, are also among the major centers of American commercial recording.

Before the advent of Vitaphone (the first sound track used for early talking pictures), which came into widespread use in 1927, any musician of reasonable skill had his choice of jobs, and the better players might combine a noontime restaurant stint with the theatre pit and a radio show in a single day and night. But talking pictures obliterated movie house orchestras, and the Great Depression found violinists, more than a few of soloist caliber, competing desperately for theatre pit work. (Eugene Ormandy, fresh from study with Hubay at the Budapest Conservatory, was unable to attain a solo career and started as assistant concertmaster to Fradkin at the Capitol Theatre in New York.) It is no exaggeration to state that the overwhelming majority of American-born and naturalized violinists, including many with international reputations as soloists, pedagogues, chamber music players, and symphony concertmasters, have worked (paid by the hour) at one time or other in the commercial field. Many gifted violinists have found themselves stranded in the commercial field for life, well paid, but all too often artistically impoverished.

The key element in lucrative commercial playing of solo caliber is unabashed ear titillation. Vibrant beauty of sound, stylish and emotive phrasing and, of course, an exceptional ability to read any and all types of music with accuracy and rapidity, are vital requisites. The vibrato-poor alumni of middle-European academicism that descended from the Joachim precepts and Sevčik-schooled technicians, were soon vanquished by the lush-toned players of the Russian and, to a lesser extent, Belgian schools. This coincided with the situation (particularly after the advent of recordings at the turn of the century) that existed in the concert hall at that time.

The supreme commercial violinists in terms of direct mass appeal were Kreisler and Heifetz, and the ravishing charm and elegance of their vignette playing became the model for commercial violinists. A drab-toned "gymnast" who spent eight hours a day mastering Paganini's finger-twisters was almost certain to be surpassed by the violinist with a beautiful vibrant sound. In earlier years it was possible for dry-toned players to "hide" in the violin section that had a concertmaster with a golden tone, but as the decades passed this became less prevalent unless a colorless player had political job connections having nothing to do with the quality of his performance. Often violinists of comprehensive musical background and intelligence lost out to players of limited training who possessed instinctive expressive gifts and a songful tone. Thus, through the years, and still today, many a violinist who has earned his livelihood in the commercial field is not a commercial violinist in the truest sense of the term, but a well-schooled player displaced from the classical field. Some of the finest commercial violinists belong to the latter category.

Like gifted college athletes from poor families who leave school before graduation in order to enter lucrative professional sports, many violinists in similar circumstances, particularly those of the 1920s and 1930s, curtailed their music studies to earn big money in the commercial field. One could easily compile a lengthy roster of such players who achieved exceptional earnings by virtue of their naturally beautiful sound and expressive talents.

Selections are always debatable, but having worked for more than four decades with the best in the field, if I were to pick the archetypal commercial violinist who was *not* an economic refugee from the classical ranks, it would be Lou Raderman.

LOU RADERMAN

Born in New York, Lou Raderman (1902-1979) began playing the violin at the relatively late age of nine. At 12 he was already earning money playing for dance schools. His formal training was meager, but he did mention having had some lessons with Theodore Spiering and Maximilian Pilzer. At 15 he was a member of the Russian Symphony in New York, and soon after began recording for RCA Victor with such stars as Caruso, McCormack, Galli-Curci, and others. When Nathaniel Shilkret was engaged as conductor for that company, Raderman became his concertmaster. Meanwhile, he held the same position for many nationally broadcast radio shows. In 1938 Shilkret left for Hollywood. Upon becoming music director at MGM studios, the monarch of the film scene, he brought Raderman to the West Coast as his concertmaster, a position the violinist held for 35 years. Raderman, a guileless, winsome personality, was one of the most natural violinists I have ever heard, equally at home in the frothy strains of *Over the Rainbow* or the tensely dramatic solos in *The Four Horsemen of the Apocalypse*. His vibrato was not much over medium speed, but he employed it with rare sensitivity, and his rhythmic instincts, which permitted him to "bend" a phrase to delectable effect without distorting its essence, recalled those of Kreisler's. Violinists with infinitely more impressive academic credentials held Raderman in enormous respect. The overwhelming majority of them, recognizing his unusual gifts, did not resent sitting behind him in the section. His solos can be heard in most of the vintage MGM films, and record collectors fortunate to possess one of the four or five vignette collections he left, will quickly note the Kreislerian lilt of his artistry.

Specialty groups in the commercial field include jazz's "hot fiddlers," Gypsy-type violinists, and bluegrass and country-western fiddlers. The obstreperous Joe Venuti (1903-1978) was the undisputed king of hot fiddlers for decades, a position later vied for by the Frenchman Stephane Grappelli (b. 1908) and the Swede Svend Asmussen. The black violinist Eddie South (1904-1962), who concocted provocative jazz of such

Lou Raderman

pieces as Kreisler's *Praeludium and Allegro*, and the more elemental Stuff Smith (1909-1965), together with Ray Nance, Benny Gill, and the Curtis Institute graduates Paul Nero and Florian Zabach, deserve mention. Among the more well-known Gypsy players in America were the remarkable classically trained Nicolas Matthey and Bela Bobai. Prominent in the country hierarchy are Chubby Wise, an originator of bluegrass fiddling in the 1940s; Scott Stoneman, who imbued bluegrass playing with classical intensity; Richard Greene, a contributor to bluegrass with Western swing; Dale Potter, inventor of double-stop devices in Western swing; Tommy Jackson, a slick country commercial fiddler; Johnny Gimble, a top player of Western swing style; Benny Martin, creator of sundry novel effects and intervals in bluegrass on an eight-string fiddle; and Mark O'Connor, a commercial fiddler with a sparkling tone and extraordinary dexterity, who came to Nashville after a childhood career as a major prize-winner in old-time fiddle contests.

LOUIS PERSINGER

At present many of the most talented pupils from around the world come to the United States for advanced training and coaching, thus reversing the former trend of Americans flocking to European pedagogues for instruction and status. Louis Persinger (1887-1966), born in Rochester, Illinois, was certainly not the first American-born teacher of quality, but he was the first to garner international renown through his leading pupils, Menuhin and Ricci. Other outstanding violinists such as Guila Bustabo, Joseph Knitzer, Miriam Solovieff, Camilla Wicks, Berl Senofsky, Fredell Lack, and Zvi Zeitlin numbered him among their teachers. At 12 he was taken to Leipzig and there was graduated with honors from the old Royal Conservatory at age 16, winning praise from the famed conductor Arthur Nikisch. But it was his subsequent study with Ysaÿe for several years in Brussels, and the summers of coaching with Thibaud, that indelibly stamped Persinger as an exponent of the Belgian and French schools. He made his American debut in 1912 with Stokowski and the Philadelphia Orchestra. In 1914 Nikisch invited him to be concertmaster of the Berlin Philharmonic, but the war exigencies convinced him to return home, and in 1915 he became concertmaster of the San Francisco Symphony. After several years he decided he had had enough of symphony life and formed a string quartet, which quickly gained recognition and respect. From 1916 to 1928 he was director of the Chamber Music Society of San Francisco and began private teaching. In the wake of the Menuhin phenomenon, Persinger was appointed to the Juilliard faculty in 1930, replacing the deceased Leopold Auer, and remained there for 36 years as a violin pedagogue and chamber music coach. He was also an excellent pianist, and collaborated with his star pupils in concerts and recordings.

As a teacher, Persinger emphasized the musical and spiritual elements in performance. He was not one to prescribe back-breaking academic toil as a way of life for his students, holding that an hour and a half of practice at one time was sufficient for maximal results. His was a rare gift for inspiring his students. But in the case of Menuhin, Persinger's failure to demand uncompromising technical discipline in favor of accomplishments on the purely musical and communicative levels, undoubtedly was a significant factor in the serious technical problems later incurred by Menuhin.

However, Persinger possessed unusual musical sensitivity and imagination. His violinistic philosophy, as exemplified in his fascinating 64-page booklet, *Why the Violin?*, in which he touches briefly upon an amazing number of technical and musical points, indicates a searching, inquisitive mind and a willingness to challenge rigid orthodoxy. The material in the treatise ranges from a discussion of the "singing" nature of the violin to the frequency of rosining the bow. The ideas and presentation of his booklet also suggest that

Louis Persinger

profound, hair-splitting analysis was not his forte. But he could be a wonderful, liberating influence upon tense, inhibited students who had been "manhandled" by professional martinets. He encouraged individuality in his pupils; thus, there is no palpable Persinger stamp in their performance.

In my youth I once heard Persinger's quartet and was impressed by the sweetness of his tone and by his lyrical musicality. All he left behind were a few duet recordings and a lecture illustration of the Mendelssohn concerto that reveal similar propensities. As a performer Persinger ranked among the best American concertmaster-level violinists of his era. Who, among those present at the time, can ever forget the obvious love and solicitation with which he tuned their violins and presided as a bastion of support at the piano for the young Menuhin and Ricci?

SOME NOTEWORTHY NATURALIZED AMERICANS

PAUL KOCHANSKI

Paul Kochanski (1887-1934) died prematurely at only 47. It is sad that an artist of his exceptional gifts, who concertized as late as 1934, has left so small a heritage of recordings. This scion of an orthodox Jewish family (his surname at birth was Kaganoff) was born in Orel, Russia, but he is generally included in the hierarchy of great Polish violinists (Lipinski, Wieniawski,

Huberman, Szeryng, et al) inasmuch as his residence, early training, and first important successes were in Warsaw. Following his initial training with his father, Kochanski studied with Emil Mlynarski, himself a pupil of Auer. Considered a prodigy, Kochanski was the first soloist with the newly founded Warsaw Philharmonic. Two years later he went to Brussels where he continued his studies with César Thomson, ultimately winning first prize with the highest distinction at the Conservatoire. Indeed, Kochanski's playing, as evinced in his recordings, is a marvelous blend of the Russian school (emerging into international prominence), sparked by Auer, and the older, grandly romantic Belgian school, as epitomized by Ysaÿe. In 1915 he succeeded Auer as professor at the St. Petersburg Conservatory, and in the mid-1920s became a professor of violin at Juilliard.

In his maturity Kochanski was greatly respected as a brilliant conversationalist and a musician of sophisticated, cosmopolitan tastes and interests—all of which is mirrored in his playing. He had an active interest in music contemporary to his time, and was an ardent champion and performer of the violin music of his friend Karol Szymanowski, as well as works of Stravinsky and others.

Kochanski left only 11 commercially circulated recordings, one a major work, the others vignettes. They reveal him as an artist who would equate (except, perhaps, for an occasional dated slide) with standards of today. Though he was older than Heifetz or Elman, his playing, among other fine attributes, reflects the new revolutionary singing propensities of the violin. Whereas the playing of Vecsey, born in 1893, and

Paul Kochanski

255

Příhoda, born in 1900, could in no way compete in quality of tone and sophistication of style with first-class modern artists, the playing of Kochanski, born earlier, would be highly respected. One need only take the time to compare Vecsey's Beethoven Sonata No. 3 disc and the non-bravura pieces played by Příhoda with Kochanski's Brahms Sonata No. 3 in order to substantiate the above statement.

Unfortunately the few Kochanski discs cannot prove conclusively whether or not he was a large-scaled player capable of giving "heavyweight" top-level performances of such masterworks as the Beethoven, Brahms, and Tchaikovsky concertos. We must therefore be satisfied with the evidence of his recordings unless we wish to rely on the contradictory reports of individuals who heard the violinist in his prime.

No matter what he plays, Kochanski enchants the ear at all times. In addition, he combines an exceptional intuitive talent for expressive phrasing with a suave musical intelligence that rarely transcends the bounds of admirable discipline. It is the discipline of romanticism rather than academicism. Needless to say, his vibrato is highly developed, capable of various speeds and colors, and his bow arm is ever fluent, as is his entire musicality. His intonation is pure and his technique facile, though it is almost always used in the service of musical cognition rather than virtuoso display. On occasion the very propulsion of his melodic outpourings will result in a sort of breathless transition from one phrase to the next, but this idiosyncrasy is not of serious consequence. His art radiates sensitivity, and he is always a provocative stylist. One can note an affinity between Kochanski and Elman in certain position changes, but the Kochanski tone is less opulent and his musical personality not as strikingly personalized as Elman's.

Kochanski's Brahms Sonata No. 3 disc enjoys the piano collaboration of Artur Rubinstein, who plays with uninhibited, romantic gusto. The opening Allegro is sensually lyric, the pace brisk, the violin-piano rapport superbly integrated as befits two artists who have performed together countless times and know each other's heartbeat. On a few occasions the piano overpowers a bit, but the cause could be in the original engineering. One can note a few slides that hearken back to the Belgian manner of the turn of the century. The G-string sound of the Adagio is exquisitely sweet, the trills fast, the double-stops vibrant—an exceptionally fluid reading. The Poco presto e con sentimento is carefully honed to chamber music disposition, relaxed and finely etched. The Presto agitato finale is alternately songful and incisive, indicating Kochanski's knowledge of the art of musical diversity. In all, the interpretation is passionate, eloquent, and poetic.

The Wagner-Wilhelmj *Prize Song* is ardently vibrant, the high E-string passages extraordinarily so. One can note vividly Kochanski's relationship to both the Russian and Belgian schools. The Rachmaninoff-Gutheil *Vocalise*, containing a few more slides than most of Kochanski's short pieces, muses dreamily and beautifully. Kreisler's *La Gitana* bears the composer's influence in the playing, but is in no way imitative, and is delightfully piquant. Sarasate's *Malaguena* is almost lascivious in sound and languorous in mood; a few brief cuts are made; the G-string and E-string themes are equally impassioned. The disc's only technical tour de force is Wieniawski's *La Carnaval Russe*, a tricky theme-and-variation work. Kochanski makes much of what is essentially musical trivia, instilling it with a flavor that is unmistakably Russian; the left hand finger pizzicatos are swift and clean; the harmonics pure, the trill-tremolos exceedingly rapid. It is not a Heifetz technique, but is still admirable. Frank Tresselt is the conscientious piano collaborator.

Kochanski's brother Joseph, an excellent pianist, collaborates in Tchaikovsky's *Melodie* and the salon-style *Chant sans paroles*. Both recall Elman. The tempos move along brightly; all is sweet but never mawkish. Pierne's *Serenade* is elevated far above its intrinsic value and invested with a silvery sheen. The Raff *Cavatina* cannot rival Elman's G-string sound, yet is exceptional, with superbly clean and vibrant double-stops. The Brahms-Joachim *Hungarian* Dance No. 1 is dashing in style; the trill-tremolos, electric. Several of the phrases are strung together without adequate "breath." The approach is quite individual.

There can be no doubt that with the death of Paul Kochanski, the world lost a violinist of redoubtable qualities. His discs are an invaluable testament to an artist every violin fancier should know.

EFREM ZIMBALIST

Efrem Zimbalist (1889-1985) was born in Rostov-on-Don, Russia. His father, a violinist and conductor at the Rostov Opera, was his first teacher. Around 1904 he was taken to St. Petersburg by his mother. Like other

Efrem Zimbalist

budding violinists of Jewish lineage, he required special permission from the czarist authorities for his parent to remain in the city—in this instance, for a single week. This was obtained through the efforts of Leopold Auer. Following preparatory work with Auer's assistant, Nalbandyan, at the St. Petersburg Conservatory, the boy was admitted to Auer's class in 1907. Biographers generally point out that Zimbalist was a "red-shirt" leader of the conservatory student strike during the abortive 1905 revolution. However, his intimate association with extremely wealthy society figures dating from shortly after his arrival in America, would indicate that Zimbalist was a realist in terms of advancing his career. Upon graduation, he won the conservatory's Gold Medal and the 1,200-ruble Rubinstein Prize. In November 1907, he made a successful Berlin debut with the Philharmonic in the Brahms concerto and a month later, his London debut. He also studied for a short period with Sevčik.

Arriving in the United States in 1911, Zimbalist made his American debut with Max Fiedler and the Boston Symphony in the relatively new Glazunov concerto. His introduction to the American music scene is related by Samuel Chotzinoff, his early piano collaborator (later brother-in-law of Heifetz, and a New York music critic), in his nostalgic autobiography *Days at the Morn.* In 1914 the violinist married the noted soprano Alma Gluck, a divorcée and mother of the writer Marcia Davenport. Zimbalist, an accomplished pianist, often served as accompanist for his wife. The couple had two children, Maria and Efrem Jr., the well-known actor. Gluck died in 1938. In 1943 Zimbalist married Mrs. Mary Louise Curtis Bok, a benefactor of the Curtis

Institute of Music, daughter of the Philadelphia publisher, Cyrus Curtis.

Zimbalist performed on and off until 1955, when he played the Beethoven concerto with the Philadelphia Orchestra. While his solo career was of longer duration than that of many other victims of the Heifetz phenomenon, it ultimately slackened. He continued to play many concerts throughout the 1920s and 1930s, after which the frequency of his public performances abated. In 1928 he became a faculty member at the Curtis Institute and from 1941 to 1968 held the post of director. Many American violinists of stature count Zimbalist among their teachers, including Oscar Shumsky, Shmuel Ashkenasi, Joseph Silverstein, and Norman Carol.

There can be no doubt that Zimbalist was one of the most sophisticated and intelligent violinists of his era. His overall career as a musician was long and honorable. He moved in the highest social circles and was the intimate of the music world's greatest figures. His ability to perform successfully such masterworks as the Beethoven and Brahms concertos placed him in a more exalted category than many highly gifted, tonally-oriented violinists whose musicianship and essential artistry were comparatively limited. As late as 1954, Zimbalist gave the premiere performance of Gian Carlo Menotti's violin concerto. During his later years he retired to the Reno, Nevada area.

In his autobiography, *Memoirs of Carl Flesch,* Flesch states:

> I must confess that (Zimbalist) interested me the least of the best Auer pupils...His playing offered no evidence of a significant personality...I regard it as an injustice of fate that (Toscha Seidel) is not considered the third in a triumvirate with Heifetz and Elman.

This was a direct slur against Zimbalist, who was invariably cited as the third. Flesch also complains about the slowness of Zimbalist's vibrato, a problem he well understood since he was plagued with a similar shortcoming. One might consider Flesch's appraisal to be prejudiced, since his relations with the Curtis Institute were strained during the period before his resignation from the faculty. He makes a point of writing that "the 84-year-old Auer and Efrem Zimbalist, who had never before taught the instrument, became my successors." Flesch also rather uncharitably states of the elderly Auer's private lessons in America, "The chief condition of admission for a prospective pupil consisted in his ability to pay $360 for six lessons." Alas, it was all too true. (At the time Kneisel, the premier teacher in America, was receiving $20 for a private lesson, one-third of the outlandish Auer fee. But Kneisel was not the reputed teacher of Elman and Heifetz.) However, regardless of Flesch's disposition, the many occasions on which I heard Zimbalist in person and on recordings generally support Flesch's evaluation.

I particularly recall a Zimbalist recital during the early 1930s. About 300 people were in attendance on a Sunday afternoon in the 3,500-seat Philharmonic Auditorium, a hall invariably filled by Kreisler, Heifetz, and the boy Menuhin. Zimbalist, a thoroughly poised, imperturbable figure, began with Bach's E-major Concerto, which he delivered with bland accuracy. He then proceeded to play Bruch's *Scottish Fantasy*, all with piano support. It was then that I understood why Zimbalist, for all his polished facility, could not sustain a solo career in competition with the top artists of the day. His playing was practically devoid of emotional projection, though he was well skilled in expressive finger devices. He would, for example, make a long Heifetz slide on the G string, and one could almost count the oscillations of his vibrato on the pallid landing note. Everything seemed on the surface of the instrument, and his vibrato was not only inherently slow and undistinguished, but ineffective in terms of producing warm-hearted sentiment, temperamental fire, sensuality of sound, or dramatic tension. Yet there were elements of his playing that one could admire greatly, such as his ability to sustain the "long bow" in lyrical phrases. The recital continued with several Zimbalist favorites: amazingly fleet, cogently phrased, crystalline renditions of the Popper-Auer *Spinning Song* (originally for cello), Hubay's *Le Zephyr*, the Glinka-Auer *The Lark*, the Chopin-Spalding *Waltz in G-flat*, No. 11, and Sarasate's *Carmen Fantasy*, in which the technical passages were of stellar brilliance and almost birdlike clarity. Interspersed were cool, glassy-toned performances of Glinka's *Persian Song* and a little Japanese trifle titled, I believe, *Kukura-Kukura*, both Zimbalist settings.

Zimbalist recorded about 89 different compositions, the most significant of which are Brahms's Sonata No. 3, Op. 108, Ysaÿe's Solo Sonata No. 1, and two movements of Hubay's Concerto No. 3. All closely mirror the impression of his live playing. He also tried his hand at composition, the most significant of his output being his Sonata in G-minor which can be heard in a highly capable recorded performance by his one-time

pupil Philip Frank, and pianist Bernard Frank. It is a congenial work containing many glints of Zimbalist's Russian past, liberally sprinkled with clever violinistic effects. Unfortunately, it also has an unrelieved meandering quality that may be one of the reasons it has never become a repertorial staple of his celebrated colleague-friends. Irrespective of how one assesses Zimbalist as a soloist, his influence on American violin art was considerable, and his overall contribution was of major stature.

NAOUM BLINDER

In the same age group was Naoum Blinder (1889-1965), born in Eupatoria, Russia, a pupil of Alexander Fidelman in Odessa and of Adolf Brodsky in Manchester. His early years included a post on the Moscow Conservatory faculty (1923-1925), and numer-

Naoum Blinder

ous solo appearances throughout the USSR and Japan. Coming to America in the late 1920s, he became concertmaster of the San Francisco Symphony in 1932. He was Stern's teacher from 1932 to 1937. The single time I heard Blinder, he impressed me as a major talent with outstanding technical equipment, broad expressive powers, a richly intense sound, and tasteful musicality. Had he been with one of the major East Coast organizations, undoubtedly his career would have attained greater scope. He left only ten recordings of short pieces.

MISHEL PIASTRO

Mishel Piastro

Among the leading pupils of Auer who were unable to sustain top-level solo careers were several who became concertmasters of major symphony orchestras. In the vanguard of these was Mishel Piastro (1891-1970), born in Kerch, Russia. He was generally included as one of the best six or seven of the pupils Auer taught in St. Petersburg. His violinist father, who had once been an Auer pupil, was his first teacher. His older brother, Josef Piastro-Borissoff, also a pupil of Auer, was prominent as a splendid technician and teacher, though his tone was less vibrantly beautiful than that of the younger violinist. Mishel studied with Auer for about four years, starting in 1906, and in 1911 won the 1,000-ruble Auer prize. Together with Elman and Zimbalist, he was one of three military-age Jewish violinists exempted from military service by the czar.

In 1914 he began a tour eastward to the Orient, and ultimately arrived in San Francisco in 1920, where he became concertmaster of the San Francisco Symphony from 1925 to 1931. Engaged by Toscanini as concertmaster of the New York Philharmonic, he enjoyed a brilliant career, winning nationwide renown through his annual broadcasts as soloist with the orchestra, performing most of the major concertos from Brahms to Miaskovsky. Piastro's broadcasts were eagerly awaited by young violinists of the era, including myself. During John Barbirolli's leadership of the orchestra (1941-1943), he became assistant conductor, but was later victim of a purge of first-chair players by the new leader Artur Rodzinski. At that time Piastro, while still concertmaster, had already been serving since 1941 as conductor and violin soloist of the highly respected Longines Symphonette, which performed for many years on radio and recordings.

Flesch says of Piastro: "Instrumentally, he is of Heifetz's class, while his personal aura is, of course, far weaker." The latter part of the statement is true, but Piastro, although a brilliant violinist of exceptional polish with a sweetly vibrant tone of medium intensity and disciplined musicianship, was certainly no competitor of Heifetz, instrumentally. His playing was smaller-scaled, but he had the instinct of a true soloist, as opposed to quite a few solid, highly regarded concertmasters who did not. His left hand expressive devices bore Elman's influence. This can be heard in the more demanding works among the 19 recorded pieces he left, such as Wieniawski's *Faust Fantasy*, *Le Carnaval Russe*, and *Souvenir de Moscou*, all made early in his career. Piastro's style possessed the heroic thrust and breadth of the best Auer pupils. Undoubtedly had he been able to concentrate purely on solo playing, his artistry would have been considerably enhanced. (The same holds true for so many brilliant concertmasters of the 1920s, 1930s, and 1940s, and for that matter, today.)

I once had the opportunity to spend about three hours privately with Piastro, reminiscing about his early days with Auer. Since he could be counted among the best tonal pupils of Auer, I asked about Auer's teaching of vibrato and tone production. Why, I wondered, in view of Auer's eminence as a teacher, did the vibratos of his pupils range from the one extreme of Elman, Seidel, and Heifetz to the other of Zimbalist, Achron, and Borissoff? He replied that Auer would discuss *usage* of the vibrato, but not its development and manner of production. Either the pupil already had a viable vibrato before coming to Auer, or he did not. Auer's lessons, he stressed, offered no clinical instruction about vibrato. And like Milstein, he stated that the most fruitful moments of his association with Auer were during the twice-weekly master classes in which he was inspired by watching and listening to the other extraordinary talents.

RICHARD BURGIN & ALEXANDER HILSBERG

Other Auer pupils of note were Richard Burgin (1892-1981), born in Warsaw, who was concertmaster of the Boston Symphony from 1920 to 1967, and Alexander Hilsberg (1897-1961), born in Russia, who was concertmaster of the Philadelphia Orchestra for some two decades. Burgin had also studied with Lotto and Joachim, and after four years with Auer he won the Gold prize at the St. Petersburg Conservatory in 1912. After concertmaster stints in Helsinki and Oslo, he came to the United States in 1923, and in 1927 combined his concertmaster duties with those of assistant conductor under Koussevitzky. He married violinist Ruth Posselt in 1940. Hilsberg, who studied with Auer for only about a year, also became addicted to the baton, and ended his music career successfully as a conductor of the New Orleans Symphony, a position he accepted in 1952. Both Burgin and Hilsberg were superb section leaders, but not in Piastro's category as soloists.

MISCHA MISCHAKOFF

A powerful member of this company was Mischa Mischakoff (Fischberg) (1895-1981), born in Proskouroff, Russia, son of a flutist. He studied with Korguyeff, himself an Auer pupil, at the Imperial Conservatory in St. Petersburg, receiving the Rubinstein prize of 1,200 rubles in 1913. Arriving in America in 1921, he was successively concertmaster of the New York Symphony (not the Philharmonic), the Philadelphia Orchestra, and the Chicago Symphony. His stature can be judged by the fact that Toscanini selected him from a large number of the finest available candidates to be concertmaster of his "all-star" NBC Symphony in 1937. Mischakoff also appeared often as soloist; his 14 recordings, capped by the Brahms

The Mischa Mischakoff String Quartet

Double Concerto with cellist Frank Miller (Toscanini, NBC Symphony), are mostly single movements from concerto staples. I heard him many times on radio as soloist and in orchestral solo excerpts. His performance was impeccable, his tone warm and solid, his rhythmic stability unshakable. It was neither highly personalized nor particularly imaginative playing, but he was certainly one of the finest concertmasters of his era. He continued his concertmaster assignments well into his 70s with the Detroit Symphony.

SAMUEL DUSHKIN

The career of Samuel Dushkin (1895?-1967) is proof positive that a violinist need not be a heaven-storming virtuoso, a member of a prime quartet or trio, or a brilliant concertmaster-soloist, to make a valuable contribution to his art. Essentially a pupil of Rémy in Paris, he also had some lessons with Auer in New York. Dushkin commissioned the Stravinsky Violin Concerto in 1931, in which he collaborated with the composer in matters of violinistic detail. From that time on, the two were intimately associated, and Dushkin played an important role in the creation of the *Divertimento*, *Duo Concertante*, and *Suite Italienne*. He also fashioned arrangements of short pieces from selected Stravinsky works. The two performed together in Europe and America, popularizing Stravinsky's music at a time when much of it was considered avant-garde and sensationalist. In music other than the novel Stravinsky compositions, Dushkin's playing might be described as no more than capable and efficient. This is borne out by his recordings. Wisely, he opted for contemporary works that did not place him in direct competition with the elite among his colleagues. In addition to Stravinsky, he performed works by Martinu, Victor Rieti, Virgil Thomson, William Schuman, and Gershwin, and he is said to have been the first to introduce Ravel's *Tzigane* to America. His 13 recordings are mostly pieces by Stravinsky, with the latter at the piano, and his recording of the concerto (with Stravinsky, Lamoreaux Orchestra) was the first of many since recorded. Dushkin was a pioneer whose efforts merit respect and emulation by enterprising violinists, who may or may not be fortunate enough to find new violin works by composers who understand the instrument and are able to exploit its lyric propensities with some degree of talent and inspiration.

TOSCHA SEIDEL

Had Heifetz not come along, Toscha Seidel (1900-1962) might well have joined Kreisler and Elman in the topmost echelon in terms of mass public acceptance during the late teens and 1920s. Born in Odessa, Seidel was yet another prodigy from that incubator of violinists. He started lessons with Max Fidelmann, an Auer pupil, and at age 12 began study with Auer himself in St. Petersburg. At 14 he shared programs with Heifetz (one year his junior), both of them winning resounding success. Seidel was dubbed "the devil of the violin"; Heifetz, "the angel." His major debut in 1915 was in Oslo playing the Tchaikovsky concerto, followed by his St. Petersburg debut a year later. After numerous European concerts, he made his Carnegie Hall debut in 1918, a year after Heifetz, again with great critical acclaim.

One of the most instinctive and exciting violin talents ever to draw a bow, Seidel possessed a thrilling tone that was sumptuous and voluptuous, motivated by one of those "meaty," impulse-type vibratos, and abetted by a sonorous Russian-style bow arm. It can be safely asserted that among presently concertizing violinists there is no violin tone to compare with Seidel's in sheer impassioned sensuality. His fiery, extravagant romanticism, dominated by a rare, completely personalized, readily recognizable tonal timbre, was vastly different from the pellucid clarity of the far more disciplined, seraphic Heifetz muse. Professionals who were familiar with his live performances still rhapsodize about the "Seidel sound." Like his sound, his musical approach and interpretations were tinged with an ingenuous Gypsy spirit and rhythmic liberties recalling Elman, but even more exorbitant in over-emotive thrust. Although his playing was of massive scale, he could also charm the listener in short pieces. Seidel's emotive slides and position changes were occasionally overused, but generally in good taste and devastating in effect. He did not specialize in Paganinian gymnastics, although his technical equipment was comprehensive and fluent. Pure intonation, marvelous singing double-stops, a brilliant trill, and a fine staccato were cardinal elements of his playing.

Courtesy I. MonDragon

Toscha Seidel

Why, then, after his triumphant early years did Seidel's career fail to sustain itself on the highest level? True, he might be considered yet another victim of the Heifetz phenomenon. But others such as Menuhin, Szigeti, Milstein, Francescatti, and later Stern, built careers while Heifetz was still in his prime. Seidel had the advantage of a start as early as 1918, an advantage not enjoyed by many important talents who reached maturity during the Great Depression. The downturn in Seidel's career can be attributed to two main factors. First, for all the aural beauty of his playing, Seidel could not be considered a profound, perceptive, all-encompassing musician in an era in which these qualities were increasingly in demand by critics and the concertgoing public. As an incorrigible romantic, musical introspection was alien to his nature, intellect, and temperament. His tone and musicality were too singular for the impersonal glories of the Bach sonatas, or even to an extent for the music of Beethoven, though his brawny Brahms concerto was impressive, as were his Tchaikovsky, Bruch, Lalo, and Mendelssohn concertos. Historically, by the mid-1930s, freewheeling violinists like Elman were gradually becoming anachronistic at the topmost level. Second, unlike the worldly wise Zimbalist, who was utterly at ease in any cosmopolitan company, Seidel was a somewhat naive, unsophisticated personality, who was most at home with the violin under his chin. I knew him very well after he had been relegated to the Hollywood milieu in the late 1930s, in which he was totally miscast and not really comfortable. During this period he played considerable chamber music, which broadened his musicianship, but his playing was far too individualistic for a concertmaster "section-leader" in commercial orchestral work. Nonetheless, many of his film score solo excerpts are memorable. His mental powers retrogressing through illness, this one-time prodigy of the violin ended his career playing in a Las Vegas show orchestra.

Around 1930, while still in his prime, Seidel performed a weekly series of CBS nationwide radio broadcasts featuring a different concerto each week. Unfortunately the transcriptions have not been preserved. Thus we cannot hear his finest large-scale work, though he did record the Brahms Sonatas No. 1, Op. 78 and No. 2, Op. 100, and Grieg's Sonata No. 3, with pianist Arthur Loesser. These were recorded during the 1930s, when he no longer performed regularly on the concert stage. In them his playing is artistically inconsistent. Thanks to James Creighton's Discopaedia Records, 17 of the short pieces among the 57 Seidel recordings have been restored. The early Columbia discs have much more surface noise than their Victor counterparts, but the dedicated listener can scarcely fail to be enchanted by such extraordinary playing. Among them the Rimsky-Korsakov *Chanson Arabe* is saturated with lush tone; *Eili-Eili*, a Seidel setting, is heartfelt and freely intoned; Hubay's *Hejre Kati* is a Romany delight; Burleigh's *Indian Snake Dance*, a piece tritely imitative of Kreisler, is forgettable. Kreisler's *Caprice Viennois* is ultra-rhapsodic, but perhaps the most tonally impressive performance, along with Elman's, after that of Kreisler. The Paderewski-Kreisler *Minuet*, once ubiquitous, is gleamingly beautiful and demonstrates Seidel's excellent digital and bowing flexibility.

Some later noiseless Victors are Saint-Saëns's *Prelude to the Deluge* and the Wagner-Wilhelmj *Albumblatt*, both broadly conceived, overtly extroverted, and voluminous in sound. *Brahmsiana*, a banal vaudevillian paraphrase of *Hungarian Dances* No. 4 and No. 5 by V. Bakaleinikoff, and the Brahms-Joachim *Hungarian Dance* No. 1, have gut-shattering G-string sound, though the latter contains some G-string notes almost too intense for the violin to project tastefully. The Mozart-Burmester *Minuet* from *Divertimento* No. 17 is rather muscular, ornate in sound, and resonantly buoyant in the flying staccato bowings.

And, of course, there is his legendary, gorgeous performance of Provost's *Intermezzo* from the film score, a recording which, for an extended period, popularized the violin for millions of listeners.

Little known to modern audiences and the younger generations of players, Seidel was one of the top violin talents of the 20th century, an artist who, irrespective of certain musical shortcomings, has much to offer violin fanciers who revel in playing of spontaneity and inner warmth, exquisitely virile sound, and grand-manner perspective. At his best, Seidel deserves inclusion, after Heifetz and Elman, in the leading triumvirate of Auer's Russian pupils.

RAOUL VIDAS

Raoul Vidas (1901-1978) was born in Rumania (of Jewish parentage, according to the noted American critic James Huneker), but was considered a French violinist since he came to Paris at age eight. After initial lessons with his father, he studied privately with the blind Henri Berthelier, a professor at the Paris Conservatoire. Vidas enjoyed a brilliant career as a child prodigy and was tremendously acclaimed in France. He made a successful New York debut in 1918, and once when Heifetz fell ill, Vidas was recruited as his substitute. As an artist and representative of the French school, Vidas stood somewhere between Thibaud and Francescatti. His playing was influenced by Ysaÿe, Kreisler, and Thibaud. The few recordings he made reveal him as a stylist of decided elegance. Like so many fine violinists who had the misfortune to be born in the Heifetz generation, Vidas, a person of gentle spirit, hampered by a serious injury to his right thumb, retired after a comparatively short adult career. When his injury healed, he tried to make a comeback in New York around 1938, including in his program (of all things!) a violin transcription of the Grieg piano concerto. He soon retired permanently, living alone with his mother in Los Angeles and devoting all his waking hours to composition. When playing privately, on occasion, he performed with the sweep, sound, and authority of an important Romantic violinist. Among his compositions were his tribute to Americana, violin-piano transcriptions of numerous Stephen Foster songs, and many complex contemporary works that were rarely performed. An affable man who loved to "talk violin," he seemed quite content to exchange the rigors of the concert and commercial worlds for his self-imposed isolation. Vidas willed his beautiful Guadagnini violin and exquisite Tourte bow to the Paris Conservatoire.

Unhappily, these instruments disappeared mysteriously, and though I sought vigorously to locate them, I could get no concrete or satisfactory answer as to their whereabouts, either in Los Angeles or Paris.

LOUIS KRASNER

Moving ahead chronologically among foreign-born Americans, we veer to the opposite extreme of the violinistic and musical spectrum with Louis Krasner (1903-1995), born in Cherkassy, Russia. Brought to America by his parents at age five, he began lessons in Providence, Rhode Island, and graduated from Boston's New England Conservatory in 1922. Subsequently, he studied in Europe with Flesch, Capet, and Sevčik. Like Dushkin, Krasner gained renown through his association with leading contemporary composers and, in 1934, he commissioned Alban Berg to write the violin concerto which he premiered April 19, 1936 in Barcelona, shortly after Berg's death. Krasner continued to introduce the hyper-romantic work elsewhere, and succeeded in winning converts to its cause in New York and Boston.

At that time the concerto was considered by some to be hopelessly avant-garde, but today, like Prokofiev's Concerto No. 1 and the Stravinsky concerto, it is in the repertoire of nearly every concertizing artist, including several from the former USSR, where 12-tone music was once an anathema. In 1928 he also premiered a Joseph Achron concerto in Vienna and Alfredo Casella's concerto in Siena and Rome, neither of which has won acceptance into the standard repertoire. The Achron (which I heard played by the composer), is an interesting, worthwhile work, unfortunately neglected. Krasner then accepted the supreme challenge of being the first to perform Schoenberg's violin concerto in 1940 with Stokowski and the Philadelphia Orchestra. Several violinists have performed and recorded the work, which reveals at once the limitations of the violin by consistently abusing its intrinsic nature as the instrument closest to the human voice. One can understand the thrill of accomplishment experienced by those violinists who have scaled the heights of cacophony, and applaud their Herculean labors. But after nearly half a century, a performance of the Schoenberg concerto, no matter how brilliant, remains a sensationalist feat appealing only to a limited audience. Krasner, concertmaster of the Minneapolis Symphony in the 1940s, plays with a dry tone production that hearkens back to the Sevčik pupils, but his playing style is aggressive, and he surmounts the concerto's massive obstacles with courage, accuracy, and poise. His handful of recordings include the Berg (Rodzinski, Cleveland Orchestra) and the Schoenberg (Mitropoulos, New York Philharmonic). And whether one does or does not like these concertos, violin art, like any other, needs its pioneers, and in this area, Krasner has made an important contribution.

HENRI TEMIANKA

Born in Greenock, Scotland (1906-1992), where his father served as cantor for the local Jewish congregation, Henri Temianka enjoyed an exceptionally diverse musical career. Both parents had come from Poland but Henri spent most of his childhood in Holland. He studied with Carel Blitz for eight years in Rotterdam and later with Willy Hess in Berlin, Jules Boucherit in Paris (whom he credits with "doing wonders for my bow arm"), and ultimately with Carl Flesch at the Curtis Institute and at Baden-Baden. In 1935, while residing in London, he became a last-minute entry in Poland's politicized Wieniawski contest, and was awarded third prize after Ginette Neveu and David Oistrakh. Subsequently he served as concertmaster of the Scottish Orchestra under George Szell and from 1941 to 1942, with Fritz Reiner and the Pittsburgh Symphony. After World War II he became the first violinist of the Paganini String Quartet, whose members performed on Stradivarius instruments once belonging to Paganini. After two decades and many personnel changes, the quartet disbanded in 1966. The immensely enterprising Temianka founded the California Symphony in 1960, a group that, despite an amazing number of personnel changes through the years, prospered and won deserved respect in the Los Angeles area under his leadership, which was honed in the strict Szell-Reiner image. A number of the world's greatest artists—Oistrakh, Menuhin, Stern, and Szeryng, among others—performed with the ensemble. Temianka premiered works of such contemporary composers as Shostakovich, Ginestera, Milhaud, Menotti, Copland, Chavez, Arnold, Krenek, William Schuman, and Castelnuovo-Tedesco. His pupil Nina Bodner won first prize in the 1982 Thibaud Competition, and Camilla Wicks and Leo

Berlin number among his former students.

Temianka was an extremely articulate man, and his many writings include the witty, semi-autobiographical *Facing the Music*. As a remarkably knowledgeable public speaker on musical subjects, he had few peers. And he was a tough-minded musician who stood up publicly to newspaper critics and survived their often scurrilous attacks.

Temianka was an unusually consistent violinist and a stylist of uncommon stature. In the many times I heard him in concert, whether in Mozart, Mendelssohn, or Chausson concertos, or Beethoven sonatas, his tone was invariably sweet, his technique facile, and his delivery polished.

His recordings number about 40, some 15 of which are Handel sonatas with harpsichord. Among the best of his 1935-1937 recordings are Pugnani's Sonata in E-major, Op. 1, No. 6 and Schubert's Rondo in A-major (the latter with chamber orchestra). One might pinpoint some anachronistic expressive slides (which are not to be heard in his postwar playing), but these works, so difficult to perform convincingly, are rendered with exceptional purity of line and sound. Other pieces are a ridiculously fast performance of Wieniawski's *Scherzo Tarantelle*, in which the inherent pulse of the music is almost lost, and a neatly phrased version of the *Polonaise Brilliante* in A-major, with much verve and crackling staccatos. The post-1960 Handel sonatas, with Malcolm Hamilton, display chaste classical grace, and the post-1970 three Grieg sonatas with pianist James Field, though evincing a noticeable slackening of his vibrato, are sensitive and idiomatic. Temianka's career was kaleidoscopic; he must be counted as one of Flesch's important pupils, and his contribution to the American music scene has been considerable.

TOSSY SPIVAKOVSKY

Without doubt, the most unorthodox, individualistic, independent violinist among the significant soloists of this era has been Tossy Spivakovsky, born in Odessa in 1907. At a very early age he was taken to Berlin, where he studied with Arrigo Serato and later with the domineering Willy Hess. However, Spivakovsky was exclusively "his own man" as an artist, uninfluenced by any specific school or colleague. At ten he made his debut, and at 18 became one of the

concertmasters of the Berlin Philharmonic for several seasons, then resigned to concentrate on solo playing. When the Nazis came to power he left Germany for Australia, and eventually identified himself with the musical life of that area. From 1933 to 1940 he taught at the University Conservatorium of Melbourne. In 1941 he moved to America, and from 1942 to 1945 was concertmaster of the Cleveland Orchestra.

Spivakovsky appeared often as soloist with the orchestra, and in 1943 scored a sensational triumph in Bartók's Concerto No. 2 with Rodzinski and the New York Philharmonic, which was nationally broadcast. I vividly recall the occasion. The Bartók ideally showcased the best elements of Spivakovsky's playing. For the moment it seemed as if he belonged to the stellar few among international stars. This success was the catalyst that enabled him, within two years, to retire from orchestral playing and pursue a solo career.

Shortly after, in the Tchaikovsky concerto, it was obvious that while he was a brilliant virtuoso, his playing was not quite of superstar stature. I heard him in many live concerts, both in concertos with orchestra and in recitals. The results in the standard repertoire were generally uneven. In a single work he was capable of interpretive logic, discipline, superficiality, stunning virtuosity, and ill-conceived musicality, particularly in such works as the Beethoven and Mozart concertos. Yet it must be said that his performances of the Beethoven sonatas were well ordered and respectful of the composer.

Spivakovsky might well be thought of as the alchemist of the violin—an indefatigable experimenter. His choice of bowings, and to a lesser extent, of fingerings, were different from those of any other violinist. It was a disturbing experience for professional violinists to view him in action because his bowings were so utterly divergent from the various traditional modes. But, these seeming aberrations worked beautifully for him. His bow grip was unusual, held a bit above the frog. This rendered his bowing exceptionally smooth, supple, and powerful, but limited in variety of textures. In the Bach solo sonatas he used a curved bow in the slow movements. It was both impressive and disquieting to hear sonorous three-note chords played unbrokenly in the baroque manner, and in the same work, vibrato employment that at times was patently romantic. His facility was tremendous in both hands. His playing of Sarasate's *Carmen Fantasy* and *Introduction and Tarantelle* compared favorably with anyone's, except

Heifetz's, in dazzling speed and clarity. But when not at his best, intonation problems would creep in. Spivakovsky's vibrato was exceedingly fast, and coupled with occasional, somewhat peculiar, sensuous slides, it gave his sound a glittery Gypsy cast that recalled salon playing but, of course, on an infinitely higher level. In contemporary music such as the concertos of Roger Sessions, Leroy Robertson, Gian Carlo Menotti, Leon Kirchner, Bartók, and Stravinsky, these idiosyncrasies did not seriously vitiate his interpretations. Indeed, his performances in these works were of extraordinary caliber. In the romantic repertoire and technical pieces his playing, though ever intensely expressive, was more convincing in shorter episodes that did not require a full range of color, nuance, and modal scale. And apart from his Bach, which was always interesting whether or not one agreed with his approach, classical compositions were not really in consonance with his sound and fervent temperament. All this can be verified by his 53 recorded works.

Spivakovsky was a violinist whose playing was never less than provocative, interesting, and entertaining, and in top form he was a superlative instrumentalist.

SZYMON GOLDBERG

Prominent among the hierarchy of post-Huberman Polish Jewish violinists, among them Paul Kochanski, Stefan Frenkel, Henri Temianka, Bronislav Gimpel, Roman Totenberg, Ida Haendel, the tragic Joseph Hassid, and the formidable Henryk Szeryng, is Szymon Goldberg (1909-1993), born in Wloclawek, Poland. He began study in Warsaw at age seven with Czaplinski, and later with Mihalowicz; at ten he became Flesch's pupil in Berlin. Following a Warsaw debut at age 12, he made a Berlin debut with Flesch's blessing at only 15 in a program of three concertos, Bach's E-major, Paganini's No. 1, and Joachim's arduous Hungarian concerto. Gaining experience as a concertmaster of the Dresden Philharmonic at the tender age of 16, he was chosen by Furtwangler four years later to be one of the Berlin Philharmonic's concertmasters, a position he held from 1929 to 1934. Replacing Josef Wolfsthal who had died unexpectedly at age 31 from the after-effects of influenza, Goldberg joined Hindemith and Feuermann in a string trio. Purged from the

orchestra by the Nazis, along with all the other Jewish members, he left Germany. During the next six years he toured mostly throughout Europe and the Far East, appearing both as a soloist and in sonata concerts with pianist Lily Kraus. Theirs became one of the notable collaborations of the era. In the course of his travels he made a New York debut in 1938, then, unfortunately, left to tour the Orient. While playing in the Dutch East Indies, he was interned by the Japanese for three years, as was Kraus. In 1946 he resumed his international concert career.

From 1951 to 1966 he was a faculty member of the Aspen Festival and a member of the Festival Piano Quartet with violist William Primrose, pianist Victor Babin, and cellist Nikolai Graudan. Goldberg became conductor-soloist of the Netherlands Chamber Orchestra in 1955, after which he played and taught in London. Returning to America in 1978, he taught at the Curtis Institute, the Juilliard School, and Yale University.

Goldberg was not a violinist of the largest scale, but in such matters as refinement and impeccability of taste, his best playing could be superb. He was certainly one of the most patrician musicians among the Flesch pupils (or any others). I recall vividly his performance of the Beethoven concerto in its unfamiliar original form with the New York Philharmonic. It was a noble effort, pristinely played, but one that set him apart from the mainstream virtuosos by virtue of its novelty.

While Goldberg's intensely vibrant yet pure sound bespoke romanticism, his musical and repertorial inclinations tended to stamp him as a classicist. He did, however, successfully record such contemporary works as the Berg concerto and the chamber music of Hindemith and Milhaud. Disdaining the use of expressive slides, his playing was warmhearted, intelligent, clean-cut, and beautifully polished. And his overall facility was formidable, if not honed in the image of the romantically-oriented, heaven-storming virtuosos.

In the Goldberg performances that I have heard, admittedly, some of his interpretations were more stylistically impressive than others. But in works well suited to his aristocratic musical instincts, his playing was impressive.

The Goldberg recordings number 47 different compositions, a large portion of which are chamber music. Among his finest efforts are recordings of the Mozart Concertos No. 3, 4, and 5, a glowing account of Brahms's Sonata No. 3 with Balsam, cultivated readings of Beethoven Sonatas No. 2, 5, 6, 9, and 10 with Kraus, and numerous Mozart sonatas both with Kraus on old 78s and with Radu Lupu on LPs. These belong in the record collection of every violin fancier.

Goldberg was one of those musicians whose artistry considerably exceeded his publicity. His playing was greatly respected by professionals.

JOSEF GINGOLD

There can be no higher goal to which a young violinist can aspire than to pattern his or her life and career in the image of Josef Gingold (1909-1995). Born in Brest-Litovsk, Russia, he exemplified a rare amalgamation of superb instrumentalism, legendary pedagogy, and human being extraordinaire. He began study of the violin at age three. At the end of World War I his family resettled in New York, where from 1922 to 1927 he studied with Vladimir Graffman, an Auer pupil. In 1927 Gingold went to Brussels to work under the great Ysaÿe for three years. During this period he studied all the masterworks of the violin repertoire, as well as Ysaÿe's own compositions. His Brussels debut included the first public performance of Ysaÿe's Solo Sonata No. 3 (*Ballade*), now a staple of the repertoire. Gingold ranks among the few top Ysaÿe pupils, and following in the footsteps of Persinger, he ultimately became the leading advocate of the master's method and style in America.

Upon his return to the United States he was faced with the stern rigors of the Great Depression. Like many other outstanding violinists, he was forced to "tread water," doing commercial work while toiling assiduously to develop his art. From 1937 to 1943 he was a first violinist in the preeminent NBC Orchestra under Toscanini, and a member of William Primrose's string quartet. Gingold was also first violinist of the NBC Concert Orchestra, an offshoot of the NBC Symphony, with whom he appeared as soloist each week for more than a year. Subsequently he became concertmaster of the Detroit Symphony, but after only three seasons was lured away by George Szell to become concertmaster of the vaunted Cleveland Orchestra, an "act of piracy" in the view of Karl Kruger, then the Detroit conductor.

During Gingold's 13-year tenure in Cleveland, he was soloist with the orchestra 18 times. In a letter to

Josef Gingold

Courtesy International Violin Competition of Indianapolis

Gingold written on Christmas Eve, 1956, Szell stated:

In this tenth of my years with the Cleveland Orchestra when we can look back on a very considerable progress, I am convinced that this type of unfolding of a variety of virtues of an orchestra would have been unthinkable without you. This broad statement is meant to cover both your superb artistry and your moral influence on the consciences of us all.

In 1960 Gingold retired from orchestral playing to join the Indiana University School of Music, where he ultimately received the title of Distinguished Professor Emeritus of Music. For 30 summers he headed the Chamber Music Department at Galamian's Meadowmount School of Music.

Gingold combined encyclopedic knowledge of the violin and its repertoire with the ability to analyze instantly any technical problem, and to demonstrate the correct procedure. His temperament enabled him to handle pupils with both firmness and compassion, and his cosmopolitan musicianship, garnered by association with such giants as Ysaÿe, Toscanini, and Szell, stamped him as a rare mentor. Above all, in a world in which horrendous competition so often warps the character of many a fine (and not so fine) instrumentalist, Josef Gingold maintained his profound sense of humanity along with the virtues of patience and generosity. He not only gave instruction—he gave of himself! These qualities, of course, had long been apparent to his students and colleagues the world over, and must account for their virtual adulation of Gingold, not unlike that special reverence reserved for giants like Kreisler and David Oistrakh.

Among those who studied with him were Miriam Fried, Jaime Laredo, Joseph Silverstein, Yuval Yaron, Nai-Yuan Hu, Eugene Fodor, Ulf Hoeschler, Joshua Bell, and other pupils holding major concertmaster posts from San Francisco to Hamburg. These include Raymond Kobler, Isador Zaslav, Yuval Waldman, Otto Armin, Jacques Israelevitch, Andres Cardenes, Richard Roberts, Carol Sindell, Herbert Greenberg, William Preucil, and Roland Greutter.

To complement his teaching, Gingold edited many solo works and studies for the violin, and his compilation of orchestral excerpts is a standard text used throughout the world. He was the moving spirit in the creation of the Quadrennial International Violin Competition of Indianapolis for which, in 1982, 1986, and 1990, he served as Honorary Chairman and President of the Jury, and represented the United States at the Queen Elisabeth, Tchaikovsky, Wieniawski, Sibelius, Paganini, and Kreisler international competitions, plus the Leventritt and Naumberg contests in New York. His 75th birthday celebration was a spectacular event widely publicized by the national press, radio, and television.

Gingold's laurels as a pedagogue and international ambassador of the violin in recent years tended to obscure his stature as a soloist. Fortunately his recording output of some 25 works, incorporating several major sonatas together with a broad sampling of vignettes, reveal him to be, in his prime, one of America's preeminent violinists, a talent of extraordinary impact. His is romantic playing marked by a blazing temperament, virtuoso technique, rich vibrant sound, and sophisticated musicianship. More than that, he was a master stylist in the most exalted tradition, whose interpretations communicate a definite personal note. He employed ingeniously those subtle expressive devices utilized by Ysaÿe, Kreisler, and Heifetz to fulfill his own aesthetic needs. While the experienced listener can detect Ysaÿe's influence, Gingold is distinctly "his own man." Lest the reader feel these statements are exaggerated, I invite him to listen to Gingold's elegant, suave Fauré Sonata, Op. 13 (1966); the brilliant Walton Sonata (1964) with pianist Walter Robert, taken from radio broadcast tapes; a variety of vignettes recorded from 1942 to 1976 in the two-record album released in honor of his 75th birthday; or the searing G-string

sound and contemporary swagger of Roy Harris's Sonata with pianist Johanna Harris. And in a 1976 album of Kreisler pieces, Gingold evinces an ultrasensitive penchant for Kreisler's lilting imagery. Historically, Josef Gingold ranks in the topmost echelon of America's brilliant concertmaster-soloists.

BRONISLAV GIMPEL

Bronislav Gimpel (1911-1979) was born in Lwow, Poland, into a family immersed in cultural activities. His grandfather created the Jewish Theatre in that city, and his older brother Jakob was an internationally prominent pianist. Gimpel's father, originally a clarinetist, also played violin and conducted the small theatre orchestra in which Bronislav played at about age eight. After first taking lessons from his father and then from a cousin of the noted violinist Josef Wolfsthal, he studied at the Vienna Conservatory of Music from 1922 to 1926 with Robert Pollak, who shortly after became Stern's early teacher in San Francisco. A child prodigy, he played in Italy and was invited to perform on the Paganini Guarnerius del Gesù which rests in Genoa's City Hall, and he played for both Pope Pius XI and the Italian king. He joined the Flesch class in 1928 but remained with him at the Berlin Hochschule for only about a year, though he is commonly regarded as a Flesch pupil. Advised by Flesch to get some orchestral experience in order to improve his musical discipline, Gimpel served in 1928 as leader of the second violins under Herman Scherchen in Konigsberg. In 1930 he became concertmaster of the Göteborg, Sweden orchestra where he remained for seven years until Otto Klemperer recruited him as concertmaster for the Los Angeles Philharmonic in 1937. In 1935 Gimpel had competed in the Wieniawski Competition won by Neveu, and was cited at the time by David Oistrakh as "a wonderful violinist with wide international experience." He was unaccountably given only ninth place, behind several violinists who were never of his caliber; so much for politics-riddled competitions!

I heard Gimpel play a broad range of concertos, including those of Brahms, Mozart, Glazunov, Mendelssohn, Wieniawski, and Tchaikovsky. He was not like Neveu as a stylist, but was rather a large-scaled virtuoso of the Heifetz, Milstein, Menuhin, Stern, Perlman order. He had a fiery temperament, and his

Bronislaw Gimpel

tone was among the most vibrant of the Flesch disciples; his vibrato, cannily controlled. Not quite of maximal opulence, his sound nevertheless was rich and multifaceted. Although the central European discipline of Flesch and Pollak was evident in his playing, Gimpel was essentially an Eastern European artist whose temperament was emphatically romantic. A performer of unflappable poise, his single concession to stress was a disposition to turn beet-red while playing. If one compares him to the very greatest artists, perhaps his imagination was a bit less vivid and his musical personality not as striking. But these things were marginal. After serving three years in the United States Army during World War II, Gimpel returned to Europe where he scored many a triumph. However, he could not reach the summit in America. For all his talents, he was not calculated to displace any of the six or eight reigning violinists. Nor did he enjoy a sponsor of Artur Rubinstein's importance, as did Szeryng.

Gimpel's recordings include the Beethoven, Brahms, Dvořák, Glazunov, Goldmark, Sibelius, Tchaikovsky, Wieniawski No. 2, Mendelssohn, and Paganini-Wilhelmj No. 1 (first movement with a slightly abbreviated Sauret cadenza) concertos, and the cycle of Bach solo sonatas and partitas. The Goldmark compares favorably with that of Milstein and of Perlman, and the others are all stunning performances in every respect. The Bach cycle may not be the most profound, but neither is it overprecious and fussy. His interpretations tend to be straightforward and conscientious, inclined more toward contemporary stylization than an amorphous striving for baroque authenticity with modern violin and bow.

Concurrent with his postwar years of international concertizing, he taught in Karlsruhe, at the University of Connecticut from 1967 to 1973, and at the Royal Academy of Music in Manchester until 1978. According to Jakob, Bronislav was the first to perform the Britten concerto in London. On occasion he conducted and played concertos with orchestra while conducting. He also performed chamber music with the New Friends of Music Quartet, the Mannes Piano Trio, and the Warsaw Quintet, and gave sonata recitals with his brother. By nature he was somewhat of a "rolling stone."

Like that other brilliant Flesch pupil Ricardo Odnopossof, Gimpel failed to achieve the career he deserved. In 1979 he met with success during a three-month sojourn in Venezuela and was reportedly in fine spirits. A short time later, only days before a scheduled sonata recital with Jakob in Los Angeles, he died of what was described in the press as a medical overdose.

ROMAN TOTENBERG

Roman Totenberg, born in 1913 in Lodz, Poland, started violin lessons at age seven. Like Szymon Goldberg, he had lessons with Mihalowicz in Warsaw, and in the late 1920s, with Flesch. Though generally considered a Flesch pupil, he also studied with Enesco. After winning the Mendelssohn prize in 1932, he toured in South America with pianist Artur Rubinstein, and concertized with the composer Szymanowski in the mid-1930s. After emigrating to the United States in the late 1930s he combined his solo appearances with teaching assignments which included posts at the Music Academy at Santa Barbara, the Aspen Institute in Colorado, and Boston University as head of the string department. In recent years he has been director of the Longy Music School in Boston.

Totenberg's career has been perhaps less spectacular than those of some of Flesch's other leading pupils, but he is an admirable violinist. I have heard him play the Mendelssohn concerto with felicity and sparkle. His performance repertoire ranges from Bach to such contemporaries as Berg, Bartók, Milhaud, Prokofiev, Stravinsky, and William Schuman. Numbering around 50 works, his recordings display his playing as medium-scaled, sweet-toned, clean-cut, warmly expressive, and tempered with sincere, intelligent musicianship. In particular, his disc of the Bloch concerto with Golschmann and the Vienna State Opera Orchestra is deeply felt, sensitively wrought, and technically brilliant.

OSSY RENARDY

Ossy Renardy (née Oskar Reiss) born in Vienna in 1920, belongs to that lamented company of exceptionally gifted string players whose careers were cut short by death or debilitating illness, either before full artistic maturity or in mid-flight. This group includes David Hochstein, Stephan Partos, Josef Hassid, Josef Wolfsthal, Ginette Neveu, Emanuel Feuermann, Jacqueline du Pré, and Michael Rabin.

Renardy began violin lessons at age five, but his early training is obscure. After his arrival in the United States he studied with Theodore Pashkus in New York. Following his Vienna debut at age 13, he won great acclaim for his Italian debut in Merano in 1933, playing the Paganini Concerto No. 1 and the Schubert A-major Sonata. In 1937 he toured some of the midwestern American states and, in 1938, made a successful Town Hall debut. In a 1939 Carnegie Hall debut he scored a triumph by playing all 24 of Paganini's caprices in the second half of his program, after having played Nardini's E-minor Concerto, Dvořák's Sonatina, Op. 100, and Lalo's *Symphonie Espagnole*. Immediately hailed as a Paganini specialist, Renardy was the first to record all 24 caprices in 1940, before Ricci. To set the record straight, Ricci was the first to record them in their original solo form. Renardy used the skeletal Ferdinand David piano accompaniments, omitted nearly all of the repeats, and made several cuts, most of them negligible. Nevertheless, it was a prodigious recording feat which skyrocketed his reputation at the time. He re-recorded the caprices shortly before his death in 1953, the tragic result of an automobile accident near Santa Fe, New Mexico, while en route to a concert. His pianist Walter Robert, who was driving, survived the crash, as did his Guarnerius violin. During World War II, Renardy served in the American armed forces.

Renardy and Ricci have a similarity in tonal texture. Both play with exceedingly vibrant finger intensity that tends to produce tautness of sound, though Ricci's tonal palette is wider in scope. One of the most impressive features of Renardy's Paganini is that he never made a fetish of stressing his vast technical

Ossy Renardy

prowess for mere vaudevillian effect, although his playing is always brilliant in character as well as disciplined in execution. He could play as rapidly as anyone, but shunned mindless speed and always respected the innate pulse of the music. The sheer neatness and flexibility of his performance is stunning. He does not play Paganini with the precipitous aggressiveness or explosive bow contact of Ricci, but his playing is devoid of the impurities sometimes occasioned by Ricci's devilish razzle-dazzle. His commitment to the music is consistently expressive.

Renardy's recordings number about 87, 50 of which comprise two sets of Paganini's caprices plus two caprices recorded for the third time with more complex piano accompaniments. In comparing Renardy's recording of Ernst's *Hungarian Airs* and Saint-Saëns's *Konzertstück* with those of Ricci, both are swashbuckling in delivery, but Ricci's sound is a bit more satisfying. The "live" performance of the Tchaikovsky concerto and his recording of the Brahms concerto with Munch and the Concertgebouw of Amsterdam (and many other performances that I heard) indicate that Renardy, for all his instrumental command, would not have joined the elite. Unfortunately the angularity of his rather monochromatic sound detracted from the poetic imagery and diversity of color demanded by distinguished performances of the romantic masterworks, and certainly was not suited to the subtleties of Mozart and Beethoven. Yet Renardy left his mark on the development of violin art, and at his best was an imposing violinist.

269

JAIME LAREDO

Jaime Laredo

Jaime Laredo (b. 1941), born in Cochabamba, Bolivia, learned to read music at age four, and at six he received his first violin. His first teacher, Carlo Flamini, urged the boy's parents to take him to the United States so as to enable him to have the best training. The family moved to San Francisco where he studied with Antonio de Grassi and Frank Houser over a five-year period. At eight he played the Mendelssohn concerto in Sacramento. His parents then took him to Josef Gingold in Cleveland for further study, and later, upon Gingold's recommendation, he began work in 1955 with Galamian at the Curtis Institute. As early as 1956 he made a Latin American tour of ten concerts, and in 1959 played a Washington recital prior to his entry later that year in the Queen Elisabeth Competition in Brussels. Funded in part by the Bolivian government and various American contributions, his expenses for the Belgian competition were offset further by the sale of the family piano. Using a Stradivarius loaned by the John Phipps Foundation, Laredo was awarded first prize shortly before his 18th birthday by a jury which included David Oistrakh, Menuhin, Francescatti, Szigeti, Grumiaux, and Galamian. He was followed by Albert Markov (second prize) and Joseph Silverstein (third), eight and nine years his elders, respectively. He was the youngest at that time (and probably still is) to ever win the coveted award. The Bolivian government accorded him a hero's welcome and issued a stamp in his honor with his name, la-re-do, cited in musical terms.

Like many another major competition laureate, Laredo found that forging a bona fide career was even more difficult. A New York recital he gave after the competition evoked mixed critical response. Yet I heard him play the Sibelius concerto the following year and found him to be a violinist of outstanding accomplishment and potential. His early recordings substantiate this appraisal. In 1961 he joined the Serkin Marlboro group which emphasizes chamber music, and this partially succeeded in diverting his career from single-minded concentration on solo work.

After his marriage in 1960 to pianist Ruth Meckler, he began to stress sonata playing, though he continued his intermittent solo appearances. Replacing Charles Treger as first violinist of the Chamber Music Society of Lincoln Center in 1973, he increased his activities in that field and later created his own chamber music series in New York. When he and cellist Sharon Robinson were married in 1976, they formed a trio with pianist Joseph Kalichstein that has since achieved prominence. Currently Laredo is conductor-violinist with the Scottish Chamber Orchestra. During a recent tour I heard him with that ensemble in a Mozart concerto which he played with admirable refinement and polish. His successful recordings with that group continue to increase in number.

Laredo's early recordings (1959-1960) display him both in the virtuoso role and as a sonata interpreter. It is youthful playing, not fully mature in subtlety, but in Sarasate's *Carmen Fantasy* he exhibits exceptional facility and daring. His tone is bright, gleaming, and ingratiating, abetted by a vibrato that is fast and close, though its range of color is not particularly wide. Brahms's Sonata No. 3, Op. 108, already indicates musicianship of a high order and warm expressivity. Like most violinists of his generation, his use of expressive slides and position changes is sparing, at times to the degree that one may feel his overall playing is not fully in accord with his inherently fervid temperament. The dance movements in Bach's Solo Partita in E-major are exuberant, and the sound is alive and vibrant with no pretense at artificial interpretive posturing. One can note a certain diminution of spontaneity in his 1976 recordings of Bach's six sonatas for violin and harpsichord with Glenn Gould (pianist), but Laredo's radiant musicality nevertheless shines through, especially in the faster movements, and his genial artistry shows substantial development.

I had the pleasure of meeting Laredo when we

served as members of the jury at the 1982 (first) Quadrennial International Violin Competition of Indianapolis, and found him to be a reserved, affable man with a ready sense of humor, and utterly absorbed in his judicial responsibilities. Now in mid-career, his reputation continues to expand, and he is one of our leading American violinists. He has succeeded the late Josef Gingold as President of the Jury at the prestigious Indianapolis event.

By the late 1930s, invigorated by the emergence of Menuhin and Ricci, American-born violinists had become a potent force in violin art. During the next several decades, the United States began to rival the Soviet Union in the production of superb string instrumentalists, a situation which continues to this day. Foreign-born American pedagogues played a principal role in their training, but following in the footsteps of Persinger, American-born pedagogues, too, have been making their mark in the foremost American conservatories and university music departments. The conflux of these two currents of American pedagogical expertise has transformed what was a backwater of violin art at the turn of the 20th century into one of the two leading international centers of violin artistry and pedagogy. Whereas for so many decades talented Americans had gone to European centers for advanced training (i.e., "finishing"), gifted young people from countries the world over now travel to the United States.

Every so often some commentator refers to the "American School" of violin playing. I believe such a sobriquet is far-fetched. What similar characteristics are there, for example, in the playing of Elmar Oliveira and Joseph Swenson that would unqualifiedly identify them as protagonists of a definitive American School? Or Dylana Jenson and Ida Kavafian? Or David Nadien and Paul Zukovsky? Or Michael Rabin and James Buswell? Or Carroll Glenn and Eugene Fodor? Or for that matter, Menuhin and Ricci, both products of the same teacher in their youth? The truth is that American playing, more than any other, represents cosmopolitan violinistic attitudes, styles, and methods. And this is vital for its continued good health and prosperity. *Should one particular outlook gain control through acquisition and manipulation of monetary grants, sheer publicity, or any other monopolistic device, the totality of American violin art will be poorer. Such a danger always lurks in the byways of the music establishment.*

With Stern's rise to stardom around the mid-1940s, a new era began to dawn in the Western violin world. The Soviets, of course, were dominated by David Oistrakh, and later joined by Kogan. And the late-blooming Henryk Szeryng (abetted by the influence of his friend, pianist Artur Rubinstein) and Arthur Grumiaux, both elegant, superb artists, deservedly achieved careers on the top level. But particularly in the United States, the ever-expanding Stern hegemony was to have a crucial effect upon the career aspirations of numerous outstanding American-born violinists for some four decades. And many a splendid violinist of soloist caliber was forced to settle for less.

OSCAR SHUMSKY

One of the most highly respected American-born violinists is Oscar Shumsky, born in Philadelphia in 1917, esteemed by such stellar colleagues as Oistrakh, Menuhin, Primrose, and a host of fellow professionals everywhere. Starting the violin at age four, his first teacher was Max Senofsky (father of Berl). He than had lessons with Albert Meiff, after which he studied with the aged Auer, later completing his training with Zimbalist at the Curtis Institute. His adulation of Kreisler, further heightened by a youthful meeting with the Viennese giant during which Kreisler accompanied him at the piano, resulted in a special affinity for performing Kreisler compositions with exceptional charm and nobility. Shumsky taught at the Curtis Institute from 1961 to 1965, and was a member of the violin faculty at Juilliard from 1953 to 1978. Among his pupils are Ida Kavafian and Philip Setzer. He is an excellent violist and has performed concerts featuring both violin and viola on the same program. He is also one of a growing number of violinists who have taken up the baton. Once a member of Toscanini's famous NBC orchestra, he decided to leave after two and a half years under the maestro's "hypnotic spell." "I had learned a tremendous amount, but felt it was time I began listening to my own inner voices." Shumsky is also a chamber music player of extraordinary caliber, and was first violinist of the Primrose String Quartet. In later years he was the violinist in the noted Bach Aria group. His advice to students seeking a career is: "...instead of becoming a chronic contestant, adjust your sights to becoming a first-class instrumentalist and musician. There have never been too many of them. This has always been my creed."

Even at 15, when Shumsky performed the Elgar and Brahms concertos with the Philadelphia Orchestra, he seemed headed for a brilliant career as a soloist. His repertoire ultimately ran the gamut from Corelli to Hindemith's *Kammermusik* No. 4. He could play with tenderness as well as elegance. Yet it was Stern who gained the top position in the American scene, along with Menuhin, and to a lesser degree the spectacular technician, Ricci, both of whom had attained international fame as young prodigies. Shumsky's press notices did not always reflect the practically unanimous enthusiasm of his professional colleagues. Nor did his playing seem to attract a mass audience. I recall Howard Taubman's critique of a New York recital in the 1940s that chastised Shumsky mercilessly. His solo career languished for several decades. It has only been since reaching his mid-60s that Shumsky has begun to garner the international prominence as a soloist that many believe should have been won 40 years earlier—a phenomenon of sorts. His early recordings, mostly on minor labels, were "lost in the crowd." However, his recent recordings of the complete Mozart sonata cycle, the six solo sonatas and partitas of Bach, and a comprehensive panorama of Kreisler originals and transcriptions, have served to inject new life into his career as soloist.

Admittedly, the two occasions on which I heard Shumsky in the 1980s were not nearly as impressive as his recordings. One was a somewhat undistinguished performance of the Beethoven concerto, not top-level either technically or musically; the other, a sparkling but impersonal rendering of a Haydn concerto. Neither was in the class of his taped "live" performance of Spohr's *Gesangsszene* and a crystalline, patrician version of the Corelli-Kreisler *La Folia*. Shumsky's music is neither characterized by impassioned drama nor a bravura "kamikaze" daredevilry. Rather, it is large-scaled, tasteful, polished, and above all, stylish playing that seems all the more persuasive in the current era when stylistic subtleties and spiritual grace are in such short supply. His tone is silken, wonderfully pliant and soft in texture, though good-sized in volume. His sound is not as sensuous or as highly individualized as that of the top romantic violinists, though it is invariably sweet and impeccably nuanced. Nor is his musical personality as marked as that of Heifetz, Menuhin, or Stern. The

Oscar Shumsky

Shumsky platform image might be described as unusually severe. He is capable of performing any type of music with eclat, but it is perhaps in Kreisler specialties, both classical and romantic, that his playing is most personalized. Shumsky's pristine sound has not the sensual rapid vibrato of a Kreisler, but he is a master of all the unique Kreisler subtleties and expressive devices, which he applies not imitatively, but with meticulous discrimination and refinement. His Bach is crystal-clear in sound and bright in character, although some purists might resent his slight rhythmic liberties in the slower movements. The Mozart sonatas are buoyant and sensitively etched. In all, Shumsky is a superb artist and one of the finest America has produced.

SIDNEY HARTH

Sidney Harth, born in Cleveland in 1925, began violin study at age four with Albert Sack, and at age nine went to Herman Rosen, an Auer pupil. From age 15 to 21, he studied with Joseph Knitzer, whom he considers his principal teacher; he later spent two years with Piastro ("he taught me a lot about bow articulation and solo projection") and played once a week in Enesco's master class at the Mannes School of Music. He also had some lessons with Felix Eyle and Joseph Fuchs. In 1949 Harth won the Naumburg Competition, made his New York debut the same year and, in 1952, his debut in Paris.

While continuing to establish a solo career, he became concertmaster of the Louisville Orchestra (1953-1959), an ensemble strongly emphasizing contemporary works. Sponsored by the Louisville Orchestra Association, he competed in Poland's Wieniawski Competition in 1958, missing first prize by only three-quarters of a point. Even as a second-place winner, he was presented with the Wieniawski medal that previously had been awarded only to the pianist Wittold Malcuszynski and David Oistrakh. Harth states: "I am not one to indulge in 'sour grapes.' Before entering such an affair, one should realize that political ramifications and overtones must inevitably play a part in the proceedings, and if one cannot be realistic about it, perhaps he should stay home" (from *The Way They Play*, Applebaum and Roth).

Harth's publicity from the Poland competition accelerated his career considerably, and he has appeared as soloist with many major orchestras. He was concertmaster of the Chicago Symphony for three years under Reiner and for seven years was concertmaster of the Puerto Rico Musical Festival Orchestra under Casals. In 1963 Harth was appointed administrative head of the Department of Music at Carnegie-Mellon University in Pittsburgh, where he founded a string quartet and conducted the Carnegie College Community Orchestra. Meanwhile he continued to strive for conducting assignments.

In 1973, attracted by the opportunity to serve as associate conductor with Zubin Mehta, he became concertmaster of the Los Angeles Philharmonic. I heard him regularly for five years as concertmaster, conductor, and soloist. Now deeply immersed in conducting, Harth strove to juggle the three activities, a Herculean task with which a full-time soloist would not have to contend. Though his efforts as a conductor were sincere and respectable, they in no way equaled his talents as a violinist. This is the case with most fine violinists who hanker to conduct the major symphonic repertoire. Top-level conducting is an art in itself. It requires many long years of apprenticeship, intellectual mastery of a multiple of scores, and vast podium experience undistracted by the daily practice grind demanded by a great violinist in the current era of an ever-widening repertoire. Under such pressure the performance of any violinist, no matter how skilled, tends to become inconsistent, though the artist himself is often oblivious to the fact.

At his best, Harth is a violinist of international stature with broad expressive powers, just a bit below the highest echelon. Actually, he has no violinistic shortcomings whatsoever. His technical resources are vast, though he is an all-around musician rather than a gymnastic specialist. While his vibrato is not of the most rapid variety, it is meticulously controlled. Thus his tone

is multifaceted as well as sweet and warm, if not uniquely individual. The scope of his playing is large, as is the man himself. His knowledge and use of expressive devices (i.e., slides, etc.) is extensive. Among his concerto performances that I heard were stunning renditions of the Elgar and Walton, a colorful Sibelius, a sensitive Mozart, a rather spotty Tchaikovsky, and a Beethoven riddled with rhythmic aberrations and diverse loose ends. His concertmaster solos were seldom less than impressive in all genres of music. Outstanding among his recordings are stylish, sensitive interpretations of sonatas by Brahms (Nos. 1 and 3), Fauré, and Schubert, Op. 162; exciting virtuoso performances of the solo Ben-Haim and Ysaÿe No. 3 sonatas; and a commanding reading of a splendid Concert Suite by Herbert Elwell. Since leaving Los Angeles in 1978 when Mehta took over the New York podium (the incoming Giulini wished to select his own associate conductors), Harth has undertaken various assignments, but at this writing has neither secured a major orchestra podium appointment nor accepted a steady concertmaster post.

BERL SENOFSKY

Berl Senofsky, whose parents were both violinists, was born in Philadelphia in 1925. After initial lessons with his father, he studied with Persinger, Stassevich and, later, with Galamian at Juilliard. Following a three-year period of military service he became assistant concertmaster of the Cleveland Orchestra, and in 1946 received the Naumburg Award which led to his New York debut that year.

In 1955 Senofsky was the first American ever to win the Queen Elisabeth Competition in Brussels, surpassing such prominent violinists as the gymnastics-oriented Russian Julian Sitkovetsky (second); his brilliant countryman Victor Pikaisen (fifth); and the Argentine Alberto Lysy (sixth). His victory secured, Senofsky made some solo appearances with major orchestras, culminating in 1958 with the New York Philharmonic and the Boston Symphony. But, strangely, his career sputtered despite a recording of the Brahms concerto that was first class in every respect. Young Americans who think it is tremendously difficult to pursue a career in their own country in the 1990s (and it is!) are fortunate that they were not vying for fame in the 1930s, 1940s, or 1950s, when opportunity, sponsorship, and public interest were at a disgracefully low ebb.

Berl Senofsky

I heard Senofsky during the late 1950s in the Brahms concerto at a time when it was said that he was experiencing domestic difficulties. His performance tended to be spotty and not overly inspired, certainly considerably inferior to his recording. However, it was apparent that he is a tonalist of stature, with an intensely rapid vibrato (a bit too rapid at times) coloring the type of sound that immediately titillates the ear. Some years later I had occasion to verify this opinion at a concert featuring his trio, in which the vibrant beauty of his tone dominated the admirable collaborations of the pianist and cellist. And his recording of the Fauré and Debussy sonatas with the virtuoso partnership of Gary Graffman, while not models of Gallic subtlety, are perspicuously clean, vital, energetic, tasteful, and refreshingly appealing. A tape I heard of him at 60 verified that he retained full command of his virtuosity and tonal resources. Senofsky, highly respected by fellow professionals, is currently chairman of the string department and a professor at the Peabody Institute in Baltimore. He was founder and organizer of the American Artists International Foundation, a juror at the Tchaikovsky, Queen Elisabeth, and Montreal International competitions, and decorated as an "Officer of the Order of Leopold" by the King of Belgium.

Aaron Rosand

Aaron Rosand, born in 1927 in Indiana, studied with Leon Sametini in Chicago, a former pupil of Ysaÿe, and Sevčik, who once commanded a pedagogical authority in that city somewhat analogous to that of Kneisel in New York. Later Rosand worked with Zimbalist at the Curtis Institute. He made his New York debut in 1948 and has been battling to achieve star status ever since, generally with more success abroad than in his own country.

However, Rosand has long since proved himself one of the leading American violinists of his generation. The scope of his playing can be described as medium-scaled; his tone is velvety, sweet, and soft-grained, and his vibrato speed ranges from moderate to rather slow. Like many violinists trained in that period, Rosand is a master of expressive devices (slides and position changes) and employs them with extraordinary suavity and impeccable taste. In works best suited to his ardent temperament, he is a stylist par excellence. His recording of Saint-Saëns's *Introduction and Rondo Capriccioso*, wisely avoiding the mindless racing of so many of his younger colleagues, captures the Gallic piquance of the work with exceptional grace. In many of his recordings, made mostly with minor league orchestras, one can pinpoint phrases of compelling beauty, whether in the *Canzonetta* of the Tchaikovsky concerto or in the piquant lyricism of the Saint-Saëns Concerto No. 3.

Recorded live and unedited, his 1970 Chicago recital, with the brilliant piano collaboration of the late Eileen Flissler (currently on CD), bids fair to keep listeners on the edge of their seats. It is playing comparable to the best of Stern and Perlman, highlighted by Rosand's superb rendition of Bloch's rugged, impassioned Sonata No. 1. The CD includes a whirlwind performance of Mendelssohn's felicitous F-minor Sonata as well as an exciting rendition of Ravel's *Tzigane*, among other works. And his 1995 release of 16 Romances for the Violin and Piano emphasizes his rare gift for expressing tenderness, and his mastery of the entire gamut of subtle, coloristic tonal devices is enhanced by artful phrasing.

Rosand has made a significant contribution to romantic violin music by seeking out and resuscitat-

Aaron Rosand

ing nearly forgotten but worthy concertos by Joachim (*Hungarian*), José White, Hubay (No. 3), Arensky, Ernst, Godard (*Romantique*), and other works of this genre. His warm-hearted recordings of Sarasate's Spanish specialties are instilled with an Iberian zest that is lacking in all too many contemporary renditions of this work. His facility sparkles. Rosand recordings exude refinement and sophistication. In recent years his recordings have once again proliferated. They include masterful performances of sonatas by Bach, Handel, Ysaÿe, Telemann, Bloch, Grieg, and Saint-Saëns, and super-stylish renditions of Heifetz transcriptions, Hebraic legacies, and the complete Brahms-Joachim *Hungarian Dances*.

David Nadien

DAVID NADIEN

David Nadien, born in New York in 1928, studied with Adolpho Betti and Galamian. He made his solo debut with the New York Philharmonic at 14, and has since appeared over 30 times as soloist with that orchestra under conductors such as Bernstein, Mitropoulos, Maazel, Steinberg, and Ozawa, and with several other major American and Canadian symphonies, receiving critical praise. He has been highly successful as a recitalist in the most renowned New York concert halls and their counterparts in metropolitan centers throughout the United States and Canada. Best known in the East, Nadien was concertmaster of the New York Philharmonic from 1966 through 1970, at which time he resigned to resume a full-time career as a teacher and solo performer. Throughout the country he is greatly admired by professional colleagues who recognize him as one of the leading American violinists of the day. For several years he has been in charge of string workshops at the Stratford Music Festival in Ontario, Canada, and at Wolftrap in Washington, D.C.. In addition to his nationwide telecasts, his playing is known to millions, anonymously, through innumerable solo excerpts in commercial phonograph and film recordings. He is, in fact, apart from his other achievements, one of the few finest "commercial" players among thoroughly schooled violinists to ever record in that field.

Nadien's expressive powers are prodigious, and his sound is supremely intense, propelled by an "impulse" fingertip vibrato. It stamps him as a tonalist of extraordinary stature, even among stellar violinists. His record-

ings include the sonatas of Franck and Debussy; Vivaldi's *The Four Seasons*; the Prokofiev Duo (with Ricci); a lengthy list of shorter virtuoso showpieces by Sarasate and Wieniawski; tonally-oriented favorites: *On Wings of Song, Humoresque*, and others, played with surpassing grace, sophistication, and ravishing sound; and the violin solos in symphonic works of Tchaikovsky and Richard Strauss with Bernstein and the New York Philharmonic.

There are those who may find his vibrato excessive and not sufficiently diversified in his recordings (with David Hancock) of the Franck and Debussy sonatas. But one would be hard pressed to find more than a small group of younger-generation violinists, including many over-publicized, post-1965 international competition winners, who can even approach his mastery in heartwarming vignettes. Elgar's *Salut d'Amour* as performed by Nadien may well bring a tear to the eye of the most stone-hearted listener.

JOSEPH SILVERSTEIN

Enormously respected by his professional colleagues, Joseph Silverstein, born in Detroit in 1932, had violin lessons from age three to age 12 1/2 with his father, a string teacher in the public schools. From 1946 to 1950 he studied at the Curtis Institute with Vida Reynolds and Zimbalist. He also worked for several years with Gingold, whom he calls "an immensely exciting, inspirational personality," and briefly with Mischakoff and Demetrius Dounis.

Joseph Silverstein

In 1959 Silverstein took third prize in the Queen Elisabeth Competition, and the following year won the Naumburg prize, which earned him a New York Town Hall recital and other appearances. Apparently not one to rely on the unpredictability and vicissitudes involved in building a solo career, he opted for symphonic work. After stints in the Denver, Houston, and Philadelphia Orchestras, he joined the Boston Symphony as a section player in 1955, and in 1962 became its concertmaster. At the onset of the 1971-1972 season, the post of assistant conductor was added to his duties. His violins include a 1773 J.B. Guadagnini once owned by Grumiaux, and more recently he acquired the 1742 "Camilla Urso" Guarnerius del Gesù.

Through the years Silverstein has achieved nationwide prominence by means of his many impressive televised appearances as soloist with the Boston Symphony. His listed repertoire includes more than 30 major concertos, ranging from Haydn to Schoenberg. He has toured Europe as first violinist and director of the Boston Chamber Players, a group which boasts several outstanding recordings, and was leader of the Symphony String Quartet. Included in his activities have been teaching assignments at the Berkshire Music Center in Tanglewood and at Yale University. However, his ultimate goal has been to establish himself as chief conductor of a major symphony, and in addition to his podium efforts in Boston, he has appeared as conductor of various important orchestras. I heard him conduct the Los Angeles Philharmonic as a neophyte in 1973. It was an unsuccessful effort. But Silverstein has gained considerable experience since then, and recently retired as Boston's concertmaster to become musical director of the Utah Symphony.

As a violinist Silverstein has no instrumental weaknesses. His facility is prodigious, and his tone, meticulously colored by a vibrato capable of several speeds, is rich and capacious. Especially convincing in 20th-century music, he can toss off the immensely difficult Schoenberg concerto immaculately, and his recordings of the Bartók No. 2 and Stravinsky concertos, and Bartók's solo sonata, invite comparison with any. In a recording of Bach's G-minor Solo Sonata, his approach is respectfully disciplined, his sound, romantically vibrant. Marginally less impressive are his performances of romantic concertos, though they are certainly first-class in every violinistic respect. In classical compositions he plays buoyantly and with crisp, "live" sound, though I once heard him in a Handel sonata that was quite charmless. Silverstein has an extremely analytical musical intelligence, and his romantic and classical playing, judging by Olympian standards, lacks the ultimate in spontaneity and imagination. Still, overall he rates very high among the prime American-born violinists.

MICHAEL RABIN

A tragic figure among American violinists was New York-born Michael Rabin (originally Rabinowitz, 1936-1972). In the quarter-century between the birth of Stern and that of Perlman, Rabin was one of the most superlative talents to emerge anywhere in the world. He initially had lessons with his violinist father, a member of the New York Philharmonic for many years, and at age nine became a pupil of Galamian, who ultimately considered Rabin his greatest pupil. At eleven he made his first public appearance, and two years later won first prize in a contest sponsored by the National Federation of Music Clubs. In 1950, at 14, he established himself as a genuine prodigy, publicly performing such technically difficult works as the Vieuxtemps Concerto No. 4 in A-minor and the Wieniawski Concerto No. 1 in F-sharp minor. He brilliantly recorded eleven Paganini caprices at age 12 (they were released when he was 14). At 15 he made his debut with the New York Philharmonic as soloist in 45-minute performances occurring four times a day, and later that year was guest soloist with the orchestra both at Carnegie Hall and in Philadelphia with Mitropoulos. Fortunately, unlike so many gifted American-born violinists of his generation, Rabin's success as a youthful prodigy guaranteed him the opportunity to attain a solo career without having to do commercial or symphonic work for economic survival. Nor was he forced to ply the treacherous international competition circuit.

I first heard Rabin in a 1954 radio broadcast playing the Glazunov concerto with the New York Philharmonic. It was obvious immediately that here was a young man of extraordinary promise whose violinistic attributes were practically flawless. Several years later, when he was about 23, I attended a comprehensive recital that, despite his burgeoning reputation, attracted only a tiny audience. In top form, Rabin exhibited all the qualities of a rare virtuoso. His Bach sonata was splendidly etched; his Fauré sonata sang sweetly and fluently; his Elgar *La Capricieuse* sported a staccato faster than that of the young Heifetz, though the lyric passages were somewhat less graceful; his Paganini caprices were impeccable. On the purely violinistic level he compared to the young Kogan. His long, powerful fourth finger would make almost any violinist green with envy. All this was abetted by an instinctive suavity of phrasing and delivery recalling only the most supreme among his colleagues. Yet I had a strong impression that he was still searching for a personal musical identity.

Rabin's tone was softer in texture than that of Heifetz, less vital and penetrating; his vibrato generally slower, although it was capable of the ultimate intensity in the high G- and E-string registers. He had total control of his vibrato, produced many shades of tonal color, and for the most part he avoided the "on-and-off" usage in a single melodic line that was to become so prevalent. His sound resembled more that of Perlman's, and his temperament was extremely warm and sensual. Heifetz's influence was strong in his general style. He used the Heifetz slides lavishly, but not in blatant imitation. Rabin was a master of expressive finger portamentos and kindred devices that he employed tastefully. Tenderness, charm and a certain gentleness of character pervaded much of his playing, along with his tremendous virtuoso flair and daring. In his prime years his performance consistently exuded youthfulness of spirit.

For all his wonderful attributes, Rabin's playing did not communicate the overwhelming personal aura and individuality of Heifetz, Menuhin, Oistrakh or Stern, either in sound or stylization. And when around 1960 he began to suffer from instability and illness, the quality of his performances declined sharply. Later he made a comeback during which time I heard him in a

Michael Rabin

rather technically spotty, uninspired rendition of the Tchaikovsky concerto, and a clean, energetic interpretation of the Brahms concerto that lacked, however, any comprehensive sense of profundity. The fabulous boy virtuoso never had the opportunity to develop into the mature artist and man. His return to the concert platform was short-lived. Rumors of drug dependency, debilitating illness, and a variety of personal pressures persisted. The official explanation for his unexpected death denied that it was self-induced, attributing it to an accidental fall.

Rabin left over 60 recorded works, major and minor, some of them recorded more than once. Among them are Paganini's 24 caprices made in his early 20s, that collectively, are fully equal to, or even possibly surpass any recorded before or since, and transcendental discs of the concertos by Wieniawski, No. 1, Paganini, No. 1 (Flesch cadenza), Glazunov, Bruch's *Scottish Fantasy*, as well as of Ysaÿe's Solo Sonatas No. 3 and No. 4. It is interesting to note that in his recording of Bach's formidable Solo Sonata No. 5 in C-major, the playing is beautifully polished and his vibrato usage is more attuned to the spirit of Bach's era than that of several topmost, romantic-oriented violinists whose Bach recordings have received the effusive praise of critics and commentators. This suggests that had his development been able to continue without interruption, he might have transcended the limitations of mere violinistic bravura and romance, and matured into an

Michael Rabin and his father

Erick Friedman

artist capable of performing masterworks demanding musical introspection of the highest order. Sadly, we will never know.

The Bach recording certainly merits re-release. Records of many medium-length and shorter pieces, such as Saint-Saëns's *Introduction and Rondo Capriccioso*, Sarasate's *Zigeunerweisen*, the Dinicu-Heifetz *Hora Staccato*, and the devilish Scriabin-Szigeti *Étude in Thirds*, are performed on an exalted level. With the exception of Perlman, I do not know of any younger generation (post-1945) violinist who can play the Chopin-Wilhelmj Nocturne, Op. 27, with a tenderness and beauty of tone comparable to Rabin's.

ERICK FRIEDMAN

Friedman's story is unusual, and a vivid example of the more pernicious aspect of the competition syndrome. By his early 20s he seemed well along the way to a promising career, with a list of recordings second only to that of Rabin—an extraordinary accomplishment for an American in the Stern era. A contract with the eminent impresario Sol Hurok was pending but never came to pass, presumably because of powerful inimical pressures. In an effort to accelerate his career, Friedman took the well-intentioned advice of David Oistrakh and, apparently tempted by the prospect of a Cliburn-like avalanche of international publicity, decided to compete in the 1966 Tchaikovsky Competition in Moscow, thereby compounding his ill fortune. There, a "loner" in an atmosphere of "wheeling and dealing," he could do no better than to tie for sixth place. It was a cruel blow that temporarily sidetracked his career. However, after a sabbatical during which time he concentrated

on scholastic subjects, he continued his violinistic pursuits, performing 50 to 60 concerts a year while fulfilling his responsibilities as a teacher. Standing about six feet three inches tall, handsome of feature and figure, Friedman always presents an imposing platform image.

In his early career, Friedman epitomized Heifetz's influence perhaps more directly than any other violinist. Whereas Kogan played strongly in the Heifetz manner, Friedman's entire musical personality was practically an extension of the Heifetz muse. As he matured he shed the most obvious reverberations of this influence, though he still profitably employs expressive position changes and the subtle horizontal devices (that are neither slides nor portamentos) that recall those of Heifetz. The soprano character of his sound, the nature and application of his vibrato, his articulation in both hands, and his stylistic inclinations as heard in those early recordings, link him to Heifetz to a startling degree. He has the equipment of a daring, top-level romantic virtuoso. While the body of his vibrant tone is somewhat lean, his overall delivery is almost invariably suave. If one is willing to overlook these similarities, the recordings are exceptionally brilliant in every violinistic respect.

A 1980 live concert recording of the Bartók Concerto No. 2 reveals Friedman to be an artist of important stature. If not exactly a striking, individualistic musical personality in his own right, he has distinctly become "his own man," though still readily recognizable as Heifetz's disciple. His pellucid, intelligently wrought recordings of the Beethoven String Trio cycle with violinist Emanuel Vardi and cellist Jascha Silberstein, rank with the finest performances of this music. The several times that I heard Friedman play in his 40s confirm the quality of these recordings.

EUGENE FODOR

Eugene Fodor, born in Colorado in 1950, started violin lessons at age seven. At eleven he made his debut with the Denver Symphony, of which his teacher, Hans Wippler, was concertmaster. As a youth he played duo violin recitals with his older brother John, who is now a member of that orchestra. Following his high school graduation in 1967, Fodor's study began in earnest when he received a scholarship to Juilliard and became a pupil of Galamian. Subsequently he studied with Harry Farbman, Josef Gingold, and finally at the University of Southern California for nearly a year with Heifetz, two days a week, each lesson lasting several hours.

I heard Fodor in the Glazunov concerto when he was about 17, but his playing, while manifesting virtuoso promise, was raw and that of a student. Working assiduously, he soon won the moderately prestigious Merriweather Post Competition in 1972. He leaped into the international limelight when he tied for second place with two Russians, Rueben Agaronian and Rusida Gvasalia in the 1974 Tchaikovsky Competition in Moscow, a contest in which no first prize was awarded. The epitome of the all-American boy from the wide-open spaces, handsome, poised, and glib, Fodor, then 24, came home to a hero's welcome. The publicity tub-thumpers found themselves with an ideal product to sell. Sponsors, mostly of minor league concert presentations throughout the country, eagerly snapped up his services. He played for President Ford at the White House and Mayor Beame in New York. RCA quickly arranged for several Fodor recordings. Television talk shows vied for his presence. Now all he had to do was win the hearts of the metropolitan music critics and cognoscenti.

Here he made a decision that was both naive and unintelligent. Apparently in an effort to counteract the current trend of violin recitals--which are almost always overweight chamber music affairs featuring three or four sonatas, containing little or no crowd-pleasing virtuoso fare for balance--Fodor went to the opposite extreme. In his 1974 Fisher Hall debut he offered a program starting with Sarasate's *Caprice Basque* and ending with Paganini's *Nel cor piu non mi sento* Variations, and includ-

ed Tchaikovsky's *Valse Scherzo* and *Serenade Melancolique*, Wienawski's *Legende*, and Beethoven's *Romance* No. 2 in F-major. Such an act of defiance towards the critics was like waving a red flag in front of bulls. Had Fodor played like Heifetz, he still would have been in for a drubbing. He was immediately deprecated as a "lightweight" not deserving of top-level contention, and failed to receive an invitation to appear as soloist with the New York Philharmonic.

In later major appearances Fodor attempted to placate his tormentors by programming some sonatas, but the harm had been done. To give the critics their due, his performance, for all its flashy virtuosity, reflected considerable artistic juvenility, and was not always consistent even in the favored portion of his repertoire. It was playing calculated to delight unsophisticated audiences.

In contrast to young Friedman, Fodor's violinistic approach is not cast in the style of their teacher, Heifetz, though occasionally there are certain similarities, particularly in articulation and aggressiveness. His tone is of medium sonority, rather spare in texture but capable of extreme brilliant intensity. However, in flowing lyric phrases his vibrato can project a feeling of tautness. It is playing invariably oriented toward brilliance and bravura utterance. Fodor's temperament is tempestuous but not innately sensuous. An important violinistic talent, his basic shortcomings are vested in the man himself, in areas of aesthetics and general culture, as has been the case with innumerable highly accomplished performers throughout the history of violin art. For some time he played on a borrowed Guarnerius del Gesù, but he has also performed many concerts on contemporary Peresson instruments.

Fodor's recordings reflect the best elements of his performance, except for an album of Kreisler pieces for which he is not stylistically equipped. His disc of the Paganini Concerto No. 1 is dashing and flamboyant, highlighted by a rapid stiff-arm staccato as spectacular as any I have ever heard. His *Nel cor piu non mi sento* Variations compares favorably with any other performance in flair and excitement. The concertos of Tchaikovsky, Mendelssohn, Glazunov, Khachaturian, and sundry shorter showpieces are all brilliantly negotiated, but below the highest artistic standards. Made in his mid-20s, the interpretations still contain vestiges of the gifted student who has not yet attained profundity of spirit and rounded musicianship. In his mid-30s Fodor was still striving to make the transition from precocious adolescence to maturity, from splashy instrumentalism to full-fledged artistry. Unfortunately, some personal peccadillos have further damaged his career.

ELMAR OLIVEIRA

Like Fodor, Elmar Oliveira's road to fame and fortune came via Moscow. Both had an older violinist brother named John, and the elder Oliveira (a violinist in the Houston Symphony) was Elmar's first teacher when he began studying at the comparatively late age of nine. Son of a Portuguese carpenter, he was born in Waterbury, Connecticut, in 1950. At eleven he played his first recital. Later he studied for three years with Ariana Bronne and then for eight years with her father, Raphael Bronstein (a disciple of the Auer Russian school), at the Manhattan School of Music. At 14 he won the Hartford Symphony Scholarship Competition, and made his official solo debut with that orchestra. His 1966 victory in the New York Philharmonic Young People's Concerto Competition earned him a solo appearance with the prestigious group. A 1973 New York recital debut brought mixed reviews. Performing on the borrowed 1708 "Empress of Russia" Stradivarius, he was cited for his facility in Paganini caprices, his "masterly" Bach, his lack of elegance in Vitali, and his insufficient drama in Beethoven. His playing in general was characterized as small-scaled and restrained. In 1975 he achieved national recognition through the G.B. Dealy Award, giving him two solo stints with the Dallas Symphony. The highly coveted Naumburg String Competition First Prize provided two Alice Tully recitals in New York.

I heard a tape of him performing short pieces, taken from a live concert of this period. Evaluating the performance by the highest standards, it was stylistically immature and tonally undistinguished. But a tape of the Glazunov concerto with orchestra, made under inferior live-concert conditions, revealed much expressiveness and inner warmth, plus a tone that was songful and solid, if not opulent. It was playing of unusual promise. Despite his contest successes, engagements were not very plentiful. Oliveira easily could have gravitated to the commercial recording jungle, as had so many gifted American-born violinists before him.

A man of unlimited self-confidence and determination, enormously fortified by his longtime close friend Sandra Robbins, he decided somewhat belatedly in his career to enter the 1978 Tchaikovsky Competition. Oliveira shared first prize with the less-talented Russian Ilya Grubert. A strange manner of selection presented dual awards to the first four places. Could such a ridiculous outcome as eight co-winners of four prizes occur mathematically? Oliveira's gold medal, the first for an American violinist in Moscow, together with that of cellist Nathaniel Rosen, created a temporary American euphoria. The pair was invited to the White House; engagements began to pour in.

Oliveira's first New York concert after his return from Moscow met with critical reservations as to the quality of his tone and the degree of his musical personality. Another recital four months later at Carnegie Hall, more successful, still met with some adverse criticism. Nevertheless, in the following years his career, in contrast to Fodor's, has been on the rise. This is both understandable and deserved.

Oliveira's tone is not one of unique personalization, nor is it of rich, lustrous vibrance. At times it can be taut and lacking in variety of color. But it is clean-cut, penetrating, and polished, and especially effective on the E string. What places him above a sizeable legion of admirable but essentially "faceless" violinists of his generation, is a fiercely impassioned personal involvement, a sense of spontaneity, and expressive powers that communicate directly to the listener. Whereas so many play with machine-like efficiency, Oliveira has studied the subtle expressive devices of Kreisler and Heifetz from their old recordings, and liberally and tastefully applies slides and position changes in his lyric playing. This adds an extra dimension to his performance. No longer can anyone rightly characterize his playing as "reserved." In fact, he now often goes to the opposite extreme, and one wishes for an occasional slackening of his drive, a bit more self-discipline and serenity.

Unlike the great majority of violinists whose recordings flatter their playing, Oliveira's do not fully reflect the impact of his live concerts. I refer specifically to his Franck and Saint-Saëns sonatas. Perhaps future recordings will offset the imbalance. Unfortunately RCA Victor did not accord him the comparatively extensive recording roster it gave Fodor and Friedman. Be that as it may, Oliveira, at his best, can produce many an exciting moment. And there can be little doubt that his career will continue to burgeon and his audiences grow.

The list of American violinists who have led or are leading solo careers, some in conjunction with other violinistic functions, continues and is long and honorable. The amount of attention given them varies individually, but all are known to professional colleagues as violinists whose accomplishments merit respect and admiration. More than a few, for a diversity of reasons, have not won the measure of sustained exposure as soloists that they deserve. The following roster is not intended to be encyclopedic, but merely representative of the tremendous reservoir of violin talent in America.

Sidney Weiss

JULIAN OLEVSKY

Julian Olevsky (1927-1985), son of a violinist, was born in Germany, and began violin study at age seven. When his family emigrated to Argentina two years later, he came under the tutelage of Alexander Petschnikoff. He made his Buenos Aires debut at ten, toured widely as a youthful prodigy, and later concertized throughout the world. Arriving in the United States at 20, he later became a citizen.

Olevsky's 60 recordings include concertos by Brahms, Bruch, Mendelssohn, Lalo, and Wienawski, the Bach solo sonata cycle, the 12 concertos of Vivaldi's *Il Cimento dell'Armonia e dell Invenzione*, 15 sonatas by Handel, and eight by Scarlatti. They show him to be a brilliant virtuoso, a fine tonalist with glowing temperament, and a tasteful musician and stylist, confirming the excellent impression I received when I heard him in concert during the 1950s. His 1955 disc of Kreisler's short numbers was re-released in 1974 by Westminster Records under the waggish title, *Putting On the Fritz*. They are easily comparable in stylistic panache to the best three or four disc compilations of this music recorded in the last quarter of a century.

SIDNEY WEISS

Sidney Weiss, born in Chicago in 1928, studied in that city with Joseph Gorner and Paul Stassevitch. His first major position was with the Cleveland Orchestra, in which he played for ten years. Later he played in the first violin section of the Los Angeles Philharmonic and in 1968 became a co-con-

certmaster of the Chicago Symphony under Carlo Maria Giulini, a post he held through 1972. From 1973 to 1979 he was concertmaster of the Orchestre National de Monte Carlo. When Giulini became music director of the Los Angeles Philharmonic, he selected Weiss as his concertmaster in preference to several well-known violinists interested in the position. He has frequently been soloist with the orchestra in concertos of Beethoven, Brahms, Prokofiev, Sibelius, the Vivaldi *Four Seasons* (the last without music), and other major works, winning critical acclaim. For many years Weiss and his pianist-wife Jeanne have performed successfully as a duo in sonata and concerto appearances. The Weiss repertoire is extensive. As a hobby he makes violins of such high quality that he sometimes plays them in public performances.

One of those violinists who has brought himself up from the ranks, Weiss is greatly underpublicized in relation to the caliber of his performance. With an intensely vibrant sound, a smartly controlled vibrato, excellent facility, cogent musicianship, a fervent temperament, and mastery of suave digital expressive devices, he ranks among the leading American concertmaster-soloists.

CHARLES TREGER

To date, Charles Treger is the only American to win first prize in the Poznan Wieniawski Competition (1962). Born in Detroit in 1935, Treger studied with Hugo Kortschak, Szymon Goldberg, and Adolf Busch (though his romantic-oriented playing reveals no trace of Busch's old-fashioned, Germanic style). At 16 he was soloist with the Detroit Symphony, and at 20 gave a New York recital in the Metropolitan Museum which was enthusiastically received. Appointed head of the University of Iowa string department, little known nationally, his Wieniawski victory came as a bolt from the blue, and resulted in the usual initial spate of concerts. The U.S. State Department, taking advantage of the situation to publicize American culture, sent him to 14 countries. He also appeared as soloist with the Pittsburgh Symphony.

In 1969 Treger was offered the post of first violinist with the Lincoln Center Chamber Music Society, and relocated in New York. In 1972, apparently seeking to regain a solo career that was clearly in decline, he gave a series of three concerts in New York titled *The Romantic Revival* that received positive reviews, but not the kind from which great careers are made. In 1973 Treger retired from the Lincoln Center group. Forming a duo with pianist André Watts that lasted for several seasons, Treger's public image was considerably enhanced. I heard one of the concerts and was impressed with his strong musical attributes, even though his highly individualistic virtuosity is not ideal for team playing. As of this writing the partnership is not operational, possibly permanently dissolved. In 1985 Treger was named musical director of the Meadowmount School of Music, succeeding Galamian in a post from which he has now retired.

On hearing Treger's recordings of the Moszkowski, Szymanowski No. 2, and Joachim *Hungarian* concertos, it is obvious that his Poznan triumph was no fluke. While the consistency of his medium-scaled playing varies, he displays a neatly facile technique, an ardent tone with a rather wide vibrato, and persuasive expressive powers. In all, here is yet another gifted American violinist, perhaps not of the highest international rank, but of admirable stature. And like so many worthy colleagues, he is sadly underpublicized.

CHARLES CASTLEMAN

Charles Castleman, born in 1941, made his first major appearance at age seven as soloist with Arthur Fiedler and the Boston Pops. Following successful youthful recitals, plus network radio and television shows, he made a debut at age 12 with the New York Philharmonic. He first studied with Emmanuel Ondříček and lists Josef Gingold and David Oistrakh as his coaches. A graduate of Harvard and the Curtis Institute which he attended simultaneously, he is now Professor of Violin at the Eastman School of Music in Rochester, New York. Castleman has also been soloist with the orchestras of Moscow, Chicago, Brussels, Philadelphia, San Francisco and, in 1981, the St. Louis Symphony, with which he gave the world premiere of the David Amram concerto, commissioned for him by the Ford Foundation.

In 1981 Castleman played the six Ysaÿe solo sonatas in Alice Tully Hall, the first New York performance of the complete cycle. With his recording of this cycle, Castleman joins a select international group of violinists who have recorded these works in their entirety. His interpretations exude flair and virtuosity. One might wish for a more heightened sense of poetry, but he does project a good measure of the freewheeling style for which Ysaÿe was noted.

PAUL ZUKOVSKY

It would be nearly impossible to name an American-born violinist more dedicated to the cause of 20th-century music than Paul Zukovsky, born in Brooklyn in 1943. Son of the author-poet Louis Zukovsky, he studied with Galamian from age seven. At 13 he made a Carnegie Hall recital debut as a prodigy, and at 17 his programs began to reflect his interest in contemporary compositions. He holds a bachelor's and a master's degree from Juilliard where he won the Loeb Prize in 1963, followed by the Albert Spalding Prize at the Berkshire Music Center in 1965, and various laurels at the Paganini, Thibaud, and Enesco international competitions. His activities have included faculty positions as a professor of violin at several major universities and conservatories.

Since there are about as few contemporary violin compositions that achieve repertorial permanence as there are full-fledged artists (as opposed to mere violinists) emerging from violin competitions, some observers would dispute the efficacy of devoting the overwhelming portion of one's career to the performance of new violin works. Yet this task must be undertaken! Many an admirable violinist who is not of topmost soloist rank finds himself partially limited to learn-

Paul Zukovsky

ing and performing contemporary works in order to obtain engagements. Still, an historic survey would indicate that stellar violinists have at one time or another performed and even commissioned new works (Sarasate, Ysaÿe, Kreisler, Heifetz, Oistrakh, Stern, Perlman et al).

Composers who ignore the inherent singing propensities of the violin, and insist upon using and abusing it for unorthodox, sensationalist purposes, are apt to find their works automatically consigned to oblivion. However, it is vital to remember that concertos such as Prokofiev's No. 1 and Bartók's No. 2, which three or four decades ago were considered impossibly avant-garde by many listeners, are now part of the standard repertoire. One must be forbearing and careful in judging new violin works. Only time can judge the true worth of a composition and, for that matter, of an artist.

It is only natural that contemporary composers and their publicists tend to overrate a violinist like Zukovsky inasmuch as he is a champion of their products. But conversely, violin traditionalists will be just as likely to downgrade him, choosing to emphasize his negative attributes and overlook the service he is rendering to the cause of violin art. True, Zukovsky's tone is commonplace and generally one-dimensional in terms of beauty. And while he plays with great vigor and daring, his emotional communication is slender. But his facility is tremendous, registering at times with almost computerlike accuracy. Works such as the Roger Sessions concerto, Hindemith's *Kammermusik* No. 4, Penderecki's *Capriccio*, and Elliot Carter's Duo for Violin and Piano are exceptional digital challenges, as are many of the works in Zukovsky's *Music for a 20th-*

Century Violinist, representing 14 composers from Babbitt to Wolpe. He has recorded all of these (except the Hindemith), along with the William Schuman concerto, the Ives sonatas, the overlong but provocative *A Mitzvah for the Dead* for violin and tape by Michael Sahl, and J.K. Randall's *Lyric* Variations for violin and computer.

As if to prove his worth as a legitimate virtuoso, Zukovsky has recorded Paganini's 24 caprices, but in an unorthodox individual manner which drastically slows down the lyric segments as well as some of the technical passages, while still maintaining propulsive bravura tempos in many of the rapid sections. The results are debatable; the natural flow of the music is vitiated, melodic phrases become ponderous and dull, and the innate Italianate heroic brilliance that exemplifies Paganini is too often rendered academic. Caprice No. 4 takes 11 minutes and 39 seconds with repeats; No. 8, 9 minutes and 51 seconds. His playing of Caprice No. 6 in ponticello is quite bizarre. Yet, one cannot deny Zukovsky's ability to play as rapidly and cleanly as anyone.

Hearing him in concert, it was easy to ascertain why he chose the contemporary path. It required only a few bars of the Adagio from Bach's E-major Concerto to realize that his awkward, stiff vibrato and his earthbound musicality were not calculated to produce transcendental artistry. But the *Kammermusik* No. 4 that followed was extremely impressive in lightning-like, glistening passagework. In his best element, Zukovsky is a violinist to be respected.

JAMES OLIVER BUSWELL

Born in Fort Wayne, Indiana in 1946, James Oliver Buswell is the son of an anthropologist father and a pianist-organist mother. At age five he began to play both piano and violin, and at seven was a violin soloist in the New York Philharmonic Children's Concerts. A year later he performed in similar concerts in Chicago and Fort Wayne. His teachers were Joseph Knitzer at the Eastman School, Paul Stassevitch at De Paul University and, starting in 1959, Galamian at Juilliard. As a Harvard student he majored in 15th-century Italian art. But the violin was his destiny. He won first prize in the Merriweather Post contest in Washington which led to a solo appearance with the National Symphony. In 1965 he played the Mendelssohn concerto in New York with the visiting Pittsburgh Orchestra under

James Oliver Buswell

Steinberg, and the Stravinsky concerto with Bernstein and the New York Philharmonic. I heard him in the Stravinsky and was quite taken with his clean-cut, vigorous performance. Nonetheless, one should not make serious artistic judgements on the basis of the Stravinsky concerto alone, no matter how well played.

In 1969 he was soloist with the Los Angeles Philharmonic in Mozart's Concerto No. 4 in D-major. His publicists had him decked out in top hat, tails, cape, and cane, in a sort of "blue-blood" image. One critic captioned his review with "The IV Buswell & the IV Mozart," and archly characterized him as a branch off the Anglo-Saxon violinistic tree that produced Maude Powell, Albert Sammons, and Albert Spalding. He displayed a small, sweet tone of smooth texture and clear intonation. But while the Rondo projected a measure of ebullience, the performance generated little suavity or sophistication of style. Nor did the rather scrappy accompaniment of Frubeck de Burgos facilitate matters.

Sometime later he dropped the "IV" from his publicity along with the stuffed shirt image, and began his artistic growth in earnest. One of his best-known recordings is Bach's six sonatas for violin and harpsichord, with the eminent harpsichordist Fernando Valenti. The interpretations are only partially convincing. The faster movements generally project the verve of an uninhibited 20th-century violinist. But in the slow movements, apparently in an attempt to blend with the inherent monochromatic sound of the harpsichord, Buswell turns his vibrato on and off to no specific purpose, except possibly to court authenticity, but the results are aurally and spiritually arid. In contrast, his recording of Vaughan Williams's boisterous and songful

Concerto Accademico is bright and buoyant.

Buswell has matured musically to a greater degree than many of his colleagues born in the 1945-1955 period, and has become a well-known figure at music festivals. He has been an artist-member of the Chamber Music Society of Lincoln Center since 1976, and its only principal violinist. Formerly a professor at the vaunted Indiana University School of Music, he was also founder-conductor of the Indiana University Chamber Orchestra.

In a recent performance of the Brahms Double Concerto with the redoubtable cellist Lynn Harrell, Buswell demonstrated that he is now a formidable artist. He collaborated with his august partner on equal terms, with a strong, vibrant sound, incisive attack, secure intonation, warm temperament, and thoughtful phrasing—the playing of a man who would appear to possess broad cultural interests.

GLENN DICTEROW

Glenn Dicterow, born in Los Angeles in 1948, is the son of Harold Dicterow, long-time principal of the Los Angeles Philharmonic second violin section, and Irina, an artist. He began violin at age eight with his father and later studied with Manuel Compinsky, Naoum Blinder, and at Juilliard, with Galamian. Dicterow first came to my attention when he had scarcely turned 16 in a program that included the Sonatas No. 3 of Leclair, Brahms, and Ysaÿe, the Bruch Concerto No. 1 and Wieniawski's Polonaise No. 1. At the time I felt that among players of his age group, he ranked just after Perlman and Zukerman. His technique was practically infallible, his tone glowingly vibrant and smartly varied, his musicianship unusually disciplined for his age, and his interpretations charged with a sense of spontaneity. My column was the first to give his potential career serious consideration, and since then I have viewed his progress with special interest.

About two years later he went to New York for further study, and in 1970 competed in Moscow's Tchaikovsky Competition. He took fifth prize behind Spivakov in a contest won by Kremer—neither of whom, in my opinion, is as well endowed with natural tonal lustre or sheer communicative power. There were the usual grumblings about the bias of East European jurors, and Dicterow, like Friedman before him, was sorely disappointed. He returned to Los Angeles, and in a "coming home" concert shared with pianist Horacio Gutierrez (who had won second prize in his category), played the Tchaikovsky concerto with Mehta and the Los Angeles Philharmonic.

It was not a night of glory for Dicterow. He played accurately and in a disciplined manner, but the wings of his temperament had been clipped and his expressive fire cooled. He had fallen into the "on-and-off" vibrato syndrome, though not to a pernicious degree (a habit he still retains). Whether this was the fault of unwise guidance from domineering Eastern advisors, or due to his own devices, it is not possible to ascertain. Perhaps both were involved. Since top managers are more interested in "winners" and publicity-generating defectors than in fifth-prize laureates, his future as a soloist was not bright.

Fortunately, Zubin Mehta took an interest in Dicterow and recruited him for the Los Angeles Philharmonic, and after a period of orchestral experience, moved him to the nominal position of concertmaster alternating with Harth, who was the principal concertmaster. During this period Dicterow's natural talents began to revive, and his appearances with the orchestra, which included concertos of Saint-Saëns, Prokofiev, Vieuxtemps, and Mendelssohn, among others, reasserted his stature as a soloist. His recordings of Wieniawski's *Polonaise* No. 1 and *Scherzo-Tarantelle* with the orchestra compare with the finest performances of these showpieces. With Harth's departure from the Los Angeles scene and Giulini's selection of Weiss as his concertmaster, Mehta brought Dicterow to New York where he is currently enjoying outstanding success as concertmaster of the Philharmonic. His eastern solo stints in the concertos of Brahms, Shostakovich No. 1, Vieuxtemps, and Prokofiev have won extraordinary acclaim. In his playing of Mozart, Dicterow does not project the ultimate grace and spiritual repose, but in romantic and contemporary works his rich sound and aggressive musicality rank him among the very finest American concertmaster-soloists.

NAI-YUAN HU

Winner of the 1985 Queen Elisabeth Violin Competition in Brussels, Nai-Yuan Hu, born in Taiwan about 1961, now resides in the United States. A pupil

of the late Broadus Erle for five years and of Silverstein for about one year, Hu ultimately became a confirmed disciple of Gingold. I first heard him in the 1982 International Violin Competition of Indianapolis. After making no more than a fair impression in the Adagio from Mozart's Concerto No. 5 and the Adagio and Fugue from Bach's C-major Solo Sonata, Hu literally "brought the house down" in a blazing performance of Sarasate's *Carmen Fantasy* that was the personification of sensuousness and subtle expressive devices. Paganini's Caprices No. 11 and No. 21 had been tossed off previously with flair and aplomb, plus extraordinary stiff-arm and flying staccatos. Later he offered a rich-toned, expressive rendition of Fauré's Sonata No. 1 and an impassioned, idiomatic Bartók Concerto No. 2, almost impeccable in execution. His vibrato ran the gamut of speeds. Only experience and a measure of polish separated him from prime artists. Here was a romantic-oriented talent of major stature. He launched into Saint-Saëns's *Introduction and Rondo Capriccioso*, and after a reasonably acceptable *Introduction*, he unaccountably ripped off the *Rondo* with mindless speed and graceless style. It was enough to reduce his award to fifth place. Given discipline and maturity, a violinist of this vast violinistic and temperamental equipment can scarcely fail to make his mark in the world. Abetted by his magnificent performance of the Elgar concerto in Brussels, Hu has taken a great step up the ladder to fame. If he can perform the masterworks of Beethoven, Mozart, and Brahms with comparable artistry, he has the potential to attain the uppermost ranks. He was also an assistant teacher to Gingold at Indiana University. It will be interesting to note the progress of his career.

ANDRES CARDENES

Another younger-generation violinist deserving of mention is Andres Cardenes. A Gingold pupil and a 1982 Tchaikovsky Competition third prize laureate, he is one of our outstanding concertmaster-soloists.

PETER ZAZOFSKY

Peter Zazofsky, born in Boston in 1954, is the son of George Zazofsky, a former assistant concertmaster of the Boston Symphony. First taught by his father and later by Silverstein, Galamian, and DeLay, Zazofsky has won laurels at many competitions. His citations include the Leventritt Award, bronze medal in Poland's Wieniawski Competition, and second prize at the 1980 Queen Elisabeth Competition. A recording of Bartók's Concerto No. 2 presents him as a player of technical brilliance and positive expressive powers, though neither his sound nor his musicality is strongly personalized.

JOSHUA BELL

Approaching the forefront by leaps and bounds is Joshua Bell, born in 1967, a Gingold disciple. One of

Joshua Bell

the most outstanding natural talents since Perlman and Zukerman, Bell first received major acclaim as soloist with the Philadelphia Orchestra at age 14, and at 18 was practically a veteran of the concert stage. He was also enrolled in a full scholastic program at Indiana University. On the basis of his successes to date, it is clear that Bell is rising to significant rank without recourse to the international competition circuit. His concert schedule is already substantial.

An exciting performer with great intensity of spirit as well as sound, Bell also has an ear for diversity. When he was 16 I heard him perform the Tchaikovsky concerto with stunning virtuosity. His poise, polish, and sophistication were beyond his years. Some months later, in recital, he played a Handel sonata with uncom-

mon charm, Beethoven's *Kreutzer* Sonata with a degree of introspection rare for his age, and a dazzling Ysaÿe Sonata No. 6. Bell is well along the way to becoming a master of stylistic variety, and is a violinist of daring and enterprise. His career continues to escalate. At this writing, he is among the premier violinists of the post-Perlman-Zukerman era. It is hoped that he will divest himself of some distracting knee-bends.

DANIEL MAJESKE, RAFAEL DRUIAN, CHARLES LIBOVE & OTHERS

Daniel Majeske, late concertmaster of the Cleveland Orchestra, made an admirable recording of Paganini's caprices. Rafael Druian's sonata recordings register stylistic piquance. Charles Libove and his pianist wife Nina Lugovoy constitute a duo of impressive stature. And while this volume is not designed to explore chamber music playing in any comprehensive manner, one can scarcely refrain from mentioning such leading American violinists in the field as Robert Mann, the late Alexander Schneider, Arnold Steinhardt, John Dalley, Earl Carlyss, Isidore Cohen, David Cerone, Daniel Guilet, Walter Verdehr, Donald Weilerstein, Stephen Shipps, and Paul Rosenthal (some are also soloists). Or their formidable international colleagues, the Italian soloists: Salvatore Accardo, Franco Gulli, and Uto Ughi; the Israelis: Shlomo Mintz, Shmuel Askenasi, Yuval Yaron, Ivry Gitlis, and Sergio Luca; the Germans: Frank Peter Zimmerman, Ulf Hoelscher, and Christian Tetzlaff; the French: Pierre Amoyal, Maurice Hasson, Gerard Poulet, Jean Jacques Kantorow, Augustin Dumay, Patrice Fontanarosa, and the late Christian Ferras; and the Asians: Toshita Eto, Yoshio Unno, Cho-Liang Lin, the Shanghai String Quartet, and Hu Kun (female violinists will be cited in the "Women's" chapter); and the various Europeans: Arve Tollefsen, Erich Gruenberg, Nicolas Chumachenco, Ana Chumachenco, Ion Voicu, Kostanty Kulka, Václav Snítil, Pavel Prantl, Tibor Varga, André Gertler, Herman Krebbers, the late Alfredo Campoli, and Antonio Brosa. There are, of course, many others deserving of mention, but I have cited only those that I have heard personally.

Peter Ilyich Tchaikovsky, icon of Russian music, for whom the famed quadrennial international Moscow competition is named

SOVIET VIOLINISTS

Avid to prove what it believed to be the superiority of the Soviet system in promoting mass culture, the Soviet government gave tremendous support to its musicians throughout the years. Arguably this support was cultivated for political ends. But whatever the motivation, a musical establishment capable of continually producing world-class instrumentalists, proved its strength since the 1937 Brussels competition when Oistrakh led a team of Soviet players that captured five of the first six places.

At a time when other, far more affluent governments callously ignored the economic welfare of their musicians, both before and after World War II, the Soviets organized their efforts in the manner of an army marching to, and determined to win, a war. They saw to it that their representatives were totally prepared musically, amply seasoned in concerts at home, and given every physical comfort available. For many years during the Great Depression and well into the postwar era, gifted, qualified Western musicians who were without hope of a concert career, or even an orchestral job paying enough to earn a decent livelihood, were prone to envy their Soviet colleagues. As late as 1960 the pay scale in many major American symphony orchestras hovered around $3,000 per year. It is no secret that in 1958, just before Van Cliburn won the piano first prize honors at the Moscow Tchaikovsky Competition, catapulting him into a golden career, he was floundering about with scant prospects for success worthy of his talents. And his was by no means an isolated case. With the proliferation of major international competitions and the realization by leading Western musical organizations of the political value of such events, private support began to materialize slowly for Western hopefuls.

The situation today is no longer one-sided, though it must be stressed that even during the most difficult years, individual young artists of the West proved their mettle by challenging and, at times, besting their Soviet counterparts. Among them during the lean years before 1965 in the Queen Elisabeth Competition in Brussels were Berl Senofsky, U.S.A., first prize, 1955; Jaime Laredo, Bolivia, first prize, and Joseph Silverstein, U.S.A., third prize, 1959; Arnold Steinhardt, U.S.A., and Charles Castelman, U.S.A. third and fifth prize respectively, 1963. Sidney Harth of the U.S.A. took second prize in 1958, and Charles Treger, U.S.A. first prize in 1962 at Poznan's Wieniawski Competition, and Shmuel Ashkenasi of Israel took second prize at the Tchaikovsky Competition in 1962. All have gone on to brilliant careers in various areas of performance. In later years Miriam Fried, Israel, Eugene Fodor, U.S.A., Elmar Oliveira, U.S.A., and Dylana Jenson, U.S.A., either defeated or tied the Russians in top-level competitions.

It would be naive to suppose that international politics have not played a role at various competitions, just as conflicting opinions of what constitutes "good playing" are held by jurors who stem from diverse musical and cultural backgrounds. Many a behind-the-scenes deal has been made to appease and satisfy the demands of national pride, deals that have victimized one or another competitor.

One of the advantages the Western contestant enjoys is knowing that if his credentials warrant acceptance, he can enter any competition. Not so his Soviet counterpart, who could compete only if he were selected by the Soviet authorities. Oistrakh himself touched upon the frequent injustices of this system. At this writing the number of international competitions has grown by leaps and bounds. The result has been double-edged. On the one hand, a number of young talents have received sizable cash awards that may well have contributed to their personal well-being. On the other hand, most of these awards do not guarantee more than a limited number of concert appearances, and certainly do not promise a significant international solo career. Oistrakh, Kogan, and now Kremer, among Soviet prize-winners, have had extended careers on the international circuits, and to a lesser degree so have Klimov and Igor Oistrakh. But other Soviet laureates of major competition were forced to settle for less, including many who had made international appearances. The oscillation of Soviet-American cultural exchange programs had some bearing on their comparative downgrading. But the truth of the matter is that the winning of a gold medal, no matter how sensationally it is publicized, does not necessarily signal the emergence of a truly, or even a potentially great artist, as opposed to a superb instrumentalist. Naturally this applies to non-Soviet laureates as well. And it is still possible for an exceptionally gifted young artist to reach the top echelon without ever having won an international competition, particularly if that individual has extraordinary sponsorship such as that of Stern or the late Karajan. It must be remembered that in the former Soviet Union, just as in the United States or any other country, there were violinists who had a natural affinity for the "political game" in self-advancement, and there were others who knew nothing but practicing the violin.

However, no music educational system, no matter how rigorous and well organized, can hope to produce consistently a flood of outstanding instrumentalists unless it has a vast reservoir of talent upon which to draw. In discussing the reasons for many Soviet violin successes, it is necessary to examine briefly a phenomenon of Russian violin artistry both before and after the 1917 revolution.

The predominant force of prerevolutionary Russian violin art stemmed from Leopold Auer (of Jewish extraction) and his Jewish pupils Elman, Zimbalist, Heifetz, Seidel, Poliakin, Piastro, and others. The wandering lifestyle imposed upon the Jewish people and the heritage of Hasidism that sparked a wider range of self-expression among the poor and persecuted masses, served to generate a spate of violinistic talent that was no less overwhelming after the Communist revolution than before.

Emulating 19th-century Liège, hub of the old

Left to right: Max Rosen, Jascha Heifetz, Leopold Auer, and Toscha Seidel

Belgian non-Jewish hegemony that culminated in the mighty Ysaÿe, Odessa and its environs became a veritable wellspring of Jewish violinists, both before and after the revolution. Among those who lived and studied there were Elman, Milstein, David Oistrakh, Boris Goldstein, Mikhail Vaiman, Samuel Furer, and a galaxy of noted musicians, writers, and cultural figures. But the Odessa contribution was merely a part of the Soviet heritage. After the departure of Auer and his star pupils, such Jewish professors as Stolyarsky, Yankelevich, Yampolsky, and later, Oistrakh, Bondarenko, Kogan, Abram Shtern, and numerous others played the leading role in training Soviet violinists of all national backgrounds. They were responsible for education of such outstanding non-Jewish violinists as Klimov, Tretyakov, Grindenko, Mullova, and many more.

In addition to the most noted violinists, a host of excellent players of the second and third categories from Moscow, Leningrad, Kiev, Kharkov, and other great centers had been trained in the leading conservatories of the USSR. The 1970s saw a steady stream of fine violinists emigrating to the West, disappointed with what they considered to be a lack of opportunity worthy of their talents and a prevailing undercurrent of anti-Semitism as expressed by the quota system. The promise of fame and fortune in the West under conditions of superior personal freedom beckoned temptingly.

Yet no matter how vast the reservoir of talent, its organization and quality of training ultimately determine the extent of its success. The Soviet music establishment systematically sought out talented youngsters throughout the country, and enrolled them in special schools allied to the leading conservatories, which combined musical and secular education in spartan curricula. Only the hardiest and most gifted could survive the arduous competition over a period of ten to 15 years.

Although Auer's influence continued under the Soviet aegis through Poliakin and other Auer pupils, it diminished rapidly after the emergence of Oistrakh. It is important to recognize a certain resurgence of the violinistic precepts of the 19th-century Belgian School in Soviet training, precepts that had been introduced into Russia by Vieuxtemps and later by Wieniawski and Ysaÿe. To this day Russian violin students study and perform extremely difficult and ultrastylistic, lesser-known violinistic showpieces by Vieuxtemps, Wieniawski, Paganini, and Ernst that have not been stressed in Western training for five or six decades. The Ysaÿe solo sonatas, only now gaining popularity in the West, were widely performed in the USSR 40 or more years ago. Even after the Western successes of Oistrakh and Rostropovich, some observers, while praising their overall artistry, felt them to be somewhat old-fashioned.

Nevertheless, the fierce concentration on sheer instrumental mastery in their training produced a host of formidably equipped young Soviet violinists, against whom only a handful of their Western contemporaries could compete successfully in purely technical feats. More than a few of these Russians, however, have publicly decried the lack of sufficient chamber music playing in the Soviet curriculum, and its single-minded emphasis on virtuoso-type accomplishment. But with the ever-increasing exposure to Western violinists and musical concepts through cultural exchange programs and recordings, the influence of such artists as Heifetz, Stern, Szigeti, and other Westerners have made a deep impression upon many Soviet violinists. Transcriptions by Kreisler and Heifetz are widely performed, and while the Kreislerian style has eluded them, a few have played Heifetz arrangements with reasonably convincing style. We have already discussed the singular Heifetz-Kogan compatibility. In the decades of the 1930s through the 1960s, there was still a wide gulf in both musical approach and instrumental production between the Soviet and the various Western sounds and styles of performance. In listening to Russian recordings, particularly symphonic solo passages played by a Soviet concertmaster, an experienced listener could (and almost invariably still can) immediately recognize the performer

to be a Russian as indicated by vibrato usage, overall sound production, phrasing, and general musicality. This dichotomy continues, especially in the Soviet players trained before World War II, but the gap is definitely diminishing.

Some Western observers have a tendency to label all of the leading Soviet violinists (except possibly Oistrakh and Kogan) as supertechnicians who possess little, if any, personal magnetism or individual style. It may be true that except for the two aforementioned, the Soviet musical personalities are not strikingly marked as compared with the most personalized players. But the same can be said for just about all of the world's current leading violinists, including a legion of outstanding violinist-musicians. Great personalities on the violin have been rare in every era, and the extremely personalized violinists of yesteryear are now out of fashion. It is far more difficult today for a violinist to emphasize his or her personality under the existing rules of stringent musical discipline, although it is certainly not impossible for an extraordinary artist. While Soviet training was rigid and tended to discourage any wide divergence from their interpretive norms (though the Russians would deny this vehemently), Soviet artists, like everyone else, represent a diversity of sound, style, and temperament, if not of basic musical values. Now that the USSR has been dissolved, musical matters are in a state of flux; it is to be hoped only temporarily, inasmuch as music has always enjoyed tremendous popular and governmental support in that country. Since we have already discussed Oistrakh and Kogan at length, let us briefly survey a broad cross section of other leading Russian violinists.

MIRON POLIAKIN

Miron Poliakin (1895-1941), nominally a Soviet violinist, does not strictly represent the so-called Soviet School although he ultimately became a member of its teaching corps and, in his maturity, concertized throughout eastern Europe.

He was born in Cherkassy near Kiev. At ten he went to study in Kiev with Vousovskaya, a pupil of Ferdinand Laub. When he was 12 he was accepted into Auer's class in St. Petersburg and studied with him for six years. One of Auer's favorite and most gifted pupils, Poliakin was often afflicted with nervousness. Not pos-

*Miron Poliakin, an
extraordinary violinistic talent*

sessing the sovereign mastery of Heifetz, the golden tone of Elman, the exciting vibrance of Seidel, or the musical intelligence and polish of Zimbalist, he nevertheless was an extraordinary natural talent who, at his best, deserved ranking among the first six to eight Auer pupils. His playing, as bequeathed to posterity through recordings, reveals a fiery temperament, a facility that if not actually immaculate, was of virtuoso caliber, a beautiful vibrant tone, and a colorful style that stamped him as a thoroughgoing romantic of the prerevolutionary era. It is said that he played far better in private than in public, and that on his best days his communicative ability in live concert could be electrifying.

Poliakin came to America in 1922, and in 1925 won a contest for international violinists. But he was essentially, despite some success, another victim of the Heifetz phenomenon. Not until Milstein's appearance was another Russian-trained violinist to establish a lasting career on the world level. Returning to the USSR in 1927, Poliakin became a preeminent figure among Soviet violinists and a principal professor at the Leningrad Conservatory, which was locked in spirited rivalry with the Moscow Conservatory. Admired as a soloist by his colleagues, including David Oistrakh, he was eventually eclipsed by Oistrakh and died comparatively young.

Consistency of performance and musical (or personal) sophistication were not Poliakin's strong points, nor were his teaching methods highly respected. As is often the case with enormously gifted instrumentalists,

his intellectual horizons were limited, quite the opposite of Oistrakh's wide range of knowledge and interests. The contemporary music of his time was almost nonexistent in his repertoire. Soroker relates in his book, *Oistrakh* (p. 115):

> Among the sharp-tongued students the following story was popular: M. Poliakin had read a methodological lecture; he got on the rostrum, spread around a pile of books with bookmarks for references. After a long reflection, he exclaimed, 'The main thing is exercises!' and left to the accompaniment of the booing audience.

Poliakin made only a dozen recordings which clearly manifest his strengths and shortcomings and corroborate the more reliable reports of those who heard him in person. Chief among the recordings is the Glazunov A-minor Concerto (1941), with A. Orlov and the USSR Academic Symphony. Inconsistent in execution, it nonetheless projects the singular broad sweep of Auer's influence. His sparkling, though not opulent, sound is particularly impressive on the E string, as are his scintillating trills and instinctual expressive phrasing. There is no vestige of the annoying "on-and-off" vibrato afflicting some of the later Soviet violinists. A decidedly personal note is heard in his playing, but it is not as overpowering as that of Heifetz, Elman, or Seidel among the Auer pupils. For all its minor imperfections, the performance is convincing, ranking below that of the few topmost performances, but high in contention among other competing versions.

The first movement of Beethoven's *Kreutzer* Sonata (1938) in collaboration with pianist Heinrich Neihaus, despite poor engineering, is a reading of excellent violin sound, good ensemble, verve, and surprisingly well-disciplined musicianship. A dramatic cadenza to the Beethoven concerto (1938) by Isaac Dunayevsky, extremely brilliant technically, shows Poliakin in top form, and is stunningly and artistically played. Tchaikovsky's familiar *Melodie* (1936), with pianist Vladimir Yampolsky, is effectively sentimental and intensely vibrant in sound, if rather naive musically, even for its genre. Sarasate's *Habanera*, with pianist A. Dyakov, is stylish, but neither consistent in tonal quality nor one of the best technical performances of the work.

Poliakin did not leave a lasting impression upon Soviet playing, but he must be regarded as an important violinist of ultra-romantic persuasion who, were it not for the dominance of Heifetz, might have enjoyed a far more spectacular career.

GALINA BARINOVA

Galina Barinova (b. 1910) was at one time known as Russia's foremost woman violinist. A pupil of V.A. Zaventnovsky in Leningrad, she won third prize in the first All-Union musical competition in 1937, and in 1949 was named a Stalin Laureate. Early in the 1950s she was given one of the two Stradivari violins belonging to the State collection, an instrument which for many years had been played by Oistrakh. On what basis this decision was made must remain conjectural, since there were so many more outstanding violinists in the USSR sorely in need of a fine instrument.

She recorded 54 compositions, all in the USSR, of which only the concerto by Mieczyslaw Karlowicz, Prokofiev's solo sonata, and several Bach sonatas with keyboard collaboration (and one for two violins, cello, and clavier) can be considered major works.

The Karlowicz, a traditional Polish favorite composed in 1902, and a typical romantic work of late 19th-century spirit and devices, is little played outside of Eastern Europe. However, it is an engaging, neatly constructed work that permits the soloist to exhibit the range of her virtuosity. Unfortunately the concerto demands a more heroic violinist than Barinova for optimum performance. Her playing suggests a hard worker of serious purpose, with no more than moderate expressive powers. Her tone, hampered by a slow vibrato, is solid but neither especially sweet nor suave. The total impact of her Karlowicz is somewhat less than that of Wanda Wilkomirska; both are patently inferior to the excellent recording of Konstanty Kulka. Though Barinova is a contemporary of Oistrakh, it was Elizabeth Gilels and Marina Kozelupova who brought honors to the USSR in the 1937 Ysaÿe Competition (third and fifth prizes, respectively), not Barinova. One can only wonder at the reason for Barinova's inflated reputation in the USSR, particularly in view of the superior talent and ability of such younger women players as Nelli Shkolnikova, Rosa Fain, Nina Beilina (all current émigrés), and the even younger Tatiana Grindenko and Viktoria Mullova, among others of both sexes.

BORIS GOLDSTEIN

Boris Goldstein (1922-1987), pupil of Stolyarsky in Odessa and Yampolsky in Moscow, was considered a prodigy in his youth. At 14 he took fourth prize in the 1935 Poznan Wieniawski Competition won by Ginette Neveu (Oistrakh took second prize), ahead of such exceptional talents as Ida Haendel (seventh) and Bronislav Gimpel (ninth). Two years later at the historic Ysaÿe 1937 Competition in Brussels, he again placed fourth in a powerful field. Though highly respected, Goldstein's career did not attain international renown. Doubtless it was Oistrakh's domination of the Soviet sphere, like Heifetz's earlier supremacy in the West, that was responsible for moderating his career. He is no longer mentioned in Russian violinistic annals or journals. Nevertheless he was a brilliant violinist whose natural gifts were close to those of Oistrakh.

His roster of some 40 recordings include concertos of Mendelssohn, Conus, Arensky, Glière, Bach, and the Soviet concertos of Rzayev and Feltzman, plus such major sonatas as Bloch No. 1, Szymanowski No. 1, Poulenc, Honegger, and Beethoven's *Spring* Sonata. How he could fare in the concertos of Brahms, Beethoven, and Mozart, or the intricacies of Bach's solo works and Paganini, is not, of course, possible to judge from his recording roster. His recordings of smaller works do not include any of the repertoire bravura virtuoso items—which is surprising for a top Soviet-trained artist.

Goldstein's recording of the Glière Concerto in G-minor, Op. 100, orchestrated by Liatoshinsky, with V. Esipov and the Symphony Orchestra of the Moscow Philharmonic Society, reveals an artist of supreme assets. The intensely Russian, 17-minute one-movement work, akin in spirit to the Glazunov concerto, deserves wider international exposure than it has received, though admittedly it is not sufficiently large in scope to be counted among the major romantic concertos. Its main themes are lyrically compelling and their exposition skillfully developed. The Goldstein interpretation is ravishing, of first-level artistry. The same can be said of his dazzling performance of the Conus concerto. His style indicates some Heifetz influence, but his comparatively soft-grained sound, projecting a smartly diversified vibrato, readily recalls that of Oistrakh, albeit without any of the latter's idiosyncrasies. The articulation of his bowing is masterful, and his sostenuto is seamless. It is highly polished, acutely sensitive romantic playing with a strong personal note--perhaps a bit less pronounced than those of the most striking international violinistic personalities, but it ranks with the topmost echelon of Soviet players.

JULIAN SITKOVETSKY & DMITRI SITKOVETSKY

Julian Sitkovetsky (1925-1958), a pupil of Yampolsky, died of a brain tumor at only 33, the same age as Ossy Renardy, another brilliant gymnastics-oriented violinist who was tragically killed in a car accident. Sitkovetsky was married to Bella Davidovich, now a Russian émigré pianist who has been forging a major career in the West.

Highly respected in the USSR, Sitkovetsky remained somewhat in the shadow of his countryman and contemporary Leonid Kogan. In 1955 he took second prize at the Queen Elisabeth Brussels Competition won by the American Berl Senofsky, a particularly bitter defeat for the Russians.

Fortunately he left behind some 35 recorded compositions which include the Sibelius, Glazunov, Paganini No. 2, and Lyapunov concertos, the Bach Solo Sonata No. 2, Tartini's *Devil's Trill* Sonata, and Mozart's Sonata K. 378, three string quartets with A. Sharoyen, R. Barshai, and Y. Slobodkin, and numerous bravura virtuoso showpieces. From these it is possible to make a broad assessment of his playing.

Sitkovetsky's performances give the impression of a violinist who did nothing but eat, sleep, and practice. Purely as a digital technician he was the equal of anyone. It is in the finer points of artistry that he fails to attain the heights. The Sibelius, recorded from a live concert of the 1950s with Nikolai Anosov and the Czech Philharmonic, is a specific case in point. Among the least impressive of his recordings, it reveals a tone that is taut and one-dimensional, and a fast, pinched-sounding vibrato. His general instrumental command is authoritative, but the intonation is all too often not right on the mark, as it is in his recorded virtuoso pieces. Emotionally the performance is matter-of-fact, and favors muscularity over tenderness and spiritual grace. Perhaps he had a bad day.

In the showpieces Sitkovetsky displays both temperament and a positive sense of style, although his sound is rather tough-grained and commonplace; the totality of his phrasing and expressivity lacks the ultimate in suavity and sophistication. His Ernst *Last Rose of Summer* étude and Paganini-Kreisler *Witches Dance* (the latter with Davidovich providing accompaniment), are superlative models of daredevil virtuosity rivaling those of the young Ricci. Fingered-octaves, double-har-

monics, and left-hand pizzicatos are tossed off like they were child's play. Paganini's *Moses Fantasy* with scordatura tuning a minor third in pitch, Lipinski's Caprice, Op. 20, No. 3, Bazzini's *Ronde des lutins*, Wieniawski's caprice, *Cadenza*, Op. 10, No. 7 and *Polonaise* in D are handled in similar fashion. Saint-Saëns' *Konzertstück*, with A. Mitnik, alternates between brilliance and stodginess, and the Saint-Saëns-Ysaÿe *Valse-Caprice* contains too many rhythmic liberties. Sarasate's *Malaguena* and *Habanera*, Bartók's piquant Sonatina, and Szymanowski's *La Fontaine d'Arethuse* are all played with extraordinary dexterity. But Sitkovetsky's E-string sound is far superior to that of his G-string. For all his marvelous fingerboard agility, he was neither a striking musical personality nor an artist to compete with the world's greatest. His son Dmitri (with Bella Davidovich), a pupil of Yankelevich in the USSR and Galamian in the USA, won the first Kreisler Competition in Vienna in 1979, at age 25. The younger Sitkovetsky is a violinist of excellent instrumental authority and studied musicianship. His tone tends to be cool and lean, and like many trained in his generation he appears to be of the opinion that subtlety consists mainly of deliberately stopping his vibrato. One can respect and even admire such playing in compositions that do not appeal directly to the emotions. But he is essentially impersonal.

MIKHAIL VAIMAN

Mikhail Vaiman (1926-1978) had an Odessa background as a Stolyarsky pupil in his youth, but was nominally a Leningrader. He first studied with his father who was later killed in World War II. A graduate of the Leningrad Conservatory, Mikhail ultimately became a leading pedagogue there. He died suddenly at age 52.

I heard Vaiman in a comprehensive recital when he was 41 and in top form. He was an exceptional violinist of the second category, comparable to the finest concertmaster-soloists in the West. Like nearly all of the Soviet violinists, he was essentially a romantic player. His recordings of the Haydn Concerto in F, Telemann's Concerto in B-major, and the Vivaldi Concerto Op. 3, No. 6, avoid any traces of romanticized exaggerations; his vibrato is meticulously chaste.

Vaiman's recordings number about 40. In addition to the concertos mentioned above, they include those of

Sibelius, Mozart No. 5, Bach No. 2, Arapov, Machavariani, and the Bach Double Concerto with Boris Gutnikov—a Tchaikovsky Competition gold medalist. Major sonata recordings are of the Bartók No. 1, Prokofiev No. 1, Beethoven Nos. 1, 7, and 10, and Ravel No. 2, all with M. Karandashova.

The Machavariani concerto, with Odyssei Dmitriadi and the USSR State Radio Orchestra, is practically a Georgian replica of the Khachaturian; a product of that period in Soviet musical life when anything suggestive of folkishness was extolled, no matter how transient or banal. Actually the concerto is a benignly exotic item cast for immediate mass consumption, about on a par with that of Kabalevsky. Vaiman's performance reflects Oistrakh's influence, but is not imitative. His violinistic equipment is commanding and his expressive powers strong, if not overwhelming. The Shostakovich Trio No. 2 with Rostropovich and Pavel Serebryakov, finds the great cellist dominating, but Vaiman plays with vigor and authority.

I found Vaiman's art more exciting in live concert than recordings. In a 1967 concert he displayed an ardent temperament and a sonorous tone abetted by bowing that was generally close to the bridge, utilizing all or most of the hair. His vibrato could project medium intensity as well as the extremes. It was healthy, sincere, expansive, exuberant, mostly intelligent playing. The Bach *Chaconne* was powerful, with virile chordal salvos; an outstanding performance. The Handel Sonata in D-major, broad in concept, live in sound, and incisively bowed, was buoyant throughout. In Prokofiev's Sonata No. 1 he lacked Oistrakh's serenity in the muted filigree passagework, but otherwise it was a masterful delivery. Beethoven's *Spring* Sonata, joyous in spirit, was vitiated by occasional overrapid vibrato resulting in steely tones, and in a few instances strayed perilously close to the "Romany" border. Saint-Saëns's *Introduction and Rondo Capriccioso* represented his only serious breach of musicianship, victim of an accelerated tempo that sabotaged the music's inherent rhythmic pulse. Yet it contained many seductive phrases. Bloch's *Nigun* was heartfelt and Tchaikovsky's *Waltz-Scherzo* displayed exceptional verve and virtuosity. Unfortunately his inferior instrument was not worthy of his artistry. Alla Zokhova (Mrs. Vaiman) contributed sensitive, sympathetic piano collaboration. In all it was a most satisfying recital.

Vaiman's playing possessed positive character, though like Sitkovetsky, he was not a striking musical personality, nor a fingerboard gymnast of the latter's

stamp. But Vaiman was superior in beauty of sound and artistic detail—one of the most well-rounded musicians among Soviet violinists.

NELLI SHKOLNIKOVA

Nelli Shkolnikova (b. 1928), born in Zolotonosha in the Ukraine, moved to Moscow at age two with her family. At age five, her father, a musician, enrolled her at a music school for children that is connected to the Moscow Conservatory. Her first instructor was Lilia Fidelevo-Kossodo, an Auer pupil. After her teacher's death, when Nelli was ten, she went to study with the noted Professor Yuri Yankelevich at the Secondary School of Music, and continued with him at the Moscow Conservatory. After receiving an Honors degree from the conservatory in 1954, she completed postgraduate studies there in 1957. During that period of studies she won many competitions in the USSR. In 1953 Shkolnikova was sent to Paris by the government to compete in the Long-Thibaud Competition. She won both first prize and the special Ginette Neveu award for the best concerto performance in the final round. This victory launched her international career, and she has since concertized in Europe, Canada, Japan, the United States, and Australia. Her second American tour was highlighted by appearances with Eugene Ormandy and The Philadelphia Orchestra in 1967. Among other leading conductors with whom she has performed are Kondrashin, Munch, Cluytens, Rozhdestvensky, Sanderling, and Masur. After 1970 the Soviet authorities confined her appearances to the Eastern bloc countries. From 1975 to 1980 she taught at the Moscow Gnessin Music Institute in the capacity of a Senior Lecturer, and in 1978 was named an "Honored Artist of the Russian Soviet Federated Socialist Republic (RSFSR)." At her first opportunity to revisit the West in 1982, she defected in West Berlin, and then went to Melbourne, Australia, where she pursued her career for some time. Currently she teaches at the noted Indiana University School of Music.

Shkolnikova's Russian recordings and tapings of live Australian performances confirm the high esteem in which she is held by her Soviet colleagues. Of the numerous Soviet-trained women violinists I have heard, her playing projects the most satisfying overall blend of technical mastery, expressive communication, stylis-

Nelli Khkolnikova

tic awareness, and artistic finesse. Her tone is warm and appealing; her vibrato, basically of medium speed, is wisely controlled and applied naturally to the spirit of the specific music she is playing. At times her performance reflects Oistrakh's influence, but it is neither openly imitative nor as highly personalized. It is playing in the Russian romantic tradition, although Shkolnikova is capable of disciplined restraint as well as propulsive brilliance; her technique is nearly impeccable.

Judging by the top aesthetic standards, one might prefer a bit more introspection and subtlety of phrasing in the slow movement of her interpretations of the Beethoven concerto and Sonata No. 8 in G-major, though both contain many passages of suave declamation. Her Tchaikovsky concerto, ardent yet admirably controlled, compares favorably with the better versions of this era. Veracini's Sonata No. 8 in E is imbued with charm and nobility; her Shostakovich Ten Preludes run the gamut from winsome lyricism to glittering virtuosity, and strong rhythmic impulse. Paganini's *Moses Fantasy* (tuned in scordatura) and Caprice No. 2 are instilled with amiable music probity rather than gymnastic emphasis. Her recordings include about 50 works of varied lengths.

IGOR BEZRODNY

Igor Bezrodny (b. 1930) was born in Tbilisi, capital of Georgia, USSR. Both parents were violinists; he began study at age six with his father. In 1937 he entered the school for gifted children affiliated with the Moscow Conservatory, and from 1949 to 1953 was a pupil of Yampolsky. He won gold medals at the Prague Kubelik Competition in 1949 and the Bach Competition in 1950 at Leipzig.

I heard Bezrodny in 1961 playing Khrennikov's Concerto No. 2, a work of vigorous, mass audience appeal, recalling both Khachaturian and Kabolevsky. But it did little for the violinist except to demonstrate that he possessed instrumental powers of a high order and a mediocre violin. (Since Khrennikov was the permanent Secretary-General of the Union of Soviet Composers for over 35 years and a deputy to the Supreme Soviet, he had no difficulty getting his works performed either by Soviet musicians or by foreign musicians seeking Soviet connections.)

Bezrodny's recordings number around 60. The single major concerto is the Beethoven along with the minor concertos of Kabolevsky and Foerster. No major violin-piano sonatas are listed, though he has recorded two Handel sonatas, the Locatelli-Ysaÿe *Le Tombeau* Sonata and Bach's *Chaconne*, as well as Ravel's *Tzigane* and Chausson's *Poème*. Throughout his recordings of many short works, it is apparent that Bezrodny is one of the more Western-oriented among Soviet violinists, and one of their finest stylists.

He has an effusive temperament, knows how to use tasteful slides and position changes for expressive purposes, and understands the role of tenderness and poetry in performance. Like most Soviet-trained violinists, he displays a prodigious facility. But his range of tonal color is rather limited. And while the sound quality is engaging, it is not a sound of compelling beauty. The root cause of this is a rapid vibrato that at times becomes too fast, vitiating the solidity of his tone.

Outstanding among his recorded brevities with pianist Abram Makarov are the Gershwin-Heifetz Three Preludes, clearly under the Heifetz influence; a heartwarming Bloch *Nigun*; a lilting Kreisler *Gypsy Caprice*; a Triggs *Danza Brasiliana* (the latter dedicated to, and first recorded by the American Louis Kaufman); a jaunty Prokofiev-Grunes Theme and Processional from *Peter and the Wolf*; and a gracefully sensitive Mompou-Szigeti *Jeunes Filles au Jardin*. From the origin of the selections it is obvious that Bezrodny's tastes are eclectic, and he is closely in touch with Western repertorial items of the 1940s and 1950s.

In recent years Bezrodny has turned seriously to symphonic conducting and currently is busily occupied with podium chores.

VALERI KLIMOV

Valeri Klimov, son of Alexander Klimov, a well-known conductor of the Kiev Opera, was born in that city in 1931. Originally a Stolyarsky pupil, he concluded his studies with David Oistrakh at the Moscow Conservatory. In 1955 he only placed sixth at the Paris Long-Thibaud Competition, but in 1956 won first prize in the Prague Spring Festival "Ondřiček" Competition, and in 1958 was awarded the gold medal in the first Moscow Tchaikovsky Competition. Following this victory he was sent abroad as soloist with the Moscow Philharmonic performing the Tchaikovsky concerto. Klimov has toured the U.S.A. several times, though not all have been top-level bookings. A personable blond man with a winning stage presence, he has appeared successfully throughout the world.

Klimov rightfully belongs in the echelon of Soviet violinists just below Oistrakh and Kogan. Polish, clarity of line, and refinement, rather than fiery temperament and bravura virtuosity, characterize his playing. He does, however, possess formidable technical equipment and warmth of sound. His vibrato, basically of medium speed, flows naturally and is smartly controlled, with no "on-and-off" aberrations. And he employs expressive slides and position changes with tasteful selection. Quite free of idiosyncrasies, his playing reflects the utmost in musical integrity, and is in many ways exceptional, but not of striking individuality.

The Klimov recordings number about 35 at this writing. They include the Tchaikovsky, Mendelssohn, Mozart No. 3, and Beethoven concertos; the sonatas of Franck, Prokofiev No. 2, Beethoven No. 3 in E-flat and *Kreutzer*, Schubert's *Fantasy* Op. 159, Bach No. 3 in E, and Handel No. 4 in D-major (nearly all are with pianist Yampolsky). Klimov's virtuoso showpiece records are limited to the ubiquitous Tchaikovsky *Waltz-Scherzo*, Sarasate's *Caprice Basque*, and *Jota Aragonesa*, and Ysaÿe's Solo Sonata No. 6. Obviously he is not one of the many Russians who make a specialty of fingerboard gymnastics. No chamber ensemble recordings are among his listings.

The Tchaikovsky concerto recording (Kurt Eliasberg, Moscow State Philharmonic, 1958) is much as I heard him in live performance—pure, sensitive, warmly affectionate but not impassioned. The finale (with none of the usual brief cuts in the repetitive rapid spiccato passages) is not truly exciting. But overall it is a sleek, fluent, fastidious interpretation.

Klimov's Mendelssohn concerto disc is one of his finest: sparkling, propulsive, and amiably expressive, an outstanding performance in every respect. And Mozart's No. 3, with Oistrakh's superb cadenza, stressing buoyance and nobility of style, is equally impressive. (Both with Maxim Shostakovich, USSR State Symphony, 1967.) His Bach Sonata No. 3, for violin and piano, cool and limpid in sound and approach, contains a somewhat joyless second movement *Allegro*. More satisfying is his elegant, stately rendering of Handel's Sonata No. 4.

After the death of David Oistrakh, when it was assumed by most that Igor Oistrakh would succeed to his father's pedagogical chair at the Moscow Conservatory, Valeri Klimov, rather surprisingly, was given the post. Whatever the reasons given by the powers that be, whether justified or not, one cannot deny that Klimov's standing as an artist qualifies him for the position.

IGOR OISTRAKH

In the post-Paganini era, the Oistrakhs have been the first example of father and son violinists to attain solo careers on the international level. Igor, born in 1931 in Odessa, first took piano lessons, then switched to the violin at age six, studying with Valeria Merenbloom. After two years he was taught briefly by his father, but was, as he put it, "very lazy." It was Stolyarsky who finally motivated the recalcitrant boy to work seriously, and at age 12 he began a ten-year

Igor Oistrakh

period of study with that master, though he was coached intermittently by his father. In 1949 he played his first major recital in Kiev, and in 1952 won the gold medal at the Poznan Wieniawski Competition. His initial European concerts took place in 1953, and in 1962 he appeared in the first of many American tours.

As the son of the great David Oistrakh, Igor enjoyed many advantages and, of course, was subject to extraordinary pressures. How onerous and frustrating it must be to hear oneself compared constantly to a universally beloved and respected father. But this was only part of Igor's burden. In addition, the powerful influence of his father's playing and its personalized style impressed upon him daily and at intimate range when David was home, could scarcely fail to engrave itself upon all of his artistic sensibilities. Imagine any young violinist striving to form his own musical personality while living with a Kreisler or a Heifetz—or an Oistrakh!

Igor has always been "the other Oistrakh," and as such he all too often has been underrated as a violinist. Yet in spite of this handicap, the younger Oistrakh has honestly earned his position among the topmost Soviet violinists against fearsome competition.

Even though it is essentially unfair to insist upon comparing Igor with David, it is scarcely possible not to do so. Igor's concept of tone production, interpretive approach, texture, and usage of vibrato, phrasing, and the important expressive horizontal movements involved in position changes and slides, are markedly similar to those of David. In fact, there are passages in which even an experienced ear can have difficulty in telling them apart. Naturally it is a prodigious feat in itself to make music that resembles so formidable an artist as David Oistrakh. However, in the process, Igor obviously sacrificed whatever potential for strong individualism he might have possessed.

As an instrumentalist, Igor is a formidable virtuoso who handles any genre of music with aplomb, though he does not specialize in the most gymnastic of the "variation" showpieces of Paganini and Ernst. His superlative recording of Hindemith's *Kammermusik* No. 4 demonstrates that his technical resources can cope readily with the most severe demands of 20th-century unviolinistic technical challenges. To his credit, unlike many of his contemporaries and colleagues, he is willing to accept this type of challenge.

At this writing Igor's recordings number about 100, including duets with his father and several collab-

orations with such colleagues as Pikaisen and Barshai, as well as the outstanding Soviet pianists Yampolsky, Makarov, N. Zertsalova, A. Ginzburg, B. Davidovich, and I. Kollegorskaya. His disc repertoire encompasses most of the basic major concertos, sonatas, medium-length showpieces, and a broad sampling of shorter works.

In assessing Igor's art, it is necessary to stress two vital factors. First, in live concert his playing is not fully consistent. Even within a single program his instrumental authority and emotional projection may vary in different works. I have heard him in several performances playing below his highest standard. Secondly, his playing is constantly beset by the "on-and-off" vibrato syndrome which vitiates his lyric flow. This shortcoming, of course, is less blatant in the music of Bartók, Stravinsky, Hindemith, Shostakovich, and most 20th-century works than it is in 19th-century, overtly romantic staples. Also, unlike David, that steady "Rock of Gibraltar," Igor at times will mar a performance by playing rapid passage segments too fast, losing the inherent rhythmic pulse of the music. A vivid case in point occurred at a concert I attended in which Igor, obviously upset by a technically inferior performance of the Sibelius concerto, quickly returned on stage offering as an encore Ysaÿe's Sonata No. 3 (*Ballade*). Played at breakneck speed, it was a technical tour-de-force, but an incongruous example of music-making.

One of the more impressive of Igor's recordings is the Tchaikovsky concerto with his father conducting the Moscow Philharmonic. It is extremely agile, pure of line, and stylistically in the finest tradition of the Soviet musical approach, ranking high among the more than 70 recordings of this work. Although not as emotionally consistent as David's interpretation, it projects warmth of spirit, and contains less "on-and-off" lyric vibrato than most of Igor's performances of ultra-romantic works.

Other outstanding discs are Prokofiev's Concerto No. 1 (Rozhdestvensky, Moscow Radio Orchestra) and Bartók's Concerto No. 2 (Rozhdestvensky, Moscow State Philharmonic). Lalo's *Symphonie Espagnole* is brilliantly idiomatic, although more sweet than sensuous. His Beethoven concerto is sensitive and thoughtful in a musical approach similar to David's (D. Oistrakh, Vienna Symphony), but again his uneven vibrato usage is sometimes irksome. His Rakov concerto and Szymanowski's *La Fontaine d'Arethuse* are strong in David's influence; Ravel's *Tzigane*, while medium-weight in tonal texture, is highly polished and ardent in sound and phrasing. Chausson's *Poème*, otherwise elegant, is impaired by "on-and-off" vibrato, as are to an even greater extent Saint-Saëns's *Havanaise*, Vitali's *Chaconne*, and Paganini's *Moses Fantasy* (no scordatura).

Ysaÿe's *Lointainé Passé* Mazurka No 3, is absolutely exquisite, and Vieuxtemps's *Tarantelle*, a breathtaking exercise in facility, dominate a superb collection of recorded brevities from the mid-1950s. Eight of Paganini's caprices, 1973 (with wife Natalia Zertsalova playing the simplistic Schumann accompaniments), are straightforward, scrupulously clean, propulsive renditions, and the Kreisler version of *La Campanella* is scintillating. Turning to the viola, Igor, also conducting the Solo Ensemble of the Moscow State Philharmonic, with Viktor Pikaisen on violin, offers a performance of Mozart's *Duo Concertante* that is neatly limned, resonant in sound, and musically alert.

In retrospect, one might say that David Oistrakh's legacy to his son has been both bountiful and deleterious. Irrespective of any shortcomings, Igor Oistrakh is an artist to be admired.

VIKTOR PIKAISEN

Viktor Pikaisen, born in 1933 in Kiev, is the son of Alexander, concertmaster of the Kiev Opera Orchestra. His mother, a pupil of Simon Barere, was a piano-accompanist at the same theater. Viktor began violin study with Joseph Gutman, a well-known teacher of children in Kiev. After the war broke out, the family was relocated in Alma-Ata, Khazhakstan, and at age nine the boy made his debut in Wieniawski's Concerto No. 2 with the Alma-Ata State Symphony. Meanwhile he continued lessons with his father. In 1946 David Oistrakh accepted him as his pupil and taught him in Moscow for 14 years, longer than any other pupil. Among his many awards were second prizes in 1957 at the Thibaud Competition and in 1958 at Moscow's Tchaikovsky Competition, and first prize in 1965 at Genoa's Paganini Competition. He has concertized extensively on an international scale but has never been in the United States.

I met Pikaisen at the Moscow Conservatory, where he has been a leading professor since 1966. A man of gentle mien, he bears a striking physical resemblance to David Oistrakh, and is a close friend of the

Victor Pikaisen

Oistrakh family. His repertoire is broad. He has performed all 24 Paganini caprices in a single concert more than 50 times, and the full cycle of Bach solo sonatas and partitas on numerous occasions. He favors recitals for solo violin, and often programs the solo sonatas of Bartók and Geminiani. Both Aram Khachaturian and Boris Tchaikovsky have dedicated major works to him. In recent years he has given many concerts with his pianist daughter Tatiana.

Pikaisen's recordings number about 40, and in addition to the solo vehicles and various violinistic showpieces, they include the concertos of Beethoven, Mendelssohn, Dvořák, and Wieniawski No. 1 in F-sharp minor.

When Pikaisen took second place to Klimov in the 1958 Tchaikovsky Competition, more than a few observers preferred his fiery, intensely vibrant performance to the polished, patrician playing of Klimov. Surprisingly, despite his long years with Oistrakh, Pikaisen is not an imitator of his mentor, and while one can pinpoint instances of "on-and-off" vibrato usage, it is not annoying.

Pikaisen's interpretations represent two distinctly different approaches. Basically he is a full-blooded romantic, an impassioned performer with exceptional virtuosity. His recording of the Wieniawski No. 1 (Rozhdestvensky, Moscow Radio Symphony) vies with those of Rabin and Perlman as a stunning tour de force of opulent sound and immaculate authority. And his Dvořák concerto (David Oistrakh, Moscow Philharmonic), with its lush tone and fervent temperament, ranks with the better recordings of this work. The Beethoven concerto, with Wolfgang Schneiderhan's lengthy, unorthodox cadenza consisting of some material unrelated to the theme and punctuated by drum beats, is vitiated by a logy, uninspired opening of the orchestral tutti (Igor Oistrakh, Central Television and Radio Orchestra). Pikaisen's performance is admirable, technically, and his high E-string sound is excellent. But there are moments of prosaic playing, and in general it is not memorable.

The dichotomy in Pikaisen's playing is most evident in his Paganini caprices and Bach solo sonatas. Here his inherent fire is deliberately curbed by his intellectual devices. The caprices are scrupulously delivered, clean and neat in detail, and one can scarcely be unimpressed with many of his attempts at originality of interpretation. Yet in the process the bravura character of the music is often sacrificed. And in the Bach, his square-cut approach inhibits the natural flow of the lighter dance segments (i.e. Gavottes, Menuettos, Bourrées, etc.). If Pikaisen were an artist of academic pursuits and cool temperament, this would be understandable. But in his obviously sincere efforts to perform Bach without any vestige of romanticism, he has adopted a quasi-cerebral musicality that is essentially studied and alien to his instincts.

The above observations notwithstanding, Pikaisen is of international stature, and one of the finest of Soviet violinists.

VLADIMIR SPIVAKOV

Vladimir Spivakov was born in 1944 in Ufa in the Soviet Ural area, after his family had been evacuated from Leningrad during World War II. He first received piano lessons from his mother, but at age seven began study of the violin with Mme. Lubovitch Siegel, also a teacher of Boris Gutnikov. Next he studied with Veniamin Sher at the Leningrad Conservatory, and at 17 was enrolled in the Moscow Conservatory where he was a pupil of Yankelevich. In 1965 he took fourth prize at the Paris Thibaud-Long Competition; in 1967, second prize at the Genoa Paganini Competition; in 1969, first prize at the Montreal International Competition; and in 1970, second prize in the Moscow Tchaikovsky Competition. Spivakov has toured extensively both at home and abroad, and during the Soviet-

Vladimir Spivakov

American political freeze was one of the very few Soviet artists permitted to play in the United States. His prestige in the Soviet Union was extremely high and his loyalty unquestioned. I met and spent some time with Spivakov during one of his Los Angeles visits, and found him to be a modest, reserved man of striking sincerity, looking younger than his years, and a strongly patriotic Soviet citizen despite his Jewish heritage.

Spivakov was not well received in his various Southern California appearances, and I concurred with this opinion. Of course he is a brilliant instrumentalist, as are so many of his countrymen, but his playing is marked by a major shortcoming—a vibrato that is consistently too fast, at times almost approximating a whinny. And for all his finger intensity, the "on-and-off" vibrato habit is one of his hallmarks. Thus his sound is either excitedly vibrant or "white," with no intermediate tempering degrees. How this has escaped major adverse commentary from the Soviet violin establishment and foreign critics must remain a mystery. He uses practically the same vibrato for a Mozart concerto as for the Sibelius concerto (both of which I have heard live), just as in a recording his sound in a Haydn concerto is scarcely less vibrant than in the Tchaikovsky concerto. There are times, naturally, when this tense vibrato is acceptable, but his tonal palette has little variety and tends to be monochromatic. Spivakov does evince a measure of individuality from his interpretations, but his tonal aberrations prevent him from ranking artistically with such violinists as Perlman or Zukerman.

In a survey of his recordings to date, the most

impressive are the Paganini-Spivakov *Witches Dance*, a dazzling performance, and his highly personalized, interesting, if unorthodox renditions of the Brahms-Joachim *Hungarian Dances* No. 16, 2, 9, and 6. Spivakov formed and presides as leader and soloist with a 27-member group called the *Moscow Virtuosi*. At this writing he is devoting much of his time and energies to conducting his ensemble in Spain.

Now in his 50s, it is too late for any appreciable change in Spivakov's tonal production and projection even if he wished to effect it. This is all the more unfortunate since his natural expressive powers and galvanic, yet controlled temperament, are superior to those of Mullova, Grubert, or just about any of the younger Soviet-trained violinists of their generation.

VIKTOR TRETYAKOV

Viktor Tretyakov (b. 1946), born in Krasnoyarsk, Siberia, is the son of a tuba player in an army band. At age six he began violin study at the Irkutsk Conservatory, and later entered the noted Central Music School of Moscow, the preparatory subsidiary of the Moscow Conservatory. In 1963 he became a pupil of Yankelevich, who taught him until his death in 1973. In 1965 he was named the laureate of young Soviet violinists, and in 1966 won first prize in the third Tchaikovsky Competition in Moscow. He has had many international tours and first appeared in the United States in 1969.

A handsome, engaging stage figure, with a bearing almost military in decorum, Tretyakov is a model "Russian" violinist, one of the more successful Soviet artists to follow Oistrakh and Kogan.

As an executant his equipment is superb, and his repertoire is broad. A dominating feature of his playing is its obvious sincerity of purpose, disciplined intelligence, and the absence of carelessness or superficiality. In live concert Tretyakov's tone is not very large-scaled, but his vibrato is strong and evenly applied. It is not the type of sound that can thrill an audience by its beauty alone, but can at times project a sense of opulence. There is an aura of formality in his interpretations of masterworks, yet he does possess a warm temperament that infuses a positive glow into those works for which he is best suited. Thus, in one of his recitals

that I attended, he generated a dynamic drive to Prokofiev's *March* that attained an overwhelming climax. But Kreisler's *Caprice Viennois*, after a promising beginning, fell victim to a plodding tempo and almost flaccid double-stops that lacked completely the vital intensity and charm demanded of the music.

The best-known of Tretyakov's recordings in the West is the Paganini Concerto No. 1 (Neimye Varvy, Moscow Philharmonic). It is a glittering performance, virile, immaculate in technique and bold in spirit. The first movement Sauret cadenza registers as a tour de force; the operatic *Adagio expressivo* may not project the ultimate drama, but does contain a good measure of intense lyricism. The finale is unusually rapid and all, including the double-harmonics, is crisply articulated. This is Tretyakov at his zenith, and the disc ranks among the finest half-dozen of this work.

Conversely, in his recording of Brahms's Sonata No. 3, Op. 108, while he obviously strives for introspection in a rendition that is quite individualized, his tempos are decidedly elastic and his tone inconsistent. His pace too often tends to plod, and passages of genuine excitement are few and far between. In Ravel's *Tzigane* Tretyakov is essentially miscast, and though the performance is efficiently wrought, it does not have the tonal richness and instinctual fire of an exceptional reading. Again, the Vitali-Charlier *Chaconne* is chaste and conscientious but lacking propulsion and diversity of pacing, and generally uninteresting.

Tretyakov's recording of Bach's G-minor Solo Sonata is outstanding, highlighted by beautifully delineated fugal patterns and eloquent chordal salvos. Also extraordinary are Paganini's Caprice No. 17, which smartly avoids dull dynamic repetition in the filigree scale passages, and Caprice No. 24, spotless in bowing inflections and purity of intonation, plus a novel forte-and-piano exposition of the left-hand pizzicatos. Even more exciting is the Paganini-Kreisler *I Palpiti*, hair-raising in its technical integrity and clarity in the awesome gymnastic challenges.

A recording of the Sibelius concerto, taken from a live performance (Alexander Dmitriev, USSR Academy Symphony) is estimable overall; the third movement is a bit labored but the Adagio contains some sensuous G-string tones.

In all, Tretyakov is one of the finest Soviet violinist-musicians.

GIDON KREMER

Gidon Kremer was born in Riga in 1947 of musical parents. His first teachers, at age four, were his father and grandfather. At seven he entered the Riga School of Music where he studied with V.A. Sturestep, and at 16 won first prize in the Latvian Republic Competition. During the following eight years he was a pupil of David Oistrakh. In 1967 he received third prize in the Brussels Queen Elisabeth Competition; in 1969 won first prize in Genoa's Paganini Competition and second place at the Montreal Competition; and in 1970 was gold medalist in Moscow's Tchaikovsky Competition. Kremer has concertized widely on an international scale, and at this writing enjoys the most prolific and successful career of all contemporary Soviet-trained violinists. This can be attributed to several factors. He was acclaimed as "the greatest violinist in the world" by the eminent conductor Herbert von Karajan. Also, as a de facto citizen of the world he has moved to the West and is, to all intents and purposes, a Soviet émigré. This has enabled him to build his career without the interference and frustration caused by East-West political antagonisms and boycotts. And in addition to the impact of his performances, he has a gift for garnering attention and publicity for himself by means of highly unorthodox musical activities. Kremer was first married to the violinist Tatiana Grindenko, 1972 gold medalist at the Poznan Wieniawski Competition, with whom he has made several duo recordings. His second wife, pianist Elena Bashkirov, daughter of pianist Dmitri Bashkirov, collaborated with her husband in recitals. (They are now divorced.)

Gidon Kremer

Kremer is probably the most idiosyncratic, controversial violinist of his generation. Except for a few glints in his early recordings, his playing reflects no direct influence of Oistrakh's sound or style. As a virtuoso he is easily the equal of any of the gymnastics-oriented Soviet violinists; his recording of Ernst's *Last Rose of Summer* (Étude No. 6) and *Erl King*, Geminiani's solo sonata, Bach's Solo Partita in B-minor, Paganini's Caprice No. 4, Milstein's *Paganiniana*, and excerpts from Rochberg's immensely difficult Caprice Variations are note-perfect gems of technical facility. However, even in these spectacular performances one can discern Kremer's shortcomings as well as his strengths, and understand why he has cleverly elected to make novelty and experimentation the cardinal components of his career.

The crux of the matter is that for all his individuality, vigor, and fervor, Kremer possesses a thin, commonplace, impersonal sound, a sound essentially indistinguishable from that of any number of second- and third-rate colleagues. His comparatively thin fingers and slowish vibrato simply cannot produce a tone of sensuous beauty. Inasmuch as sensuality is not an integral element of his performance, he cannot compete directly with tone-oriented artists of the first rank. Since there are so few of them among contemporary international soloists, Kremer's lack of tonal opulence has not proved an insuperable handicap.

Some observers tend to associate Kremer's artistry with that of Joseph Szigeti, who forged a major career despite the competition of such great tonalists as Heifetz, Kreisler, Elman, and Menuhin, among others. I believe this to be fallacious. Any Kremer-Szigeti similarity is merely superficial. Both have sought repertorial novelty and have been champions of works originally shunned by others. But at this point resemblances cease. Szigeti, in his prime, could elevate masterworks such as the Beethoven, Brahms, and Mozart concertos with a spiritual grace and inner nobility quite beyond any of the routinely efficient interpretations of these works by Kremer, although Kremer is the superior technician. I cannot help but compare a recent international telecast of Kremer's playing of Vivaldi's *The Four Seasons* with the English Chamber Orchestra, an overpropulsive, lean-toned, graceless romp, with the lofty elegance Szigeti could impart to a simple Handel sonata. Apart from comparisons with Szigeti, Kremer is unable to achieve the tonal intensity and luster necessary for impassioned performances of the great romantic concertos of Tchaikovsky, Sibelius, Bruch, Lalo, and others. Even in his recordings of such works as the Bartók Sonatas No. 1 and 2, and the Shostakovich Sonata Op. 134, which he plays with sensitivity and elan, the slenderness of his tone is always apparent to a professional ear. And because of his unsightly body contortions and deep knee bends, it is more satisfying to hear Kremer in recordings than to watch him on the concert platform.

Kremer's fierce independence is well-suited to the talents he possesses. Thus far, avant-garde compositions for the violin have gained little favor with audiences, but there has always been a potential audience for contemporary works that do not assault the ear or insult the intelligence. In his search for material, Kremer has unearthed such curiosities as Milhaud's *Ox on the Roof* arrangement, a saucy, nose-thumbing confection recalling the jazzy 1920s; several wry, forgettable pieces by Satie; Beethoven's undistinguished *Twelve Variations on a Mozart Theme*; the early (1897), immature sonata by Ravel (not the familiar sonata with the Blues movement); and a slight morsel purportedly written by Charles Chaplin for *Modern Times*. And in his zeal for novelty he has taken up such rarely performed romantic gambols as Vieuxtemps's *Fantasia Appassionata*, which he has recorded. A recent ploy that won Kremer an enormous amount of attention was his inclusion of cadenzas by the Soviet avant-gardist Alfred Schnittke in his performance of the Beethoven concerto. Apparently operating on the proven theory that any publicity, good or bad, is desirable, Kremer stoutly defended his action against a barrage of criticism. Actually the cadenzas, aside from being alien to the style and spirit of the concerto, contain little to cause indignation among musically more permissive auditors. They employ a scarcely cohesive collection of insignificant pizzicato pluckings, rambling double-stops, chordal salvos, and dexterous digital flights that bear scant relationship to the concerto's basic themes. In some of the climactic bars the violinist is assisted by drum beats and surging billows of sound from the orchestra's string players. Kremer is currently presenting a concerto by Schnittke, and no doubt will continue to build his career along these lines while retaining as much of the basic repertoire as he requires to balance his program.

Kremer can be an extremely interesting artist in "off-beat" and little known works. Yet even at best, while his playing may be exhilarating, it is hardly exalted, and not calculated to touch the heart.

OTHER SOVIET VIOLINISTS

Many a Soviet virtuoso has lived and died, either unknown in the West or known only to a few Western colleagues. One of these was that elegant stylist of the "old school," Shmuel (Samuel) Furer, born in 1909, who was more or less a casualty of the Oistrakh hegemony. More than a few never received the recognition they deserved.

One who has recorded at least 80 widely diverse works, including Soviet exotica, Western brevities, and chamber music, is Eduard Grach (b. 1930), an Oistrakh pupil who is little known abroad. The late Boris Gutnikov (1931-1986), a winner of the 1962 Tchaikovsky Competition, performed in the West with rather indifferent success. As I heard him in the Tchaikovsky concerto, he was a brilliant instrumentalist with strong tonal attributes, but projected no particular personal aura. Mark Lubotsky (b. 1931), an Oistrakh pupil, now a professor at the Amsterdam Conservatory, boasts a formidable, top-level recording of the Britten concerto.

ALBERT MARKOV

Albert Markov (b. 1933), now living in the United States, is a fiery player of rhapsodic bent, who took second honors to Jaime Laredo in the 1959 Queen Elisabeth Competition. A smooth, lyric performer, his music-making is not profound, and "on-and-off" vibrato usage mars his delivery, particularly in his recording of the Kvernadze concerto, a sort of Georgian reflection of the Khachaturian concerto. He is, nevertheless, a sensitive, entertaining stylist, and his recordings of Paganini's *Moses Fantasy*, with one of the final variations played pizzicato, is quite dazzling. His transcription, *Second Rhapsody on Gershwin Themes*, is a blazing tour de force, cleverly conceived and stunningly executed. Markov's son, Alexander Markov, whom I have heard, is an outstanding violinistic talent, and at 18 was winner of the 1982 Paganini Competition. Young Markov has recorded the 24 Paganini caprices.

VICTOR DANCHENKO

Victor Danchenko (b. 1937), now a Canadian citizen, was born in Moscow to a musical family. In 1955 he graduated from the Central Music School, then entered the Moscow Conservatory where he studied with David Oistrakh, eventually gaining a doctoral degree in a post-graduate course. In 1957 Danchenko won the Gold Medal in the International Competition of the 6th World Youth and Student Festival in Moscow. A prize winner in the 1961 Long-Thibaud Competition, he received a medal in 1967 for the best rendition of a Ysaÿe work from the Ysaÿe Foundation in Brussels. A concertizing soloist of long experience, Danchenko has toured internationally and recorded numerous works on the Melodiya label and for the Soviet National Radio "Gold Foundation." He is a versatile violinist of impassioned temperament, with an intensely vibrant sound and virtuoso facility. He is eminently respected as a pedagogue, and many of his pupils have appeared widely as soloists. Since emigrating in 1977, he has been on the staff of the Toronto's Royal Conservatory, a visiting professor at the Cleveland Institute of Music, a faculty member of the Meadowmount and Encore Summer Schools, and in 1992 he was appointed to the Peabody Conservatory faculty. In 1994 Danchenko was invited to join the teaching staff of the Curtis Institute.

VLADIMIR LANDSMAN

Vladimir Landsman (b. 1942), now living in the West, in a live performance dispatched the Tchaikovsky concerto with sure-fingered agility, but with no more than routine interpretive powers and no particular individuality. Oleg Kagan (b. 1946), an Oistrakh pupil, winner of the 1965 Sibelius Competition and second prize winner in the 1966 Tchaikovsky Competition, is a violinist-musician of respectable stature. His recording of Beethoven's Sonatas No. 4 and No. 5 (*Spring*) with pianist Sviatoslav Richter, offers playing of sound, alert musicality, a straightforward approach, and clean-cut delivery, but lacks any exceptional subtlety. A fast, occasionally fluttery vibrato is a key element in his tonal production.

BORIS BELKIN

Boris Belkin (b. 1948), a Yankelevich pupil now living in Italy, appears to have more powerful contacts than some of the other artist émigrés. Onstage as I saw him, he sported shoulder-length hair and affected a cocky, quasi-Paganini stance. Belkin's recording of Paganini's Concerto No. 1 is far better than the live performance I heard. His tone is small though warmed by a fast vibrato, and he has a sense of drama and verve that so many of his generation lack. Technically his playing is sometimes labored. A violinist of romantic persuasion, he plays the Tchaikovsky concerto in both live and recorded performances with flashes of brilliance. But his performances overall do not project top-level artistry.

VADIM BRODSKY

Vadim Brodsky, born in Kiev (1956), is a violinist of superb technical equipment, vibrant sound, and fervent temperament--one of the leading Soviet-trained players of the post Oistrakh-Kogan era. He was the winner of the 1977 Wieniawski Competition and a laureate in several other major European competitions, including the 1974 Tchaikovsky competition in Moscow. Currently Brodsky concertizes principally in Poland, Italy, France, Germany and, on occasion, in the United States. His recordings embrace many major works of the repertoire. They include the complete Ysaÿe solo sonatas and a CD of the Saint-Saëns Concerto No. 3 which compares favorably with any on record. He lives in Rome. Andre Korsakov (b. 1950), second to Miriam Fried in the 1971 Queen Elisabeth Competition, recorded a Wieniawski collection including the extremely difficult "Original Variations," Op. 15, with admirable verve and panache. His digital equipment is outstanding and his pure tone can be impassioned. However, his performance does not denote big-scaled authority or scope.

Vadim Brodsky

PHILIP HIRSHHORN

Philip Hirshhorn, a Vaiman pupil now living in Brussels, was a winner of the 1967 Queen Elisabeth Competition. A recording of the Saint-Saëns-Ysaÿe *Valse-Caprice* made at that time displays him as a brilliant virtuoso whose playing is vitiated by an inordinately fast vibrato. Pavel Kogan (b. 1952), son of Leonid Kogan and Elizabeth Gilels, a Yankelevich pupil, is a violinist of superior attainments. In a live performance of the Brahms concerto, he exhibited excellent command and a disciplined thoughtful manner though his interpretation did not reflect a strong personal note. In a recording of the dark, tension-packed concerto by Franco Mannino, a challenging, difficult contemporary work, young Kogan displays a decided flair for the modern idiom; his technique sparkles and his tone is intense and penetrating. He is presently forging a career as a symphonic conductor, a profession for which he has considerable training and background.

VIKTORIA MULLOVA

Viktoria Mullova (b. 1959), a Kogan pupil, winner of the 1982 Tchaikovsky Competition and a previous winner of the Wieniawski and Sibelius Competitions, emigrated to the West in order to aggrandize her career. In two comprehensive recitals which I attended, she displayed outstanding technical equipment plus clarity of intonation and musical line

Pavel Kogan

that recalls her eminent master. She handles big-scaled works such as the Bartók No. 2 and Shostakovich No. 1 Concertos with impressive instrumental command. But her tone, while bright and fairly vibrant, tends to be one-dimensional, limited in color, and cool. Her performances of Paganini's *Nel cor piu non mi sento* Variations and the entire *La Campanella* movement from Concerto No. 2 was a scintillating tour de force, as is her recording of the Paganini Concerto No. 1. Bach's Solo Partita No. 1 in B-minor, cleanly wrought, was musically immature. And in the Brahms Sonatas No. 1, Op. 78 and No. 3, Op. 108, the meagerness of her expressive powers would indicate that Mullova's chief virtues are purely violinistic. Nonetheless, her career continues to burgeon.

DANIEL SHINDARYOV

Daniel Shindaryov (b. 1924), now of Los Angeles, is a performer of extraordinary spontaneity. He has

Daniel Shindaryov

sought to infuse his playing with the best precepts of Western musicianship while sharpening the stunning virtuosity inherited from his Soviet training. A former concertmaster of the Bolshoi Ballet and Opera orchestra, Shindaryov has blossomed into a soloist of multifaceted tonal expressiveness. He possesses the rare gift for exciting his audiences.

Tapes of the 1978 Tchaikovsky Competition indicate that co-winner Ilya Grubert (b.1954), a Yankelevich pupil, is a well-trained violinist of undistinguished sound and moderate talent. Oleh Krysa, an extremely polished artist, is now a professor at the Eastman School of Music in Rochester, New York. Ilya Kaler, a virtuoso of formidable stature, has recorded, among other works, Paganini's Concertos No. 1 & 2.

ABRAM SHTERN

Abram Shtern, born in 1919 in the Ukraine, started the violin at age seven; at age ten began study with David Bertich Lifshitz, (a pupil of Auer), and eventually was his assistant from 1945 to 1951. Shtern toured the Soviet Union as a soloist with the Kiev Philharmonic and various chamber groups, and also performed throughout the countries of the Soviet bloc and Cuba. He was concertmaster of the Kiev Opera and Ballet Theatre orchestra from 1947 to 1989. Shtern's recordings of the great violin ballet solos which I have heard, are remarkably beautiful. He became a professor at the Kiev Conservatory in 1976. Among the violinists he has coached are Ilya Kaler and Ilya Grubert, each a gold medalist at a Tchaikovsky Competition, as well as Zinovi Vinnikov, Polina Kotliarskaya, Pavel Vernikov, and Sergei Krilov. Shtern emigrated to the United States in 1990, and since has performed and taught there; his master classes have included engagements in Germany, Israel, and Italy. Violinists from many countries come to him for coaching.

EDUARD SCHMIEDER

Eduard Schmieder was born in 1948 near Lvov in the former Soviet Union. His first teacher was Akiva Zemmel. He made his debut at age seven with Bach's A-minor Concerto; at nine he played the Mendelssohn concerto in public. Heard by the noted violinist, the late Mikhail Vaiman, he was taken to Leningrad to study with Vaiman and his assistant. Later he became a longtime private pupil of David Oistrakh. In 1968 he suffered a serious heart condition, and illness has continued to plague his solo career. His pupils have won numerous laurels in major international competitions. Emigrating to the United States in 1979, he has become

widely prominent for his total commitment to pedagogical exploration and practice; his professorships have included Rice University and the University of Southern California. Currently Schmieder divides his teaching between Southern Methodist University in Dallas and the Paris Conservatoire; his masterclasses and appearances as a juror for competitions are international in scope. He has received critical acclaim as conductor of chamber music orchestras in France, Germany, Israel, Russia, and the United States.

Nina Beilina and Tatiana Grindenko are cited in my chapter on *Women and the Violin*.

VADIM REPIN

Notable among the current young generation is Vadim Repin, born in 1971 in Novosibirsk. His early training was with Zakhar Bron, who studied with Igor Oistrakh at the Moscow Conservatory. Repin started violin at age five, had lessons at a children's music school, and in 1977 began study at the "specialized" secondary music school at the Novosibirsk Conservatory. At nine he played Wieniawski's Concerto No. 2 and Paganini's Caprice No. 16 in concert.

In 1982 he won first prize at the Wieniawski Competition, and at 13 his repertoire included concertos of Mozart, Bach, Tchaikovsky, Mendelssohn, Khachaturian, Wieniawski, Khrennikov, and the Beethoven *Romances*, together with many virtuoso showpieces. At 15 he performed the Paganini Concerto No. 1 with the Sauret cadenza.

A recording made when he was only 13 stamped him as a genuine child prodigy with the powerful tone of a mature artist, incredible facility, and uncommon communicative instincts. Repin tosses off Ysaÿe's Solo Sonata No. 6 with stunning virtuosity, instills the Tchaikovsky-Bezekirsky *Meditation*, Op. 42, No. 1 with an impressive warmth, and plays the quixotic Schumann-Kreisler *Fantasia* in C-major, Op. 131 with considerable charm. His vibrato usage, on occasion, is afflicted with the "off-and-on" habit in lyric passages in this recording. Now in his 20s, I heard him in a superb Tchaikovsky concerto lacking only that degree of sophistication necessary for super stardom. It is impossible to determine whether or not his playing has individual profile or is steeped in emulation. But Repin's career merits close scrutiny. It is hoped that he will develop into a great artist rather than merely just another superb instrumentalist.

MAXIM VENGEROV

A tremendously impressive young virtuoso is Maxim Vengerov (b. 1974?), also a former pupil of Bron; a violinist whose extraordinary talent and instrumental command marks him as a potential successor to D. Oistrakh, L. Kogan and B. Goldstein. At age 15 his recording of Ernst's *Last Rose of Summer Variations* ranks with the most dazzling performances of this étude ever recorded, and his immaculate recorded performance of Schubert's Sonata, Op. 159, *Grand Fantasy* displays an innate musicianship and an instinct for phrasing of rare sensitivity. His tone is rich in timbre and cogently varied.

In view of the tremendous emigration of leading violinists from the Soviet Union, it will be interesting to see whether post-Soviet Russia will produce violinists of the number and calibre of the previous decades.

Maud Powell, America's leading violinist in the early years of the 20th century

Women and the Violin

Any survey of the role of women in the history of violin playing must of necessity be analogous, in many respects, to surveys of their role in all cultural and professional endeavors. And, of course, the existing social mores and practices of the specific age into which she was born greatly determine the potential for success of any individual woman who finds herself in direct (or even indirect) competition with men. Thus, when one considers that mastery of the violin requires a degree of continual toil, sacrifice, and fanatical dedication demanded by few other occupations, the enormity of the challenge faced by women who seek to attain the Parnassus of violin art becomes the more apparent.

There are those who would deprecate the efforts of women violinists by pointing out that no woman can be included among such immortals as Corelli, Paganini, Joachim, Ysaÿe, Kreisler, Heifetz, or others of comparable rank in their respective eras. This, however, is quite a superficial attitude if one takes the trouble to evaluate violin art in all its many fields and facets—not merely the highest realm of concertizing virtuosity. It is true that for more than a century after the beginning of the age of modern violin playing (generally dated from Corelli), women's participation and contributions were modest—in keeping with their repressed position in society. But as social freedoms for women expanded, so did their penchant for the violin. And as we shall see, their future is unlimited.

In discussing the comparative merits of women violinists as opposed to men, it is often said that there are psychological differences between the sexes. Much has been made of the so-called feminine nature—that women are more sensitive, delicate, refined, spiritual, intuitive, etc..

Of course there are fundamental differences between men and women and they can be debated ad infinitum.

But for all practical purposes, it would appear that together with social factors, the most readily accessible evidence involves physical, rather than psychic, phenomena. As with men, women's temperaments run the gamut from sensuality to placidity; some have strongly pronounced personalities, others reflect quasi-anonymity; some play with emotional projection, others, dry scholasticism.

There are women who play with brash, expansive aggressiveness, others with gentle reticence; some project positive intellectual force, others superficial musicality. And who can deny that woman's traditionally docile, dependent image in society, particularly in the 18th and 19th centuries, tended to encourage "ladylike" playing?

Body size and weight alone are not decisive factors, as proved by the success of such small men as Elman, Huberman, Ricci, and numerous others, although some fragile or petite women may be limited in sheer muscular application. However, there are observers, including this writer, who believe that the bone structure, plus the breadth, thickness, and distribution of flesh on the left hand finger tip pads of *individual* men give them an advantage in producing the ultimate resonance and richness (but not necessarily intensity or decibel power) of tone.

By the beginning of the 20th century, leaving aside the very greatest male personalities of the violin, it was becoming increasingly difficult, and often impossible, for even experienced professional competition judges to tell the difference between gifted male and female contestants—particularly if the principals played behind a curtain. This trend has continued to increase by leaps and bounds and, while this chapter is confined to women violinists, similar criteria apply to women cellists and violists.

On the purely digital level, women have generally been handicapped by smaller hands, so that in works demanding inordinate stretches, such as the Paganini caprices and concertos, they were alleged to be at a disadvantage. Today, however, there are women who have recorded the entire cycle of the caprices and the complete Paganini Concerto No. 1 (with Sauret's cadenza) and other gymnastic-oriented works of Paganini and Ernst. Let us remember, too, that in the context of the higher standards of musicianship demanded in the modern era and the greatly expanded repertoire, the role of specialized spellbinding digital extravaganzas has diminished substantially.

The number of important talented women who upon marriage have retired in mid-career is legion. A good wife was (and often, still is) expected to put her husband and family before all else. How many gifted ones have disappeared before their potential was fully developed! Even in researching the careers of accomplished women players, the number who are listed with a birth date but no death date is exorbitant, because somewhere along the way, the career-versus-family syndrome forced them into comparative or complete anonymity.

Historically, piano lessons were considered a necessary adjunct to the education and proper upbringing of the genteel daughters of the nobility and rising bourgeoisie. Not so the violin. In fact, there was widespread prejudice against women playing the violin.

George Dubourg, writing in 1878, said: "The common objection is that it is ungraceful—a more solid objection, perhaps, is that they do not naturally possess the physical grasp, so essential to the requirements of playing." Then he adds: "The ladies in Boccaccio's *Decameron*, however—and who shall charge them with want of grace?—played on the viol, a bowed instrument requiring from the performer a similar position and handling to those exacted by the violin."

This was indeed a charitable pro-female gesture for a man of Dubourg's time, but not really accurate, since the neck-shoulder holding of the violin and the erect standing position of post-Corelli concert soloists were not employed in Boccaccio's time.

The entire question of "want of grace" of women violinists seems the more ridiculous in an era which saw nothing graceless in the appearance of long-bearded men violinists. It is interesting to note that in 1893, only 15 years after Dubourg's observations, G.B. Shaw wrote: "Young ladies who can play much better than the average professional 'leader' of 20 years ago are discoverable with a little research in sufficient abundance nowadays (chiefly because Madame Neruda proved at that time that the violin shews off a good figure)."

In reviewing the careers of 18th- and 19th-century women violinists, it is considerably more difficult to attempt to assess their talents than those of their male contemporaries. Whereas most men violinists created compositions which reveal the extent of their technique, general style, and musical taste (or dearth of it), we have no similar heritage from women—at least of a comprehensive nature. In discussing women as performing artists, we are forced to rely upon the testimony of observers and critics who all too seldom write with unadorned rhetoric, or display convincing professional violin expertise.

One of the earliest women violinists on record was Mrs. Sarah Ottey (b. about 1695— ?, English), who also performed on the harpsichord and bass viol. Burney makes no attempt to assess her ability.

A violinist known only as *La Diamantina* (b. about 1715— ?) was described by the English poet, Gray, who heard her in Rome about 1740, as "a famous virtuoso, playing upon the violin divinely."

Catherine Plunkett (b. 1725— ?, Irish) played in London and Dublin with "great success" about 1744 and then disappeared from the scene.

Madalena Lombardini Sirmen (about 1738-1798, Italian) was said to have had "such an eminence in violin playing as enabled her, in some degree, to rival Nardini." If this is true, it is interesting to recall that Nardini was alleged to have been more noted for his tone than his technique (though his compositions are certainly comparable, technically, to those of his contemporaries). Lombardini was said to have been a pupil of Tartini who, in 1760, wrote her a lengthy letter of quaint instructions on how to study and practice technical fundamentals. After successfully touring Europe and winning plaudits in London, she married a violinist, Ludovico Sirmen, and they concertized together. She also became a singer. Unlike most of her women colleagues, she composed nine concertos and several sonatas (once published by Hummel in Amsterdam) and, perhaps in the interest of female posterity or sheer nostalgia, violinists of both genders will seek them out and perform them.

Teresa and Marie, the Milanollo sisters

Regina (Sacchi) Strinasachi (1764-1839, Italian) was a virtuoso of "the highest degree of talent," for whom Mozart wrote his famous Sonata in B flat, K. 454. The story is told that he did not get around to committing the music to paper until the night before he was to perform it with her before the royal court in Vienna—an aberration which caused the lady much distress. The performance, however, proceeded smoothly, though the Emperor Josef II discovered that Mozart had used a completely blank, dummy score (because he didn't have time to copy the piano part) and had played entirely from memory.

"Signora" Paravacini ("Signora" was the only first name given, b. 1769 —?, Italian) was a pupil of Viotti who was heard by Napoleon's Empress Josephine in Milan, and brought to Paris as instructor for her son Eugene Beauharnais. Abandoned by her fickle royal patroness, Paravacini was aided by Italian residents of Paris to return home, and she continued a career which won her a reputation of distinction.

Other well-known women players of this period were Luiga Gerbini, pupil of Viotti (b. 1790 —?, Italian); Madame Filipowicz, pupil of Spohr (b. 1794 —?, Polish); and Caterina Calcagno (b. 1797 —?, Italian), who, as a child of seven, was said to have had some lessons with Paganini. Following a brief but extremely brilliant career, she disappeared from the concert stage after 1816.

The first of the important women players born in the 19th century was Teresa Milanollo (1827-1902, Italian), a pupil of Lafont, Habaneck, and de Bériot. She had a younger sister, Marie, whom she taught and who was said to have been a player of equal skill. As girls they toured Europe. Marie died in 1848 at age 16, and Teresa went on to attain a full-fledged career. Though she lived until 1902, she retired from the concert stage in 1857, at only 29, when she married a French army officer. According to a German critic writing in 1854:

> Milanollo is a great artist, and in many things so great that few can be compared with her—all the enormous difficulties achieved by Paganini with which he almost set the world on fire, are produced by this extraordinary girl with the greatest ease—her effects are pure and legitimate, though she can also call forth, in their turn, 'smiles and tears.' She does let the instrument comparatively weep in the *Elegy*, but her playing never becomes too tearful; for this reason she plays Ernst's Elegy better than Ernst himself... .

A sober analysis of this romanticized rhetoric would suggest that the critic was prone to substitute nebulous impression for violinistic expertise, but there is sufficient evidence to believe that Milanollo was a superior violinist. It is interesting to note that the Czech, Bertha Brousil (b. 1838—?), who toured Europe and played for Queen Victoria, was called "the Bohemian Milanollo" in Germany.

Perhaps the dominating woman violinistic personality of the 19th century was Wilma Maria Francisca Neruda (1839-1911, German), subsequently known as Norman-Neruda and Lady Hallé, through her marriages to Ludwig Norman and Sir Charles Hallé. Her career was eminently international, and she was often referred to as "the woman Joachim" (they played the Bach D-minor Double Concerto together in 1892). So reliable an observer as Flesch said: "She played wholly in Joachim's spirit...although I could not hear a truly personal note, her playing (in three Beethoven sonatas) left an extraordinary profound impression on me." Hanslick, too, spoke glowingly of her playing as a child: "notwithstanding the smallness of her hands," and Vieuxtemps induced her to be concertmistress for a series of orchestral concerts in London.

Neruda's career as a soloist was triumphant, and in later years she organized a successful ladies' string quartet. In 1876 she was given a superb 1709 Strad by a group of titled patrons, and in 1896, a committee composed of royalty, statesmen, and eminent musicians formed a public subscription and presented her with a palazzo at Asolo, near Venice.

*Wilhelmina Norman-Neruda,
Lady Hallé, often called the
"female Joachim," was once
selected by Vieuxtemps to be
concertmistress of his orchestra,
a signal honor for a woman in
that era*

*Leonora Jackson, Boston
born, a pupil of Joachim,
noted American violinist
of yesteryear*

In the last quarter of the 19th century, women began to win honors in direct competition with men. Teresina Tua (1867—?, Italian) won first prize at the Paris Conservatory in 1880. Nettie Carpenter (1865—?, American) also won first prize at the Paris Conservatory in 1884. Arma Senkrah, an American whose real name was Harkness (1864-1900), won the Paris Conservatory first prize during that era (year not mentioned).

Irma Saenger-Sethe (1876—?, Belgian), who was later favorably compared with Neruda, won first prize at the Brussels Conservatory in 1891. Marie Soldat-Roeger (1864-1955, German), who won the Mendelssohn prize at the Berlin Hochschule, became especially noted for her performance of the Brahms concerto, and later formed a celebrated ladies' string quartet which engaged the interest of Brahms himself. Charlotte Ruegger (1876—?, Swiss) won the Brussels Conservatory first prize, and later composed a concerto, sonatas, solo pieces, and studies for the violin.

Sophie Jaffe (1872—?, Russian) won first prize at Paris in 1892, and according to Flesch, "though not the most musical of violinists, she was certainly the greatest virtuoso of her time—as a talent, she was among the elite." Jaffe retired from the concert stage after a sensational early career because it is said she inherited a fortune.

Gabriele Wietrowitz (1866—?, Austrian) ranks among the most gifted of Joachim's pupils, later formed a ladies' string quartet "which rivaled any of the male organizations." Leonora Jackson (1878—?, American) won the Berlin Hochschule's Mendelssohn prize, and toured with Paderewski and Patti.

Camilla Urso (1842-1902, French), a pupil of Massart, enjoyed a formidable international career as a soloist, and was called "the greatest of woman violinists"

*Teresina Tua, Italian violinist,
pupil of Massart and winner of
the first prize at the Paris
Conservatory in 1880*

311

Camilla Urso, French violinist, pupil of Massart, a violinist of international stature before the turn of the century

by the American critic Huneker. Urso spent many years in the United States, and her successor Maud Powell memorialized her in 1918 by stating: "When I first began my career as a concert artist I did pioneer work for the cause of the American woman violinist, going on with the work begun by Mme. Camilla Urso. A strong prejudice then existed against women fiddlers, which even yet has not altogether been overcome."

There were other accomplished women violinists of the 19th century, but since this essay is by no means intended as an encyclopedia of names, they have been regretfully omitted.

We now come to players whose careers were substantially in the 20th century (though some were born in the latter part of the 19th century), and we can now rely upon firsthand testimony in evaluating their violinistic powers, as we have reached the age of phonograph recording.

Of the nearly 1,700 violinists listed who have made phonograph records, about 300 are women. Numerically, Suzanne Lautenbaucher (1932—) leads feminine recordings with 157. The large majority is confined to baroque and classical works for violin solo with chamber orchestra collaboration (though she has also recorded the Beethoven and Brahms concertos and the complete Bach solo sonatas). Marjorie Hayward (1885-1953) has 126, ranging from trivia to string quartets and major violin-piano sonatas. (She apparently was British.)

Erica Morini (1906—1995), with 108, is the nominal leader among major women players. Edith Lorand, a noted salon-type artist, has 89; Yvonne Curti, with 88, offers strictly trivia, limited to piano accompaniments. Ida Haendel, with 83, is second to Morini among the more internationally recognized players.

Maud Powell recorded the most of the great ladies of yesteryear with 71, and while her listings descend to such concoctions as Vieuxtemps's *Yankee Doodle* Variations, she was a top-ranking artist of her time, whose premature passing occurred only five years before electric recordings, so that the masterworks in her repertoire died with her. (Powell was discussed in the "American Violinists" chapter). Renée Chemet (1888 —?) has 64, nearly all vignettes with a few medium-grade works. Elsie Southgate (1889-1946) has 63 flufferies; Isolde Menges has 62; Mary Law (1890-1919) has 50; Rae Eleanor Ball, a polished vignette player of yore, has 48, including some Edison cylinders. Marie Hall has 31. Jelly d'Aranyi has 54, mostly small- and medium-grade pieces, plus duets with her sister, Adila Fachiri, and a few trios. She has no recording of Ravel's *Tzigane*, which was dedicated to her.

Among the top-notch moderns: Camilla Wicks has 28, Johanna Martzy, 25, Ginette Neveu, 19, Guila Bustabo, Eudice Shapiro, and Joan Field, 14. Such worthy players as Patricia Travers and Edith Peinemann have only three and two, respectively. Wanda Wilkomirska, Lola Bobescu, Michele Auclair, Claire Bernard, and Huguette Fernandez have sizeable rosters. Kyung-Wha Chung and Anne-Sophie Mutter are the leading contemporary female recording violinists at this writing; Midori, Kyoko Takezawa, Sarah Chang, Mayumi Fujikawa, and Masuko Ushioda are outstanding names among a growing list of Asian ladies who currently grace the listings.

Guila Bustabo was the first woman to have recorded the Paganini Concerto No. 1 (the one-movement Wilhelmj edition with the Sauret cadenza). I have heard an excellent, if small-scaled, live performance of the entire work with the Sauret cadenza by Teiko Maehashi. Others, too, now perform the opus, and one or two performances have been recorded by lesser-known women. Just recently I heard a live performance of the complete Paganini Concerto No. 1 (Sauret cadenza) that was stunning, both technically and stylistically by 17-year-old Leila Josefowicz. And Viktoria Mullova's Paganini Concerto No. 1 CD is superb.

The entire Bach solo sonatas have been record-

Teiko Maehashi, Japanese violinist whose small hands do not prevent her from performing the Paganini Concerto No. 1 (and Sauret cadenza) with virtuosity and dashing musicality

Marie Hall, prominent English violinist in the first quarter of the 20th century

ed by Martzy and Lautenbaucher. It is hoped some enterprising collector will present an LP by the American, Dora Valesca Becker, highly regarded in her time, who left 16 pieces made on Bettini cylinders.

Perhaps the earliest-born woman recording violinist was Maud Powell, who left a prolific number of discs which prove her to have been a player of much temperament, digital facility, and expressive power. She was undoubtedly the finest American violinist, male or female, before the ascendance of the (transplanted to America) modern-age Eastern European players and their American descendants.

Marie Hall (1884-1956, English) represents an anachronistic style in recordings of a facile (by turn-of-the-century standards) Paganini *Perpetual Motion*, some dry-toned vignettes, and an horrendous 1916 recording of the Elgar concerto (with the composer conducting) that can only serve to embarrass her memory. However, it may be that Hall, like Erica Morini in later years, was one of those players who, on the live concert platform, communicated a personal spark to audiences that was never quite captured in a recording.

Kathleen Parlow (1890-1963, Canadian) was the first of the Leopold Auer female pupils to attain fame. Her discs reflect a cool-ish temperament (reminiscent of Zimbalist), and like so many other players who

recorded in this era, are riddled with over-abundant slides in poor taste. Yet her general style begins to hearken to the modern era. Her trill is extraordinarily rapid. A small volume, *Kathleen Parlow, A Portrait*, written by her cousin and friend Maida Parlow French, cozily relates a skin-deep version of the violinist's personal and artistic life.

Isolde Menges (1893-1976, English) was considered by Auer to be one of his most gifted pupils, and was perhaps the first woman to record such masterworks as the Beethoven concerto, the *Kreutzer* Sonata, and Bach's *Chaconne*. She concertized in the United States and Europe but her home was in England. Menges founded a quartet in 1931 that bore her name, and

Kathleen Parlow in London, 1905, pupil of Auer

313

Steffi Geyer, Hungarian violinist, pupil of Hubay

became a professor at the Royal College of Music in London. The Menges recordings show her to have been a player with excellent instrumental equipment, a robust sound, buoyant style, and a sensitive ear for dynamic variance—a forward-looking 20th-century violinist.

Steffi Geyer (1895-1958, Hungarian), a Hubay disciple, was a child prodigy who never really achieved advanced artistic maturity. Her discs reveal a solid fundamental technique, an over-wide vibrato, and a moderate violinistic personality. Hubay's Concerto No. 4,

Renée Chemet, French violinist

Op. 101, is dedicated to Geyer, and she was a special favorite of Bartók in his early years as a composer.

Renée Chemet (French) was dubbed "the female Kreisler." Her vignette playing is highly poetic, though her tone is characterized by an over-rapid, tense vibrato which takes some getting used to. A Saint-Saëns

The sisters Adila Fachiri and Jelly d'Aranyi

Rondo Capriccioso disc and another of Wieniawski's *Polonaise Brilliante No. 2* (with major cuts) reveal digital dexterity, but many of her slides and position changes border on the ludicrous.

Jelly d'Aranyi (Hungarian, 1895-1966), a grandniece of Joachim, called a "picturesque personality" by Szigeti, lacks elegance and tonal lustre in her disc vignettes, but was an industrious, enterprising musician for whom Ravel wrote his *Tzigane*. Two sonatas by Bartók and Vaughan Williams's concerto are dedicated to her, and she was one of the first to re-introduce the Schumann concerto in a controversial episode (with Menuhin and Kulenkampff) in 1937. Her interesting life story is narrated in *The Sisters d'Aranyi* by Joseph McLeod.

Cecilia Hansen (1898 —?, Russian-Danish), a leading Auer pupil, won first prize at the Petrograd Conservatory in 1914. Statuesque, blonde, and attractive, she projected a stunning platform image. Avoiding most of the old-fashioned excesses of pre-20th century playing, her nine recordings reflect sturdy musical discipline and cleaner intonation, while emulating the broad sweep of the best Auer disciples. Vieuxtemps's

Leah Luboshutz, a pupil of Ysaÿe, was a violin faculty member at the Curtis Institute in Philadelphia.

Thelma Given, pupil of Auer

Rondino, the most demanding opus of her recordings, reveals admirable instrumental command and a solid, resonant tone; however, she omits the tricky, rapid scale passages in thirds about midway through the piece. Though her playing is scrupulously clean and stylistically alert, it is neither impassioned nor exciting. In contradistinction to the numerous male violinists who have married their women piano collaborators, Hansen married her pianist Boris Zakharoff.

By the late 1920s, her career had waned. Flesch stated: "She has a charming personality without being in any way outstanding as a fiddler," an evaluation which may be over-harsh, but would seem to be essentially accurate, since Hansen's career did not ultimately sustain or develop to the very top rank.

I have heard no recordings (if there are any) of the Australian-Irish violinist, Alma Moodie (1900-1942), who, according to Flesch: "must be regarded as the most outstanding female violinist of her time, a worthy successor to Norman-Neruda...between 1920 and 1930, she stimulated modern compositions for the violin in a similar way as Joachim, Sarasate, and Ysaÿe had done before her. Amongst other works, the violin concertos of Hans Pfitzner and Ernst Krenek, as well as many sonatas for violin alone, owe their existence to her art." Moodie gave the premiere performance of Stravinsky's *Pulcinella*

Suite for violin and piano in 1925, with the composer at the keyboard.

Other prominent women violinists born in this era were Leah Luboshutz (1886-1965), May Harrison (1891-1959), Adila Fachiri d'Aranyi (1886-1962), Irma Seydel (1896 —?), and Thelma Given (1898 —?).

ERICA MORINI

Among a myriad of brilliant women violinistic talents, the career of Erica Morini (Austrian) dominated the second quarter of the 20th century with but a few serious competitors. She was a pupil of Sevčík and Rosa Hochmann-Rosenfeld. In an era which stressed opulence of sound and modern sophistication of style quite foreign to her somewhat antiquated training and musical ethos, Morini achieved success by virtue of her polished, well-balanced interpretations, profound musical sincerity, and scintillating instrumental virtuosity. Her violinistic personality was decidedly individual and, surprisingly, in no way reflected the influence of any of her top-flight male colleagues. Morini's repertoire was neither overly large nor adventurous by modern standards, but her instrumental mastery of the essential classical and romantic (to Tchaikovsky and Glazunov) masterworks was sovereign. Other women, some with richer intensity of sound and more sheer imaginative flair, have rocketed to prominence and then vanished from the scene (or settled for less because of complications in their personal lives). But Morini "put it all together" where a host of others failed, and eminently deserved her hegemony as the uncrowned "Queen of the Violin," in that now burgeoning niche in our world reserved for women violin virtuosos.

I first heard Morini in live performance in 1936, in a recital that included the Brahms Sonata No. 2, the Glazunov concerto, several of her perennial favorites, such as Mozart's Minuet (from Divertimento No. 17), Wieniawski's *Capriccio-Valse*, and the Waltz from

Erna Rubinstein, Hungarian violinist, pupil of Hubay

Erica Morini succeeded in sustaining a long, successful concert career and preserving her individual identity as an artist.

Sarasate's *Faust Fantasy* (each featuring her crisp, sparkling staccato) plus Paganini's *Moses Fantasy*, which concluded the program.

One immediately received the impression that here was a woman who seemed content to play like a woman (in the most exalted sense of the term), unlike so many others, who subordinated their femininity, hectically striving to play like a man. Her playing was ever secure technically; her intonation, pristine, and her articulation, precise. It exuded an aura of chasteness, and the cool timbre of her silken tone with its modest vibrato, hearkened back to an earlier era. Her interpretations generally possessed a certain reserve of character, and were literal and conscientious, shunning any vestige of juvenile effusiveness or egoism. Yet Morini could also play with propulsion and bravura brilliance when demanded by the music, but always in her own preferred context—never in a violinistically competitive sense. Perhaps it was her willingness, yes, insistence

upon being herself, that was responsible for much of her warm reception from the public.

Morini was the first woman to record a sizeable list of the great concertos: Beethoven, Brahms, Tchaikovsky, Mendelssohn, Bruch, Glazunov, Mozart, Bach, and Wieniawski, along with major baroque, classical and romantic sonatas, and numerous short pieces. True, it would be difficult to conceive Morini in such lush expansive canvases as the concertos of Elgar, Walton, Bartók, or even Sibelius. Unfortunately, though her recordings certainly represent a facsimile of her playing, somehow they do not project the communica-

Ruth Posselt Burgin, American violinist of distinction, wife of the late violinist Richard Burgen

316

tion of Morini in live concert.

Other prominent and exceptionally gifted women violinists of Morini's general age group were Erna Rubinstein (about 1906-), Ruth Posselt (1914-), Frances Berkova (1898-1982), Sada Suchari (1908-), Ibolyka Zilzer, Kayla Mitzel, Sylvia Lent, Edith Lorand, and the USSR's Galina Barinova (1910-). Mention must be made of Giaconda de Vito (1907-), whose recorded interpretation of the Brahms concerto is both sensitive and poetic, and her technique, exceedingly clean-cut. De Vito's playing in this recording is comparatively small-scaled; her vibrato, rather slow and, like Morini, her style was not influenced by the lustrous Russian School of playing that had risen to dominance during her formative years.

Ginette Neveu was a supreme colorist of the violin who died tragically in a plane crash at age 30.

GINETTE NEVEU

Since the advent of Morini, one of the most spectacular woman violinistic talents to emerge was Ginette Neveu (1919-1949, French), whose career was tragically cut short at the age of 30, along with that of her pianist-collaborator brother Jean, in a plane crash. At only 15 years of age, Neveu took first prize in the Wieniawski competition in 1935. (David Oistrakh, age 27, was second). In listening to the all-too-few recordings left by Neveu, the enormity of her gifts registers so vividly, it is obvious that she deserves to be ranked among the uppermost violinists, male or female.

A Flesch pupil, Neveu had scarcely attained full artistic maturity at the time of her demise. She was a supreme colorist, as opposed to a host of outstanding violinists who may possess beauty of sound, but whose tonal projection and vibrato are essentially one-dimensional. Neveu was a painter of exquisite musical soundscapes. Each note was accorded individual consideration and respect--an integral part of the whole. Her interpretations are alive with myriad nuances and a variety of dynamics. Though her stylistic ethos was ineffably French and she was immensely effective in music of Gallic idiom, her art transcended nationalistic boundaries. Intellectual discipline is ever present, but never fettered by cerebral academicism.

On the technical level Neveu's equipment was easily capable of handling any challenge presented by the masterworks, though her facility was not of the overtly bravura heroic genre. One could point out that her tempo in the third movement of the Sibelius concerto is excessively slow, and even the first movement, to a certain extent, lacks virtuosic propulsion. However, her sound and phrasing in lyric passages are of compelling beauty.

Neveu's Brahms concerto succeeds in projecting both tension and intensity of sound without yielding to hysteria. The outer movements make no concessions in tempos and are marked by exceptional drive and audacity. Some of the slides are a bit dated; there are, unaccountably, several badly rushed bars a few lines before the end of the Adagio, and a recurrent tendency to rip off the second half of the bow in slashing passages. But in all, it is a strongly individual and absorbing interpretation, unmistakably French in character, palpably romantic, yet thoughtful and subtle in phrasing.

Her Debussy sonata, in impeccable consort with Jean, is an adventure in luminescent, poetic music-making, and demonstrates her surpassing ability to diversify her vibrato, thus producing a kaleidoscopic range of tonal shadings. The Neveu intonation was pellucid and her passagework scintillating, as exceptionally manifested in Suk's Four Pieces, Op. 17, with its glittering *Burleska*. Her recording of Chausson's *Poème* displays an intense spiritual force, and Ravel's *Tzigane*, though gloriously impassioned and opulent in sound, is elegantly French in style as intended by the composer, rather than a riotous Gypsy carousal. All of Neveu's sterling qualities were manifested in her performance of the

317

Beethoven concerto in a nationwide broadcast from Boston, which immediately established her in the United States as an artist of international stature.

Some time after the plane catastrophe, her mother, Mme. Neveu, wrote a sad, rather pitiful little book about her departed children; a volume more oriented to poignance than comprehensive, perceptive biography. Meanwhile, the small heritage of Neveu discs continues to illuminate the artistry of an extraordinary violinist.

IDA HAENDEL

Ida Haendel (1928- , Polish), like Neveu, a Flesch pupil, is also a top-flight soloist who has recorded a long list of the major concertos including those of Beethoven, Brahms, Tchaikovsky, Mendelssohn, Bruch, Sibelius, Glazunov, Lalo, Wieniawski No. 2, Walton, and Britten. Her shorter recordings run the gamut from Kreisler bonbons to such virtuosic works as Sarasate's *Carmen Fantasy* and *Zigeunerweisen*, Paganini's *Caprice* No. 24 (Auer) and *Moses Fantasy*, Bazzini's *Ronde des lutins*, two Wieniawski *Polonaises* and Ravel's *Tzigane*, among numerous other pieces of every type—a major violinist in a major repertoire.

Haendel's instrumental equipment is comprehensive and capable of meeting all of her interpretive requirements.Her tone is warm and robust, though not quite opulent, and is fortified by a well-controlled vibrato. One can occasionally note the Heifetz influence in her expressive slides. On the interpretive level,

Haendel's performance is cogent, cohesive, and polished. Even in her moments of comparative abandon, a sense of discipline prevails. At her best she can afford pleasure to, or even delight, the critical listener.

Handel has written a book, *Woman with Violin*, an intimate (up to a point) account of her life dating from her childhood in Poland. Along with a wealth of personal anecdotes and details, the autobiography, though somewhat self-serving, contains much of interest as a testament dealing with many of the special problems and vicissitudes confronting a woman of uncommon talents, who seeks fame and fortune in the stratosphere of the international concert world. (The book has her birth date as 1928; Grove's Dictionary lists it as 1924).

GUILA BUSTABO

Guila Bustabo (1919- , American), a pupil of Persinger, Enesco, and Hubay, has had an unusual and checkered career. Following her initial successes in the United States, she elected to perform in countries of the European Axis periphery during World War II, though she did return to perform in the United States in the late 1950s.

In certain respects Bustabo was an amazing tal-

Ida Haendel, Polish-born violinist, a polished artist of international stature who, like Morini, has enjoyed a lengthy career.

Guila Bustabo, American-born violinist, pupil of Persinger, Enesco and Hubay

Frances Berkova, American violinist, pupil of Auer, Flesch, and Sevčík, retired early in her career as a soloist.

Saundra Berkova-Maazel, daughter of Frances Berkova, first cousin of conductor Lorin Maazel, also retired early in her career as a soloist.

ent. (A compendium of her earlier recordings, *The Bustabo Legacy*, was issued in a limited edition by her uncritical admirer, Thomas Clear, an amateur record collector.) These discs, transferred to LPs from 78s, vividly recall her New York Philharmonic radio broadcast of the Dvořák concerto in the late 1930s, which I heard. Made during her early 20s, this set contains the Paganini No. 1 Concerto (single movement Wilhelmj edition with the Sauret cadenza), Sibelius and Bruch concertos, and includes short pieces by Sarasate, Kreisler, Nováček, Suk, and Paganini's Caprice No. 5.) In the realm of sheer technical facility, Bustabo, in her youth, equalled that of any woman I have ever heard. The Caprice No. 5 (played in spiccato) is a digital phenomenon, performed with kamikaze audacity, at a speed rivaling such finger-and-bow gymnasts as Ricci, Rabin, Perlman, or Renardy. And her Sauret cadenza of the Paganini (slightly abbreviated) is nearly as spectacular, as are Sarasate's *Zapateado* and *Habanera*.

Bustabo's temperament was impetuosity personified, lending her performance an immediate impact of excitement. But this temperament often bordered on the hysterical, a quality mirrored in her over-tense and over-rapid vibrato, imparting an aura of juvenility to her playing. Her tone was impassioned

but brittle. Nevertheless, many of the lyric passages, particularly in her concerto recordings (made with the Berlin State Orchestra under Zaun, and the Concertgebouw under Mengelberg), though over-emoted, reveal a positive penchant for expressiveness. One is quickly sated with her excesses, yet greatly impressed by her raw, unpolished (if flawed) talent.

It is interesting to compare these performances with those of two concerto recordings made in Bustabo's later years: one, a cliche-ridden concoction by her friend and mentor Wolf-Ferrari; the other, a rambling narrative by Otmar Nussio (written in 1959), both recorded in Europe. Most of her technical equipment is still intact; the hysteria has relaxed into normal expressivity, and her vibrato is no longer excessive; but oddly, the essence of the playing, despite its instrumental brilliance, is often comparatively noncommittal. The old aggressive, if superficial, spontaneity has been replaced by a respectability that offers considerable meritorious playing, but fails to attain any notable stature.

Among the women violinists born between 1915 and 1935 who have achieved prominence as soloists or chamber music players are: Eudice Shapiro (1915-), Lola Bobescu (1920-), Fredell Lack (1922-), the late

319

Fredell Lack, American violinist, combined the roles of soloist, teacher and parent with admirable success.

Carroll Glenn (1922-1983), Frances Magnes (1922-), the late Johanna Martzy (1924-1979), Anahid Ajemian (1926-), Patricia Travers (1927-), Joyce Flissler (1929-), Nora Grumlikova (1930-), and Saundra Berkova Maazel (1933-1978), a bonafide child prodigy with an enormous talent and potential that, sadly, was unfulfilled in maturity for personal rather than musical reasons.

WANDA WILKOMIRSKA

Wanda Wilkomirska (1920-1992, Polish), a striking musical and platform personality, was an interpreter

Wanda Wilkomirska, Polish violinist, an artist of unusual individuality and spiritual force

of unusual spiritual force. She was most impressive in music of such composers as Szymanowski, Shostakovich, and Prokofiev, in which her endemic leanness of sound does not seriously detract from the performance. However, Wilkomirska was much less convincing in music demanding sheer beauty and richness of tone as a vital element. An interesting if paradoxical artist.

CAMILLA WICKS

The career of Camilla Wicks (1929- , American), a pupil of Louis Persinger and Henri Temianka, has been victimized by interruptions. In her youth, blessed with an exceptionally engaging appearance, notable instrumental mastery, and an aggressive temperament that was ideally suited to big-scaled romantic works, her future seemed unlimited. The early Wicks recording of the Sibelius concerto, characterized by extraordinary drive, intensity of sound, clarity of line, and bravura virtuosity, served to thrust her into the limelight. Apparently marriage and family superseded her career for some years. Later, in the mid-'60s, an impressive disc of a difficult concerto by Klaus Egge, a Norwegian composer, served to re-establish her international reputation, after which little more was heard from Wicks.

Camilla Wicks, American violinist, whose career has suffered interruptions; however, she continues to play with splendid virtuosity.

*The late Carroll Glenn,
American violinist, who enjoyed
a salutary career both as a soloist
and in concert with her pianist-
husband Eugene List*

*Nina Bodnar, American
violinist, 1981 winner of the
Thibaud Competition in France*

In more recent appearances the violinist has displayed most of the technical skill and drive of her younger years in commendable performances of the Brahms and Glazunov concertos, and other works. The Wicks muse may not particularly stress introspection, but hers is robust playing of glittering, vibrant extroversion.

Suzanne Lautenbacher (1932- , German) has a discography prodigious in size, featuring playing that is dry in sound, academic in style, and beset by a woefully slow vibrato.

Among the leading Soviet women players of this era are: Marina Kozolupova (1918-), Elizabeth Gilels (1919-), wife of the late Leonid Kogan, medalists in the 1937 Ysaÿe Competition in Brussels, and Rosa

Fain (1929-), winner of the 1949 Wieniawski Competition in Poznan.

Women violinists born after 1935 who have, or are in the process of achieving substantial careers, include: Edith Peinemann (1937-), Nell Gotkovsky (1939-), Iona Brown, a brilliant chamber orchestra concertmistress and soloist, Pina Carmirelli, Stoika Milanova (1946-), Tatiana Grindenko (1946-), Claire Bernard (1947-), Cornelia Vasile (1949-), Kaja Danczowska (1949-), Edith Volckaert (1949-), Christine Edinger, Ani and Ida Kavafian, Miriam Fried, Mihaela Martin, Dylana Jenson, Anne-Sophie Mutter, Nadja Salerno-Sonnenberg, Ida Levin, Nina Bodnar, Sylvia Rosenberg, Stephanie Chase, Maria Bachmann, Ana Chumachenko and Jane Peters. Some of them have won or received high honors in international competitions.

KYUNG-WHA CHUNG

At this writing, one of the most active concert and recording woman violinists is Kyung-Wha Chung (1948- , Korean), who numbers among her teachers Galamian, Szigeti, and Szymon Goldberg. Chung is a consummate virtuoso with a fiery, almost ferocious temperament, though her slender tone, intensely vibrant, mirrors her slight physique and, at times, her tigerish tension produces tautness of sound. Chung's romanti-

*Iona Brown, British violinist—
a chamber orchestra conductor
and soloist*

*Kyung-Wha Chung, Korean
violinist of international rank*

*Mayumi Fujikawa, Japanese
violinist, an outstanding
representative among the
proliferating number of
Asian artists*

cism is often forced rather than natural which accounts for her comparatively unmoving performances of concertos by Bruch, Tchaikovsky, and Dvořák. Nor does she possess the breadth, subtlety, and variance of tonal color necessary for elite interpretations of such grandiose canvases as the concertos of Elgar, Walton, Bartók, or Sibelius. Yet Chung's accomplishments deserve recognition and much respect for the sheer range of her repertorial mastery. The Chung instrumental command and self-discipline, plus her boundless energy, are amazing, and suggest an iron-willed character. And one must single out her disc of Vieuxtemps's Concerto No. 5 for its superb articulation and heroic bravura style.

In the rapidly mushrooming list of outstanding contemporary Asian women violinists, including major international award recipients, are: Masuko Ushioda (1942-), Takako Nishizaki, Mayumi Fujikawa (1946-), Teiko Maehashi, Yoko Sato, Shizuka Ishikawa, Yuuko Shakawa, and Sung Ju Lee, among others.

MIRIAM FRIED

Miriam Fried (1946-), born in Rumania, emigrated to Israel where she began study of the violin, and ultimately won first prize in Israel's Tenth Anniversary Violin Competition in 1958. Later she studied with Josef Gingold and Ivan Galamian in the United States.

In 1971 she was the first woman ever to win the coveted Queen Elisabeth of Belgium International Competition; she also won first prize at the Paganini International Competition in Genoa in 1968. Fried is a big-scaled virtuoso with highly-charged romantic inclinations. Her tone can project the utmost vibrant intensity, yet she is capable of admirable self-discipline and intellectual perception. An unedited recording made live at the Queen Elisabeth Competition, while not antiseptically perfect, contains a stirringly impassioned version of the Sibelius concerto, and an interpretation of

*Nadja Salerno-Sonnenberg, 1981
winner of the Naumburg Violin
Competition—a gifted but
eccentric artist*

322

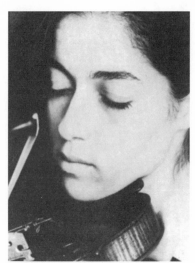

Miriam Fried, Israeli-American violinist, first woman to win first prize in the prestigious Queen Elisabeth of Belgium Competition

Chausson's *Poème* that reflects a spirit of spontaneity and personalized musicality.

NINA BEILINA

Nina Beilina (1937-), a Russian Jewish émigré of formidable violinistic stature, evinces exceptional power, drive, propulsion, and instrumental command,

Nina Beilina, Soviet emigré violinist, a well-rounded artist of ultra-serious purpose

and an unusually sturdy bow arm, but her emotional projection tends to be stern and unaffectionate. She seems dedicated to the credo that even the slightest ves-

tige of overt sentiment in performance constitutes a misdemeanor.

TATIANA GRINDENKO

Tatiana Grindenko (1946- , Russian), winner of the 1972 Wieniawski Competition at Poznan, a pupil of Yuri Yankelevich, is one of the most provocative and independent musical personalities of Soviet-trained violinists. A live recording of the Brahms concerto made during the Poznan contest reveals her to be a big-scaled virtuoso with tremendous instrumental resources and as explosive a sound and attack as one is likely to encounter. Her Kreisler cadenza is a triumph of virtuosity. At times her naturally fast vibrato becomes over-rapid and stiff, but the innate drive of her playing, occasionally tempered by glints of comparative relaxation, is calculated to engage the constant attention of the listener. And one might add that the vibrance, solidity, and voluminousness of her tone are far superior to those of her ex-husband Gidon Kremer. Grindenko is also a

Tatiana Grindenko, winner of the 1972 Wieniawski Competition in Poznan

devotée and performer of experimental and avant-garde music. In general, her highly emotive playing projects more of an individual note than many of her Russian colleagues.

SYLVIA MARCOVICI

Sylvia Marcovici (1952-), a Rumanian Jewish émigré with solid instrumental resources, a superior instinct for romantic musical expressiveness (and an unnaturally high bow arm), seems to be an unfor-

Photo David Weiss

Sylvia Marcovici, Rumanian-born violinist, who possesses a glowing tone and extraordinary lyric expressiveness

tunate example of arrested artistic development. The exceptionally gifted Rumanian-trained Marcovici, impressive in her early appearances, needed a few years of top-level Western training to help fulfill her high potential. Apparently she has neither sought nor obtained this, since her recent concerts have reflected no perceptible degree of musical maturation. One can only hope her artistic momentum alters radically before her career is irrevocably downgraded.

DYLANA JENSON

Dylana Jenson (1961- , American), whose teachers have included Manuel Compinsky, Josef Gingold, and Nathan Milstein, tied for second place in the 1978 Tchaikovsky Competition at only 17. Jenson, a strapping young woman, enjoys a distinct physical advantage over many of her colleagues; her technical facility, power, temperamental flair, and poise marked her as a singularly big-scaled talent even before her teen years. Whether she possesses such qualities as poetic insight, imagination, and subtlety on the highest level, remains

Dylana Jenson, American violinist, second-place winner at the 1978 Moscow Competition

to be determined. Due to a lack of patience in career development and improper guidance, the early part of her career has been attended by a certain amount of controversy and adverse publicity. Her recordings of the Sibelius concerto and Saint-Saëns' *Introduction and Rondo Capriccioso*, while still retaining vestiges of immaturity in matters of pacing and interpretive detail, are vital, expansive, and stylistically alert.

ANNE-SOPHIE MUTTER

Anne-Sophie Mutter (1963- , German), a protégé of Herbert von Karajan and a pupil of Aida Stucki, made her international recording debut at age 15 with the Mozart No. 3 and No. 5 Concertos, displaying an extremely pellucid sound, a chaste, literal style, exceptional left hand finger dexterity, and a marvelous trill. Two years later, in a recording of the Beethoven concerto, her vibrato had solidified and become more intense in a meticulously clean but rather stodgy, unimaginative, overlong 48-minute interpretation. Yet her Kreisler cadenzas contain flashes of unusual bravura brilliance. All of the above, along with a top-level performance of the Brahms concerto, were recorded with von Karajan.

In her post-Karajan performances, Mutter's interpretations seem to be much freer and more personalized. In a live concert about a decade after her original Beethoven recording, this was substantiated by her performance of the first two movements of the concerto which were admirably paced, tonally compelling, impeccably clean, and intelligently phrased. However, the Rondo finale was performed as if Mutter had never heard of that joyous dance form as she raced unconscionably in what was practically a Presto, and dashing so breathlessly through the Kreisler cadenza that it was almost beyond recognition.

Essentially her playing is powerfully etched and large-scaled, and her tone, propelled by a fast vibrato (that occasionally is vitiated by tremulousness), is generally pleasing to the ear.

Her recording of Lalo's *Symphonie Espagnole* (with

Anne-Sophie Mutter, German violinist of international stature

Ozawa) communicates considerable Iberian flavor and contains more subtleties of phrasing in this work than most of the current players. In her recording of the Mendelssohn concerto with von Karajan, the final movement is a bit too slow and measured to capture the maximal elfin spirit. A recent live performance confirmed this shortcoming. Mutter's three Brahms sonatas and the Franck sonata (with pianist Alexis Weissenberg) are impressive instrumentally, but not fully personalized. Like so many of her generation, she is quite sparing in the use of expressive slides and position changes, and while she is alert to the necessity for variance of tonal color, it is to be hoped that she will continue to expand her range in this area.

Nevertheless, Mutter has deservedly advanced to the top echelon of the under-35 generation at this writing.

IDA KAVAFIAN

Ida Kavafian was born around 1953 in Istanbul of Armenian parents, and came to America as a child. She studied with Mischakoff for three years, Galamian for two, and Shumsky for four. In 1974 she won the Loeb Prize at Juilliard, and then was active as the violinist in the noted Tashi chamber group initiated by pianist Peter Serkin, which concertized widely and boasts numerous recordings. Concurrently she has been striving to establish a career as a soloist.

At 29, in the interest of furthering her solo status, she entered the 1982 International Violin Competition of Indianapolis, and was awarded second prize. As a juror I could see immediately that she was among the most polished and experienced players of the 44 participants. She had made noticeable progress from the time I heard her in recital about a year prior to the competition.

Like so many younger-generation players, she excelled in 20th-century music; her brilliant performances of the Bartók solo sonata, Ravel's sonata, and Prokofiev's Concerto No. 1 stamped her as a virtuoso of uncommon accomplishment. Yet her solo Bach was overly stoic, her Mozart *Andante* from Concerto No. 4 wanting in subtlety, and her Saint-Saëns *Introduction and Rondo Capriccioso* somehow lacking in sentiment and affection. A year later, in another recital, my opinion of her Bach and Mozart was reaffirmed but she had obviously made further strides. A performance of Ysaÿe's Solo Sonata No. 6 was dazzling, and her fingered octave passages were delivered with a dash and surety equal to any I have heard. Superb by any standards, her Ravel sonata and *Tzigane* were intense in G string sound, stun-

Ida Kavafian, American violinist, a leading representative of the contemporary generation

Ani Kavafian and her sister Ida, both admirable performers, continue the violinist-sister tradition of the Milanollos, the d'Aranyis and others.

ning in facility, and alert to the dictates of style. Her post-18th-century music-making had gained in emotional projection though she still cannot be characterized as a movingly romantic player. But even if Kavafian does not win your heart, she can be an exciting violinist and one to admire. No doubt if she were a foreign defector her opportunities for a solo career would have been greatly enhanced. Ida Kavafian is now the violinist of the celebrated Beaux Arts Trio.

ANI KAVAFIAN

I have heard her sister Ani Kavafian, born around 1948, only on a disc of Kreisler favorites. They are played with clean agility, graceful phrasing, cool sound, and limited sensuality. One cannot presume to make a serious evaluation of her artistry on such meager evidence. She enjoys a fine reputation as a chamber music performer and all-round musician.

STEPHANIE CHASE

I heard Stephanie Chase, a Sally Thomas pupil (also a 1982 Tchaikovsky Competition third prize lau-

reate), in a sensitive performance of Mozart's Concerto No. 5 and a recital which included a workaday Beethoven Sonata in C-minor and a scintillating Prokofiev No. 2. At her best, Chase is a violinist of considerable communicative talents.

The post-1935 era could possibly include Carmenzita Lozada (Filipino) and Huguette Fernandez, a prolific chamber orchestra recording artist. But let the reader be reminded that in general, it is often difficult to obtain the birth date of contemporary women performers. It must be stressed that throughout the world there are many more estimable women violinists whose names have not been cited in this essay.

Through modern-age recordings, we are able to hear more women players in a wider diversity of musical vehicles than ever before. It behooves men to take cognizance of the fact that in direct competition in the international contest syndrome which now dominates instrumental concert life and survival, women are playing a far greater role than ever before in violinistic history. While no accurate statistics are available, the number of women engaged in serious violin study is mushrooming as compared to men. A few seasons back it was indicative that the touring Suzuki group of youngsters from Japan had eight girls and only two boys.

Women have become internationally prominent in the field of violin pedagogy, and grace the faculties of conservatories and universities in most countries.

Photo Christian Steiner

Dorothy DeLay, Juilliard Institute pedagogue, teacher of numerous luminaries

Linda Cerone, pedagogue at The Cleveland Institute of Music; also prominent as a soloist and chamber music artist

Among them are: Dorothy DeLay, Margaret Pardee, Sally Thomas, Linda Cerone, Almita Vamos, and Ariana Bronne in the United States; Kato Havas and Eta Smith in England; Aida Stucki in Switzerland; Elizabeth and Zinaida Gilels, Olga Parkhomenko, and Aneta Zvaigzne in Russia; and Lyndall Hendrickson in South Australia. Any really comprehensive survey of worthy women pedagogues and teachers, institutional and private, would fill several pages.

Almita Vamos, violin professor at Oberlin Conservatory. Many of her pupils have been laureates in international competition

Such anachronisms as "Women's Symphony Orchestras" are few, as the ability of women continues to become more respected and recognized by their male colleagues. Several of the major string quartets include one or more women (or all). In the USA, women concertmasters of major orchestras have been proliferating. Chamber orchestras and other chamber ensembles boast of an increasing number of women, even in

Sally Thomas, pedagogue at Juilliard School and Mannes College of Music; long-time assistant to the legendary Ivan Galamian, and teacher of many internationally-known violinists

Lyndall Hendrickson, Australian pedagogue, who has established her own violinistic dynasty in Adelaide

Margaret Pardee, professor at the Juilliard Institute in New York

Ariana Bronne, eminent New York violin pedagogue and performer

Germany (though at this writing, the Berlin Philharmonic, the Vienna Philharmonic, and the Vienna Symphony include no women at all).

The last bastion of male hegemony in symphony orchestras is middle Europe. During a trip to Prague when Czechoslovakia was still known as a communist country, I noted that the Czech National Philharmonic included no women. Upon inquiry, a spokeswoman of the organization told me rather shamefacedly that the orchestra did have a woman harpist who was accepted by the male contingent, but only because she was married to one of the men in the orchestra. I asked how such a situation could exist in a nominally communist state (Russian and Polish orchestras have many women). She said it was tradition, and an extremely difficult problem to solve. I then inquired whether a woman could

Eta Smith, prominent teacher in Leeds, England, mother of violinist Maureen Smith

not win a position in a fair audition. She hastened to inform me that auditions were open to all, and that the contestants played behind a curtain. Then she told me with pride of a young woman violinist who easily bested her male rivals in the audition, and bid fair to break the male monopoly. "But," she added ruefully, "the young woman decided not to take the post because she did not want to be placed in the awkward position of being the only woman among the rank-and-file sections, and felt she had made her point by having won in the auditions."

Women have been entering the fiercely competitive world of professional violinists in unprecedented numbers. Outside of middle Europe, there are few opera, ballet, or symphony orchestras that do not employ women violinists, as for example: the Philadelphia Orchestra with four, and the Los Angeles Philharmonic and Orchestre National de France, each with at least one-third of the total. And many excellent women violinists have entered the lists (i.e., jungle) of the various commercial recording fields. Thus, historically women violinists have been winning the right not only to become artists, but just as important—if not more so—they can now hope for economic independence as the result of their blood, sweat, and tears sacrifice for the violin.

There is every reason for these trends to continue and proliferate. Women violinists, after three centuries of evolutionary struggle, are finally coming into their own.

Historic Carnegie Hall in New York as it appeared in 1907—to perform here is the goal of every aspiring musician

Whither Violin Art?

The essence of life is struggle--the new struggles against the old, the old against the new, and the inevitable result of struggle is change. This applies to the development of violin art as it does to any other element of social or cultural endeavor. As we go forward into the 21st century we can look back upon an era of striking changes, undoubtedly some for the better, at least in the collective sense, and some which are less enviable. For example, in the latter category, it is often pointed out that the most illustrious artists of yesteryear were unique "Personalities of the Violin"—that the individual character of their sounds and styles and expressive inclinations was distinctive and readily recognizable. Conversely, it is averred that current stars, though they may be remarkable instrumentalists and well-disciplined musicians, are scarcely identifiable, individually, and lack the extreme personalization and interest of past luminaries. I agree with this evaluation.

There are a variety of reasons for this. A glimpse into the past reminds us that such artists as Kreisler, Huberman, Elman, Szigeti, Thibaud, Wieniawski, and Paganini (among many others) had no formal violin training after the age of 12 or 13. Thus, each developed his own style, preferred repertoire, and musical philosophy, each was singularly different from the others, each formulated his own idiosyncrasies. Then, too, there were various national schools of violin playing and training, each with powerful historic roots, each in competition with the others, each claiming fanatical adherents. Today violin art has become almost fully internationalized. There still may be an afterglow of certain national traits, but these are far less extreme than in the past. The proliferation and availability of recordings, particularly in the re-creation of masterworks, has also played a major role in influencing current interpretations and,

ultimately, neutralizing the element of individuality. And our world is far more impersonal and less appreciative of overt sentiment as a vital factor in musical communication. When was the last time a violinist's performance actually touched your heart?

Many current violinists are aware of the importance of personalization in carving out an individual niche for themselves in winning the affections of the concertgoing public. But all too often they attempt to achieve musical 'personalization' by indulging in juvenile deep knee bends, torso-twistings, and unsightly facial grimaces, as well as questionable musical practices such as grossly distorting rhythms, pandering to audiences who are not old enough to have known the unforgettable platform charisma and 'class' of such giants as Kreisler, Francescatti, Heifetz, Oistrakh, Szigeti, Enesco, Grumiaux, Szeryng, and, yes, the young Menuhin. These artists (and many another) did not stoop to, or feel that it was necessary to resort to 'punk' haircuts, public vulgarity, or tasteless eccentricity to gain international notoriety.

However let us not put all the blame on the aberrants among contemporary violinists. As in any previous era, they inevitably must be affected to a greater or lesser degree by the values, mores, and atmosphere in which they live. We can scarcely expect them to be impervious to the onslaught of a culture fueled by media-driven sexual exploitation and the idolatry of mediocrity and mindlessness. Admittedly, it takes a strong-minded, dedicated youngster to resist this sea of negativity. Fortunately we have a fair number of these admirably accomplished players among our developing talents. Despite desperate competition among them for professional concert appearances, or positions that approximate a reasonably secure livelihood (a few years back some 325 violinists applied for two openings in the San Francisco Symphony, many of them competition laureates and/or established professionals), they continue to toil incessantly for careers that are, at best, highly uncertain.

The "Competition Syndrome" has snowballed to a degree unprecedented in the history of violin art, offering hope to large numbers of players who do not have private 'clout' to abet their careers. Many flit from competition to competition in the quest for glory, concert engagements, and monetary rewards—often to their artistic detriment. It is generally accepted that such competitions are 'a necessary evil.' Some of these competitions deserve praise for the integrity of their operation; nevertheless, it is no secret that others are riddled with inequities, and even obvious injustices. The latter sometimes award gold medals to players who are essentially mediocre and do not merit a career of importance. Even the most honorably-run competitions only rarely produce a violinist of stature, one who will assuredly and deservedly achieve a permanent career on the topmost international level. Basically the major competitions pander to 'decathlon' violinists who may be very sturdy performers in many genres of music, but who are not necessarily outstanding in any of them. They become so totally involved in mastering and maintaining the difficult competition repertoire (which varies but little in the major contests) that they do not permit themselves the time for the aesthetic growth and maturation necessary to develop into full-fledged artists. And today there are so many competitions, that in spite of the wide presence of admirably accomplished young violinists, there are simply not enough of them with truly singular gifts to 'populate' all these events. At best, a young violinist should view entry in a major competition as tantamount to buying a ticket for the state lottery, and not take a loss (or even victory) too seriously. Those who are overly sensitive to losing in several successive contests may become psychologically crippled, and their talent subsequently mutilated. Yet, were competitions to be abolished, many fine young players would have no way to sustain hope for establishing a career, or have access to a major showcase in which to display their talents. And, of course, it is true that competitions can considerably 'toughen' a candidate for the rigors involved in struggling to obtain a career. Happily, there are still a comparative handful of gifted young artists who enjoy private support that enables them to forge a career without the need to resort to the 'competition syndrome.'

For the overwhelming majority who never became laureates (and, in many cases for most laureates, too), the best guarantee for economic survival as a life-long professional is to become a fine all-round violinist and musician—highly proficient as a soloist and chamber ensemble player, a strong orchestral violinist both in the symphonic and chamber orchestra repertoire, and a teacher capable of handling students possessing a diversity of temperaments and talents, along with acquiring the instrumental flexibility and instantaneous response required for commercial work. This is, needless to say, a tall order requiring many years of dedicated work, but those who demand this degree of expertise from themselves will have by far the best chance of finding a professional niche somewhere in the broad perspective of violin art. Of course, to be realistic, let us not forget the element of *LUCK!* At this writing the financial support for music and musicians from government and private sources is declining, potentially limiting professional opportunities for all musicians.

Publicity provides much of the lifeblood of a career, in certain cases more than does the performer's artistic stature. Paganini understood this, and even though he possessed genius, he craftily utilized every possible means to publicize himself. In our time, Stern, Menuhin, and Perlman have been masters at garnering publicity to sustain their careers. But publicity can often be employed to lionize players who do not merit all of the claims made on their behalf. A recent case in point was the allegation by a world-renowned conductor that one of our younger generation violinists is going to set new standards for violin playing in the 21st century, and a world-renowned violinist-violist proclaimed this person to be the greatest violin talent in 50 to 75 years!

While this violinist possesses phenomenal technical co-ordination, energy and agility, it would not be difficult to disprove the remarks of the two prominent musicians on the artistic level. What could have impelled these gentlemen to utter such hyperbole? Should not leading musicians bear some responsibility to art when making remarks that are calculated to influence concert-going public? Why should any young artist be victimized by publicity gone amok?

We are currently witnessing two phenomena--the rise of women as direct competitors and equals of men in all facets of violin art, and the emergence of Japanese, Korean, and Chinese violinists proliferating in large numbers on the international violin scene. The profusion of outstanding young Asian artists is legion; scarcely any competition, major or minor, does not have as many as half, or even more, entrants of Asian descent, whether born in Asian countries or in the West. Once it had been introduced in Japan, Korea, China, and Taiwan, the violin rapidly became popular. A sprinkling of Western teachers went to reside there. (One of my own mentors, Professor Robert Pollak of Vienna, played, taught, and recorded in Japan for several years in the early 1930s.) Many of the teachers in mainland China were taught in countries of the Soviet bloc until the Russo-Chinese political split in 1960. As the number of serious Asian violinists grew, they migrated to Europe and America in abundance for further training and inculcation of Western violin art. Yoshio Unno, one of Japan's most prominent violinists, has said, "Despite my Japanese roots, I feel that violinists born, bred, and trained in the Orient have special problems in becoming attuned to the subtle, intimate nuances of the Western musical aesthetic." This is quite obvious in the case of indigenous Asian violinists who have had little or no exposure to training, living, and being in head-to-head competition with their contemporaries in the West. However, the most talented among those who have enjoyed this opportunity rank high on the international level, and have won many of the major international competitions. Japan has also contributed importantly with the Suzuki method which, irrespective of the pros and cons of Professor Suzuki's system, has stimulated wide public interest in the violin and inspired further training of those youngsters who possess genuine talent.

In recent years, since the demise of the destructive "Cultural Revolution," Western teachers have flocked to mainland China offering scholarships to the most gifted. The number of violin students in China is unprecedented anywhere, and since their government's policy has been comparatively lenient in permitting their best young musicians to study in the West, the results have been, in many instances, quite amazing. The main problem is that no matter how many of these formidable players may wish to return home, opportunities in China for economically fruitful careers are practically nonexistent and audiences are very limited compared to the number of violinists who merit a career. Salaries for teachers and orchestral players are meager, and having tasted life in the West, notwithstanding all the economic adversities for musicians, most prefer to remain here except for occasional visits home to their families.

Why is it that so many violinists of Asian descent, whether born in or outside of the Asian countries, are achieving outstanding prominence and expertise? They come from cultures that have long traditions of reverence for education and the hard-work ethic. Families are closely-knit and children from infancy are taught to respect and obey their elders, and to adopt their elders' values. As with so many Jewish and Italian families of yesteryear who were either immigrants from Europe or first generation Americans, Oriental parents urge and support their talented children in the quest for excellence in music as a highly desirable means of gaining entrance into the mainstream of Western society. Their hard-work ethic demands self-discipline and the desire to excel in difficult undertakings. And many of them are people of fiery temperament. All of these qualities are of vital significance in helping to produce musicians of high accomplishment. Not only in music, but in medicine, science, law, business, and other pursuits requiring exceptional self-application and diligence, the Asians register an exceptional percentage of successes. It appears certain that the current influx of Asian violinists into the collective reservoir of significant string players is not a historically temporary occurrence, but one that will play a permanent role.

Few would assert that the number of worthy string compositions meriting repertorial permanence has kept pace with the contemporary development of highly capable instrumentalists. Many a current composer (though fortunately not all) has scorned the concept that the violin, viola, and cello are essentially instruments of song. Too often they concoct compositions that employ these instruments as purveyors of percussive effects and aleatory sounds of every description, to the exclusion of lyricism as a salient ingredient. Indeed, there are some performers who spend untold hours mastering such music in order to obtain engagements through the influence of numerous composers who attempt to force string instruments in directions that are alien to their nature. For all such attempts, even by composers who have earned repute in other areas of music, these works are mostly transient efforts. Melody itself, of course, can be no guarantee that a composition deserves repertorial permanence, or even a second hearing. But it is fair to say that those string compositions which consist of significant lyric material, if inspired and masterfully constructed, will be most likely to gain repertorial permanence.

The crop of excellent young violinists whom I

have heard is bountiful and impressive. Among them in the 21-30 age bracket (at this writing) are Gil Shaham, Vadim Repin, Maxim Vengerov, Antje Weithaas, Alexander Markov, Kyoko Takezawa, Anne Akiko Meyers, Christian Tetzlaff, Kyung Sun Lee, Elissa Lee Kokkonen, Leonidas Kavakos, Evgeny Bushkov, Misha Keylin, Pamela Frank, Erez Ofer, Higai Shaham, Pavel Berman, Robert Chen, Cory Cervocek, Tedi Papavrami, Jasmine Lin, Catherine Cho, Sigrun Edvaldsdottir, Latica Honda-Rosenberg, Pavel Sporcl, Adele Anthony, Stefan Milenković, Stephen Copes, Barthomiej Niziol, Yuan-Qing Yu, Sergei Krilov, Gabriel Croitoru, Jean-Marc Philippe, Isabella Lippi, Elisa Barston, Sheryl Staples, Jennifer Koh, Michael Zuber, Patricia Sunwoo, Ivan Chan, and Scott St. John. Among the 12-20 set are Leila Josefowicz, Sarah Chang, Julian Rachlin, Stefan Milenkocí, Renée Paule Gauthier, Julia Fischer, David Garrett, Ju Young Baek, Tamaki Kawakubo, Hilary Hahn, Juliette Kang, James Ehnes, Bracha Malkin, Soovin Kim, Rachel Barton, Tai Murray, Huei Min Lee, Yura Lee, Anna Malkin, Karen Gomyo, and Yoon Kwon. No doubt there are others that deserve mention. My apologies!

In summing up the situation, it is clear that we must be prepared to accept new standards for assessing violin art, whether or not we as individuals enthusiastically approve of these new standards. The clock cannot be turned back. The era of the "Great Personalities of the Violin" has passed, as have the social environments and cultural atmosphere that bred them. We see no more Paganinis who can compose 24 immortal caprices before the age of 25, or a Vieuxtemps who can produce three major concertos by age 18, or an Ysaÿe with the uniquely individual virtuosity of his six solo sonatas, or a Kreisler who so magically captured the Viennese spirit and ethos in his wondrous vignettes. No matter how strongly those like myself who were immersed in this tradition may wax nostalgic for the wonderful 'good old days' of violin art--those days are gone. Instead, we perceive a broad vista of talented and highly accomplished violinists, greater in sheer numbers than ever before. Collectively less impressive in ravishing tonal beauty and individualized style than the most illustrious of their predecessors, many among them possess incredible facility and musicianship of a high order. It is to be hoped that from this current abundance of accomplished young artists and their successors, there will arise those who will be capable of sending the listener out of the concert hall spiritually as well as aurally enriched by an unforgettable experience.

A PARTIAL PICTORIAL SURVEY OF GIFTED YOUNG VIOLINISTS WHO ARE AMONG THE VANGUARD LEADING THE MARCH OF VIOLIN ART INTO THE 21ST CENTURY

Photo David Weiss

Gil Shaham with Lawrence Foster

Leila Josefowicz

Courtesy of Chang Family Collection

Sarah Chang

Photo David Weiss

Maxim Vengerov

Kyoko Takezawa

Courtesy International Violin Competition of Indianapolis Photo Anderson Studios, Inc.

Christian Tetzlaff

Photo David Weiss

Vadim Repin

Photo David Weiss

Midori with Zubin Mehta

Photo David Weiss

Julian Rachlin

Antje Weithaus

Pamela Frank

Leonidas Kavakos

Photo Don Huntstein

James Ehnes

Photo J. Henry Fair

Elissa Lee Kokkonen

Courtesy International Violin Competition of Indianapolis Photo Garry Chilluffo

Juliette Kang

Photo Steve J. Sherman©

Robert Chen

337

Courtesy International Violin Competition of Indianapolis Photo Garry Chilluto

Stefan Milenković

Hilary Hahn

Photo David Weiss

Photo J. Henry Fair

Cory Cervocek

Anne Akiko Meyers

338

Photo Steve J. Sherman ©

Misha Keylin

Photo Christian Steiner

Catherine Cho

Photo Sigridur Bachmann

Sigrun Edvaldsdottir

Jasmine Lin

Photo Leopold Oosterbynck

Rachel Barton

Photo Henry Grossman

Anna Malkin

Photo David Weiss

Tamaki Kawakubo

Photo Neal R. Keach

Bracha Malkin

Photo: Yoshi ONO

Karen Gomyo

Photo Jolana Kutman

Huei Min Lee

Courtesy IMG Artists

Yoon Kwon

Yura Lee

341

Bibliography

Applebaum, Samuel and Sada, *The Way They Play*, Vols. 2 (1973) and 3 (1975), Paganiniana Publications, Inc., Neptune City, New Jersey.

Applebaum, Samuel and Roth, Henry, *The Way They Play*, Vols. 5 and 6 (1978), Vol. 7 (1980), Vol. 10 (1981), Paganiniana Publications, Inc., Neptune City, New Jersey.

Auer, Leopold, *My Long Life in Music*, Frederick A. Stokes Company, New York, 1923, 1925.

Bachmann, Alberto, *An Encyclopedia of the Violin*, Da Capo Press, New York, 1966, 1977.

Brodie, Fawn, *Thomas Jefferson, An Intimate History*, W.W. Norton & Co., New York, 1974.

Chotzinoff, Samuel, *Day's at the Morn*, Harper & Row.

Creighton, James, *The Discopaedia of the Violin*, James Creighton, University of Toronto Press, Toronto and Buffalo, 1974.

Davenport, Marcia, *Too Strong for Fantasy*, Charles Scribner's Sons, New York, 1967.

de Courcy, G.I.C., *Paganini, The Genovese*, Norman: University of Oklahoma Press, U.S.A., 1957.

De Saussine, Renée, *Paganini*, McGraw-Hill Book Company, Inc., U.S.A., 1954.

Downes, Olin, *Olin Downes on Music*, Simon and Schuster, New York, 1957.

Finck, Henry T., *My Adventures in the Golden Age of Music*. This 1971 Da Capo edition is an unabridged re-publication of the first edition published in New York and London in 1926 by Funk & Wagnalls Company.

Flesch, Carl, *Memoirs of Carl Flesch*, translated by Hans Keller, Rockliff Publishing Corporation, Great Britain, 1957.

Gingold, Josef, *Private Notes* (unpublished).

Ginsburg, Lev, *Ysaÿe*, edited by Dr. Herbert Axelrod, Paganiniana Publications, Inc., Neptune City, New Jersey, 1980.

Itzkoff, Seymour W., *Emanuel Feuermann, Virtuoso, a Biography*, The University of Alabama Press, University, Alabama, 1979.

Kirk, H.L., *Pablo Casals*, Holt, Rinehart and Winston, New York, Chicago and San Francisco. Published simultaneously in Canada by Holt, Rinehart and Winston of Canada, Ltd. 1974.

Lahee, Henry, C., *Famous Violinists of Today and Yesterday*, L.C. Page and Company, Boston, 1899.

Lawrence, R.D., *Pearls of Wisdom* interview, *The Strad*, 1989.

Lochner, Louis, *Fritz Kreisler*, Macmillan Publishing Co., Inc., New York, 1951.

Magidoff, Robert, *Yehudi Menuhin, The Story of the Man and the Musician*, Doubleday & Company, Inc., Garden City, New York, 1955.

Martens, Frederick H., *Violin Mastery*, Frederick A. Stokes Co., New York, 1919.

Martin, George, *The Damrosch Dynasty*, Houghton Mifflin Co., Boston, 1983.

Persinger, Louis, *Why the Violin?*, Cor Publishing Co., Massapequa, New York, 1957, 1965.

Piatigorsky, Gregor, *Cellist*, Doubleday, Garden City, New York, 1965.

Plaskin, Glenn, *Horowitz, a Biography*, William Morrow and Company, Inc., New York, 1983.

Primrose, William, *Walk on the North Side, Memoirs of a Violist*, Brigham Young University Press, Provo, Utah, 1978.

Pulver, Jeffrey, *Paganini, The Romantic Virtuoso*, Da Capo Press, New York, 1970.

Rolfe, Lionel Menuhin, *The Menuhins: A Family Odyssey*, Panjandrum/Aris Books, San Francisco, 1978.

Rooney, Dennis, *Courage & Ability* profile, *The Strad*, April, 1989.

Saleski, Gdal, *Musicians of a Wandering Race*, Bloch Publishing Company, New York, 1949.

Schickel, Richard, *The World of Carnegie Hall*, Julian Messner, Inc., New York. Published simultaneously in Canada by The Copp Clark Publishing Co., Ltd., 1960.

Schwartz, Boris, *Great Masters of the Violin*, Simon and Schuster, New York, 1983.

Shaw, George Bernard, *How to Become a Musical Critic*, Introduction and editorial, Hill and Wang, New York, 1961.

Sheppard, Leslie and Axelrod, Dr. Herbert R., *Paganini*, Paganiniana Publications, Inc., Neptune City, New Jersey, 1979.

Soroker, Yakov, *David Oistrakh*, Lexicon Publishing House, Jerusalem, 1982.

Spalding, Albert, *Rise to Follow*, Henry Holt and Company, Inc., New York, 1943.

Szigeti, Joseph, *Szigeti on the Violin*, Frederick A. Prueger, Publishers, New York, 1969.

Szigeti, Joseph, *With Strings Attached—Reminiscences and Reflections*, Alfred A. Knopf, New York, 1947.

Taubman, Howard, *Music on My Beat*, Simon and Schuster, New York, 1943.

Thomas, Theodore, *A Musical Autobiography*, edited by George P. Upton, Da Capo Press, New York, 1961; original two-volume work published by A.C. McClurg & Co., Chicago, 1908.

Ysaÿe, Antoine and Bertram Ratcliffe, *Ysaÿe: His Life Work and Influence*, William Heinemann Ltd., London, Toronto. Republished by Scholarly Press, Inc., Michigan, 1978.

Index

Bolshoi Ballet and Opera orchestra, 141, 304
Bonaparte, Princess Elise, 12
Bondarenko, Pyotr, 150, 289
Borodin, Alexander, 193
Boston Chamber Players, 276
Boston Pops, 282
Boston Symphony, 35-36, 89, 106, 110, 171, 181,
    211, 215-216, 240, 244, 247, 257, 260, 273,
    276, 286
Boucher, Anthony, 11
Boucherit, Jules, 263
Bouillon, Gabriel, 177
Boulanger, Lily, 243
Boulanger, Nadia, 184
Bour, Ernest, 206
Breeskin, Elias, 176, 248
Bress, Hyman, 30
Brieff, Frank, 193
British Symphony Orchestra, 98
Britten, Benjamin, 302, 318
Brodsky, Adolf, 82-83, 188, 258
Brodsky, Vadim, 303
Bron, Zakhar, 305, 306
Bronne, Ariana, 280, 327
Bronstein, Raphael, 280
Brosa, Antonio, 286
Brown, Eddy, 93, 105, 242, 244, 245
Brown, Iona, 321
Bruckner, Anton, 34
Brussels Conservatory, 21, 93, 203, 311
Brussels String Quartet, 28
Brussels Ysaÿe Competition, 210-211, 288
Budapest Royal Conservatory, 244, 252
Buitrago, Jean, 242
Bull, Ole, 2, 15, 17, 60, 62, 63, 84, 170, 238
Burgin, Ruth Posselt, 316
Burgin, Richard, 105, 260, 316
Burmester, Willy, 17, 51, 79, 89, 104, 262
Busch, Adolf, 52, 97, 157-158, 171, 282
Busch, Fritz, 154, 156-157
Bushkov, Evgeny, 333
Busoni, Ferruccio, 22, 94-96, 98, 171
Busotti, Carlos, 98, 100
Bustabo, Guila, 118, 254, 312, 318-319
Buswell, James Oliver, 271, 283-284

Byrd, Henry, 98, 100

Cadman, Charles Wakefield, 7, 42, 241
Calcagno, Caterina, 310
California Symphony, 263
Cameron, Basil, 215
Campoli, Alfredo, 45, 147, 286
Canino, Bruno, 226
Cantelli, Guido, 246
Capet, Lucien, 97, 263
Cardenes, Andres, 267, 285
Carillo, Julian, 178
Carlyss, Earl, 286
Carmirelli, Pina, 321
Carnegie College Community Orchestra, 273
Carnegie Hall, 37, 70-71, 90, 101, 104, 154, 156,
    161, 188, 191, 198, 215, 246, 261, 269, 276,
    280, 282
Carol, Norman, 257
Carpenter, Nettie, 238, 240, 311
Carter, Elliot, 283
Cartier, J. B., 46
Caruso, Enrico, 32, 43, 46, 85, 88, 226, 253
Casadesus, Robert, 119, 122-123, 125
Casals Festival, 143
Casals Orchestra of Barcelona, 56
Casals, Pablo, 28, 21, 28-29, 50-51, 53-54, 56-57, 97,
    109, 191, 197, 230, 234, 251-252, 273
Casella, Alfredo, 263
Cassado, Gaspar, 164, 243
Castagnone, Riccardo, 206-207
Castelnuovo-Tedesco, Mario, 111, 211, 216, 226, 263
Castleman, Charles, 30, 282, 288
Central Music School, 210, 300, 303
Central Television and Radio Orchestra, 299
Cerone, David, 286
Cerone, Linda, 327
Cervocek, Cory, 333, 338
Chamber Music Society of Lincoln Center, 270, 284
Chamber Music Society of San Francisco, 254
Chan, Ivan, 333
Chang, Sarah, 312, 333-334
Chanot, George, 22
Chaplin, Charles, 302
Charleroi Conservatory, 202

Poulet, Gerard, 286
Powell, Maud, 62, 104, 215, 238, 240-242, 284,
  312-313
    American premieres of, 241
    American tours of, 242
    birth/early years of, 240
    Dancla and, 241
    death of, 240
    recordings of, 242
    string quartet of, 241
    Turner and, 242
    Victor Company, 241
Poznan Wieniawski Competition, 281, 292, 297, 301
Prague Conservatory, 61
Prague Kubelik Competition, 295
Prague Spring Festival "Ondříček" Competition, 296
Prantl, Pavel, 286
Premier Premier Prix, 35
Press, Michael, 28, 82
Preucil, William 125, 267
Previn, André, 196, 225-227
Příhoda, Váša, 17-18, 67, 256
Primrose String Quartet, 271
Primrose, William, 43, 74, 113-115, 134, 197, 265-
  266, 271
    book by,
      Walk on the North Side, Memoirs of a Violist
      (Primrose), 134
Professor Yuri Yankelevich, 294
Prume, Francois, 202
Puerto Rico Musical Festival Orchestra, 273
Pugno, Raoul, 21
Pulitzer Prize, 248
Pulver, Jeffrey, 10

Queen Elisabeth Competition, 125, 143, 150, 211,
  267, 270, 273-274, 276, 285-286, 288, 293,
  301-304, 322
Quiroga, Manuel, 29

Rabin, Michael, 17-18, 29, 67, 147, 190, 205, 216,
  220, 224-225, 269, 271, 276-278, 298, 319
    birth/early years of, 276
    death of, 276
    debut of, 276
    Heifetz/influence on, 220, 277

    illness of, 269
    virtuosity, 277
Rabinof, Benno, 246-274
Rabinof, Sylvia, 172
Rachlin, Julian, 333, 336
Rachmaninoff, Sergei, 13, 43, 150, 193, 207, 226, 256
Raderman, Lou, 253
Rados, Ferenc, 173
Raff, Joachim, 7, 21, 89, 224, 226, 242, 256
Rakov, Nikolai, 146, 297
Ravel, Maurice, 96, 100, 111, 119, 124, 149, 160,
  170, 196, 206, 216, 234, 260, 274, 294-295, 297,
  300, 302, 312, 314, 318, 325-326
RCA Symphony, 110-111, 113
Reiner, Charles, 181, 183
Rejto, Gabor, 114
Reményi, Edouard, 7, 62, 82, 239
Rémy, 239, 244, 260
Renardy, Ossy, 17-18, 67, 118, 169, 269, 293, 319
Repin, Vadim, 305-306, 333, 335
Rethberg, Elisabeth, 244
Reynolds, Vida, 275
Ricci, Giorgio, 169, 171
Ricci, Ruggiero, 30, 67, 70, 90, 118, 133-134, 167-173,
  188, 193, 216-218, 255, 269, 271-272, 275, 293
    birth/early years of, 168
    debut of, 168
    Glory of Cremona, 173
    playing style of, 170
    recordings of, 169-172
    scope/repertoire of, 176
    violin of,
      1734 ex-"Gibson" Guarnerius del Gesù, 169
Richter, Hans, 36
Richter, Sviatoslav, 149-150, 303
Ries, Hubert, 64, 137, 155-156
Riga School of Music, 301
Rimsky-Korsakov, Nikolai, 28, 96, 136, 150, 183,
  193, 262
Robbins, Gerald, 231
Robbins, Sandra, 280
Robert, Walter, 267, 269
Roberts, Richard, 267
Robertson, Leroy, 265
Robin Hood Dell Orchestra, 136
Robinson, Sharon, 270
Rochberg, George, 196, 301

Violin Virtuosos – From Paganini to the 21st Century
BY HENRY ROTH

Book design by Nigey Lennon and Esther Roth.
Art direction, typography and production by Ken Boor of The LA Type.
Typeset in QuarkXPress on Macintosh Centris.
The text face is Janson Text 10.5 point; chapter titles are in Oxford.
3000 copies were printed on acid-free, 60 pound natural stock
at McNaughton & Gunn in Saline, Michigan.